The Ruble

THE RUBLE

A Political History

EKATERINA PRAVILOVA

OXFORD
UNIVERSITY PRESS

OXFORD
UNIVERSITY PRESS

Oxford University Press is a department of the University of Oxford. It furthers
the University's objective of excellence in research, scholarship, and education
by publishing worldwide. Oxford is a registered trade mark of Oxford University
Press in the UK and certain other countries.

Published in the United States of America by Oxford University Press
198 Madison Avenue, New York, NY 10016, United States of America.

CIP data is on file at the Library of Congress
ISBN 978-0-19-766371-4

DOI: 10.1093/oso/9780197663714.001.0001

Printed by Sheridan Books, Inc., United States of America

In memory of my teacher,
Boris Anan'ich
(1931–2015)

Contents

PART IV *Ruble, Wars, and Revolutions*

Acknowledgments

WHEN I TOLD my friends that I was writing a history of Russian money, some shrugged their shoulders and felt sorry for me. Others were very excited to hear about the project and welcomed my idea, and I am grateful for their enthusiasm. I am also grateful for the opportunity to prove that studying money, especially the ruble, can be fun and rewarding.

It would be impossible to name everyone who has helped me in research and writing. I especially appreciate the generous support offered by Princeton University, my academic home since 2006, and the John Simon Guggenheim Memorial Foundation, which funded my sabbatical year in 2018–2019 and paid for several trips to the archives in Moscow and St. Petersburg. In Russia, many archivists and librarians were very welcoming, friendly, and helpful. My special gratitude goes to an expert in Russian numismatics, historian Andrei Bogdanov of the Goznak's Museum of Money in St. Petersburg. He introduced me to the museum's extraordinary collection and responded to multiple questions and queries. Anastasia Poverin, Maria Starun, and Azat Bilalutdinov helped me to collect and systematize materials in libraries and archives, which was especially important when COVID-19 made traveling difficult, if not totally impossible. Thomas F. Keenan, Princeton University's Slavic librarian, has been indispensable in tracking down rare publications and locating sources that I was desperate to find. Kristen Kapfer worked to improve the text of the manuscript at its early stage.

I was lucky to be able to present the concept of the project before COVID-19 put academic meetings on hold. The feedback that I received from my colleagues at the Russian history kruzhok at Columbia University, the German Historical Institute, and the Centre for Modern Russian History at the Higher School of Economics in Moscow was essential for shaping the concept of my research. Presenting this work at the Shelby Cullom Davis Center for Historical Studies at Princeton University was a privilege. I am grateful to the Center's then director Angela N.H. Creager for the opportunity to brainstorm the politics of the ruble with my Princeton colleagues. Graduate students, but most important, Geoffrey Durham and Friedrich Asschenfeldt, have read and commented on the chapters of the manuscript and provided their insights. I was glad to find out that my interest in the fate of Russian money during the First World War and the revolutionary era was shared by William Rosenberg. I benefited enormously from reading Bill's chapters from a forthcoming book on the Russian economic and social crisis and comparing our interpretations of this period. Anne O'Donnell offered excellent advice, and we had many conversations about finance, property, and economy in the revolutionary era. Stephen Kotkin's opinion about my version of the early history of Soviet finance meant the world to me (of course, he does not bear responsibility for any of my mistakes). Harold James, Stefan Eich, Yanni Kotsonis, and Francis Wcislo read the entire manuscript in its pre-edited, more extended version and wrote extensive comments and suggestions that I followed faithfully. I admire their academic comradeship and owe them for the project's significant improvement in concept and argument. Finally, Susan Ferber of Oxford University Press has helped me to turn the manuscript into a book. I am grateful for her hard work, patience, and professionalism.

Many other friends and colleagues have supported me in ways I cannot even explain. Naming everyone would take dozens of pages. My conversations with Igor Fedyukin, Katia Deminsteva, Ilya Vinitsky, Monika and Helmut Reimitz, Anna and Michael Meerson, and Tatiana Borisova have been especially important. Igor Khristoforov, my husband and a fellow historian, knows about imperial money and banks no less than I do, and I often sought his advice in research and writing. My parents, Natalya Vasilievna and Anatoly Mikhailovich, have always been my most enthusiastic supporters. Even though the history of money isn't their subject, they tried to understand what exactly I was studying, and I did my best to explain.

This book is dedicated to the memory of my teacher, Boris Vasilievich Anan'ich (1931–2015), who spent more than three decades of his academic life studying the life of Serguei Witte and exploring Russian imperial finance. Boris Vasilievich was a fantastic adviser—very kind, warm, and endlessly generous. Everyone admired him, and he inspired many of his students to study economic and political history. He was also a great storyteller, and Serguei Witte, whom Boris Vasilievich often called simply "Count," became a household name for us, while the history of the gold reform, Russia's foreign loans, and its economic expansion appeared riveting and exciting. My interpretation of the gold standard and Witte's policy may differ from Boris Vasilievich's account. Still, I know that he would have been excited to hear it, as he always welcomed the most daring experiments of his students and colleagues. Without him, this book could not have been written.

The Ruble

Introduction

THE RUBLE'S STORIES

CAN MONEY HAVE a story? Russian writers thought it could. Nikolai Novikov's comic autobiography of a 25-kopeck coin (1778), Nikolai Bestuzhev's *A History of a Silver Ruble* (1820), *The Adventures of a Blue Assignat* by Evgenii Grebenka (1847), along with numerous other works, focused their narratives not on people but on the imaginative life stories of kopecks and rubles, coins and notes. The money's journey spotlights the virtues, sins, fortunes, and misfortunes of people who hoarded coins and forged, stole, lost, exchanged, or gave paper rubles away. The long life cycle of money underscores humans' fragility: rubles are resilient to crises, diseases, and starvation while people suffer and perish in poverty. Money seems passive, a silent witness to the deeds and misdeeds of men, but it is not; it is the invisible driver of petty tragedies, intimate dramas, and grand historical processes. The pre-revolutionary stories, most famously Leo Tolstoy's epic *The Forged Coupon* (1904, publ. 1911), are often dominated by moral didactic and reflections on the corrupting influence of money on human nature. Soviet "travelogues" and fairytales about money, such as Serguei Mikhalkov's *The Adventures of a Ruble* (1969), straightforwardly deliver an ideological message about the advantages of the Soviet financial order over imperialist economies. In any case, both the old and the new hagiographies of the ruble exploit the anthropomorphic nature of money. Rubles come to life, like people, and die—some of them graciously, being melted into ornaments or burned in a bonfire in front of an imperial palace, others with jeering and mockery, as the despised Soviet "monetary signs" that, after the monetary reform of 1921–24, lost their value and were replaced by "good" *chervonetz*.[1]

Such metaphoric parallels between humans and money are age-old. Sociologist Nigel Dodd's *The Social Life of Money* spotlights both the temporality of money ("money is a process, not a thing") and its embeddedness in the fabric of society.[2] Other scholars have highlighted the peculiar duality of money: it is at once a quintessentially fungible commodity devoid of any personal characteristics, yet it acquires a wealth of meanings—social, gender, generational, political, religious, and national.[3] Thus, paradoxically, while the history of modern society is often told as a process of simplification and flattening—"making up people" to fit standardized categories—money appears in a palette of subtle meanings and identities.[4] One can write a history of the dollar, the złoty, or the franc as a biography of a currency, with a focus on its role in politics, its financial career, or the aesthetic or material qualities of coins and banknotes. This book is a political biography of the Russian paper ruble, from its inception in the mid-eighteenth century to the reform of 1921–24. It considers money not only as a passive product of economic and constitutional organization, but also the active means of enacting (or preventing) changes in the political and legal structure of the state and society.[5]

Any biography is bigger than one person's life story. Even when focusing on the extraordinary and unique lives of individuals, biographies spotlight the fates of whole generations, social groups, or nationalities. Similarly, a political biography of the ruble offers an opportunity to explore the political life of modern money, to reveal and explain the reasons for similarities and divergences between national currencies. The nineteenth century, known as a century of nationalism, brought an unseen universalization to the sphere of finance. It gave the world the modern idea of a monetary standard and international monetary unions that partially suspended national particularisms in the sphere of finance. In the 1860s–80s, the gold standard spread across Europe and North America and then reached beyond these two continents, creating an illusion of a financial concordance based on a common monetary language. By the beginning of the twentieth century, adherence to the gold standard came to be seen as a virtue, while deviance from it was synonymous with failure. In economic history and the history of money, exceptionality often means abnormality, while the uniformity of criteria, standards, and rules is considered a higher good. Yet, despite the name, the principles of monetary standards were less "standardized" than it may seem. John Maynard Keynes noticed it in 1913, when he wrote about the futility of the attempts to follow the British model.[6] But if financial models of the monetary standards differed, their political constituents demonstrated even more variety. Much can be found looking at how domestic politics and the specificity of political organization affected the monetary regimes in the silver- and gold-standard world. The Russian case is especially revealing.

Historians have long debated the idiosyncrasy of the Russian state and political culture. Some have tried to normalize Russia's story by searching for non-European points of comparison and questioning the universality of the applied criteria of normalcy. Others have resisted smoothing over the story of autocracy and totalitarianism. Russian particularism in the sphere of finance has usually been bluntly called "backwardness." Russia followed many European institutional patterns, but its currency remained inconvertible through most of its history. It was the last European great power to join the gold standard system despite its gold reserve being the largest in Europe. Russia avoided the turmoil of the nineteenth-century European revolutions and remained an autocratic empire, yet a strong liberal movement simmered for decades, producing original, if oftentimes impractical, ideas. Russian society was attentive to European intellectual exchanges and was amazingly receptive to economic ideas coming from the West, yet many of the economic and political projects that were discussed in clubs, academic journals, and bureaucratic offices remained unfulfilled. The Revolutions of 1917 that followed the devastation of World War I swept away the old state with its monetary system, but the contours of the new state that emerged on the ruins of empire bore the indelible features of its predecessor, and the new socialist ruble replicated its imperial ancestor. Without implying some inherent specificity (or pathology) of the Russian state and its society, *The Ruble* shows how they evolved in the context of Russia's political, financial, and intellectual relationship with the West and the East.

In tracing the evolution of the ruble and the debates around it, this book translates the meaning of financial institutions and terms such as "convertibility," "exchange rate," "monetary standard," "independence of the bank of issue," and others into the language of politics. The political meaning of these terms was not the same 200 years ago as it is today. In the eighteenth century, when Catherine the Great introduced Russia's first paper money, called "assignats," paper notes were not considered real money but the "representative signs" of currency. To ensure the credibility of assignats, the state promised to make them exchangeable for copper and silver coins that were kept in the storage rooms of state Assignat Banks. But after the government discovered the ease of using paper money to cover extraordinary wartime expenses, it started issuing paper notes that were not "backed up" by the metal collateral. Due to various factors, but mostly overprinting, the value of assignats began to fall, and the government took up a new means of supporting their value—through references to the sublime power of the ruler. Thus, the idea developed that in an autocratic state, the value of paper money hinges on the sanctity of the sovereign's promises rather than a material collateral. Assignats came to be seen as a projection of absolute authority.

Not everyone welcomed the idea of autocratic money. In the 1780s, Russian politicians versed in the economic ideas of the Enlightenment coined a concept of money as the representation of national wealth. It assumed that the nation owned the bullion reserve, and the government could not issue monetary signs that did not correspond to the value of this common asset. This idea was clearly very radical: it imposed limits on autocratic privileges and even indirectly suggested the political sovereignty of the people. But how could it be possible to restrict the authority of the monarch? One way to do so was to demand the inviolability of the bullion reserve and the convertibility of assignats to specie. This arrangement made both economic and political sense: the reserve, as well as the convertibility of paper notes, was considered to be the best conditions of credibility not only domestically but also internationally. Therefore, a government seeking capital and investments would be interested in maintaining the reserve. However, simply holding a metal reserve equivalent to the amount of paper money in circulation did not guarantee the observance of the "rule of law" in finances. Sooner or later, the government (or the ruler) could succumb to the temptation to overprint. Therefore, proponents of the nation's right to money suggested complementing material collateral with institutional guarantees, namely, the creation of an independent private (joint stock) bank of issue. Economists contended that in addition to the metal reserve, an independent central bank could back up currency with short-term bills of exchange that reflected actual commercial transactions. Such a bank was thought to represent the productive part of society and would release banknotes in the amount reflecting the demands for money in the economy.

The appearance of assignats, which coincided with the Westernization of Russian intellectual life and Russian society's embrace of the Enlightenment, opened up questions of the state's indebtedness to its own subjects. Russian thinkers compared the paper money's convertibility to the right of political representation, while a banknote was seen as a mandate for participation in governance. The bullion reserve appeared crucial for maintaining the accountability of government and the separation of powers, and allegiance to a monetary standard was analogous to the rule of law. Furthermore, in Russian liberal nineteenth-century parlance, an independent bank that guarded the reserve, issued banknotes, and ensured their convertibility to specie stood for a parliament. This entire intellectual edifice rested on a presumption that the government derived its power of money issuance from the sovereign people, not vice versa.

The conservative theory that developed in parallel and in reaction to the liberal doctrine asserted that the request for additional material and constitutional guarantees of the paper ruble's value contradicted the logic of imperial rule. In the monarchal state, the monarch's pledge and honor were sufficient to support the value of money and the credibility of the state. Maintaining the reserve was seen as an unnecessary restriction of the state's financial authority that infringed on the tsar's sacred duties—to wage the war against enemies of the empire or Christian Orthodoxy and to protect the Fatherland. Russian conservatives were very unhappy with the rigor and doctrinaire nature of the liberal theory that, in their opinion, was very inflexible. They thought that the government of a growing empire required the freedom to issue paper money when it saw fit. Since the proponents of the nominalist theory associated monetary liberalism with the imaginary "West," this theory acquired a nationalist bent. It developed into a concept of the "people's ruble" that emphasized the Russian population's unconditional trust in any kind of monetary signs issued by the state. Therefore, while liberals were embarrassed by the ruble's inconvertibility, nineteenth-century nominalists considered it almost a virtue. The story of the Russian ruble deserves to be told if only to illustrate how Russian monarchists invented the indigenous paper standard and turned it into official ideology. No other country has ever produced such an odd ideological construct.

In the nineteenth century, as Russia turned into an active borrower on the international market of capitals, it had to somehow respond to the expectations of solvency. Therefore, economic conservatism further transformed the liberal idea of convertibility into something associated with monarchy rather than a constitutional right. These conservative financial ideas that combined autocracy with the concept of a monetary standard were original and not seen elsewhere in Europe. While liberals envisioned an independent bank that on behalf of the people held the reserve and ensured convertibility, conservatives considered it a royal asset that was meant to compensate, in the eyes of Russia's creditors, for the lack of constitutional guarantees. If, as political scientist Stefan Eich has argued, money "can help to create and maintain the precondition for . . . democratic politics," it can also work in the opposite way.[7] The Russian monetary system was designed to maintain autocracy.

Having rejected "Western" notions of good currency that were considered
incompatible with the monarchal doctrine, the Russian imperial government invented its own vision of economic success and financial stability that
matched the political principles of the autocratic state. After all, if political
stability means the absence of revolutions, from this point of view, Russia
until 1905 looked like an oasis of tranquility. Of course, this tranquility was
misleading and could only be achieved through political repressions and censorship. In finance, conservative stabilization assumed fixing the ruble's rate
and preventing its fluctuation. But, similar to the visibility of political order
that concealed widespread discontent, this stability of money was to a great
extent maintained with the help of political and administrative measures. The
Russian ruble was "fixed" on the silver standard in 1839, meaning that one
paper credit ruble was equivalent to a silver ruble, and it switched to gold
in 1897. Both reforms assumed an increase in bureaucratic surveillance over
commercial activity and were predicated on the centralization of state power.
In the mindset of the imperial administrators, the threat of instability came
from the unpredictable and unruly market that was associated with speculation and the perils of bankruptcy and ruin. Of course, the government did
not attempt to completely paralyze commercial activity and credit networks.
But, while business and commerce were expected to develop, money had to
remain solely within the purview of the state.

These attempts to destroy the influence of the market while aspiring
for economic growth may seem staggering. After all, isn't money one of its
key components? Historians of money have by now dismantled the myth
of money's emergence from trade and exchange, and the origin story of the
Russian paper ruble gives further evidence of money being created rather than
naturally born.[8] Yet although the state claimed its monopoly on the production of money, it could not fully control the economic behavior of society and
its attitude toward the ruble. To the chagrin of Russian administrators, when
the ruble's rate was unstable, people invented their own alternative measures
of account, such as the "coin ruble" of the 1830s and the "bread rubles" of the
Civil War. And if the government failed to supply the market with notes or
coins that were in high demand, local communities started printing their own
marks to compensate for the deficit of cash.

But the most apparent constraint on the state's ability to control the
ruble was its constantly fluctuating value. The problem of rate emerged simultaneously with the appearance of the assignats, and it represented more
than a strictly economic issue. The ruble's rate, as much as it represented
the projection of Russia's commercial activity, was seen as a reflection of

Russia's geopolitical standing or, more generally, Russia's civilizational inferiority or superiority. Throughout the nineteenth century, debates over how to interpret the rate continued. The ruble's falling rate affected the ability to buy imported commodities that, along with the introduction of European ideas, symbolized the Westernization of Russian elites. After the abolition of serfdom and the removal of most restrictions on credit and investment activities, Russian society plunged into the new realities of capitalism, and the ruble's rate turned into one of the key parameters of everyday life. However, the majority of Russia's peasant population did not consume imported goods or buy shares, and nationalists stressed this while trying to present the ruble's rate as a form of Russia's dependence on the West. Economic factors, such as the revenue from the export of grain or the costs of paying for foreign loans, mattered, but the rate was not exclusively a financial category. When Russia's relations with the European great powers were especially frayed after the Russo-Turkish War (1877–78) and the Berlin Congress, the government pretended that it ignored the falling rate, considering the ruble's demise in the wake of Russia's victory a humiliation. A few years later, the situation was reversed. The same people who had suggested measuring the ruble's value in pounds of wheat bread instead of francs or pence declared that the low rate of the ruble was an assault on the emperor's honor. Economists were also trying to figure out which factors—the amount of printed money, Russia's trade balance, the size of its foreign credit obligations, or the successes of Russian army on the battlefields—affected the ruble's standing.

Conversations about rate, convertibility, or the authenticity of money often revealed preoccupations with ethical and ideological matters and fundamental issues of honor, dignity, and trust. When Catherine the Great vouched for the convertibility of assignats and pledged to preserve their value, she endorsed the perception of rubles as the ruler's promissory notes. The promise of exchange for specie printed on each assignat and, later, credit ruble enhanced this connection; when the assignat's rate fell, writers lamented the "humbled" state of the ruble, referring to the dual meaning of the word *dostoinstvo* as both dignity and nominal value. The honor argument appeared in different contexts and meanings. In 1862, for example, the government, with inadequate preparation, rushed to resume the exchange of paper rubles for gold, referring to its duty to fulfill the promises of the deceased tsar (Nicholas I). However, in 1876, on the eve of the Russo-Turkish War, nationalists argued that the honor of protecting the Slavs from the Ottoman Turks was more important than the dishonor of the ruble's falling rate. In 1896, when news of the projected devaluation of the ruble got into the press, critics of the reform characterized it as a violation of the honor code, comparing the government to an untrustworthy merchant. The ruble, which is supposed to be neutral and fungible, often appeared in an anthropomorphic form—as a person, with soul, honors, and dignity. The "honor" arguments especially dominated the conservative discourse. Nationalist critics of political economy offered a heavily romanticized vision of monetary relations, blaming liberal economists for their heartless, mechanical approach to money. True, the liberal version of trust stressed transparency and control, science, and evidence, which offended the sensibilities of their opponents.

What appears important in the context of the ruble's story is that monetary ideology and patterns of financial policy were always embedded in larger systems of ethics, culture, epistemology, and history.[9] Consequently, the rift between conflicting ideologies was much deeper and more substantial than often thought, and it was not limited to institutional preferences. If, as Austrian sociologist Karl Mannheim wrote, conservatism (and likewise, liberalism) represented "styles of thought," then the analysis of money offers a perfect opportunity to explore these modes of thinking.[10] The choice of the vector for monetary policy was often justified by historical and philosophical references. For instance, in the first half of the nineteenth century historians and policymakers were immersed in a debate over the existence of leather (or skin) money in pre-Mongol Rus'. This seemingly peripheral question in fact had enormous importance. The nationalist proponents of Russia's indigenous paper standard, who refused to measure the ruble's worth in silver or foreign currencies, argued that Russia had introduced a prototype of paper currency centuries before it appeared in Western Europe. They presented fiat money as a culturally advanced form because it required abstract thinking while the use of coins and banknotes tied to a metal reserve, betrayed a more primitive form of economic judgement. The historical debate first and foremost concerned Russia's relations with the West and the role of the state as the driving force of cultural and economic progress. The argument about Russia's role and civilizational superiority expressed in its (doubtful) precedence in inventing fiat money corresponded to the nationalist view on Russian language and its development. Arguing for the priority of the state in determining the amount and value of monetary signs, nationalists also asserted the government's right to purge foreign words and introduce a new Russian vocabulary based on indigenous roots.

The ruble, therefore, served as a compass that helped to locate Russia on the economic and political map of the world. Parts of the Russian Empire also belonged to the financial "West." The Kingdom of Poland and the Grand

Duchy of Finland at different periods of their existence enjoyed monetary autonomy, while their currencies were oriented toward their European neighbors. After the failed revolutions of 1831 and 1863, Poland lost its currency, along with constitutional privileges and autonomy. In 1860 Finland was allowed to introduce its own monetary sign, and in 1876, it switched to the gold standard, thereby creating a source of constant embarrassment for Russian liberals and nationalists. All major monetary reforms—the silver reform of 1839–43, the introduction of the gold standard in 1897, and the Soviet *chervonetz* reform of 1921–24—aimed to facilitate the inclusion of borderlands into the ruble domain. While standing on the economic "East" from its own Western borderlands, Russia enjoyed the status of a civilizational "West" in relation to its own Orient, the Asiatic borderlands and protectorate territories. After the introduction of the gold standard, Russian government looked down on the silver-based currencies of Bukhara and Manchuria and tried to make the population switch to the "superior" gold-backed rubles. Administrators considered the expansion of the ruble domain as a part of Russia's civilizing mission and were genuinely puzzled over why the local population did not want to abandon their "inferior" money in favor of the "better" ruble. The ruble was not always a good (and cheap) tool of imperial management and integration, but the ideological reasons for turning it into the only currency of empire outweighed all practical considerations.

While trying to spread rubles to the remote corners of the Empire or even beyond its borders, the government was often responding to the conflicting demands of local elites, regional authorities, Russian merchants, and diplomats. The politics of money was, therefore, not limited to state governance; different actors used the ruble argument in bargaining with the state. Money was a universal language for communicating grievances and expressing expectations—not only between regional authorities and the center, Russian and non-Russian elites, but also between various social groups and the government. Russian society was deeply stratified into estates and classes, and bargaining between the government and the people during the imperial and the early Soviet period often occurred along these lines. Merchants and noblemen, and sometimes peasants or those who spoke on their behalf, expressed visions of their own ideal ruble and the parameters of the socially just monetary system and asked the government to act as the arbiter in these relations, to prescribe, discipline, police, and prohibit. More often than not, they disagreed, arguing that the economic behavior of other social groups was detrimental to the fate of the "common ruble." These debates, starting with the campaigns against luxury in the 1780s, when merchants accused noblemen of causing the inflation, to the anti-peasant sentiments during World War I and the Civil War, when peasants were blamed for hoarding money, demonstrate how social actors used the ruble rhetoric to manipulate the state and how the government used those demands to justify or postpone unpopular reforms.

Not all social interactions surrounding the ruble took the form of peaceful bargaining. Sometimes they evolved into different forms of conflict and resistance, drawing the masses into political participation, sometimes inadvertently and unpredictably for the state. The women's riots of 1915, in reaction to the deficit of small change, certainly could not match the violence of the Copper Riot of 1662 caused by the replacement of silver coins by copper, but these riots were equally spontaneous and expressed the moral economy of money as people understood it. The social protest in response to monetary policy rarely escalated to the level of rebellion, but, as anthropologist James Scott underscores, the "weak" can use other weapons and means to express discontent.[11] The silent refusal of peasants to sell grain for depreciated rubles during the Civil War of 1918–21 is an example of this form of resistance, but so too are counterfeiting in the villages of Old Believers, which reached an unseen scale during the financial crisis of the 1860s, and the widespread refusal to take gold coins after the reform of 1897. These and other episodes show that people perceived the unwritten rules of monetary circulation as the indispensable elements of the tacit contract between the state and society. In the seventeenth century as well as in the first years after the revolution, people treated money as a public good that the state had to provide. In their eyes, money was society's property that the state had agreed to manage. The authorities did not share this attitude. Policymakers often spoke about the obligation of the tsar's subjects to accept depreciated money and therefore share the burden of financing the state. The denial of the people's claims was symptomatic of the deep political cleavage that separated the rulers from the ruled, a cleavage that ultimately triggered mass discontent. The February Revolution of 1917 at once exposed the extreme politicization of financial problems. Workers and soldiers who had hoped that the fall of the tsarist government would improve their condition blamed the new republican authorities for their failure to salvage the ruble and stop inflation that eroded the social achievements of the revolution. After the October coup, the new socialist power openly declared that the ruble was the weapon of class war used to expropriate wealth from the enemies of the proletariat. When the Civil War and the violence of class purges brought the socialist republic to the brink of the catastrophe, the government turned to the reconstruction of the financial and administrative system. Astonishingly, this reconstruction included the return of the imperial ruble based on the pseudo-gold standard that assumed the centrality of the state and constraints on the free market of credit. A revolution in finance did not happen.

———

The history of the ruble is told here in different registers. One line of inquiry focuses on intellectual trajectories—the imaginary lives of the ruble reflected in the projects of reforms, pamphlets, newspaper articles, treaties, and academic books. Through these texts, the book traces the evolution of two approaches to money: as a socioeconomic institution and the mandate for rights, and as a proxy of power and the source of obligation. These two concepts corresponded to two worldview—one cosmopolitan and focused on the rule of law, another isolationist and predicated on the primacy of power. The analogy became obvious: a proposition of a financial reform aimed at restoring convertibility, along with establishing an independent bank of issue, was deemed equivalent to a demand for a political constitution and the limitation of autocracy. Therefore, this line of inquiry reveals previously unknown trends and sources of Russian liberal and constitutional thought. Including the ideas of financial constitution and the rule of law expands and enriches understanding of the Russian tradition of constitutionalism.

Not only did the type of texts dedicated to the ruble vary but so too did the professional occupations and political profiles of their authors. Journalists, ministers, and professors of political economy argued over their priority and expertise in solving financial problems. In the era when political economy came into vogue, especially in the 1860s–90s, many deemed themselves able to converse about the rates of exchange, trade balance, and credit policy. The government was very perceptive about changes in public opinion and believed that its swings could affect the ruble's standing. Therefore, as the massive volume of correspondence between ministers and journalists shows, controlling newspapers and cultivating good relations with writers and editors constituted one of the key areas of activity at the imperial Ministry of Finance. Battles over the ruble took place in clubs, learned societies, and public meetings attended by well-dressed women and students. The ruble's imaginary "adventures" in novels, poems, and short stories mirrored the most routine and bizarre features of the social life of money and its place in society.

A second line of inquiry in the ruble's story is the materiality of money. While people experienced the results of big shifts in monetary organization and economic policies, the most immediate and visible effects came with the physical changes of bills and coins—new images, shapes, and textures. As it grappled with the economic problems of rates, convertibility, and credit, the government was also preoccupied with the mundane tasks of ensuring the authenticity of bills, their resilience to counterfeiting, and their material quality, all of which were seen as key elements maintaining popular trust in currency. That was especially important because in the world of money based on standards or replete with imaginary units of account, a banknote or a coin was supposed to straddle the space between the matter of money and the imaginary value that it designated. In Russia, this dichotomy was expressed in language. For example, the "silver ruble" (*rubl' serebrom*) as a legal tender was represented not only by paper notes but also by copper coins that bore an inscription "1 (or ½, 2 and 3) silver kopeck," reflecting the financial alchemy that could turn one metal into another. After the introduction of the gold standard in 1897, and its resumption in 1922, the paper ruble was made gold (*rubl' zolotom*) in actuality (with gold coins minted in new denominations) and figuratively. All these changes were reflected in the design of money, with special attention paid to formulating the values and the promises. The logistics of making money also created physical horizons for political decisions. The Bolshevik government, overwhelmed by inflation and unable to satisfy the demand for cash, was forced to use tsarist money with two-headed eagles and tsars' portraits until the end of the Civil War and the normalization of currency.

Through the analysis of texts, ideas, policies, and practices, the political history of the Russian ruble creates an alternative vision of the emergence, growth, and collapse of the Russian Empire, through the crisis of the revolution, to the end of the Civil War and the beginning of the New Economic Policy (NEP). The rhythm of the story appears quite conventional, punctuated by the accessions and death of rulers, the sequence of wars and reforms, the dynamics of expansion, and the formation and the dissolution of the imperial domain. Yet, by telling this story from the point of view of Russia's national currency, this book refutes many myths and stereotypes while clarifying important phenomena and processes. Among many things, it addresses the problem of autocracy and explains the economic implications of an unlimited political power. It discusses the genealogy of constitutionalism and redefines the meanings of liberalism and conservatism, as well as the notions of economic development and backwardness. It also reconsiders the significance of the Revolutions of 1917 and questions the radicalism of revolutionary changes in the spheres of economy and governance.

———

The book's chronological narrative is arranged in four parts. Part I: "The Age of Assignats" begins with Catherine the Great's main financial reform: the introduction of assignats and the creation of Assignat Banks (Chapter 1, "Assignats: From Paper Substitutes to Paper Money"). The story of the assignats' birth reveals a conundrum that many other countries of eighteenth-century Europe faced at that time, namely, how to reconcile the political ideas of the Enlightenment with the financial exigencies of imperial expansion and growth. For Russia, this problem was even more complex because, unlike its European counterparts, the Russian monarchy had not developed the mechanisms of borrowing from domestic elites, which would have required political bargaining. Thus, paper money, secured by a collateral in copper coins, appeared as the first instance of the state's domestic debt. By introducing assignats in 1769, Catherine II inadvertently subjected the Russian monarchy to scrutiny. From the very moment new money was released into circulation, her courtiers were plunged into a debate about the nature of money and the essence of the sovereign's rights and obligations. Trying to figure out how to frame these relationships in political terms and how to boost Russia's political credibility as a rule-of-law monarchy without affecting its financial means, Russian thinkers advanced a notion that was novel and radical even for pre-revolutionary Europe: they designated the empress's subjects as the owners of the bullion reserve that backed up the value of paper money and described paper assignats as the ruler's debt to the people. However, as the analysis of this financial policy demonstrates, institutional arrangements—most importantly, the status of Assignat Banks—contradicted these lofty ideas. The government continued to print money excessively, and the paper ruble's value vis-à-vis its metal equivalent and other currencies plummeted.

Chapter 2, "Autocracy or Representation?" explains how the Napoleonic Wars sealed the fate of Russia's constitutional and monetary reforms. It traces the development of the political concepts of money in the first quarter of the nineteenth century—the period of Alexander I's reign, when intensive debates about the virtues of constitutional rule over unlimited monarchy unfolded against the background of near-constant warfare, which brought the ruble to the brink of collapse. In the minds of Russian reformers, the two issues—monetary and political—represented two sides of the same coin: a constitutional reform presupposed the introduction of a financial rule of law, while financial stability was unthinkable without limiting the power of monarchy. Mikhail Speransky built this dual principle into his reform plan of 1809 which was introduced in a severely truncated form, without a free Silver Bank or a representative legislature. The conservative opposition to Speransky's reforms, which prevailed on the eve of Napoleon's invasion in 1812, annulled his monetary innovations, including, most important, the silver standard, and proclaimed the ideas of a metal-based ruble incompatible with monarchy.

Chapter 3, "The End of Assignats," focuses on the 1830s through the 1850s, the period known through Alexander Pushkin's poetic works and Nikolai Gogol's stories, which are replete with money riddles and metaphors. Indeed, the monetary system of post–Napoleonic Russia looked as phantasmagoric as Gogol's tales, with several currencies—paper and metallic—circulating in parallel and creating perplexing systems of measuring and counting. In an attempt to fix this anomaly, the government in 1839 initiated a monetary reform that ended the era of assignats and introduced a new kind of paper currency: silver-based credit rubles. Chapter 3 decodes the meaning of the reform by focusing on the philosophical and political views of its main ideo-logue, Egor Kankrin [Georg Cancrin], who translated the political principles of Nicholas I's ideology of Official Nationality into the language of money. Along with Kankrin's project of the reform, the tsar and his functionaries briefly considered a model based on the Bank of Poland and its convertible złoty banknotes. However, the Polish alternative, which evoked Poland's constitutional past and its financial independence, had no chance of being adopted. Moreover, the monetary reform, conducted according to the tsar and Kankrin's plan, opened the way for the financial russification of Poland through a gradual introduction of rubles. Although the reform based the ruble on silver, it conspicuously rejected the principles of state accountability for the issuance of paper money.

Unable to withstand the pressure of the Crimean War, Nicholas I's mon-etary system collapsed even before the tsar's demise, and Russia entered the era of the so-called Great Reforms with an inconvertible ruble. Part 2, "Autocratic Capitalism," opens with Chapter 4, "Paper Money in the Era of the Great Reforms," which asks whether the scale of the monetary reforms of the 1860s matched the radicalism of the changes in society, law, and the rural economy (including the emancipation of peasants). Did the waves of Westernization, liberalization, and decentralization that reformed Russia's public institutions and even its structures of everyday life transform the ruble as well? Although the financial reforms of the 1860s rebooted the credit system, and the government receded from several areas of financial activity, leaving more space for private initiative, the political principles of Russia's monetary economy remained untouched. The key element of the reform, namely, the de-governmentalization of money and the transformation of the

State Bank into an autonomous institution, was left out of the reform plan; at the same time, the projects introducing a representative legislature were rejected in the final stage of their preparation. Still, the ideological and cultural effect of the Great Reforms could not be undone. Russia entered the age of capitalism, and attitudes toward money and wealth changed dramatically. Russians traveled, invested in bonds, and mortgaged lands in private banks, bought shares, and anxiously followed the movement of rates. While financial publicity and popular monetary literacy dramatically increased, Russian society came to see the ruble through different political and social lenses. The depreciation of Russian currency contrasted starkly with people's elevated expectations of economic prosperity.

After an unsuccessful attempt to restore the ruble's convertibility in 1862–63, the government embarked on a program of gradual financial restoration, amassing gold in the State Bank and slowly preparing for another reform. This process ended abruptly in 1877 when Russia entered another war with the Ottoman Empire. Chapter 5, "Ruble's Wars," focuses on a remarkable period in the ruble's life, when, after the end of the Russo-Turkish War, the Ministry of Finance, which pursued financial austerity and the ruble's restoration, was attacked by conservative and nationalistic journalists who enjoyed the patronage of the tsar and succeeded in removing the minister of finance, Nikolai Bunge. In the absence of political parties, newspapers and their editors assumed the role of the leaders of public opinion. Among the various components of state national identity, the nationalists singled out currency as a symbol of Russia's distinctiveness, turning the ruble's inconvertibility into a virtue. Conservative criticism of "Western" financial principles revealed not only growing discontent among nobility and commercial elites with the government's stringent policy but also elites' anxiety over the prospect of joining the monetary realm of Western Europe, which in the 1870s had switched to the gold standard.

Part III, "The Gold Reform," tells the story of the reform's prelude, preparation, and realization. Chapter 6, "Witte's Rollercoaster," foregrounds famed financial reformer Serguei Witte. Witte joined the government under the flag of conservative and nationalist policy, which in financial terms meant inflationism. His plan to increase the volume of paper money was linked to the economic appropriation of Russia's borderlands through the construction of waterways and railroads, the resettlement of peasants, and the development of the agrarian economy. Although Witte, disappointed with the financial efficiency of inflationism, became an ardent supporter of the gold standard in 1895, he did not abandon his political stances. The gold reform of 1897 pursued the same objectives as those advocated by Witte's earlier conservative mentors, such as the concentration of the government's power over the production of money. As Witte reasoned, the gold ruble represented a better tool than a paper ruble to accomplish the objective of imperial expansion.

Chapter 7, "The Autocratic Standard," offers a radical reconsideration of the monetary reform of 1895–97 and emphasizes the centrality of political mechanisms in determining the financial results of monetary innovations. The gold reform manifested a new iteration of financial nationalism that was fully compatible with both the orientation toward the West and the creation of favorable conditions for foreign investments. To explain the meaning of the gold standard in Russia, the chapter analyzes the mechanisms of the country's transition to gold, including Witte's efforts to tame newspapers, negotiate with recalcitrant journalists, control public debates, and impose the use of gold coins in commerce. Witte's legislative proposals show that, although his version of the gold standard looked similar to other models introduced in Europe and elsewhere, the political ramifications of the new monetary regime gave it a completely different meaning. Established by a royal decree in violation of all legislative procedures (and dubbed a "monetary coup d'état"), the gold reform projected the autocratic principles onto finances. The transition to gold secured the ruble's rate against constant fluctuations and increased the influx of foreign capital. However, in the absence of institutional and political guarantees, such as political representation and the State Bank's independence from the government, the ruble's standing and Russia's credibility came to depend on the size of the gold reserve. The reform therefore created new anxieties and threats. Chapter 8, "Practicing the Gold Standard," begins by analyzing the practical and logistical application of the reform—the introduction of gold coins and the elimination of paper cash of small denominations. As a result of the reform, the social pyramid of the monetary system turned upside down: wealthy people were expected to use paper banknotes, while simple folk had to operate with silver and gold coins. Predictably, there was a great deal of discontent, especially in the agrarian sector. The new system's vulnerability became even more apparent when Russia attempted to introduce the gold ruble into the Eastern "realm of silver," that is, Bukhara and Manchuria, where the population stubbornly continued to value the ruble by its reputation and purchasing power, not according to its gold "content."

The ruble's main weakness, paradoxically, was rooted in Russia's fixation on gold. Unlike other countries that suspended convertibility at times of crisis, Russia could not afford to give up the standard without jeopardizing its ability to borrow money abroad and pay for its obligations. Chapter 9, "The

Gold Syndrome," opening Part IV, "Ruble, Wars, and Revolutions," begins by analyzing how the fixation with the size of the gold reserve affected Russia's financial policy during the crisis of the Russo-Japanese War and the revolution of 1905. In 1905, Russia switched to constitutional rule, but the representative State Duma did not receive any prerogatives in the monetary sphere, and the ruble's fate remained fully under the government's control. This feature of Russia's political order backfired in 1914, when Russia entered the First World War. Chapter 10, "War and the End of the Gold Ruble," examines the political constituents of Russia's financial crisis during the First World War, such as the government's conflicts with the State Duma over the gold reserve, and the problems of mobilizing the population under the banner of financial patriotism. From an economic viewpoint, the Russian imperial government followed the standard script for managing war finance. Explaining why the Russian ruble suffered from the war more than the currency of any other belligerent countries requires factoring in politics alongside purely economic reasons. The issue of the ruble became even more politicized after the February Revolution of 1917, which brought down the tsarist government. The ruble became a trophy of a class war in which various actors—liberals and socialists, industrialists and bankers, workers and peasants—blamed each other for the ruble's demise.

Chapter 11, "A Revolution That Did Not Happen," tells this paradoxical story and describes the Bolsheviks' failed attempt to create a new socialist currency. War communism, a bewildering experiment in the eradication of money, resulted in its de-governmentalization. The state lost the monopoly on the production of money, but money hardly went away. The New Economic Policy (NEP) was therefore an attempt to regain control over the currency and to reconstruct the pre-1914 monetary order. The reform of 1921–24 bore many traces of Witte's gold standard—for example, the centrality of the state and the obsession with the size of the gold reserve.

The explanatory power of a political biography of currency is in changing the angle of analysis and shifting focus from the well-known political events and the conventional notions of politics to the hidden mechanisms of political reforms and processes. With the ruble as its vantage point, the book explains substantial and subtle causes of great historical events and processes. The ruble's story zooms in on the everyday financial politics of businessmen, politicians, and administrators, and zooms out to a wide view of economic structures and political institutions. It explains how and why certain political conditions, models of governance, and political participation generated similar models of financial policy and organization. Following the literary works of Russian writers who chose to tell their stories in the voice of a ruble bill or a coin, the ruble's story offers a sweeping historical picture drawn in subtle brush strokes and with attention to detail. Like other political biographies, the biography of the ruble recounts the extraordinary turns in its life and fate and, at the same time, reveals the persistence of common mechanisms and patterns.

PART I

The Age of Assignats

I

Assignats

FROM PAPER SUBSTITUTES TO PAPER MONEY

Love and Profit

Russia's first paper money, issued in early 1769, looked plain and unimpressive. In the center of the assignats, which were printed on yellowish A8-size sheets of paper with wide margins, there was a short text indicating the assignat's value in rubles and promising the exchange of these paper notes for "circulating coins." Above the text hung two stamped ovals with almost indiscernible images: one was a rock in the middle of a storm-tossed sea, another an eagle astride a pile of objects apparently symbolizing commerce.[1] Perhaps the most remarkable feature of the assignats' design was a grammatically weird phrase watermarked on the top and bottom of the assignat sheets: "Love for the Fatherland works for the benefit of thereof."[2] Its first part—"Love for the Fatherland"—sounded very familiar. A synonym of civic virtue, it represented the key expression in the political vocabulary of Catherine II's Russia. This phrase was imprinted on the coronation medal hastily made in September 1762 to celebrate the empress's accession to the throne after the coup that had cost her husband's life. "Love" justified the very fact of the unlawful seizure of power. References to "love" appeared in Catherine's numerous decrees and instructions, intended to stir patriotic feelings in the souls of the "sons of the Fatherland" and to explain and justify new dues and obligations. At the same time, Catherine II commonly appeared as a "mother" of the "fatherland" (*mater' otechestva*). In the political rhetoric of Catherine's reign, metaphorical kinship compensated for the lack of the empress's blood ties to the Romanov dynasty. Furthermore, in December 1768, when Catherine announced the production of assignats, Russia was already at war with the

Ottoman Empire; hostilities had been declared on November 18, 1768, but the military campaign only began in January 1769. The enigmatic words "unharmed" (*nevredima*) and "[it] guards and protects" (*pokoit i oboroniaet*) in the stamped ovals above the rock and the eagle conveyed the patriotic symbolism of Russia's first paper money.

The second element of the formula about love—"works for [the Fatherland's] benefit"—tied the patriotism of the empress's subjects to the more pragmatic reasons of profit and common good. Indeed, even if the assignats were meant to play the role of patriotic propaganda leaflets, their financial constituent remained central. The austere design of assignats, which, unlike Catherine II's ornate coins or sumptuous nineteenth-century credit rubles, likened them to private promissory notes (*veksel*), as if the Fatherland were demanding a loan from its offspring. But if this was a bill of credit, then who impersonated the Fatherland, the potential benefactor of people's love and sacrifices? Watermarked inscriptions on the left and right sides of the assignat referred to the "State Treasury"; the coats of arms of the four tsardoms that had formed the Russian Empire (Moscow, Kazan, Siberia, and Astrakhan') in the assignats' corners represented the monarchy. For a loan document, this designation of a debtor was quite unclear. In eighteenth-century-Russian vocabulary, the State Treasury referred to the entirety of the state and the sovereign's financial wealth, not a particular institution. In fact, as the Manifesto on the release of assignats affirmed, the assignats were issued on behalf of two Banks (one in Moscow, another in St. Petersburg) that were established specifically for the purpose of administering the circulation and exchange of paper money. The handwritten signatures of two senators, the Bank's director, and a board member of the Bank that sealed the promise to exchange assignat for coins suggested a double liability of the "treasury" and the Banks. In short, the status of assignats was somewhat unclear, and their design betrayed this uncertainty. What was an assignat? A certificate of the state's debt or a demand for new dues from the populace? A proxy for metal coins or a new kind of credit paper for the needs of commerce? A mandate for participation in financial governance or a token of allegiance to the throne?

In 1769 almost no one could answer these questions with certainty. Attempts to define the nature and role of paper money in Russian finances and governance inadvertently questioned the consistency of the commonly accepted but legally undefined categories of the Russian political system (such as "treasury," "people," and "state") and necessitated the reconceptualization of the government's and the monarch's relation to its subjects. This modest and visually unappealing sheet of paper played, perhaps, a bigger role in the development of political discourse in Catherine's Russia than any pamphlets, memos, or projects that circulated in the Russian court. The paradox of the assignats was hidden in the obscurity of their meaning: they were at once an invitation for the empress's subjects to participate actively in economic and political life and also a declaration of unlimited autocracy.

Autocracy and Money

Launching the issuance of paper notes was a risky enterprise. In the 1760s, paper money was still a novelty in Europe, and the first experiments did not go well. The political risks of issuing paper notes were even more serious than the financial ones. In medieval and early modern Russia, as elsewhere in Europe, money was seen as a token of legitimacy, a material symbol of the sublime power, similar to the "royal marks" that, according to popular belief, every true sovereign bore on her or his body. Authenticity appeared as the main quality of both money and power, hence the parallel between forgery and royal imposture that was ubiquitous in political rhetoric during this period of intense political struggle.[3] The failure of this financial endeavor could, therefore, undermine Catherine's precarious position on the throne and question the authenticity of her claims of power.

Authenticity in relation to money could mean different things: first, a legitimate origin (i.e., the person minting the coins has a legitimate power to do so) and, second, the sameness of the value (the material and cost of the coins) and their declared nominal worth. The latter quality could be suspended if trust or authority compensated for the lack of material genuineness. However, in early modern Russia, manipulations of the material qualities of money had direct implications for the prestige of authority, while the full weight of coins indicated the pureness and integrity of monarchal power. The most explicit manifestation of this attitude was the popular response to the monetary reform of Tsar Alexei Mikhailovich (1645–76). Reformers planned to model the Russian monetary system on Western European examples, which legitimized the circulation of "imaginary" money whose value was determined by the sovereign. The reform introduced new coins of various denominations, including copper coins in the nominal value of silver money.[4] The substitution of copper for silver in domestic trade, which allowed the government to procure significant sums for its military campaigns in the West, produced enormous discontent and resulted in the so-called Copper Riot of 1662. The government had to roll back the reform and return to the original standard of coinage. Forty years later, Peter the Great reenacted the ideas of his father, introducing

Western standards of coinage for high-denomination money (a silver ruble equal to a thaler and a gold chervonets the equivalent of a ducat) along with copper kopecks. Minting coins of large denomination and bigger size did not simply offer a convenient new medium for trade but also allowed imprinting the state emblem and other signs of royal authority on both the face and the reverse side of the coins. At the same time, manipulations of the weight and matter of coins served a fiscal purpose: the nominal value of copper coins minted from one *pood* (16 kg) of copper grew from 12 rubles 80 kopecks to 40 rubles.[5] The state, therefore, deliberately exploited its minting privilege to fund the Northern War (1700–21). In stark contrast to the early modern European governments that relied heavily on credit at home and abroad, the Russian state did not use these mechanisms until the mid-eighteenth century. That means that, in addition to taxes and various kinds of dues levied on the population, coinage offered the single most effective, though politically precarious, way to procure extra revenues.

When war broke out, cannons (except those that commemorated past victories) were melted into coins, a reminder that money was the state's main weapon.[6] Yet Peter the Great's reform, including the successful introduction of copper kopecks, signified an important rupture between the old understandings of authenticity and new ideas of value; the latter came to reflect the relationship between the state and society rather than the materiality of coins. Peter I expressed interest in John Law's ideas of enhancing economic development through the multiplication of money and the expansion of colonial trade, and in 1721, that is, after the crash of Law's colonial company and the Banque Royale in France, he invited the Scottish economist and entrepreneur to Russia. The tsar promised to grant him a noble title and the order of St. Andrew, 200 serfs and 100 personal guards, and total freedom in the realization of the most daring projects, such as the colonization of the Caspian seashore and the development of cities and maritime trade. Law did not come. However, he had several admirers in Russia, including prince Ivan Shcherbatov, who translated Law's treatise *Money and Trade Considered: With a Proposal for Supplying the Nation with Money* (1705) and drafted a plan to found a joint-stock bank with the right of issuing paper money.[7]

Radical changes in Russia's monetary system inevitably caused resentment. As with all of Peter's reforms, which in people's religious imagination were magnified into the upheavals of the moral and spiritual principles of life, changes in money standards evoked deep discontent. Coins bore Peter's "sacred" image and an inscription resembling icons, and this religious connotation enhanced the rhetoric of purity and honor that appeared most prominently in *The Book on Poverty and Wealth (1724)* by Ivan Pososhkov, Russia's first self-trained economist and master of coinage. A "Moscovite progressivist," as historian Nikolai Pavlov-Sil'vanskii called him, and a moderate critic of Peter the Great's Europeanization of coinage, Pososhkov tried to persuade the tsar to return to the ideals of the "old purity" of silver and gold so that Russian money could "excel all foreign coinage and earn the praise of all both in the quality of the workmanship and in the fineness of the silver." He likened the fineness of precious metals to the purity of the Christian faith. At the same time, Pososhkov agreed that the nominal value of copper coins was to be defined by the sovereign, whom his subjects revered "as they [revered] God," and it should not depend on the coins' material value: "On whatever thing we see His Majesty's superscription, that thing we treat with all honor and respect." Pososhkov advocated the debasement of copper coins as the source of the tsar's revenue inasmuch as they lacked the appearance of silver: "Their face value shall not be, in the foreign manner, that of the actual value of the copper, but as His Majesty shall decide."[8] Pososhkov's system suggested that the tsar's power rested on the preservation of the purity and authenticity of silver money, with full authority to determine the value of copper change.

Thus, in the early eighteenth century, money came to be seen both as a projection of sovereign power and a fiscal tool allowing the state to procure resources when taxes and other revenues did not suffice. Periodic expansions and contractions of copper mass, which were accompanied each time by the melting and reminting of coins, worked as a peculiar mechanism of state borrowing. In this sense, copper coins, which the economists of the eighteenth and nineteenth centuries often considered "monetary marks" not deserving to be called "money," paved the way for the introduction of assignats.[9] Both served and appeared as substitutes for the real silver currency. When Catherine the Great introduced paper assignats, the new paper money was perceived as representing copper coins, which, in turn, represented silver.[10]

The semantic and financial evolution of paper assignats somewhat followed the same trajectory, from a direct substitution of one matter by another to the indirect representation of value, a model that made room for the use of credit. Initially, assignats simply stood for copper coins, which they literally replaced. The Manifesto of December 29, 1768, announced the introduction of assignats and justified the reform by citing the inconvenience of using heavy copper coins and transporting them across the country (1,000 rubles in copper coins weighed around 2,250 pounds);[11] it also referred to the examples of foreign banks issuing "printed notes of obligation" for public circulation.[12]

The law contained Catherine's vow—on behalf of herself and her heirs—that the assignats would always remain convertible into specie. Everyone could receive, in exchange for the paper bills issued by two newly created Assignat Banks in St. Petersburg and Moscow, a corresponding number of coins in copper (and very briefly, until 1770, also silver). The silver ruble remained the main unit of value; copper coins played the role of small change; and paper assignats represented a convenient substitute for both.

When the initial 1 million-ruble assignats were printed, the exact amount of metal money was put into storage in the Assignat banks as collateral. The Empress's Manifesto presented the reform as a radical innovation but one that was not intended to affect or invoke royal authority. Copper coins stored in canvas bags in the basements of the Assignat banks sufficed to ensure popular trust in the assignats; the substance of currency changed but not its essence. The government accepted assignats for all tax and state payments, which was also supposed to ensure popular trust. Therefore, initially, the role of paper money was quite modest. Assignats—light and easy to produce—facilitated the transfer of funds between state agencies across provinces and simplified the collection of taxes that were usually paid in copper coins and carried across the country to the capitals. In other words, the enormous (and

FIGURE 1.1 Assignat Bank in St. Petersburg. Arch. Giacomo Quarenghi (1783–1790). From *Gosudarstvennyi bank: kratkiii ocherk deiatel'nosti za 1860– 1910 gody*. St. Petersburg, 1910.

growing) size of the empire and the centralization of revenue collection in the eighteenth century made it almost necessary to create a lighter and easier medium of payment. Assignats also made it easier for noblemen, who generally spent their time and money in cities, to receive revenues from their serf estates in the provinces. However, since the issuance of assignats locked up an equivalent amount of coins in the reserve, the new paper money could not provide extra resources. The status of assignats was unclear. They appeared as promissory notes but, unlike other credit obligations, were fully backed up by metal money. Both the assignats and the metal coins they represented originated from the state that functioned simultaneously as creditor and borrower. The transformation of assignats from paper substitutes into credit money required at least some sort of an institutional separation between these two roles.

This transformation began to occur, albeit piecemeal, in practice when local and provincial government offices started requesting assignats in amounts exceeding the value of copper coins collected in state revenues, that is, taxes. Since transferring coins to the Assignat Banks was difficult and inconvenient, and the Banks did not have enough space to store copper, offices were allowed to keep coins in local storage as collateral for paper money received from the Assignat Banks.[13] In January 1771, the empress's decree prohibited offices from claiming assignats at the deposit of expected revenues that they had not yet collected. Nevertheless, this practice persisted, and in 1772, the amount of assignats requested by government offices was twice the value of copper that they possessed (in other words, they borrowed the money against future taxes). The Russo-Turkish War and a plague epidemic in the early 1770s made the transportation of revenues collected in copper coins even more difficult. As the Bank's director, Count Andrei Shuvalov, noted, "There hardly was a single government agency that did not owe great sums to the assignat banks."[14] Although assignats helped the government to overcome the crisis, the practice of procuring easy cash persisted, producing, as an unsigned memo from 1772 suggested, a wrong pattern: "Against the mental [conceived] value of paper notes circulating in the public, the banks count imaginary monetary capitals." The initial connection between the copper backup reserve and paper representatives, the signified and the signifier, was thus severed. The quantity of assignats in popular circulation began to increase disproportionally, "discrediting" the status of paper money and undermining the "popular trust" built into the foundation of the Assignat Banks.[15]

The Assignat Banks kept an exact count of the paper assignats issued to the government (its separate agencies) and to the so-called Cabinet responsible for managing the empress's personal spending against the value of the copper coins at the disposal of these institutions. The Banks' balance sheets presented assignats as the government's debt to the Banks. Later, after the creation of a centralized network of provincial treasuries, the debts of various agencies were consolidated as the State Treasury's debt to the Assignat Bank. The idea of paper money serving as debt may appear illusionary, but it nevertheless was the first manifestation of a new attitude to money as a mechanism of credit. It was not a coincidence that in 1769, the year following the introduction of assignats, Russia concluded its first foreign loan, with Dutch bankers De Smeth. A country with no "credit history," Russia had offered its income from customs on the Western border as collateral for a loan.[16] The mechanisms of private credit, the instrument of mortgage and collateral that had developed in Russia's economy in the seventeenth and early eighteenth centuries, were finally penetrating the sphere of public finance. The Russian Empire was joining the ranks of European countries that lived from international and domestic borrowing, but the institutional arrangements of public credit were not quite the same in Russia as elsewhere.

The idea of debt for assignats rhetorically assumed the existence of two autonomous entities: creditor and debtor. The notes of the Bank of England, for instance, represented the crown's obligations to private creditors incorporated into a Company of the Bank of England—a private institution run on private funds. The Swedish Riksbank, founded in 1688, stood under the exclusive control of the legislature of Sweden, the Riksdag. Therefore, monetary policy and the issuance of paper money reflected political arrangements between the crown and the parliament, two distinct political entities. Catherine II was highly familiar with the principle of the separation of powers in finance: her famous "Instruction to the Legislative Commission" (1767) praised independent banks "which, by their credit, having established new signs of value, have increased also the circulation in these states."[17] In accordance with the leading concepts and practices of the day, the empress instructed that "in order that in monarchical governments such establishments may be securely relied on, these Banks should be . . . independent of all magistracies, . . . so that all people may have the utmost confidence and assurance that the sovereign will never offer to meddle with the money, nor injure the credit of such establishments." Did the empress follow this principle in organizing the Assignat Banks? In some sense, yes. According to their statute, the Banks were "not dependent on any government [institution]," were governed by a board "under my Own [i.e., the empress's] supervision," and reported "about [their] actions to no one but Myself."[18] Thus, the banks were separate from the administration but stood under the empress's supreme command. This meaning of "independence" fully fit Catherine's interpretation of constitutional and administrative principles. In a similar vein, she interpreted the separation of powers as a separation of administrative functions under the umbrella of her indivisible monarchical authority. The culture of double standards that characterized the Russian Enlightenment allowed for this particular coexistence of ideas and practices standing in sharp contradiction with each other.

Even a small shift in the understanding of the nature of money and credit, that is, the interpretation of assignats as state obligations, had important political consequences. In 1770, Catherine's courtiers discussed a suggestion coming from the Bank's director Andrei Shuvalov, who thought the Assignat Banks could "vouch" for Russia's state foreign loans, that is, offer their bullion reserve as material collateral. The debate regarding the use of the banks' guarantees and resources to secure Russia's credit abroad reflected two competing views concerning state obligations. Ivan Chernyshev, one of Catherine's closest advisers, declared that state loans were based on the empress's personal vows, therefore "using the bank's warranty [for state loans] was inappropriate for the persona of Her Imperial Majesty, because the bank is not [to pledge on behalf of] Her Majesty who had established it, rather Her Majesty [is to pledge] on behalf of the bank, should it need to borrow money." Catherine disagreed: she perceived Russia's foreign loans as state obligations rather than her personal debts, and she expressed the "desire" that "people trust not the persona of the ruler, but the state itself," therefore confirming Peter the Great's principle of separating the state from the personality of the monarch.[19] Shuvalov's proposal did not come to fruition at this point, but the discussion of it highlighted the growing divergences in thinking about money that would become clearer in subsequent debates. At the heart of this debate was a definition of royal authority, its attitude to society, and the role of money and banks in balancing the interests of both.

In Catherine's time, the question of the nature and limits of royal financial authority and credibility stood at the center of financial debates in Europe, especially after the crash of John Law's infamous financial "System" in France.[20] The collapse of John Law's financial pyramid delivered a crushing blow to the financial credibility of the French monarchy; it also raised the question of what should define the nominal value of money—its material worth or the ruler's word.[21] Although at the beginning of his enterprise, Law claimed that the credit of his paper notes rested solely on "the assurance to be paid," he ended up staking the stability of his system on the sovereign will, and when it started falling apart, he relied on state enforcement of the value of already inconvertible banknotes. Despite this misfortune, the French monarchy continued to live off loans, strengthening its dependence on local elites and inadvertently fostering ideas of political participation that gradually undermined the foundation of the monarchy.[22] Therefore, historians consider the development of public credit in pre-revolutionary France as a precipitating factor in political regime change. Scholars also portray the spectacular success of the British system of public credit as an outcome of the Glorious Revolution and the growth of representative institutions. The Parliament's backing of public debt allowed the state to borrow at a much lower interest rate, therefore contributing to the emergence of Britain's fiscal-military state.[23] But even in the states where representative institutions were less powerful than the British parliament, they still came to play a central role in building financial apparatuses and public credit. For example, in Sweden, the Riksdag essentially controlled the Bank and its issuing policy, the principles of which were often defined in competition between various political parties.[24]

No representative institutions of that sort existed in eighteenth-century Russia. Does this mean that the concept of state debt and public credit was devoid of any political connotation? Quite surprisingly, in the absence of an alternative center of political power, Catherine's financiers resorted to political concepts that were much more expansive and even potentially subversive. For example, a suggested *Reglament* (Charter) to the Assignat Banks presumably drafted in the late 1770s to early 1780s, introduced the notion of "the State all-people's treasury" in relation to the metal coin reserve of the Assignat Banks. As the *Reglament* explained, this "all-people's treasury," presumably distinct from the regular treasury of the state, was so named because "each of Our subjects carrying state assignats has a share in the capital of these banks, along with Our state offices . . . when they have the same state assignats." Encroachment upon the integrity of the people's treasury would be considered an assault not only on the ruler's interest but also "the property and the wellbeing" of all the empress's subjects.[25]

The idea expressed in this statement—that an assignat is a certificate for a share of national wealth—sounds extremely radical for pre-1789 European political thought. That someone thought about people's participation in the national wealth may appear accidental and almost improbable in the context of monarchal Russia, and yet there could be no other interpretation of the statements expressed in this document that represented, perhaps, the first manifestation of the idea of popular sovereignty, albeit in financial terms. From the late eighteenth century until the revolution of 1917, Russian political thinkers and economists repeatedly turned to the concept of paper money as a mandate for political participation in the common imperial household. In the absence of elected legislative institutions, this idea received more weight in Russia than in the West, although its roots can probably be found in European political philosophy. Memos and drafts that originated from the office of the procurator general Alexander Viazemskii, Catherine's key financial adviser, are replete with references to European books, concepts, terms, and institutions. The thinking of Andrei Shuvalov, the director of the Assignat Banks, also seems to have been very much influenced by French sources. A son of a famous financial *projecteur* of the Elizabethan era, count Andrei, a poet and socialite, spent several years in France in the early 1760s, where he befriended Voltaire. Catherine's enlightened bureaucrats were fully immersed into the intellectual life of Europe and the European debates on credit and finance.

"The idea of attaining people's trust under autocratic rule . . . does not have examples in history, and this idea belonged to no one other than Her Majesty," wrote Shuvalov in 1786, reflecting on the history of assignats. According to Shuvalov, back in 1768, nobody understood the role of banks, "and in general, it was considered a futile enterprise. . . . At first, people did not want to believe that paper money could successfully exist in Russia, and then they considered [the Bank] as a free-of-charge trunk for copper money."[26] This statement, referring to the widespread doubts in the compatibility of autocracy and a stable paper-based monetary system, was meant to emphasize the peculiarity of Russia's enlightened monarchy. The idea that a political regime defines monetary order apparently came from Montesquieu's *L'Esprit des Lois (1751)*. The philosopher declared that in despotic countries, the representative link between things and money does not exist, and therefore, money cannot play its role properly.[27] Montesquieu also specifically named Russia as an example of a despotic country that cannot live under the normal regime of exchange, pointing out that its political laws were incompatible with commerce.[28] Catherine II and her enlightened courtiers tried to wash away the stigma of despotism; therefore, their efforts were directed not only at fixing the currency problems but also at improving the political image of the Russian financial system. It is also possible that they wanted to distance themselves from the image of the prodigal ruler associated with the French monarchy and severely criticized by the economists of the Enlightenment.

Montesquieu, writing about the relationships between government and credit institutions, described three kinds of paper bills: "a circulating paper which represents money," a bill that represents a company's current or future profit, and "a paper which represents a debt." While the first two kinds of paper money were "advantageous for the state," the third category "can never be so" "for only a rich state could sustain such a paper". Which of the three categories of paper notes did Russian assignats belong to? Initially, assignats circulated as the representatives of money; even while increasing the emission of paper notes, the government maintained a 1:1 balance between coins and assignats. In 1774, the empress passed the law declaring that the amount of paper issued was not to exceed 20 million rubles, but even this modicum of self-restraint did not last long. People continued to trust assignats that the government accepted in tax payment, and the exchange for coins remained uninterrupted for several years. However, the bullion reserve no longer matched the volume of paper money, and on the market, the assignats could be redeemed with a discount.[29] Thus, the initial idea of using assignats as a substitute for copper coins became obsolete. Did assignats belong to the second category of "papers," those that, like the notes of the Bank of England, stood for an existing or expected commercial profit? No, since the Assignat Banks that issued and exchanged assignats were not, strictly speaking, credit institutions connected to commerce and production. Therefore, assignats represented "state debt." To transform the nature of money, the Russian government had to reconsider the organization of the Assignat Banks and their relation to the state.

In 1783, Shuvalov received the empress's approval to prepare a reform of Russian finance "following the example of the great European states that not as much by coins, but mostly by public credit have increased their wealth."[30] The first step toward organizing the credit system and maintaining people's trust in the Bank consisted of normalizing the Bank's relations with the State Treasury and establishing a plan for the repayment of the state's debt for assignats, that is, the amount released above the proportion fixed in the law. Another goal of Shuvalov's plan was to link banks to commerce and trade, introduce "bank obligations," and invite merchants and entrepreneurs to open bank accounts to facilitate commercial transactions and the transfer of funds.[31] An important element of this plan was the institutionalization of "argent de Banque" (Shuvalov used French financial terminology) that "will stand above the assignats." [32]

In 1786, Shuvalov, with the help of a few other of Catherine's high officials, put together these thoughts to propose a large-scale bank reorganization.[33] Remarkably, unlike Shuvalov's preliminary memos that aimed to bring the bank closer to commerce and industry, this project placed strong emphasis on helping the government pay its assignat debt. By 1786, the debts of the treasury and the Cabinet combined had risen to 30 million rubles, plus 10 million rubles of anticipated expenses and needs. This sum exceeded the state's annual revenues that the report considered a virtual security for treasury debts.[34] Paying back the entire sum, even in installments, would be too hard for the treasury and would necessitate the introduction of new taxes. Defaulting on this debt was impossible, because it would have ruined the government's reputation and people's trust in the banks. Therefore, the report offered an alternative combination: the Assignat Bank would lend 22 million rubles to nobility, via a newly established State Loan Bank, and 11 million rubles to merchants or cities, who would pay it back in twenty or twenty-two years with interest. Money earned on these loans would be used to redeem about half of the treasury's "assignat" debt to the Bank, which would gradually withdraw and destroy excessive assignats. The government would still be liable for the remaining debt, which it would pay back in installments, also with interest.

The main problem with this scheme was that it required yet another increase in the amount of issued assignats. In 1786, the volume of assignats in circulation reached 46 million rubles, which was already twice the limit established by law in 1774. Instead of simply legitimizing the existing issue, Shuvalov and his coauthors suggested raising the cap to 100 million rubles, of which about a third was intended for the loans to nobility and cities. Interestingly, the proposal did not mention how the amount of paper money should correspond to the bank's bullion reserve. It said, however, that the Assignat Banks, merged and renamed the State Assignat Bank, should make an effort to acquire gold and silver, instead of copper, to align its practice with European norms.

Thus, this reform project consists of a mixture of various, even somewhat contradictory, ideas. The idea of increasing the amount of *numeraire*, that is, paper money in circulation, as a way of stimulating trade and production betrayed the influence of mercantilism. Shuvalov and company were convinced that the shortage of money promoted usury, whereas pouring *numeraire* into circulation would do no harm. They wanted both to turn the Bank into something bigger than an exchange office and to change the nature of assignats from the simple substitutes of coins into banknotes linked to commerce and trade. However, if the financial assets of European banks consisted of promissory notes related to commercial transactions, Russian banks provided credit to the serf-owning nobility, who mostly splurged money on consumption rather than production. The reform, therefore, substituted a significant part of the bullion reserve in copper coins with the immovable property of noblemen, that is, the serf peasants.[35] As for the remaining, unbacked share of assignats, its value was meant to rest on an intangible asset—the empress's pledge and honor. The reform project therefore revealed a significant change in the political philosophy of monetary policy, namely, the reconsideration of the nature of monarchal obligations and the means of securing the value of currency. The value of paper money that used to be fully backed up by copper would instead hinge on three assets—the dwindling bullion reserve, the souls of serf peasants mortgaged in banks, and the empress's word and honor.

Remarkably, Alexander Viazemskii, a frugal general procurator and the only one of Catherine's advisers who spoke against the suggested reform, warned the empress that the increase in the amount of issued assignats would break the "sanctity" of her promise and distort the essence of the monetary system. Even more important, Viazemskii emphasized that the issue was illegal, because money stored in the Assignat banks belonged to the entirety of the "state" and not only the "treasury." This idea looks familiar—it appeared in the project of the *Reglament* for Assignat Banks that designated the exchange fund as the "people's treasury," in contrast to the government's treasury. In Viazemskii's interpretation, the "state" encompassed both society and the government (as opposed to the treasury alone). To support this opinion, Viazemskii referred to the Manifesto of 1768 that had justified the introduction of assignats by the needs of state credit "and the good of each and every one of the monarch's subjects." In contrast to this idea of the ruble as a common good, the project of the new monetary law favored only the needs of the government treasury and nobility; it indulged luxury and undermined "public trust" for the sake of narrow and minute interests.[36] According to Viazemskii, the project perverted the original idea of assignats and could cause damage not only to the monetary system but also to the social and political foundations of the monarchy.

The first debate about the nature of money between Shuvalov and his coauthors, on the one side, and Viazemskii, on the other, shows the contours of future controversies between the two camps—those who saw no danger in the expansion of monetary mass beyond a limit secured by the bullion reserve and their opponents, who argued for the contraction of paper issue. Remarkably, Shuvalov and Viazemskii shared the Enlightenment spirit of cosmopolitanism and reform, and both seemed to agree on the main point regarding the responsibility of the government and the crown to pay back its debt. As Shuvalov wrote to Catherine in 1789, the redemption of assignat debts was essential "for the dignity of the state in front of your [i.e., empress's] people and all of Europe."[37] Therefore, in the sphere of political philosophy, their disagreements were subtler than in matters of economy. The two men diverged in the interpretation of the ruler's power to change the nature of national currency. In this sense, their debate echoed European discussions of the mid-eighteenth century that also centered on the role of public authorities and economic "circumstances," that is, markets, in defining the value of money. The Enlightenment writers denied rulers the capacity to establish money's value—a claim suggesting that the state had limited power over economic forces.[38] Montesquieu, among others, insisted on the principle that money's worth (he certainly meant the coins) reflected its material value rather than the conditional, imaginary value imposed on it by the ruler. Maintaining the bullion reserve in an amount corresponding to the value of paper money was an extension of the same principle. This practice may appear economically useless and even absurd (why should the bank keep this enormous mass of copper?). However, in the eighteenth century, anchoring money's value by the solid matter of bullion reserve, in contrast to grounding it on the sovereign's promises, was seen as the most efficient way of checking the absolute ruler's power to issue money. In the absence of political guarantees, the bullion reserve played the key role of an anchor and a restraint on arbitrariness.

The second issue that divided Viazemskii's and Shuvalov's positions concerned the state and the crown's attitude to nobility. Viazemskii's worries about the consequences of tying the fiscal interests of treasury and nobility at the cost of inflating the national currency turned out to be prophetic. The loan to nobility, which was supposed to help the treasury redeem its debts in twenty years, evolved into a long-term financial dependence between the government and the landowning estate. Since serf owners mortgaged their estates at the State Loan Bank, which was subsidized by the State Assignat Bank, the ruble's fate came to be strongly associated with the state's policy of crediting landowning nobility. One author, writing in the 1880s, expressed the common opinion that "assignats had been released at the security of . . . noble estates."[39] Even after the extinction of assignats, the liquidation of the State Loan Bank and the emancipation of peasants, the idea of paper money embodying the connection between nobility and the crown continued to circulate and culminated in the creation of the Noble Land Bank in 1885, almost a century after the reform of 1786. The consequences of the initial arrangement went beyond rhetoric and ideology. State banks enjoyed a monopoly on the market of credit, offering nobility, along with the loans at the security of estates, an opportunity to deposit money at high interest. Constantly in debt, the state treasury actively borrowed money deposited by nobles at these institutions. As a result, nobles and the state were locked in a vicious circle of financial obligations that could be maintained only as long as the state secured its monopoly on the production of paper money and preserved serfdom.

In 1786, Viazemskii could not predict how the system of state-noble financial relations would evolve in the decades to come, and his objections
were mostly grounded in arguments of ethics and morality. He was fighting a
losing battle: the bank "reform" sanctioned a de facto existing policy of inflation employed to fund the development of the serf economy as well as Russia's
increasing imperialist ambitions. In 1785, Catherine's Charter to the Nobility
reconfirmed her policy of privileging the ruling estate, and Shuvalov's plan of
monetary reform simply offered financial grounds for the nobles' privileges
secured by the Charter. It is no coincidence that the authors of the 1786 reform plan were lavishly rewarded for their work, with one receiving several
serf villages in Ukraine.[40] The reform also signified an important shift in the
interpretation of monarchal duties and the ideology of money. The rhetoric
of the law promulgated on June 28, 1786, the day of the twenty-fourth anniversary of the coup d'état that brought Catherine to the throne, reflected
this change. The empress swore by "the autocratic authority given by God
and by the sanctity of the monarchal word for ourselves and for the heirs of
the Russian Imperial Throne" not to exceed the limit of 100 million rubles
assignat released in circulation.[41] Catherine's Manifesto enacted the practice of pledging the credibility of state paper money, and this idea of using
the sovereign's honor and prestige as a security was developed in subsequent
monetary reforms.

The emphasis on the personal prestige of the ruler had much to do with
the success of Catherine's financial, social, and administrative reforms and
with Russia's rising geopolitical status, which were all associated in European
public opinion with the name of the enlightened empress. The reform stressed
that few monarchical regimes had been able to support the credibility of
assignats, and the key to Russia's success had been Catherine's firm adherence
to the principles of financial policy. However, this model of monetary issue
encapsulated the paradox of absolutist rule: the personalization of responsibility subjected monarchal power to an ever-present danger of reputational
losses incurred by the fall in value of paper currency. Besides, in the monarchical "scenarios of power," replete with the rituals of oath-taking, it was
usually the sovereign's subjects who took the oath, not vice versa. Although
Catherine's pledge was not sealed by religious ceremonies, the mere fact that
she rhetorically vouched for the value of assignats created a source of concern and anxiety. All subsequent emissions of assignats were declared by the
monarch's special supreme order upon the proposal of the general-governor

(and later, the minister of finance).[42] The emphasis on trust and honor was also manifested in the ritualization of mundane procedures, such as the public burning on the square in front of the Senate building, of old assignats exempted from circulation.

"Why Does the Ruble Fall?"

Continued emissions of assignats and the decrease of their rate on the market spread anxiety and created a deficit of coins. In 1789, between 500 and 1,000 people came every day to the State Assignat Bank in St. Petersburg to exchange assignats for coins, and the bank, despite longer working hours, could not satisfy the demand.[43] To maintain exchange operations, the bank needed to have at its disposal 6–8 million rubles in coins annually. Fearful of the disruption in exchange, the government sent a secret order to provincial governors requesting that they deliver half (or at least a third) of their excise income in metal. This request only created a vicious circle of exchanges: to pay taxes in copper coins, people went to the bank and redeemed assignats for coins that were meant to satisfy the copper hunger. The Bank received exclusive rights to purchase all copper produced in Siberia for the needs of the exchange, but the real problem lay not in the productivity of copper mines. Rather, the Russian Empire was spending beyond its means, prioritizing geographical expansion over the internal development of production, commerce, and culture. Between 1786 and 1795, military expenditures consumed from 67% to 100% of Russia's ordinary revenues.[44] The government, however, looked elsewhere for the reasons for the ruble's fall. Count Alexander Bezborodko reckoned that the main problem was in the publicity of assignat emissions. In a sharp reversal from Shuvalov's statement that "the more [the state] trusts society, the bigger is the public's trust to it. Good deeds and good intentions do not need a veil," Bezborodko called for secrecy in finance.[45] Public trust, as he thought, had nothing to do with the amount of paper money in circulation; it was the news about the issuance of assignats that made people anxious. Therefore, Bezborodko suggested preserving the secrecy of money issues: "the enigma of the proliferation of paper [money]" was seen as the key means to preventing the bank runs.[46]

Was it possible to keep the "enigma" of paper money secret? Hardly. The fluctuation of the assignats' value affected not only their exchangeability for copper and silver; for Russian nobles spoiled by the habits of Western-style consumption, much more obvious and painful was the ruble's fall vis-à-vis European currencies. The ruble's standing in the world market was expressed by the rate at which Russian bills of exchange were discounted at the European bourses in Amsterdam, London, Hamburg, and Paris. As Ivan Novikov, a bookkeeper and author of popular textbooks on finance, explained in his brochure *The Key to the Calculation of Rate*, the rate expressed the "price of the ruble."[47] However, if for the noblemen the stability of the ruble's rate defined their ability to enjoy the luxury of Western goods, for merchants, the ups and downs (mostly downs) of national currency, which devalued Russian goods on the world market while raising the prices of foreign goods, brought financial losses and the threat of bankruptcy. The fluctuations in the ruble's international exchange rate began in the mid-1770s, when the influx of assignats shook the balance between the size of the bullion reserve and the amount of paper money in circulation. The government called on experts to investigate the causes of the rate's fall, but, with the exception of economist Timofei Klingstaet, who attributed the demise of the ruble's exchange rate to the multiplication of assignats, Russian officials believed that the ruble's value had fallen due to the excess of luxury import, to contraband, and to foreign speculation.[48] Merchants' petitions seconded this view. They held the nobility accountable for contaminating other classes with the pernicious habit of excessive consumption and the fall of the ruble's rate, and they begged the government to take measures against the importation of foreign goods, especially luxury items, that sucked money out of the country.

The merchants' critique of Russian "lovers of floppery"[49] highlights an important feature of Russian debates on money: the ruble's rate was often associated with the economic behavior of social estates, while various interest groups often manipulated the government's concerns over national money to receive privileges. Merchants blamed nobles for the lifestyle and consumption that had transfigured the Russian economy. The fall in the ruble's rate certainly depreciated Russian goods; however, the inability of Russian industry, agriculture, and commerce to compete with European counterparts hardly resulted merely from the nobles' preference for European stuff. The Westernization of lifestyle was the consequence of Russia's political and economic Westernization; the "cost" was paid by nobles, serf peasants, merchants, and the state.[50]

Russian commercial elites, therefore, attempted to use the government's anxiety over the ruble's fall to wangle privileges. Their suggestions for fixing the rate included, along with traditional measures against illegal trade and smuggling, the prohibition of the importation of luxury items and "unnecessary foreign commodities."[51] The list of "unnecessary" items encompassed "wines, Champagne and Bourgogne," "rum" that people drank "as a fancy," pasta, noodles, cheese and "delicacies," as well as "canaries and larks," coconuts, gloves, "feathers (we have a lot of our own)," "silk stockings (we have our own manufacture in Moscow)" and many other items. Anchovies, sardines, lemons, oranges, oysters, mussels, and other goods not harvested or made in Russia were supposed to be heavily taxed. In other words, merchants wanted the government to abandon the regime of free trade and engage in a more protectionist policy. Remarkably, English merchants who exported Russian goods rather than bringing in foreign commodities, responded to the inquiry into the ruble's fall in an entirely different manner, indicating that the exchange rate had fallen due to the excess production of paper assignats and copper money and to the depreciated quality of silver and gold coins.[52]

Of the two versions of the story behind the fall of the ruble's exchange rate, the government naturally preferred the one that explained the phenomenon through external influence rather than its domestic monetary policy. In 1793, Russia introduced new duties and prohibited the import of several categories of luxury goods. The exchange rate indeed improved a little; however, in the long run, the statistics of money printing and the exchange rate show a strong correlation between the assignats' depreciation and the value of the ruble abroad. In 1787, one ruble was rated at 39 Dutch stuivers or 41 English pence; in 1790, it cost 30 stuivers or 31 pence, and in 1793 only 25 stuivers or 26 pence. The assignats' rate to silver rubles showed similar dynamics. After the Manifesto of 1786 that allowed the volume of paper money to increase from 46 million to 100 million, the silver ruble's value to assignats rose to 103 kopecks in 1786 and to 115 kopecks in 1790. By 1793, the mass of assignats had increased to 120 million, and the silver ruble's cost to 135 kopecks assignat.[53] The correlation between the two rates' fluctuation was not always straightforward. In addition to the increase of domestic (assignat) debt, Russia was actively borrowing money abroad, and the increasing annual payments for foreign obligations, along with the rise of military spending, also contributed to the ruble's depreciation on the international market. It is important to note, however, that the government often treated these two issues separately and was reluctant to admit that the ruble's international standing depended on its credibility at home.

In 1796, when Catherine died, one silver ruble "cost" 142 kopecks assignat, and after 1796, the gap between the value of the silver ruble and the ruble assignat, which was meant to be its "representative," kept growing. Catherine's son Paul I, embarrassed by the falling rate of the assignats and debasement of money, ordered the public burning of almost 6 million newly printed rubles assignat just after his accession to the throne. This took place in front of the

Winter Palace, the royal residence of his detested mother.[54] The burning of assignats symbolized Paul's deliberation "to eliminate . . . any kind of paper money and to never have it" again.[55] However, Paul I's plan to liquidate the assignats or at least to restore their convertibility was doomed. Shortly after resuming the exchange of assignats, the government had to suspend it and restart printing assignats with even greater intensity.[56]

Catherine II's monetary policy established the institutional principles and, most crucially, the ideological tenets of the Russian financial system. These principles were not yet clear in 1768, when the empress signed the manifesto introducing assignats; the understanding of the meaning of assignats and the financial opportunities and political costs associated with paper money evolved gradually in the 1770s and 1780s. Catherine's dignitaries who stood behind the reforms, as well as the empress herself, were very familiar with contemporary European theories but applied them selectively. They bypassed, for instance, Montesquieu's warning that the sovereign's power over money is limited by the borders of the state and, even within the state, it is checked by economic conditions.

Russian assignats in many respects resembled other paper money of early modern Europe, such as the notes of the Bank of England, that originated as a king's war debts.[57] They differed in one important respect: while the King of England borrowed money from a private bank, Russian assignats, in the absence of creditors at home, appeared as the state's debt either to itself or, as the Catherine's courtiers believed, to its people. Shuvalov and others tried to present the Russian assignats as analogous to their European counterparts and used the elevated rhetoric of the treasury's obligation to the empress's subjects, as if the State Assignat Bank represented the public and stored the nation's wealth. Bezborodko, in a memo written for Paul I (presumably in 1797), bluntly declared that "the assignats . . . are nothing but the sovereign's loan from their subjects."[58]

It is impossible to overestimate the ideological importance of recognizing assignats as a form of state borrowing from the population. Even though this recognition was not made a public declaration, it became a commonplace in the late eighteenth- and early nineteenth-century writings about money. In contrast to the monarchs of major European countries who had been chronically indebted to their vassals, bankers, corporations, and other subjects, Russian tsars never borrowed from their own people until the nineteenth century. It is an altogether different question of why Russian monarchs could not or did not want to borrow from the population; either the subjects were too poor, or, most likely, the ideology of autocratic paternalistic authority did not allow that kind of dependence. In any case, the assignat debt was the first domestic debt of the state, and its recognition had profound political implications. No longer was the financial relationship between the state and the public seen as one-directional. As Michael Kwass writes about eighteenth-century French finance, "Borrowing tested public confidence in the monarchy and may have paradoxically reinforced democratic habits of political participation internal to corporate groups."[59] Due to the absence of corporate credit communities or institutions that entered into negotiations with the crown, assignats could not bear the same meaning. However, the idea of the state's (or the monarch's) indebtedness endowed the state's creditors with some political agency. Theoretically, the entirety of the population turned into the empress's creditor. This rhetoric contrasted sharply with institutional realities: the Assignat Bank was no more than yet another office of imperial administration that played no role in defining the principles of issuing money. Nevertheless, the idea of the Bank as an institution representing the nation's wealth, which had made its first appearance in the 1770s and 1780s, came to play a central role in the nineteenth-century liberal discourse about money.

Autocracy or Representation?

THE POLITICAL PHILOSOPHY OF MONEY IN THE AGE OF NAPOLEON AND AFTER

Skin Money

The subjects of the Russian tsar Alexander I lived on three continents, and often they used different money. Some carried coins in their pockets and never encountered paper money; in other provinces, metal money was a rarity. From 1817 until Russia's sale of Alaska in 1867, the workers of the Russian American Company received their meager salaries in pieces of tanned leather branded with the company's seal that featured a Russian two-headed eagle and the signature of the company's director. Assignats were in short supply in Russian America, while coins imported from the mainland quickly disappeared from circulation.[1] Therefore, in 1816, the Russian administration in America started issuing its own private money called "*marki*" that in design and colors resembled paper assignats. Printed on the skin of sea animals, Alaska's most precious commodity, and delivered to the colony from St. Petersburg, leather rubles and kopecks circulated in Sitka, Kodiak, the Aleutian Islands, and the Russian possessions in California. Backed by nothing other than the military and administrative power of the Russian colonial authority in America, leather money represented the quintessential example of the currency of power, a projection of the unlimited authority of the tsar's colonial proxy. The extraction economy of Russia's colony in Alaska assumed the restriction of the free market of goods and labor for the conscripted natives: the company's stores monopolized trade selling simple merchandise at high prices for "marks" while the economically enserfed Aleut and Alutiiq hunters were forced to work for the company delivering precious sea otter pelts that were sold to Chinese tradesmen in Kiakhta. Foreigners did not take Russian skin money, preferring more liquid means of exchange: furs, foreign coins, and alcohol. The economic model of the Russian American Company, therefore, represented a miniature state that maintained active commercial exchange with the world while imposing isolationism in the domestic economy with the help of money based on military, economic, and administrative domination.[2]

By the early nineteenth century, Russian territorial possessions had expanded dramatically, and each new acquisition sharpened rivalry with neighboring empires, prompting another war or conflict. Continuous warfare and violence inevitably affected the standing of the Russian currency, changing both the worth of the ruble and the political nature of the Russian monetary system. At the same time, Russia claimed a more visible and active role in European political, intellectual, and economic life, borrowing ideas and emulating the practices of its Western neighbors. All these factors led to a change, incremental and subtle, in the perception of the nature of money. What was money: the mechanism of exchange and credit, or the tool of power, governance, and coercion? The answer to this question often involved the way money came to life as well as the material form of its existence. That is why the seemingly random case of Russian leather money in America is

FIGURE 2.1 1-ruble mark, Russian American Company. Courtesy of Division of Work and Industry, National Museum of American History, Smithsonian Institution.

important. Around the same time that Russian American skin rubles came into circulation (1816–17), the Russian government decided on its monetary policy and the concept of state money based on authority rather than trust and credit. Coincidentally, the argument about leather money played a key rhetorical role in changing the direction of financial policy. The Russian American Company was a cartoon image of the Russian Empire: imbued with Western ideologies of commerce and progress, led by a handful of liberals based in St. Petersburg, and dependent on violence and extortion. The company's formative years coincided with the heyday of liberalism and reformism in Russia when the rhetorical flirtation with the ideas of constitutionalism promised a major change in the empire's organization. These years were also marked by Russia's ongoing wars in Europe (the anti-Napoleonic campaigns) and Asia (the wars against the Ottoman Empire and Persia). The financial exhaustion of fighting wars and maintaining the empire contributed to the government's choice in favor of the nationalist and isolationist monetary ideology.

This chapter explains how and why the ideas of money based on popular sovereignty and a limited state power that appeared in the early years of Alexander I's reign yielded to the conservative ideologies of a closed state and the concomitant concept of a nominalist currency. The polarization between these two visions of money—one oriented toward the market and popular political participation, and another toward essentializing state power and obligations—reached its pinnacle on the eve of Napoleon's invasion that led to the debacle of the liberal program of reform. This period is unique in that the two opposite ideologies precisely mirrored each other, politically and economically. The liberal concept of money entailed formation of an independent bank, adherence to the silver standard, constitutional government, and rule of law. This concept rendered money an extension of citizens' political rights. Its conservative counterpart prioritized the flexibility (or arbitrariness) of paper currency, the state prerogative on the production of money that was the attribute of unlimited autocracy, and the ruble as a token of obligation. The juxtaposition of "silver" and "paper" (or leather) was not simply material and symbolic. In addition to political underpinnings, the two concepts of money were based on radically different interpretations of Russian history, language, and cultural specificity. As time passed, the distinctions between these two concepts became less pronounced. But even decades later, staunch liberals and devoted conservatives continued to refer to the initial early nineteenth century ideas that encapsulated the essence of the two visions of money and political order.

Money, Sovereignty, and Constitution in Early Nineteenth-Century Liberalism

The accession of Alexander I to the throne after Paul I's murder in 1801 was met with euphoria. The new monarch's reformist zeal and liberal ideas produced an illusion that everything, including self-limitation of autocratic power by a constitution, was possible. The young tsar, trained by a republican writer Frédéric-César de La Harpe and educated in the best tradition of the European Enlightenment, gradually but decisively ousted the old elites and brought new people to the court and bureaucracy. Inspired by Alexander's words, his friends started feverishly drafting plans and projects of reform that aimed at resolving the practical problems of state governance in an ideologically different and radical way. Russian intellectuals and politicians shared a feeling of belonging to the world of post-revolutionary European politics. Economists and political philosophers Adam Smith, Henry Thornton, J. C. L. Sismondi, and Jean Jacques Rousseau, among many others, became household names. Russians took up debates over economic theories and the questions of monetary policy, along with the issues of constitution and political liberties, as topics of dinner conversations.

"Money had no value other than in relation to people's labor," wrote retired admiral and newly converted liberal Nikolai Mordvinov in December 1801, just a few months after the coup that had brought Alexander I to the throne. This opening sentence to the project of the "labor-encouraging bank" reversed the key concept of money that had tied the value of assignats to the sublimity of monarchal power and grounded it in human capital.[3] In Mordvinov's view, if the amount of money in circulation corresponds to the amount of goods produced by the national economy, "then gold, silver and any other metal or paper coins possess authentic and stable value, and if it does not [correspond], then the worth of gold and any other kind of currency is lowered." Notably, Mordvinov's concept departed from the simplistic interpretation of the intrinsic value of coins juxtaposed to the abstract nature of paper notes: all kinds of money derived their validity from the productive force of the national economy. The wording of the phrase about the falling value of money—literally, the denigrated dignity of currency—suggested the moral superiority of a well-balanced monetary system. It also tacitly recognized that money originated from people's labor rather than the state's authority; the state merely played an auxiliary function in producing assignats and regulating the exchange and, therefore, it could not voluntarily ascribe value to money without breaking the moral laws of order.

The radicalism of Mordvinov's thought consists not merely in the novelty of his proposals for labor banks and the reconsideration of the notion of money. What might have amazed Alexander I, the intended addressee of the project, was the underlying political philosophy that endowed the people, rather than the government, with political sovereignty. The young emperor was excited by the radicalism of such plans. Similar ideas appeared in two short memos, "On the fundamental laws of the state" (1802) and "On the spirit of government" (1804), written at Alexander's request by a thirty-year-old-son of a priest, recent seminary graduate, and self-taught philosopher Mikhail Speransky, who was serving as personal secretary to the tsar's close friend count Victor Kochubei. According to Speransky, the government derived its power from the people who had yielded to it the prerogative of law enforcement and subsidized the government with human and material resources for the formation of the army and financial capital.[4] Therefore, if a representative legislature was to express the political will of the people, the money represented the nation's (and not the government's) wealth. Translated into the language of money, the principles of the people's financial sovereignty required the recognition of the derivative or representative status of paper money and its convertibility to metal coins, which served as a proxy for economic goods and transactions.[5] The nominal value of assignats could not exist separately from the subject that it represented: the national economy.

The reformers' preoccupation with the nature of money had a prosaic explanation. Russia was drawn into the anti-Napoleonic Coalition Wars in Europe while fighting its own battles in the south, straining its financial resources to the extreme and compensating for the lack of funds with an abundance of printed money. In 1801, there were 221 million rubles of paper assignats in circulation; in 1806, this number had risen to 319 million, in 1808 to 477 million, and by 1810, to 579 million rubles.[6] Indeed, the system of state revenues, 60% to 70% of which relied on taxes collected from peasants and excise duties, was outdated and inflexible, and the treasury's gains were also significantly diminished by the fall of the ruble's rate. In 1810, the Russian state received as its "ordinary" income half as much money as it spent; the lion's share of the state's resources was consumed by war, and the deficit of revenues was covered with a "loan from the Assignat Bank" of 127 million rubles ("loan" was a euphemism for the influx of newly printed rubles).[7] The ruble assignat's rate continued to fall, and in December 1810, a paper ruble was worth a fourth of its silver counterpart. The disintegration of the national currency became a norm of everyday life. All goods and services assumed double prices—in assignats and in silver rubles.[8]

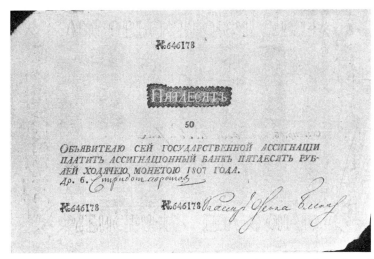

FIGURE 2.2 50-ruble assignat, 1807. Courtesy of Division of Work and Industry, National Museum of American History, Smithsonian Institution.

Most countries in early nineteenth-century Europe also faced the problem of falling currency as warfare and economic crises in England, France, and Austria led to the politicization of the money question. In Russia, however, the government tried to enact monetary reform at the same time it was reforming its system of governance. Therefore, the issue of money came to be seen through the lens of the political reform, and vice versa. Because money was much more than a financial issue, the master plan of currency reform did not originate from the offices of the ministers of finance.[9] The *Financial Plan*, drafted in November 1809 by Mikhail Speransky, who skyrocketed to positions as a secretary of the state and the tsar's key adviser, formed a central element of a large-scale reform plan that included, among other things, the separation of powers, the introduction of a hierarchy of elected representative institutions with the legislative State Duma on the top, and the reform of state service.[10] Russia, in Speransky's view, stood on the brink of major changes and challenges, and while Napoleon imposed a new political and legal order on conquered Europe, the Russian tsar was supposed to benevolently grant reforms from on high. Constitution, the rule of law, and a new currency formed the foundation of Speransky's system.

To fully appreciate how transformative Speransky's plan was, his project of monetary reform must be considered alongside the political meaning of his initiative.[11] In addition to constraining the ability of a ruler and his courtiers and ministers to exercise their legislative and executive power in full, Speransky's projected reform of money and banking deprived the sovereign of his privilege to control financial resources. To be sure, Speransky's financial plan pursued a set of pragmatic goals and did not explicitly target autocracy. To restore the standard of value distorted by the fall of assignats, Speransky suggested establishing the silver ruble as the main unit of measure and payment. The government had to acknowledge that assignats represented "state debt," withdraw them from circulation, and burn them publicly. In lieu of assignats, Speransky suggested the introduction of new "credit notes" issued by a newly created independent joint-stock Silver Bank.[12] Merely withdrawing excess paper money and setting up the bullion reserve would not solve the problem, because the success of the reform would depend on the government's commitment to the rules. Without changing the principles of the production of money, the reserve could only temporarily restrain the government from sliding into an uncontrolled monetary emission. Therefore, the ultimate goal of the reform was the de-governmentalization of the issuance of money, while the independent bank served as a financial counterpart for the elected State Duma.

The idea of an independent bank encapsulated the essence of liberal thinking about state, money, and society, and Speransky's project put down on paper thoughts that were on the mind of a few other economists and politicians.[13] The political constitution needed to be complemented by a financial constitution of some sort, and the link between the two constitutions held together Speransky's grandiose plan of reforms. Speransky planned to enact his *Financial Plan* in the aftermath of a major political step that aimed to transform Russia's despotic autocratic regime into a constitutional (or, as he called it, "true") monarchy through the separation of powers and the introduction of a hierarchy of representative institutions, from the local to the national level.[14] Speransky hoped that the *Financial Plan* would be the first item on the agenda of the projected institutions, legitimizing the plan by the consent of the legislative "estate."[15] The *Financial Plan* imposed significant commitments on the government, including the obligation to correct and maintain the standards of the monetary system. In other words, Speransky envisioned the establishment of a "rule-of-law" ruble, as opposed to the whimsical ruble of despotic monarchism.

The radicalism of Speransky's suggestions becomes clear when considered within the context of early nineteenth-century debates about state, banks, and money. The war constituted the single most significant factor of financial policies and debates in Napoleonic Europe that allowed for a tremendous increase in the state's role in finance. In 1797, the Bank of England suspended its specie payments, providing for the stability of national finance and the possibility of securing emergency loans. The suspension saved Britain from major financial shocks, but it also shook the balance of power between the Bank and the government. As the relationship between the Bank of England and the government became less distant, many contemporaries started questioning the Bank of England's independence.[16] Similarly, la Banque de France, Napoleon's famous creation of 1800, underwent a radical reform in 1806 that did not affect the structure of its private joint-stock capital but imposed immediate government control over its governance.[17] In other words, the idea of bank independence gradually, even though temporarily, lost ground in wartime Europe.

Against this backdrop, Russian liberals' thinking about banks and money look especially radical. Speransky did not specify the principles and guarantees of the bank's independent organization, but the gist comes through in the writings of one of his closest political allies, Nikolai Mordvinov, who proposed the establishment of a Free Russian Bank (1809). Mordvinov saw the Bank not simply as a private corporation representing an alliance of bankers and the government but also as a decentralized network of credit institutions financed by all free members of Russian society. Like Speransky's suggestions, Mordvinov proposed eliminating state assignats and passing the right of issue to a Free Russian Bank that was supposed to embrace all social estates.[18] Peasants, landlords, and merchants were invited to deposit their capital, receive interest, apply for credit, and, most important, participate in the bank's management, either directly or indirectly through elected representatives. The level of participation depended on the size of the individual's bank deposit: every local bank had to define which sum would be equivalent to one vote. Therefore, as Mordvinov wrote, "everyone would manage his capital by himself," since the national bank would have a large network of local branches, each governed by local representatives. Only those who chose to deposit their funds anonymously would have no vote (the principle of representation required openness, trust, and transparency). Interestingly, the government had no right to deposit treasury funds in the Free Bank, and the tsar could only participate in it as a "private individual." The government was supposed to accept the Free Bank's banknotes, printed on the same paper as current state assignats, for all state payments, so that the new banknotes could gradually replace state paper money. As a result, mutual trust would bind the government, the tsar, and the people in the "closest union."[19]

Mordvinov's idea of the Free Bank encapsulated the meaning of money as a form of representation. Thus, the transition from inconvertible state-issued assignats to the convertible banknotes of the Free Bank offered either a substitute for or an extension of a political reform—a transition from bureaucratic autocracy to popular monarchy with representative institutions. In 1813, after Speransky's dismissal and exile, Mordvinov returned to his idea of a financial republic in the form of a Free Bank. In this new project, Mordvinov aimed to achieve the social and territorial unity of the empire through the network of provincial banks: "Every province must have its own bank, and every inhabitant of a province must participate in the formation of the capital of his bank." This literally reproduced Speransky's idea of a hierarchy of representative institutions. Banknotes issued by the local cells of the national banking system would reflect the amount of wealth produced by each estate, and the problem of money overprinting would be solved. Ultimately, "all parts of Russia would be united by the bonds of trust and mutual help" through financial participation in the national economy and governance.[20] Writing about banks Mordinov undoubtedly expressed constitutional ideas in the language of finance.

Mordvinov's vision of the Free Bank was a financial utopia in its purest incarnation: public capital collected through local banks was supposed to satisfy almost all state needs and eventually replace taxes.[21] The state seemed to be withering away, since self-governed provincial banks would assume most economic functions and subjects of the Russian emperor could participate in governance. Mordvinov attempted to resolve multiple problems at once—the problem of political representation, imperial governance, cheap local credit, the sustainability of large noble landholding, serfdom, and many others—and it is remarkable that he used the reform of banks and the monetary system to repair the most vital flaws in all spheres of social and political life. The metaphor of unity, frequently used by Mordvinov, proved to be very versatile. The "unity of currency" meant the identity of value between all forms of its existence (metal and paper) and its ability to represent the total wealth of the nation (Speransky defined these qualities as "authenticity"). "The unity of currency . . . connects all thoughts, feelings, wishes and rights, no matter how different they are," wrote Mordvinov, adding moral overtones to this financial formula.[22] The "unity of the country" assumed not only social and national cohesion but also the unity between the throne and the people. Representation was the key to achieving both forms of unification.

Mordvinov's projects were a sort of political daydreaming rather than practical solutions to a problem.[23] He merged Speransky's pragmatic ideas into a financial utopia that encapsulated the spirit of liberalism in Alexander I's early reign. Such financial reform could seemingly save the tsar from the necessity of surrendering autocratic power through a constitutional reform. However, despite his ostentatious commitment to change, Alexander I was not willing to agree to a radical limitation of his privileges—political or financial. Neither the *Financial Plan* nor Speransky's plan for political reform reached full fruition. The idea of an independent Silver Bank with a right of issue was dropped, along with the establishment of a representative State Duma, like other constitutional plans the tsar often initiated and then revoked.[24] Truncated political-administrative reform helped create a separate and specialized legislative body in the form of the State Council (1810), whose members, instead of the elected deputies, were chosen and appointed by the emperor. Speransky had to limit his financial aspirations to a more modest program, namely, to replace the institutional guarantees of controlled emission with government promises to redeem the "assignat" debt. In both cases, the monarchy and the administrative government ultimately evaded external public control, while the representatives of the public or capital received no power.

Despite the backlash against his larger program, Speransky attempted to realize one of his most cherished ideas—the "unity" of the legislative process, which limited the ability of ministers and courtiers to obtain the tsar's approval for their initiatives without consulting others. The new order introduced in 1810 mandated that all legislative projects go through consultations and discussions at the State Council prior to being submitted to the tsar. Similarly, the currency reform restored the "unity" of the ruble by reducing paper and metal money to a common silver denominator of value. The logic of monetary reform expressed in a Manifesto of June 20, 1810, put silver above paper assignats, as the reform of governance established the supremacy of law over administrative orders.[25]

Speransky's initiatives that were often perceived as daring innovations in fact returned to much of the original thinking about assignats. Another law drafted by the state secretary unambiguously called the assignats "state debt guaranteed by the entire wealth of the state." Catherine II's court bureaucrats had defended this view as a condition of the state's credibility, but by 1810, the attitude toward assignats had changed. When the Manifesto of February 2, 1810, declared that the government considered the existence of excessive assignats a problem, the political establishment perceived it as madness, as if a person seeking to improve his financial reputation was publicly declaring that he was on the brink of bankruptcy. "The said Manifesto, by removing the veil that should have been only lifted in front of the government, incurred harm instead of bringing relief," wrote Nikolai Rumiantsev in response to Speransky's measures.[26] The same Manifesto also announced that the redemption of assignats required the sale of state properties "that had always served as a security for assignats," therefore retrospectively changing the status of assignats and the nature of the state's obligation.[27] Speransky was apparently following the example of the French revolutionary government that invented both the idea of backing up money with national property (biens nationaux) and redeeming obligations through the sale of state land domains.[28] It is therefore remarkable that Speransky chose to follow this example. Like the French National Assembly, the Russian government found itself in a situation where it had nothing else to offer to the bearers of assignats than the value of its own property.[29] Not surprisingly, the results were similar: the Russian government was able to sell only a fifth of state properties intended for the redemption of assignats. Nevertheless, the ideological impact of this reform was quite substantial: the assignats were no longer considered the personal obligations of the tsar but were bound to the state's material assets.

Despite the apparent technicality of Speransky's monetary measures, they bore tremendous ideological meaning. Speransky considered "authenticity"—both material (resilience to counterfeiting) and financial (ability to represent value)—to be the key quality of money.[30] The whole system hinged on the principle of symmetrical representation: "credit notes" represented the silver bullion reserve at the bank, which, at the same time, reflected the capital involved in commercial transactions. Assignats, in contrast, did not fit this model since they had lost the ability to represent wealth (as Speransky put, "Assignats are based on presumption and possess no authenticity").[31] As Speransky's closest ally, Nikolai Mordvinov, expressed a few years later, the assault on the authenticity of the value of money destroyed not only the people's trust in the government and its obligations but also the moral standards of trust in all relationships. When the ruble falls, "laws lose their strength, virtue is deprived of constancy, and vice is justified and acquitted."[32]

This attitude toward money left very little space for the sovereign. The liberal model, with all its emphasis on presentation, was more technical and depersonalized than the autocratic system that prioritized honor over material guarantees. Catherine II, ruling in the spirit of "despotic aristocracy," had pledged her personal honor for the credibility of Russian assignats.[33] In contrast to the empress's top-down relationship between ruler and subjects, Speransky envisioned these relations as mutual. The state debt originated not from the vows but from the initial delegation of power and the contract. Interestingly, this approach allowed Speransky both to oblige the government to follow the laws and to justify the increase of taxes and the introduction of other extraordinary obligations for the sake of financial well-being and common good. In other words, the state's obligation for the debt of assignats was supposed to be reciprocated by the obligation of the tsar's subjects to pay increased taxes and participate in loans.[34]

Each financial instrument that governments use to collect revenues—taxes, foreign or domestic loans, and issuance of money—has a defined political meaning, and each assumes a different form of political participation and social inclusion. In the liberal discourse of the nineteenth century, issuing assignats came to be considered the worst form of extracting resources, because it represented a hidden tax that was not based on consent and fell unevenly on various estates, exacerbating social inequality. Government forces everyone to take depreciated assignats, silently expropriating value.[35] In contrast to assignats, domestic loans and the income tax were both grounded in the idea of transparency and voluntary participation. Speransky, therefore, tried to find a way of replacing the issuance of paper money with fiscal mechanisms that invited the political participation of all classes, such as the income tax. In the early nineteenth century, the income tax, which had originated in Britain in 1799, was seen as a novelty and a politically radical measure, especially for Russia, where taxpaying was a stigma of lower social origin. Therefore, when Speransky, in addition to raising taxes on peasants, initiated the introduction of income tax targeting landowning nobility in a form that relied on the peer control of local noble assemblies and a conscious reporting of revenues from estates, it was seen as an assault on the privileges of the ruling elite. Nobles, even those who most vocally opposed the measure, nevertheless paid the tax, which in 1812 brought in 5.5 million rubles.[36] When the war was over and patriotic zeal waned, tax collection fell drastically, and the tax was abolished in 1819.

In sum, the financial results of Speransky's measures were rather modest. The effects of many of his initiatives were undone by the war and the resistance of the minister of finance, Dmitrii Guryev, who sabotaged their implementation.[37] However, such early experiments were remarkable when considered within the broader framework of Speransky's financial and political reform. Speransky's measures entailed a different attitude toward public finance, understood not in the narrow sense of the state's fiscal activity but more broadly as a socioeconomic and political ground for interaction between the state and the people. In liberal discourse, monetary reforms came to be seen as either preceding or following constitutional changes, whereas conservative discourse debunked the principle of representation as either invalid or inapplicable to

Russia. In monetary debates between liberals and their opponents, one could choose either to admit the principle of representation or deny it.

Russian Conservatism and the Invention of the "Paper Standard"

Russian conservative thinkers contrasted traditionalism and nationalism with the cosmopolitan zeal of liberal reformers and juxtaposed the unity between the tsar and his people with the falsehood of political representation. The question of currency was indeed not the central point of the conservative agenda in Europe, but because financial reform in Russia was so closely connected to the political transformation of autocracy, it became a matter of political debate. While liberals could draw their arguments from a large reservoir of liberal economic theory, conservative nominalism—that is, the doctrine that reserved for the state the right to determine the value of money—had not yet produced an equally authoritative and abundant literature. Russian conservative thinkers improvised, grounding their arguments on historical examples and political concepts.

In the era of Alexander I, ideological debates between liberals and nationalists were mainly limited to the upper crust of the political elite and represented the flipside of the scramble for power at the imperial court. The epicenter of conflict was the fight between Mikhail Speransky and his opponents, who used political polemics and intrigues to get rid of the mighty state secretary. Financial innovations served as one of the main pretexts and reasons for the attack against Speransky. Of all principles of monetary reform, the conservatives primarily attacked the idea of the silver standard, convertibility, and the concept of paper money as state debt. For them, paper money based on trust and belief in the sovereign power of the tsar provided more security. Moreover, Speransky's opponents presented the paper standard as a historically superior form of currency.

The centrality of the historical and philosophical arguments in favor of the existing system is striking. For instance, the minister of finance Alexei Vasiliev's denunciation of the principle of convertibility rested on a peculiar historical interpretation of the evolution of money. He claimed that the development of the monetary system had widened the gap between the material and imagined (nominal) value of currency. Vasiliev tried to present the depressing fact of the ruble's fall and the dissolution of the standard of value as a result of intellectual development from primitive valuation based on matter to a more superior form, grounded in "intellect and trust." Certainly, the introduction of paper money in early modern Europe had been preceded by a turn to the use of abstract, not material, units for the calculation of value. However, while his interpretation of the mental revolution that had preconditioned the appearance of paper money certainly made sense, Vasiliev drew conclusions that did not logically follow from this observation. "With a stroke of a pen, a piece of gold can become less valuable than a piece of paper." The "magic" power of "inscriptions" rested on assurances that one can exchange paper money for "any kind of need," while the government appeared as a magician who could endow assignats with this quality.[38]

Vasiliev's reasoning about the virtual value of money may appear completely logical and rational from a twenty-first-century perspective, while the liberals' reliance on the value of bullion reserve may seem archaic. However, if the political underpinnings of both paradigms are considered, the bullion reserve served as a proxy for economic productivity and commercial transactions, while the abstract money of the conservative nominalist theory was contingent on the ruler's (immaterial) authority and the sovereign's (material) being. "What gives value to money?" According to historian Nikolai Karamzin, it was the government's willingness to accept tokens, no matter what they were made from—wood, leather, gold, or paper. Karamzin's famous conservative manifesto *Memoir on Ancient and Modern Russia* (1811)— written at the request of the tsar's sister, Grand Duchess Ekaterina Pavlovna, but meant for Alexander's eyes—highlighted the fallacy of contemporary liberal monetary theory and, most important, the preference for a metal standard.[39] "If the sovereign offered us marked chips, and ordered that they circulate instead of rubles, . . . we would accept the chips as well."

To support his thesis, Karamzin deployed a historical argument—the alleged existence of leather money in pre-Mongol Rus'. Remarkably, it was not the historical arguments that had shaped his vision of current economic problems; instead, Karamzin's political battle against Speransky's monetary reforms affected his writing about the Russian medieval economy. Describing the development of the economy in pre-Mongol Rus in his magisterial *The History of the Russian State*, Karamzin asserted that "our ancestors got along from the ninth to the fourteenth centuries without metallic coins of their own, using only leather scraps, which were sealed by the government and called *kuny*, that is, *assignats*; and they traded with the East and the West, with Greece, Persia and the German Hansa."[40] According to Karamzin, *grivna*, which many historians thought were the main silver coin of the Rus' state, represented a "counting unit" and had no intrinsic value. "The Treasury, being moderate in the emission of leather money, had been able to maintain their value until the [khan] Baty's invasion; after the invasion, *kuny* lost their value because the Mongols did not accept them in lieu of silver."[41] The eventual disappearance of leather money and its replacement with silver "had detrimental consequences for domestic trade, because it suddenly reduced the amount of money in circulation" and even caused the reappearance of the real skins of martens and squirrels as the means of exchange, therefore throwing Russia back to the age of barter.

In Karamzin's account, branded leather money symbolized the civilizational superiority of pre-Mongol Rus' compared to the barbarous Mongols, who used metal and were unable to grasp the abstract character of money. "Leather assignats were replaced in Russia by silver and copper coinage during the most turbulent and barbaric periods of our servitude to the khans."[42] This phrase from Karamzin's *Memoir on Ancient and Modern Russia* unequivocally compared Speransky's efforts to introduce silver to the policy of the Mongol khans, while Speransky's alleged admiration of Napoleon at the time of the looming invasion strengthened the parallel.[43] Indeed, Napoleon's financial reforms—the establishment of the Bank of France and the stabilization of currency after years of revolutionary turmoil—served as an example to Speransky and many subsequent Russian financial reformers.

Karamzin used a seemingly impeccable argument that the ability to value things based on convention, rather than matter, indicated a higher level of civilization. Therefore, the existence of leather *kuny* put Russia centuries ahead of Western European countries and at the same time neutralized the embarrassment of the fallen currency.[44] He also stressed the priority of national interests: the value of conditional money rested on social consensus inside the country rather than on an agreement with other states. However, at the center of Karamzin's theory was the role of the state in regulating the amount of leather assignats in circulation. Based on this example, the government under the wise policy of the current ruler could cure the problem of the ruble's falling rate just by reducing the number of assignats.

A devoted monarchist, Karamzin believed that no material proof, such as the bullion reserve, was necessary to ensure the government's credibility, and the promise to pay to the bearer a certain amount in coins printed on the assignats should not be interpreted directly as a state obligation. Many conservative thinkers after Karamzin would argue for the removal of this phrase from Russian assignats and state credit bills in recognition of the fact that the value of paper money emanated not from their material backing and convertibility but from the sovereign's authority. Assignats were real money, not debt, because people accepted them as such. "Despite the fact that assignats came in the form of promissory notes, we did not consider the sovereign our debtor, we did not expect him to pay for the papers, we did not study the treasury's condition, being satisfied that assignats obtained for us everything we wanted," asserted Karamzin.[45] Denouncing the idea of debt that eighteenth-century politicians considered central for maintaining the credibility of assignats, Karamzin also rejected the idea of the people's, or the nation's, existence as an autonomous entity and the owner of national wealth.

Karamzin's reference to Russia's past should not obscure the fact that his views on money resembled certain European concepts of monetary reform. Joseph de Maistre, Karamzin's political alter ego and another influential conservative politician at the court of tsar Alexander I, penned a project that offered a similar financial reform in the Kingdom of Piedmont. In 1798, a few years prior to his arrival in St. Petersburg as an ambassador to Russia, de Maistre wrote a memo for the king suggesting that the government "could and should deliberately institute and consistently maintain a system of inconvertible paper money."[46] He asserted that the circulation of paper money rested on public trust and the sovereign power, and rejected the idea of the government's debt. According to De Maistre, paper money represented "credit by the nation to the nation."[47]

Although both men belonged to the narrow circle of Russian conservative politicians at Alexander's court and even competed for the emperor's attention, Karamzin did not necessarily borrow from de Maistre. More likely he drew these ideas from the contemporary pool of European conservative economic thought. A possible source of Karamzin's inspiration could be Johann Gottlieb Fichte's famous treatise *The Closed Commercial State* (1801), which propagated economic isolationism for the sake of domestic, internal development. One of the key "decisive measures" for the achievement of the state's self-sufficiency was the introduction of inconvertible national currency and the withdrawal of gold and silver: "The world currency that is found in the hands of the citizens, viz., all gold and all silver, must be brought out of circulation and converted into a new national currency, a currency—this is to say—that would be valid only in the country, and yet would be exclusively valid in it."[48] Fichte emphasized the necessity of coercive measures in order to assert the monopoly of the new money that must originate from the government, "the one who manufactures and gives out this money and provides it with general validity by announcing that it will henceforth be the only means of exchange."[49] According to Fichte, the government should not use its monopoly on money printing indefinitely, but instead of external restraints and public control, the monarch should "irrevocably bind itself and all his successors, with every new monarch renewing this obligation upon attaining the throne."

The introduction of this new kind of money, according to Fichte, eliminated the anxiety of contemporary financial policy. The new money could not fall, because unlike paper money that circulated along with metal coins, it would be the sole means of exchange, and it could not be compared or related to other signs of value.[50] Thus, Fichte's system aimed to change the entire model of semantic relations between things and the signs of value. Money must not have intrinsic value; it "is in and of itself absolutely nothing, it only represents something due to the will of the state."[51] The ultimate outcome of both Fichte's plan and Karamzin's program extended beyond the realm of economy. By creating the sole means of economic communication and excluding all others, Fichte strove to build a new foundation for the national unification of the German nation. Money, like language, came to symbolize the unity and the spirit of the community while allowing the state to forge and control the nation.[52]

The linkage between language, money, and nationalism was not an exclusive feature of German Romanticism.[53] Karamzin distinguished himself as an ideologue and an active participant in a radical reform of the Russian language. The dispute involved the members of Alexander Shishkov's nationalist circle, "The conversation of the lovers of Russian language" (1811–16), and their opponents, the literary cosmopolitan circle "Arzamas" (1815–18), led by Karamzin.[54] In 1813, Shishkov became the president of the Russian Academy, whose main product was the compilation and the publication of the *Dictionary of Russian Language*. Karamzin's polemics with Alexander Shishkov revolved around questions of nationality and the provenance and future of the Russian language.[55] If Shishkov took ultra-nationalist positions, claiming that the Russian language was a distorted version of Church Slavonic, Karamzin, while disapproving of borrowings in principle, preferred Western borrowings to Shishkov's neologisms derived from Church Slavonic. Petr Viazemskii described Karamzin's cosmopolitan nationalism through an analogy with money: "One can say about our language that it is both rich and poor at the same time. There are not enough words to depict the subtle tints of thoughts and feelings. . . . It is not appropriate to borrow foreign words from neighbors; however, Dutch guldens are in great demand, and no one is squeamish about it. That is the point, that a skilled writer may, if he is in need, use Dutch guldens. Englishmen do the same thing."[56]

Thinking about language, Karamzin preferred simplicity to the fake abundance of artificial vocabulary that overflowed with excessive derivatives from the Church Slavonic or foreign languages. In this sense, his position in regard to language is different from the "self-referential"[57] epistemology in Fichte and, in fact, even contrasts Karamzin's own objections to the imposition of Western standards of value (silver or gold) and the excessive printing of paper notes. Karamzin's view of money was also more moderate than Fichte's radical isolationism and, perhaps, closer to de Maistre's stance, which did not assume complete autarky, despite its focus on inconvertibility. His nationalism was likewise more moderate than that of Alexander Shishkov. However, the nationalist message remained explicit in his writings about language and money. Like Fichte and another "monetary nationalist" and staunch advocate of paper money, Adam Mueller,[58] Karamzin saw national currency as a foundation of national unity, a self-sufficient means of communication that held the nation together. Therefore, his denial of the superior status of silver as an international standard against which Russia should measure the value of its national paper currency both internalized the mechanisms of regulation and suggested a superior role of the state in monetary policy.

The "People's Ruble" and Other Alternatives to the Rule-of-Law Currency

As Napoleon's army approached Russia's borders, Speransky's political defeat became imminent. Shortly before his fall in March 1812, the minister of finances, Dmitrii Guryev, who had initially assisted the state secretary and then joined the camp of Speransky's enemies, blocked one of his last initiatives at the State Council. Speransky suggested establishing annual "legal rates" between silver and paper money for private credit transactions. According to Mordvinov, the ultimate goal of the introduction of legal rates was to facilitate the adoption of the silver standard and the extension of assignats' circulation in Russia's western provinces, where they were almost absent due to the proximity of Europe and the development of foreign trade.[59] Guryev, who was Speransky's and Mordvinov's opponent on this issue, suggested that instead of facilitating the use of Russian silver coins, the government should make the acceptance of assignats mandatory for all subjects of the emperor. The inhabitants of the western provinces, claimed Guryev, tried to escape the burden of paper circulation, which fell heavily on the shoulders of other subjects in Russian core provinces. Guryev accused 6 million subjects of the western borderlands (primarily Jews) of treason that ultimately caused the fall of Russian paper currency and destroyed the monetary unity of the empire.[60]

The question of the assignats' acceptance in the western provinces touched on two crucial questions of monetary reform. The first concerned the definition of money either as an obligatory institution imposed from above or as an instrument of the market. The second dealt with the use of currency for imperial financial integration. Speransky's *Financial Plan* motivated the adoption of the silver standard, among other things, by the necessity of integrating the western provinces that were oriented toward Europe and silver. The government had to fix the imperial currency prior to its expansion westward; in this sense, the imperial core had to adjust its standard to that of its western European borderland. As for Guryev, he always stood for the unconditional inclusion of national borderlands in the imperial monetary system based on the "paper" standard.[61]

In March 1812, Mikhail Speransky was exiled to Nizhny Novgorod and a few months later was sent even further to Perm'. In the strained political atmosphere of Napoleon's impending invasion, Speransky's purge was presented as an act of retribution for his treacherous admiration of the nation's enemy. A formal reason for the accusation was that Speransky "by his financial affairs tried to ruin the state and, through taxes, to incite hatred against the government." Speransky believed that the real reason was his plan for political reform, which had been interpreted as a malicious attempt to limit the tsar's authority.[62] It seems that nobody regretted the departure of the reformer who had imposed new taxes on the rich and, due to the reduction of state expenditure, deprived many dignitaries of pensions and other financial benefits. A member of Speransky's team, Ludwig Heinrich von Jacob, complained that he, along with Mikhail Balugianskii, who also worked on Speransky's *Financial Plan*, had been accused of *Jacobinism* (note the pun) and faced "a great deal of mockery and hatred."[63] Soon after Speransky's fall, things began to change: on April 9, 1812, the government adopted Guryev's project and made both the acceptance of paper money and counting by assignat ruble mandatory not only for state and tax payment but also for all private transactions in all provinces of the Russian Empire, thus reversing Speransky's earlier law (1810) that had designated silver as the main standard of currency. In practice, this meant that, if a contract was settled in silver, the contractor could not reject a payment in assignats. The designation of assignats instead of silver as the main legal tender also bore a strong political message, forcing people to rely on the declared value of money. Guryev's claim—that all subjects of the Russian tsars must be bound by the common obligation to use paper money—reversed Speransky's idea that assignats were the state's debt to its citizens. The contrast between these two visions reflected the opposition between imperial subjecthood and citizenship as two different forms of political participation.

Napoleon's invasion precipitated the failure of Speransky's liberalism and his technocratic program of reforms greatly inspired by Napoleon's financial innovations. Not only the war but even more Russia's victory over Napoleon cast doubts on economic theories foundational to Speransky's system. People started wondering if something else, apart from the bullion reserve and financial austerity, could support Russia's credibility.[64] After all, Russia was not the only country experiencing financial difficulties during and in the aftermath of the Napoleonic Wars. The war in a certain sense suspended the principles of monetary circulation based on a tangible collateral and firm institutions.

Another factor that cast doubt on what was thought to be the European principle of monetary economy was the tremendous cost of Russia's military campaign in Europe. The "patriotic" war of 1812 inflicted horrible losses on the national economy due to violence, devastation, and specifically, Napoleon's massive counterfeiting of assignats; however, it did not cause such acute and immediate financial difficulties as the victorious continuation of the anti-Napoleon operations in 1813. Military campaigns beyond Russia's borders required payment in gold and silver that Russia did not have and had yet to purchase.[65] The common goal of Europe's victory over Napoleon necessitated concessions, and Russia's minister of finance, Guryev, negotiated with Prussian minister Heinrich Friedrich Karl von Stein various agreements for issuing "federate" money that would be used by the armies of allies (Russia, Prussia, and England) for purchasing food supplies and other provisions.[66] Although none of these proposals involving European money succeeded, according to an agreement with Prussia concluded in 1813, Russian assignats were made acceptable in Prussia. This agreement may have helped the Russian army, chronically short of hard currency, support itself during the campaign, although soldiers and officers often ran into difficulties paying in assignats.[67] But when the war ended, this mass of paper assignats, along with millions of counterfeited notes, threatened to flow back to Russia and decimate the ruble's rate "at the moment when victories gave [Russia] an unquestionable right to glory, esteem and wellbeing."[68] To prevent the deluge of assignats, Guryev delayed the dispatch of funds to the Russian troops in Prussia who, according to Mikhail Barklay de Tolly's report, were on the brink of starvation.[69] Anticipating "terrible consequences" for private wealth and the state economy, the minister of finance begged the tsar to approve yet another kind of Russian paper bond—specifically for the exchange of 50 million assignats that turned out to be in Europe. As Guryev pointed out, since there was no

way to find a corresponding sum in hard currency, the new bonds were supposed to be guaranteed by His Majesty's word.[70]

Alexander I wisely bypassed the idea to release new obligations bearing
his name. However, the contradiction between the deplorable condition of
Russia's finances and her recent political and military triumph made many
patriots believe that the standing of the currency did not reflect the real
state of the economy. This idea appeared in Senator Dmitrii Troshchinskii's
bombastic declarations addressed to the commander-in-chief, Mikhail
Kutuzov: Russia, despite her heavy losses, would emerge before the aston-
ished world in all greatness and glory and prove that her "wealth and power
are inexhaustible because they originate from the abundance of our land
and do not depend on the exchange for the ridiculously precious metal."[71]
Even the member of the future Decembrist circles Nikolai Turgenev, trained
in Germany in the spirit of liberal economics, in 1813 admitted that the "recent experience had shown . . . that Russian assignats cannot absolutely fit the
theory of paper money of other states; this is not because our assignats are
different from paper money in other countries, but because the *internal resources of Russia are not yet fully known*,"[72] This combination of economic liberalism and belief in the potency of natural riches was poetically encapsulated
in Pushkin's *Eugene Onegin*: Onegin reads Adam Smith and believes that the
states "can dispense with gold, when in the land itself they hold the simple
product ready given."[73]

Nikolai Turgenev's doubt about the universality of the principles of monetary circulation was not in line with Karamzin's thinking about money as the
extension of state authority. In contrast to Karamzin's ideas of money imposed
by the state from above, Turgenev suggested issuing special wartime assignats
to represent the "obligations of the government toward the people" who bore
the hardship of war and requisitions.[74] The war was indeed the most important factor that called for the reconsideration of the relationship between the
state and the people. The "people's war" of 1812, in Turgenev's interpretation,
endowed the Russian people with rights distinct and equal to the government.
However, the conservatives reversed this relationship. "The state is nothing
else than the individuals that compose it; people and the state are the same
thing," states an 1816 memorandum found the papers of Andrei Razumovskii.
Therefore, to request the payment of state debts for assignats was equivalent
to saying "I pay myself my debt." The state's spending, especially its military
expenses, represented the state's "sacrifices"; everyone was obliged to share
the financial burden of war.[75] Shifting the emphasis from the state's debt to
the people's duty resulted in the creation of a peculiar nationalist concept

of the "people's ruble," which encapsulated Russia's uniqueness while also allowing for a greater presence of the paternalist state in finances and national economy. Russian assignats came to resemble the proverbial leather money from Karamzin's history books. Coincidentally or not, at the same time that Russia accepted this monetary ideology, the new governor of Russian America introduced leather money as the ultimate instrument of Russian economic domination over its colonized population in Alaska.

The Russian government accepted the conditional value of assignats as a new national ideology that distinguished Russia from other countries, while the Russian ruble came to be seen as a unique currency to which the laws of liberal political economy did not apply. To understand the true meaning of the Russian monetary system, "one should address the folk ways of thinking about state assignats," wrote Victor Kochubei, Speransky's former boss. (Kochubei had introduced Speransky to the tsar in 1806 and had therefore paved his way to power; but after Speransky's fall, Kochubei shifted to conservatism.) In fact, peasants, who constituted "the greatest part of the people," did not notice the decrease in the value of paper rubles. "Having no need for the silver ruble, people do not care about its value and do not measure the value of its products in silver," asserted Kochubei. His report, written in response to a plan for monetary reform by Swiss economist Francis d'Ivernois (1813), pictured an ideal landscape of bucolic Russia living in the golden age of pre-monetary exchange: "In the modesty of its thoughts, they [the people] come near to the most just understanding [of money], and measure their wealth in bread."[76] The simple folk value assignats as "the real money granted by the supreme authority of the tsar" and treat them with "holy faith." Any major reform, such as the devaluation of assignats proposed by d'Ivernois, would shake people's faith and weaken their esteem for the government, therefore threatening the stability of the entire "edifice of state power."[77]

Kochubei's romantic portrayal of people's affectionate attitude toward rubles somehow aligned with the notion of Russia's backwardness. Arguing against the idea of introducing credit notes instead of assignats, Kochubei wrote that "Russia, for many good reasons, in its institutional organization cannot fully follow the examples of European countries." Among these "good reasons" were economic underdevelopment, the untrustworthiness of tradesmen, the absence of commercial laws, the inefficiency of the judicial system, and, most important, the lack of "enlightenment" among people, which made the circulation of promissory notes and other "credit papers" impossible. Therefore, only assignats, papers based on the "firm promises" of the state rather than on credit, could circulate normally.[78]

The ideal image of simple folk who fully and unconditionally trusted the tsar's paper money combined the nationalist adoration of peasant life with the critique of the arrogance of the commercial elite. Interestingly, Kochubei's theory of the "people's ruble" reversed Karamzin's and Vasiliev's earlier ideas about assignats as the expression of a superior form of economic thinking, which required an ability to comprehend the abstract concepts of value. If Karamzin praised the Russian people for the invention of imaginary money, Kochubei emphasized its backwardness. Both, however, wanted to prove that Russia did not need the convertibility of paper money and an independent bank. In later debates, the opponents of monetary and bank reforms often used the argument of Russia's underdevelopment, while the adherents of reforms criticized the government for "making peasants backward" and denying them the possibility of using money based on credit rather than the government's law.[79]

In conservative rhetoric and official ideology, the ruble assignat had turned into a true "people's currency," the material embodiment of the bond between the tsar and his subject. However, it seems that despite the wide acceptance of assignats, "the people" did not value them very highly and counted a ruble assignat as a quarter of a silver ruble.[80] In addition, as Dmitrii Guryev reported, the influx of counterfeited assignats brought in by the Napoleonic army "instilled prejudice" against them among peasants who were seeking silver instead of paper money. To restore the "simple people's trust in assignats," the government urged all state offices to accept and exchange all counterfeited assignats without delay and to show "mildness and lenience" toward their bearers.[81]

The government's anxiety about the attitude to assignats suggests that, despite the rhetorical emphasis on the irrelevance of rates, it could not totally ignore the assignats' fall. Minister of Finance Dmitrii Guryev, who after Speransky's exile enjoyed freedom in administering Russian finances, hoped to raise the rate by simply reducing the amount of paper money in circulation. In 1818, the government gradually started withdrawing assignats from circulation while simultaneously replacing old assignats with newly designed assignats manufactured at a new state-owned money-printing factory named the Expedition for the Production of State Papers (EZGB, Ekspeditsiia Zagotovleniia Gosudarstvennykh Bumag). In addition to traditional elements (serial number and pledge to exchange to hard currency, sealed by two signatures) the new assignats featured the two-headed eagle with an imperial crown. This was both a departure from the previous modest form and a recognition of the assignats' status as real money rather than a representation of hard currency.

Between 1818 and 1823, 252 million out of 836 million rubles assignat in circulation were withdrawn through an exchange for silver at a current rate and were destroyed.[82] This costly operation made the government seek resources abroad and float a loan in Europe. Nikolai Turgenev laughed at such an irrational and absurd policy: "The financiers, who had lent money to us, could not believe that the government would . . . burn the millions that it had borrowed, in order to replace the interest-free debt [of assignats] with a debt burdened by interests. . . . In what mental derangement was the Russian government when it ventured upon such an absurd measure?"[83] True, the destruction of the millions of assignats without changes in the mechanisms of their issuance could not improve the monetary system; the rate of assignats to silver increased by merely 6 kopecks (from 1:3.79 to 1:3.73).[84] It is noteworthy that Russian economists of that time recognized that one cannot fix a system distorted by inflation simply by withdrawing bad money. As Nikolai Demidov wrote in the late 1820s, "fallen currency" essentially represented counterfeited money, and its authenticity could not be restored by reducing its amount. The government should "replace counterfeited money with the authentic money," since merely exempting a certain amount of assignats from circulation would raise the prices of goods but not the value of money.[85]

———

"Words are the conditional signs of thoughts," wrote Petr Viazemskii in 1826 (a distant relative of Catherine II's procurator general Alexander Viazemskii, Petr was a poet, and a close friend of Alexander Pushkin). "Some of them have in our eyes real value, acquired through time and use; others are being introduced forcefully, and their value is conditional. [When] the state does not have enough metal coins, it recurs to assignats. [When] language does not have enough indigenous words, it recurs to composite or fake words."[86] In a piece published in *The Moscow Telegraph*, P. Viazemskii used the metaphor of paper assignats to comment on the famous dispute around the Russian language between the conservative archaists and the cosmopolitan innovators. The issue at stake was much larger than either the development of language or the problem of monetary reform: the role of the state in cultural and economic life, and the relationship between state and society. Who can and should define the direction and character of language's progress? In Viazemskii's view, the conservative policy of reforming the language by artificially creating new words from Church-Slavonic roots produced "fake coins that cannot prove their authenticity in the furnace of taste." The authenticity of words, as well as the authenticity of money, was to be defined through social consensus rather than an order from above. "When is an assignat valid? When the one who put it in circulation holds responsibility for it, and either with force or by some other means makes others count it for what he wants them to count." Coins and assignats were the "representative signs of things" created by the "society of equal people" to facilitate trade and contractual relations. "A *representative sign* has no value outside society, but inside the society its value is firm and indubitable."[87]

Extending the parallel between money and language, Viazemskii suggested that society, in a similar manner, should be able to generate new words that have currency and are accepted by everyone. Nationalists did not welcome foreign borrowings: "It is not allowed to take foreign words: from such a loan, the national conceit would suffer. . . . But what can be done?" How to cure the shortage of words "for the expression of thoughts and concepts"? Viazemskii's solution to the language problem came from the analogy with monetary emission: to fill up the vocabulary with new words that would reflect national consensus rather than the opinion of a few. The ability of the "representative signs"—words and money—to represent true values, meanings, and thoughts was the most essential quality; the absence of such an ability voided their status altogether.

Viazemskii's choice of metaphor and its connection to the idea of representation betrayed his deep familiarity with Enlightenment philosophy and contemporary philosophical debates in Europe. It also reflected Russia's peculiar intellectual climate in an epoch when literature, scholarship, and public service were not yet compartmentalized into different occupational clusters. A famous poet, journalist, and literary critic, Viazemskii alternated state service with freelance work in journals. From 1818 to 1820, he was a member of a reform team that worked on the elaboration of constitutional plans, including the famous "Constitutional Charter" of 1820 that remained unsigned despite Alexander I's declared commitment to the reform. Viazemskii's major personal contribution was the translation from French to Russian of Alexander I's constitutional speech in Warsaw, which required the invention of constitutional vocabulary that was still a novelty in Russia.[88]

Most likely, Viazemvskii's epistemological vision of money as language and a form of political representation was drawn from the works of Jean-Jacques Rousseau, who famously lamented the inability of words to convey man's thoughts and to live up to the visual sensations of the world as well as the inability of money to express the true value of things. He similarly asserted the impossibility of the representation of sovereignty through parliament.[89] While not sharing Rousseau's pessimism in regard to political representation and his admiration of direct democracy, Russian intellectuals picked up the epistemological juxtaposition of language, money, and parliament and used it to advance new ideas peculiar to the Russian situation. Viazemskii's discontent with the state regulation of language and culture mirrored Russian liberals' dissatisfaction with the state's monopoly on issuing paper money and making laws: both assaulted the people's sovereignty in the cultural sphere as well as in politics and finances.

After Alexander I's death, the Decembrist Rebellion, and the political reaction that followed, ideas of constitutionalism and financial rule of law were seemingly consigned to oblivion, at least in official discourse. Russia's commitment to an autocratic paper standard, a result of ideological choice and necessity, excluded the possibility of constitutional and financial reform. The ideas of monetary reform moved to the periphery of attention, while liberal thinkers fell under the prosecution of authorities for too literally interpreting the government's invitation to participate in the process of reforms. What could not be reversed was the firmly established understanding of money as a part of a system of governance and the alignment of financial ideas with philosophical, epistemological, and political concepts. The flexible intellectual climate in which discourse about language and history could stand in for money and constitution allowed the debate to continue.

The first quarter of the nineteenth century was a crucial period for the formation of financial ideologies. Until Alexander I's reforms, tensions between conservative "nominalists" and liberal "monetarists," the two visions of money that corresponded to political and epistemological views, had not been clearly articulated. The beginning of political debates about the future of the Russian monarchy and ways to reconcile the lofty and widely popular liberal ideas of constitutionalism with the existing principles of monarchal rule stimulated the crystallization of the two opposing ideologies. In Russia, as elsewhere, the main question was the origin of money and its nature. In the elevated atmosphere of Alexander I's early reign, the discussion about whether the state could preserve the monopoly of designating the value of national currency often turned into a conversation about the relationship between the state and society and touched on the issues of citizenship, morality, and culture. The debates expanded the rhetorical boundaries of talk about money that came to include the problems of language, rights, and constitution.

3

The End of Assignats

Platinum Assignats

In 1822, workers washing sand at a private gold mine in the Ural Mountains noticed grains of white metal. As it turned out, the substance contained alloys of platinum. Within the next few years, other fields with platinum were discovered, and Russia suddenly became the world leader in platinum production.[1] The only other country that produced platinum at that time was Colombia.

Platinum was an unlikely candidate for a new kind of currency metal, since it was precious, rare, and unwanted. The process of minting was costly and the results not completely satisfactory, because platinum coins looked very much like silver ones and were therefore susceptible to counterfeiting. However, the discovery of platinum happened at a time when Russia's currency system lay in ruins and nationalism was on the rise. The idea of founding its own currency model, one not necessarily based on accepted European standards, may have seemed attractive to Russian officials, and the St. Petersburg Mint produced the first experimental coins in 1827. Nicholas I liked the coin so much that he immediately approved the design.[2] Yet, because so little platinum was on the world market, defining the coin's value was difficult. Egor (Georg) Kankrin, the minister of finance appointed after Guryev's departure in April 1823, sought advice from someone very familiar with the mining, geology, and economy of South America: German scientist, philosopher, and traveler Alexander von Humboldt. Kankrin asked Humboldt to help him determine the rate of platinum coins vis-à-vis silver.[3]

Humboldt did not hide his skepticism regarding Kankrin's plan of making money out of platinum: other countries would not accept platinum coins, and the currency would have to remain "provincial." Russia could certainly mine plenty of platinum and turn it into coins, but this domestic money would be "no other than the same paper money, but heavy and inconvenient."[4] Humboldt recommended that the government use platinum to make medals and insignias, so that His Majesty could award Russian and foreign scholars with memorable gifts other than traditional golden rings and snuffboxes.[5]

Kankrin did not follow Humboldt's advice. Perhaps Nicholas's fascination with the new coins was too strong, or his hope to establish a standard by which Russia would overcome the West distracted him from the obvious fact that, without international acceptance, platinum was no better than paper assignats. Responding to Humboldt's skepticism, Kankrin insisted that state institutions would accept platinum coins "not according to nominal value," that is, as assignats, but according to their intrinsic value, like gold and silver. However, since there was no market beyond Russia's borders, the "intrinsic" value of platinum was set fairly arbitrarily by the decree of April 24, 1828, which announced the introduction of new coins in platinum made from the same mold as silver coins but featuring the inscription "3 silver rubles."[6] The coins also stated that they had been made of "pure Ural platinum." Like other coins of that period, they bore the image of the two-headed eagle.

The issuance of platinum coins ignited the interest of Simon Bolivar, and Humboldt was even invited to counsel the Colombian "dictator" on platinum money. Nothing came of it, however, and Russia remained the only country to ever use platinum as regular currency. Kankrin, it seems, was very excited about the future of new money and, as he mentioned in his letter to the scientist, "took measures to spread the coins in Asia," that is, in Persia.[7] However, these plans remained in the realm of fantasy. The production of platinum in Russia increased, but the demand for it outside Russia remained low. In 1832, Baron Meiendorf reported to the government that in Paris, a *pood* (16 kilos) of Colombian platinum was sold for 5,238 rubles, while the Imperial Mint in St. Petersburg paid the Demidovs' mines, the main suppliers of Ural platinum, 9,472 rubles for the same amount of raw metal.[8] The government reacted by simply prohibiting the import of platinum, and because the nominal value of Russian *platinnik* was almost twice as high as its value on European markets,[9] smuggling platinum to Russia and making it into coins became increasingly profitable. In other words, Humboldt's prediction about platinum assignats proved correct. By the late 1830s, the coins started to disappear[10] and in 1845 they were exempted from circulation. People were given six months to exchange their platinum coins and after the deadline passed, the government recommended that holders of the former money "find the most profitable way" to use them.[11]

The coinage of platinum was an experiment, and the government did not go far in trying to remake an entire monetary system that rested on assignats. More than a numismatic curiosity, however, Russian platinum coins represented a very particular nationalist ideology of monetary policy, one that denied the role of international monetary markets in defining the value of money. Kankrin believed that the value of money rested on the power of the sovereign and the "moral" bonds between the tsar and the people. The story of platinum is therefore a remarkable attempt to invent Russia's own standard and to turn the deficiency of capital into a benefit. It defines the financial ideology of Nicholas I's reign (1825–55) better than more celebrated events.[12]

Money, Trust, and Evidence

Egor Kankrin, unlike his predecessor Guryev, was an experienced manager and a very opinionated economist who wrote several treatises on political economy. Confident in the fallacy of the inflationist policy, he was also a vocal critic of liberal political economy and the financial ideas that had inspired it. He was a cameralist, or an advocate of state-centered technocratic ideology in economics.[13] At the same time, Kankrin's technocratism somehow coexisted with a romantic economic nationalism that stressed paternalism, the morality of the pre-industrial economic order, and a belief that the national spirit defined economic existence. While Kankrin agreed that paper money was an evil, he thought it could "survive much longer in a nation which lags behind the general European culture . . . than in countries of high culture."[14] Russia belonged to the category of nations fairly isolated from the rest of the world; Russians valued their paper currency more than foreigners did, and, while the exchange rate of the ruble assignat fell on European markets, its domestic rate diminished to a much lesser extent. Patriotism, popular trust in the state, isolation, and backwardness ensured the stability of paper money.[15] This statement certainly manifested a departure from liberal theory that, as Kankrin believed, could work in no society.[16]

Conservative economic theory often relied on the argument of morality, culture, and the spiritual connection between the sovereign and his people as opposed to the inferior forces of the market. As Kankrin wrote in his first, programmatic memo to Alexander I after his appointment in 1823, assignats did not represent the state's debt but were rather a kind of "mental money," a system of moral credit that originated from the government and then permeated society and relations between individuals. Russian assignats represented a superior kind of money because "the consorted warranty of the entire people . . . is much stronger that any metallic fund, which cannot add anything [to it] and, in general, is unable to raise the assignats above their worth." Be it copper, silver, gold, or even the legendary wootz steel, metal cannot support the value of paper if it does not enjoy public credit.[17] These ideas may not appear new, but Kankrin's ideology of Russia's cultural distinctiveness, more poignant and pragmatic than Karamzin's earlier cosmopolitan nationalism, represented one of the first manifestations of a new philosophy that later became known as Official Nationality.

Though the newly professed ideological centrality of the nation and Kankrin's economic nationalism are rarely compared, the connections between these two pillars of Nicholas's reign are profound. Kankrin's memos, declarations, and legislative proposals arguably laid the groundwork for the ideology and policy of Official Nationality. Kankrin's idea of the national distinctiveness and moral ties that held an economic nation together also assumed the centrality of the state and predated the doctrine of "official nationality," formulated in 1833 by Nicholas I's minister of education Serguei Uvarov.[18] The philosophical and epistemological foundation of both doctrines put forward the newly invented concepts of trust and authenticity. The centrality of the rhetoric of trust in conservative doctrine requires explanation since the preponderance of trust is usually associated with liberal ideas of political participation. Trust also represents the cornerstone of the credit system in market economies of which Kankrin was a staunch opponent, and the difference between the two interpretations of trust—economic and monarchical—was subtle but essential.

In Kankrin's notion of money's authenticity, reliance on the silver standard appeared dishonoring and incompatible with the dignity of the monarchy because it allowed for the existence of doubt. Nikolai Karamzin applied the same concept of indubitable truth to his treatment of historical sources, constructing a streamlined historical narrative of the emergence of the Russian state, including the development of its monetary system. In the 1820s through the 1840s, the juxtaposition of material and immaterial proofs became a key issue in the debates over the principles of historical authenticity, in which Serguei Uvarov, also a historian, played an important role. In the 1820s, Russian historians developed methods of historical source criticism thereby questioning the official narratives of the emergence of the Russian state. Conservative historians responded by condemning these attempts and contrasting the notion of historical truth based on criticism and doubt with the concept of authenticity originating in the blind trust of the state and its

version of history. One of the central episodes of this controversy concerned
the story of "leather money"—the alleged medieval "assignats" made from the
skins of wild animals.

Although evidence of leather money's existence was very thin and nobody except for Karamzin had seen it, until the late 1820s historians did not
doubt the validity of Karamzin's theory. Between 1828 and 1835, historian
Mikhail Kachenovskii published a series of articles on the monetary system
of the early Kievan state. Applying a method of textual analysis, Kachenovskii
argued that the monetary system of Kievan Rus' consisted only of metal
coins: silver coins, known as *grivna*, could be exchanged for the metal coins
of smaller denominations, which were named after the prototypes of money,
kuny and *belki*. Kachenovskii protested the attempts at modernizing the Rus'
state and medieval monetary system through the parallel with assignats. Rus'
was sufficiently advanced to abandon skins and tails but not civilized enough
to start thinking in abstract values. Silver and gold currency represented an
intermediary stage in the development of money.[19] Kachenovskii's arguments
against the existence of leather money, therefore, flew in the face of official
historiography and ideology in two ways.[20] First, Kachenovskii questioned
the trustworthiness of early medieval chronicles, none of which had survived
in an original form, and the existence of the Kievan Rus' state as Karamzin
had pictured it. Second, he called historians to think freely and assess the historical possibility of facts instead of blindly trusting their sources. In total, it
amounted to a subversion of the master narrative about the development of
the Russian state and economy.[21]

In the early 1830s, Kachenovskii's works were heavily criticized by nationalist historians, and in 1835, the minister Uvarov removed him from
his professorship in Russian history at St. Petersburg University. Although
Kachenovskii had a few followers, his "skeptical school" faded into oblivion,
while the dominant nationalist school, sponsored and promoted by Uvarov's
ministry, grew in influence. As Uvarov formulated the credo of this historical
worldview, "historical truth" was not based on the critical analysis of sources
and scientific inquiry into evidence but on national consensus. Truth was what
people, guided by the state and religion, agreed on. The nationalist conservative emphasis on belief and consensus, as opposed to the materiality of evidence and critical analysis, bore a very important political and philosophical
message that appeared in Kankrin's interpretation of paper money grounded
on faith and power and in the political doctrine of Official Nationality. Paper
money did not require proof of its value, and no one could doubt the validity
of sovereign promises.

Kankrin was not, however, an impractical romantic thinker fascinated only with the ideas of nationalism and cultural uniqueness. His nationalist economic theory was conveniently turned into a pragmatic model that became known as the "Kankrin system." In addition to strict protectionism and anti-industrialism, this model included three other deeply interconnected elements: the state's monopoly on credit operations, the status quo for assignats, and total secrecy regarding state finance, money, and credit. Kankrin openly detested private banks and their profit-seeking activity. As he wrote in a treatise published two years before his appointment as a minister of finance, private banks issuing banknotes "should perhaps not be tolerated, on the same ground that one does not tolerate charlatans, universal remedies and other arts that speculate on the credulity of the public."[22] The minister believed that, because private banks were driven by profit, they deserved zero confidence; therefore, governments should try to abolish private banks and replace them with reliable state credit institutions "acting not only under control but under the government's management."[23] Setting aside Kankrin's indignation with profit-seeking capitalists, his attitude toward private banks and the preservation of the treasury banks' monopoly had a very practical explanation: it allowed the state to draw money from the national economy without pouring newly printed assignats into circulation.

This is how it worked. State (or "treasury") banks, which had no competitors on the market, accepted deposits and paid high (5%, and 4% after 1830) compounding interest to their clients, who could withdraw their money at any moment. Noble landowners could take out long-term mortgage loans (of 15, 28, and 56 years) on the security of their serf estates. In other words, the government was pumping money from the accounts of all depositors to the accounts of noble borrowers. Most important, along with the landowners, the state treasury was one of the main borrowers of capital from those banks, simply using money sitting in the accounts of individual clients and organizations to cover gaps in state revenues. Enormous sums of money that accumulated in banks, instead of being invested in production and commerce, were spent on the current needs of the state and on nobles' consumption. The de facto prohibition on the crediting industry and entrepreneurship helped preserve money in the accounts of treasury-owned banks.[24] According to Kankrin, only government institutions deserved the trust of the tsar's subjects.

The treasury's borrowing from the deposit accounts in state banks represented the easiest and most convenient alternative to foreign loans and the emission of assignats. This secret borrowing did not require public announcements and therefore did not immediately affect the ruble's rate and convertibility.[25] Although politically convenient, this kind of domestic borrowing by the government was very expensive and inefficient because the government paid very high interest on deposits in order to keep money in the banks. Crucially, it necessitated the preservation of a state monopoly on the issuance of money, a monopoly that turned out to be closely tied to the entire system of credit through a vicious circle of state borrowing. The government always ran the risk of being unable to pay back millions of rubles deposited in banks and subject to "immediate" withdrawal. In such a case, it could only secure its financial liability by printing more paper money. Sometimes, the government had to bypass borrowing from banks because the amount of money available in the banks had fallen dangerously low and paying back clients could be problematic.[26]

Thus, both Kankrin's anti-bourgeois rhetoric and his policy of diverting funds away from industry concealed the very simple and pragmatic goal of financing the state through secret borrowings from its subjects' pockets. It was also closely connected to the principles of the monetary system. Every year, when reporting the success of his financial policy at the Council of State Credit Institutions, Kankrin stressed that the amount of assignats in circulation remained unchanged. In the early nineteenth century, such stability looked miraculous. In fact, when a group of reformers tackled the problem of state banks in 1858, they discovered that the state was on the brink of bankruptcy and unable to pay back its debts.

The semblance of a perfect financial order sharply contrasted with the public perception of economic reality. People wondered why, if the amount of assignats remained the same, the ruble's rate was constantly fluctuating. Why did the state prioritize assignats over silver and gold coins that were circulating along with paper money? Why was the economy of Russia grounded on money that had lost its "dignity" and value? Kankrin interpreted the Russians' affection for assignats as a national trait, but to close observers, the strange cult of a fallen money seemed like a metaphor for political crisis, decay, the perversion of values, and the loss of authenticity.

Taming the Rate

Guryev's withdrawal of assignats had created a deficit of money, which was quickly filled with silver, gold, and foreign coins that in some areas even outnumbered the national currency.[27] The state, however, did not accept coins as payment for taxes and dues, therefore artificially creating a constant demand for assignats. Merchants, tax farmers, and local authorities petitioned the government to allow them to pay taxes and other state dues in silver, but until the late 1820s, the government declined those demands, fearing that the acceptance of metal coins would further lower the rate of assignats.[28] Only in 1827 did the government start accepting coins for certain state payments in several provinces. Thus, paradoxically, the government denied the acceptance of silver and gold money, insisting on the acceptance of paper money and thereby encouraging the fluctuation of the assignats' "price."[29]

For this reason, among others, people preferred to be paid in assignats rather than in silver, which, as Pushkin put it, represented the "legacy of fathers" in contrast to the mundane utilitarianism of the "bunches of assignats."[30] Nikolai Gogol made almost all of the protagonists of his short stories and novels pay in paper. For instance, Chichikov of *Dead Souls* persuades the owners of the deceased peasants to sell him the peasants' souls by promising payment "only in assignats." The parallel between people who exist only on paper and paper money accentuates the fictitious quality of both. Stepan Probka, the dead carpenter of the greedy landowner Pliushkin, hides "the state's" (*gosudarstvennaia*), that is, the assignat, by sewing it into his canvas pants. Gogol used the feminine adjective "the state's" as a noun because the censor had scratched out the noun "assignat," leaving only the possessive behind.[31] The corrupt police officer in "The Nose" glorified the virtues of the assignat, which could not be compared to anything else: "this thing . . . does not ask for food, does not take up a lot of space, can always fit into a pocket, and if you dropped it—it would not break."[32] Assignats always appeared crumpled and in "bunches"; the artists from Gogol's "The Portrait" traded their talent for these "bunches."[33] In Dostoyevsky's *The Double*, assignats, the fake substitutes of money, underscore the effect of absurdist duplicity and mystification.[34] As the doppelganger of the main character, Mr. Goliadkin, steals away his life and money, assignats are characterized as the ruble's imposter. For Dostoevsky, Gogol, and other writers, assignats were a metaphor for the perversion of values in Russian life, where bribery ruled and old believers baked assignats into bread—the traditional honorary gift—to ease the repressions by corrupt officials.[35] Perhaps the most explicit and sarcastic take on the cult of the assignat, an anonymous mock manual called *The Art of Bribe-taking* (1830), recommended to its readers "of all state monetary signs, to choose assignats because they come from hand to hand without noise and clatter; easily change for silver and gold, even with a profit; take little space and fit into everything: a pocket, under a necktie, in boots, under the sleeves' cuffs." In this world, each assignat had a nickname: "a 5-ruble assignat we call a tomtit, a 10-ruble one—a bullfinch, the 25 and 50 ruble are white doves, a 100-ruble [assignat]—a dandy, or a dusky redshank, for its size and pretty ornament, and a 200-ruble assignat—a trout, for the colors of its inside."[36] The "poetic" language of bribe-taking, the manual suggested, made the whole business easy and enjoyable.

Russia's monetary system struck outside observers as a world in which everything was turned upside down. Astolphe Marquis de Custine, who visited Russia in 1839, was shocked to discover that "in Russia, the silver money represents the paper, although the latter was created and is legally authorized only to represent the silver."[37] "It is, perhaps, the only example in the history of finances," remarked Custine in his famous travelogue *La Russie en 1839*. It is extraordinary in the view of Custine and others, that it was the silver ruble, not the assignat, that was constantly fluctuating. Indeed, the official *Commercial Newspaper* [*Kommercheskaia Gazeta*] announced the rates in a form that indicated the prices of gold and silver rubles, for instance, "Gold ruble—3 ruble 62 kop.; Silver ruble—3 ruble 51 ½ kop.," as if assignats represented a *sui generis* currency.[38] The ruble was an elusive category, a speculative unit whose value was subject to multiple local and subjective factors.

Starting in 1817, the State Council annually approved the "tax" rate of exchange for the ruble silver to assignat, which was slightly different from the "stock-exchange" and "custom-duty" rates of exchange that oscillated between 1:3.5 and 1:3.6.[39] In addition to these state-approved rates of assignat-to-silver exchange, the market produced so-called popular rates that depended on the place, amount, purpose, time of transaction, and, especially, the means of payment. Assignats, gold coins, silver rubles, and copper and silver kopecks of different denominations all had different prices.[40] Merchants calculated the prices of goods in imaginary units called "coin rubles" or simply "moneta" according to which one assignat constituted around one-fourth of a ruble. However, to adjust prices to the current rate, they added "*lazh*," that is, an adjustment for paying in assignats, silver rubles, gold coins, and sometimes even copper. *Lazh* allowed merchants to avoid frequent recalculations of prices caused by the local fluctuation of the ruble's standing, the availability of currency, season, and other factors, such as the collection of taxes that increased the demand for assignats. For example, in Moscow in 1839, the imaginary "coin ruble" constituted 4.25 ruble assignats. Listing the prices of goods, merchants indicated "*lazh* on assignat," which in early January 1839 equaled 20 kopecks bringing the actual silver to assignat rate to 1:3.54 (1: 1.2 x 4.25 = 3.54). In St. Petersburg, the "coin ruble" constituted 3.75 ruble assignats, *lazh* was 6.5 kopecks, meaning that the rate was close to 1:3.52.[41] However, not only ruble assignats had prices. A typical price listing, like the one for grain in Moscow in late January, indicated the "price" of a silver ruble (4.30), gold half-imperials (22 rubles each, which is 4.4 for one gold ruble), and "*lazh* on assignat" (in this case, 21 kop.).[42]

The existence of the *lazh* certainly added complexity to accounting, as evidenced by the manuals for housekeepers.[43] In Kankrin's interpretation, the popular rate, or *lazh,* was a trick invented by merchants with an intention to deceive simple people. Official propaganda stressed the narrative of deception calling on merchants to list all prices in assignats or silver rubles without *lazh.* In March 1839, the newspaper reported on a patriotic move by tea and wine traders in Moscow who had agreed not to include *lazh* in their calculation of the goods' prices.[44] The names of traders who had agreed to sell goods at the rate approved by the government, without *lazh*, appeared regularly in the pages of the *Commercial Newspaper* and other publications, along with the government's warnings that traders participating in the exhibition of manufacturers in May 1839 must list the prices of their goods without *lazh* and according to the government's rate of 1:3.6.[45]

Assailing the vicious practice of using *lazh,* the government referred to the interests of simple peasants who were not able to comprehend the meaning of the rate and were deceived by greedy merchants, but the main reason for the government's discontent was apparently a different one. The popular rate emerged in response to a particular situation in Russia's monetary system in which the main unit of value was unstable and multiple kinds of money, including foreign coins, circulated in parallel. In other words, the abstract "coin ruble" was a product of the market—the chimera that Kankrin perceived as incompatible with Russia's traditional economy.[46] Moreover, the market-based currency unit contradicted the logic of monarchal rule, according to which money was a creation of the sovereign's will and could not originate on its own. As recalled by Konstantin Fischer, who served in the Ministry of Finance under Kankrin, "The tsar wanted to issue a decree prohibiting *lazh,* but Kankrin responded that after such a decree, *lazh* would definitely double. The tsar felt offended. 'You shall see,' he said, 'I am going to show that in Russia, there is still autocracy.'"[47]

The government's discontent with the existence of popular rates somehow contradicted Kankrin's assertion regarding the primary role of trust and people's thinking about assignats in defining their standing. Its reaction to the popular rates also points out that this abstract "people" stood for very particular social categories; the "people" were the taxpayers and the consumers and producers of agricultural goods, while merchants and industrialists, who

tried to adapt prices to the fluctuation of the ruble's value, did not fall into
this category. Most important, in the ideal national monetary system, based
on consensus between the government and society, the government was nevertheless supposed to dominate. The monetary reform initiated by Kankrin
aimed at eliminating popular rates and putting an end to the fluid and unstable situation of having multiple monies.

"The national means of payment, instead of their primary destination to
be the tools of trade and other needs of social life, had themselves become the
objects of bargain,"[48] stated the State Council's report on the projected reform
that intended to turn rubles from merchandise into a solid currency. The series of measures undertaken between 1839 and 1843 ended with the abolition
of the old assignats and the issuing of new "state credit bills," which remained
in circulation until the early 1920s. The reform began with the *ukaz* of July
1, 1839, which reversed the relation between paper assignat and silver and
restored the priority of the silver ruble as the main measure of value.[49] The
assignats were again—as in 1810—degraded to the level of "auxiliary" tokens
that could be exchanged in local treasury offices for silver rubles at the rate of
1:3.5 and in the maximum amount of 100 rubles.

The political meaning of the monetary transformation was apparent from
the very beginning of the reform process. Its first step, the definition of the
exchange rate, made clear that the value and status of the ruble had to depend
solely on the sovereign's will. The popular rate valued one ruble assignat on
average as one quarter of a "coin" ruble, plus *lazh*. The stock-exchange rate
oscillated between 1:3.5 and 1:3.6, while the tax rate in 1839 equaled 1:3.6.
Therefore, the government had to decide which rate it was going to fix for
good. When the State Council, a consultative legislative body created by
Speransky, discussed the rate, the majority of the legislators suggested fixing
it at a tax collection rate of one silver ruble to 3.6 rubles assignat. Kankrin,
supported by three other members, insisted on accepting the current stock-
exchange rate of 1:3.5. The government probably could have gone either way,
but Kankrin used his personal access to the tsar to persuade him to take
his side. When the members of the State Council met again to discuss the
issue, Kankrin presented the tsar's personal note approving the 1:3.5 rate, and
the legislative assembly could do nothing but vote on the tsar's choice. The
whole issue was, therefore, turned into a political scandal over the power of
the tsar and the role of the State Council in the legislative process. Kankrin
interpreted the State Council's efforts to continue discussion after the manifestation of the sovereign's will as a "tremendous insult of the supreme authority. . . . The Council is a consultative body, to which the tsar sends only

what he wants [to send]." Thus, the question of monetary reform once again invoked the problems of rule of law and authority. In the end, the Council voted according to the tsar's will. The ruble's rate depended neither on the forces of the market nor on the opinion of the legislative body but only on the monarch's word. All further decisions on the reform, such as the intro- duction of new credit notes and the withdrawal of assignats, originated from correspondence between Nicholas I, Kankrin and his opponents as well as the debates in a secret committee presided over by the tsar.

Draped in the rhetoric of legality and order, the restoration of the assignats' convertibility at the 1:3.5 rate represented the state's recognition of its inability to raise the value of paper money. The government did not con- sider devaluation as overly embarrassing or shameful, counting on the public to forget it, but the operation would certainly not pass unnoticed.[50] Vasilii Kokorev sarcastically commented that the announcement of the Manifesto of July 1, 1839, followed the wedding day of Nicholas I's daughter. Traditionally, such events were marked by a display of the monarch's mercy, and everyone expected that the tsar would pardon the Decembrists.[51] Instead, the "gracious manifesto" declared the bankruptcy of the state.[52] More seriously, the de- cree was announced shortly before the opening of the annual fair in Nizhnii Novgorod, the most important commercial event of the year. Merchants la- mented that many contracts had been already sealed under the old conditions, and the introduction of the new system threatened to inflict significant fi- nancial losses. Marquis de Custine, who was in Nizhnii Novgorod at the time, described a remarkable encounter between the provincial governor and the representatives of the commercial elite. In response to the merchants' complaints about the unexpected change in the ruble's status, the governor declared that a delay in the implementation of the government's measure would have brought much more ruinous consequences for the country than the bankruptcies of a few individuals.[53] The reform affected all social groups in different ways. Alexander Nikitenko, a writer who also worked in a censorship office, observed in his diary that those who were in state serv- ice overnight became poorer; their salary, previously calculated in assignats, was converted to silver rubles in a 1:3.6 ratio instead of the announced rate of 1:3.5.[54] The reform also led to a significant increase in food prices. The govern- ment reminded merchants that they had to recalculate prices at the new rate of 1:3.5, but very few complied.

Another decree, issued simultaneously with the law on the silver standard, announced the opening of the so-called deposit offices in the state Commercial Bank, where people could exchange their silver coins for special temporary deposit certificates—a new kind of state papers with a nominal value in silver rubles and exchangeable at any time for coins at par. Deposit certificates acquired unprecedented popularity, partly due to convenience but mostly because of the fear of a looming reform and the total secrecy that surrounded it. Somebody spread a rumor that the government would soon stop accepting coins, and people rushed to the bank to convert their savings in silver and gold into new paper certificates. Describing crowds of people carrying bags of coins besieging the building of the state Commercial Bank on Sadovaia Street, observers remarked that such a scene could only take place in Russia. In the first thirteen months after their opening, the state deposit offices received 26 million rubles in silver.[55]

Kankrin's Plan and a Polish Alternative

Establishing a fixed exchange rate for paper and silver rubles and releasing new "deposit" money did not appear to be a permanent solution. After all, the government's goal was to make people forget the fall of state paper money. How to proceed with the reform remained an open question that could be resolved only through personal communications with the tsar. Kankrin certainly enjoyed the almost unlimited trust of the emperor, but he was not the only person who courted the tsar's attention and offered plans of reform.[56] Among these proposals, the most radical came from Prince Franziszek Drucki-Lubecki, the former minister of finance in the autonomous Kingdom of Poland, who tried to persuade the emperor that the reform could not move forward without the creation of a new bank of discount and issue.

Kankrin's plan of fixing the Russian monetary system on the silver standard assumed minimal innovations.[57] The minister suggested exchanging assignats for deposit certificates that would in turn be redeemable for silver accumulated in the treasury banks' vaults. However, he also proposed increasing the amount of the certificates to 170 million and setting up a silver reserve fund in one-sixth of this amount, thereby changing the status of the certificates and diluting their metallic backing.[58] The idea of immobilizing a substantial amount of wealth in the bullion reserve seemed strange to him, and Kankrin planned to have only 10 million rubles in coins in the reserve,[59] holding the remaining 18 million rubles in treasury bonds. Therefore, the deposit certificates were supposed to change their ratio to metal from 1:1 to 1:17. It remained unclear what would happen to those 50 million rubles in coins brought by the public to exchange for deposit certificates. The minister's avoidance of this question gave the impression that the government would simply pocket that money after turning the deposit certificates into the new kind of state currency.

This plan looked like blatant state fraud, and Nicholas I, perhaps under the influence of his advisers, rejected Kankrin's proposal. Quite unusually, the tsar personally wrote a memo criticizing Kankrin's approach and emphasizing the government's honor and the "sanctity" of its promises. The deposit certificates, as the tsar noted, were issued as the direct 1:1 substitute for silver, and their full exchangeability represented a "inalterable, sacred condition," which had made them so popular with the public. They turned into a token of "trust in the Government and its word," and the change of their status, therefore, could undermine people's belief in the "government's honesty." Silver brought by the public did not belong to the government; the state was merely its "keeper."[60] The tsar's somewhat theatrical gesture gave everyone a signal to attack Kankrin's cunning plan. It also launched a debate over the notions of honor and trust. Alexander Chernyshev, minister of war, described Kankrin's plan as an encroachment on "other people's property" and "inconvenient, unjust, not compatible with the government's dignity."[61] The most ferocious accusations came from Franziszek Drucki-Lubecki, who unequivocally called Kankrin's plan a speculation and drew parallels between the ministry's policy and unscrupulous merchants who try to find ways to enrich themselves even in bankruptcy.[62]

Kankrin and Drucki-Lubecki were political rivals, and their stances concerning the principles of the relationship between the state and society were diametrically opposed. But what stood out in Drucki-Lubecki's critique of Kankrin's proposal was his references to trust and knowledge. Drucki-Lubecki emphatically stressed the persistence of public memory. Contrary to Kankrin's claims regarding the trust in state money, "the public remembered" the government's promises to limit the issue of assignats, and it also remembered that the government broke these promises. "The public" was conscious that the assignats bore an inscription promising their convertibility into "current money," without specifying the metal of coins, but that they remained unconvertible for most of their existence. "The public remembered" that the government had changed the amount and value of copper coins several times; the public could thus conclude that the combination offered by Kankrin did not secure the stability of the standard.[63] "The public knew" that in all well-governed states there were banks of issue, independent of the institutions that dealt with state incomes and expenditures, and that the amount of banknotes issued by these banks was backed by the value of mortgaged properties. It was aware of the experience in other countries, which had successfully dealt

with their currency problem by establishing strict legal norms shielding the
process of money-making from the abuses of power. Kankrin's plan to replace
assignats with deposit certificates represented, therefore, not simply the rejection of all norms and rules established through the experience of other
countries, but an open fraud. "What would people think? What would they
say? What would those who hold in their hands, instead of real money, the
certificates given to them by the government have to do? What would Europe
of the nineteenth century say about that?"[64]

The ferociousness of Drucki-Lubecki's attack on Kankrin could also be
explained by his desire to achieve his own goals of monetary reform and bank
organization that he had designed at the tsar's request.[65] This plan, in sharp
contrast to Kankrin's, replicated European practices of monetary policy. The
most obvious model was the pre-1831 organization of Polish finances. Even
though it was very unlikely to succeed, the Polish alternative to the plan for
monetary reform in Russia deserves our attention for two reasons. First, although the concept of a free bank may have seemed dead after Alexander
I's reign, it reappeared in Drucki-Lubecki's plan. Second, after Alexander
I granted political and financial autonomy to the constitutional Kingdom
of Poland, Russian politicians viewed this western European borderland of
the empire either with jealousy or with fear, anticipating that Poland's experience might spread into Russia. The suppression of the Polish rebellion in 1831
seemed to have dashed notions of the import of the constitution. The plan
for monetary reform therefore represented a camouflaged attempt to use the
Polish case for the political transformation of imperial finance.

Let us take a closer look at the Polish model. The Kingdom of Poland,
established in 1815 on the principles of constitutionalism and political autonomy within the empire, ran its finances independently, operated its own
autonomous budget, and had the right to issue its own currency, the Polish
złoty. In practice, the kingdom did not fully exercise the constitutional rights
it had been granted by Alexander I; the Polish Sejm gathered irregularly.
Therefore, the kingdom's financial autonomy acquired particular importance
and compensated for the lack of political rights. The Polish monetary system
was tied to the German measure of weight (the Cologne mark) and relied on
the silver standard; while rubles could freely circulate in Poland, the Polish
national monetary system had no connection to the Russian one. As the head
of the Commission of Finance and Treasure (equivalent to the Ministry of
Finance), Drucki-Lubecki played a major role in governance. The tsar's support helped him push through important initiatives, including the establishment of the Bank of Poland in 1828, which Kankrin strongly opposed. The

Bank of Poland (Bank Polski) issued banknotes that, unlike Russian assignats, were exchangeable for silver 1:1 according to their nominal value. The amount of banknotes in circulation could not exceed the size of the Bank's assets, which consisted of the bullion reserve and various securities. The banknotes, in effect, fulfilled the role of paper money and thus greatly facilitated the kingdom's currency exchange without distorting or inundating the monetary system.[66] The financial organization of the kingdom in certain ways realized the aspirations of Russian liberal economists. Although, as the Lubecki's opponents asserted, Bank Polski came into existence without the Sejm's sanction and was not a private organization, it differed from its Russian state-run counterpart, the Assignat Bank.[67] Its banknotes were tied to the Bank's own assets rather than to the treasury or to state property, and the Bank maintained a close relationship with the developing industry of the country and its agrarian economy and commerce via a flexible system of short-term credit. Perhaps even more important was the ideological role of the Bank, which came to be associated with the kingdom's financial autonomy and independent growth.

The suppression of the Revolution of 1831 deprived Poland of its independent financial management system, and Drucki-Lubecki was forced to move from Warsaw to St. Petersburg, where he sat on various committees and played the role of Kankrin's main opponent. Strangely, Nicholas I allowed the

FIGURE 3.1 100-złoty banknote, Bank Polski. 1830. Courtesy of Giesecke+ Devrient Stiftung Geldscheinsammlung.

former minister of the formerly autonomous Poland to criticize the imperial minister of finance's plans and projects. The two ministers represented two conflicting ideologies: one referring to the experience of all European civilized states and arguing for the separation of the bank credit system from the fiscal system, the other claiming the "superiority" of the Russian financial organization over the European models. These two approaches were predicated on different views regarding industrialization and economic growth. Poland's Western-oriented economy experienced tremendous growth, but Russian industry, despite the appearance of state-supported technological innovations and flourishing trade, was slowed down in its development by restrictive rules and the absence of credit. Drucki-Lubecki rightly attributed Kankrin's reluctance to undertake deep reforms of Russia's monetary and credit system to the belief that holding back the development of industry and banking would help avoid the "inconveniences of overproduction" and bankruptcies that "America and England were now experiencing."[68]

Drucki-Lubecki's own plan for monetary reform in Russia reproduced the dogma of liberal monetary theory: money should reflect the actual state of the economy; therefore, its production by an independent bank must correspond to the volume of commercial transactions and be secured by the bullion reserve. The bank must be able to exchange its notes for "papers or things that can be conveniently and at any time turned into current money, such as promissory notes, public funds, stock shares and the like."[69] The project outlined a plan for transforming the State Commercial Bank into a new credit institution whose domestic and international reputation would be supported by its total "independence from the Ministry of Finance."[70] Lubecki's plan to found a new independent bank therefore aimed to deprive the state of its privilege of being everyone's banker and, at the same time, to link new state credit bills to the needs of commerce and industry. Obviously, while drafting it, Lubecki kept in mind the improved version of the Bank of Poland that actively supported burgeoning economic growth in the country with a well-developed system of short-term credit.[71]

Drucki-Lubecki's proposal also hinted at the need for a large-scale transformation of the entire credit system of the empire. One of Drucki-Lubecki's supporters in the so-called Secret Committee that considered the reform project, Prince Illarion Vasil'chikov, pointed out that when the state monopolizes the market of credit, it cannot resist the temptation to pick the pockets of its subjects. This practice, as Vasil'chikov noted, obstructed and delayed repayments, jeopardizing the entire system of credit. The possibility of the state defaulting on loans from the treasury banks could ruin its political reputation and trustworthiness because the payments for the private individuals' deposits were "guaranteed by the Monarch's word."[72]

According to Modest Korf, an official who kept the informal account of the debates in the secret committee on monetary reform, the bank reform was Drucki-Lubecki's obsession, one that was shared in theory by many "state men of that time"—except, of course, Kankrin.[73] However, Kankrin's aversion to private banks was insuperable, and the idea of transplanting the experience of a rebellious borderland to Russian soil did not pass. As Korf observed, due to "some strange fatalism, [this idea] could not reach its realization, and after the death of its creator [Drucki-Lubecki], it sank into oblivion."[74] The trail of documents left through the preparation of the monetary reform shows that the idea of an independent bank was eventually dropped from the reform agenda.[75] This outcome is not surprising since the creation of the bank did not fit Nicholas I's own vision of the reform.

The Tsar's Money

The story of the two competing projects and the tsar's role as an arbiter conveys an impression that the tsar intentionally staged this competition in order to present his own triumphal solution to the ruble question. The plan of monetary reform outlined by Nicholas I suggested issuing a new kind of paper money named "state credit bills" that would replace both the assignats and the deposit certificates and would be convertible to silver rubles at a 1:1 rate. While discussing how to proceed with this reform, both the tsar and the members of the secret committee were particularly concerned with two aspects of the credit bill issuance: first, to what extent and by what means should the government back up the new paper money, and second, should the government publicly announce its intentions and explain the technicalities of the reform in a manifesto? Both questions concerned the nature of the relationship between state and society as well as the notion of trust. Nicholas I's personal involvement in the introduction of the new monetary system led to discussions of moral and political issues of honesty and deception, such as whether the operation itself was a kind of trickery, and whether the public would perceive it as a deceit.

In practical terms, the government had to decide how to back up the new paper currency. The tsar thought that issuing the new money would not necessitate maintaining the 1:1 metallic bullion reserve, as was the case with the deposit certificates. The credit bills projected by the emperor were supposed to be backed at a ratio of 1:6. However, the bullion reserve for the new credit rubles was to be built mainly from silver that people exchanged for deposit certificates.[76] Kankrin cautiously remarked that "the public may think that this operation was conducted at its expense" and indeed that the tsar's plan concealed "some sort of a fraud."[77] The tsar responded that the sum of silver taken into the fund of credit rubles would be equivalent to the amount of certificates used to pay state taxes. That silver would no longer represent the "property of the public" and would turn into the state's possession. In other words, the public, while paying taxes in certificates, would unknowingly commit its silver to the new fund. This operation, as the tsar noted, would not require any "sacrifices" from the treasury; the bullion reserve would form "easily and as if by itself," and the government would avoid accusations of fraud and dishonesty.

At the same time, since the bullion reserve backed up only one sixth of the credit bills issued, the government was anxious to complement the material guarantees of the credit ruble's credibility with intangible ones. Discussing how to communicate the promises of credit bills' convertibility to silver in a manifesto in 1843, the members of the secret committee proceeded from the rather modest expression that the value of the ruble was ensured "by the reserve capital and all means of the state treasury" to the more extended "by all properties and means of the treasury," arriving finally at the formula that secured the value of paper money by the "entire patrimony of the state."[78] From a juridical point of view, the phrasing of this pledge was very vague, because Russian property law did not assume the existence of such a category as "patrimony." It remained unclear, for instance, whether this "patrimony" included private possessions of the tsar's subjects along with state (treasury) property. This extensive interpretation of "patrimony," that is, as embracing private domains, relieved the state of its obligation vis-à-vis the public. The most ironic aspect was that the very idea of guaranteeing the credibility of money with material collateral had originated in revolutionary France, and the formula of "state patrimony" that was printed on credit rubles unmistakably evoked the parallel with revolutionary "*biens nationaux.*" Nevertheless, the term stuck. It even survived the turbulence of the nineteenth and twentieth centuries, and in 1922 it appeared, in a slightly modified form, on Soviet ruble banknotes backed by "the entirety of the republic's wealth," in contrast to the gold chervonets of the same year, which bore the inscription "entirely backed by gold."

Offering the entirety of Russia's wealth as collateral for paper money seems absurd due to the fictitious nature of this indemnity: unlike the gold ingots or even the treasury's land possessions, state patrimony was not redeemable.

FIGURE 3.2 5-ruble state credit bill, 1847. From *Russian Ruble: Milestones in History*. The State Bank of Russia, virtual museum.

There was, however, another trick that helped the state secure itself, even if only in theory and imagination, from bankruptcy. In a radical departure from the previous norm and practice of counting assignats as a part of the state debt, the new credit bills were not registered in the Book of State Debts.[79] In the eyes of contemporaries, this was trickery: if the assignats represented a state debt, then the state credit rubles that replaced them had to have the same quality, even though the devaluation reduced this debt by 72%.[80]

So, what was the credit ruble—a "credit" money or fiat currency? Contrary to the connotations of the ruble's new name, it had no connection to the credit system. The State Assignat Bank, which had mediated the printing of assignats, was abolished, and a new unit in the Ministry of Finance took this task on itself. The reform eliminated the administrative duplicity that had existed since 1769, since the Assignat Bank was a governmental structure controlled by the government rather than a bank. But the Bank's disappearance confirmed the principle that in Russia, money was a creation of the state and not a product of market and credit mechanisms. The new money was in no sense connected to credit, and the use of the term "credit" was a misnomer.[81] The government monopolized the entire process of money making from the printing of bills at the Expedition for the Production of State Papers to their exchange for silver at the Expedition of State Credit Rubles. Anyone willing to receive silver coins for paper money could come to the latter Expedition's office in St. Petersburg or Moscow between nine o'clock in the morning and one o'clock in the afternoon (or noon on Saturday). This arrangement did not make exchange very accessible, but it preserved the ruble's de jure convertibility.[82]

The final and symbolic stage of the reform was the relocation of the bullion reserve from the vaults of the state Commercial Bank to a special building constructed in the stronghold of autocracy—the Peter and Paul Fortress, which also served as the main prison for political criminals and the burial vault of tsars.[83] It took a full week in December 1844 to move coins and ingots worth 70 million rubles across the city. The solemn ritual involved the members of the Council of Credit Institutions, who had been invited to testify for the trustworthiness of the government, and, importantly, twenty-four merchants—representatives of the stock-exchange committee headed by the court banker, Baron Alexander von Stieglitz.[84] The reserve was seen as the state's special asset. Unlike the bullion reserve of European central banks, the state remained in full possession and control of the gold and silver that backed up the rubles that it issued. In this sense, Nicholas I invented the treasury's bullion reserve, a unique institution that did not exist anywhere else in Europe.[85]

Russia's monetary system, created as a result of the reform, represented a remarkable hybrid.[86] On the surface, Russia's silver standard resembled that of its European counterparts. Coincidentally or not, in July 1844 the British government passed the notoriously stringent Bank Charter Act, also known as the Robert Peel Act, which tied the issuance of banknotes to the size of the bullion reserve and signified the theoretical victory of the so-called bullionist school over its opponents' more flexible and decentralized model. Russian reform fell into the same trend exploiting the splendor of the bullion reserve as the token of stability. Yet the political content of the reform made it radically different because the bullion belonged to the state and the crown. This contradiction was perhaps not even apparent to Russian functionaries; for instance, the Ministry of Finance's *Commercial Newspaper* interpreted the Peel Banking Act of 1844 "as a beginning of a new system that must liberate the country's monetary obligations from the dependence upon private credit institutions and subjugate them directly to the government's administration." The reform of the Bank of England indeed centralized the banknote-issuing activity in England by taking away the rights of issue from multiple provincial banks and prescribing that the entire sum of notes issued by the Bank of England be backed up by "securities, coin and bullion."[87] However, as the Bank was a private joint-stock company, the status of its capital and relation to the state did not change. The Bank of England did not depend on the state;

the directors of the Bank were, in Walter Bagehot's words, "trustees of the public, to keep a banking reserve on their behalf."[88]

The political difference reflected the specificity of Russia's autocratic state where money and laws originated from the sovereign. In 1832, the Commission for the Codification of Russian Laws, headed by Speransky, who had been returned from exile in 1826 and offered a chance to exculpate his liberal sins through active participation at the Decembrists trial, finally produced the Code of Laws of the Russian Empire. Thus, the regime, which had eliminated almost all civil and political freedoms and had acquired the reputation of a bulwark of anti-constitutional and anti-revolutionary forces in Europe, declared its allegiance to legality. In the spheres of law and money, the government produced the rules, swore to obey them, but tolerated no control over the legality of its actions. Russian state credit bills embodied the Fundamental Laws of the Russian Empire, the indivisibility of power and accountability alike. In this sense, they did not differ from the assignats that they replaced. The contradictions between the ostensible rhetoric of renewal and the persistence of the old institutional settings were blatant. Credit bills looked very different from the modest, one-sided assignats. Colorful and ornamental, they featured a long excerpt from a manifesto announcing their issuance, printed three times in different fonts, which for a country with a low literacy rate looked unnecessarily verbose and excessive. Yet despite the visual difference between assignats and state credit bills, even decades after the reform, people continued to use the term assignats in relation to the new kind of state paper money. In 1845, the government was surprised to discover an entire production of old assignats in Bogodorskii uezd, Vladimir province that had apparently begun in 1843, when the new credit rubles came into existence. "The impudence of counterfeiters had reached such a degree that one of the assignats bore the signature "cashier Vokhonskii" (after the village's name Vokhna)," reported the police.[89]

How financially stable was the system? On the surface, everything looked perfect. Russia gave the impression of the most politically and economically stable country, secured from the European revolutionary frenzy by an impenetrable shield of police, censorship, and military force. Kankrin refrained from new issues of credit rubles, and they remained fully convertible into silver; the exchange fund looked solid, although gradually a certain amount of metal was replaced with interest-bearing securities, and the share of credit rubles covered by the metal reserve was reduced from 48.8% in 1845 to 35.7% in 1850.[90] Another noticeable change was the gradual increase in the share of gold in the reserve, which had consisted almost exclusively of silver. Two

factors facilitated the accumulation of metals in the economy: the discovery
of alluvial gold in the early 1830s and the regime of free silver and gold mining,
introduced back in 1812. In the 1830s and 1840s, Russian Siberia experienced
a gold rush. The threefold increase of gold production (from 378 *poods* a year
in 1831–1835 to 1076 *poods* in 1841–1845)[91] resulted from the booming development of private mining.[92] In 1828, the government raised the "mining duty"
in Siberia from 10% to 15%, and in 1840, up to 24%, thereby securing a steady
influx of gold from private mines into the treasury.[93] The manifold increase in
gold production did not contribute correspondingly to the growing presence
of gold in economy because of the inferior status of gold coins in the monetary system.[94] Until the discovery of American gold in 1858, Russia remained
the world's leading producer of the yellow metal, and yet, paradoxically, the
government forbade even the payment of taxes and state dues in gold coins
until 1833.

Maintaining the balance between the size of the reserve fund and the
amount of paper money in circulation helped the government preserve a
façade of financial stability and irreproachable credibility even though
Russian budget was chronically in deficit (in total, between 1832 and 1861,
the deficit amounted to 1 billion rubles). In reality, while refraining from
money printing, the government resorted to other means to cover budgetary
deficits, first, by continuing to borrow from state-owned banks. By 1860,
the State Treasury had borrowed more than half of the private deposits
(521.4 million out of 1,012 million rubles). To compare, in 1860 all Russian
budget revenues equaled around 386 million rubles with expenditures
counted at 438 million.[95] Second, it issued interest-bearing treasury bonds,
for the first time, in 1831, when the state banks' resources were running very
low. A big foreign or domestic loan could not proceed without a "public
announcement," which could stir unwanted conversations and create the
impression of Russia's active preparation for war, and the issuance of paper
money was not considered an appropriate solution.[96] The government repeatedly went back to the emission of treasury bonds, redeeming previous
emissions with new ones in order to, as Kankrin asserted, maintain the
public's habit of using them as money. Indeed, the bonds that were not officially named as paper money became such a ubiquitous phenomenon of
financial life that they circulated along with the credit bills. Remarkably, the
government did not want people to consider treasury bonds its debt because
this could "shake the public's trust in them." For this reason, treasury bonds,
like state credit bills, were not registered in the State Book of Debt. In addition, Russia continued to borrow money abroad. In total, during the twenty

years of Kankrin's tenure in the minister's office (1823–43), the amount of state debt more than doubled.[97]

The End of the Polish Złoty

Nationalism can take different forms: one is the assertion of national uniqueness vis-à-vis others, and another is the claim to dominance over other nationalities and territories. Nicholas I's nationalism encompassed both versions of this ideology, and the idea of monetary self-sufficiency accompanied attempts to eliminate the diversity of currencies in the empire. It was logical that the first manifestation of this policy was the gradual elimination of Poland's monetary autonomy. Poland's experience inspired the Drucki-Lubecki proposal of liberal financial reform, which was abandoned in favor of a conservative variant. Moreover, the monetary reform of 1839–43 paved the way for Poland's financial integration into the Russian imperial system.

The plans for curtailing Polish financial autonomy appeared immediately after the revolution of 1831, but the assignats' unstable rate prevented the realization of these plans, since the złoty was a much more stable and reliable currency. As the kingdom's viceroy, Ivan Paskevich, observed, tying the złoty to the paper ruble made no sense. "In Russia, the ruble itself . . . ceased to be a real ruble after the fall of our assignats," wrote Paskevich about imperial currency. The viceroy, who had played a key role in suppressing the Polish revolution of 1831, with pride compared the banknotes of the Bank of Poland, which represented "the capital that must always be, and always is, present at the Bank," to the Russian assignats, which were "based on state credit" only, that is to say, on something intangible and unstable.[98] Considering the superiority of the Polish currency to the ruble, the Ministry of Finance had to maintain the złoty as the basic unit of accounting in the Kingdom of Poland, and the proposed "integration" of the monetary systems was limited to the production of coins with a double ruble/złoty denomination.

The monetary reform of 1839–43 paved the way for a more aggressive policy of monetary centralization. In this sense, the celebrated silver standard reform was also an imperial reform that embodied the main elements of the dominant ideology. In January 1841, the Russian silver ruble was declared "the single denomination and legal tender" in Poland; all government and private accounts were required to be held in rubles, and the holders of the banknotes of the Polish Bank were ordered to exchange them for the new "banknotes in Russian rubles," with inscriptions in Polish and Russian and a new Polish national emblem. All old monies, with the exception of the dual language Russian coins, were to be reminted as Russian rubles.

Thus, in 1841, the unification of the two monetary systems seemed to be essentially complete, with one notable exception: Russian paper rubles did not circulate in Poland, while the banknotes of the Bank of Poland could not be accepted in Russian provinces.[99] This relative isolation of the kingdom's monetary system remained unchallenged until the 1848 revolutions in Europe caused a financial crisis in the western provinces of the Russian Empire. In March and April 1848, the governors of the western provinces (Volyn, Vilno, Grodno, Kovno, Minsk, Kurland, and others) complained about a sudden "lack of trust" in credit rubles among the population. People rushed to exchange paper rubles, reasoning that in such circumstances, "it's safer to have hard currency than the signs that represent it." Rumors spread that the credit rubles would soon "fall like the assignats during the war of 1812" and would subsequently be declared void, as had recently happened to the assignats. The government shipped an increased amount of silver to the western provinces, instructing local authorities not to disrupt the exchange and to publish announcements rebutting the rumors in all major newspapers.[100] Secret instructions, however, advised opening exchange offices only three days a week and not accepting more than 100 rubles from one person. Against the backdrop of the ruble's falling credibility, Polish convertible banknotes were in very high demand. In circumstances critical to Russian currency and administration in the western provinces, Viceroy Paskevich made the unilateral, secret and illegal move of permitting government offices in the Kingdom of Poland to accept payments in Russian credit rubles.

As the Bank of Poland's governor Benedict Niepokojczycki argued, the influx of credit rubles beginning in 1848 drained Poland's metal reserves to the point that they could no longer supply metal to the bank. The 1848 revolution, as local officials lamented, was soon followed by "the Hungarian campaign, then the Eastern Question returned to the fore, and soon there was the Danube campaign and the Crimean War." Russia's large military presence in Poland meant that the region was awash in credit rubles. In 1854 alone, the Polish Treasury processed approximately 71 million silver rubles' worth of paper rubles, an amount that many times exceeded the amount of Polish banknotes in circulation, issued for merely 10 million rubles.[101] The financial crisis that unfolded in the empire as a result of the Crimean conflict led to an inundation of ruble bills throughout the empire, including Poland. When the open exchange of credit ruble bills for coinage was suspended in 1854, the banknotes of the Bank of Poland remained the only means of payment convertible to hard currency. The demands for exchange increased dramatically, and the Bank of Poland was running out of metallic reserves, being unable to proceed with payments for state foreign loans.[102] Poland found itself on the brink of bankruptcy inflicted by the kingdom's integration into the monetary system of the empire.

The Crimean Disaster

The Peter and Paul Fortress depot, which since 1844 had held Russia's gold reserve, had been hastily built. Workers applied plaster on wet walls, and in the damp air of the building, the plaster very soon came off, exposing ugly bricks; the iron grids and doors rusted; and moldings on the exterior walls collapsed. In 1856, the building stood empty. With the gold and silver reserve gone, the building's custodians left the windows open for a few months to dry out the rooms, and in June the Ministry of Finance finally began renovating the depositary.[103]

Where did the gold go? The main cause for emptying the rooms of gold and silver was the Crimean War. Anticipating the worst, the government prepared a plan for relocating the Mint to Petrozavodsk and the Expedition for the Production of State Papers, which manufactured credit rubles, and the metal reserve to Moscow. The capital city was not endangered, and the plan was never fully put into practice. However, the Ministry of Finance ordered the move of 105 million rubles in gold and silver to Moscow, claiming to open a new branch of the Expedition for the exchange of credit rubles. In March 1854, boxes with gold and silver were put on carts provided by a "patriot" citizen, Kharichkov, delivered to the train station, and then sent to Moscow, where they were stored in the armory in the Kremlin until February 1859.[104]

The remaining gold and silver from the Peter and Paul Fortress was simply spent by the government on paying off its debts in Europe, purchasing goods, exchanging credit bills, and other necessities.[105] In peacetime, the government could use bills of exchange for transferring money, avoiding carrying heavy gold bars across the borders. However, after the outbreak of the war, the rate of Russian bills of exchange fell, and the government, as well as merchants and bankers involved in international trade, had to revert to the old means of paying in gold. The administration of the Central Post Office reported that in only two months, private individuals and institutions sent 4.5 million rubles in gold to Europe. Gold started rapidly leaving the country, while people rushed to convert their paper credit rubles into hard currency. The government panicked. In February 1854, it prohibited the export of gold, and

this prohibition dropped the ruble's rate of exchange by 10%–19%.[106] Over
the following months, tons of gold would nevertheless cross the border, and
the government would be anxiously watching the movement of gold coins
and bars. The crisis following the Crimean War was marked by anxiety over
disappearing metals and by attempts to find the elusive gold and silver, in the
pockets of allegedly roguish tax collectors and even on the ears and chests of
Tatar women who, as the Kazan treasury office reported, used the coins as
jewelry.[107]

The real reasons for the disappearance of coins had nothing to do with the
cultural traditions of Russia's Muslims. When in 1857 Alexander II asked his
minister of finance why the reserve fund dwindled, Petr Brok referred to both
the extraordinary war spending and, most important, the critical situation
with Russian paper currency.[108] Since the beginning of the crisis, all treasury
revenues had been collected only in paper rubles, and the Mint had become
the only supplier of metal money. Paper rubles were abundant, but they cost
much less than they were supposed to. Russia's extraordinary expenses during
the war had reached the sum of 538 million rubles, of which 400 million
rubles were obtained through the massive emission of credit bills.[109] The ratio
between credit ruble and bullion fell dramatically. In 1854, the bullion reserve
covered 43% of credit bills, while in July 1857, this ratio fell below the 15%
approved by the law.[110] In 1857, as Brok attested, individuals and institutions
were still exchanging up to 1 million rubles every month, emptying the
Expedition of the State Credit Bills' depositories. In August 1857, the Mint
stopped supplying the Expedition with coins.[111] The exchange of rubles for
gold turned into a privilege accessible to a small number of individuals whose
requests could not be ignored; it was quite normal to deny this right to the
"broad mass of the dark public."[112] De facto, the ruble became inconvertible in 1854, when the first restrictions on the exchange were introduced, although the government did not issue an official declaration suspending the
exchange.[113] Whenever Russia's convertible ruble ended—in 1854, as some
economists thought, or in 1858, as claimed by the government experts—the
country entered the era of financial uncertainty and instability symbolized by
the presence of gendarmes at the gates of the Expedition of the State Credit
Bills, called in to protect the institution from an anxious mob.[114]

PART II

Autocratic Capitalism

4

Paper Money in the Era of the "Great Reforms"

The Gales in the North

In early October 1860, the London *Times* reported terrible gales that "last appear to have swept with equal fury the whole of the coast of the north of Europe; and the havoc among the shipping, especially in the Baltic, where the storm seems to have spent its full force, has been truly awful." Telegrams furnished "a most fearful list of disasters" that included sixty shipwrecks. Among the casualties of the storm was the steamer *Arctic*, commanded by Captain Bowes, which was on its usual passage from Hull and Grimsby to St. Petersburg. The *Arctic* built just a year earlier and "a favorite vessel on the station," sank near Lemvig, off the coast of Jutland, taking the lives of four passengers and two crew members.[1]

The shipwreck of a British steamer would not have concerned top Russian officials had it not been for the *Arctic*'s cargo. Among other things, she carried equipment for money printing and templates with engravings and rolls commissioned by the Russian imperial government from the American Banknote Company in New York for the production of new, improved state credit rubles. The box, Captain Bowes reported, "went down with the vessel," along with a printer from the company, who had accompanied the cargo.[2] A few days later, when divers retrieved it from the bottom of sea, saltwater had already ruined the engravings.

This collaboration between the imperial government and an American company represented perhaps one of the most explicit and symbolic signs of the new epoch in finance that had begun with Alexander II's accession to the throne in 1855. The newly commissioned money had to convey the

spirit of the rule and simultaneously make credit rubles more technologically advanced and less susceptible to forgery, which plagued the Russian
monetary system in the 1850s.[3] The sketches of new paper rubles, made at
the emperor's request in 1859, featured the stylized portraits of historical and
folk "types" along with architectural landmarks of cities and inscriptions
in national languages—Polish, German, Georgian, Swedish, Finnish and
"Tatar" (Arabic). The choice of cities—Moscow, St. Petersburg, Helsingfors
(Helsinki), and Warsaw—may have suggested the autonomous status of
Russia's western borderlands. The emphasis on the multiculturalism of the
Russian Empire marked a departure from the old design and ideology, although aesthetically, the new design was a failure. The folk figures looked fake
and unnatural, and there was, perhaps intentionally, a mismatch between the
stylized figures and the landscapes: a design with the image of Warsaw featured figures in "Moscovite clothing," while a Helsingfors sketch had a portrait of a girl with grapes not grown in Finland.[4]

In any case, imagery and aesthetics were not seen as the key factors in
determining paper money's resilience to counterfeiting, which hinged almost entirely on the technological sophistication of the money-printing
process. From this point of view, Russia lagged behind other countries. The
Expedition for the Production of State Papers (EZGB), with its old manual
work technologies, proved to be unfit to produce new high-quality paper
money. Therefore, in tune with the cosmopolitan spirit of the new rule, the
Expedition's management decided to order the engraved plates for Russian
credit rubles from one of the world's best-known companies specializing
in the production of paper money and securities: the American Banknote
Company in New York.[5] The company was also supposed to supply the EZGB
with new equipment, materials, and specialists. Ultimately, the EZGB's management anticipated entirely remaking the production process and the introduction of a new technology called siderography.[6] The contract with the
Americans was sealed in July 1859, and in September 1860 a box with plates
and rolls for making ruble bills, along with machines and other materials, was
shipped to Russia.

After the shipwreck destroyed the precious templates, the government
once again decided to change the design. Instead of the stylized images of different nationalities, the new credit bills of the denominations of 5 rubles and
more were to bear the portraits of Russian rulers who had become "famous in
national history," namely, Prince Dmitrii Donskoy, tsars Mikhail Fedorovich
and Alexei Mikhailovich, Peter I, and Catherine II.[7] The rejection of the previous "ethnographic" design coincided with (but was probably not caused by)

the Polish rebellion that erupted in early 1863 and ultimately led to significant shifts in attitude toward non-Russian nationalities in the empire and the final liquidation of Poland's financial and political autonomy. The new design also seemed technically less prone to counterfeiting; it was believed that artisan engravers, who were usually good at copying ornaments, did not have the skills to make engraved portraits. The Committee of Finance also reasoned that it would be better to avoid using any "typical or allegorical figures" representing abstract notions, so as not to give grounds for interpreting them in political terms. Therefore, the portraits of historical rulers were considered the safest choice.[8]

The collaboration with the American Banknote Company did not go as planned, and ultimately, the Committee of Finance decided that it would be safer to prepare new plates at home. The Expedition paid for the "secret" (patent) of making machines and paint to print money and for the services of mechanics and engineers. However, even though the design and templates were made in Russia, the Russian credit rubles that appeared several years later, in 1866, bore a striking resemblance to US dollars that featured the portraits of American prominent historical figures in ovals, just like the portraits of tsars. This was hardly the most important result of the collaboration. Following the American company's example, the Expedition for the Production of State Papers was turned into a government-owned business enterprise that received orders from the government via the State Bank, enjoyed relative economic autonomy, and could even earn a profit. The new management was built on the American company's model, with a director at the top and a group of technical experts in leading positions, an improved system of financing based on the proceeds from orders instead of budgetary allocations, a free labor force instead of serfs and conscripts, minimal red tape, and initial investments from the government. All these factors were meant to allow the Expedition to "develop and stand on the level of the best foreign enterprises" of that sort.[9] As a result, the Expedition for the Production of State Papers turned into an exemplary factory, with workers participating in the company's profit—an unheard-of model in pre-emancipation Russia. The technology of money printing improved significantly, even though a few years were required to enact all the changes. However, the scourge of counterfeiting did not go away. It turned out that the problem was rooted not in the shape of letters or the finesses of engraved ornaments but in the political and ideological standing of the state and the state currency that embodied it. The proliferation of fake money was a symptom of deeper and more serious problems in the Russian financial system.

FIGURE 4.1 5-ruble state credit bill (reverse), 1866, from the new series with the portraits of tsars and princes. The outcome of collaboration between the Expedition for the Production of State Papers and the American Banknote Company. Note the resemblance to the US dollar. Private collection.

FIGURE 4.2 50 dollars, legal tender note, United States, 1862. Courtesy of Division of Work and Industry, National Museum of American History, Smithsonian Institution.

The sunk ship and the redrawn rubles highlight an era when the old principles of the pre-reform order were yielding to new practices and mechanisms, yet the radicalism of changes in the economy and society was often compromised by the resilience of the political regime. As the portraits of tsars replaced the figures of random artisans and peasants, the ideas for reforming Russia's financial institutions changed from more expansive plans to cosmetic makeovers. The Western patterns, whether studied, selectively adopted, or rejected, left imprints on the patterns of reforms. Although the institutional reforms often disappointed experts in public finance, changes in the popular view of money, its nature and function, indicated that the post-reform politics of money would be drastically different from what had come before.

The Ruble and the Coming of Capitalism

The post-Crimean crisis of the late 1850s and early 1860s differed from the earlier crises of assignats, even though it evoked memories of the post-Napoleonic era, when the paper ruble cost 25 kopecks. This crisis unfolded in the midst of a political transformation that was perceived as a radical renewal of Russia's state, economy, and society. The banner of reform was Russia's rapprochement with the West, an attempt to catch up with Europe as it was taking up gold as the dominant currency standard. Despite the Russian ruble's allegiance to the silver standard,[10] both the government and the population were longing for the yellow metal. Russia's production of silver dropped to only 800,000 rubles a year, while the production of gold increased to 20 million rubles. In addition, the idea of a pan-European monetary union based on gold was widely discussed at the time. Still, due to Russia's negative trade balance and the growing payments for loans, the lion's share of the gold that Russia produced did not stay in the country, and existing proposals to switch to a gold standard remained utopian.[11]

Another distinctive feature of the post-Crimean monetary crunch was the new standards applied to the measurement of the ruble's value. The credit ruble's value in silver did not tumble as much as its price on the foreign markets; however, in the 1850s and early 1860s, both the government and the public were primarily concerned about the credit ruble's standing vis-à-vis European currencies and the rate at which Russian bills of exchange were discounted in Europe. This rate depended on several factors, including the political and economic prognosis (the bills were the promises of future payments), the trade balance (i.e., the demand for payment made in rubles) and the amount of the state's obligations. Both the preference for gold and the anxiety about the rate of exchange symbolized the end of Russia's economic and political isolation. The government of the new tsar, Alexander II, threw the Russian market wide open for foreign traders and investors and lifted barriers that had protected the Russian currency and industry from external influences. In 1857, the government radically changed customs tariffs and switched from strict protectionism to a regime of free trade. In 1861, the State Council lifted a ban on the import and export of credit rubles, essentially allowing the circulation of credit bills as commodities in Western financial markets (and, coincidentally, allowing for the massive import of counterfeited money from Europe).

The elimination of the ban on export turned credit bills into a commodity that had its own price and value that depended on the rubles' availability and demand.[12]

For Russia's affluent public, Alexander II's economic reforms began with the removal of financial restrictions on international travel and emigration. Russian nobles streamed to European cities in search of new things and experiences, and the ruble's falling rate affected their ability to maintain a European style of consumption abroad and in Russia. According to official data, in 1850, only 8,000 travelers crossed the European border of the Russian Empire. In 1855, the number of people leaving Russia for Europe doubled; in 1858, it was already close to 70,000, and the following year, 110,000 travelers crossed Russia's western border. They carried with them bills of exchange and gold, or, with the help of private bankers, they transferred money from their Russian accounts to Europe. The rate of exchange thus became an important factor in the lives of noble and middle-class Russians. Newspapers assumed the new habit of informing the public about the fluctuation of the "rate of exchange," explaining in elementary terms how the rise and fall of the credit ruble vis-à-vis francs or pounds sterling affected its ability to purchase goods in Paris and London. Every educated person was expected to watch the rate because, as Gavriil Kamenskii, the agent of the Ministry of Finance in London suggested, it was "the most perfect instrument in the observatory of the political and commercial world. Physicists have not yet been able to invent such a sensitive tool."[13]

The growing attention to rate also indicated major changes not only in financial policy but also in the public attitude toward value, property, and the sources of wealth, processes that can be described as the coming of the age of capitalism.[14] As explained by Mikhail Katkov of the *Moscow Bulletin* [*Moskovskie Vedomosti*], arguably one of the most influential journalists of this time, in the early nineteenth century, property consisted of immovable properties and goods, but in the late 1850s, Russia's economic landscape looked drastically different. Tangible valuables started yielding their place to intangible resources of many kinds (securities, bonds, shares), while the role of the ruble became more abstract—the measure of value rather than a value itself. The emancipation of peasants in 1861, the redemption operation that converted the value of peasants' predominantly natural obligations and lands into state-issued bonds, and the general monetization of the economy all changed the meaning of the ruble's rate, while the emergence of dozens of banks and joint-stock companies created new forms of wealth. As the *Herald of Industry* [*Vestnik Promyshlennosti*] reported in the midst of Russia's first joint-stock fever in 1858, "There is no more money in St. Petersburg. St. Petersburg has become very poor. That is to say, very rich. The capitalists of St. Petersburg have exchanged millions of their credit rubles for hundreds of thousands of other papers, bigger in size, better looking and offering such enticing and lustrous hopes; they have traded and continue trading money for stock shares. . . . To repeat: rich people in St. Petersburg do not have money anymore; only poor people have money."[15] Wealth came to be accessed not in the amount of rubles in pockets or on bank accounts but in the availability of capital that depended on multiple factors, including the rate of exchange. Therefore, the fluctuation of the ruble's rate was very troublesome. "One cannot watch the fall of the exchange rate without anxiety," wrote Katkov.[16]

Katkov's personal attention to the ruble's rate symbolized an interesting twist in nationalist ideology: his nationalism did not undermine the importance of Russia's international financial reputation and its place in the world economy. "Russia is not different in this regard from other states; the circulation of credit bills and patriotism have nothing in common, and the rate of exchange does not refer to the degree of patriotic feelings," wrote Katkov. In the new worldview of cosmopolitan nationalists like Katkov, old ideas of the Russian ruble as unique and different from other currencies did not find support. Katkov openly rejected the long-standing belief in the "trust to the credit bills as a characteristic feature of the Russian people originating from its unconditional trust to the government." As he pointed out, "In fact, there [was] nothing particular about it."[17] For Katkov, financial patriotism consisted in sharing concerns about the ruble's status on the world market and nagging the government to undertake necessary reforms rather than isolate the Russian currency in the bubble of a "closed state."

If the public worried about whether it could afford imported goods, the government's concern about the ruble's exchange rate amounted to a true obsession, as if it were a matter of sovereignty or geopolitical prestige. To support the falling exchange rate in 1857, the government started systematically selling bills of exchange (for credit rubles) in St. Petersburg so that they could be discounted in European cities; the government's agents subsequently redeemed those bills with gold obtained through foreign loans or simply transported to Europe from Russia.[18] Between May 1 and November 1, 1861, the government spent about 25 million rubles to artificially maintain the exchange rate, while the total cost of the operation, from 1857 to 1862, amounted to 120 million rubles.[19] This transfer operation maintained a decent exchange rate at the expense of inflating the prices of goods in Russia

and draining the gold reserve.[20] Observers interpreted the attempts to keep
the rate up as the signs of Russia's anxiety about its prestige abroad, or "fake
patriotism" that signaled the government's wrong and old-fashioned understanding of the rate's meaning. The criticism was not, perhaps, totally fair.
After all, many governments in financial crisis practice interventions of that
sort. However, in the 1850s, when free-trade liberalism was a dogma, government intrusion looked inappropriate. Economists claimed that, in a country
with free trade, the fluctuations are normal, while the efforts to conceal them
resembled "makeup on the face of a sick person, or stilts under the legs of a
short man."[21]

Liberalism's New Face.

By supporting the rate, the government tried to fix financial problems by
means that liberal economists described as coming from the "dark age of
mercantilism." The liberal spirit of reforms contradicted the needs of the financial restoration; the government did not want to restrict financial activities and freedoms even if they had a detrimental effect on the state of the
economy. When in November 1860 the new minister of finance, Alexander
Kniazhevich, suggested curing the problem of fleeing gold by introducing a
special tax on Russian subjects living abroad, the government rejected this
measure, despite the numbers cited by Kniazhevich as proof of the enormous
loss of gold incurred by tourism and emigration.[22] The refusal to cure financial crises with repressions and restrictions signified not only an important
turn in the economic worldview of government officials and economists but
also an attempt to reconsider the state's role in credit and monetary relations.

It would be a mistake, however, to interpret the meaning of the changes
simply as an ideological shift. In contrast to Nicholas I, who was confident
in his ability to grasp economic matters, Alexander II did not meddle in
finances, leaving them to the new bureaucratic group of experts-technocrats.
The pool of experts involved in the special commissions to prepare and elaborate financial reforms included many who were young and theoretically
savvy and possessed both academic training and bureaucratic experience.[23]
Most of them had authored scholarly books or numerous articles on money,
banks, and statistics. These young academics without rank or state positions
rubbed elbows with the representatives of the St. Petersburg elite in fashionable "circles" and salons. Fedor Terner nostalgically described a unique atmosphere when ideas for reforms emerged in informal meetings and discussions
among elite bureaucrats, grand dukes, and ambitious young economists at the

gatherings of the Imperial Geographical Society and the so-called economic soirees at Vladimir Bezobrazov's apartment. Ministers often dropped by to listen to academic talks that were frequented by public intellectuals, activists of the *zemstvo* (self-government) movement, and scholars.

While sitting on governmental committees, new "experts" continued writing on financial matters, but their works targeted a much wider audience. Nikolai Bunge, Evgenii Lamanskii, and Vladimir Bezobrazov became regular contributors to the daily *Stock Exchange Bulletin* [*Birzhevye Vedomosti*], the monthly *Russian Herald* [*Russkii Vestnik*]. The new weekly edition of the *Economic Index* [*Ekonomicheskii Ukazatel'*] with a supplement, *The Economist* [*Ekonomist*] played an especially important role in propagating new liberal ideas and inculcating new economic thinking in Russian society. The journal's contributors believed that ignorance and the dominance of old, outdated concepts represented the main obstacles to financial improvement. "Due to the backwardness of politico-economic education, the majority still look at money through the lenses of mercantilism, thinking that . . . money acquires value . . . at the whim of the authority that makes it."[24] The new economic outlets aimed to combat both old theories about the state as the sole source of money and new myths about money widely disseminated by newspapers. Terner recalled a "public discussion" on money held at the concert halls of the *Passage*, St. Petersburg's fashionable department store, that turned so "passionate," with people screaming and shouting over one another, that its moderator, Lamanskii, had to end the meeting.[25]

As in the early nineteenth century, liberals insisted on the government's withdrawal from the production of money. There was, however, a new element in liberal financial ideology of reform that reflected the spirit of the Great Reforms era. The reforms of the late 1850s–60s allowed for more active participation of all social estates in administration and justice through new elected institutions of self-government and new courts. In the financial sphere, credit institutions could play the role analogous to zemstvos or the justices of peace and jury courts. In 1858, Yulii Gagemeister expressed the common belief that private credit institutions connect "material successes with the moral achievements" of society. Credit is the "most precise measure of civilization; it is at the same time the strongest means toward the moral education and ennoblement of people." Therefore, Gagemeister concluded, "in a state where the people are ready for political and industrial liberty, credit institutions must be granted freedom as well."[26] This idea—that the development of credit is a marker of political maturity and at the same time a way to achieve that maturity—sharply contrasted with earlier stances regarding the backwardness of the Russian population and its inability to grasp the abstract meaning of credit.

As Gagemeister claimed, the absence of an independent bank of issue signified the government's distrust toward its own people in financial matters, just as the absence of parliamentary institutions showed its distrust in their political abilities. "Political liberty" and representation were, therefore, strongly associated with financial representation. V. Dubenskii, the author of an essay "What Is Money?" (1859), doubted that the term "money" could even be applied to credit rubles printed by the government and not connected to the system of credit. Only the banknotes of an independent bank could enjoy this status. "If the bank falls under the auspices of the government, or if it belongs to the government," its banknotes lose any guarantee of acceptance and therefore turn into "fake money." Dubenskii unequivocally accused governments, whose task was supposed to be limited only to "stamping" and "verifying" the value of coins, of abusing these prerogatives and, essentially, counterfeiting.[27]

The Bank Reform and the Catastrophe of 1863

The first and most important step in the direction of the state's gradual withdrawal from spheres where private capital and commerce were to play a key role was the reform of state, or "treasury," banks. Treasury borrowing from state banks had been a life-saving measure that kept Russian credit rubles and state budgets afloat while benefiting the banks' clients with high interest rates and discouraging them from business investments. This model imposed a particular mode of relations between the state and society, one that was based on secrecy and that transformed people into passive, lazy rentiers who were indifferent to the fate of their capital. Evgenii Lamanskii described the typical client of a state bank who "does not care about the bank's operation. He knows that the interest on his capital must be there, and he is not interested in how the bank gets the money."[28] Observing the two lines of clients in the state banks' offices, Lamanskii often asked himself, "What kind of notion of credit and the meaning of banks does this mob have, when these people come to get *their own* money?"[29]

An additional flaw in the state credit system was that the state banks could not contribute to economic development. For instance, in 1853, the State Commercial Bank accumulated 200 million rubles (or 800 million francs)—a sum equal to the capital of the Bank of France multiplied by eight. However, while the Bank of France used a capital of 100 million francs to conduct commercial operations for 1,500 million francs annually, the State Commercial

Bank's commercial operations amounted to no more than 37 million rubles (148 million francs). Even very wealthy countries could not afford such a waste of capital, wrote Ludwik Tęgoborski in a memo addressed to the tsar and the Grand Duke Konstantin, the tsar's brother and the leader of the reform team in the government.[30] The "idleness" of capital, however, was a necessary condition of maintaining more or less balanced state budgets without the issuance of paper money because it offered the government quick and easy credit.

In 1857, the minister of finance Peter Brok attempted to eliminate the excess "idle" money in the state banks' deposit accounts by drastically decreasing the interest rate.[31] This unilateral and abrupt change in banking policy coincided with a burst of commercial activity and Russia's first-ever stock fever. Depositors rushed to withdraw their money and invest it instead in company shares. The outflow of capital from state banks soon turned into a mass exodus: millions of extra credit rubles printed during the war and deposited into bank accounts were pushed out onto the market.[32] Between June 1857 and July 1859, the banks' cash reserves dropped from 150 million to 13 million rubles. The remaining 13 million rubles could be found only in provincial offices of the Commercial Bank, while the offices in St. Petersburg and Moscow had no cash at all.[33] The dynamics of withdrawals indicated that the state banks would soon run out of money, and state bankruptcy, which threatened to ruin the entire monetary system, seemed almost unavoidable. As Alexander Guryev, a member of the State Council and son of the former minister of finance, observed, to satisfy the demands of the banks' clients, the state would have to print hundreds of millions of credit rubles: "One cannot think without horror about the scale of such an emission," which was equivalent to the "death of our finances."[34]

The decision to start the bank reform by lowering the interest rates targeted the consequence of the problem rather than its source.[35] The reform, therefore, had to start with institutional changes, repairing the "false foundations" of Russia's money and credit. "The impending bankruptcy of banks subjected the domestic and international credibility of the state to an extreme danger," concluded a special commission summoned in June 1859 to determine how to proceed with the reorganization of state banks.[36] The commission included a bunch of young economists, such as liberal free-traders and reform-minded bureaucrats, and suggested abolishing the old treasury-owned banks as well as converting domestic debts into interest-bearing state bonds and centralizing state credit activity in a radically transformed Commercial Bank that would offer credit to industry and, at the same time, issue banknotes. The reform aimed not simply to prevent state bankruptcy, but to transform the economic relationship between the public and the state, making both the government and the people responsible for the political implications of financial actions. The conversion of idle bank deposits into interest-bearing state bonds was meant to instill in citizens the habits of making "independent and free choice in the use of capital," while the creation of a new, independent bank with the right of issue, as well as a system of local banks with representatives of local landowners elected "without taking into account their social estate" would complete the entire politico-financial edifice. According to Lamanskii, who later claimed authorship of the new system's main idea, the reform bore the "highest moral importance": "each capitalist, receiving his income and keeping the capital, can manage his material wealth independently and on his own choice. . . . The habit of looking for the most profitable investment of capital among people, even among its highest classes . . . will give rise to the feeling of independence and personal responsibility—qualities that are sorely lacking in the material as well as the moral aspects of Russian life, and without which neither civic virtues, nor moral greatness or common well-being . . . may exist."[37]

Lamanskii's idea of linking civic virtues with financial reforms and building a hierarchy of self-governing banks strongly resembles Nikolai Mordvinov's early nineteenth-century financial projects. The new context imbued this idea with new meaning. For Lamanskii, being an active capitalist and investor was synonymous with being a citizen. It was also the opposite of the passive subjecthood of the treasury banks' depositors. Written in March 1859, when the zemstvo reform (1864) was not even fully conceived and the emancipation of peasants (1861) was still in preparation, the project betrayed the spirit of the early reform era, when financial independence and participation were seen as political rights. Lamanskii suggested that the future State Commercial Bank should resemble the central banks of European countries, particularly the Bank of France, and envisioned the gradual replacement of state credit bills with banknotes that would be issued "not arbitrarily, but in exchange for promissory notes," thereby matching the amount of money with the scale of commercial transactions.[38] The credibility of new banknotes would be supported both by the bullion reserve and by payments that would come in during the process of discounting promissory notes.[39]

In short, there was nothing very original to Lamanskii's idea of bank reform and his desire to prevent the government's and treasury's direct involvement in credit and the production of money. Yet, in each period, the dream of a free bank acquired new layers of meaning and importance. In the 1850s–60s,

Russian society, drawn into the whirlpool of entrepreneurial and commercial activity, discovered the form of joint-stock corporation as an extension of decentralization into the sphere of finances and the economy, a metaphor for self-government and public participation, embodying the spirit of unity and civil society. The lawyer Semyon Pakhman, for instance, interpreted the development of joint-stock companies as a sign of a deep transformation in Russian society: the old society was limited to the educated elite, while the new sociability emerging in the form of the joint-stock corporation—"most original manifestations of the indigenous social element"—encompassed the entirety of the people.[40] "Social freedom—this is the integral principle of a joint-stock association," based on the principles of "freedom, publicity and responsibility," concluded Pakhman.[41] Thus, the idea of a joint-stock bank issuing new money resonated with this excitement about economic freedom and entrepreneurship that swept Russian society in the late 1850s.

To the disappointment of the young reformers, the minister of finance, Alexander Kniazhevich enacted the commission's reform, but decided to skip the central point of the bank reform's agenda, namely, the privatization of the bank of issue. Instead, he focused merely on the technical, although important, suggestions of the commission's report. Pavel Migulin later claimed that the decision to leave the main feature of the bank's organization intact was made at "Alexander II's personal insistence."[42] The government consolidated domestic debt and converted it into state bonds, eliminated multiple treasury banks, and concentrated state credit operations into one bank renamed the State Bank.[43] This reform prevented state default, but it left the entire system unchanged in its political foundations and let the state bureaucracy run the country's credit and monetary economy. The State Bank, established in 1860 under the control of the Ministry of Finance and the Council of State Credit Institution, assumed many new functions that corresponded to its new mission "to invigorate trade and strengthen the credit monetary system."[44] The two functions, however, were not linked to each other. As a commercial credit institution, it provided loans, accepted deposits, and discounted bills of exchange; at the same time, the bank serviced the needs of the State Treasury and the government in general. On its creation, the bank received 15 million rubles in capital that it could claim as its "property." Nevertheless, since the major share of the bank's profit was directed toward the redemption of state debts and the maintenance of the bank's reserve, its management was not motivated to raise profit or respond to the demands of the public.[45] The State Bank enjoyed much greater autonomy than its predecessors. Its director and the governing board could make decisions that were not directly related to the interest of the Ministry of Finance and the State Treasury. However, no concrete rules guaranteed the bank's autonomy, and, in practice, everything depended on the individual minister of finance and his willingness to control the bank. The Russian State Bank's dependence on the government was the major flaw in its organization, which, as many experts believed, distorted the rational ideas underpinning its foundation. The state's monopoly on the production of money remained secured and undisturbed.

Despite its unwillingness to undertake major structural reforms in finance and governance, the government did not abandon its efforts to restore the convertibility of credit rubles. The gap between the value of silver and paper rubles was not large (12%), and the restoration of parity seemed realistic. In 1861, Lamanskii, as deputy director of the newly created State Bank, drafted a proposal in which he again suggested combining the restoration of convertibility, modeled on a similar operation in England in 1819, with a reorganization of the State Bank into an independent joint-stock emission bank like the Bank of France, whose banknotes would eventually replace state credit bills.[46] Yet again, as in 1859, the final program of the operation approved by new minister of finance Mikhail Reutern omitted everything that concerned the Bank's autonomy. Of the initial intention of monetary reform, only the resumption of paper rubles' exchange for gold and silver remained intact, but without the institutional transformation it assumed a different meaning.[47] The new, truncated scheme solely emphasized the ruble's convertibility, while the main, driving factor behind it was the fulfillment of the sovereign promises to restore the currency balance, without which "the government would lose public confidence."[48] Therefore, the decision to proceed with the restoration of convertibility without securing the stability of the monetary system was not accidental. In fact, it betrayed a very peculiar political philosophy of money that, despite the reformist spirit of the rule, remained unchanged: money continued to be associated with sovereign power.

The analogy with Speransky's *Financial Plan* (1809) explains how the refusal to de-governmentalize the bank of issue was linked to the failure of constitutional ideas in the early 1860s. As was the case during Alexander I's reign, discussions about the issues of monetary reforms unfolded in parallel with debates on major political transformations in the press, in society, and in the government. A constitution introducing the political representation of estates was deemed a logical consequence of the emancipation of peasants and an integral part of the reform of self-government and administration. In 1861, Petr Valuev, the minister of the interior and one of the key figures in Alexander II's government, suggested transforming the bureaucratic State Council into

a prototype of a parliamentary institution by inviting in elected representatives of estates. Remarkably, Valuev used the arguments of the state's financial
credibility as an ultimate argument to convince the tsar of the necessity of
limiting his own power: "One stroke of a pen of Your Majesty would suffice
to abolish the entire Code of Laws of the Russian Empire, but none of your
order can either raise or lower the price of government securities on the St.
Petersburg stock market."[49] In other words, Valuev suggested that only a constitution could strengthen financial credibility, and the tsar's sovereign power
did not extend into the sphere of finance. In the context of the early 1860s,
when everyone was preoccupied with the ruble's rate, the argument about an
unruly stock exchange that was not susceptible to the state's control was very
powerful. Under Valuev's plan, the constitutional reform of the legislature
was supposed to be accompanied by the introduction of a "united government" and the income tax, which seemed to be a natural extension of political
representation. The emperor rejected Valuev's proposals.[50]

By excluding the institutional component of the monetary reform—
the introduction of an independent bank and a new law on the issuance of
banknotes—the government reduced the essence of the monetary reform
to restoring the autocrat's financial reputation and preserving his honor.
Considering the procedure of re-opening the exchange of credit rubles in
May 1862, Mikhail Reutern insisted that Alexander II himself should announce this measure. As he argued, credit bills had been introduced by a tsar's
manifesto of 1843, while another manifesto in 1858 announced the suspension
of their convertibility. Therefore, it was all the more important that the tsar
solemnly announce the "healing measure, which with God's blessing will start
the new era, and . . . show that Russia wants to fulfill its obligations, . . . not
being afraid of tremendous sacrifices" in accordance with the "wise tradition"
of preceding reigns.[51] The emphasis on convertibility was, therefore, an ideological departure from the liberal plans, demonstrating the government's allegiance to the political philosophy of Nicholas I's rule. As the *Russian Herald*
explained, convertibility alone would have no meaning if the nature of the
paper ruble, "its essence and meaning," did not change: "Convertibility is a
derived property, a quality of a secondary and not of the first nature. . . . To
accept the secondary quality for the primary quality . . . is to sacrifice the
main meaning of a thing; it means not to want the real thing but something
that resembles it."[52] The Ministry of Finance's plan of monetary reform, that
considered the restoration of the ruble's convertibility a starting rather than
an end point in the process of financial improvements, therefore, reversed this
logic. The only preparatory measure the government and bank undertook was

the procurement of a foreign loan of 15 million pounds (100 million rubles) through the bank of Rothschilds of London to fill the State Bank's exchange fund.[53]

In May 1862, the office of the State Bank in St. Petersburg opened the exchange of state credit bills for gold and silver 10% below their nominal value and promised to gradually raise the credit ruble's rate until it reached parity with silver rubles. In the meantime, Rothschild's gold bars packed in boxes began to arrive at the State Bank, which sent them directly to the Mint. Between May and October 1862, 826 *poods* (one *pood* equals 16,38 kilograms) of gold from the gold reserve, plus 465 *poods* sent by the Rothschilds, were melted and coined into Russian gold half-imperials and delivered to the exchange offices.[54] The Rothschilds' gold continued to trickle in when, in January 1863, the Provisional National Government in Poland launched a revolution against the Russian Empire, forcing the government to drain the funds intended for the exchange operation. The bags and boxes of gold moved in the opposite direction, to the West. Having spent 60% of the Rothschild loan along with millions of rubles from the reserve fund on the counterinsurgency operations in Poland, in August 1863 the government had to limit exchange to silver only and was then forced to suspend it entirely in November 1863.[55] The announcement of the exchange's suspension in November 1863 came from the State Bank and not the tsar.[56] During the entire operation, the Bank managed to withdraw about 72 million credit rubles out of 707 million rubles in circulation, but it paid dearly for them. In one day, November 1, 1863, after the State Bank restricted the exchange of rubles even for promissory notes, the ruble's rate vis-à-vis European currencies fell 8%.

The suspension and subsequent fall of the ruble's rate hurt everyone, not only the state. Katkov's newspaper rushed to explain the consequences of the fall: "Imagine . . . that you have ordered a certain merchandise from Paris. It costs, let us say, 4,000 francs. If you managed to buy a bill of exchange for that sum at 4 pm on November 1, this bill cost you . . . 1,007 rub 50 kop. If you, however, missed this moment and showed up at 5 pm, this bill cost you . . . 1,090 rub, that is to say, you lost . . . 82 rub 30 kop."[57] In an instant, the Westernization of Russian society and consumption became much more expensive, as the ruble again turned into an inconvertible currency.[58] In contrast to the period between 1812 and 1839, when the assignats-silver rate remained flexible and fluctuated widely, the post-1863 inconvertible credit ruble was de jure equal to the silver ruble, although de facto its value fluctuated. This meant that if someone wanted to change a silver or a gold coin to credit rubles in the State Bank or treasury office, he would be paid at a 1:1 (1:1.03 for gold)[59] rate, even though the market value of silver and gold differed significantly. In contrast to the pre-1839 situation, the compulsory rate of the credit ruble unavoidably led to the disappearance of metal money. The political and moral significance of the catastrophe of 1863 was enormous. Afterward, the government abandoned its attempts to restore the ruble's convertibility in one fell swoop and changed to the policy of gradual restoration and improvement, while the credit rubles remained inconvertible until 1897.

Was this outcome inevitable? At the beginning of the operation, the Bank had 175.5 million rubles in gold in its reserve fund, which covered one quarter of 707 million credit rubles in circulation. This ratio exceeded the one-sixth norm established by Kankrin, which supported the convertibility of credit rubles until the mid-1850s. However, in 1862–63, the circumstances were very different: Russia was devasted by a recent war and the Polish rebellion.[60] Further, Kankrin's financial system relied on secrecy and blind trust, whereas in 1862–63, everyone could learn about the condition of the Russian economy and the state budget from various published sources. Probably, the spirit of 1861—a large-scale peasant emancipation reform conducted by the government—convinced reformers of the possibility of repairing the monetary system "from above" by one forceful act. Everyone believed that, after the elimination of serfdom, the economy would blossom, but the reformers' optimism was unjustified.[61]

Writing in the immediate aftermath of the termination of exchange in November 1863, Vladimir Bezobrazov, one of the brightest young economists, expressed a thought that might have seemed like economic heresy to the bureaucrats. Bezobrazov pointed out that the size of the gold reserve, despite its importance as an auxiliary means of support, could not guarantee the stability of the monetary system. Under normal circumstances, banknotes should be backed up by real commercial transactions and work as the means of credit (a model now called the "real bill doctrine"). The exchange fund played a mere supporting role, and the bureaucrats' belief in the paper-to-gold ratio made no sense in a system of credit money. Drawing from the works of European economists, Bezobrazov juxtaposed state assignats to the banknotes and the different ways these two kinds of money come into existence. State assignats are issued as the means of payments, while banknotes originate as the means of credit; state assignats represent the needs of the government, while banknotes reflect the demands of the public. Therefore, in line with earlier Russian economists, Bezobrazov asserted that convertibility to gold alone means very little if the nature of the money remains the same.[62]

Considering the reasons for Russia's financial crisis of 1863, most nineteenth-century economists and historians agreed with Bezobrazov's assessment. The financiers of the 1860s believed that the convertibility of paper money had been both a sufficient condition and a means of restoring financial stability. They overestimated the power of the government to regulate the monetary system in a country that was no longer isolated from European markets and the credit economy. The reformers borrowed the mechanism of resuming the exchange from Britain, which restored its gold standard in 1821 after several years of inconvertibility. However, they overlooked one important distinction. In the case of Britain, the banknotes' rate had grown gradually, prompted by the rapid development of the economy and trade, and the government simply formalized and confirmed the factual restoration of the exchange.[63] In 1862–63, the Russian government attempted to restore the exchange at parity but did not want to wait until the national finances and economy improved. As banker and public figure Avraam Zak described the reformers' mode of thinking, "Statesmen at the financial ministry of that time were inspired by an optimism that was unusual for that kind of serious business."[64]

Among other characteristic features of this period, Zak noted the moral lens through which the reformers perceived their tasks: "Almost every minister . . . starting from Knyazhevich, . . . considered the question of the exchange rate as a matter of their own dignity."[65] Fully immersed in the ideas of the European political economy and social sciences, the reformers continued to think in the old categories of pledges and promises; they saw trickery in the inability to give people gold for paper, whereas the government misled its population by artificially supporting the rate of exchange, thereby providing a false impression of wealth while the economy stagnated and capital fled the country. Russia had experienced even more dramatic devaluations of paper money in the past, but they had never incited such a crisis as in the 1860s because "the society had not been deceived in its thinking about the value of things."[66] "We were afraid that the fall of the currency rate would injure us in the eyes of Europe,"[67] concluded the historian of the Great Reforms Alexei Golovachev, accusing reformers of excessive preoccupation with honor and reputation and with disregarding institutional problems.[68] The reformers of the early 1860s perceived the numbers of the ruble's exchange rate as a barometer of confidence, whereas "trust or distrust played no role in this situation," concluded economist Illarion Kaufman.[69] The declarations of the ruble's convertibility continued to be perceived as obligations resting on the personal promises of the tsar.

Strangely, the reformers failed to notice tensions between the "objective" laws of political economy and non-economic factors such as trust and belief. They spoke the languages of capitalism and autocracy, not seeing the mismatch between the two. For instance, in his memo to the Grand Duke Konstantin of 1857, Mikhail Reutern tried to explain that the Russian economy was subject to the work of certain universal economic laws (for instance, that the government cannot make the economy absorb more money that it needs), but at the same time presented the restoration of the monetary system as the fulfillment of the personal obligation of Constantine's father, Nicholas I. "This measure is just because it has been promised by the Sovereign's decree, and one should not play with His name. If paper money has not yet fallen completely, it is because the Russian people trust its Government firmly; and one should not reward this trust with ruin."[70] Public trust and personal reputation were not yet separated. For example, at the most critical moment of the 1863 exchange when the Bank started running out of gold, Baron Alexander Stieglitz, its first director, supplied the Bank's exchange offices with money from his own funds.[71] However, when the attempt to resume exchange failed, Stieglitz refused to provide his signature for the credit bills, which, according to the law, promised to exchange paper notes with hard currency. He did not want to harm his own reputation by participating in this trickery and certify an obvious lie.[72] The state credit bills issued between 1861 and 1866 appeared with the signature of the Bank's deputy director, Evgenii Lamanskii.

The obsessive desire to monopolize risk and to bear the entire responsibility for possible failures might have appeared the least logical feature of the autocratic governance. Yulii Gagemeister, commenting on the political meaning of currency, referred to the example of the United States, where "banks had gone broke due to the excessive issue of banknotes, where bills had lost value, incurring tremendous losses to the public, but where, in spite of that, the state was going forward with long strides, and the wealth was increasing in an unseen progression."[73] In Russia, however, the depreciation of paper money had an entirely different meaning. Whereas the fall of US private banks could not have shaken the credibility of the government, in the Russian Empire, "the supreme power [of the tsar] guarantees [the value of] state credit bills, and their fall had a much greater meaning than in America."[74] Financial disturbances cast a shadow on the prestige of royal authority. Therefore, Gagemeister concluded, as did many of his peers, true monetary reform must assume the transfer of the emission right and the responsibility of the tsar's government to an independent credit institution—a bank that would possess living ties with the economy and trade.

In 1866, the minister of finance, Mikhail Reutern, wrote to Alexander II, "Here [in Russia] the government enjoys more trust than any private person or a public organization."[75] It is true that in the 1860s, the government abolished several burdensome functions and institutions. The elimination of the state's monopoly on credit allowed dozens of new credit institutions to emerge, including the first joint-stock bank, which opened in 1864. However, the government preserved its monopoly on the production of money.[76] The failed attempts to restore the ruble's convertibility and to reform the State Bank showed that, in essence, the state did not want to withdraw from this sphere of public finances. The ideology of state-driven liberal and progressive transformations originated in the era of the Great Reforms, when the government took upon itself the formidable task of eliminating the centuries-long institution of serfdom. Liberal reforms granted from the throne might have produced a cognitive and ideological dissonance, but the reformers justified the state's intrusion through the traditions and collective mentality of the population.

Money and Financial Publicity

The government's obsession with its financial reputation expressed in the numbers of the ruble's rate was roused in part by a sudden increase in the quantity of financial information. The removal of old censorship laws and the new spirit of "openness" that followed years of secrecy demonstrated Russia's commitment to transparency and cooperation with foreign investors. At the same time, it produced new threats and challenges. The era of publicity unfortunately coincided with a serious crisis in Russian finance, and official statistics could not always inspire optimism among foreign investors and bankers. Information about its gold and silver reserve put Russia in a "very embarrassing" position in the eyes of foreigners, who read these numbers as the "barometer . . . of credit," wrote Ludwik Tęgoborski. The Russian government had to choose between revealing the critical state of resources and suspending the publication of any data, and it was unclear which would produce the worse effect.[77]

The exchange crisis of 1862–63 revealed that the government could not yet determine which information helped maintain financial stability and which threatened it, what could and could not be said in public. The new budgetary rules of 1862 made the publication of the budget mandatory for the first time. In 1864, the State Financial Control started publishing its reports, which showed the application of the state budgets with the actual revenues and expenditures. The State Bank released its weekly, monthly, and annual balances and reports, complementing the overly general but informative reports of the Council of State Credit Institutions. Newspapers eagerly grasped the opportunity to comment on and interpret this new information about finances. The avalanche of information sharply contrasted with what was available in the reign of Nicholas I, when the annual speeches of the minister of finance at the Council of State Credit Institutions represented the only source of knowledge available about Russian money and credit.[78] Ironically, one of the factors that increased the costs of the failed exchange operation in 1863 was the government's excessive openness. The bureaucrats who designed the operation to restore the convertibility of the ruble in 1863 decided to inform the public that the State Bank would exchange credit bills at an ascending rate, and they even provided the schedule for the changing prices of gold. Indeed, people rushed to the bank to sell gold in order to buy it back a few months later for a much lower price.[79] Unnecessary publicity based on false notions of honesty and honor was a grave mistake that contributed to the failure of the exchange operation.

The obsession with reputation and its influence on the rate of exchange also generated anxiety about public information regarding Russian finances. In 1859, Yulii Gagemeister, director of the Credit Chancellery at the Ministry of Finance, publicly revealed his fears about Russia's impending default and commented on Russia's "poverty." A French banker struck by Gagemeister's declaration reported it to St. Petersburg, and Alexander II demanded Gagemeister's immediate removal from his position.[80] If such declarations could perhaps have gone unnoticed earlier, in the late 1850s, they were thought to threaten the stability of the ruble. The government wanted to be honest and increased financial publicity, yet it also strove to control the flow of information and public representation of its financial policy. An obsession with honor and reputation made the government compromise on the declared allegiance to liberal principles and introduce unofficial financial censorship. As Fyodor Terner recalled, in 1862, the minister of finance, Mikhail Reutern, asked Vladimir Bezobrazov, who contributed to Katkov's *Moscow Bulletin*, to write articles supporting the government's financial initiatives while Terner monitored publications on financial matters in the Russian press. Bezobrazov was appalled by the offer and responded that he could write favorably only about measures he approved. Terner, while not in principle against working with the press, was repulsed by the word "censorship," which Reutern used to describe his new job.[81]

Apparently, Reutern ultimately obtained Bezobrazov's consent, but the deal did not work out as planned. In 1863, the *Moscow Bulletin* received an

unofficial warning from Minister of Interior Petr Valuev for an article that
mildly criticized the Ministry of Finance's handling of the exchange operation in 1863 and described conditions under which the exchange could be
completed as planned. Valuev, in response to Katkov's indignation, admitted
that even though the government appreciated his "independent, but noble
and useful" style, state censorship would treat articles on financial matters in
a special way.[82] Indeed, for several months until November 1, 1863, Katkov did
not publish anything on money, following "the advice of people who see in the
silence of the press the circumstance most favorable for finances." Then, when
the exchange was terminated, Katkov's newspaper took pains to explain the
causes of the crisis to readers and how to deal with its consequences.[83] Valuev
responded immediately, this time, conveying "special gratitude" to Katkov
from the minister of finance "for the *Moscow Bulletin*'s articles on the issue of
the bank crisis."[84] Katkov's further correspondence with Valuev suggests that
the journalist was obliged to send drafts of his articles on monetary issues for
Valuev's and Reutern's approval. In late December, Valuev returned another
draft from Katkov (or rather Bezobrazov, who apparently penned the articles)
and assailed him for promoting "theories that have brought and are bringing
Russia to ruin." Valuev called these views "bookish" and false and described
them as not respecting "people's unshaken belief in paper money." While not
openly prohibiting the publication, Valuev requested softening the passages
indicated by the Ministry of Finance.[85] Whether this type of relationship
between the newspaper and the minister continued after 1863 is unknown.
But this pattern of relationships between the government and the press established in the early 1860s persisted until the fall of the empire.

The government's control over the press could not, however, reach beyond
the empire's borders. The publication of an article in a January 1864 issue of
the *Revue de Deux Mondes* by Louis Wolowski, a well-known French economist of Polish origin and an active participant in debates over European monetary and bank policy in 1860s, threw many people into despair. His article
opened with the phrase "Russia is poor" and analyzed the state of Russian
finances after the bankruptcy of 1863. The main indicator of Russia's deep
crisis, according to Wolowski, was the enormous increase in the amount of
state credit bills and the decrease of the bullion reserve. With the size of the
Russian economy equal to a third of the national economy of France, the
amount of paper money in Russia was three times greater (900 million francs
in France versus 3 billion francs in Russia).[86] Nothing in Wolowski's article
was a new revelation, since he used numbers from the official statistics, but it
produced an unprecedented reaction. "They got scared. One response to the

article was immediately followed by another. It has touched the most sensitive chord. . . . All the official press shuddered, from *The Moscow Bulletin* to *The Nord*," wrote Nikolai Ogarev, an émigré socialist and co-editor of the famous radical periodical *The Bell*.[87] The avalanche of articles denouncing Wolowski's interpretations and the accusing him of collaborating with Polish revolutionaries was further proof of the Russian government's acute sensitivity to critiques of its finances, which could drop the rate of exchange and drag Russia into another cycle of financial troubles.[88] Ironically, Wolowski had borrowed the main phrase of the article, "Russia is poor," from an article published in 1862 in the Russian periodical the *Russian Herald* [*Russkii Vestnik*]. What could be said in Russian, however, could not be translated to French and appear in a well-read European magazine. The entire discussion around Wolowski's article was conducted in French and was intended for Western audience.

The government saw Wolowski's essay not only as an expression of anti-Russian sentiment or economic criticism but also as a subversive political act. This fixation on financial reputation showed that the government considered finance to be solely the government's sphere of activity . But by claiming monopoly on monetary policy, the government also assumed full responsibility for its failures. When, in the aftermath of the 1863 financial crisis, several newspaper writers blamed speculators and capitalists for the greediness and lack of patriotism that led to the collapse of the exchange operation, their voices were immediately silenced by the chorus of journalists and experts who placed the full responsibility for the unsuccessful reform and the ruble's fall on the government.[89] "Private individuals are incapable of fighting the ghost [of excess paper money]. The war can only be fought by the state alone,"[90] wrote Mikhail Katkov in the *Moscow Bulletin*. The *Stock Exchange Bulletin* [*Birzhevye Vedomosti*] expressed a similar opinion: "The regulation of the monetary system may not be left to society alone; to the contrary, public interests must be protected against losses produced by monetary chaos, and the government must take upon itself this responsibility."[91]

The idea of the government's fault and responsibility was grounded in the interpretation of credit rubles as evidence of the state's indebtedness to society for the mass of inconvertible paper rubles. In 1865, Russia's leading newspaper, the *St. Petersburg Bulletin* [*Sankt-Peterburgskie vedomosti*], received an official "warning" from the Ministry of Interior—a disciplinary notice that could be followed by the newspaper's closure—for "expressing opinions not compatible with the interest of state credit." The newspaper was reprimanded for discussing whether the government was allowed to sell or mortgage state properties that served as the collateral for the credit bills. The article referred to the common interpretation of the meaning of words printed on every credit ruble bill, namely, the state's obligation to exchange paper rubles for gold or silver guaranteed by the "patrimony of the state."[92] The *St. Peterburg Bulletin* was neither the first nor the only outlet to express this view. The *Stock Exchange Bulletin* also reminded readers that the treasury owed more than 500 million rubles to the State Bank (for the unbacked credit rubles), arguing that it should first pay the old debts to society before creating new ones.[93]

The official *Northern Post* [*Severnaia Pochta*] sponsored by the Ministry of the Interior responded to the *Stock Exchange Bulletin*'s suggestion with a diametrically opposed interpretation of the credit ruble's pledge printed on every ruble bill. It blamed liberals for confusing two different terms— "state properties" and "state patrimony," that is, the formula adopted for the Manifesto in 1843. According to the government's newspaper, the formula included both private and state properties; therefore, the responsibility "for the state debt" lay "not with the treasury, but with the people." Apparently, this understanding of the people's command of wealth and power did not extend to rights and was strictly limited to debts and obligations.[94] By raising the question of a mutual relationship between state and people and responsibility in the monetary sphere, the *Northern Post*'s article only let the genie of the constitutional debate out of the bottle. The discussion of a seemingly theoretical issue of what constituted the collateral for credit rubles ended with a conversation about sovereignty, representation, the nature of private and state property, and the limits of state power. The *St. Petersburg Bulletin* objected to the official newspaper's vision of the people holding the responsibility for the domestic debt, since such an interpretation excluded the possibility of state bankruptcy or the very possibility that the government could fail repay its domestic loans to the people. Society is responsible for paying taxes, and only this part of private wealth can be seen as belonging, along with state properties, to the "entire wealth of the state." If the state that collects taxes lacks money to pay its obligation, this does not mean that it can shift its responsibility onto the people. The *St. Petersburg Bulletin* noted that "in theory," it is not the people's wealth that forms part of the state wealth; rather, the state "owes its origin to the people's labor and productivity; hence, in constitutional states, the representatives of people's interests control the disposal of state property." The newspaper claimed that it did not want to antagonize the relationship between the government and society and believed that, despite the absence of representative institutions in Russia, they could achieve solidarity.[95] Nevertheless, this olive branch did not save the newspaper from an official warning and the accusation of subverting the credibility of the state. Even Mikhail Katkov, who was often at odds with the *St. Petersburg Bulletin*, was appalled by the government's reaction: "Is state credit indeed such a flimsy thing that it can be affected by an ungrounded, false or even absurd opinion of one or another independent newspaper?"[96]

The conversation about the nature of credit rubles that continued into the late 1860s and 1870s inevitably led to analysis of the relationship between the state and its subjects. In the era of the "Great Reforms," the debate over the mutual relationship between state and society reached its apogee. Most liberals continued to perceive the state if not as an adversary, then at least as an alien or external element. Reiterating the question, "What is money?" the *Stock Exchange Bulletin* concluded that, of the three main functions of money—to be the measure of value, the means of exchange, and the security of transactions—only the third needed the state's participation and mediation. In practical terms, the government's task of producing money should be limited to the coinage of gold currency, which should work as the "relative unit of value." "Money has predominantly private economic meaning," state interests should never trump private interests, and the government should not interfere in other spheres of the monetary system outside its primary responsibility of producing the measure of value. The government "is incompetent in this sphere, as the amount of paper money must reflect the current needs of commerce and remain flexible. The two principles formulated by liberal newspapers—the freedom of banks and the gold standard—outlined the expectations of the business and intellectual elites.[97]

Frustration with the failure of the reform and the dashed hopes for restoring the Russian currency grew stronger after a successful reform in Finland. Until 1860, the autonomous Grand Duchy of Finland remained fully integrated into the ruble domain; in 1860, Finland introduced its own currency (*markka*), and in 1865 it successfully switched to the regime of metallic monetary circulation. Finland floated a loan with the Rothschild house in Frankfurt, and in November 1865, Alexander II's decree declared "metallic money" (i.e., silver) the main measure of value, thus decoupling the Finnish markka from the ruble.[98] Remarkably, the imperial Committee of Finance approved this measure despite admitting that it would have very "unfavorable" economic and ideological effects on the Russian financial system.[99] The monetary reform in Finland followed other significant political changes, including, most importantly, the 1863 resumption of the Diet of Estates, a national parliament that had not met since 1809. As Johan Vilhelm Snellman explained in his report to the imperial Committee of Finance, "The metallic fund of the Bank of Finland constitutes the property of the nation."[100] In 1867, the Bank of Finland, which issued paper banknotes that could be exchanged for silver marks, was put under the Diet's supervision. Therefore, even though the Bank remained a state institution, the idea of bank independence was realized in the form of parliamentary control.[101] In the meantime, Russian reformers failed to either enact constitutional reforms or introduce the rule of law in finances.

Against the backdrop of mostly successful and celebrated transformations in the sphere of law, local governance, education, and rural economy, the monetary reform, along with the constitution, represented the major failures. However, the environment in which the State Bank operated drastically differed from the pre-reform era. In the 1860s–70s, the Russian media and the growing body of Russian professional economists closely and anxiously watched the activities of the Ministry of Finance and the State Bank. The "solidarity" of the State Bank and the treasury and their disregard for the needs of trade and industry remained the greatest concern for economists and journalists.[102] Critics of the government's policy were particularly concerned with the political and legal aspects of the continued printing of credit rubles, namely, that the Ministry of Finance and the State Bank could (and did) issue paper money secretly and at will.[103] Mikhail Katkov painstakingly deciphered the Bank's balances and revealed that the Bank's "temporal" emissions allegedly aimed to support the cash deposit of its branches, and it had done so at the government's demand.[104] Katkov called these emissions "illegal." In his interpretation, only measures that "maintain the value of the credit ruble" could be considered in compliance with the law: "Anything that undermines that value, even if it is legal from a formal point of view, should be considered illegal." Katlov concluded, "The bank's emission of credit rubles would have been rightful only if it had had the real character of a bank's emission, that is to say, if it had been called for by the demands of the market."[105] The idea of financial rule of law was firmly established in liberal economic ideology and rhetoric.

Slavophile Capitalism

Even at the times of its greatest popularity, liberalism represented only one of several theoretical and political trends. The high economic and social costs of reform produced discontent that fueled the revival of conservative ideas. Industrialists, while welcoming structural reforms, complained about the unfavorable conditions of the free-trade regime as well as the radicalism of financial measures, such as the lowering of the deposit interest rate in state banks and their subsequent elimination. Moscow merchants and nationalist intellectuals vented about their discontent with the government's tariff policy and the growing presence of foreign businesses in the pages of several periodicals, most important, the *Herald of Industry* [*Vestnik Promyshlennosti*], the *Stockholder* [*Aktsioner*][106] and the *Trade Almanac* [*Torgovyi Almanakh*]. Urging the state to better protect national industry, economic conservatives of the 1860s also protested the proliferation of the "Western" theories of money brought by a group of young, cosmopolitan economists nicknamed "*They*" (*Oni*). Nationalists suspected "*them*" of conspiring with Russia's enemies, who were envious of her successes, and of propagating the dogma about the impropriety of the government's issuing paper money for state needs. According to the conservatives, the unpatriotic idea of the de-governmentalization of money was meant to limit the financial power of the supreme authority and therefore its ability to wage wars.[107]

Nineteenth-century economic nationalism never represented a homogenous movement. In the 1860s, several nationalists, such as Katkov, combined laissez-faire reformism with nationalist ideas, but this oxymoronic combination did not last long and disappeared after the Russo-Turkish War and the Berlin Congress of 1878. Cosmopolitan nationalism differed from the stances of more radical conservatives. In the 1860s, Katkov often clashed with the bulwark of protectionism, the *Trade Almanac*, over the question of whether Russia had too much (or not enough) paper money in circulation, while for the old-believer industrialist and railroad capitalist Vasilii Kokorev, the *Herald of Industry* appeared too cosmopolitan.[108] Economic nationalism and protectionism were not totally incompatible with aspirations for financial rule of law and the restoration of the ruble's stability, but if, in 1858 and 1859, the *Herald of Industry* appeared more or less sympathetic to the government's activity and shared its cosmopolitanism, it grew more critical in the early 1860s, protesting the directions and methods of the monetary reform. Moscow merchants who financed the outlet did not share the government's obsession with the ruble's convertibility to gold which, under the regime of free trade, would be carried away from the country.[109] In general, the program of "Slavophile capitalists" resembled early nineteenth-century economic nationalism. It did not amount to Fichte's isolationism, but it reinforced the ideas of moving away from international metal currencies and measuring the purchasing capacity of national money by domestic standards. Nationalists claimed that there was nothing wrong with the low exchange rate of credit rubles: it was not that the ruble was cheap, but rather that gold and silver were expensive.[110] Contributors to the *Trade Almanac*, such as Alexander Shipov, even thought that a gradual decrease in credit rubles had been beneficial to Russian exporters and especially domestic producers, who needed special governmental attention and support in the wake of the peasants' emancipation.[111]

The writers of the *Trade Almanac* reproduced almost verbatim earlier ideas of economic nationalism that became a staple of conservative thought: the state credit ruble symbolized the unity of the government and the people, a unique standard of value that differed from "foreign" silver and gold.[112] They were infuriated by the assertions of the Russian state's bankruptcy in credit rubles and repeated Nikolai Karamzin's claim later reiterated by a famous historian and one of the founders of Russian Panslavism, Mikhail Pogodin, namely, that the state did not owe anything to anyone.[113] References to the proverbial money of the ancient Rus' made of the ears, tails, and muzzles of wild beasts reappeared again as an argument in favor of the state's unconditional authority to issue money in any matter it saw fit and of the "true popular thinking about money."[114]

Along with the old concepts of money, the economic nationalism of the late 1850s–60s generated new ideas and projects. The main new element of the conservative agenda of monetary reform was the substitution of the bullion reserve, as a collateral for paper money, with railroads. In its general contours, this idea curiously resembled one of the trends in Western economic thought, namely, the "real bills doctrine." Its main proposal was to replace the restrictive mechanism of the passive gold fund with a productive collateral reflecting the state of commerce and industry. However, the similarity was only superficial: railroads, unlike the bills of exchange, were not liquid, did not stand for real or potential economic profit, and could not reflect the demand for money. The concept of railroad money, as with many other conservative ideas, emphasized the moral and ideological aspects of the economy and, not coincidentally, originated from the writings of historian Mikhail Pogodin. One reason for Pogodin's plan was the rumors of the planned foundation of the Russian Railroad Company (Glavnoe Obschestvo zheleznykh dorog, or La Grande société des chemins de fer russes) with international (Russian, Polish, British, German, Dutch, and French) capital and French management, which offended the patriotic feelings of many Russian industrialists and thinkers. Pogodin, therefore, wanted to solve two problems at once: to release the government from the need to search for gold, which represented Russia's enslavement by Europe, and to fund the construction of railroads. The "railroad assignats" would therefore have better, more solid and valuable collateral than credit rubles: they would match the value of the assignats, and, unlike gold, would bring real profit and wealth.[115]

Pogodin's "railroad assignats" soon turned into a favorite idea of all writers and economists who opposed the government's drift toward the Westernization of finances and the gold standard. It appeared simple and attractive: the new paper money "will be represented and backed up by the railroad itself, up to the last kopeck. One only needs to declare that they [the new paper money bills] will be accepted along with credit rubles and circulate as money."[116] Pogodin, angry at the government for blindly following the advice of Western "science" that had been brought to Russia along with vaudeville and comedies, blamed the authorities for ignoring a natural, national cure to the ruble problem. The opening of the exchange in 1862 was an example of the government's doctrinairism: "They have now made a loan to exchange assignats [credit rubles] for gold, but why? nobody wants this gold?" wrote Pogodin in April 1862, predicting that the gold would end up in the coffers of "Jews."[117]

Despite his aversion to the laissez-faire doctrine and its embodiment in British capitalism, Pogodin tried to find theoretical support for his idea of railroad assignats from the guru of British free-trade ideology, radical liberal Richard Cobden. In a letter to Cobden, Pogodin formulated the key points of his views on currency. Quite remarkably, these points closely followed Nikolai Karamzin's earlier ideas about the uniqueness of Russian money and the Russian people's indifference to gold or silver accompanied by a boundless trust in the state. Echoing Karamzin (although not referring to him), Pogodin invoked ancient leather money as the ultimate argument: "If the government decided to issue martens' muzzles with the Imperial coat of arms, they would immediately become for us more valuable than gold. The government should use this trust before it gets weaker or changes to engird Russia with railroads as if with ferrules, to print special assignats that would circulate along with other credit bonds."[118]

Cobden remained unimpressed by Pogodin's scheme and, apparently, misunderstood his intention to use railroads assignats in lieu of foreign capital. Jean-Joseph Proudhon did not respond to Pogodin's letter with the same content (or perhaps Pogodin chose not to publicize this part of the correspondence). However, the response of the Russian nationalist press was much more sympathetic. The idea of railroad assignats appeared in several publications, along with the critique of the government's monetary policy. In 1867, Nikolai Danilevskii, a naturalist and philosopher who later became famous for his Slavophile manifesto *Russia and Europe* (1869) and his vehement critique of Darwinism, published a series of articles on a theme straying from his main area of expertise but very important for the conceptualization of political nationalism. Danilevskii's "The Fall of the Credit Ruble," which appeared in the *Trade Almanac*, endorsed Pogodin's idea of anchoring the Russian ruble to railroads—a valuable, productive, and, most important, domestic resource—and criticized cosmopolitan economists in the government who had borrowed their free-trade ideas from England while neglecting Russian national interests.

While unanimously supporting the idea of railroad assignats, nationalist writers could disagree about the details. Some authors wanted to use them as a way to raise money for future railroad construction, while others suggested using already built and functioning roads instead of a gold exchange fund.[119] The common point was replacing absent (and, as the authors thought, useless) gold with a resource that would be productive and beneficial for everyone. One of the first start-ups of the "Slavophile capitalists" was the construction of a Trinity Railroad from Moscow to the Trinity Monastery, which was intended to carry, among other passengers, Orthodox pilgrims. The project was initiated by the writer, economist, and publisher of the *Herald of Industry* Fedor Chizhov who "resolved to wrest Russian railroads from the hands of foreigners."[120]

Alternative Money

While writers and politicians debated the ideological principles of financial policy, another battle for the ruble was taking place in Russian provinces. Cities, villages, and trade fairs were flooded with counterfeit credit rubles of various origins. According to Mikhail Reutern's report, counterfeiting had ceased to be a crime with the goal of gaining "illegal profit" and became a cause that aimed "to shake the financial means and the credit of the state."[121] Police interrogations found that the massive production of counterfeit rubles organized by Polish émigrés after the suppression of the 1863 rebellion indeed sought "to disorganize state finances through the emission of these notes" and to support exiled Poles in Europe and elsewhere.[122] Russian authorities claimed that the production of counterfeit money originally began in London with the Polish Revolutionary Government (Rząd Narodowy).[123] Apparently, it quickly spread throughout Europe and was part of a network in Paris, Aberdeen, Brussels, Warsaw, and Le Havre, with depots and transition points in many other cities and multiple agents (many of whom were women) to carry the false money across the border.[124] The police changed the methods of investigation, offering lavish rewards to informants and police officers in European cities. Widely publicized arrests and trials perhaps helped improve the reputation of the government in Europe, but they barely decreased the quantity of bad money inside Russia.

The police agents' bulletins that recorded rumors and registered the general mood in Russian cities sounded the alarm. People complained about the disappearance of silver coins and the influx of counterfeit rubles. "There is a rumor in the city that even in the offices of the State Bank one can get false credit papers. The distrust to our credit institutions is growing more and more, and the rate [of the credit ruble] to the silver ruble is falling," stated one report. "People are wondering, why is our paper ruble valued so low abroad? This is very clear: it is because there are so many counterfeit papers [i.e., paper rubles], so well made, that it is hard to distinguish the true ones from the fake ones. They are being brought into the country in great amounts and immediately exchanged; soon, we will have more counterfeit money than the real assignats."[125] Fake money came, however, not only from abroad; cases of counterfeiting were registered in almost all provinces of the empire, and the sites of manufacturing usually did not coincide with the sites of dissemination.[126]

The chief of the Moscow gendarme administration was startled. The main center of counterfeiting was situated "not on a borderland of the state, but near the capital"—in the Guslitsy village of the Bogorodskii district, and it spread bad money to the core provinces and the "remote corners of the state." Guslitsy was an Old Belief community that had around 40,000 inhabitants who made their living by growing hops and weaving. It was also a center of Old Belief icon painting, book miniatures, and copper casting—crafts that made many local peasants into true artists. No wonder the counterfeited bills local engravers produced were of excellent quality, almost indistinguishable from real money. Several families from twenty-five villages of the Guslitsy community were involved in producing false bills. An intricate network of communication extended as far as the Expedition for the Production of State Paper in St. Petersburg, where one of the villagers' brothers served as a janitor and kept them apprised of all changes and innovations. For instance, Guslitsy artisans knew well in advance about the new credit bills with tsars' portraits issued in 1866 and had no difficulty counterfeiting them. Indeed, in 1868, the chief of the Moscow gendarme administration reported the spread of counterfeit bills of the new issuance that were disseminated in various provinces, mainly outside Moscow.[127] Guslitsy peasants destroyed the government's last hope that the introduction of new credit bills—printed on paper made of hemp fiber, with a new, intricate design and complicated American technology—would change the situation. New handmade bills quickly spread around the country through a "systematic and regular" network that included the famous trade fairs in Nizhnii Novgorod, Kharkiv, Kursk, Kazan', Orenburg, and Don.[128]

"The authorities have been unable to extirpate this evil," admitted the chief of the Moscow gendarmes.[129] The names of the main eighty-six counterfeiters from Guslitsy were well known to the police, who could not catch them red-handed. Their workshops and tools were well hidden (as the police believed, in underground labyrinths), and no one in the village would reveal their whereabouts. Agents who came too close to the secret sites risked their lives: one police agent and one guard were killed, and the house of a villager who was suspected of helping the police was burnt down.[130] The communities of Old Believers, trained by decades of persecution and living under the control of authorities, were almost impenetrable by outsiders. "Notorious fanaticism and the unity of the entire communities in villages where the nests of counterfeiting were located . . . served . . . as a strong bulwark against . . . prosecution by officials," stated the report of Ivan Putilin, the legendary head of the St. Petersburg detective police.[131] Without satisfactory evidence of counterfeiting, the cases could not be brought to court, and even if police could secure an indictment for distributing false money, the jury either acquitted counterfeiters or sentenced them to several months of detention. Insolent counterfeiters who were confident of their safety did not even try to hide from the police. Only after the Moscow gendarmes established a special observation point in Guslitsy did they become more cautious. Foiling the Guslitsy enterprise required joint efforts from the police of Moscow and St. Petersburg as well as the Ministries of Finance and the Interior, including Ivan Putilin, who appeared in Guslitsy disguised as the brother of a local priest.[132] Finally, in December 1868, the police were able to arrest engraver Ivan Loginov and, after forty-eight hours of searching, found the necessary proof of his complicity: an engraved stone sunk in a river. In January 1869, after months of living undercover in Guslitsy, Iurevich, an agent of the Ministry of Finance, was able to arrest another engraver, Semyon Zotov, an old master who had trained generations of artisans and made several plates for counterfeit bills.[133]

Despite the success of the Guslitsy operation, the problem of counterfeiting did not disappear. After the arrests of Loginov and Zotov, the production of false money continued in other villages in the same district.[134] New centers appeared near Moscow, in Baku, and in Tobolsk, and false money continued to trickle in from abroad. Even state money-making was ultimately not sufficiently secure. In 1868, an employee of the Expedition for the Production of State Papers, Ivan Vetkhov, who boasted about the ease of obtaining blank paper to make money, stole blank sheets for 100-ruble bills worth 25,000 rubles at the instigation of police agents.[135] The police brought Vetkhov's case to court, but as a result, the police agents also found themselves in the dock: the instigation to steal, even with the goal of revealing criminal actions, was equivalent to complicity. Vetkhov's case was not unique. While trying to catch criminals red-handed, police often became involved in criminal business. Lawyers were outraged by the police actions; the Ministry of Finance warned local authorities against using tactics that "tempted and probably even created crimes" and therefore discredited the government.[136] However, the practice of police provocation continued because of the desperate need to bring forgers to court and prevent the spread of counterfeiting. At the same time, the police simply stopped arresting and prosecuting money changers who disseminated false money, since the specificity of Russian penal laws meant that it was almost impossible to procure an indictment in court, and the arrests only alerted counterfeiters and spurred them disguise their factories.[137]

While dealing with mixed records of success and failure with individual cases of counterfeiting, the government struggled to elaborate a general strategy of prevention. The main principles of policy in this sphere had remained unchanged since the eighteenth century: a presumption of innocence in relation to all bearers of counterfeit bills, and even the exchange of false money for genuine, was supposed to prevent the spread of fear and distrust. The government was a hostage of its own monetary policy. Since the standing of the ruble rested on people's confidence and trust in the government, it feared damaging this trust by refusing to accept false credit rubles. Moreover, the legislation offered rewards for information about counterfeiting and amnesty to people involved in forgery if they were willing to denounce their accomplices. As a result, savvy criminals often denounced their less experienced and naïve comrades in the business and could walk away with a reward (up to 1,500 rubles).[138] Despite some successes by police authorities,[139] Western provinces of the Russian Empire were awash in bad money carried across the border. The situation became serious enough that the governors of Kyiv, Warsaw, and Kalish provinces sent private detectives to London, thought to be the main center of counterfeiting. This démarche resulted in a rather nasty scandal involving the central administration and the governors, who accused the Ministry of Finance of being unable to prevent the flood of counterfeit money.[140]

For the government, the detrimental effects of counterfeiting were not limited to financial losses. It distorted the very idea of paper money as a state-issued representation of value whose acceptance was based on people's trust in the government. As the Ministry of Finance observed, the acceptance of counterfeit money "is based not on the premise of its authenticity, but mainly on mutual trust between individuals participating in the exchange, which is absolutely incorrect and not conforming to the meaning of money in the state."[141] Counterfeiting questioned the reputation of the state as the sole bearer of trust and authority, and shifted the emphasis to trust between people rather than the individual and the state. This could work both ways. Police authorities were amazed to find that the inhabitants of Guslitsy often knowingly accepted counterfeit bills, even at a reduced price; the counterfeit money circulated locally as an alternative means of payment, a surrogate money within the community of counterfeiters. In other instances, people did not pay attention to the authenticity of the means of payment until rumors about bad money made them boycott all state credit bills altogether.

The government had to admit that it was itself partly responsible for the distortion of its own monetary doctrine. One of the consequences of the postwar financial crisis and the ruble's fall vis-à-vis its silver counterpart was the disappearance of full-weight silver coins, which constituted the main means of transactions for peasants and workers. As a result, the vacuum of state-issued change coins was filled with privately issued marks and surrogates. In 1860, the Ministry of Finance declared that it would refrain from banning private marks until finances were normalized. Perhaps the most widespread and best-known example of private money was the marks issued by Serguei Maltsov, a Russian tycoon whose industrial estate spread over the territories of three provinces (Kaluzhskaia, Orlovskaia, and Smolenskaia). The Maltsov factory employed more than 100,000 workers, had its own railroad and a telegraph network, and was famous for technological and social innovations. Contemporaries preferred to call Maltsov's enterprise a "republic," an "America in Russia," emphasizing the democratic style of Maltsov's management. However, this republic had evolved and flourished before the abolition of serfdom; it was a miniature model of the autocratic system, the rule of one man, albeit a progressive one. Maltsov enjoyed the full confidence and perhaps even love of his subjects, and this attitude extended to all his initiatives. A visitor to the capital of Maltsov's state (Diatkovo) observed that the money he had printed possessed unshakable credibility. In fact, Maltsov's bills, which bore his name, replaced state credit bills in three provinces. Initially issued for local transactions within the factory, they gradually spread beyond this area, and their issuance certainly exceeded the goals of facilitating exchange. Maltsov's money appeared in various denominations, including 1-, 2-, 3- and 5-ruble bills, and they competed with state-issued bills. Even tax collectors had to accept Maltsov's money, which they could exchange elsewhere for state credit bills with a mere 1% discount.[142] The withdrawal of Maltsov's money could ruin his business and destabilize the economic and social situation in several provinces. Further, the local population was convinced that the state had approved their circulation, and the fall of Maltsov's currency could detrimentally affect the status of state-issued paper bills.

In 1868, the Ministry of Finances decided to stop the proliferation of alternative monetary units, a move that can be seen as another attempt to centralize finances. However, the prohibition of Maltsov currency also symbolized one important feature of the Russian reforms of the 1860s—namely, the attempt to shift emphasis from individual trust-based relations to trust in institutions. Maltsov's money was backed by his own reputation and personal fortune, which exceeded the amount of the "bills" issued many times over. Unfortunately, no institution could control and guarantee the solvency of Maltsov's business, and, therefore, the well-being of his former serfs, turned free subjects of the emperor. No law in Russia prohibited the issuance of private money, nor was there a law that allowed its existence. "No doubt, people may put confidence in each other in financial matters without expressing it in one or another legalized form, but in such a case they deprive themselves of the protection of law," stated Reutern. Agreements of that sort should be based on "free will," but in cases like Maltsov's, workers had no choice but to accept the money. Maltsov's private money was based on authority and wealth. Therefore, the issuance of private money had to be prohibited.[143]

Reutern was adamant about exterminating private currencies, but not everyone in the government shared his view. The minister of justice, Konstantin Pahlen, argued, for instance, that the right to issue private notes should be granted "to all Russian subjects." Anyone willing to issue private monetary units should simply inform the local governor about the amount of issue, denominations, and the place these notes could be exchanged for state credit bills. The issuer should also place an "exchange fund" consisting of state money or securities at the disposal of the local administration and order the printing of notes at the Expedition for the Production of State Papers, which would guarantee them against counterfeiting. In other words, private money should mirror the system of state credit bills and compensate for their deficit. In fact, the governors of the Southwestern and Northwestern regions had already approved a similar model, where various notes and marks circulated in lieu of the lacking coins.[144]

The debate between the opponents and the proponents of private money revealed an interesting ideological paradox. Private money in Russia stood for the ideological legacy of serfdom: a system that substituted an entire structure of local administration, police and judicial authority, and financial management, all concentrated in the figure of one landowner. The abolition of serfdom and the creation of a free labor market necessitated the development of a monetary economy, but the financial means for this development were limited. As a result, many former owners of serf estates and factories tried to compensate for the lack of state-issued money by issuing their own local notes.[145] Herein lay the contradiction: the abolition required replacing the networks of personal authority with institutions, and private money appeared to deviate from that principle. At the same time, the main principle of the Russian state monetary system was, in essence, no different from the private money of landowners. Arguing for the extermination of private money, the minister of finance inadvertently confirmed that in Russia, only one kind of "private" money could exist. Responding to Pahlen, who had referred to the practice of European banks that issued banknotes and "bearer checks," Reutern remarked that banks issued notes under the security of the bills of exchange. That is, behind every banknote stood a commercial transaction, and, therefore, the banknotes were the means of credit. In contrast, private money "serve[d] not the tools of credit, but the means of payment": "their amount depend[ed] on their [the owners'] needs, rather than the demands of local trade and industry." Ironically, this phrase repeated verbatim the common characteristic of state credit rubles that were not based on "credit." State credit bills backed by the tsar's honor and the dwindling gold reserve were, in some sense, the private money of the Russian emperor.[146]

Consideration of Maltsov's case was complicated because Maltsov's family was well connected to St. Petersburg high society. His wife was a friend of the estranged wife of Alexander II. Several members of the government were tied to Maltsov's family in some way. Nevertheless, in 1870, the State Council voted to prohibit the issuance of private money. Maltsov's bills continued to circulate for several years before they were gradually exchanged and withdrawn.[147] In the 1870s, Maltsov's business slowly decayed. His relatives, unhappy with the dwindling income, declared him insane and took over management of the enterprise, which the state treasury purchased in 1885.[148]

The story of Maltsov's money and the unprecedented spread of counterfeiting is very revealing. The government rejected the idea of

demonopolizing the issuance of the means of exchange; in practice, however, the proliferation of alternative money dissolved this monopoly, threatening its financial sovereignty and financial stability. The government was
convinced that counterfeiting was responsible for "the unexampled fall of
our credit rubles' rate" and the "distrust of the state-issued papers not only
abroad, but also within the Empire."[149] Indeed, in 1867–68, at the height of
the struggle with counterfeiting and private money, the ruble rate was quite
low, despite all efforts to keep it afloat. However, it is questionable whether
counterfeiting lowered the rate. The dynamics of the rate fluctuation and the
surge of counterfeiting suggest that the ruble became the object of forgery
more often when it was weak. It was not the material quality of the ruble's
bills, nor the intricacy of their design, but the economic vulnerability of
Russian currency that made it especially susceptible to forgery and fraud.

5

Ruble's Wars

"It Is money that They're Burning!"

Although making paper notes resilient to counterfeiting might seem the most difficult aspect of money production, it was no less tricky to destroy the defective and old notes or withdraw them from circulation at the end of their life cycle. The Bank of France used a chemical method; banknotes were soaked in a special soda solution for four days and turned into a paper mass recycled for the making of cardboard. More common was the practice of burning money. Most banks did this discreetly, but in Russia, the extermination of paper money, unless the bills were defective or counterfeited, was a public ritual.

The citizens of St. Petersburg were accustomed to the spectacles of burning assignats and credit rubles. In the eighteenth century, these ceremonies were arranged with great pomp, with announcements of the events made in the city's neighborhoods.[1] In the nineteenth century, the ritual of burning money became more mundane: money bills taken out of circulation were destroyed in the furnaces of the State Bank on Sadovaia Street in the presence of members of the Bank Council, the representative of the St. Petersburg joint-stock committee, and sometimes, "foreign guests."[2] Locals could observe the ritual in the yard of the State Bank through the cast-iron grid fence designed by virtuoso architect Giacomo Quarenghi. Thick, bitter smoke emanated from the furnaces, clouding the Bank's yard and the surrounding streets. Hot ashes and flaming pieces of money flew around, and merchants from the nearby markets and stores complained about damage caused to their merchandise. Money, in other words, did not burn well.

The construction of furnaces at the Bank as well as the furnace at the Expedition for the Production of Paper Notes, did not ensure complete and accurate destruction of paper notes. In June 1883, a peasant woman, Filippova,

FIGURE 5.1 The public burning of credit bills at the yard of the State Bank, 1851. From G. Timm, "Publichnoe sozhzhenie vetkhikh kreditnykh biletov 24 ianvaria 1851 goda v St. Peterburge." *Russkii khudozhestvennyi listok*, 1851, no. 5.

FIGURE 5.2 The public burning of credit bills at the yard of the State Bank in 1870. From *Vsemirnaia illustratsiia*, 1870, no. 68.

brought six burned scraps of 10-ruble bills to the bank. The law permitted the exchange of damaged paper money if the serial numbers remained intact. It turned out, however, that these bills had not caught a spark from her kitchen stove or miraculously survived a domestic fire; they had flown up from the chimney of the Expedition's furnace, and Filippova had found them and brought them to the bank for exchange. The management of the Expedition started an investigation of this case and eventually ordered the construction of a new, improved furnace with a revolving drum and a special chimney that was meant to catch all unburned particles, allegedly, modeled on a furnace used by the Bank of Austria. The trial of the new machine in 1888 ended in disaster, however. The entire yard and the Expedition's buildings were covered in ashes, while the bills inside the drum were not even fully destroyed.[3] Experiments with various models of furnaces were no more successful. In 1892, the State Bank commissioned engineer V. L. Pashkov, who had built waste-burning furnaces for the Winter Palace, to construct a new furnace.[4] Pashkov's "money crematorium" proved little more effective than the previous ones, but for lack of a better alternative, it remained in place.[5]

The problem of getting rid of paper money may appear to be a mundane issue when set against the history of high-end money-making technology. Yet in the 1880s, the image of burning money and of old ladies behind the Bank's fence on Sadovaia Street crying "It's money that they're burning!" turned into the symbol of the government's financial policy after the end of

FIGURE 5.3 Furnace for paper money built in the 1890s. Early twentieth century postcard.

the Russo-Turkish War of 1877–78.[6] Under the fire of nationalist criticism and amid public discontent, the State Bank exempted and burned millions of paper rubles issued during the war. In fact, the scale of the operation was greatly exaggerated, but the image of money consumed in flames stuck nonetheless. Economists interpreted the purifying fires on Sadovaia as a necessary reckoning with the legacy of a senseless war—the price to be paid for Russia's nationalist fantasies and imperial ambitions. Conservative journalists exploited the image of burning money to reveal the anti-national and anti-popular policy of liberal doctrinaires who blindly followed Western models and did not understand the uniqueness of the Russian economy. The cleavage between the two views grew more profound and marked a new phase in the ruble's history. Yet for anti-inflationists and nationalists, the Russo-Turkish War represented a political landmark: either the end of the era of economic reforms or the beginning of Russia's own march toward prosperity.

A Debtor Empire

The financial disaster of the Russo-Turkish War was expected and even welcomed. When on October 1, 1876, minister of finance Mikhail Reutern came to see Alexander II at his summer residence in Crimean Livadia, he found the atmosphere there "very militant." The specter of another war against Turkey, brought about by the pressure of public opinion and political intrigues in the tsar's family and court, was becoming more and more real. Alexander II explained that although he had tried "to solve the issue in peaceful way," it was not working out. He had called Reutern from his countryside retreat to prepare a memo on the financial means for war. The minister of finance declared that no resources were available and that the government would have to revert to printing paper money. More important, Reutern explained to the tsar that his economic and social reforms had made Russia more susceptible to the influence of international markets. Therefore, the war could deliver a crushing blow to Russian finances by destroying the "foreign capitalists' trust in our future."[7] Alexander II thought that Reutern's words "humiliated" Russia.[8] For the emperor, the war and money existed in parallel universes. The empire's dignity could not depend on the trust of foreigners or the availability of credit: it was defended on battlefields and in diplomatic negotiations.

Political events preceding the political crisis in Russia in the fall of 1876 suggest that politics and finance were much more closely connected than the tsar imagined. On the one hand, the hostilities in the Balkans and the revolts of

Slavic peoples, bloodily suppressed by the Ottoman authorities, placed Russia in opposition to the "barbarous" regime. A protector of Christianity and civilization in the East, Russia projected itself as a great Western power offering its support to the suppressed Slavs. Reutern, however, saw the world from a different viewpoint. Nations, in his view, belonged to two categories: "nation-creditors and nation-debtors." The economic development of the nation-debtors depended on the influx of foreign capital. "As history shows, the states that fall behind others in terms of civilization, must borrow from other, more educated nations not only knowledge and inventions but also capitals,"[9] he wrote in the preamble to one of his last pre-war financial projects. Russia's well-being and its development over the previous twenty years had been made possible by the arrival of foreign money. Even in peacetime, Russia did not have enough capital for industry, trade, and agriculture and had to borrow from others. How could it spend such enormous sums of money on war if its livelihood depended on foreign capital? Russia would be doomed to compensate the lack of capital by printing new paper money and therefore lose forever any hope "to return to the status quo, not to mention the improvements of our monetary system."[10]

Perhaps what sounded so offensive to the tsar and his courtiers in Reutern's rational reasoning was an unmentioned but probably intended parallel between Russia and its enemy, the Ottoman Empire. Seen from a financial point of view, both Russia and Turkey fell into the same group of "nation-debtors." Although Turkey had floated its first international loan only in 1854, to pay for the Crimean War against Russia, it could not bear the burden of debts, and in 1875, the Ottoman government declared bankruptcy on all foreign loans. Curiously, Turkey, unlike Russia, did not have a permanent paper currency. Treasury notes (*kaime*) bore interest and represented a form of domestic debt, and only temporarily did they circulate as paper money (1852–62 and 1876–80).[11] The nineteenth-century Turkish financial system was based on silver and gold coins, so, at first sight, it looked healthier, if not more modern, than the Russian one. Russia's experience was different. Diligently making payments on all foreign loans, even under circumstances of dire financial crises, it defaulted on its own domestic obligations and increased the circulation of unbacked and inconvertible paper money.

The impending war threatened to make both empires insolvent. European politicians and financiers, shocked by the recent Ottoman bankruptcy, watched the competition between the two empires and saw Russia's finances as comparatively much better. However, in the words of Anatole Leroy-Beaulieu, one of the most influential writers about Russia, the "beautiful edifice" of Russian finance, "built with such skill, was made of flimsy and un-stable material that has neither solidity nor resistance." A budget that rested on paper money was "like an icehouse whose polished blocks remained intact and solid in the cold; but when the spring and the thaw comes, the house edifice falls and liquefies under the sun."[12] Russia's monetary system would bend under the pressure of war, and Russia's future development would be hindered for a quarter or half a century. Thus, even "the triumph of Russian armies" would turn into a new source of financial losses.

This was the idea that Reutern tried to deliver to the tsar. By launching the war, the government put itself in the position of a "competitor" vis-à-vis its own national economy by "spending people's savings" and "taking from trade, industry and agriculture" capital that was so urgently needed.[13] Russia just could not afford another war, especially for the sake of other nations' interests. But if Reutern saw the danger of indignity in bankruptcy and the ruble's fall, the tsar thought of the reputation of the state in terms of a man's personal honor: "In the lives of states, as in the lives of private individuals, there are moments when one must forget about everything and defend one's honor."[14] As Reutern recalled, the tsar perceived himself as being "obliged by the issue of honor," so the mercenary tone of Reutern's arguments may have appeared repulsive and inappropriate.

The war symbolized a rupture with the policy of the Great Reforms, which had aimed to normalize Russia's economy. By 1875, the State Bank had accumulated a solid sum of roughly 309 million rubles in gold (compared to 78 million in 1867), which corresponded to 763 million credit rubles (697 mil-lion in 1867).[15] This was one of the largest gold reserves kept in central banks at the time,[16] and restoring the exchange appeared plausible. In 1876, the Expedition for the Production of State Papers issued 25-ruble credit bills with a design that closely resembled the banknotes of the Bank of England.[17] The same year, the government mandated the collection of custom duties in gold, gold-based securities, and currencies or gold-mining certificates.[18] The accu-mulation of gold per se did not significantly improve the ruble's standing, but it was hoped that these measures would help the government build a solid ma-terial foundation for a gold-based monetary system. In the 1870s, almost all of continental Europe switched to the gold standard, and the Russian Ministry of Finance was eager to follow.

The war threatened to put an end to Reutern's frugal policy of saving money and preparing the resumption of convertibility. Declaring war was not simply a geopolitical move but a deliberate choice against the gold standard and the financial rapprochement with Europe. Yet in 1876–78, everyone despised and condemned such financial pragmatism. Talking about money was deemed indecent and unpatriotic. "All this is unpromising and stupid," commented Prince Dmitrii Obolensky on Reutern's efforts to find a solution to the financial crisis of the impending war. "I know that we have no money. I know that the generals are bad. . . . But this does not matter, because the main question is, What are we?" Unlike the practical Englishmen, whose national policy is built on material interests, Russia's policy "is entirely un-selfish." "How to explain that 'man does not live on bread alone' and that without national pride, the man, and society, are pathetic. . . . How to explain it?"[19] Even the liberal *Voice* [*Golos*] called on its readers to "put up" with the inevitable, namely, the printing of paper money and the ruble's collapse, while the *Herald of Europe* [*Vestnik Evropy*] discussed other forms of financial sacri-fice that Russia could bear "to support Russia's honor and protect the greatest interests of her future."[20] The motto of the anti-financial, anti-pragmatic spirit of the war was concisely formulated in the words of a proverbial peasant *mu-zhik* and recounted by a populist nobleman Alexander Engelhard. Unlike a "Petersburg functionary," a Russian peasant was not fearful of war and its hardship: "There is no money? Why do we need it? If we run out of money, the tsar will give the order to make more."[21]

The relatively short, year-long Russo-Turkish War—the first war fought after the emancipation of peasants, with a new army of conscripts instead of recruits—turned out to be one of the most expensive wars to that date. Russia's victory cost 1 billion rubles—at least twice as much as the Crimean disaster and it had more detrimental effects on the Russian economy than the previous war.[22] The Ministry of Finance estimated that the war necessitated printing almost 500 million extra paper rubles, in addition to making one foreign and three domestic loans.[23] The credit ruble's value in "metal" fell from 78.5 kopecks (in 1877) to 62.5 kopecks (in 1883), but during the war, it even reached the minimum of 50 kopecks.[24] More significant was the ruble's fall vis-à-vis foreign currency. At the mobilization of troops, the value of the ruble was 29 or 30 pence, which dropped to 27 pence at the declaration of war. During Russia's unsuccessful attempts to storm the Turkish fortress Plevna, the ruble sank to 22.5 pence. The "Plevna rate" became proverbial and even got into the *Encyclopedia Britannica* as an illustration of how pol-itics and public opinion affect the currency rate.[25] When the Russian army emerged victorious, Reutern resigned, leaving the daunting task of restoring finances to his not very capable successor, Samuel Greig. The ruble rose a little (up to 26.75 pence) and then collapsed again to the lowest point of 22.125 pence.[26]

Yet the financial consequences of the war paled in comparison to its impact on policy and ideology. The paradoxical de-pragmatization of financial policy, that is to say, the declaration of the priority of non-financial, non-economic interests over economic goals, brought nationalist writers and journalists to the forefront of economic debates. Financial bureaucrats in the governments of Alexander II and Alexander III tried to resist this trend, cautiously restoring the elements of the pre-war financial order. In the paradoxical world of post-war politics, the government of the conservative tsar often proved to be the bearer of reformist spirit and pragmatism while "society" was pushing toward reaction.

The Politics of Resentment

Why did this victory cause such an abrupt reversal in financial ideology? One of the reasons was Russia's diplomatic fiasco at the Berlin Congress, which reconsidered the results of the initial peace agreement between Russia and the defeated Turks. Russia's diplomatic humiliation by the European Great Powers contributed to the extreme politicization of the credit ruble issue after 1878. All elements of liberal economic policy, including the gold standard, came to be seen as the import from the obnoxious West. The most obvious symptom of the slide toward nationalism and the rejection of Western concepts was a sudden and almost miraculous transformation of Mikhail Katkov's views on paper rubles, gold, and the state's role in the monetary system. The change of the *Moscow Bulletin*'s credo after the completion of negotiations in Berlin in September 1878 was so abrupt that other newspapers doubted that the same person was still writing the editorials.[27] If in January 1878 Katkov lamented the high costs of war and the hard consequences of Russia's financial overstretch, in November, he celebrated the invigorating effect of the war on the Russian economy and the "non-material capital" created by "an unseen rise of Russian national spirit."[28] Katkov explained his conversion as a departure from an erroneous passion for Western theory. Even the extra half billion credit rubles did not appear as "poisonous" to him as the liberal press presented it: the ruble's value consisted in the ability to purchase Russia's "own bread," which had not changed as a result of the war.[29] Following the denunciation of the importance of rates came the denial of the meaning of gold and a sharp reversal of Katkov's attitude toward the State Bank.[30] In the early 1870s, Katkov was the first journalist to uncover the State Bank's hidden issuance of credit rubles. Back then, he had called these emissions illegal and considered the excess of credit rubles to be Russia's main illness; after 1878, he called the abundance of paper money a blessing.[31]

Katkov had always been a nationalist, but until the Berlin Congress, his worldview combined nationalism with economic liberalism. In the 1850s and 1860s, he was a devoted free-trader, but his post-1878 nationalism leaned toward the most extreme Fichtean version of a "closed state." His new ultra-nationalist critique of Russia's dependence on foreign capitals and the Western principles of monetary policy was a reaction to the contradiction between Russia's self-awareness as an empire and its low standing in the world of international finance. Ironically, Katkov echoed Reutern's thought about the world being divided into the two camps of nation-creditors and nation-debtors, although he came to the opposite conclusion. As he put it, when measured by Western standards, the Russian ruble was on a par with the Turkish *kaime*.[32] Katkov found the comparison humiliating and could not tolerate the world's treating Russia's finances as it did those of Egypt or Turkey.[33] Russia's defeated enemy offered an example of the West's financial and political dominance. After the Ottomans' default in 1875–76 and its debacle in the war, the Turkish government was forced to partially surrender its financial sovereignty when the Ottoman Public Debt Administration, which included the representatives of European countries, took over the management of imperial foreign debt and obligations.[34] In 1881, the Ottoman Empire switched to a "limping" gold standard that also accommodated the empire's payments to its debtors.

The post-1878 economic nationalism assumed, first and foremost, the rejection of the universality of financial and institutional criteria applied to the assessment of economic solvency and well-being. Petr Valuev, a chairman of the Committee of Ministers, doubted that the quantity of paper bills played any role in the fluctuation of the ruble's international value or that it had any effect on the domestic market. If "Western" theories said the opposite, then they were just inapplicable in Russia, the only country that "by the conditions of space, means of communication, habits and mores was . . . destined for a paper monetary system."[35] More important than space and cultures was the nature of Russian autocratic rule: "The financial system of a country must correspond in its peculiarities and its political organization."[36] Valuev's words, written in 1880, were strikingly similar to Nikolai Karamzin's seventy years earlier. However, in the early 1880s, the context was different. Political economy had developed into an academic field, and Russian economists perceived themselves as the members of a larger European academic community. By declaring Russia's uniqueness, nationalists, in the words of economist

Illarion Kaufman, waged an "anti-science" war. The proponents of Russian isolationism also described the confrontation as an opposition between the two camps: the "economists" and the "practitioners," the latter represented by journalists and conservative politicians.[37] The two trends—the professionalization of political economy as a discipline and as the sphere of expertise, and the development of "popular" writings on economic matters—ran parallel, making possible a paradoxical situation in which the dominant opinion about financial issues came to be shaped by a handful of conservative political journalists.

The debate was splashed across the pages of newspapers, popular literature, and fiction. At its core were questions of national dignity, patriotism, and Russia's relations with the West. Was the standing of the national currency relevant to the empire's reputation? By denying the importance of the ruble's international standing, nationalists inverted the idea of prestige and made it self-referential. Perhaps one of the best illustrations of this distortion of self-assessment based on self-defined criteria was given in Mikhail Saltykov-Shchedrin's short play "Conversation between a Boy in Pants and a Boy without Pants" (1881). The boy in pants, representing Germany as the proverbial ideal of order, and his Russian half-naked interlocuter discuss the benefits of paper money. The former says that if he takes a paper bill to a bank, he will get "real money"—gold or silver—in exchange, while the latter proudly declares that he invented an "[as]signatsia" for which "the exchange office issues the bearer a punch in the face!" In Saltykov-Shchedrin's parody, the Russian boy stands for the Russian political establishment and its inventiveness and contempt for the people and for the enviable quality of being proud of things that others find embarrassing.

The Bureaucratic Rule of Law

In political rhetoric, the opposition between theory and practice often stood for the liberal-conservative controversy. However, in matters of monetary policy, the contours of economic liberalism were becoming increasingly blurred. If in the 1860s the gold standard was unquestionably associated with political liberalism and came packaged with well-defined political and economic reforms, the relation between monetary and political reform became much more complex and less straightforward in the 1880s. Conservative critiques of the plans for monetary reform continued to associate monetary reform with the limitation of autocracy, but in fact, this was often an exaggeration.

In 1879–81, Alexander II's government, while tightening its grip on political control and anti-revolutionary repression, was also considering plans for moderate reforms, including the introduction of representative legislative institutions (the so-called "constitution" of Mikhail Loris-Melikov). The bureaucratic reformism of the post-Turkish war was not driven by the spirit of renovation or modernization but aimed at plans securing administrative order and improving governance. Among other things, the program of bureaucratic reformism presupposed a gradual restoration of the pre-war monetary policy. In late December 1880, minister of finance, Alexander Abaza, secured approval from the Committee of Finance for an imperial decree (signed by Alexander II on January 1, 1881) that unequivocally described the wartime issuance of paper rubles as the State Treasury's "borrowings" from the State Bank and obliged the State Treasury to "pay its debt" in the amount of 400 million over a period of eight years.[38] Certainly, the State Bank still belonged to the Ministry and could not therefore stand for an autonomous public; as Katkov sarcastically remarked, paying the treasury's debt to the Bank was equivalent to moving money "from one pocket into another."[39] Still, simply acknowledging the issuance of credit rubles as "debt" was important. Even more significant was the decree's provision that prohibited new issuances of paper money and required the establishment of "more righteous relationships between the State Treasury and the Bank."[40] In an atmosphere strained by rumors about the impending constitutional reform, contemporaries perceived the law of January 1, 1881, as a euphemistic financial constitution. Petr Valuev, who was not sympathetic to the law, thought it "not the theoretical withdrawal of bills from circulation, but a restriction, an indirect and hidden one, indeed, of the autocracy's right to govern expenses."[41] The idea of limited paper issuance and the government's financial responsibility was, therefore, perceived as a financial match for the constitutional projects of Alexander II's late reign, promoted by the powerful minister of the interior, Mikhail Loris-Melikov, with the active support of the head of the financial ministry, Abaza. Until 1891, the law of January 1, 1881, remained the main ideological and legal constraint that helped the government resist the temptation of the printing press. The subsequent ministers revered the law as the guarantee of and commitment to financial austerity and improvement. It was a financial bureaucratic pact, a self-limitation imposed by the government upon itself.

Alexander II's assassination in March 1881 and the turn of the regime from moderate reformism to conservative reaction had a strong, although not immediate, effect on monetary policy. The new spirit of Alexander III's reign was manifested in minor details, such as the change of the font for the tsar's initials portrayed on the obverse side of credit rubles: Alexander II's elegant "Latin" *A*, embellished with curls and flourishes, was replaced with a "Slavic" **A**, bold and squared.[42] Nationalism, which had previously been the domain of conservative journalists and public politicians, was becoming the new ideology of the government, while the ideas of constitutional reform that had circulated prior to Alexander II's assassination were decisively rejected. The dismissal of the political reform's main proponent, Mikhail Loris-Melikov, meant Abaza's inevitable departure. The new tsar's Manifesto of April 29, 1881, which announced the inviolability of autocracy and the termination of constitutional projects, dropped the ruble's rate and was followed by Abaza's resignation.[43] However, Abaza's deputy minister, Nikolai Bunge, who did not belong to the group of constitutionalists in the government, enjoyed Alexander III's personal trust and was able to secure a ministerial position.

Bunge, a professor of political economy at Kyiv University, one of Katkov's ex-allies, and a former young expert of the 1850s–60s reform team, was appointed a deputy minister of finance in 1880.[44] The appointment of a university professor as minister had no precedent and could have been seen as a choice in favor of "science" and "theory" rather than "practice." At the same time, Bunge's lack of administrative experience left him unprepared for political games and competition. The *Moscow Bulletin* reacted to Bunge's appointment with a series of articles in which Katkov revealed the antinational, liberal plans of the new minister "in tune with the professed theory of establishing a 'legal order' [constitutionalism] in Russia."[45] In fact, Katkov significantly exaggerated Bunge's radicalism. While making the restoration of the Russian currency a priority, Bunge knew that it was going to be a long process involving a sequence of reforms in all spheres of the economy. He also felt that the state should hold on to the most important functions, including credit and the monetary system. The difference between his stances and those of Katkov and others lay in the interpretation of the state's role: Bunge considered the state a supra-class political and managerial system, while to his conservative opponents, the state institution was a tool in the hands of the tsar that distributed, according to the logic of autocratic rule, the burden of taxes and, even more important, the profits of the empire.

Bunge's main asset was the tsar's personal sympathy and support. For this reason, however, he competed with another, much more powerful agent of political influence, the less economically savvy but more politically cynical journalist Vladimir Meshcherskii. Meshcherskii's articles in his state-sponsored newspaper *The Citizen (Grazhdanin)* echoed Katkov's editorials, sometimes twisting and even strengthening their message. In addition to expressing himself publicly, Meshcherskii enjoyed the privilege of writing to the tsar personally, and his letters conveyed the messages of his articles in a more intimate and straightforward way. Given that Alexander III did not want to delve into financial matters, the centrality of the financial theme in Meshcherskii's letters to the tsar is striking.[46] In his persistent attacks on Bunge and the Ministry of Finance, Meshcherskii emphasized three main ideas. First, he described Bunge's obsession with Western financial theories and consequent neglect of the real needs of industry and agriculture (as Meshcherskii wrote to the tsar, Bunge had never been "a *Russian* minister, but only a professor of political economy.")[47] Second, he portrayed Bunge's financial policy as aimed at the destruction of the landowning nobility. Third, Meshcherskii pointed out that the ministry's policy of financial austerity and its refusal to print money went against Russia's geopolitical interests and, overall, was incompatible with the principles of autocratic rule. In the mid-1880s, the Afghan crisis, or the Panjdeh incident of 1885, put Russia on the brink of a conflict with Great Britain, while the so-called Bulgarian crisis spoiled Russia's relationship with Germany and Austria and even spread the fear of an "all-European war." The specter of war certainly strengthened nationalist stances.[48] Playing on Alexander's nationalist sentiments, the tsar's confidant tried to persuade him that his ability to protect Russia's national interests was constrained by the Ministry of Finance that limited the tsar's power to dispose of the printing machine. The ministry "will force Russia to renounce the policy of action and may compromise the dignity of the Russian Sovereign, His Word, His policy and bind him at the moment when all Russia would expect from him the full freedom [of action]." Denying Bunge even the status of a liberal, Meshcherskii described the Ministry of Finance as a "nest of ultra-radicals" and the "ultimate enemies of monarchal rule in Russia" whose goal was to force the government to "provide a constitution."[49] "Russia's financial policy stands in contradiction to the policy of the entire government and, being formed of two currents—a constitutional and an anarchist one—explicitly undermines the foundations of autocracy," wrote Meshcherskii to the tsar. It obstructed the efforts of other "ministries to strengthen authority and extirpate the old passions for liberalism."[50] Meshcherskii's unsophisticated and straightforward letters to Alexander III echoed Katkov's portrayal of the Ministry of Finance as "an opposition to the government not outside, but within the government itself."[51]

Bunge remained the main target of Katkov and Meshcherskii's attacks for the entire five years of his tenure, until they succeeded in removing him and orchestrated the appointment of their protégé Ivan Vyshnegradskii. The political configuration under which journalists and a few courtiers played such a powerful role in creating a public discourse of money may appear unusual even for an autocratic regime. A few years after his resignation from the ministerial position, Bunge described the specifics of the Russian political system: "In Russia, there are no parties in the Western European sense. There are the views of different circles and, in particular, of the newspapers, which have risen in importance in recent years as spokesmen for the mood of these circles."[52] Indeed, the opinions expressed in Katkov's *Moscow Bulletin* and Meshcherskii's *Citizen* on major financial issues could be read as the opinions of a particular political circle that affected the policy of the government in a most direct way. In the words of historians Boris Anan'ich and Raphail Ganelin, "M. N. Katkov's influence on Alexander III and the government's policy in the '80s was so significant that in bureaucratic circles, *The Moscow Bulletin'* editor and his entourage were seen as a second government that existed along with the legal one."[53] Under autocratic rule, the tsar's personal attention was the main political asset, and the choice of financial measures was often determined by the ability of competing groups to persuade the tsar.

Under continuous attack in the press, Bunge laid out a series of financial measures that continued Reutern's policy of normalization and in the long run could prepare the ground for a large-scale monetary reform. Although Bunge was convinced that Russia would sooner or later settle on the gold standard, the contours of the reform were still very unclear. In the 1880s, nobody could say what represented Russia's main monetary unit. Russia was still officially following the "silver standard": contracts and deals featured only fictional silver rubles and were paid in state credit bills, while gold coins had the status of commodities. Russia paid in gold for earlier loans that had been concluded in silver, therefore placing international financial credibility above fiscal interests and even legal provisions. Domestically, however, gold remained a numismatic curiosity.[54] The Russian monetary system de facto operated on the paper standard: Russian legislation continued to enforce the "compulsory rate" of 1 credit ruble being equal 1 silver ruble or to 1 ruble and 3 kopecks in gold, but no one wanted to pay in gold at such a rate. Reutern had tried to fix this anomaly by allowing the use of gold at a market rate in commercial transactions, therefore creating conditions for keeping gold coins inside the country. His suggestion, which came a month before the beginning of the Russo-Turkish War, was certainly untimely and was rejected.[55] In December 1882, Bunge recovered Reutern's pre-war proposal regarding the use of gold in private transactions and all treasury payments, but the second attempt to legalize gold in the Russian economy failed as well. The project, approved by the Committee of Finance, was rejected by the State Council.[56]

Reutern's and Bunge's attempts to change the attitude toward gold and its status in the country did not bring significant results. Some measures, such as the introduction of custom payments in gold, even produced backlash. In 1880, a customs officer from Arkhangelsk reported that goods remained in storage, incurring additional fees because Russian merchants could not find gold for the payment of customs duties.[57] At customs' request, the State Bank started shipping gold coins to its local branch and selling them at the stock exchange price so that importers could purchase coins and pay custom duties.[58] The flow of gold shipped in various directions increased significantly, while the regional branches were made to report the sales of half-imperials to the Bank's central office: the state was pumping gold through the Bank and customs while also increasing the purchases of gold from private banks, gold miners, and foreign suppliers.[59] This did not mean that gold became more present in public finances; in fact, the same gold simply circulated through various state offices. In other words, the effect of this measure was negligible. In 1885, the Ministry of Finance took another important step toward transforming the perception of gold from its image as a precious but raw metal to one of real money. A new Monetary Code changed the alloy of Russian "half-imperials," which, due to a slightly higher gold content in comparison to the gold coins of the Latin Monetary Union, were massively exported to Europe and melted. The new law adopted the European (lower) standard and, at the same time, strengthened the political importance of the gold coins. The new "half-imperials," worth 5 rubles, and the 10-ruble "imperials" featured a profile image of the tsar, which was a sharp contrast to the old faceless coins with large digits on the obverse and the two-headed eagle on the reverse. Alexander III picked a new design with a raised portrait and an inscription of the tsar's title in a stylized Old-Russian font; the same design was adopted for silver coins.[60] If the old coins were thinner, bigger, less attractive but easier to read, the new ones represented true "state monuments" that allowed "even the most remote peoples of Russia to see the features of their beloved Monarch."[61] According to Bunge's memo to the State Council, the tsar's wish to change the design was the primary reason for issuing the new Monetary Code.[62] If this was really the case, then Bunge managed to use Alexander III's vanity to sneak in a major coinage reform that brought Russia closer to gold-standardized Europe.

This international financial trend, on which Russia depended so heavily, and the Ministry of Finance's policy left no doubt that Russia should move toward gold, but it remained unclear when and how Russia would adhere to the gold standard. Should the government continue its efforts to raise the rate of the paper ruble to parity with its gold equivalent by withdrawing excess paper rubles and accumulating gold? Or should it give up these efforts and instead stabilize the rate and fix it at a certain level, thus devaluating credit rubles as Kankrin had earlier devaluated assignats? The government's policy of withdrawing paper money and refraining from paper issuance suggested that it preferred the first option for restoring the paper ruble's original value. However, the realization of the 1881 law on the repayment of the State Treasury's debt to the State Bank for the wartime emissions of credit rubles did not proceed as intended. After the first repayment of 400 million rubles, the treasury continued transferring money. However, only 87 million credit rubles of this sum were burned, and the remaining sum was settled on the Bank's accounts. The image of the State Bank daily burning rubles in its yard was blown out of proportion by the conservative press. The plan to withdraw already released credit rubles proved to be an illusion. Alexander Abaza wittily remarked that paper money was like water poured into wine, impossible to extract.[63] Bunge came to the same conclusion. If in 1881 the withdrawal of paper bills had been a way to eliminate the negative effect of the wartime emissions, in 1885, the fall of the ruble's rate was a fait accompli. Prices were adjusted to the new rate, and the reduction of the mass of paper rubles could not raise it any more.[64] The repayment of the treasury's war debt and the bonfires on Sadovaia Street lost financial meaning and turned into a symbolic demonstration of the government's commitment to financial stability shown in the annual state budget. Grumpy Petr Valuev remarked in his diary that the state budget for 1883 was approved at 778 million with a deficit only due to the payment of 50 million to the Bank: without the payment, it would have been a surplus of 27 million.[65] Were the reputational losses due to the state budget's deficit less significant than the gains from fulfilling the obligation? No one could tell, but having declared its intention of paying the debt for wartime credit rubles, the government decided to fulfill it.[66]

The Nobles' Ruble

The discontent with the government's policy of monetary recovery was not limited to a group of influential journalists and nationalist politicians. Bunge understood well that the clash between "practice" and "science," autarky and cosmopolitanism, or the ideologies of paper and gold revealed an increasing political and social divergence in society. Both Katkov's and

Meshcherskii's editorials expressed the discontent of Russia's landowning nobility as well as that of Moscow's merchants and producers, over the "anti-national" financial policy of the past twenty years. Bunge recognized that the ideology of the paper ruble represented more than the raving of uneducated reactionaries; it was a conscious choice predetermined by economic interests—and this recognition was a hugely important step. His assessment differed, for instance, from Illarion Kaufman's view of Katkov's supporters as the greedy "dregs" of commercial society that flourished in an economy inflated by paper money.[67] In Bunge's words, people who opposed the restoration of the credit ruble's rate—domestic producers, merchants, and real estate owners—benefited from the rise of prices and the abundance of money. On the other hand, the fall of the ruble's rate and the rise of prices hurt the interests of state officials and employees as well as that of financiers, who were interested in a monetary reform. Bunge admitted that these two positions were irreconcilable, and he unequivocally sided with the proponents of reform. He warned that the monetary reform would not pass without "sacrifices" and that the government's task was to ensure that the burden of the reform was spread evenly among classes.[68] In this sense, Bunge's above-class vision of the state contradicted the official ideology of rule that found its new ideal in the revival of the landowning nobility. This notion regained strength in conservative journalism and generated a number of ideas for the reform of local government, credit, and finances. Therefore, if earlier nationalist economists had characterized the paper, inflationist ruble as the "people's ruble," in the 1880s, inconvertible state credit bills came to be associated with nobility and its interests. Most vividly, the nobles' claim that the government's monetary policy must take their interests into account appeared in the debates over the state-owned land mortgage bank for the landowning nobility.

The linkage between land credit and monetary policy began in the assignat era. The fall of paper money originated with and later continued to be significantly influenced by the state's policy of crediting the landowning nobility.[69] Catherine the Great's decision to unleash the emission of assignats in 1786 coincided with the opening of the new Loan Bank [Zaemnyi Bank], and a significant share of assignats was offered in loans to landowners. By 1859, 60% of the noble landownership, or 44,000 noble estates with more than 7 million serf peasants, had already been pledged in state-owned banks.[70] With the elimination of treasury banks in 1859 and the peasant emancipation in 1861, landowners were left without access to cheap state credit. The government sanctioned the creation of private joint-stock mortgage banks and mortgage societies, but, against the nobles' expectations, the state did not interfere with their credit activity.

Even at this early stage, the state's withdrawal from the sphere of crediting noble landownership was often met with anxiety due to the instability of the ruble's rate and the precariousness of the security market.[71] The government stayed aloof from the demands of the nobility to open new state banks or to issue special "land bonds" using the nobles' land in lieu of the gold reserve.[72] However, another way to increase the influx of investments into newly founded land credit societies was to make them attractive to foreign investors. To enter the European market of securities, credit societies could issue "metal bonds" with denominations in gold rubles and a parallel indication of their nominal value in foreign currencies. Russian law prohibited deals in metal currencies, but the government was willing to make an exception here and allowed the emission of "metal" bonds. These bonds could be traded on the foreign stock exchange; they had better chances to accumulate funds but imposed on their borrowers an obligation to repay debts in gold rubles.[73] Using this scheme, Russia's largest mortgage organization, the Society of Mutual Land Credit, which had been created in 1866 by a group of the wealthiest aristocratic landowners, issued its securities in "metal" and earned the nickname "the Gold Bank."[74] The Society was active across the empire and, along with several other land credit societies and banks, served a growing number of borrowers.

The ruble's collapse in the aftermath of the Russo-Turkish War pushed more than 7,500 of the Society's borrowers to the brink of bankruptcy. The market value of gold "half-imperials" increased to 8 rubles 30 kopecks in credit bills, and the interest rate jumped from 7% to 8.9%. As a result, after the war, the Gold Bank's borrowers owed twice more than before. The Society of Mutual Land Credit appealed for assistance, hoping that the government would buy it and transform it into a new state credit institution. Bunge declined the request, claiming that the government was not going to interfere in the system of private banks and could only "direct it toward common good."[75]

The Society of Mutual Land Credit's story revealed in miniature the potential pitfalls of the state-issued paper money system, namely, that the government had to bear responsibility for the fall of currency. The arguments made in support of the claims for the state's assistance differed and sometimes contradicted each other; for instance, the representatives of the Kazan' branch of the Society stressed the hereditary nobility's merits and accomplishments that had earned the government's protection, while others emphasized the government's guilt, not merely in letting the ruble fall but in creating conditions under which this fall could affect landowners' well-being.[76] "Metal" borrowers thought that the state, not an abstract market, was responsible for what had happened to their capital and to the ruble. Since the Russian ruble was a state-issued currency, the state had to absorb the cost of the ruble's fall. However, the most demonstrable proof of the state's responsibility for the ruble's fate and consequently the fate of "gold" borrowers was the promise, printed on each credit ruble bill, to exchange paper for gold. Vladimir Okhotnikov, the marshal of Penza's provincial nobility, argued in a series of articles published in Meshcherskii's *The Citizen* that the government must dismantle the Society and make a newly founded State Noble Land Bank to convert the borrowers' obligations at the nominal rate of 1 "metal" (i.e., gold) ruble to 1 credit ruble. In other words, it must take on itself the difference between the total sum of the nobles' obligation calculated in gold and paper. This operation would cost the government about 100 million rubles, which should be raised with the help of a domestic loan. Responding to the hypothetical outcry against social injustice—"Why should peasants pay for the noblemen's debts?"—Okhotnikov observed that financial equity was a myth: peasants paid for railroads that they never rode and for other enterprises. "But are not landownership and nobility the same all-state values as the construction of railroads, fortresses and others? No, gentlemen, . . . 'nobility' is as necessary for Russia as all other institutions of the Russian state; its support and assistance are the state's responsibility."[77] Okhotnikov therefore reproduced an inverted logic claiming that the nobility, not the ruble, represented the "common good" worthy of sacrifices. One of the dominant motifs that ran through most publications on the issue of noble credit in the 1880s was the compensation for damages inflicted on the nobility by the reforms of the 1860s, including the abolition of serfdom. Okhotnikov described the financial assistance that he expected from the state as the "emancipation" of nobility, and he justified it by the sacrifices born by the nobility and the violation of their property rights in 1861.[78]

Even though the Society's problem originated from the instability of paper rubles, which, in turn, was the outcome of war, nationalist journalists often used the story of the Society's borrowers as an argument against the gold standard and in favor of using land as a collateral for credit rubles. Vladimir Meshcherskii pressed on the tsar the idea of combining state-financed land credit for the nobility with a partial replacement of credit rubles by new land-based money.[79] The concept of the "land ruble" was thus associated with both a particular economic vision and a social and financial policy that prioritized the interests of the nobility over other estates. Noble debtors were longing for a new, state-owned land bank that could offer loans at lower interest rates—which in fact would mean returning to the pre-emancipation era in credit but with loans secured by land rather than with peasants' souls.

Bunge, who had participated in the credit reform of the late 1850s and early 1860s, did not want to dismantle the existing system of private credit institutions and place land credit in the government's hands. The minister emphasized that the creation of affordable credit for landowners should not occur "at the expense of burdening other classes of society."[80] Instead, he suggested the creation of a new State Land Bank that would function along with private banks and serve the needs of nobles and peasants alike. In this battle, he lost: Bunge's proposal of an all-estate Land Bank that was supposed to draw funds from its commercial profits and not rely on state subsidies did not go through, and he had to settle for the institutionalization of a special privileged bank for hereditary nobility that existed separately from a land bank for peasants. The creation of the State Land Bank for Nobility was conceived of and seen by the public as a primarily political measure rather than a measure related to credit and the economy.[81] The Manifesto announcing the Bank's creation was issued on April 21, 1885, which marked the centennial anniversary of Catherine the Great's Charter to the nobility and imitated the empress's rhetoric of the appreciation of the first estate's "service" to the Crown and the Fatherland. The Manifesto unequivocally declared the departure from the policy of the late 1850s and early 1860s that had led to the impoverishment of the nobility, and it promised to reward the nobility for the "sacrifices" made for the emancipation of the serfs.

The new bank offered loans only to hereditary nobles on conditions that were much more favorable than those made by the State Land Bank for Peasants.[82] In 1890, the State Land Bank for Nobility took up the management of the Society of Mutual Land Credit, whose 5% "metal" bonds had already in 1887 been converted into 4.5% bonds with "the government's pledge."[83] In Bunge's initial project, the State Land Bank was not supposed to claim the government's financial support; however, the Russian Land Bank for Nobility received subsidies from the State Bank.[84] These subsidies, similar to Catherine II's grants to the Noble Loan Bank in 1786, immediately increased the amount of credit rubles in circulation. After a steady reduction of circulating paper money from 907 to 878 million rubles in January through March 1886, between April and November 1886, the amount rose to 946 million rubles. As Alexander Chuprov, the chronicler of the *Juridical Review*, observed, "The natural explanation of such a sharp turn is the opening of the Noble Bank."[85]

Along with the institutionalization of the State Land Bank for Nobility came the final shutdown of the independent Bank of Poland in 1885. The sad irony of this coincidence was that the Bank of Poland, in its commercial organization, embodied the ideals of well-organized agrarian and commercial credit. Unlike Russian land banks, it issued loans for the purposes of land improvements, such as the purchase of machines, materials, and fertilizer. Therefore, the Bank of Poland's banknotes represented an example of "good" paper money that was tied to "production" rather than consumption.[86] Bunge was not, indeed, fully responsible for the Bank's disappearance, which had become a fait accompli in 1870, but the fact that it was completed on his initiative during his tenure in the minister's office betrayed his forced compliance with the growing nationalist and conservative spirit of the rule.

Conservative nationalists of the early 1880s argued for a financial policy that included indulging nobility, absorbing the costs of imperial expansion, and eliminating credit institutions based on commercial interests. This ideology may seem devoid of any economic rationality. However, what would appear completely illogical to any trained economist was perfectly logical from a political point of view. This ideology encapsulated a dominant vision of autocracy based on the union with nobility and nationalist centralization. Nationalist "practitioners" and their academic opponents spoke different languages without a chance of understanding each other. That explains the bewildering effect that this fierce debate about money and credit produced. The editorial article of the *Economic Journal* in 1886 characterized the clash between the reformist bureaucracy and reactionary politicians as "an unprecedented debate" that ignited public interest in financial matters.[87] Neither purely literary nor academic, this battle ended with Bunge's defeat and resignation in December 1886.[88] Katkov and Meshcherskii succeeded in toppling the tsar's minister by presenting his policy as anti-noble, anti-autocratic, and constitutional even though Bunge himself did not profess such ideas. The "constitutional" argument was a lethal political weapon of conservative rhetoric. Bunge responded to the accusations of disloyalty by arguing that he had never written a single line about a constitution; his goal, as well as that of his predecessors, had been to prove that well-ordered financial management was possible under an "autocratic monarchy" and not solely under constitutional rule.[89] But it did not matter. When any element of financial policy could be easily translated into the language of political reform, one did not have to say the word "constitution" to be seen as a constitutionalist.

While denying the allegations of anti-state policies, Bunge was not lying. At its core, the idea of increasing the state's role in economic development did not contradict his vision or even allegiance to the metal standard. As conservatism became more radical, Russian liberals also moved to the right and embraced state-centric ideas. As Bunge wrote in his memo on the state annual budget for 1886, "The state cannot remain a spectator of what is going on in the national economy. If in the West . . . the influence and the participation of the state in the national economy is gradually increasing, it is all the more necessary in Russia, where without the government's initiative, much proves to be impossible, and without the government's supervision, it may become pernicious."[90] The new minister of finance, Ivan Vyshnegradskii, who was appointed to the position as a result of a long-term campaign led by Katkov and Meshcherskii, would have agreed with this statement. His "program" was not, surprisingly, antagonistic to Bunge's policy. After Katkov's death in 1887, Vyshnegradskii returned to the plan for the financial measures launched by his predecessor. The treasury continued paying its debt to the State Bank and refrained from new emission, while the State Bank continued to accumulate gold in storage and prepare for the future reform.[91]

The Merchants' Ruble

When Ivan Vyshnegradskii became minister, he declared that the restoration of the paper ruble's full metallic value was not only impossible but also "undesirable," both because Russia had lived with this rate for too long and because all prices and credit relations had already adjusted to the existing ratio. Vyshnegradskii's plan therefore consisted of stabilizing the relationship between gold and paper currency at the normal rate of 1.5 credit rubles = 1 gold ruble.[92] The stabilization was not possible without the normalization of the status of gold because no one could imagine a balanced relation between two legally unequal units. Thus, the strategy of the reform looked like the legalization of gold as a means of payment, followed by the devaluation of the credit ruble. In addition, the government embarked on a policy of strict austerity and an even more intensive accrual of gold. Vyshnegradskii's system focused on the suppression of import and the encouragement of grain export, even to the detriment of domestic consumers. The Ministry of Finance also conducted a successful conversion of Russian foreign loans, which allowed the reduction of annual payments in gold currency and, when market conditions permitted, the purchase of quantities of gold in Europe. During Vyshnegradskii's tenure, Russia's gold reserve increased by 281.5 million rubles to 581 million rubles.[93]

Unfriendly German newspapers interpreted Russia's frantic appropriation of gold resources as a sign of preparation for war.[94] In fact, the Russian government was preparing for another endeavor. Unfortunately for Vyshnegradskii, while his economic measures had almost succeeded in laying the groundwork for the adoption of the gold standard, he failed politically. He enjoyed neither the strong confidence of the tsar nor political support in court. Largely for this reason, he failed to gain approval for one of his most important measures: the legalization of gold in commercial transactions. On this issue, Vyshnegradskii faced strong opposition not from journalists, courtiers, or discontented nobility, but from the representatives of the commercial elites.

While the opposition of the landowning nobility to the introduction of gold was understandable, the Russian bourgeoisie's resistance to the introduction of gold in transactions may seem perplexing. In Europe and America, the transition to the gold standard was often met with resistance by agrarian elites who preferred the flexibility of bimetallism. In both populist critique and attacks by landowners, gold currency appeared as an attribute of commercial and industrial interest—that is, bourgeois money. In Russia, however, the main proponents of the gold reform were the imperial bureaucracy (or, rather, its economic sector) and the economists. Russia's middle class, except for a small part representing a West-oriented business elite, turned against the initiatives of the Ministry of Finance.

In 1888, Vyshnegradskii raised for the third time the idea of permitting gold in domestic commercial transactions and treasury payments, unequivocally presenting this measure as preparation for the resumption of exchanging credit rubles for gold and leaving no doubt as to the impossibility of any other resolution of the ruble question. Russia had no financial future without the gold standard, and the rejection of his proposal would only postpone the reform. With numbers showing the movement of money in the State Bank's accounts, Vyshnegradskii's secret proposal to the government and the tsar demonstrated the dire deficit of capital that could only be compensated by the influx of foreign investments.[95] Russian industry needed gold and foreign money; however, foreigners were reluctant to invest because they could not count on receiving their revenues in a stable currency. The legalization of transactions in gold could fix this problem.

Despite the scale and significance of his initiative, Vyshnegradskii wanted to keep it confidential. Someone, however, leaked his project to the press. On February 4, 1888, the *Stock Exchange Bulletin* announced the impending introduction of gold in transactions, quoting from the minister's secret project.[96] As the minister complained to the tsar, to his "great chagrin, the question of primary state importance, through channels unknown to me, was made public and caused an enormous commotion."[97] The news was republished, with some distortions, in European newspapers, causing confusion at stock exchanges. Two days later, the credit ruble's rate fell to 52.6 gold kopecks.[98] Meanwhile, the Moscow Stock Exchange Committee requested that the Ministry of Finance discuss this measure with the representatives of the business community.

The Ministry of Finance had previously consulted with the representatives of business elites. Nikolai Naidenov, head of the Moscow Stock Exchange Committee, in his memoirs described his participation in a number of commissions in the 1860s and 1870s, preparing laws on bills of exchange, bankruptcy, commercial courts, labor laws, and, perhaps most important, customs tariffs.[99] Even though some ministry officials had initially been biased against "ignorant merchants," in the 1860s and 1870s, Mikhail Reutern actively sought input from the "merchant estate," and the relationship between the government and the community, as Naidenov characterized it, was "propitious."[100] However, neither Reutern nor Bunge invited merchants and bankers to discuss the plans for monetary reform; the money issue had always been seen strictly as the government's business. Naidenov was known to staunchly oppose the reform, and Katkov quoted him as the voice of the national business elite in his articles directed against Bunge's financial measures. Vyshnegradskii was therefore not keen to discuss the gold issue solely with the Moscow elite, and he tried to at least neutralize the Moskovites' opposition by inviting to a discussion the representatives of other stock exchange committees who might be more sympathetic to the measure. It did not help. At the conference with the representatives of several regional stock exchange communities, all participants of the debate with only two exceptions, spoke against the introduction of gold and other measures aiming at stabilizing the ruble's rate. The conference revealed the almost unanimous aversion of the Russian commercial elite to the introduction of gold.

When the conference took place in March 1888, the credit ruble's value had reached a record low of 50 gold kopecks, plunging 10% in just a few days.[101] Shockingly, the representatives of the stock exchange committees still continued to claim that the ruble's rate had no meaning for Russia's national economy and did not reflect the ruble's real value. Eschewing the discussion of economic processes that may have led to the ruble's downfall, they repeated almost verbatim the rhetoric of Katkov's editorials and even the arguments of early nineteenth-century financial conservatism. The idea of the "people's ruble" was once again resurrected, since the population trusted the government and believed in the value of a credit ruble that was secured by the entire wealth of the Russian state. Ivan Alafuzov, the owner of an enormous industrial empire specializing in textile and leather production, declared that not just peasants but even 80% of merchants had never heard of the exchange rate and judged the ruble's value by its ability to purchase goods. The government should hide the very idea of the paper ruble's exchangeability to gold because it could shake people's belief in paper.[102] Evgenii Shultz, a banker from Odessa, echoed this thought: "There is nothing wrong in keeping people unaware of the ruble's fall, because the ruble's rate is not equivalent to its real value."[103] "Who needs the gold ruble," asked Konrad Banza, co-owner of the Moscow-German trade giant Wogau & Co., which sold its goods both domestically and internationally.[104] Max Rathauz, a lawyer and a banker from Kyiv, responded, "As long as we can . . . build railroads on credit rubles, we don't need the gold ruble."[105] Only the state had to hold on to its gold reserve in case of war, claimed Ivan Alafuzov, who had built his fortune on military orders.[106] Alafuzov and others, apparently, mistook the exchange fund for a security reserve that the government could use as needed.

Among the very few who spoke in favor of the ministry's suggestion to stabilize the ruble's rate through the legalization of transactions in gold was Avraam Zak, a banker and an active leader of the Jewish community. As the director of the St. Petersburg Discount and Credit Bank (Sankt-Peterburgskii Uchetno-Ssudnyi Bank), Zak represented the St. Petersburg Stock Exchange, which was supposed to play a key role under the new arrangements by defining the current rate of exchange in transactions with gold. In fact, this practice already existed. The Statute of the St. Petersburg Stock Exchange established the bourse as a self-governing body ruled by a Committee with a chairman, and an elected Assembly of eighty members. Twice a week, the chief broker, chosen and appointed by the minister, submitted the bulletins of rates to the ministry.[107] The procedure of quoting exchange rates was not strictly regulated: the rules, based on "existing custom," prescribed that the rate represent the mean between the lowest and the highest rates quoted during the day.[108] However, when the rate was especially volatile, it could be defined through negotiations among "interested persons."[109] The absence of strict rules made the practice susceptible to various external influences.[110] Thus, a handful of powerful bankers in St. Petersburg, including Avraam Zak, played a key role in determining the ruble's standing.

In the 1880s, the Stock Exchange remained fairly autonomous vis-à-vis the Ministry of Finance. Avraam Zak and the St. Petersburg Bank for Discount and Credit participated in several financial operations on behalf of the

Russian government, including the arrangement of state loans.[111] Zak's bank also profited from the State Bank's operation with gold; when in 1881, the State Bank had to sell a certain amount to gold to support the falling rate, Zak, among other bankers, purchased this gold and later sold it at a profit.[112] Naidenov was also no stranger to the bureaucrats of the Ministry of Finance, but his discontent over the dictatorship of the St. Petersburg Stock Exchange may have played a role in the rejection of the legalization of gold. Other corporate organizations of Russian businessmen also expressed discontent with the role of the St. Petersburg Stock Exchange in "establishing the cost of the exchange unit—the rate of the credit ruble—for Russia's international commercial relations."[113] The petition of the Society for the Advancement of Russian Industry and Trade (Obshchestvo sodeistviia russkoi promyshlennosti i torgovle) emphasized the non-Russian ethnic composition of the St. Petersburg joint-stock committee, which allegedly comprised mostly Jewish and German bankers and businessmen.

The Russian business elite was deeply divided along national and regional lines, and a split was manifested in industrial specialization, the specifics of corporate organizations, and the structure of incomes.[114] The old-Russian Moscow of producers of textiles and merchants, with banks oriented mainly toward discount operations, contrasted with the cosmopolitan financiers of St. Petersburg, where banks earned their profit on operations with funds and securities.[115] Regional and national differences translated into commercial interests and were ultimately exposed in the businessmen's opinions regarding the place of gold in Russian finances. In addition to Avraam Zak, the main supporter of Vyshnegradskii's suggestion was Ivan (Jan) Bloch. A railroad magnate, banker who represented the Warsaw Stock Exchange Committee, and expert at the Minister's Council, Bloch published numerous academic and statistical works on Russian finances, including the magisterial *The Finances of Russia in the Nineteenth Century*, which came out in 1882.[116] Zak and Bloch represented the cosmopolitan German-Jewish-Polish business elite of the capital city and Russia's western provinces and were therefore interested in a financial rapprochement between the empire and the West. In contrast, the Moscow elite did not share the enthusiasm about the arrival of foreign capital. "If foreign capitalists come to Russia, it would be to our detriment," pointed out Nikolai Naidenov, the most outspoken opponent of the legalization of gold. Their arrival would create competition that Russian commercial elites wanted to avoid.[117]

Bloch's defense of the government's position also echoed traditional liberal arguments. He repeatedly quoted Nikolai Mordvinov's early

nineteenth-century stances regarding the government's obligation to maintain the stability of the national currency as the "measure of everything."[118]
Another liberal rhetorical tool was the reversal of conservative pseudo-
populist discourse about "the people's ruble." As Bloch explained, simple folk,
more than anybody else, suffered from the instability of the ruble's rate, which
affected domestic prices and allowed predator merchants and speculators to
control the grain market. It was therefore immoral not to undertake certain
measures because there was a "dark mass of people that suffers but cannot understand the reason of the suffering."[119] Moreover, it was impossible to hide
the ruble's fall from the people: "There will always be the enlighteners."[120]
However, the social effect of monetary instability was not limited to the lower
strata of the Russian population. In the presence of his peers—merchants and
bankers—Bloch declared that without the stability of the national currency, a
country could not develop a mature class of merchants. Deeds and contracts
were subjected to higher risk, and only speculators ventured into the blurry
area of business, while the "best people" stayed away from it.[121] Thus, in
Bloch's rhetoric, the issue of the ruble acquired an important social dimension, explaining rural poverty and the absence of the middle class in Russia.
Bloch was also the first participant in the debate to exit the conventional vicious circle of rhetorical arguments and connect the ruble's rate with the main
criteria of well-being—the index of child mortality—which was linked to the
low wages of workers and to poor nutrition.[122]

Bloch did not explain how the link between child mortality and the ruble's
rate worked, but his speech stood out because Bloch used numbers, while
others resorted to non-quantitative political and ideological arguments. The
neglect of numbers in the assessment of the development of trade, agriculture, and industry was a distinctive feature of Russian debates on the ruble
issue. Writers and speakers, professionals and dilettantes interpreted and
re-interpreted the same set of data—the volume of money issuance, the export and import of goods and gold, and the rates of exchange. The ruble and
the monetary system existed in a world not connected to the economy but
heavily loaded with ideological meaning. The concept of the "people's ruble"
could not have any empirical backing or content, and Bloch's attempts to link
the stability of the currency to child mortality was a way to debunk the anti-
gold arguments.

Bloch and Zak's arguments in favor of gold were trumped by the overwhelming opposition of provincial commercial elites. In the face of unconditional rejection of his initiative by the business community, Vyshnegradskii
quietly abandoned the project, which was supposed to be an important step

in Russia's transition to the gold standard. Vyshnegradskii's defeat, which followed Bunge's failure to resist the creation of a Bank that favored the interests of nobility at the expense of the national currency, underscored the reality that the problem of the ruble's fate was primarily political and social. The extreme politicization of the gold issue was not a uniquely Russian phenomenon. In forcing through the monetary reforms, policymakers had to make a choice between two irreconcilable options and prioritize the interests of one that sought to preserve the weak fixed currency and isolationism, over another that expressed a commitment to the international standard, which limited the state's ability to support domestic producers. As political scientist Jeffrey Frieden writes, the policymakers "must decide which groups in society—consumers, debtors, international investors, manufacturers and farmers—will be helped and which hurt by the real exchange rate. There is no obviously 'right' decision for both sets of choices."[123]

The specificity of the Russian case was that the group of people interested in a stable ruble was very small, limited to the administrative bureaucracy, economists, and a tiny but influential community of bankers in St. Petersburg and the Western provinces. Bunge intended to pursue a policy that favored cosmopolitan commercial elites. His initial program combined the declaration of the government's commitments to the international principles of monetary policy and a particular social policy that prioritized the interests of the urban educated classes over the interests of the nobility and local, mostly textile, producers. The political realities of Alexander III's reign, however, imposed limitations on the realization of this program. As a result, Bunge's financial policy combined financial cosmopolitanism with an economic policy that privileged landowners over other social groups. Taking over the Ministry of Finance, Vyshnegradskii declared the reorientation of its policy to strict protectionism combined with budget austerity. Like Reutern and Bunge, he believed in the benefits of attracting foreign capital to Russia, which required the reorganization of its financial system.[124] The commercial elites, who welcomed the change of trade policy and protectionist measures, strongly opposed the monetary improvements, and their resistance thwarted the possibility of legalizing transactions in gold. For them, gold was an unnecessary link in the chain of exchange between paper money and goods. Instead of the de-commoditization of gold proposed by the government, they offered its de-monetization and commoditization.

The government had to maneuver between the two irreconcilable goals of shielding the Russian economy from the detrimental effects of a weak currency and preserving its nationalist agenda. During Vyshnegradskii's tenure as minister, Russia increased its gold reserve by 75%, and more than 50% of the gold fund that later became the main anchor of the monetary reform, was acquired in the nine years preceding the transition to the gold standard in 1897.[125] In the attempt to increase the bullion reserve, Russia was buying gold even when its price skyrocketed due to the increased demand in Austria-Hungary, which was also preparing its transition to gold.[126] Remarkably, Russia was able to make these purchases without resorting to foreign loans. Money for gold purchases could only be taken from budget surpluses: therefore, Vyshnegradskii concentrated his efforts on increasing the profitability of the Russian revenue system, which included raising indirect taxes and stimulating grain exports. Between 1888 and 1891, state revenues exceeded spending due to a series of good harvests, while exports trumped import by almost 50%. Both phenomena were almost unseen in the history of Russian finances.[127] Simultaneously, the Russian government continued not only collecting tax duties in gold at an increasing rate but also stimulating the production of gold inside the country. In total, these measures brought an enormous increase in the stock of gold.[128]

The disastrous famine of 1891 caused hundreds of thousands of deaths and demonstrated the tragic consequences of Vyshnegradskii's policy of stimulating grain export at the expense of domestic needs, but even this massive crisis did not divert the government's path to the gold standard. In October 1892, the government proudly reported to the European press that the combined funds in gold of the State Bank and the State Treasury constituted 604.5 million gold rubles, or 2 billion francs, which significantly exceeded the combined stocks of the Bank of France and the Bank of England.[129] This news, which appeared in the midst of the monetary conference in Brussels, shocked European economists and financiers.[130] The accumulation of gold by a country that almost demonstrably refrained from the principles of the gold standard spoke volumes about the contradictions inherent in its financial, political, and social policies.

PART III

The Gold Reform

6

Witte's Rollercoaster

Patterns and Contingencies

The so-called international gold standard of its classical age (1880–1914), as often described by economists, resembles a vortex. Britain, France, the United States, and Germany formed its core. Economically advanced, these countries were most faithful to the rules of the standard. The less economically developed members of the gold club, such as Brazil, Colombia, Argentina, and Chile, suffered from political instability, experienced a shortage of investment, and primarily depended on exporting raw materials—coffee, rubber, nitrate, and copper. Staying on the gold standard often exceeded their means, and they repeatedly slipped out of the system into the regime of inconvertibility. The economies of Italy, Portugal, Spain, and Austro-Hungary were far better off, but for various reasons, their allegiance to the standard was either inconsistent or incomplete. A group of Northern and Western European countries, including Denmark, Norway, Sweden, Belgium, the Netherlands, and Switzerland belonged to the advanced periphery. And there was Japan—a latecomer with meager resources that was strongly committed to the standard. As the vortex analogy suggests, the closer a country was to the ideal core, the easier it was for it to remain within the system. Those on the margins had a harder time holding on and paid higher costs for keeping their currencies on gold. The benefits of staying within the system were sometimes unclear, but the losses associated with expulsion appeared staggering.[1] Economic historians have meticulously explored factors that affected the transition to gold from either bimetallism or inconvertible paper money. Economic factors that pushed countries to the standard (the high transaction costs of currency exchange, the fluctuating price of silver, industrialization, etc.) are thought to be the most important, although the motives of countries that joined early

in the process differed from the factors that triggered the latecomers' transition. If before 1880 the allegiance to gold was a matter of choice, after 1880 it
was almost an inevitability. Every nation that wanted to participate in global
commerce and the international market of capital had to adhere to the gold
standard. Economists have also acknowledged the importance of "historical
contingencies" that erode the mythology of an almost automatic transition to
the gold standard.[2]

The last European great power to join the gold standard, Russia might
appear to confirm the pattern of economic determinism. Despite the overall
resistance of Russia's elites, the Russian monetary system eventually adopted
gold. However, this determinism is misleading: the story of Russia's gold reform suggests that Russia was not simply driven into the vortex of the gold
standard system. Political factors and ideologies played central roles in the
decision to adopt the standard. Russia did not sleepwalk into the system, and
its transition was neither easy nor straightforward.

Even though the golden age mythology had been debunked, in economic
literature and common imagination the "classical" gold standard still often
stands for prudence and rationality, while its alternatives are often deemed
irrational. The gold standard appears a holistic ideology that assumes financial austerity and self-restriction, liberalism and international cooperation. However, a closer look at the intellectual and political landscape of
nineteenth-century Europe shows that the criteria of economic rationality
and their political markers remained fluid. Russia's financial policy of the
1890s, especially in the years preceding the adoption of the gold standard,
showcases this phenomenon, namely, the combination of measures aimed
at stabilizing the ruble's rate with inflationist ideologies and projects reminiscent of John Law's infamous enterprise. This improbable mixture was the
result of a search for conservative currency stabilization—an alternative to
the gold standard, and the person who tried to implement it in practice was
minister of finance, Serguei Witte, who became known as the author of the
gold reform of 1897. Witte's initial vision of financial rationality defied the
link between monetary stability and austerity, thereby violating the "scientific" criteria of monetary economy. A former top manager of the private
Southwestern Railroad and a member of the ultra-conservative nationalist
"Holy Squad," Witte was notorious for his almost complete incompetence in
key theoretical questions of political economy, which was a significant change
after the two minister-professors (Bunge and Vyshnegradskii). Witte's financial policy in 1892–95 represented an attempt to rationalize economic nationalism, to turn Meshchersii's and Katkov's delusional ideas into an economic

system while at the same time continuing Bunge's and Vyshnegradskii's policy of strengthening Russia's currency. When these attempts failed, Witte dropped inflationism while retaining the core of his politico-economic views. This rollercoaster of policies and ideas was astonishing, and in the end, Witte alienated his former allies without creating new ones. Throughout these changes, Witte demonstrated his firm allegiance to the ideas of autocracy, empire, and nationalism. Russia's transition to the gold standard was not predetermined, and the political circumstances of this reform amounted to much more than a historical contingency. In fact, the opposite is true: the gold standard represented a contingency, while the political program of strengthening the economic power of the state and using monetary govern-ance to expand the empire was the pattern.

Indeed, economic factors mattered. Due to the size of Russia's foreign debt, the rising costs of its repayment, and the necessity of borrowing even more and attracting foreign investments, Russia needed to stabilize its currency. Yet in the imagination of Russian nationalists like Witte, the gold standard did not represent the only way to stabilization, and stabilization was seen not simply as an economic objective. In 1892–95, when Witte successfully tamed the ruble's rate and prevented its wild fluctuations while also trying to finance imperial projects with newly issued Siberian rubles, and in 1895–97, when he tried to impose the gold standard, he pursued the same goal of continuing to put the monetary system in the government's strong grip. The "bear squeeze" tech-nique that Witte invented and used to prevent the speculation with rubles on European markets nicely characterized his attitude to monetary regulation. Another unchanging element of Witte's system was economic nationalism and imperialism. Russia's view of the monetary regime defied the central idea of the early gold-standard cooperation, namely, the partial suspension of mon-etary sovereignty. To the contrary: Witte's gold ruble appeared as a tool of imperial aggrandizement and a centerpiece of his economic system based on nationalism, protectionism, and imperial expansion. As this chapter shows, the principles of the gold standard implemented after 1897 evolved in the years preceding the reforms that are often dismissed as an embarrassing and abnormal prelude to the reform, but this period is central to understanding the specificity of the Russians' thinking about money and power.

Gambling on Rubles

Economic nationalism represents a remarkable example of an ideology that constantly changed in substance while explicitly declaring allegiance to the same old ideals. If Katkov's editorials of the late 1870s and early 1880s suggested that patriotism meant indifference toward the ruble's standing in Europe, then in the late 1880s, the attitude, at least in the political establishment, was reversed. The credit ruble came to be seen as an embodiment of national pride and sovereignty, and its vulnerability represented a grave concern for nationalists. The almighty ober-procurator of the Synod, Konstantin Pobedonostsev, who was Alexander III's mentor and longtime correspondent, wrote to the tsar in 1886 regarding the ruble's rate as "the issue of primary importance to Russia," calling the rate's fluctuation a "national disaster," "disgrace," and "shame." "Even" small states such as Serbia and Romania, or Austria with its "pathetic and ruined finances," did not experience such painful and distressing falls. Pobedonostsev attributed the fluctuation of the ruble's rate to foreign influence—stock exchange speculation in Berlin, supported by "our state bankers Stieglitz, and then Zak and Co."[3] Ironically, Avraam Zak was one of the few representatives of the Russian elite who spoke in favor of stabilizing the ruble on the basis of gold. Apparently, Pobedonostsev and Zak differed in their views on the causes of the ruble's falls and the remedies for stabilization. What is certain is that the ruble's fall increased the costs of paying off Russia's foreign loans, whose value rose from 1.7 billion rubles in 1866 to 4.5 billion rubles in 1886.

Why did the ruble's rate fluctuate? A few economists attributed the ruble's volatility to factors "within the state,"[4] but it was much more common to believe that the national currency fell victim to a cunning plot by Russia's enemies and a speculation spree with Russian currency and securities on the Berlin exchange in 1886–87. Indeed, a series of measures that culminated in the so-called *Lombardverbot* (the German government's prohibition against accepting Russian securities as collateral for loans by the Reichsbank) caused the fall in price of the Russian bonds and the decline of the ruble's rate.[5] As a result, the speculation with rubles on the Berlin Bourse, although not intentionally orchestrated by Bismarck's government, came to be seen in Russia as a part of German economic warfare. In reality, the circumstances of this episode were less political and more prosaic. The speculation in rubles did not differ from any other kind of stock speculation that involved forward contracts with securities. Forward contracts for the purchase of currency usually ended in settlements a few months after the deal, when a buyer paid either the entire sum of the contract or, more commonly, only the difference between the price at the time of the contract and the price at the moment of the settlement. Between the two dates, both a buyer and a seller were trying to either lower or raise the price of currency using various means—media, rumors, or other non-economic factors. In addition, stock gamblers were engaged in more complex speculative combinations, for which the Russian ruble represented an ideal object. Most of the deals were fictitious and did not involve cash, so the scale of speculation could reach very significant numbers. One source suggested, referring to the *Berliner Börsen-Courier*, that as much as 15 million rubles had been "sold" in only one day.[6] Since certain deals were arranged in physical payments and one of the contracting parties could, in principle, request the full sum in cash, paper rubles packed in bags were carried across the border to Berlin for the dates of the monthly settlements of speculative deals. Russian bankers played a crucial role in these deals, either as agents supplying Berlin clients with cash or as contractors.[7]

The very fact that the ruble turned into the favorite prey of Russian and European speculators is not in itself surprising. Paper currencies were quoted as commodities, and in this capacity, they were subject to all kinds of deals and contracts. As economist Vlasii Sudeikin observed, "The general rule of stock exchange speculation is to gamble with the most unstable security, since there are more chances to win on the fluctuation of rates. Our credit rubles belong to the category of the most fluctuating objects."[8] However, in Russia, stock exchange speculation was not seen as a normal economic phenomenon. Nikolai Novoselskii, a conservative publicist whose memos were widely read by top bureaucrats, specifically emphasized that speculation suspended the "economic laws of demand and supply" in relation to credit rubles.[9] Thus, ironically, economic nationalists turned into advocates of the free market; in their view, however, the free market did not include stockbrokers. The stock exchange came to be seen as an anomaly rather than a necessary element of the financial system.

In the overdramatized depiction of speculation, Russian writers imagined "train cars full of paper money sent from Russia to Berlin in order to lower our ruble's rate."[10] The dynamics of the ruble's fluctuations did not always support such accusations, but the public nonetheless blamed German stockbrokers and speculators. Russia's strained relationship with Germany contributed to the escalation of paranoia around the Berlin Stock Exchange. In February 1888, three postal clerks, who had been accused of stealing 120,000 rubles' worth of valuables from a shipment sent to Berlin, were acquitted by a jury of the Moscow court after a defense attorney, Nikolai Shubinskii, praised the act of theft as retribution for the speculation in Russian paper currency. The liberal press was shocked and outraged by the attorney's "eloquence"; conservatives expressed indignation over yet another acquittal. Kostantin Pobedonostsev, who used the occasion to remind Alexander III about his intention to "limit the jury court," also pointed out that Berlin was indeed "the center of stock exchange speculation that sucks money from our people."[11] Arguably, in Russian public opinion of the 1880s, Berlin was associated with gambling in Russian paper money, while the St. Petersburg Stock Exchange was perceived as the auxiliary to the Berlin Stock Exchange.[12] The Russian ruble was under siege. Vladimir Meshcherskii, who several years earlier had denied the importance of international rates, wrote in one of his letters to the tsar that the speculation was tantamount to "economic war against Russia" and "a mean insinuation against You, against our Ruble."[13]

The Ministry of Finance undertook its first anti-speculative measures in the late 1870s, but only in the mid-1880s did it address the problem more systematically. These measures had both symbolic and practical meaning. In 1885, the St. Petersburg Stock Exchange was obliged to publish quotes in Russian, not in French, and in 1887, the format of the quotes changed to show the prices of foreign currencies in rubles, not the ruble's price in foreign currencies. As an editor of a handbook of rates of exchange pointed out, this small reform "turned the ruble . . . into the measure of value for foreign currencies."[14] Among other means to foil the "plots" of enemies of Russia's credit and currency was the control of public media. The Ministry of Finance's "secret agents," dispatched to Berlin and Vienna, were responsible for "influencing the German press" by publishing informational leaflets, preempting and preventing the spread of rumors, and delivering favorable information about the state of Russian finances directly to banking houses and the Stock Exchange. The agents promised "immediate and palpable outcomes" from their campaign, but these efforts did not bring about any significant improvements.[15] More important, while trying to prevent private profiteering on the ruble's fluctuation, the Russian government itself plunged into stock exchange gambling, secretly buying and selling rubles.[16] The government's attempts to outplay speculators by their own means did not help stabilize the national currency. Moreover, Vyshnegradskii's own policy of increasing the gold reserve contributed to a tremendous increase in the ruble's rate fluctuations he was trying to prevent. Massive purchases of gold paid in credit rubles not only caused the prices of both gold and rubles to swing up and down but also made Russian paper cash available in large quantities on European markets.[17]

In late August 1892, Vyshnegradskii lost his ministerial position to his closest assistant, Deputy Minister Serguei Witte, who had used his boss's failing health to advance to power.[18] Witte came to the government with a background different from Bunge's and Vyshnegradskii's academic past: he had been a manager at a private railroad company. In the 1880s, Witte participated in the monarchist anti-revolutionary organization "The Holy Squad" and regularly wrote articles for Katkov's the *Moscow Bulletin*. His political views were staunchly nationalist, in contrast to the technocratic progressivism of the Ministry of Finance. He also did not subscribe to the principles of liberal-bureaucratic propriety, and tackled the problem of speculation in a completely different way. While his predecessor shied away from intervening in the market mechanisms, Witte initiated a project to "strengthen state control over the stock exchange," which followed a public announcement in January 1893 prohibiting speculative operations with the ruble.[19] According to his plan, the government assumed control over the internal working of the business community so as to regulate the access of dealers to the stock exchange and to observe the essence of operations through the inspection of the broker firms' books. Witte's unprecedented claim that the Ministry of Finance had the right to audit the books of private firms violated financial privacy and encroached on the internal practices of private financial organizations and banks.[20] Even the bureaucratic establishment was shocked by the severity of Witte's anti-speculative crusade. Commenting both on the "principles of the unlimited intrusion of bureaucrats upon the particulars of private entrepreneurship" and on the "dreadful bureaucratic surveillance" that killed initiative and prevented economic growth, the state secretary Alexander Polovtsov called this policy "state socialism." In his opinion, Witte's approach was even more dangerous than the socialism of "certain individuals," presumably revolutionaries.[21]

Ironically, to justify such an unprecedented measure, Witte drew a parallel between the government's right to control financial activity for the sake of protecting the ruble's rate and the power of police authorities to peruse private correspondence for the sake of the public good. Indeed, other measures intended to prevent speculation on the ruble's rate clearly fell into the category of policing. For example, the introduction of customs duties on the export of credit bills aimed to control the movement of paper currency across the border. The tax itself was minuscule and had no fiscal meaning (0.01% of the total sum), but it was supposed to reveal the outflow of paper money.[22] Additionally, it made all future contracts on the purchases of Russian currency risky, if not totally impossible, because the government was aware of the amount of credit bills in cash available in Berlin for the termination of deals.[23] There was only one rub in this plan: paper money was usually transferred across the border by mail, and by the rules of the Universal Postal Convention signed by Russia in 1891, senders were not obliged to indicate the value of shipments. Subjecting credit rubles to duty taxes changed their status: taxable goods could not be sent in envelopes, and the senders were forced to transfer money orders openly via post offices.[24] Yet to fully exclude the mailing of money in letters, the Ministry of Finance issued a secret instruction obliging post offices to check the envelopes and report all shipments of credit rubles, with the names of senders and indications of sums and destinations. When the head of the Warsaw post administration refused to comply with this obviously illegal request to violate the privacy of correspondence, Witte instructed him to get this information "unofficially."[25] Passengers carrying money in their luggage were also told to report the amount of money taken abroad.[26]

The most important phase of Witte's anti-speculation campaign took place in the fall of 1894, when stock dealers in Paris and Berlin used the news of Alexander III's terminal illness to bring down the ruble. Witte gave his agents the order to buy all cash credit rubles available on the market in Europe, and when the time for settlement came, the buyers were instructed by the government to request payment in full rather than only the difference between the price at the time of the contract and the price at the moment of the settlement. Speculators were unable to procure cash to honor their forward contracts because the export of credit rubles was prohibited. Desperate, they pleaded with the minister to sell them the necessary amounts of rubles at a much higher price. After this incident, stock exchange gambling with Russian currency permanently ceased. The vast area in the hall of the Berlin Bourse that had been occupied by brokers specializing in Russian rubles remained empty for a while, perplexing visitors and prompting questions.[27] Witte became known for inventing the "bear squeeze"—a technique for cornering the markets by controlling and manipulating the price of commodities—a term that reflects his brutal, coercive, manipulative methods.[28]

Witte perceived the fight against speculation as his own personal crusade. As Polovtsov remarked, "He got mad about the speculation."[29] In the end, his policy proved to be quite successful, and the fluctuation of the ruble's rate was dramatically reduced within a few months. Perhaps one of the most visible and significant outcomes of this campaign was the strengthening of his personal authority, which helped him earn the support of the new tsar, Nicholas II, and oust political adversaries and competitors. Witte acquired a reputation as the savior of the Russian ruble and the rescuer of the Russian currency from financial predators. The final episode of Witte's anti-speculation crusade involved the former minister of finance and the actual head of the Department of Economy of the State Council, Alexander Abaza, the author of the financial pseudo-constitution of January 1, 1881. As Witte recounted this story, soon after his appointment to the ministerial position in 1892, he received a request for a large loan from Odessa banker Alexander Raffalovich, who was short 900,000 rubles—a debt he had incurred conducting an operation on behalf of his client, Abaza. As it turned out, in August 1890, the minister of finance Vyshnegradskii had discussed with Abaza the government's strategy of restraining the ruble's sudden growth via the sales of gold. The entire operation was supposed to be kept secret, with the realization of gold arranged in small portions and alternated with the periodic sale of paper rubles to hide the government's intentions and to lower the rate slowly.[30] Abaza enthusiastically supported the minister, and when the government began selling gold, he asked his banker, Raffalovich, to perform the same operation on his behalf. Raffalovich was perplexed by Abaza's instructions, which went against the tendencies of the stock exchange, and Abaza revealed to him the source of his intelligence. The ruble's rate continued to grow for several months before beginning to descend, and Raffalovich, who had initially trusted Abaza's knowledge and speculated with his own funds along these lines, could not tolerate his temporary losses. He panicked, swung from one strategy to another, and eventually went bankrupt, while Abaza, having sold gold for 2 million pounds sterling, earned approximately 700,000 rubles on the margin of rates.[31]

Events may not have played out exactly as Witte described them in his report to the tsar and in his memoirs. Raffalovich's testimony about the speculation was Witte's main evidence against Abaza, and Witte built his entire case around this one document.[32] In his penitential letter to Alexander III, Abaza admitted his mistake but stated that his earnings had been greatly exaggerated. Eventually, Abaza had to resign, clearing the way for Witte's rise. It is quite possible that Witte exaggerated the scandal in order to be rid of Abaza, who, in his capacity as chairman of the State Council's Department of Economy, could have blocked the new minister's initiatives. The importance of this episode is its exposing a range of new attitudes toward the paper ruble. Russian bureaucrats perceived credit bills simultaneously as an asset, a commodity, and a symbolic "public good." For Witte, the ruble was also a means for building his political power, since his political gambling helped him become a top government figure. Another, long-lasting effect of the campaign was that Witte's attack on speculation propagated a new vision of financial markets and a new attitude of the state toward financial entrepreneurship. If in the late 1850s Russian economists celebrated the first stock exchange rush and the subsequent crisis as a sign of Russia's "normality," Witte perceived speculation as a deviation and therefore followed the logic of nationalists, who portrayed speculation as a factor impeding the normal functioning of market mechanisms.

Russian bankers did not share this attitude. One of the most remarkable manifestations of their aversion to the minister's vision was a memo written by Adolph Rothstein in February 1893, after the ministry launched its first attack against speculators and the government established the State Bank's monopoly on the sale of foreign bills of exchange. Rothstein, director of the St. Petersburg International Commercial Bank and Witte's closest adviser, questioned the minister's conviction that fluctuations in the rate of exchange could result from such temporary and superficial factors as agiotage and speculation. "In essence, all fluctuations conform to the real state of things" and reflect major economic and political trends, wrote Rothstein. Witte's policy of regulating the rate was meant to replace the workings of those "big" forces of the market with administrative tools, essentially allowing the minister of finance to monopolize the regulation of the ruble's rate. "One authority or one person is given the means to take into his hands and provide the regulation of the rate? . . . But what role would belong to the imponderable move- ment of public opinion, that of serious businessmen, and not speculators?" If under normal circumstances the fluctuation of the rate of exchange could be attributed to the whim of the market or chance, under the new regime, "with the State Bank regulating the level of exchange," all fluctuations would be ascribed to the minister of finance's whim. All minor fluctuations would rise "to the proportion of state action."[33] The policy of "fixing the rate by authority" threatened to incur many problems associated with the "loss of the free market" and the derangement of credit.[34] This measure, yet again, imposed on the minister "the moral responsibility for the general results of the private banks' activity, a responsibility that will not be adequate to reality."[35]

Rothstein's intervention did not affect the minister's plan, and the attitude toward unregulated market as a pathology remained unchanged even after 1895, when Witte gave up his early ideas and started preparing for the transition to gold. In an important public statement concerning the gold ruble reform, Witte criticized the erroneous views on the fluctuation of the rate of exchange as a "natural" and "inevitable" economic phenomenon that could not and should not be regulated.[36] Under the banner of protecting the ruble, Witte introduced a series of measures that launched a policy of increasing the state's role in the sphere of credit. He was unable to subject private banks to the government's ultimate control because the State Council did not allow the ministry to close private banks, referring to the principles protecting the freedom of the "banking business."[37] However, his attempts signaled an important and significant shift in the government's policy already visible after 1881. The idea of a stable currency as the property of a liberal constitutional regime was no longer relevant, even though opponents continued to present it that way. The government's policy of monetary reform was no longer associated with the principles of the freedom of commerce and credit.

The Imperial Ruble

Witte's efforts to curb speculation unfolded in parallel with the notorious projects of financing the construction of the Siberian Railroad through issuing so-called Siberian rubles and the State Bank's reform, which was supposed to allow for an uncontrolled printing of paper money.[38] How could these two contradictory trends coexist in one's person head? How can the idea of maintaining the ruble's stability be reconciled with the inflationist expansion of the money supply? Historians usually point to Witte's theoretical naïveté, his illiteracy in questions of monetary policy, his past closeness to nationalist journalists, and the influence of his deputy minister of finance, Professor Afinogen Antonovich. While all these explanations are important, they overlook an important element: Witte's plans of 1892–94 had the same rationale as the anti-speculative measures. Both represented the extension of economic nationalism that combined the idea of state-guaranteed stability of the currency and the concept of using the ruble as a means of governance. Witte not only tried to insert a note of pragmatism in the utopian conservative agenda but also added new meanings to the nationalist idea of currency. One of his most shocking and notorious innovations was the concept of the imperial ruble.

Like many other of Witte's innovations, the idea of using the issuance of the ruble for the purposes of imperial expansion was not entirely novel. In the 1860s, Russian nationalists tried to find alternatives to the ruble's gold backing, the most popular being land and railroads. In the 1870s–80s, after Russia extended into Central Asia, credit rubles came to be seen as a means of furthering the empire's economic expansion, thereby securing the value of paper issues with the potential benefits of imperialism. Several ideas dominated the imagination of Russian nationalist writers: reversing the flows of Amu-Darya and building canals connecting the Russian Central Asian steppes with the Baltic Sea, the development of the Russian North, and the integration of Siberia into European Russia either by reversing the flow of the great Siberian rivers Ob' and Yenisei or with the help of a Great Siberian Railroad.[39] These projects combined the idea of absorbing extra paper money and thus repairing the Russian monetary system on its own, indigenous way, with the most impudent projects of colonization. Imperial imaginations offered images of waterways "through which goods will pass from India to Moscow," deserts "swelled with water," fertile lands in the Caspian region populated by Russian settlers instead of the Turkmen nomads, and fisheries of the Russian North. "The more the government spends paper rubles, the more it gets in gold and silver," wrote a champion of one of these projects, Yakov Yankevich.[40] Another enthusiast of imperial expansion, renowned Sinologist and chair of the Department of Oriental Studies of St. Petersburg University Vasilii Vasiliev, called on the government to print more money to finance the resettlement movement. He believed that only the state, with its capacity to produce currency, could accelerate development and revive the deserts by giving jobs to the millions of people working on the construction of great projects and the production of gold.[41] All these projects rested on the idea that paper credit rubles would become beneficial if they are used for "productive purposes." Their realization promised not only to free Russia from its dependence on the international markets of capital but also to liberate it from its reliance on imports, since imported goods like cotton and silk could be produced locally and therefore allow for the accumulation of gold and the repayment of foreign debts.[42] The idea became a staple of right-wing journalism. Among others, Serguei Sharapov's nationalist newspaper the *Russian Cause (Russkoe Delo)* propagated the plan for printing money for the construction of the Siberian Railroad and explained this operation through a theory of "imaginary capital," that is, the transformation of fictitious money into real value through its investment in state public projects.[43]

Professor Afinogen Antonovich from Kyiv University gave this idea a scholarly imprimatur. In his book *The Theory of the Paper Monetary System* (1883), Antonovich classified paper money into "bad" money issued to satisfy consumption (this included military needs) and money issued by the state for productive purposes, for example, ameliorative projects in agriculture and railroad construction. Twisting the principle of the liberal monetary doctrine that reserved for independent banks the function of issuing bills on the security of commercial transactions, Antonovich claimed that productive paper money issued by the state would be no worse than the banknotes of European credit institutions.[44] In fact, state money, if managed wisely, would be much better than that issued through private banks because "private interest contradicts public interest." "The state, as a representative of common interest and as a legal personality . . . has the right and responsibility to regulate private interest according to the needs of the common wellbeing of current and future generations."[45] Therefore, Antonovich concluded that the state could and should enforce particular patterns of productive economic behavior with the help of direct or indirect intrusion, tariffs, credit and, most important, state-owned enterprises (railroads) funded with the help of state-printed paper money.[46]

The concept of productive money was quite appealing to Witte, a former chief manager of a private railroad, an admirer of Slavophilism, and a member of an ultra-conservative monarchist brigade. Soon after becoming a minister, he took up one of the most popular ideas—the construction of the Trans-Siberian Railroad. Plans to build a road across Siberia to the Far East had been debated since the 1860s, but the government lacked the financial means to carry out these projects.[47] Given Alexander III's stinginess, the project, revived in 1891, could have remained on paper forever.[48] Witte's plan to finance railroad construction with the help of "Siberian credit rubles" seemed to offer a relatively easy solution to the problem. The proposed Siberian credit rubles in the amount of 150 million would have had a status equal to regular credit rubles. Like the earlier projects of the nationalists who proposed using railroads, instead of gold, as a collateral for paper money, Witte suggested that one of the lines serve as a security deposit for the new kind of paper currency. Justifying the increase in paper money in circulation, the minister referred to the ongoing development of the borderlands, namely, the industries and commerce of the South, Caucasus, and Central Asia that had increased the demand for money. The idea that the demand for money depended on territory and population was a key element of the ideology of the "imperial ruble."[49] At the same time, Witte's 1892 memo *On the Means of Constructing the Great Siberian Railroad* heavily relied on Antonovich's theory of paper money and the idea that the "value of paper rubles in circulation is defined . . . by the productive work of the paper ruble."[50] In 1893 Antonovich was appointed deputy minister of finance, and Witte recruited nationalist writer and journalist Serguei Sharapov to popularize the idea of the Siberian rubles in a series of articles called "The Foundations of the Russian Monetary System" (1893).[51]

Economists and bureaucrats watched Witte's initiatives unfold with bewilderment and horror. All kinds of parallels came into mind. Bunge asked, "What would have happened to France's credit system, had its 1.3 million-franc Bank of France bonds been secured by the productive work on the Panama Canal?"[52] Siberian money seemed a bizarre fantasy of Witte, who did not understand the ethos of administrative order and disregarded the established conventions of financial governance. Witte was frustrated that the law of January 1, 1881, put a brake on the mechanism of the money-printing autocracy, and not a single extra paper ruble unbacked by gold was released between 1881 and 1892.[53] Fed up with such a limitation on his financial power, he put forward a suggestion, based on "formal reasons," that annihilated the law of 1881.[54] For a businessman who had only recently been thrown into the world of bureaucracy, the matters of honor and obligation the government had taken upon itself in 1881 meant very little, and locking up gold in the reserve fund made no sense. He used the concept of the "productive ruble" to juxtapose his financial pragmatism to the legalism of bureaucrats and armchair economists. He also cited the example of other European banks of issue that enjoyed, as he saw it, greater financial freedom. "Our State Bank, in fact, is totally deprived of the right of issue," pointed out Witte.[55]

Witte's plan to increase the volume of paper money and to change the principles of monetary policy from financial austerity to indulgence culminated in the proposal to reform the State Bank that suggested merging the Bank with the State Treasury to increase the Bank's existing assets and granting the Bank an almost uncontrolled right to issue new banknotes in addition to the existing credit rubles.[56] These banknotes, which the Bank's clients were to receive under the security of bills of exchange, were supposed to compensate for the deficit of paper money and provide for the "elasticity" of the monetary system.[57] The project assumed strengthening the Bank's dependence on the Ministry of Finance and liquidating all existing mechanisms of control over issuing paper money. Thus, the future bank was a peculiar hybrid. It resembled European central banks of issue, yet in contrast to these banks that functioned under the supervision of their shareholders or parliaments, the Russian State Bank was meant to be free from any public control. As the reform project explained, "Establishing fictitious control over the activity of government institutions is tantamount to the propagation of distrust in the activity of one of the most important bodies of state governance. The Russian people do not need these fictions, and one should not pay attention to the opinion of Western theoreticians."[58] The Witte/Antonovich project of bank reform therefore suggested that state and society were one thing, inseparable and indistinguishable, and this approach imposed a particular concept of money, economy, and credit. Witte's methods of dealing with speculation as well as his policy toward business and the stock exchange exemplified a decisive turn toward the absorption of the market by the state, and the plan for State Bank reform continued this trend.

Witte's "monstrous" plans "terrified" the bureaucracy, observed Anatolii Kulomzin, one of the country's most experienced bureaucrats.[59] Certainly, the projected reform went against all principles that Witte's predecessors, starting with Reutern, had been slowly imposing on autocratic governance.[60] Whereas they had tried to disassociate the State Bank from the State Treasury, separate their accounts, and make the government (treasury) pay for its credit ruble debts, Witte (or Antonovich) suggested merging the two institutions. If the ministers, following Speransky's ideas, had tried to compensate for the lack of shareholder control over the bank's activity by inviting the representatives of commercial elites, Witte perceived this as an annoying obstacle and a su-perfluous ritual. The solemn ceremonies of inviting the members of the stock exchange and foreign guests to check the gold content of the State Bank's coffers might have seemed bizarre and outdated, but for bureaucrats Bunge and Lamanskii, these symbols mattered. Even more offensive was Witte's sug-gestion of eliminating from the Bank's Charter the obligation to exchange bills for gold. Although the Bank had not been able to fulfill this obligation since 1863, the promise symbolized the government's commitment to the re-sumption of the ruble's convertibility, while its disappearance could harm the Bank's financial reputation and suggest that "our government had abandoned any attempts at the restoration of the monetary system." Witte, however, was not interested in symbolism.

Witte's Conversion

The monstrous project of reforming the State Bank was not realized in its original plan. In the fall of 1893, Witte suddenly gave up his original idea of investing the Bank with the right to issue special banknotes, and by the end of that year, he seemed to have abandoned his initial inflationist plans.[61] Not all elements of Witte's program disappeared, however. The new Bank's statute, issued on June 6, 1894, envisioned a monetary regime based on administra-tive centralization, leaving the State Bank under the direct guidance of the minister of finance. In early 1895, Witte went even further in reversing his earlier views and declared a renewal of the government's policy targeting the adoption of the gold standard.

Anatolii Kulomzin attributed the salutary effect of Witte's conver-sion to the "educational" efforts of Nikolai Bunge and to the publication in Russian of J. E. Horn's book *Jean Law: ein finanzgeschichtlicher Versuch* (1858). Ivan Shipov, whom Bunge had recommended for the important po-sition of deputy director of the ministry's Credit Chancellery, translated the book, and Bunge wrote a preface in which he portrayed, without naming them, Witte's plans for the emissions of "productive" money in his anal-ysis of John Law's bubble. Bunge ridiculed Law's idea that the increase of

paper money in circulation could stimulate the production of goods and resources that would serve as collateral for paper currency. Such a policy could
only contribute to the growth of the state; therefore, John Law appeared as
a precursor to Henry George's socialism, while the parallel between Law's
Royal Bank of France and J.-J. Proudhon's *La Banque du Peuple*, which
was supposed to issue bonds at the security of any fruits of labor, hinted
at Antonovich's ideas for State Bank reform. Thus, Bunge suggested that
Witte's plan would not only inflate the financial system but also affect the
nature of the state and its relationship with private capital. Comparing John
Law to socialist ideas was a bit of a stretch, though Witte's policy of state intervention often evoked such allusions. A rebuke to state socialism expressed
earlier, although privately, by Polovtsov was a strong argument against the
inflationist course of reforms. Another argument was the ultimate failure
of Law's colonial projects, which, in Bunge's analysis, called to mind Witte's
Siberian enterprise.[62]

Bunge's edition of Horn's book on Law was in Witte's personal library,[63]
although it is doubtful that a single book could play such a decisive role in
suddenly changing the minister's opinion. Contemporaries, commenting
on Witte's conversion, referred to his intuition, his wit, and his phenomenal political flexibility as well as the impact of the dominant bureaucratic
ethos and his growing experience running imperial finances. Other important factors were the failure of the State Bank's reform, implemented in a
truncated form, and, finally, the death of Alexander III, one of Witte's most
devoted supporters. The disgraced Antonovich resigned from the ministry,
and Witte began to fill staff positions with young technocrats, including Ivan
Shipov.[64] On March 5, 1895, Nicholas II signed an edict in Witte's name on
the "strengthening of the gold-exchange fund," which was increased by 98 million rubles, from 277 to 375 million.[65] At the same time, Witte reanimated
the plan for legalizing transactions in gold, and this fourth attempt (after the
failures of Reutern, Bunge, and Vyshnegradskii) to gain legislative approval
for the measure ended in success.

Witte's conversion from nominalism to monetarism and to the ideology
of the gold standard may have appeared striking and unnatural. It certainly
disheartened his former allies who, like Vladimir Meshcherskii, continued
to believe that Witte had fallen victim to a Freemasons' plot. In a letter to
Witte, Meshcherskii bemoaned the drastic change in the minister's personality, a "spiritual metamorphosis": "Your sincere friends admit with sorrow
that you have become unrecognizable; the sacred flame [in you] is dying
out, you do not listen, you are always busy, . . . you see deceit everywhere."

"There were days when you were interested in the cause of the State Bank as the key to Russia's renaissance, and now what?" Meshcherskii predicted the ultimate political and personal failure of the reform and the minister. Even if he succeeded in passing the gold transition, he would lose in the end. "It will torment you, it will cause you constant anxiety, it will turn into your Achilles' heel, it will be the prison of your spirit, your creativity; it will tear you away from all living questions, it will only bring you closer to the . . . people of gold, banks, Jews and Masons; against your will, it will make you vulnerable to any geopolitical threat; the question of gold will become for you more important than the questions of Russian foreign policy, and the fear of the gold's drain abroad will paralyze your activity and your personality."[66]

Another former ally turned opponent, Serguei Sharapov, also thought that Witte's transition from nationalism to monetarism was indicative of his complete loss of independence. "It is no secret that the gold currency was not S. Yu.[Witte]'s invention; it was palmed off to him in a ready form, as they give musical scores to a singer." Sharapov also confessed the love-hate relationship that "drew" him to Witte: "While loving and cherishing him, I was ready to hate him for wasting those strengths that had been given to him." Witte had made sudden political reversals in areas other than the currency reform: "Look, how he is tossing about! One day he is for the [peasant] commune, another day he is against it; one day [he] is . . . for the *zemstvo*, another day he's against it. One day he expands credit and dreams about doing much good for all Russia with the new State Bank, then he crushes this Bank for the sake of the currency."[67] However, it was perhaps the absence of this "ideological" core that made Sharapov and others hopeful. One day, he and others thought, Witte might flip back, renew the ideas of the State Bank's reform based on the foundation of a nationalist and inflationist economy, and dispel the specter of gold.

Sharapov and Meshcherskii were wrong in interpreting Witte's sudden conversion as a sign of weakness. To the contrary: only a person so confident in his abilities to control authority could admit his past mistakes. Katkov had previously undergone a similar conversion, albeit in the opposite direction, without losing a fraction of his power. Witte, apparently, was somewhat embarrassed by his early ideas and attributed them to bad influences and lack of experience.[68] Rebukes of Witte's past interest in inflationist ideas continued to haunt him for many years, and thus it became important for him to stress the continuity between his policy and that of his predecessors and to present the first two years of his tenure in the minister's office as a short intermission. For instance, he referred to Ivan Vyshnegradskii's "plan of 1887," which had

mapped Russia's transition to the gold standard, and he even mentioned a certain "manuscript in which his [Vyshnegradskii's] ideas on this matter were articulated." "It fell to my lot to realize the plan outlined in 1887,"[69] he declared
at the State Council's meeting. No one knew which manuscript Witte was
alluding to (or whether it existed at all). It is important to stress that Witte
presented the gold standard reform as following a certain script: it alleviated
the burden of his personal responsibility and, most important, allowed him
to present the gold reform as a legacy of Alexander III's reign. This legacy was
especially important in convincing young Nicholas II to believe in Witte's
new theories. It is no coincidence that some opponents of the reform in bureaucratic circles contested this continuity.

What Witte's old and new opponents did not notice was that, despite
his conversion from inflationism to the idea of the gold standard, the core
of Witte's thinking about money and banking remained the same. His concept of the gold standard rested on the principles of the centrality of the
state in the monetary system and the use of money as a tool of imperial expansion. After the gold reform of 1897, the State Bank remained under the
minister's control, while the issuance of gold-based currency depended not
on the demands of the market, but on the discretion of the minister and the
size of the gold reserve. Witte's reversal from paper to gold did not affect his
commitment to pragmatic nationalism and his view on financial stability that
hinged on the authority of the state. At its political core, Witte's vision of stability replicated Nicholas I's official nationality and the ideas of conservative
nationalists who tied the fate of the ruble to the inviolability of monarchal
power and national unification. Stability, in his mind, meant ruling out the
influence of the market and strengthening state control.

The Road to Gold

One more circumstance that had to be considered within the context of
Russia's monetary reform was the mood of the international financial community. In 1893, the decision of the British government to suspend the free
coinage of silver in India dropped the price of silver by 20%, and the value
of silver in the Russian currency fell to 50 gold kopecks, which, paradoxically, was below the value of the credit ruble (66 gold kopecks in 1893).[70] The
Russian currency system, which was still legally tied to silver, lost its pivot.
That year, the Russian government followed other countries in suspending
the free coinage of silver coins; the Mint stopped accepting silver from
producers and prohibited the import of silver.[71] Yet, legally, Russia was still on

the silver standard, and several proponents of silver monometallism suggested that instead of introducing a new gold-based system, Russia just had to revive its silver ruble. In 1895, when the scarcity of money became a major issue, the Russian government, under the conditions of strict secrecy and confidentiality, purchased a load of silver in London worth 3 million pounds and commissioned the French *Monnaie de Paris* to mint silver rubles. Explaining the choice of a foreign mint, Witte mentioned that the St. Petersburg Mint was too busy with the coinage of gold money, but there may have been another reason.[72]

While most Western countries had already tied their currency to gold, the gold standard was not the only option. Despite all odds, in 1894–95, the idea of bimetallism experienced an unexpected revival. After three unsuccessful attempts to reach an international agreement at international conferences (1868, 1878, and 1892), in February 1895, the British parliament considered calling yet another international monetary conference to discuss the fate of silver. The German Reichstag adopted a similar resolution and encouraged the government to consider the effect of silver's fall on the German economy. The bimetallic controversy moved to the center of political debates in the United States, where presidential candidate William Jennings Bryan represented the interests of bimetallists. Perhaps most important, France, one of Russia's main financial allies in Europe, also attempted to shift the Russian government toward bimetallism, that is to say, the stabilization of currency and restoration of convertibility to silver and gold. Although France had de facto switched to the gold standard, it still possessed one of the largest shares of silver currency in Europe, and politicians and economists of different beliefs campaigned for the return to bimetallism.[73] During Nicholas II's visit to Paris in 1896, Jules Méline, who was the prime minister (President du Conseil), approached the tsar with the proposition of considering the bimetallic reform and later submitted a plan or memo via his ambassador in St. Petersburg.[74]

Reports by Arthur Raffalovich, the agent of the Ministry of Finance in France, provided a detailed analysis of the prime minister's proposal.[75] Méline's argument repeated the standard rhetoric of bimetallists: the spread of the gold standard had already reduced the availability of gold by half, and it would eventually lead to scarcity and the exhaustion of its resources, the abasement of the prices of products, and the "upset" of Europe's relationship with the countries of the Far East. The effects of the post–gold-standard crisis would hit Russia, an agrarian country, harder than others, causing "general misery."[76] According to Raffalovich, none of these assertions was true. There was no sign of gold's exhaustion; agricultural prices had fallen because of the enormous development of markets; the construction of railroads, canals, and other means of transportation; and other factors not related to the fall of silver. Méline, who combined his position of prime minister with the post of minister of agriculture, spoke regarding the needs of the rural producers in France, who were interested in the maintenance of silver. However, in Russia, "the state had already taken upon itself significant sacrifices in order to help indebted landowners and alleviate peasants' taxes."[77] Therefore, the Russian government did not share the concerns of agrarian politicians in France. Raffalovich interpreted Méline's efforts to convince Russia to adopt bimetallism as an attempt to create an outlet for silver in Europe and to prevent the further fall of silver prices. After Bryan, "the champion of bimetallism and, at the same time, the ally of revolutionary elements," lost the US presidential election, the policy's chances almost entirely faded, and the transition of Russia, "with its immense territory and 120 million inhabitants," to the gold standard would deliver "another blow to international bimetallism."[78] The number of countries interested the "rehabilitation" of silver was shrinking. France, with its 3 billion francs of the white metal, was, apparently "afraid to serve as a receptacle of the white metal of the world" and wanted other countries to alleviate this burden.[79] Russia did not have to play this role.[80]

Witte probably did not need Raffalovich to explain the dangers of bimetallism to him.[81] For Russia as well as for other latecomers, choosing gold was a choice of geopolitical orientation. Gold came to be associated with the "West" and civilization, silver was the attribute of the Orient, while bimetallism appeared to be an attribute of a bygone era. As Alexander Guryev, an expert and copywriter in Witte's ministry, put it, with the return to silver, "we would have joined China, Japan, Siam, Persia, Mexico, Peru, etc. However, we need to get closer not with these countries but civilized Western European countries that have adopted gold monometallism."[82] The fate of silver was sealed. Not only did it fall out of use not only as a metal of currency but also as a material for jewelry and other goods. "Silver jewelry is a sign of 'mauvais genre': a simple steel chain, or better a black string, or watches made of blue steel are preferred to a silver chain and silver watches. The same is true for other kinds of jewelry: everyone wants gold and nothing can overcome people's passion for it." "It is even difficult to find a silver spoon in a first-rate hotel," wrote Pavel Migulin in 1896. Silver had yielded its place to "melkhior," or nickel-silver alloy, and aluminum. In 1896, in the middle of the debates on the gold reform, art historian Nikodim Kondakov published a government-sponsored volume of *Russian Treasure Troves* that contained the first comprehensive survey of early medieval Russian and Byzantine gold treasures of the eleventh through the thirteenth centuries. An extraordinary scholarly achievement, this edition, lavishly decorated with gold chromolithographic plates, also bore an important political message, showing that early Russia belonged to civilizations of the East and West bound by gold.[83]

7

The Autocratic Standard

ECONOMIC HISTORY, AS a genre, often appears depersonalized. The main characters of its dramas are frequently markets, states, governments, groups of producers, banks, and communities. Yet many key turns in the history of economy have resulted from individual actions—laws betraying the whims of monarchs, reforms enacted by ministers or courtiers, mistakes or frauds committed by unscrupulous investors. Political histories of finance, in contrast, tend to overestimate the role of historical figures, especially when these individuals make claims for their undisputed leadership and the authorship of reforms. Serguei Witte definitely belongs to the latter category. Throughout his bureaucratic and political career, he presented himself as a savior of the Russian ruble and the father of Russian industrialization.[1] The gold reform came to be known as "Witte's reform," while the new gold coins were scornfully called "*Witte-kinder*" and "*Matildore*" (after his wife Matilda). Witte unambiguously called the monetary reform of 1897 his "greatest achievement," attributing to it the transformation of the Russian economy and the beginning of Russian industrialization. In his memos as well as his three-volume memoir, Witte created the picture of a holistic, perfectly elaborated system that extended over all key institutions of economic development, from railroads to banks, with the gold ruble representing a centerpiece of this system. Historians have invested much effort untangling the net of facts, lies, speculations, fairytales, and testimonies that originated from Witte's writings as well as the critique of his reforms.[2]

In contrast to Witte's triumphal version of the reform, his "system" was plagued with contradictions. The ostensibly pro-bourgeois financial policy accompanied gross violations of the interests of the bourgeoisie that repaid him with indifference or direct resistance. Declarations of the importance of private entrepreneurship bluntly contrasted with his open distrust of private initiatives. And his version of nationalism allowed for energetic encourage-ment of foreign investments.[3] Witte argued for the importance of institutions and believed in technocratic professionalism, yet he hired relatives and friends for key positions at the Ministry of Finance and operated the entire monetary system of the empire as a private business.[4] Contemporaries and historians have long been mesmerized by his "greatness" and his unmatched intellect, yet Witte's weaknesses as a politician and a bureaucrat were far too apparent, and his shocking ignorance in economic matters were noted.[5] Witte's gold reform perfectly encapsulated the contradictory nature of his policy. Most scholars admit that the reform was necessary and timely in launching Russia into the era of industrialization, but it was also one of the most unpopular reforms in modern history, pushed through amid general discontent and producing widespread resistance. However, the reasons for this discontent, apart from "public ignorance," "inertia," and anxiety over the high costs of the reform, remained unclear.

Generating a narrative of his heroic fight for the ruble constituted an essen-tial part of Witte's political strategy. This chapter shows that the preparation for the gold reform started with Witte's regular meetings and almost daily exchange of letters with Alexei Suvorin, the editor of the *New Time* (*Novoe Vremia*), in his persistent attempts to create positive coverage in the media. Witte's stories about his fight against reactionaries and retrogrades con-cealed his attempts to silence opposition, as well as downplay the maneuvers and political intrigues that led to the adoption of the gold standard. While Witte's official memos and reports written by a staff of well-trained officials and hired academics create an impression of an urgent, salutary, perfectly rea-soned, and progressive measure, the reality was drastically different. Long analytical memos and reports resulted in a handful of laws that were brief, vague, technical, and open to interpretation by the minister and the tsar. Therefore, what often appears to be a contradiction between a reform that served "as a vehicle . . . for the Europeanization of Russia" and its implementa-tion that demonstrated "the most un-European assertion of autocracy" can be explained as a discrepancy between the rhetoric and the methods rather than allegedly progressive content and an undue form.[6]

This chapter tells the story of how the reform was carried through—from Witte's attempts to control the press to his manipulation of the leg-islative process. In many ways these techniques resemble the "bear squeeze" that Witte used against German speculators in 1894. Certainly, Witte's re-form was not the first or the only instance of a transition to gold that was pushed through in a politically dubious way. In France, the 1873 reform originated from the miscalculations of policymakers who overlooked and misrepresented the consequences of the suspension of silver coinage.[7] In the United States, the demonetarization of silver was snuck into Congress and almost passed through unnoticed in the Coinage Act of 1873 until the consequences of this bill—the designation of gold as sole legal tender, with the subsequent change in the price of silver—became obvious.[8] The transition to gold often appeared as a conspiracy among financial groups and politicians. But the Russian case stands out. Like the silver standard reform of 1839–43, the reform of 1897 was made on behalf of and in the interests of the autocratic state, the tsar, and its minister and against the will of the majority of the elites. The autocratic standard that resulted was a model unseen anywhere else in the world.

Devaluation or Normalization?

In the 1890s, the idea of gold was in the air, but nobody understood what the gold standard meant in practice. Would gold rubles simply replace paper? How could this be carried out? In February 1895, Witte secured approval from the Committee of Finance to transfer 116 million gold rubles, equivalent to 173 million credit rubles, from the State Treasury to the State Bank's reserve fund. This seemingly innocent move produced an unexpected reaction. In March 1895, the *Berliner Börsen-Zeitung*, reacting to the news of the gold reserve's increase, predicted that the ministry would introduce the gold standard by fixing the existing rate of 1 gold ruble = 0.67 credit ruble. In Russia, the influential *New Time* promptly reprinted this news and noted that the impending "devaluation" [*deval'vatsiia*] would lead to "horrible upheavals in all our financial and economic affairs."[9] The article's title, "67 Kopecks instead of 100," seemed like a threat of losses and impoverishment, as if the government, by introducing the gold standard, was going to rob everyone of 33 kopecks from each ruble. The article caused a sensation. Much of Witte's efforts in the months leading up to the reform were dedicated to undoing the harm caused by critical publications in the press and trying to form a favorable public opinion about the gold standard.

Newspapers and their editors were the key figures in Russia's political establishment outside the imperial court and bureaucracy, and taming the press was at the top of Witte's agenda. In pushing forward the reform, he faced opposition from the *New Time*, an immensely popular and commercially successful newspaper; it was led by of one of the stars of Russia's press, Alexei Suvorin, a provocative editor and a moderate conservative whom many,

including Witte, considered to be Katkov's successor. Witte had started his
political career writing articles for Katkov's *Moscow Bulletin* and witnessed
Bunge's downfall under the pressure of the conservative press, so he spared
no effort cultivating a relationship with the press and attempting to control
public opinion. As the vast unpublished correspondence between Witte and
Suvorin suggests, their relationship was mutually beneficial, although the two
men did not like or trust one other. Suvorin frequented the minister's residence, where he could obtain confidential information and news, whereas
Witte valued and used Suvorin's talent and influence.[10] It may have surprised
the minister when the *New Time* suddenly pounced on Witte's reforms
in 1895. The word "devaluation" that appeared in Suvorin's commentary
launched an unpleasant debate over the ruble's future. "The curious word *devaluation* appeared before the public as an ominous specter," recalled economist Vasilii Lebedev. Very few people understood the meaning of the term.
Did it come from Latin *valva* (door)? "Then *devalvatio* would mean taking
doors off their hinges," Lebedev surmised with sarcasm. The word did not
exist in French, and only German *Devaluation* and *Devaluierung* offered an
equivalent. Devaluation, thus, meant "fixing the value of paper money against
the value of a precious metal on the level to which it had fallen."[11]

"Devaluation" seems to have been a topic of conversations between Witte
and Suvorin for some time, as Witte mocked Suvorin's preoccupation with
it. Inviting Suvorin to stop by and chat about "more interesting matters
than the *devaluation*," he noted that "one gentleman understood this word
as my (Witte's) request to dismiss General Val' [Wahl]," the head of the St.
Petersburg city administration and police (in Russian, devaluation is read as
de-val'vatsiia).[12] Suvorin's attack, however, was no joke. To neutralize its effect, Witte asked the journalist for a chance to respond to the frightening article about "67 kopecks" with a letter explaining the essence of the impending
transformation.

The "letter to the editor," entitled "Gold or Silver?" and signed with a letter
"V" [Vitte], reminded readers that Russia remained on the silver standard
but that the value of the silver ruble, against which the credit ruble had to
be measured, had fallen below the value of paper money. Therefore, measuring the ruble's value in gold could not legally be considered a devaluation.
Summarizing the future reform, he explained that the paper ruble would remain the same, while the gold ruble would be debased by one third.[13] Suvorin
published a note alongside Witte's letter in which he disagreed with this
opinion and requested that the plan for the future reform be made openly.
"Such a first-rate state issue as the introduction of a new monetary unit

cannot be carried out without an all-round discussion from different points of view—state, public and private; this is a common cause for all ministries and all [groups of] interests."[14] Two days later Suvorin expressed his own opinion in an editorial that criticized the minister for keeping such a major transformation secret. Unlike other financial issues, "devaluation is a state matter" that needed to be discussed with the entire country, interests big and small."[15] After the publication, Witte rushed to calm the editor down. "We are not talking about devaluation at all. Frankly, I don't even understand what you mean by devaluation," he wrote in a private note sent to Suvorin the same day. Witte's goal, however, was not to convert Suvorin but to offer him a different vocabulary for future publications. The right word was "the *normalization* of monetary circulation."[16]

The range of acceptable terms also included "stabilization" and "fixing the rate." Apparently, similar instructions were given to other newspapers, a few of which did try to convince their readers that the legalization of gold was an innocent step that did not mean devaluation.[17] Suvorin did not comply. Devaluation mattered because it meant that the state refused to fulfill its financial obligations. "Devaluation begins when the government refuses to accept credit rubles at the same price as silver rubles and gold rubles ... or when it accepts metal currency instead of credit rubles at a higher, compared to its nominal value, rate." Therefore, the legalization of transactions and state payments in gold at an existing rate seemed to be the beginning of an open process of devaluation. In all his editorial "letters," Suvorin adopted the role of the "majority"—people unfamiliar with financial theory but affected by financial decisions and reforms. The main leitmotifs of his publication were openness and the request for public discussion. Comparing the significance of the monetary reform to the peasant reform of 1861, he emphasized: "The emancipation of the peasants directly affected only a part of peasantry and the estate owners. The circulation of gold and devaluation ... directly affects all Russian subjects, without exception."[18]

Suvorin offered his newspaper as a forum for people of different opinions to speak freely, or at least so he claimed. In March and April 1895, a steady flow of articles on devaluation and the legalization of gold appeared almost daily. In addition to some, apparently genuine, "letters to the editor" from a "retired professor" who suggested the introduction of a new monetary unit or from Russia's most devoted defender of bimetallism, Lev Raffalovich,[19] Suvorin published articles offered to him by Witte, such as one by Adolph Rothstein, director of the St. Petersburg International Commercial Bank and Witte's key adviser in monetary questions.[20] Stirring the public, Suvorin almost succeeded in preventing the State Council's approval of the law on the legalization of transactions in gold.[21] When the State Council nonetheless approved the law, Suvorin congratulated the minister, albeit with some sarcasm: "I wish devaluation were the dismissal of General Wahl, and the constitution the invitation of the Grand Duke Constantine to sit at the Committee of Finance. . . . But it has been a pleasure to be your honest enemy, whom you did not take hostage, as it has been a pleasure to be your honest ally in other questions."[22]

Dignity Games

The legalization of transactions in gold at an actual rate was a preparatory measure for the reform that aimed to make the gold ruble a legal tender and transform the rules of issuing money. Witte tried to keep the details of the reform secret, yet he had to obtain the State Council's approval and the tsar's consent to move forward. No one in the government was familiar with Witte's project that he planned to summarize in a speech at the State Council's session. Trying to conceal the particulars of the reform, the minister asked Suvorin to refrain from writing about the monetary reform until after the speech's publication.[23] They seemed to have struck a deal: Suvorin waited to receive Witte's speech and be the first to publicize it, and the *New Time* kept silent on financial issues."[24]

The State Council speech proved a rhetorical bombshell that began with a scorching critique of the Russian monetary system. "Paper notes that circulate here instead of money represent a constant reminder of the powerlessness of the state treasury," and they "work . . . only by virtue of coercion, or the government power expressed in them, as if this power were coined into money and put in circulation, even though this contradicts its nature and demeans its dignity." The minister even refrained from calling the state credit rubles "money," describing them as the "sad" legacy of Russia's past misfortunes and poverty. The emphasis on dignity was supposed to highlight the widening gap between Russia's rising economic power and the poor state of its monetary system. Responding to the "loud defense" of the "impaired" money by a "small group of people" who explained the Russian people's attachment to credit bills as patriotism, Witte called the reference to popular trust and patriotic feelings "absurd" and "inappropriate." Patriotism could not conceal the true scale of losses the population suffered from bad finances, nor could it ensure the independence of domestic prices from external valuation of the national currency. Moreover, the abuse of patriotism could be politically dangerous.

"The majority of our population with all humility endure all blows that fall on them, because, thank God, they have not yet learned how to blame and criticize the government." This last sentence suggests that this "humility" was not equal to patriotism and that with no notice, people's patience could be exhausted.[25] The speech presented the need for monetary reform to protect the regime's stability.

Witte's speech concluded with a very brief overview of the principles of the coming reform. Carefully avoiding the word "devaluation," the minister suggested that the reform was supposed to fix the credit ruble's rate at the existing level and avoid any changes in the appearance of the existing paper currency. Instead, all changes would involve only the gold coins, which "the majority of the population is not familiar with." That is to say, the credit ruble remained the same, while the gold coins would be replaced with new debased 10-ruble coins. The reform was to be conducted in such a way that nobody would notice it: all prices, wages, costs, and estimates that had been tradition-ally expressed in credit rubles would stay the same. It looked as if the paper ruble had never changed its worth while the gold ruble had, but this did not really matter as very few people used gold coins. Witte's devaluation differed from Kankrin's direct devaluation of assignats in 1839 because it was masked by the debasement of coins.

The speech may have made a very strong impression on the members of the State Council, especially since the lofty rhetoric made the defense of the status quo seem treacherous. However, nobody outside the State Council knew about the reform plan for months. The dam of silence burst on March 15, 1896, when Suvorin's the *New Time* published an article that articulated and explained the plan of the monetary reform. Written by Witte's associate Alexander Guryev, the piece stated that the ministry had designed the reform in such a way that its impact on day-to-day commercial, credit, and other ec-onomic relations was supposed to be barely noticeable. The most important innovation was the opening of the exchange, meaning that everyone could bring paper credit bills and exchange them for gold without restrictions and delays. The new rules for issuing paper rubles stipulated that the State Bank would no longer print money at the treasury's request, and half the amount of the credit bills' worth had to be backed by the gold reserve, which in 1896 constituted 750 million rubles in gold. If the amount of credit bills exceeded 1 billion rubles, all excess bills were to be backed by gold at a 1:1 ratio. Almost nothing was said about the institutional arrangement of the reform. The contradictions between meaning and scale of the reform and its legal and po-litical arrangements were glaring.

The reform announcement relieved the "torturing nervousness" and put an end to "rumors and guessing, fears and anxiety."[26] The day after the publication of the *New Time* article, the big hall of the Free Economic Society's building on Zabalkanskii Avenue in St. Petersburg was overcrowded. The society held public lectures and meetings every month, but for this event on monetary reform, the mansion could not accommodate the audience—generals and officers, senators, professors, retired bureaucrats, bankers, students (male and female) and, of course, journalists.[27] Transcripts of the speeches and discussions there appeared in all major newspapers, along with numerous op-eds, comments, and satirical pieces. According to the *Stock Exchange Bulletin*, "The issue of monetary reform saturates the air of the capital city. People talk about it everywhere, in learned societies and private gatherings; everyone is preoccupied with it, even ladies."[28] The Ministry of Finance tried to lead and monitor the public campaign, but the debate soon slipped out of its control.

As Witte himself admitted, "All of thinking Russia was against the reform."[29] The reform did not look the way many had anticipated, but everyone had a different vision of the ideal plan. It appeared formidable and too simple at once. Guryev's series of articles in the *New Time*, strengthened this impression. Guryev stressed that the reform was an "enormous cultural and historical step that also has political meaning." Culturally, it represented Russia's chance to "join the world culture, which is impossible without joining the world monetary economy." "Modern culture is being spread not by the ideational searches of crusaders and missionaries but by people's economic interests."[30] Guryev's emphasis on money as a means of "cultural communication" echoed the idea both of a common international language (Volapuk and Esperanto) that had become popular in Russia during that period and of adopting the Gregorian calendar, because Russia, due to its adherence to the Julian calendar, was always twelve days "behind" Europe. In Guryev's words, Russia's financial powerlessness was "spelled out" on each of its inconvertible credit rubles in a language common to everyone, a modern financial "Volapuk." This was a national disgrace that put the country behind many less developed and less geopolitically significant states.

The rhetoric of backwardness and *ressentiment* in relation to money was used to support different, even contradictory, views. If in Guryev's (and Witte's) representation, it was a disgrace that Russia, because of its paper standard, had to behave like a "goodie-goodie" and listen to the condescending praise of foreigners in order to get loans, nationalists thought that it was a disgrace to adopt the Western rules of the game. In yet another dimension of the

debate over honor and dishonor, the ministry's claims of financial stability
and well-being did not align with the main principle of the reform, namely,
the devaluation of the ruble. Fixing the existing paper-gold ratio at 1:1.5 was
not the only possible way to the gold standard; there was also the option of
resuming the exchange for gold at parity, as was attempted, albeit unsuccessfully, in 1862–63. The critics of Witte's hidden devaluation wondered why the
government, boasting of its gold reserve, did not want to restore the ruble's
full value. In the debate over devaluation, issues of poverty, dignity, and justice once again came to the forefront.

As in the 1830s and early 1860s, the state was suddenly represented
as having the social attributes of a person, such as honor and reputation.
"Devaluations, whether direct or indirect [i.e., the debasement of the gold
ruble], are, in essence, what the merchants call 'breaking the ruble' [i.e., bank-
ruptcy]. People resort to it only in a state of complete financial ruin, not
during financial and economic successes,"[31] wrote one of the reform's critics.
The comparison between devaluation and the bankruptcy of merchants was,
apparently, widespread: "Any devaluation is a hidden theft. A merchant who
pays his creditors half of his debts, even if his own reputation remains un-
tarnished, is considered bankrupt."[32] The dignity argument turned out to be
quite efficient and widespread, and the government could not ignore it. One
of Witte's political enemies, Ilya Cyon (Tsion), wrote about devaluation as
"fraudulent bankruptcy" because "nothing had made it inevitable," and, of
course, he also referred to the merchants' code of honor.[33]

The defenders of the reform responded by referring to economic rationality and common sense. In Russia, "nobody believes in the inscription on
the credit bills" that promised gold for paper notes.[34] In other words, lofty
words made no sense because the ruble had been inconvertible for so many
years that a new generation had grown up without any memory of its convertibility; if no one is dispossessed or deceived, then there is no disgrace.
Alexander Guryev, using the *New Time* to deliver the ministry's point of view,
protested against the very use of the concepts of dignity, honor, and injustice.
"Neither does the fixation [of the existing rate] give any 'honor' to the government, nor the devaluation cause any 'dishonor.' The government's 'honor'
consists merely in acting in accordance with the demands of the public good.
The 'honor' of a trader, a merchant or a rentier, and the 'honor' of state authority are the category of different dimensions." In fact, the government
could find the extra 300 million rubles needed to conduct the exchange at
parity, but it would turn into a "disaster for people." "To earn the 'merchant
honor' is easy, but we do not want it, because it would be a great dishonor for

the government and would lead to people's ruin. This is why it is laughable for us to hear these passionate speeches about 'Russia's honor that costs more than 300 million rubles.'"[35]

Arguments against devaluation varied, and the reform was criticized from both the left and the right. Ironically, nationalists found a new reason to attack the gold standard and the resumption of exchange. Having previously rejected the meaning of gold altogether, they advanced a new vision of a gold reserve of 750 million rubles as a national treasure, the apple of the nation's eye, which could not be squandered in exchange operations and had to be preserved for future generations.[36] This meant that paper money had to exist independently of the gold fund; otherwise, as soon as the State Bank opened its exchange office, the gold would fall into the hands of speculators and foreigners and flow away.[37] The gold standard was portrayed as an insidious invention of foreigners trying to swindle "our gold from us as soon as it is released.[38] "How on Earth! *Our* gold fund, which has cost us such enormous sacrifices! The fund that has already rendered us truly great service at the moment of complications in the East, the true guard of our freedom of actions, the menace to enemies, the trusted friend in misfortune," exclaimed a certain representative of "provincial Russia."[39] Sergei Sharapov formulated this idea in an even more straightforward way: "The resumption of exchange threatens to empty our gold reserve, which . . . protects Russia in case of war; in other words, this is an indirect encroachment upon Russia's political sovereignty."[40]

The argument that Russia would not be able to "keep" its gold domestically, would lose the reserve, and would end up suspending the exchange was very widespread. The reform's defenders deployed the eloquence of theory and statistics to prove that gold cannot "flow abroad," draining the fund after the opening of the exchange operation. Instead, they claimed that gold was supposed to flow back and forth, and that the national central banks used discount policy to attract gold if they needed to replenish their resources. Guryev tried to inculcate the idea that there could be no "English, French, Russian gold but only the gold of the entire family of civilized nations."[41] Speaking at the Free Economic Society meeting, Guryev protested against the very principle of the dramatic "personification" of money in Russian discourse: "We often hear the expressions 'securities go away,' 'the gold is being taken,' 'the ruble falls,' etc., but nothing like that exists in reality, and everything is based on economic factors: if people see profit, they do something, and if they don't see it, they don't do it."[42] Money as an abstract thing has no nationality or social class, no feelings, no honor or dignity.

The Russian public, however, proved more resistant to the idea of de-nationalized socially neutral money. Sergei Sharapov even proposed the creation of two currencies, one for domestic purposes (the paper ruble) and the other a gold-based currency for international operations, which should not bear the same name.[43] Money was also strongly associated with classes, estates, and occupations: the paper ruble was perceived as the property of the agrarian class and peasants, while gold was associated with the bourse and financiers. The imposition of gold coins made the impression of an "aristocratic" reform: peasants would most likely avoid using gold, other than to save it in clay jars.[44] Conversations about the future reform often evoked the old clichés about muzhik, his love for the tsar's "blue ticket," and the superstitious fear of the reform allegedly prompted by the exchange rate of 1:1.5 (meaning that 1,000 gold kopecks cost 666 kopecks)[45] The ministry, however, was not going to give up and yield to the old habits of the people. As we will see, after the enactment of the reform, the government strengthened its policy of obtruding gold coins and withdrawing paper bills of small denominations.

The Gold, the Bank, and the Constitution

Witte's reform project entrusted the State Bank with the main function of issuing state paper money. In 1894, the Bank underwent a reorganization along the principles designed by Antonovich in the period of Witte's flirtation with inflationist ideas, and the monetary reform did not assume any new reorganization of the Bank's structure and functions. Therefore, there was an inherent tension between the institutional arrangement of the issuance of money and the ideology of the reform. In a legislative proposal submitted to the State Council but not shared with the press, Witte emphasized the difference between the status of existing credit rubles issued by the State Bank for the State Treasury and the new status of credit rubles as banknotes issued "exclusively for the needs of the Bank as [a] credit institution, that is, for commercial operations." Liberal economic theory suggested that the main quality of banknotes consisted of the strong dependence between the number of banknotes emitted by the bank and the commercial demand for money. Therefore, the gold reserve was meant to play an auxiliary role, while the main anchor of the emission operation was supposed to be of bills of exchange and short-term securities.

If Witte had intended to follow this principle, he would have had to reconsider the entire organization of the State Bank. Instead of expanding short-term credit operations that could back up credit rubles, the new bank statute of 1894 provided possibilities for long-term credit at the security of all kinds of illiquid and hard-to-sell assets, including grain in elevators and agricultural machines.[46] Given the predominantly agrarian focus of the State Bank's activity, the new Russian ruble very much resembled the notorious "bread ruble" of the conservative press. In recognition of this fact, Witte admitted at the Committee of Finance meeting that "credit bills will be backed exclusively by gold rather than the bill holding,"[47] and the declared goal of aligning the emission of paper money to the Bank's commercial activity was abandoned. Although Witte imagined the future Bank as a mechanism balancing commercial demand and the supply of money, due to the specifics of its credit policy and organization, the Bank was unable to play this role. Some economists even denied the post-reform credit rubles the status of banknotes, calling them "gold certificates" or "treasury notes," since the reform failed to provide the link between the credit economy and currency.[48]

While designing the reform, Witte's academic advisers often referred to the Robert Peel Bank Act of 1844 in England as an example of an emission system that had proven its stability. The act required 100% coverage by gold of paper banknotes and resulted from an academic and political standoff between the supporters of two doctrines, one emphasizing the primacy of the metallic reserve (currency school) and the other giving preference to the bills of exchange (the banking principle). The deficiency of a system based entirely on the metallic reserve became obvious by the late nineteenth century. The law immobilized a significant amount of metallic currency while not allowing for the flexibility of the currency system. Every time there was an economic need to change the ratio, the government had to suspend the law.[49] Germany, which followed Robert Peel's law in establishing a legal ratio, complemented it with a "self-acting" mechanism that allowed for automatic regulations of the quantity of money without the government's intrusion; banknotes issued above the established limit were subjected to a special tax.[50] In France, there was no law that fixed the gold to paper ratio; the system was deemed legal as long as banknotes remained convertible. In Russia, adherence to the gold standard was strongly associated with financial discipline, and therefore the Robert Peel Act, which had also resulted from a fear of paper money, was seen as a good model for imitation, restraining the issuance of uncovered paper notes and providing order. However, in England the economic downsides of the law, such as the immobilization of gold, were compensated for by an enormous development of cash-free payments through clearing houses. In Russia, the amount of cash-free payments was negligible, making the system entirely dependent on the gold reserve.

There was yet another aspect of the State Bank's organization that affected the spirit and the goals of the gold standard reform. Both Antonovich's and Witte's initial concept of the State Bank reform rested on the idea of centralization and the Bank's embeddedness in the state bureaucratic system. The reform strengthened the Bank's dependence on the minister of finance in all spheres of its activity, and if Witte perhaps regretted yielding to Antonovich's views on the Bank's credit policy, he remained convinced of the necessity of keeping the State Bank under the umbrella of the Ministry of Finance and preserving the government's monopoly on printing or minting money. Thus, one of the central ideas of the gold standard, namely, the independence of the banks of issue and the government's withdrawal from the day-to-day involvement in the process of making money, was not implemented in Russia. The institutional and political novelty of the new system was reduced to a declaration that the State Bank would not print money at the treasury's demand. This came as a surprise to many experts, who attributed the failure to take this step to a lack of government commitment to the rules of issuing money.[51] "We all know what the State Bank is: it is just another department of the Ministry of Finance," said Alexander Zalshupin at a Free Economic Society meeting. The credit and monetary systems of all countries rested on trust, "but here, in Russia, there can be no trust while the State Bank remains the left pocket of the State Treasury."[52] An economics professor of St. Petersburg University, Vasilii Yarotskii, remarked that the nature of money indeed remained the same: the credit bills were still going to be "state" credit notes, not banknotes, because "the entire business is still going to be in the hands of the Ministry of Finance, to which the Bank serves as an auxiliary institution, a department of some sort."[53]

The history of Russian monetary policy offered very little hope that the government would stick to its promise not to overprint. Perhaps the most obvious proof that the volatility of Russia's monetary policy had to be contained by legal norms was Witte's own past commitments to nationalism and inflationist ideologies. At one of the Free Economic Society's sessions, Serguei Sharapov read aloud Witte's unpublished article written for Ivan Aksakov's ultra-Slavophile newspaper *Rus'* at the time of Witte's obsession with inflationism. Nationalists cited Witte's words as proof of the transient character of the current fashion for Western monetary theories.[54] Petr Struve tried to present Witte's conversion in a different light, namely, the manifestation of the "dialectic of economic development,"[55] but the fear of the possibility of yet another turn from "ultra-Westernism" to "dead Slavophilism," as Struve characterized these trends, loomed large. The system of monetary emission and control was designed to entirely concentrate power in the minister's hands. Economist and journalist Dmitrii Pikhno from Kyiv, one of the very few university professors to publicly support Witte's project, privately wrote to Witte to criticize the institutional regulation of the emission operation, which seemed the "weakest" element of the projected monetary system: "Of course, you, personally, having made energetic efforts toward the restoration of the metallic system, will not want to kill your own child, even under more or less strained financial circumstances. But will the next minister, for whom the well-ordered monetary circulation may represent a temptation to use this resource, hold the same view? . . . Everything in the past speaks for the seriousness of these concerns."[56]

The preservation of the government's leading role in the monetary economy was not an oversight or a legacy of the previous era. Witte intentionally designed the reform to allow the minister of finance to control the issuance of money. While his belief in inflationism waned, his thinking about the centrality of administration in economy strengthened. Responding to the popular idea of transforming the State Bank into a joint-stock company, Guryev juxtaposed the greedy interests of a private company to an all-encompassing, unbiased vision of the state: "The state, an eternal institution, can and must have in mind the future, and sometimes sacrifice the present for the sake of the future."[57] The state stands above classes and the narrow interests of parties, and its power should not be restricted in favor of a certain company or group of people. The independence of central banks was a fiction, a liberal illusion: "Be it a privileged [private] bank or a state bank—it will do what the government wants it to do. And the government wants what the circumstances require. In this sense, it is absolutely irrelevant what kind of government it is." This last remark referred to widespread concerns that a stable monetary system cannot exist in a monarchal state. Guryev particularly stressed the fallacy of this idea because it explained "the pessimistic view of the future of our gold standard."[58] Be it a republic or a monarchy, the government must have supreme authority over the production of money.

One slip of a pen, however, revealed the inconsistency of Guryev's claim. Arguing against the "separation of powers" as the means to "protect the interests of monetary economy from the encroachment by the State Treasury," Guryev noted that none of Witte's predecessors had deliberately abused the printing press: "Did the declarations of wars depend on the Ministry of Finance?" "There is no doubt that if the opinion of a minister of finance had been strong enough, . . . we would not have become involved in any war, except for the Patriotic War [of 1812]."[59] By asking (and answering) this question, Guryev, perhaps inadvertently, pointed to the real source of Russian monetary disorders: autocracy. In an autocratic state, unlike in constitutional regimes with prime ministers and parliaments, no one can stand between the monarch and his minister, so it is the tsar who has the last word.

Guryev's rather unsuccessful attempts to downplay the political meaning of the reform reflected widespread anxiety and doubts about the autocratic government's ability to maintain the standard. Witte's model of a bureaucratic gold standard, with the State Bank placed under the minister's sole control, defied the underlying political aspect of this monetary system. In the public imagination, the gold standard was still associated with constitutionalism, because a free bank was perceived as the financial prototype of a parliament. It was widely believed that the gold standard could only remain stable if it was supported by political institutions independent of the government. Suvorin, sensitive to the public mood, alerted Witte of this popular link that tied the ruble's fate to the constitution. In his interpretation, public conversations conveyed doubts about the ability of autocracy to maintain the new standard:

> People are mostly worried that the rate of the new ruble will not stay for long and that there can be no complete trust in us in Europe because we are not a constitutional state. . . . They also say that the metallic standard opens the gates to the constitution. It is not Kankrin's time anymore; now everyone has an opinion, and all are more or less discontent. Because the autocratic government in the past 50 years had to resort to two devaluations, it has proven its inability to govern. Therefore, any minor fluctuation of the new ruble's rate is bound to provoke disorders.[60]

Witte was certainly aware of the potential effect of the reform's failure or success on the image of autocracy. Therefore, unlike Mikhail Reutern, who in 1862 had talked Alexander II into announcing the resumption of exchange in a Manifesto that was followed a few months later by the announcement of its suspension, Witte suggested launching a reform by a tsar's edict, a form appropriate for laws of low significance. "By its subject, this law belongs to the sphere of routine legislative activity and does not offer enough reason to declare it from the eminence of the throne to the country and people in a form of a manifesto."[61] Witte consciously aimed to minimize the political meaning of the transition to gold and the resumption of exchange. Besides, the entire reform was supposed to be expressed in one short edict; the rest, apparently, could be regulated by a series of administrative acts. This model went against the tradition that tied the fate of the ruble to the prestige of the monarchy. "You want to downplay the importance of the reform. But is it desirable? . . . . The project of a monarchal edict has a somewhat technical character and will hardly be understandable to the mass public," wrote Dmitrii Pikhno to Witte. This was perhaps exactly what Witte wanted: to make the reform invisible.[62]

Instead, Witte's manipulations had the opposite effect: everyone noticed the contradiction between the lofty rhetoric of Russia's Westernization and modernization, on the one hand, and the attempts to de-politicize the issue of money, on the other. In an article in the *New Time* announcing the reform on March 15, 1896, Guryev, writing on behalf of the ministry, bluntly declared that the reform "did not entail the question of a constitution," and yet he described it as a major move toward the West.[63] However, this kind of monarchical Westernization—Peter the Great's type of reform—did not already seem possible in fin-de-siècle Russia. Even the journalists and experts on Witte's payroll could not always maintain the prescribed de-politicized line of arguments. Among the speakers recruited to defend the gold standard in the Free Economic Society, Vasilii Kasperov portrayed the reform as a "liberating step" and emphasized that, in the countries on the paper standard, governments regulate the flows of money and its amount and value. Under the gold standard system, nothing stands between the market and the individual, who can coordinate his or her economic activity with global economic processes. Therefore, as Kasperov observed, "The people can tell their government: take on the foreign policy and administration, issue laws, collect taxes, but give us the possibility to calculate our economic resources." "The metallic standard, the invariability of the measure of value, is one of the . . . foundations of the economic freedom of the people, one of the civil rights."[64]

Witte's conservative opponents also relied heavily on the argument of the gold standard's incompatibility with the existing political order. Most famously, Serguei Sharapov, in his book *The Paper Ruble* (1895), introduced the concept of "absolute currency," which suggested that a measure of value should not be adjusted to a certain material unit, that is, gold. The idea of abstract, or absolute, money rested on the old conservative explanatory model: the "inherent value, the purchasing capacity of the paper ruble is based on the moral principle of popular trust to the one, strong and free autocratic power that holds in its hands the governance of the monetary system."[65] "Morality," the "love and trust" that held together Russia's finances, was juxtaposed to Western models, in which the bigwigs of the bourses wrested the power of money-making from the government and passed it to the joint-stock bank.

Thus, in the conservative critique, the gold standard continued to be associated with constitutionalism.

The gold ruble debates revealed a broad spectrum of opinions, ranging from the defense of the gold standard as civil right and the symbol of popular sovereignty to the idea of the inconvertible ruble as a pillar of autocracy. There was widespread discontent with Witte's attempt to restrain public debates and reduce the reform to technicalities. While demanding public discussion of the ruble issue, Suvorin emphasized that this did not necessarily mean the parliamentarization of the debate. However, the ghost of parliamentarism was present. The meetings and debates at the Free Economic Society resembled "a parliament, although without the representation of interests but with the representation of . . . trends."[66]

This last remark highlighted another unique feature of Russia's transition to gold. If in European countries the adoption of the gold standard followed after long parliamentary debates, in Russia, the discussion was limited to the sphere of academic societies and newspapers. In the 1890s, the debate between the proponents of gold monometallism and bimetallism continued in Europe and in the United States: in 1894, an international congress of bimetallists took place in London, while national organizations, such as the Bimetallic League in England (1892) or the Deutscher Verein für internationale Doppelwährung, propagated the ideas of bimetallism at home and abroad.[67] Nothing similar existed in Russia. Petr Struve was surprised that there was "no bimetallic or pro-silver movement among our landowning class."[68] (In response to Suvorin's lamentation that nobody had asked the nobility, someone retorted that out of ten very educated noblemen, not one could support a conversation about currency.)[69] The political immaturity of the Russian landowning nobility, which did not protest against the reform, was striking because in other countries, such as Austria and the United States, agrarian opposition to the gold standard represented perhaps its most serious obstacle. The few authors writing on behalf of the landed nobility argued that the reform would ruin Russian export agriculture, but the ministry promptly responded to these concerns with statistics showing that the exporters' gains from the weak ruble had been greatly overestimated.[70] Neither industrialists nor the representatives of the stock exchange committees, who in the late 1880s had protested against the legalization of gold, managed to mobilize themselves in the few months between the announcement of the reform and its enactment and speak out about the gold standard. As Hofschtetter remarked, the reform "caught us off guard. Society revealed itself to be unprepared for the difficulties of this complex question and did not know how to approach the reform."[71] The cacophony of theories and contradictory opinions left everyone confused and unsure what exactly to expect from the reform.

The only organized resistance to the reform came from the professors of financial law at St. Petersburg University: Leonid Khodskii, who was also the chairman of the third department of the Free Economic Society; Vasilii Lebedev; Vasilii Yarotskii; Andrei Isaev; and a few others. The works of these economists exemplified a rising trend in the field that gradually subsumed the dominance of liberal economics and has subsequently been characterized as "populist" and "antimonopolist." A few of these economists participated in politics and were prosecuted by the tsarist police, and although the degree of their leftist radicalism differed, they shared an interest in the social and moral issues of contemporary capitalism and in the development of rural industry and the agrarian economy.[72] Unlike American "antimonopolist" political groups, Russian populist economists did not consider bimetallism an option. Khodskii admitted that the "ever-fluctuating paper currency" exacerbated the burden of growing state dues and military expenses on peasant households.[73] In principle, he approved of the idea of currency reform and adherence to the gold standard.[74] However, Witte's reform neglected the needs of the rural economy. Speaking of the reform, Khodskii, like many other critics, wondered why, if the government had managed to collect such a mass of gold, it continued raising taxes and did not use the funds to improve public education and raise peasant literacy. The government of a wealthy country had to put the interests of the population above its geopolitical interests and financial prestige.

Khodskii's speech at the Free Economic Society meeting launched a discussion about whether a country transitioning to the gold standard had to first meet certain standards of economic well-being or whether the reform itself was a means to improve the economy. Khodskii's view was rather pessimistic: Russia's deficit-free budgets of the 1890s spoke to the success of financial administrations rather than to economic growth. Russia remained too poor for the gold reform. The "poverty" argument could not be dismissed. Vasilii Kasperov, representing the Ministry of Finance, responded by claiming that, without the reform, an economic rise would not happen.[75] In a similar vein, the *Stock Exchange Bulletin* invoked a popular parallel between the gold ruble reform and the emancipation of peasants: it would have been useless to cultivate civic consciousness among serfs before abolishing serfdom, and it would be foolish to try to raise the economy without removing the main obstacle for its development.[76] Thus, the discussion of the gold standard revived the old question: is Russia poor? How could the attractive numbers of deficit-free budgets be reconciled with the poverty and misery of the population or with the statistics of peasant tax arrears? Does finance have primacy over economy and production, or should it be other way around? Experts expressed this dilemma in a language of political economy that distinguished between the national economy and the economic well-being of the people.[77] Khodskii agreed that financial growth does not necessarily reflect the rise of popular incomes, but he claimed that it had to be seen as "an important criterion of the effectiveness of state activity."[78] The state represented only a part of the whole system of the national economy, and there could be no wealthy country if its people lived in poverty. The gold reform did not take into account the factor of "popular well-being" and therefore could not be accepted in its current form.[79]

The populist trend exemplified by Khodskii and the "professorial opposition" remained marginal in the debates on the reform. In this context, Russian debates on money differed dramatically from the American debates unfolding at exactly the same time, on the eve of the 1896 presidential election. In the United States, the upholders of bimetallism represented the antimonopolistic populist tradition and argued for "government regulation of the financial structure" as a means of maintaining equal economic and political rights. Silver was associated with national and public interests, while gold signified the rule of private capitalist corporations and international finance. The upholders of gold considered the populism of bimetallists as a threat to private property rights, while the critics of the existing gold-based monetary system claimed that money should represent a tool of social and political regulation rather than merely a market instrument.[80] In Russia, the social and political landscape of the monetary debate was almost reversed: capitalists were either indifferent or argued against the gold standard, along with economists from academia and a few populists, while the government was pushing through a state-ruled gold standard.

In total, short and intense debates on the reform raised the problems of law and the relationship between the people and the state, the issue of dignity and obligation, and the question of constitutionalism, poverty, and culture. It was therefore not surprising that its participants picked up Suvorin's comparison between the emancipation of peasants in 1861 and the gold reform, highlighting the imbalance between the reform's scale and the public's involvement in the process of the reform. The secrecy and political intrigues surrounding the transition to the gold standard looked appalling, as if the existing tradition of publishing the projects, memos, and materials of expert commissions, even informing newspapers of the dates and time of the commissions' gatherings, had suddenly been abandoned.[81] People demanded more than public debate: one of the participants suggested that the government conduct an *"enquête,"* that is, it should send out questionnaires regarding the reform and listen to different opinions.[82] The idea of compiling *"enquêtes"* on the issue of the Russian ruble quickly gained popularity. It entailed not simply giving the floor to the representatives of various groups of interests and regions but also collecting and publicizing financial information about the state of Russian finances.

Demands for disclosing information about Russian finances showed that Witte's policy of taming the press had backfired. The Ministry of Finance's methods for manipulating foreign and national media had been well known; official government newspapers such as the ministry's mouthpiece, the *Herald of Finances*, as well as "independent" journalists on the government's payroll covered the flourishing state of the Russian economy with an enthusiasm that raised suspicion. It was no secret that Witte did not spare funds to secure the favorable opinions of the European press when Russian bonds appeared on the international (most important, the French) market. He also worked hard to cultivate good relationships with Russian journalists, and each newspaper, it seems, required special treatment.[83] As a result of Witte's efforts, the editors of most major newspapers—the *Stock Exchange Bulletin*, the *News and Stock Exchange Gazette*, *St. Petersburg Bulletin*, *Kievlianin*, and others—supported the reform, but having faced growing opposition to the gold ruble, they had to allocate space to those who had opposing opinions. Among the newspaper giants, only Suvorin stood in staunch opposition, and Witte made every effort to minimize the harm caused by Suvorin's witty critique through regular meetings and correspondence. It may seem therefore strange that Witte entrusted to Suvorin, who did not hide his aversion to the gold reform, the most delicate tasks and shared with him the most valuable information.

> Most respected Alexei Sergeevich, all French newspapers say that I allegedly prohibited Russian newspapers from discussing the law on gold money. You know that this is a lie. I never did anything of the sort and did not even intend to do so. This lie was set going by telegrams from Petersburg. . . . Please be so kind as to refute this fib in your newspaper.[84]

This short note reveals the minister's distress over the unfavorable attitude of the press and the plentiful rumors about the reform. One of the most revealing in this episode regard a humble eight-page letter to Suvorin that Witte wrote on March 24, 1896. Witte asked "if there is an occasion to guide his readers away from . . . wrong thoughts" about the reform?. He listed various rebukes and rumors—about hastiness, secrecy, and not listening to "professors" who had all turned against the reform—that had appeared in the press. He then offered possible responses to these insinuations and spelled out phrases and thoughts that Suvorin, apparently, was supposed to deliver with all his "sincerity and talent" to his readers. Finally, Witte asked the journalist to respond to the most troubling rumor concerning his own attitude to the tsar:

> If you are going to write about it yourself, please pay attention to the following mean trick. It's fine to say that the minister of finance is good or bad, but why recur to low insinuations? However, this is the weapon that is being used: the enemies of Russia have instilled in _him_ [i.e., the tsar] a thought [about the reform], that he [Witte] wants to use the tsar's youth, he wants to destroy the tsar's money and replace it with bank money—that he has given himself over to Jewish bankers.[85]

Given the most intimate style of this correspondence, Witte perhaps expected Suvorin to treat him and the reform favorably, all the more so because, as Witte remarked, he was preparing for the crucially important discussion of the reform at the State Council scheduled for late April. However, on April 10, the _New Time_ appeared with Suvorin's own editorial conveying a commonly held sense of uneasiness and confusion. "Tell me, why isn't the reform of currency popular?" Nobody knew what exactly was wrong with it, but many either "instinctively" or "half-consciously" felt that with the reform, "everyone loses something." Even if every large-scale reform happens without sacrifices, in this case, people did not know what their sacrifices would be for. Again comparing the emancipation of serfs with the reform of the gold standard, Suvorin emphasized that the two were of relative scale. However, the emancipation "was an ideological, a deeply ideological reform. It was about freedom." People who had lost something due to the emancipation at least had a "moral consolation." In contrast, the currency reform "does not have a humanitarian component, and its political sense is elusive." This is why even those people who supported devaluation and were ready to bear the burden of the transition spoke out against Witte's reform; they did not know how it would be arranged and conducted. Suvorin ended by demanding the publication of all projects of the reform and the materials of its discussion within the Committee of Finance.[86]

Four days after this editorial, Suvorin was called to the office of the minister of the interior, Ivan Goremykin, who supervised both the political police and the public press, to be reprimanded. As Suvorin remarked in his diary, "Witte has complained."[87] Goremykin, however, explained that there were more significant reasons for giving Suvorin a warning:

> Last Thursday, His Majesty told me that he was fed up with all this chatter about *devaluation* and that if he had been in my shoes, he would have taken measures against this chatter about devaluation. But I did not take any steps. Let them speak. I allow for critique of all kinds as long as it is sensible. But I cannot tolerate articles like yours. Because one can make anything laughable.[88]

It is remarkable that Suvorin's article, which did not directly criticize the reform but spoke to more subtle issues—its ideological irresoluteness and the failure of the minister to recruit people who could have been his allies had he addressed the public more openly and sincerely—provoked Goremykin's fury. Interestingly, the article did not ruin Suvorin's relationship with Witte, whom he visited again on May 1. Witte told him that the tsar had read the summary of the debates at the Free Economic Society and had asked the minister of the interior to put an end to it.[89] The Society's president, Count Petr Geiden, received a memorandum attacking the indecency of "demonstrations" and public talks about the reform attended by students, young women, and people who were not members of the Society.[90] All critique, from both the left and the right, had to be muted.

Thus, the emperor's comments regarding the talks on devaluation sanctioned the shutdown of the debate, which had lasted only four weeks. Witte's obsession with public opinion, indicated by the thousands of rubles spent on press coverage and paid to experts for their positive evaluations, accompanied a conspicuous neglect of the popular response to the reform. Witte, as experienced state official Vladimir Gurko suggested, made an important distinction between "public opinion" and "public activity," the latter assuming the power and ability of an autonomous public to act on its behalf. "Public opinion was important to Witte not in itself, but as an indication of what course of action to follow, not as a factor of public life, but as a means of accomplishing his own definite ends." Therefore, more than any other minister before or after, Witte "was alive to the tremendous influence of the press on public opinion, and he endeavored to be on the best of terms with press luminaries and representatives, using all manner of tactics to this end. . . . On the other hand, he never hesitated to muzzle the press if its opinion did not fit in with his plans."[91]

This is exactly what happened with the gold reform: Witte conducted the reform despite public resistance. People who spoke against the reform were certainly aware that their protests would not help and that Witte would push it through. There was something troubling in the feeling of fatalism and powerlessness in the face of the government, and this political feature came across almost as a feature of the national character. Popular writer and publicist Konstantin Staniukovich described the consensus on the inevitability of the reform in his fictional dialogue between a "foreigner" and a certain "Russian friend":

> So, the project would not go through? Public opinion and the majority of learned economists are all against it.—In response, a Russian gentleman looked at me with eyes wide open:
> – Why wouldn't it? ... One must be grateful that it has been allowed to discuss this question publicly, and therefore the public was prepared. But it could be done in a different way.
> – How so?
> – Like this, milord. One beautiful day, just announce an already made decision, and that's it.
> – These Russians are very strange people.[92]

"Le coup d'état monétaire"

In following through with the reform, Witte pursued an already familiar path of bureaucratic negotiations. Both the Committee of Finance and the State Council demanded that Witte elaborate the reform of the State Bank, its separation from the Ministry of Finance, and the disentanglement of treasury funds from private commercial funds in the Bank's balance, before proceeding with the monetary reform. At the State Council, the upholders of the state's "dignity" also spoke against the reform, as did those who believed in the benefits of the gold standard in theory but thought that Russia was not ready for it yet.[93] The State Council voted to postpone further discussion of the project until after the end of the festivities and the holiday in honor of Nicholas II's coronation. However, it became clear to Witte that under no circumstances would the State Council vote in favor of the plan.[94] Goremykin assured Suvorin that the reform would not go through, hinting at the tsar's support in this matter.[95]

Contrary to Goremykin's predictions, Witte scored a victory in the competition for the tsar's attention and support. His most cunning invention was to split the reform into several stages that were much easier to sneak in: first, the devaluation, then the law on monetary emission and the resumption of exchange that would legitimately put the ruble on the gold standard. Instead of wrestling with the demagogues at the Council, he persuaded the tsar to summon the Committee of Finance under His Majesty's chairmanship and discuss the seemingly minor issue of minting new coins with the same gold content as the existing ones, but with a new denomination. Thus, instead of debasing gold half-imperials and imperials of 5 rubles and 10 rubles, Witte suggested simply re-coining them with a new number: 7 rubles 50 kopecks, and 15 rubles. However, approving the new design of the gold coins meant approving the devaluation in principle, while the fact that the tsar had agreed to chair the meeting legitimized the entire reform. After all, as Grand Duke Mikhail Nikolaevich, the chairman of the State Council and Nicholas II's grand-uncle, declared at the Committee of Finance's meeting, the tsar, "as a sovereign autocrat, could have resolved the issue and signed the decree in any sense, based on the minister's memo." True, Nicholas II responded, he had already "made up his mind before the meeting," and then added, "The measure suggested by the minister of finance had been approved by my father, and I decided to carry it into effect."[96] So the ruble's fate was sealed.[97] Alexander Polovtsov, who described this meeting in his diary, added an interesting vignette about this historical event. The draft memo of the Committee's session motivated the minting of new coins with the tsar's image on them, as if the tsar's name had been compromised by the discrepancy between the nominal value (5 rubles) and the "real value" (7 rubles 50 kopecks) of the gold coins. In fact, nothing like that was said at the meeting, and Polovtsov insisted on the removal of this phrase, commenting that "servility has to have its limits."[98] Ironically, he thought it was against the rules to forge the meeting's minutes but considered it legitimate to conduct a major reform that bypassed the legislative chamber that had turned against it.

De facto and de jure, the edict on the new coins made continuing the discussion of devaluation redundant. As Witte boasted to Suvorin, "If before the decree he [Witte] had been waiting for the State Council's benevolence, after the decree, the Council will be waiting for his [Witte's] benevolence." Witte celebrated the decree as his personal victory, whereas Suvorin perceived it as his own debacle: "This is devaluation. Whatever you write, nothing can be done. . . . And, still, it is a shame to lose."[99] Indeed, all participants in the reform process, supporters and opponents alike, treated the Russian ruble as the main prize in a political scramble.

After the new coinage act, the reform was not yet complete. Its main part, the description of the new order to make money on the basis of the gold standard, still had to be discussed and approved. The State Council met once again in February 1897 to continue the discussion of the reform's plan, but in fact, it only heard Witte's boastful declarations. Witte rejected the Council's requests that he reconsider the minister of finance's standing vis-à-vis the State Bank and his role in the process of money production. When Vladimir Verkhovskii brought up the argument that to entrust the issuance of money to the State Bank under its current organization "meant leaving the emission operation to the mercy of fate and creating the dictatorship of the Minister of Finance," Witte responded that separating the State Bank from the ministry would "undermine the mightiness of the state."[100] The ruble's fate and the fate of the reform, in Witte's explanation, was entirely his own personal responsibility. "I have been constantly telling His Majesty the Emperor that I take upon myself the maintenance of the fixed rate not only in normal times, but also in strained political situations. . . . But who would be responsible for the firmness of the rate in the case of the State Bank's separation from the Ministry of Finance?"[101] The State Council's meeting ended with yet another postponement of the further debate and decision. This was exactly what Witte wanted.

After the end of the State Council's session that had left the currency question unresolved, the Ministry of Finance sent out a telegram to European newspapers announcing, "The State Council . . . has sanctioned the opinion of the members who share the Minister of Finance's view. Therefore, the decree of January 3 has been confirmed and the monetary reform of the Minister of Finance has been established firmly and irrevocably."[102] This was simply a lie, and as it turned out, journalists were aware of it. Edmond Théry, one of the proponents of bimetallism and the editor of the influential *L'Economiste Européen*, quoted the minister's telegram and accused Witte of committing "*le coup d'état monétaire*" (a monetary coup d'état). The term captured the unconstitutionality of Witte's actions and compromised the entire meaning of the new order. A "durable" monetary order assumed that the emperor's edict was supposed to reflect the decision of the legislative State Council, which would give it the "power of the law." "All financial acts of the government have to be irreproachable from a moral point of view; it seems that M. Witte wants to entice Nicholas II into a shady enterprise that is very dangerous for Russia's credit," wrote Théry.[103]

Despite Witte's success with the devaluation edict, it must have seemed improbable that he would pass another crucial law on the rules of emission without the State Council's approval.[104] However, contrary to public demands to discuss and pass legislation on monetary emission, this major law also appeared in the form of a royal edict following a personal report from Witte to the tsar.[105] A half-page-long edict, as troubling in its laconism as the law on devaluation, stipulated that the Bank would not print money for the treasury, and at least half of the issued 600 million rubles had to be backed by gold; as for the credit rubles printed above this limit, they had to be matched by gold rubles at a 1:1 ratio.[106] The law of August 29, 1897, which put the Russian currency on the gold standard, was presented as a routine bureaucratic instruction and was not even publicized. The official *Herald of Finances, Industry and Trade* briefly mentioned it in an article on the change of the State Bank's accounting forms, published two weeks after the edict's confirmation.[107]

The Russian emission law of 1897 came to be considered one of the strictest in Europe, in the sense that it required a greater percentage of gold coverage of paper money than in other countries. The extra gold was meant to compensate, in the eyes of Russia's creditors, for the lack of political guarantees and legal provisions. The most striking element of the law on money issuance was that, despite the existence of material, tangible restrictions, it granted total control over the monetary emission to the minister of finance. Characteristically, the initial draft of rules on emission, prepared inside the bureaucratic apparatus of the Ministry of Finance, straightforwardly declared that the "general command of the issuance and withdrawal of credit bills belongs to the minister of finance, who gives the [State] Bank instructions on this matter." The article disappeared from the final version of the rules only because it reiterated the principle formulated elsewhere in a more detailed and bureaucratic form.[108] Thus, the content of the legislative acts on the gold reform reflected the ways in which the reform was enacted. The "dictatorship" of the minister was a projection of the tsar's personal authority that had made the reform possible.

Witte's concept of the gold reform, therefore, was a far cry from the idea of a "standard" as a means of regulating the state and its impact on the market and the national economy. Implanted into the political system of autocracy, it failed to limit the tsar's and the minister's power to encroach on the stability of the national monetary system. The first signs of the political vulnerability of Russia's gold standard appeared almost immediately after the reform during the financial crisis of 1898–1902 when the State Bank distributed significant sums of money in long-term loans to industrial enterprises and private banks at the tsar's request. A significant portion of these loans that came to be known as "extra-legal loans" or loans "made on supreme [i.e., the tsar's] orders" were never repaid, and these losses endangered both the State Bank's role as an emission institution and the sustainability of the ruble.[109]

Why were these loans considered a threat to the gold ruble? [110] After the gold reform, the State Bank merged its commercial and "public" accounts; as a result, the exchange gold fund that had existed as a separate entity was dissolved in the Bank's capital. Therefore, the tsar's granting of subsidies to his favorites encroached directly on the integrity of the gold reserve that supported the ruble. Even government bureaucrats such as Petr Saburov thought that "the gold that secures the exchangeability of credit bills, that serves as the foundation of our gold currency, should be separated into an inviolable fund so that everybody can ascertain its security on the basis of published balance sheets."[111] Saburov prophetically observed that an economic crisis or a political turmoil might wash away the gold reserve if it were not protected. Witte angrily rejected Saburov's suggestion referring to the primacy of "practical needs" over theory. He also resisted the State Controller's attempts to audit the Bank's issuing activity, citing the privacy of the Bank's clients, whose capital, on paper, was not separated from the gold reserve. This was, however, a lie, as Witte routinely broke the rules of financial privacy.[112] As a result, the Bank's operations that directly affected the gold reserve and the ruble were sealed from the public and remained impenetrable even by other agencies, essentially leaving the Bank's assets at the minister's and the tsar's disposal.[113] After Witte's departure from the ministry in 1902, this system continued to operate under his successor. Witte related how in 1905, when Russia was on the brink of political crisis and bankruptcy, the minister of finance, Ivan Shipov, declined the tsar's request to give 2 million rubles from the State Bank to general Vladimir Skalon. Nicholas II, however, simply told his minister to execute the order, and the loan was issued. As Witte reasoned, this incident ruined Shipov's bureaucratic career, and after a few months in the office, Shipov left state service for good.[114]

As the story of the extra-legal loans from the State Bank suggests, the new monetary system lacked one of the most crucial elements: institutional resilience and depersonalization. Its stability depended on the goodwill of the minister and the tsar. It was "Witte's system" both in origin and in principle, and it seemed that the minister did not care how it would work after his departure. As one observer pointed out, "It is undeniably very flattering for S. Yu. Witte to open the exchange, that is to say, to accomplish what neither powerful Reutern nor academic Bunge or a man of great mind, Vyshnegradskii, could do."[115] Paradoxically, Witte's obsession with gold somehow overlapped with a complete indifference to the durability of the system, as if he did not want it to last.

Practicing the Gold Standard

The Expulsion of Paper

"Much nonsense is talked about a gold standard's properly carrying a gold currency with it. If we mean by a gold currency a state of affairs in which gold is the principal or even, in the aggregate, a very important medium of exchange, no country in the world has such a thing." Thirty-year-old John Maynard Keynes, in his first book on money published in 1913, sarcastically criticized European policymakers (above all, the Germans) who wanted to model their gold-based currency on the British example, yet, he claimed, they did not understand the sense of it and were "more impressed by the fact that the Englishman had sovereigns in his pocket than by the fact that he had a checkbook on his desk." Attracted by the "superficial aspects" of the English system, "they were thus led to imitate the form rather than the substance."[1] Keynes snobbishly observed that all these attempts were doomed to fail because the England's gold standard was impossible to recreate, and the countries, especially the debtor nations, had to give up on imposing gold coins. In contrast to the slavish imitations of the English model, Keynes advocated for the "gold-exchange standard" that allowed countries to hold smaller gold reserves. Under this system, gold, often in the form of foreign currency or bills of exchange, was used mainly in international exchanges. Such was, for instance, the case of Japan, which adopted the gold standard soon after Witte's reform.[2] In another example of a gold standard regime without gold coins, Austria-Hungary switched to gold in 1892, but it never opened the exchange.

For Witte, the adoption of the gold standard was a matter of personal pride and Russia's international prestige. Therefore, not surprisingly, he wanted to develop a first-rate gold-standard system rather than a spin-off model.[3] For that reason, all Russians, from peasants and petty traders to aristocrats, had to carry coins in their pockets, instead of paper bills. His intolerance of paper was so high that he decided to expand the circulation of silver coins because gold coins could not be minted in low denominations.[4] Silver and gold were meant to exist in different dimensions, and therefore the silver ruble could make its comeback, along with new gold coins, into the pockets of the Russian people. The only rub was that issuing silver rubles required purchasing silver abroad, since Russia did not have its own sources and therefore paid for silver in gold.[5] This did not seem very logical, but many of Witte's innovations could not pass the test of rationality.

What was wrong with this picture? Witte tried to impose England's gold standard model onto a Russian economy that had completely different social parameters. Overall, the poverty of the Russian public, the absence of coins that had to be almost forcibly imposed on people who had largely not seen gold for almost forty years or had never seen it at all, made the realization of this plan difficult and painful. The introduction of coins began immediately after the legalization of transactions in gold in 1895. On September 20 the clients of the State Bank in all its regional and central offices, after requesting money in loans or bill discounts or after simply withdrawing their funds from regular accounts, received payments in gold coins, which they could exchange for paper credit rubles in the same office at a different desk. As the managers of the Bank's branches promptly reported, many first-time clients walked away while others were shocked by the sudden change of the rules.[6] Of the 33,100 rubles in gold paid out in the Kyiv office on the second day of the operation, 32,715 rubles were immediately exchanged for paper rubles in the same branch. On September 22, of 177,230 rubles handed out in gold, only 70 rubles were taken by the clients, and the rest of the gold coins were returned right away.[7] Neither the attempts to convince people of the safety of operations with gold nor the information leaflets and posters that were mailed, handed out, or hung up at railroad stations and in townships seemed effective.[8] In October, private banks were forced to join the campaign of spreading gold coins and reducing the circulation of paper rubles. The central office stopped shipping paper money to its local branches, enforcing the rule that they should operate with the amount of incoming bills and force their clients to accept gold coins or gold deposit certificates.[9] The imposition of the new practices during the high season of harvest and grain trade, when the demand for money was always strong, inevitably created tensions and anxiety. In November, the head of the Rostov-on-Don branch reported: "We have reached the limit of the obtrusion of gold upon the clients, which we should not cross."[10]

Witte understood the working of the gold standard quite literally as the circulation of gold money. As the *Stock Exchange Bulletin* put it, the government wanted to teach people the "long-forgotten language of gold currency."[11] What is more, the presence of gold coins in wealthy people's safes did not count: the Ministry and the State Bank instructed that gold "can become the means of payment only when it catches on among non-wealthy folks."[12] The State Bank pumped gold through its network, trying to saturate the economy with metal. Witte's supporters reported that the Ministry of Finance fought "the war against papers [i.e., credit rubles]," not "without success: the papers retreated from the positions that they used to occupy, yielding to the pressure of the white and gold metals that began to show up in circulation."[13]

In May 1897 the State Bank started withdrawing the paper bills of lower denominations (1, 3, and 5 rubles), freeing up space for silver and gold coins. As one of the memos claimed, "Without this vacuum, metallic circulation would not stick." Paper money of small denominations constituted an enormous share of monetary circulation: in 1897, the sum of 1-, 3-, 5-, and 10-ruble bills equaled 548 million rubles or 51.2% of the total amount, of which the smallest, the 1- and 3-ruble bills, represented about 40%.[14] This was the quintessential "people's money," the main means of local trade and economy. Local State Bank agencies and treasury offices received instructions that payments of less than 25 rubles had to be made strictly in coins, while all payments exceeding this sum came only in credit bills. For affluent members of society, the growing amount of coins was a nuisance; manufacturers reacted to it by producing special boxes for coins to replace or complement porte-monnaies for paper bills.[15] But for poorer folk, it was a shock. A young worker's monthly salary of 20 rubles could be paid just in two or four gold coins; a more skillful worker's wages could go up to 100 rubles, but he would still pay for daily expenses using a few rubles that now appeared only as metal coins.[16] In parallel, the ministry approved the increased issuance of the credit ruble in large denominations (50 rubles, 100 rubles, and 500 rubles). Therefore, the entire social system of monetary circulation was reversed: "small folks" primarily used silver and gold, while rich people had the privilege of using paper, including credit ruble bills of the new highest denominations (100 and 500 rubles).[17]

While preparing for the imposition of coins, the ministry anticipated popular resistance. Creating a vacuum of small money through the withdrawal of the most popular bills was a "harsh" measure that would inevitably produce a "painful impression" especially on workers', soldiers', and officers' wages, when "big sums of money would be carried in wagons along the most dreadful

FIGURE 8.1 7 ½- ruble gold coins, 1897. These coins were produced only in 1897 after the ruble's devaluation. They were equivalent to 5-ruble gold coins minted under Alexander III. Private collection.

FIGURE 8.2 10-ruble gold coins, 1902. Private collection.

FIGURE 8.3 500-ruble state credit bill, 1898. Designers of the new 500-ruble bill reproduced the sculpture of Peter the Great by Mark Antokolskii (1872) without his consent. In 1900, Antokolskii asked the Ministry of Finance to send him "four samples of the reproductions of his work" so he could pay his creditors. The Ministry did not understand the hint and responded that it could not send him the copies of bills (RGIA, f.560, op.22. d.219). From *Russian Ruble: Milestones in History*. The State Bank of Russia, virtual museum.

roads."[18] In June 1897, the district administration of Buguruslan (Orengburg province) begged the State Bank to resume the supply of small bills because the local postal service, which operated as the main agent of money transfer, could not send and deliver the equivalent amount of money—mainly salaries to low-rank officers—in silver coins. A director of the New Flax Factory in Kostroma reported that the factory's buyers traveled miles to village fairs and farms to buy raw flax from peasants, with most transactions consisting of a few rubles and paid in 1- and 3-ruble bills. Buyers carried amounts up to 10,000 rubles, so the introduction of silver rubles in large bags weighing more than thirty-five pounds turned the transportation of money into a nightmare. These and dozens of other requests from factories, garrisons, gold mines, and railroads to send small bills were denied by the State Bank, which enforced the policy of introducing metallic monetary circulation.[19]

Discontent over the new money was widespread, not just among peasants and workers. As the director of one of the branches suggested, the urban population did not like coins either, allegedly because European clothing without big pockets could not accommodate money. Administrators suggested providing small canvas bags to the bank's clients to carry coins.[20] Ultimately, the distribution of coins depended on a multitude of factors, most important, the level of wealth. In 1899, the director of one local State Bank branch responded to the central office's instruction to enforce the acceptance of silver and gold coins with the observation that it was "unthinkable to achieve the same degree of saturation with metal money as had existed with small paper bills."[21] Gold spread faster than silver, and the State Bank continued withdrawing and burning credit rubles. Between 1897 and October 1899, the amount of credit rubles in circulation dropped from over 1,000 million to 540 million rubles (below the norm stipulated by the law on emission), while the value of gold and silver coins reached 668.4 and 145.5 million respectively. Therefore, as the ministry reported, "reality exceeded expectations," and the "goal of all efforts of the last year—the introduction of gold coins—has been achieved."[22] Ironically, when the ministry's secret directive to stop enforcing the acceptance of gold and to encourage people to take bills leaked out to the press, it caused chaos, because many saw it as a sign that the bank was running out of gold.[23] Such was the paradox of the new system, which suddenly created new dangers and anxieties.

The introduction of gold and silver coins required rebooting the entire system of the production and movement of currency, bringing almost insurmountable obstacles. Among other things, the administration had to invent mechanisms to maintain the supply of gold. Russia's major mines were located in remote permafrost areas in Siberia, and gold-mining, contrary to popular belief, remained the domain of small producers rather than large entrepreneurs. The state had a monopoly on purchasing gold, and illegal gold extraction and trade were severely prosecuted. After the reform, the government decided to give up its monopoly right and eventually introduced the "freedom of gold circulation." In 1898, it allowed the duty-free export of foreign mining tools, machines, and chemical materials and also removed certain dues and restrictions, which reduced the costs for gold producers.[24]

Logistical problems also complicated supplying the treasuries, offices, and regional and local branches of the State Bank with gold coins. It soon became clear that the postal system could not take on the transfer of the hundreds of millions of rubles in gold that had to be delivered across the country.[25] In September 1896, the government introduced the cash-free transfer of money via post and telegraph offices. This enabled anyone to send money, without physically sending coins or banknotes in envelopes, from any post office in hundreds of towns and villages across the empire.[26] The new means of transferring money, especially through telegraph, sped up circulation, a key method for reducing the demand for paper cash. However, this new financial network could not solve the problem of cash distribution. The creation of special

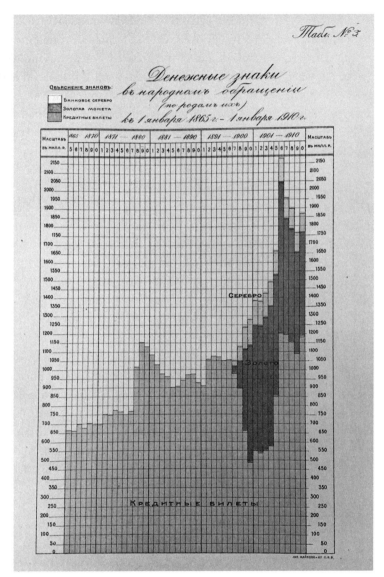

FIGURE 8.4 The structure of monetary base. Note the drastic increase in the volume of gold coins (dark gray) and the decreasing number of credit rubles (light gray at the bottom) in the late 1890s-early 1900s. From *Gosudarstvennyi bank: kratkiii ocherk deiatel'nosti za 1860–1910 gody*. St. Petersburg, 1910.

"distribution centers" in 1899 helped minimize the movement and concentrate coins in areas of great demand and supply; however, the problem of transportation remained quite serious.[27] Bags with silver and gold were supposed to be loaded onto freight cars that were sealed, covered with iron, and attached to regular passenger trains. In reality, gold often traveled in wooden wagons with wobbly doors and walls or with crooked wheels. Trains were often delayed, and freight cars were unhooked and left unattended. Safety was always an issue, especially when uncooperative railroad workers pulled the cars off to the side rails; in one such case, three unarmed cashiers were left to watch a car with a load worth 3 million rubles.[28] In the first years after the reform, the transfer of gold across the country and even across the city remained a novelty that caused a sensation. In August 1899, the *St. Petersburg Newspaper* informed its readers of the departure of cars with gold coins to Rostov-on-Don and Buzuluk and even indicated how many cashiers accompanied the transports. The release of this information to the press prompted an official prohibition of publication of any news about gold cars' movement.[29] However, even without newspaper reports, rumors about the movement of gold spread quickly. Horse-driven carts with red flags were accompanied by special guards, while train cars with gold were usually marked by official seals and the presence of gendarmes.[30] The authorities could not decide whether it was safer to implement as many security measures as possible and therefore increase gold's visibility, or to observe secrecy and transport money in passenger cars without any fuss.[31] The State Bank's governor, Serguei Timashev, once noticed on a street an open landau carriage loaded with large canvas bags and accompanied by four horsemen. Obviously, metal rubles were heavier, bulkier, and more difficult to store and relocate. From a logistical point of view, the reform looked like a return to the medieval economy, with coins stored in leather bags, hoards, and basements, rather than a transition to a modern system of currency. At the same time, the abundance of gold, as economist Pavel Migulin commented, "imparted the reform with a special shine and publicity."[32]

The contrast between the shine of Russia's gold and the poverty of its population was further exacerbated by the crisis that broke out after the reform. In 1899, the world economy was hit by another recession, relatively mild, prompted by the eruption of the Boer War. In Europe, the negative effects of the crisis were mostly over by 1901, but the Russian economy took a deep dive from which it didn't recover until 1902. The monetary reform therefore gave a particular tone to the debates of that period, which Pavel Migulin called the "battle for gold." The recent reform also affected the optics through which Witte and the government perceived the events: everything was seen through the prism of the gold reserve. Inasmuch as the State Bank had enough gold in its vaults, things did not seem so bad since the amount of yellow gold served as an indicator of well-being. In September 1899, Witte reported to Nicholas II that "at the moment, Russia is the country that possesses probably the biggest gold reserve in relation to the volume of monetary [credit] circulation"; 983.4 million rubles of gold significantly exceeded the 300 million required by the emission law.[33] In Witte's interpretation, the current crisis was no more than an illusion produced by unscrupulous journalists and alarmists who spread "false rumors." As of November 1899, Witte simply recommended working with the press to create a favorable public opinion.[34] The Committee of Finance reported to the tsar that the illusion of the severity of the crisis was created by certain individuals who projected their own personal difficulties onto the state of the national economy.[35]

In the meantime, the Russian countryside was devasted by a series of bad harvests that compounded the consequences of falling grain prices. Landowners as well as financiers blamed the gold reform for the "scarcity of money." Indeed, the disappearance of paper rubles, which were in high demand in times of hardship, produced the effect of a "cash deficit." Finally, the Ministry of Finance had to admit that the crisis resulted not from the incautious behavior of stock exchange gamblers, as had been claimed earlier, but from the long-standing problems of the economy, specifically its rural sector. Russian agriculture was the foundation of the entire state economy, and while the façade of state finance had received a facelift, production remained old and backward. For this reason, the series of bad harvests showed that Russia simply did not produce enough goods to exchange for the products that its economy needed.[36] This situation reopened the question of what should come first: stabilization of the currency or economic improvement. The crisis, in other words, called to mind money's embeddedness in the complex system of economic relations, which Witte, who prioritized state finance over other spheres of economy, had neglected. The introduction of the gold standard was made possible due to the reorientation in the 1880s of the Russian agrarian economy from the domestic market to export; therefore, Witte owed the success of the gold reform to the Russian peasantry. The Russian economy was locked in a vicious circle: the maintenance of the gold standard required the stability of export, which in turn distressed peasants and strained the condition of rural economy. The reform also perverted the principles of assessing economic well-being. Witte judged economic health by the state of the gold reserve. It would take two wars (the Russo-Japanese and the First World War) to demonstrate that the appearance of government finance, the size of the gold reserve, and even the exchange rate do not reflect the wealth or poverty of nations.

Was the depth of Russia's crisis a result of the gold reform? It was hard to tell. The constant increase of Russian exports for the sake of gold contributed

to the drop in grain prices, but at the same time, the development of railroads
and the restructuring of global markets brought down prices globally. Witte
tried to persuade the public that the gold standard in fact alleviated the effects
of the crisis. He asked Suvorin to stress this point particularly in his articles in
the *New Time*: "The devil knows what would have been happening now on
the capital market if the reform had not been completed—the exchange rate
would have collapsed, and the discount rate would have risen to 8%–12%."[37]
Witte also claimed that neither monetary policy nor global market trends affected the peasant economy, which, as he wrote in his report to the tsar, "was
in a state of natural economy and little depended on the movements of the
grain market."[38] In his portrayal, the agrarian crisis resulted from a bad coincidence of meteorological conditions that hit various provinces three years
in a row. However, he also began to realize that monetary stability could not
come without a stable economy, and he did not approve of Vyshnegradskii's
policy of "starvation" for the sake of export and the accumulation of gold.[39] In
tacit recognition of this fact, in 1902, not long before his departure from the
minister's office, Witte created a special committee "for the investigation of
the needs of the agrarian economy" and invited the representatives of forty-
nine provinces to speak up about the economy of rural Russia.

The question of currency was not supposed to be on the committee's
agenda, but Serguei Sharapov's intervention changed this plan. Sharapov,
Witte's long-time opponent, decided to use this opportunity to let the representatives of the agrarian sector express their opinion about the gold ruble.
He sent out copies of his open letter to Witte in which he criticized the gold
reform to committee members in every province. Although Sharapov's idio-
syncratic manner and aggressive rhetoric did not work in his favor, and many
representatives declined to discuss his memo, several provincial committees
responded, most of them expressing a growing conviction that peasants and
landowners had to bear a disproportionally high cost of the gold reform.[40]
The policy of increasing exports but preserving protectionist customs duties
increased the financial burden on the agrarian economy.
Complaints of the "high prices" for everything except agricultural products
were ubiquitous, as were references to the deficit of money, while almost
nobody seems to have noticed any advantages of the stabilized rate. The reform, it seemed, produced effects similar to those of Kankrin's reform, when,
against common sense and economic logic, living became "3.5 times more
expensive" and prices rose, while people often continued counting in the
old units.[41] Likewise, contrary to Witte's expectations that people would
not notice the reform, the general feeling was that the ruble was not the

same. "We have to sell 1.5 times more to get the same money," claimed the participants.[42]

Most of the speakers hesitated to connect the reasons for the 1898–1901 crisis to the reform per se, but they recognized that the general financial policy of the government, which prioritized industry and railroad construction and stimulated grain export at the expense of domestic consumption, was detrimental to the state of the agrarian economy. The feeling of uncertainty that had been so acutely manifested during the pre-reform debates in 1896 ruled here as well. The juxtaposition of local committees' reports with refutations by the Ministry of Finance and the expert opinions of economists creates an impression of two parallel economic realities. Landowners and peasants complained about the "absence of money" and the impossibility of obtaining credit, while Witte and others responded that "banks were full of money, which, however, does not get into business." Agriculture was not able to benefit from the availability of capital created by adherence to the gold standard because of the low productivity of agriculture; therefore, the investors' money went elsewhere.[43] People complained about the disappearance of cash, which caused both the reappearance of surrogate money in the form of coupons and the return to barter.[44] In contrast, experts who were also among the committee's representatives claimed that after the reform, the per capita amount of cash in circulation increased from 9.63 rubles to 11.17 rubles.[45] Sharapov's supporters demanded a reconsideration of the currency question and a return to the silver or even paper standard; if this was impossible, they asked the government to reduce mortgage debts by the proportion of 1.5, the rate at which the ruble had been devalued.[46]

Historians and economists disagree in their assessments of the economic and social effects of Witte's gold ruble reform. Critics of the reform cautioned against overemphasizing the impact of the reform on the scale of economic growth, attributing the rise of economic indices in the 1890s and 1900s to other factors.[47] They also pointed out that the enormous cost of the reform, which burdened the Russian population, mostly the peasants, with taxes and dues was the result of the tremendous growth of Russia's foreign debt. "The Russian peasant could complain even more justly than the American farmer . . . that he was crucified on the cross of gold for the benefit of bankers and industrialists and for the prestige of his country," noted historian Theodore von Laue. Von Laue, however, concluded that "the high price of the gold standard was also the high price of Russian backwardness," and Witte bore no responsibility for that.[48] Other scholars agreed that Russia "had little choice but to adopt the gold standard in order to benefit from the expansion

of world trade and investment."[49] The gold standard and the resulting stabilization of the ruble's rate improved its reputation worldwide and provided
favorable conditions for foreign investments to such an extent that, as Olga
Crisp has noted, "during the single year of 1898, the amount of foreign capital
invested exceeded that of the whole period 1851–1892."[50] This may be true,
although historians of other countries that had joined the gold standard in
this period cannot determine with certainty that economic growth was the
consequence of monetary reforms, or whether the global industrial growth of
this period made the maintenance of the gold standard possible.

　　Russia's gold standard reform is often associated with big shifts in economy
and finance—the stabilization of currency, the growth of foreign investments,
the increase of foreign debts. Yet if these changes did not become visible
until several years after 1897, the reform had palpable and immediate effects
on the everyday life of the Russian population. The biggest change was the
disappearance of low denomination paper rubles and their replacement by
coins. For an economy in which the majority of the population operated on
a daily basis with sums much less than 10 rubles, this meant almost complete
metallization of money. The brutal methods of imposing the gold ruble and
the disregard of its consequences for rural people left the impression that
the state was benefiting at the expense of simple folk. The political and social consequences of the reform were indirect and unclear: could the peasant
disturbances of the early 1900s be partially attributed to Witte's policy of
forced industrialization and the "monetization" of the rural economy? Was
Witte's unpopularity among industrialists and his failure to recruit them to
his cause an indication of his political defeat? In any case, the negative perception of the reform at home contrasted with its enthusiastic acceptance in
the West. For Russia, as elsewhere, the gold standard worked as a "seal of approval" and attracted investments. It was also an indispensable attribute of
empires, and Russia wanted to fit this role.[51]

　　One of the factors that in the end allowed society's reconciliation with
the gold ruble was the apparent absence of alternatives. Critics of Witte's
policy did not offer an alternative program for a monetary regime; the pre-
reform paper standard seemed outdated and inappropriate, and everyone
agreed on the need for improvement. The censure of Witte's system by both
liberals and democrats concerned its methods and its timing rather than the
need for reform. After the introduction of the gold ruble, the anti-gold platform attracted mostly right-wing politicians with repugnant reputations. The
quintessence of their program was expressed in the notorious *Protocols of the
Elders of Zion*—an antisemitic hoax first published in Russia in 1903 that

coincided with intensified attacks against Witte and his financial reforms. Perceptive readers were supposed to recognize the references to Witte's policy in the ideas of the alleged Jewish-Masonic plot. Although a substantial part of the Protocols, including large sections dealing with finance, budget, and loans, had been plagiarized from Maurice Joly's *The Dialogue in Hell between Machiavelli and Montesquieu* (1864), all the paragraphs concerning money were original. They claimed that the monetary reform was a consequence of the plot aimed at pumping out gold from national economy into the hands of Jews and then replacing money with labor-based notes.[52] Thus, the cult of gold was associated with constitutionalism, a progressive income tax, and the establishment of a Masonic order. Needless to say, the abysmal quality of this text that even in the eyes of potential sympathizers looked crude and ridiculous did not contribute to the success of the anti-gold standard campaign. As time went on, the gold standard became a fait accompli, and only reactionary radicals dared to call for its dismantling.

The Gold Ruble in the Realm of Silver

Since the national currency is a tool of governance that reaches further than the government's decrees or administrative orders, all currency reforms of the nineteenth century were aimed at perfecting this tool and spreading the ruble's influence. The imbalance of Russia's domestic system had often prevented the expansion of the ruble zone, such as the monetary integration of Poland and the liquidation of its financial autonomy. Likewise, the introduction of the gold standard, in Witte's own words, eliminated the "single" financial obstacle to the integration of Finland, which had switched to gold in 1876. In 1898, Witte received from Nicholas II carte blanche for the preparation of monetary unification, but the project was mired in bureaucratic slowdowns until December 1903.[53] The problem of Finnish monetary unification with the empire was raised again in 1905–6, in the context of political revolution and the conflict around Finland's constitutional autonomy.

In the East, the scenarios of monetary reform and integration looked different. Central Asia and the Far East, where Russia was trying to spread its economic and political presence, belonged to an entirely different universe of money based on silver. Russian authorities saw local monetary regimes as inferior and were certain that the population of Bukhara and Manchuria would prefer "better" money to their indigenous currencies. The gold standard, as the reform propagandists claimed, signified the civilization of the West, while silver came to be seen as an attribute of oriental backwardness. Incorporating borderlands into the ruble zone was an important part of Russia's civilizing mission on par with spreading the Russian language. The indigenous population, however, could not appreciate the benefits of using paper money backed by a gold reserve in a far-away Russian capital. Russian authorities paid a very high cost for this project, which they justified by the political advantages of maintaining Russia's symbolic presence in the region. In the end, the ruble remained a marginal and unpopular currency, underscoring the fact that the gold standard rests either on social consensus and the market or on political domination. If none of these elements are present, the standard does not work.

From the very beginning of its conquest of Turkestan, Russia had been trying to squeeze out local currencies, exempting local coins (silver *kokan*, the currency of the Kokand khanate, and *tenga*, the coins of Kashgar and Bukhara) and reminting them. The exemption and exchange of local silver coins for rubles at an increased rate cost the Russian Treasury a hefty sum but brought about no results. Silver coins kept coming from the neighboring Khiva and Bukhara khanates, where local rulers enjoyed the lucrative right of coinage. Therefore, as the Ministry of Finance admitted, the monetary integration of Russia's territories in Central Asia could be achieved only after these two semi-autonomous khanates were absorbed into the Russian monetary system.[54] Of the two, Khiva was more dependent on the empire, and its unification with Russia in 1893 did not seem problematic "from the political [or] from the financial point of view."[55] Yet in the more autonomous Bukhara, Russia's standing was dependent on the emir's authority over the local population. The experience of Russia's monetary reform there showed that political pressure was sometimes not enough to change economic practices and preferences. In Bukhara, the government faced a phenomenon that it could not explain from the point of view of "rational" economic behavior: people preferred the local currency, even though it had lost its value, to the better and more "expensive" ruble.

The Bukharians' tenga was made of pure silver. Until the late 1880s, Bukhara had been importing silver ingots (*sycee*, or *iamb* in Russian, from Chinese *yuanbao*) from China. When in 1888 Russia completed the construction of the Trans-Caspian railroad, European silver started flowing in in greater quantities. In the early 1890s, Chinese sycees were thus almost completely replaced by European silver ingots coming from Russia and the countries that had switched to the gold standard.[56] Rumor had it that the emir, whose personal purse was not separate from the state treasury, profited from speculation with the ruble and the tenga.[57] At the same time, the reorientation of the Bukharian economy made it susceptible to global monetary trends. In 1893, when the price of European silver fell due to the suspension of silver coinage in India, the Bukharian tenga also lost its value vis-à-vis the Russian ruble. Many Bukharian and Russian merchants faced bankruptcy, and the Russian government decided to intervene, suggesting that emir Said Abd al-Ahad Khan suspend the coinage of silver coins, at least temporarily. The emir reluctantly complied with the suspension and the obligation to prevent the import of foreign silver coins, but he asked the government to keep these arrangements secret.[58]

In the following years, Witte's Ministry of Finance continued negotiations with the tenacious ruler and the Ministry of Foreign Affairs, which pretended to protect the emir's rights and power. The misunderstanding between the different parties involved in the negotiations originated from a somewhat uncomfortable fact: the "crisis" of the tenga had been caused by the arrival of the Russian railroad and of Russian traders and currency. At the same time, the crisis concerned only merchants dealing with Russia: the tenga "fell" in relation to the Russian credit ruble, while its value remained stable at home and vis-à-vis other silver currencies in the region. The Russian annexation reoriented Bukhara's trade routes northward, as several textile giants of the central region firmly established themselves to buy cotton there and carry silver and other goods from Moscow. In 1895, Bukhara and Khiva were absorbed into the imperial customs system. Thus, the Bukharian economy became dependent on Russia, but the economic and political ties between the empire and the protectorate state were not strong enough to allow the replacement of one currency by another.

The ruble and the tenga had to coexist, and their mutual relations kept changing. Local actors played on the volatility of the ruble's price and even enhanced its fluctuations. Emir Said Abd al-Ahad Khan, who had been educated in Russia, appreciated the European lifestyle and regularly made trips to Russian capitals that required expenses be paid in rubles.[59] For instance, as reported in May 1895, he called "the 12 wealthiest merchants and ordered them to deliver to him 500,000 rubles in exchange for tenga" at a fixed rate—100,000 had to be brought in immediately and the remaining 400,000 by November 1895. Such an operation immediately raised the price of rubles on the market, incurring losses for merchants during the high season of cotton trade. As the head of the Bukharian branch of the State Bank reported, the emir's demand was probably connected to his planned trip to a mineral water resort in the Caucasus and the construction of a new palace that began in 1895.[60] The emir's whims represented perhaps the most unpredictable and uncomfortable contingencies of the market, but Russian authorities perceived speculation as an extra-market factor that had to be eliminated by administrative or political

methods. When in the spring of 1896, on the eve of the cotton-buying campaign, the ruble fell vis-à-vis the tenga, Russian merchants begged the administration to fix the rate. Merchants and Russian officials explained that the ruble
rose and fell in relation to the tenga through the speculative operations of local
"sarrafs" (bankers) and the emir himself. Local merchants, however, responded
that the ruble fell due to the low commercial demand for rubles and the scarcity of tenga. As they explained, bankers were unable to regulate the rate at
their whim because "the rate is established by the *bazar* itself."[61]

The stabilization of the credit ruble's value and its transition to the gold
standard convinced Russian authorities of the impeccable superiority of a
Russian currency based on solid material foundations. Russian authorities and
merchants measured the tenga's rate to ruble by the cost of silver in Moscow
minus an import duty levied in European silver. However, the Bukharan population saw matters differently. For them, the value of silver money depended
not on the material value of silver but on other political, economic, and social
factors such as trust, convenience, and purchasing ability. In other words, it
was the local market that defined the relative standing of the tenga and the
ruble. Despite the administrative and political pressure exercised by Russian
authorities and Bukhara's administration, the ruble "fell" again in September
1897, underscoring the irrelevance of the gold standard beyond the realm of
the Western monetary economy.[62] Russian merchants complained, citing the
enormous losses caused by the ruble's fall in Bukhara.[63] The managers of the
State Bank's branch in Bukhara had to witness the situation passively: "The
Bank cannot fight with the emir because it does not have tenga in its storages."
The emir controlled the market by releasing or withholding tenga, and
Russian authorities could not even estimate the real amount of silver coins at
his disposal.[64]

Plans to stabilize the tenga's (or the ruble's) standing differed in the degree of coercion exerted on the government of Bukhara. One plan assumed
the issuance of a new coin that would stand for both currencies: a Russian
tenga with the emir's portrait and inscriptions in both Russian and Tajik, in
its material quality close to Russian 20 kopeck coins.[65] France minted similar
coins in Tunisia, and the bilingual złoty existed in the Kingdom of Poland.
The plan was nevertheless rejected as a deviation from the ultimate idea both
of Bukhara's gradual integration into the monetary realm of the empire and
of its "assimilation with our Central Asian provinces."[66] Besides, bilingual
coins harkened back to medieval Rus's occupation by Mongol khans when
Russian coins with the Mongol inscription of the khan Tokhtamysh's name
had signified the subordinate status of Russian princes.[67] In the orientalist

imagination of Russian officials, the link between sovereignty and coinage seemed more direct and immediate in Asia than in the West. The supreme power of a Muslim ruler was publicly expressed in two acts: exalting his name during Friday public prayers and imprinting his name on coins. Therefore, issuing coins with double inscriptions could, according to Russian officials, produce the impression of the emir's right to issue Russian money. The opposite would also be true: depriving the emir of his minting privileges would signify the loss of his sovereignty.

The Ministry of Finance stood for the most radical solution. To control the monetary system and gradually replace tenga with rubles, the Russian government had to purchase the entire stock of silver tenga from the emir, force him to denounce his coinage privilege forever, and open the exchange of Russian rubles at a fixed rate.[68] In a certain sense, this operation resembled the forceful introduction of gold coins in the Russian provinces, as if creating an artificial deficit of money would allow the ruble to spread. In another parallel between reforms, Witte thought that the emir's authority rested solely on Russia's support, so he interpreted the reform as a "purely" financial measure. Diplomats at the Ministry of Foreign Affairs and local Russian authorities, for their part, protested against depriving the emir of the "most important attribute of his authority" and expropriating his property as a private individual.[69] Weakening the emir's authority would take away "the possibility of executing various measures with the active support of Bukhara's government and would give the emir the pretext to evade the fulfillment of our requests under the excuse of the loss of his authority in the country."[70] As Turkestan's Governor-General Vrevskii observed, even if the emir agreed to surrender his coinage right, there would be no guarantee that the population of the Bukharan khanate would tolerate the mandatory acceptance of Russian rubles, which had very modest presence in the country.[71]

The negotiations with the emir, who wanted to know what he personally stood to gain from the reform, dragged on for several years until a deal was struck in 1901.[72] The Russian government took hold of all stock of the emir's silver coins, which were transported from the fortress in Old Bukhara to the office of the State Bank in New Bukhara, eight miles away from the location of the headquarters of the Russian authorities. On September 1, 1901, the State Bank opened the exchange of tenga for rubles at a fixed rate of 1 tenga = 15 kopecks.[73] The Russian government stressed that the high cost of the exchange operation was its "sacrifice" for the stability of the tenga's rate; the authorities emphasized that the tenga "cost" 10–11 kopecks, while the government was purchasing it for 15 kopecks.[74]

The clumsy and inconvenient arrangement of the exchange operation highlighted Russia's marginal financial presence in the region. Every
morning, except on Sundays, two carts, accompanied by three bank clerks
and six *dzhigits* (armed horsemen), carried 60,000–80,000 credit rubles
and 10 bags of tenga that weighed more than 900 kilos from the office of
the State Bank in New Bukhara toward Old Bukhara—the main *bazar* of
the country. The *dzhigits* protected the bank's mobile cashier as the proces-
sion made its way through the narrow streets of the city, which were often
clogged for hours with camels, donkeys, and horses pulling carts with clumsy
and broken wheels. On several occasions, the cashier also had to withstand
violent attacks by mobs stirred by rumors, such as one that the emir had sold
Bukhara to the Russian tsar. At 3 P.M., the carts with money headed toward New Bukhara, only to repeat the journey the next morning.[75] When the
silver coins were heated on frying pans, the procedure revealed that up to 25%
of the tenga coins exchanged for rubles turned out to be fake or debased.[76]

Even though on paper Russia had taken control of the Bukharan monetary system, the practicalities of the exchange process suggested that the financial power of the Russian state remained limited. On the one hand, for
example, Italian economist Lorini, an admirer of Witte's financial reforms,
celebrated the inclusion of the Central Asian territories in the ruble zone as a

FIGURE 8.5 The State Bank branch in New Bukhara. From *Gosudarstvennyi
bank: kratkiii ocherk deiatel'nosti za 1860-1910 gody*. St. Petersburg, 1910.

real breakthrough that allowed several stages in the evolution of the monetary system to be skipped and raised territories "almost barbarian in the matter of the monetary standard . . . to the economy of credit, almost perfect." "This is a real conquest, complete, triumphal, accomplished by [the] Russian paper ruble" that penetrated deep into the region, down into the "heart of Persia and China."[77] On the other hand, travelers observed that years after the reform, Bukhara continued using its coins: "Only when merchants need rubles for Russian trade do they purchase . . . 100- and 500-ruble bills and make transfers to the banks of European Russia."[78] Therefore, Lorini's conclusion regarding the power of the Russian tsar over one-quarter of the world, established with the help of Russian railways and the ruble, was an overstatement. Indeed, the number of tenga in circulation gradually decreased due to the reduction of the minting operation and the material deterioration of coins, but the monetary vacuum was filled not with rubles but with other silver money, such as the Persian *qiran* (*krany* in Russian).[79] Outside the capital, credit rubles were accepted often with discounts, if at all.[80] The State Bank's officials explained that the spread of the ruble was unthinkable under the current administrative and political regime and in the absence of any, even the most primitive, roads and means of communication.[81] As one of the reports from Bukhara suggested, if the government wanted to spread the ruble, it had to "abandon the policy of non-intrusion in the domestic issues of the Bukhara khanate."[82] If it did not, all efforts would be in vain.

Perhaps these references to political conditions were simply meant to hide the ruble's limited economic power in the region. Its presence remained marginal not only in semi-autonomous Bukhara but even in the territories under the full sovereignty of the Russian tsar, most notoriously in the Trans-Caspian province. Having introduced a ban on the circulation of Persian qirans, the government there soon had to revoke it because of its adverse influence on trade.[83] Unlike the silver qirans, which were convertible to rupees and other currencies, the gold-based ruble remained practically inconvertible. As one of reports noted, "If a merchant takes a ruble, he does not know what to do with it."[84] Eventually, the authorities had to recognize that, in order to maintain commerce and at least a minimal presence in the economy of Afghanistan and Persia, it had to allow the circulation of local money.[85]

Rubles in Manchuria

The intricate routes of silver coins and ingots that crossed the Eurasian continent in various directions reveals an interesting story of imperial successes and failures. Russian expansion into Central Asia ushered silver from Europe, which was switching to gold, into the provinces of Turkestan and Bukhara, where European silver was minted into tenga and other coins. Then the Russian State Bank started exchanging tenga for rubles, acquiring a load of silver coins. Finally, in 1904, silver coins from Bukhara were loaded onto trains and sent to St. Petersburg. The Imperial Mint then melted them into silver ingots, which were promptly dispatched to the Far East. The Ministry of Finance asked the State Bank's branch in Bukhara to speed up the process so that the mint could work without interruption. Between November 1904 and December 1907, the St. Petersburg Mint received almost 16 million tenga coins, worth 2.3 million rubles.[86] Thus, European silver that had probably originated from colonies in the East traversed the continent several times, reflecting the pulsating rhythm of the attempts at monetary reforms and, oftentimes, their retractions.

Where did these silver ingots go, and why did Russia, which was so proud of its gold monetary system, need so much silver? The silver ingots made their way to Manchuria, another region where Russia struggled to introduce its ruble. In the 1890s, Russia's imperial ambitions spread farther to the east from Turkestan and the Central Asian protectorates. Witte entertained the idea of both strengthening Russia's presence in East Asia and penetrating economically into North China by building a shortcut line of the Trans-Siberian Railroad via Manchuria (1897) and leasing the Liaodong peninsula (1898). Behind the mundane question of which currency to use to pay for the railroad's construction materials and labor stood a range of political and economic problems.

The Chinese monetary system was based on silver that circulated in ingots (*yuanbao*; in Russian, *iamby*) that were shaped like cups or, Russians thought, like shoes, and they weighed 4.5 pounds each. Every merchant carried pocket scales to measure and chop off amounts as needed. The government did not have a minting monopoly, and multiple private mints and agencies, including the Russo-Chinese Bank, produced their own ingots.[87] In several provinces and port cities, Mexican dollars (*piastres*) circulated along with the chunks of silver; in the South, British silver "dollars," issued in Hongkong and Shanghai, started to squeeze out local currencies. Copper "chokh" (*qian*), round coins with a square hole in the middle that were carried in bundles and separated by knots into small stakes, were mostly used in small market trade and slowly began to disappear in the 1890s.[88]

To compensate for the lack of currency, in 1890, provincial authorities started minting their own silver coins equivalent to Mexican dollars and cents and accepting them in tax payments.[89] In Manchuria, the so-called Jilin (Girin in Russian) dollars, which were coined starting in 1896–97 by the *tsian-tsiun* (governor) of Jilin province, spread very quickly. With the tsar's permission, another mint was opened in the administrative center of Manchuria Shenyang (Mukden) in 1896.[90] Witnessing the development of silver coinage in China, the representatives of the Russo-Chinese Bank proposed coining special silver Russian-Chinese dollars of the same value as Mexican and provincial dollars, with bilingual inscriptions. The Chinese Eastern Railroad's administration, however, preferred to rely on local silver currency and doubted that the new Russo-Chinese money could compete with local dollars in a country where the population was very conservative and authorities would use any means to prevent the spread of a new currency.[91]

The government's reluctance to accept dollars—a convenient, but, as they claimed, financially and politically disadvantageous means of payment— rested on two assumptions. The first was that currency stands for authority, and it was therefore necessary to banish money that competed with rubles. The second was that the metallic value should define the trading value and the purchasing capacity of money. Officials thought that, in relying on dollars, they strengthened the authority of Chinese governors at the expense of the Russian state because dollars made on the standard of Mexican dollars cost 98 kopecks, while their material value in silver equaled only 92–93 kopecks. Railroad engineers, more familiar with the practices of the local economy, did not share this viewpoint. The ruble's value in China, they claimed, rested only on its exchangeability for local dollars. The fact that these dollars contained 10% less silver than their nominal value did not mean anything. For people who used them to pay taxes and purchase goods, dollars cost more than rubles despite the ruble's theoretical superiority. "All calculations that are meant to prove the disadvantages of purchasing dollars that contain 10% less silver than is paid in exchange, do not make any sense," because the railroad purchased dollars not to melt them but to use them exclusively in contracts with a population that did not accept other currencies.[92] The argument that "gold is better than silver" did not work, and consequently the ruble's value was assessed according to its exchangeability to the "inferior" silver.

The situation changed dramatically after the Boxer Rebellion, which ended in the de facto Russian occupation of Manchuria. On July 21, 1900, Nicholas II signed a decree prescribing that all contracts and payments in Manchuria were to be made in credit rubles of lower denominations and silver kopecks, which could be exchanged at any time for local silver currency at the Russo-Chinese Bank's exchange offices.[93] The Jilin Mint suspended its activity, but, contrary to the government's expectations that paper rubles would replace local dollars and quickly spread throughout the region, the population rushed to exchange their paper rubles for silver dollars, and the ruble's rate fell. The demand for dollars was so immense that not a single dollar could be found in Harbin. In December 1900, the ministry terminated the coercive imposition of Russian currency, allowing contracts in dollars, and the Jilin Mint resumed its activity with the help of the management of the Chinese Eastern Railroad.[94] The ruble remained the main means of payment on the railroad, of which all three of its branches were set on Russian lands. In short, the ruble became railroad money.

British journalist Bertram Lenox Simpson, writing under the pen name B. L. Putnam Weale, mocked the "defeat of the traveling ruble." Russia "was vainly attempting, in a most puerile fashion, to kill the minted dollar in Manchuria" and to spread instead "the famous paper money . . . stamped with the effigy of an omnipotent Czar, symbolic of Russia's victory all over the country." Even though the administration pumped millions of rubles into Manchuria, the ruble did not stick: "No sooner is paper received than prompt measures are taken to cash it in for something more finite than a mere piece of parchment." People did not trust the ruble because they were not used to paper money, and the idea of a gold or silver reserve that stood behind it was irrelevant: "A Chinaman is inordinately a lover of the tangible," concluded Putnam Weale. In fact, the omnipresent ruble did not enjoy any trust outside trains and stations: "It is condemned, like everything else Russian in Manchuria, to the dreary existence of a railway life."[95]

Putnam Weale's dismissive assessment reveals more about the tense economic competition in the region than about the causes of Russia's failings. In fact, other countries competing for financial dominance in the silver East closely observed Russia's experience in Bukhara and Manchuria and drew lessons from it. At the same time that Russia was struggling to impose rubles, the US Commission on International Exchange considered the introduction of the gold-exchange standard in silver-using countries: China, Mexico, Panama, and the Philippines. Russia's negative experience in Manchuria seemed to have played a role in designing the "American plan for China." The plan, compiled by Jeremiah W. Jenks, started with the creation of an entirely new, uniform, and integral national currency in China. It preserved the primary role of silver in the economy, although the value of silver was meant to be fixed in relation to a certain gold unit. Gold, as a metal "not suitable" for the economic conditions of China, was not supposed to play any serious role in circulation, and the gold reserve was meant to be held under the control of foreign experts and officials in Europe.⁹⁶ Thus, instead of the gold-based banknotes of foreign issue imposed by the Russian government, the US commission envisioned a much milder form of controlling Chinese finances. Silver, in other words, played the role of gold-based banknotes, and its ratio to gold was supposed to be established through an international agreement.

One of the major premises of the plan was to gain the approval of other countries for the creation of a new system of money in China that would inspire no "international jealousies." Referring to the efforts of the United States and other empires to normalize the monetary systems of the colonies (the United States in the Philippines, Great Britain in the Straits Settlements, France in Indochina), the commission argued for the benefits of creating a "uniform ratio" of silver to gold in "oriental countries" and claimed that "the representatives of all the powers," including Russia, "accepted in a general way as desirable and practicable the suggestions made by the Commission of the United States."⁹⁷ It seems that the tone of the Russian State Bank's official response to the Commission's inquiry was overall positive.⁹⁸ However, when presenting the American initiative to the tsar, Serguei Witte gave it a rather negative assessment. As Witte pointed out, silver continued to operate as a currency standard in certain "Asian" colonies of the Western empires, which therefore could be interested in such an agreement. "Russia is not interested in . . . this program because all Asian possessions of Russia have been unified, in the sense of monetary circulation, with the empire."⁹⁹ Even in relation to Russian Central Asia, this was an overstatement. A few months after Witte's boastful report, Russia faced a tremendous financial crisis in Manchuria and the Liaodong associated with the fall of the Russian gold-based ruble vis-à-vis the local silver currency. In any case, the US plan for the currency reform in China was doomed, as was the international agreement regarding silver-gold parity. Competing empires—Great Britain, Japan, Russia, and the United States—each tried to impose their vision of the future currency system, even if within the narrow limits of a "zone of influence."

The precarious position of Russian currency became obvious when, immediately after the eruption of the Russo-Japanese War in February 1904, the ruble's rate to Chinese silver dollars fell by 25%. The government panicked because the war might pose a danger to Russia's gold-based currency, which could seep through the open border and threaten the integrity of the bullion reserve. Konstantin Golovin, a former state official and a journalist, suggested converting the entire territory of Russia's Far East region of 3 million square kilometers into a special financial zone where gold would be entirely replaced by silver and the gold exchange suspended. This would require

concentrating all available silver coins in one region and purchasing an additional 100 million rubles in silver bullion (i.e., increasing the amount of silver
by 30%) from the United States, which "had plenty of it." The new minister of
finance, Vladimir Kokovtsov, rejected the proposal as incompatible with "the
Empire's dignity," the principles of the gold-based economy, and the "entire
policy of monetary circulation, which lately has been aimed at the Empire's
unification with its borderlands."[100] In fact, emergency measures undertaken
by the government against the drainage of gold created a special zone east
of Lake Baikal, where monetary circulation was limited to credit rubles of
the lowest denominations (1, 5, and 10 rubles), which had been effectively
banned from circulation for several years.[101] The gold did not drain; instead,
the government experienced an entirely new problem. To support the value
of the "gold" ruble in Manchuria, the government had to ensure its convertibility to silver, which the Russian authorities simply did not have. Ironically,
the problem of the bullion reserve, which Russia had been trying to build
throughout the nineteenth century, reappeared. After almost all the silver
at the St. Petersburg Mint had been melted, the government had to revert
to purchasing silver in Europe and shipping silver tenga from Bukhara to St.
Petersburg and then to Manchuria.[102]

The ruble's fall vis-à-vis the Chinese silver dollar was both embarrassing
and disheartening. As the official history of the war explained, "The reason
for the ruble's instability and its extreme sensibility to external events was
contained in the fact that . . . it was not sufficiently supported by full-weight
silver, because the silver reserve at our disposal in Manchuria . . . turned out to
be not equivalent to the mass of paper money that had been thrown onto the
market."[103] Thus, the problem of the bullion reserve arose again. This time, it
was silver, not gold, that was missing. The Russo-Chinese Bank had run out of
silver and suspended the exchange, referring to the absence of silver in Europe.
The military commandment in Manchuria asked the government to send 640
tons of silver from the capital, but the government had to refuse this request,
explaining that the prices of silver on the world market would skyrocket if
Russia attempted to purchase this volume of silver in bulk. The administration continued to believe that it was the lack of silver, in addition to rumors
spread by "bad people," not a lack of authority and military power, that had
brought down the ruble. On April 6, 1904, in a remarkable article addressed
to simple folk unfamiliar with monetary theories, the *Harbin Herald* tried
to explain to readers that rumors that a paper ruble allegedly "cost less than
a silver one" were spread by liars and swindlers. The ruble was not like those
paper notes printed by Chinese private banks and offices: "The Russian state,

when it issues paper rubles, puts in an equal amount of silver and gold, in the presence of high officials from other countries and bankers from capitals, who count how much gold is kept in the bank. . . . This is why [the words are] printed on Russian paper money that the Russian state exchanges, without limit, its paper money for gold coins. . . . Therefore, the rate of the Russian paper ruble cannot fall. A paper ruble and a silver ruble are one and the same thing."[104]

Thus, even in addressing the population of a country with an entirely different monetary system and understanding of the signs of value, Russian authorities reproduced the same philosophy that constituted the essence of Russia's gold standard. The ruble's rate began to grow slowly when the Russo-Chinese Bank in Harbin finally started exchanging rubles at an abnormally high price for silver ingots shipped to Manchuria from Hamburg.[105] It was fully restored only after the end of the war, which cost Russia 2.5 billion rubles in treasury spending, territorial losses, including the leasehold of the Liaodong peninsula and one branch of the Chinese Eastern Railroad, and a political crisis. The actual costs of the war, including the costs of domestic and foreign loans and interests, was estimated at three times higher than that.[106]

The international gold standard system, as historians now portray it, did not represent a single seamless realm but instead was a tiered structure consisting of several subsystems. Below the level of the classic gold standard, there was a tier of "gold-exchange" countries. These countries created yet another layer of monetary regimes in the areas of their economic dominance.[107] Russia's gold standard system also evolved as a multi-layered structure that included a core area running on gold, borderlands with different backgrounds and statuses, semi-independent countries and protectorates, and finally, "areas of influence," such as Manchuria. Russia's efforts to impose the gold ruble as a legal tender in Manchuria (without introducing gold) followed a similar procedure that was also meant to prevent the spread of competing currencies. However, in the end, Russia lost in the geopolitical, military, and financial competition for dominance in the Far East, and the Japanese yen became the region's dominant currency.[108]

The story of the attempts to impose rubles in Asia in the aftermath of the gold reform proves that the gold standard represented more than a set of financial rules and practices for the regulation of domestic monetary circulation and international exchange. The gold standard was a mode of governance, a system of control and administration that had both social and territorial dimensions. While introducing Russian rubles in colonies, the government faced the same problems and obstacles it encountered in establishing other forms of cultural and economic dominance. The fact that Russia was unable to make this system work in Central Asia and Manchuria shows the extent to which Russian authorities prioritized the political aspects of monetary policy over the economic and cultural factors that they perceived as contingencies. Tracing the earlier years of Witte's policy and his infatuation with the idea of using paper rubles as a means of imperial expansion reveals his remarkable consistency. If in the early 1890s Witte, following the pattern of nationalists, was going to build the Trans-Siberian Railroad with inflationary currency, a few years later the same railroad was supposed to work as an agent for spreading Russian gold-based rubles. In the end, Russia's imperial ambitions resulted in the Russo-Japanese war, followed by the revolution that almost ruined its gold currency. Russia's gold standard was, therefore, not only autocratic but also imperial.

If in economic terms the Russian experience of the transition to the gold standard was not so different from that of other countries, it represents a unique example of an unlimited monarchy that switched to the gold standard. Two elements—the factor of "empire" and the factor of "autocracy"—influenced both the content of the reform and the way it was accomplished. The introduction of the gold standard in Russia certainly imposed restrictions on the ability of the government and the tsar's power to make money: the emission law of 1897 was the first public commitment of that sort, and its form differed from the previous bureaucratic pact of 1881.[109] Nevertheless, in the absence of any mechanisms of control, it represented a self-imposed and self-enforced commitment by the government to its foreign creditors and investors rather than to its own society. As further developments will show, the government favored its international credibility over its credibility at home. Therefore, the internal criticism of the gold standard and widespread discontent with the methods of its realization did not matter. The gold standard was a model of an outward-looking financial policy "for export."

Politically, the reform strengthened the state's role in finance and the economy. The gold standard in Russia was supposed to activate certain market mechanisms, such as the inflow of investment, but, at the same time, it put under strict state control other important institutions of market economy, including banks and the stock exchange. In 1900, the Credit Chancellery of the Ministry of Finance headed by Witte's relative took over the main functions of the stock exchange, namely, the quotation of securities and currencies as well as the regulation of companies' access to the stock market.[110] In the words of Russian economists, the stock exchange lost its autonomy when the "imperious reformer . . . laid his hands on the security market." As they noted, "S. Yu. Witte was the Russian autocratic regime's flesh and blood. He was not gifted with an understanding and a will that could have called to life and revival the forces of civic initiative and economic freedom."[111]

Was Russia's example exceptional? The concept of the "standard" suggests uniformity and universalism, yet each country that joined the common march to gold between the 1860s and the 1910s came to it in its own manner. Despite the similarity of underlying economic norms, there was no single political scenario for these transitions; some of them were more democratic or consensual, others more authoritarian. The resulting regimes also differed in the degree of state's involvement. As acclaimed economist Milton Friedman argued in 1961, while the core idea of the standard's meaning may be the same, differences in institutional arrangements produce very distinct models. Under the regime of the "real gold standard," gold coins circulate in the economy, but the state is not involved in monetary regulation. The "pseudo gold standard" assumes that the state maintains control over the monetary system and establishes the rate.[112] The Russian case is an example of the regime closest to this standard due to the excessive participation in the monetary system by a State Bank owned and managed by the government. The institutional and political outcome of the reform therefore suggests that, among factors that affect the sustainability of the gold standard system, the specifics of the country's political regime play the most important role.[113]

PART IV

Ruble, Wars, and Revolutions

9

The Gold Syndrome

The Humbert Safe

I was walking along a long, broad corridor with high ceilings. Light was streaming from somewhere above me.

On the right and the left, and in the depths of the corridor, there were big iron-hinged doors. The doors were not solid but blacksmith openwork. I looked through the grate of the doors near me and saw a large hall with many cabinets standing along the walls. On the floor, there were piles of gray bags.

No, not this way. This is silver. Let's go to the gold, I heard a voice say behind me.

On the left, a key clanged in a padlock, a bolt clattered and a seal with the imperial eagle fell on the tiled floor. The seal was broken. The doors were wide open.

I stepped over a threshold and found myself in a grandiose, vast and high hall. Bookcases five to six *arshin* tall stood tightly along the walls. All shelves were filled, in neat rows, as it seemed to me in the twilight, by thick books with gold edges.

Someone's kind hand touched an invisible button, and suddenly the little embers of electric chandeliers hanging down from the arched ceilings flashed out and glowed.

Electric light, reflected by the mysterious cases, filled in the hall with a gold luster.[1]

This story, resembling "Ali Baba and the Forty Thieves," appeared on the pages of the *St. Petersburg Newspaper* in mid-March 1905, when St. Petersburg was seized by the turbulence of revolution and the Russian army was fighting a losing battle against Japan. The newspaper correspondent was among several other journalists invited to tour the gold depository of the State Bank. Newspapers competed in their colorful descriptions of the impregnable magnificent halls filled with gold, built of stone and concrete. Most reporters chose a fairytale style for their narratives; it was hard not to, given that the "bricks" were made of gold and the piles of coins were, quite literally, heaped by a shovel.

The gold kept in the State Bank deposit came from various parts of the world. A grid separated Russian coins from the coins of Germany, Spain, England, Belgium, Chile, and Finland.

> " 'Which gold do you want to look at?' asks S[erguei] D. Gan [director of the department of the credit bills and gold reserve].
>
> 'Japanese, let's see Japanese,' several voices respond." . . .
>
> "I pick up one of the bags, open it, and Japanese gold coins, the size of our 10-ruble coins but thinner, with amazingly beautiful and refined ornamentation, pour on the table."[2]

The gold was then counted and put back into seamless leather bags. The interest in Japanese gold betrayed more than the taste for oriental

FIGURE 9.1 The State Bank gold storage rooms. From *Gosudarstvennyi bank: kratkii ocherk deiatel'nosti za 1860-1910 gody*. St. Petersburg, 1910.

exoticism: Russia was fighting against an unfamiliar enemy, and the reasons for this war remained obscure to many.

The Russo-Japanese War waged from January 1904 to August 1905, was the first conflict fought after the introduction of the gold standard, and so past proponents and opponents of the gold standard judged it as a test of the new system's sustainability. Japan had adopted the gold standard just a few months after Nicholas II signed the decree that completed the gold reform in Russia. Japan used the indemnity received from China, defeated in a Sino-Japanese War in 1895, to build its gold reserve.[3] In March 1897, Japan passed the new currency law, and on October 1, 1897, it made the *yen* convertible into gold.[4] The war factor had played an important role in justifying the Russian gold reform of 1897. The unfortunate experience of the previous Russo-Turkish War, which had left Russian finances in ruins, supported the dogma of war economics that one can score a victory only with the help of a significant gold reserve and healthy currency; neither a special military reserve fund nor taxes or loans could compete in terms of convenience with the immediate expansion of monetary circulation, which, it was believed, could be contracted back to its original size after the war's end.[5] In 1900, Witte reported to the tsar that, thanks to the gold reform, "Russia has never been as well prepared for a big all-European war as now." If necessary, it could issue as much as 1 billion paper rubles without shaking its monetary system; after the end of the war, it would easily return to its normal condition.[6]

The size of the gold reserve was, of course, mesmerizing. When the war began, all experts declared that, financially and economically, Russia was much better prepared than Japan. It seemed that the statistical numbers reflecting the condition of the monetary economy in Russia and Japan needed no commentary: the gold of Russia's State Bank covered 150% of its paper circulation, compared to 50% in Japan. In Russia, 60% of the monetary circulation was in metal, whereas in Japan, gold coins amounted to only 35% of the total volume.[7] According to French journalist Raphaël-Georges Lévy, in February 1904, the Japanese financial authorities demanded that everyone who possessed gold coins or jewelry deliver them to the Bank. The emperor and empress set an example by sending their old jewelry from the palace, and they were followed by other dignitaries and officials. The gold raised across the country during the patriotic campaign was melted and expedited to the United States as collateral for the loan. The United States in turn used this gold to pay France for the purchase of the Panama Canal. The gold ingots came to Paris at the moment when Russia floated its war loan, and the Japanese gold, at least partially, landed in the deposits of the Russian Treasury.[8] Even if this story of the gold's round-the-world journey is no more than a fantasy, it is very revealing. Gold had no nationality, and its turnover during the wars, driven by nationalism and imperial ambitions, followed amazing routes.

With its massive gold reserve, Russia, as Lévy and many others observed, had nothing to fear, whereas Japan found itself in a very dangerous financial situation. Indeed, in Russia, 905.8 million rubles of gold covered 608 million paper rubles, with a hefty sum to spare. Nevertheless, even the government realized that the possibility of expanding paper circulation could not be defined arithmetically. Minister of Finance Vladimir Kokovtsov estimated the "reasonable" limit of expansion at only 200 million rubles.[9] In March 1904, the potential cost of war was still estimated at 700–800 million rubles (it would exceed that number threefold). By the end of 1904, the State Bank had already issued 270 million extra paper rubles, which were partially balanced by the slight increase of the gold reserve with the help of the first war loan.

Some experts suggested that instead of trying to maintain the convertibility to gold, the government should suspend the exchange and then resume it after the war's end, a common practice in all major European countries.[10] However, both the acting and the former ministers of finance (Kokovtsov and Witte) rejected this plan, declaring the preservation of convertibility "the first and most important task of financial administration." "The suspension of convertibility leads to the most serious, sorrowful consequences for the wellbeing of the state," Kokovtsov believed; convertibility affects the credibility of the state, which, in turn, produces significant losses.[11] Witte agreed: "Some people think that with the suspension of exchange, the gold locked in the Bank's storage stays intact, whereas the continuation of exchange, in view of the increased demand for gold, may lead to the loss thereof, and the suspension of exchange ultimately becomes inevitable when the gold reserve has already disappeared. This opinion is undoubtedly wrong."[12]

England, France, and other countries had experienced the suspension of exchange during times of financial hardship caused by wars, but Russia was different. Due to the size of Russia's foreign debt, the suspension could raise the costs of its maintenance and drop the ruble's value. Gold would have trickled away through other channels—the increased payments for loans and imported goods. The ministry's strategy was therefore to borrow gold abroad, put it into the exchange fund, and print paper rubles to pay for the war in the amount backed by this reserve.[13] As Russia's authorities emphatically stressed, they used borrowed money not to pay for war expenses but only to keep the appropriate size of the gold reserve intact. Thus, maintaining the gold reserve and convertibility came at the high cost of increasing Russia's already significant foreign debt. As the minister of finance asserted, "The burden of payments for loans in any case is incommensurable" with the costs of suspension.[14] To raise additional funds for the war, in April 1904, the Russian government started negotiating a loan in France. At the very same time, Japan also embarked on foreign borrowing in the United States and Britain. The conditions of Russia's first (of three) wartime loans were much more favorable than Japan's loan; however, unlike Japan, Russia was not new on the European money market and, compared to Russia's previous borrowings, this loan cost much more than usual.[15] As for Japan, the loan was a huge breakthrough and a sensation. The second loan soon followed, and then two more loans with extremely favorable conditions. The phenomenal success of Japan's loans of 1904–05 was not due to the size of its gold reserve, which was dwindling, but to the victories of the Japanese army.[16] Similarly, the story of Russia's borrowings in 1904–05 shows a correlation between the ability to raise loans and the news of military debacles, political disturbances, and reforms.[17] The revolutionary movement and social unrest, which erupted in January 1905 and unfolded at a horrific pace throughout the country, further destabilized the already shaken state of Russian finances. Russia's creditors grew wary and started wondering whether the impressive gold reserve, the largest in Europe, could save the country from bankruptcy and collapse.

To support the government's credibility, the Russian Ministry of Finance and the State Bank dutifully published budget numbers and the statistics of monetary circulation. Nevertheless, as a correspondent for *The Times* (of London) observed, "The business world, with hardly any exceptions, put very little trust in them at all."[18] In mid-March 1905, *The Times* published a two-part article by journalist Lucien Wolf under the title "Is Russia Solvent?" Using numbers drawn from official publications, Wolf proved that Russia balanced its budgets only with the help of foreign loans.[19] Russia's trade balance was inactive and her foreign obligations enormous, while the value of assets—such as state-owned railroads—was overappreciated: "For years past, Russia has been living beyond her means, and .... her foreign obligations are literally paid out of underfeeding of the people," he claimed, underscoring the connection between revolutionary upheavals and Russia's illusion of wealth.

> As she is situated today, Russia is marching directly to insolvency. Her national balance-sheet leaves her every year deeper in debt. Her liabilities to the foreigner are more than her people can bear, and she has practically nothing to show for them. Her gold reserve is a colossal

Humbert safe, the vaunted millions of which are unconsciously lent by her dupes for their own further deception.[20]

Except for this last phrase, Wolf's article did not touch on the issue of the gold reserve; it was meant to show the deceptiveness of budgetary statements and the promises of economic improvements. As he put it, "The truth . . . is that figures are not what they seem." But the article's main thrust was much more complex and ambitious than simply the ubiquitous calls to turn down Russia's further demands for loans: Wolf was suggesting that foreign investors could use loans to push Russia toward the reforms: "That ruin cannot be long postponed if the existing system, political as well as financial, is allowed to remain fundamentally unchanged. While the army remains faithful to the bureaucracy, the suffering people may be held at bay, but Russian bayonets are powerless in the foreign money market." Therefore, investors could use Russia's dire need for funds to make "the Tsar and his advisers . . . take radical steps to set their house in order. Peace abroad, far-reaching political reforms at home, and a system of rigid financial retrenchment would in the course of time put a very different complexion on the national balance-sheet."[21]

Wolf's article could not be left without a response, given, as prominent journalist Sir Henry Norman had noticed earlier, "the fanatical importance Russia attaches to the maintenance of her financial reputation"[22] and the government's attempts to procure further loans in Europe. But Kokovtsov's reaction was as immediate as it was inadequate. In his letter to *The Times*'s editor, the minister of finance seized on the comparison of the gold reserve with the Humbert safe. Wolf's phrase referred to the scandalous case of Thérèse Humbert, a French fraudster who borrowed money against an alleged inheritance from a mysterious American benefactor. For twenty years, Humbert and her family continued taking out loans to pay for their previous borrowing, and when the fraud was finally discovered, Humbert's legendary safe was found to be empty. The comparison sounded very offensive because it hinted at the government's policy to fill the gold reserve with foreign loans and then borrow again using the gold fund as a collateral. However, this was not critical to the article's argument. Entirely missing, or consciously overlooking, the "formidable case" that had been made against Russia, one that required "explanations upon many capital points,"[23] Kokovtsov, in response to Wolf's article, invited the representative of *The Times* to "come to St. Petersburg to see and verify personally the gold reserve kept in the vaults of the State Bank."[24]

Instead of improving the situation, the minister's response made matters even worse. It demonstrated a strikingly primitive understanding of the mechanisms of trust, as if they were based solely on the size of the gold reserve, whereas Wolf had pointed out that to improve its credibility, Russia had to begin constitutional reforms. Wolf's message, as the other newspapers' reactions show, was well understood by everyone except Kokovtsov, whose reading of it demonstrated that the government treated the gold as a substitute for constitutional arrangements.[25] "Mr. Kokovtsov did not understand the meaning of this witty and spiteful joke and made the entire world laugh at his telegram," remarked Vladimir Lenin, at the time an exiled leader of the Bolshevik wing of the Russian social-democratic party and editor of a short-lived Bolshevik periodical, *Onward*. "English bourgeois, laughing at the silly minister, started chewing over for him this not very complicated thing,"[26] namely, that they distrusted the government not because they did not believe in the gold reserve but because no legal representative institution in Russia could ensure its preservation.

The Times declined Kokovtsov's invitation to tour the Bank, explaining that Wolf's article did not doubt the existence of the gold reserve and simply stated that it could not be considered an expression of Russia's wealth and credibility.[27] Embarrassed, the Ministry of Finance extended the invitation to the reporters of other foreign newspapers and news agencies.[28] Kokovtsov also instructed the Bank's director, Serguei Timashev, to invite the representatives of a few Russian newspapers that were "worth the attention." However, because "newspaper folks always lie and confuse everything," Timashev was to provide them not only with a table showing the amount of treasury and Bank gold in the main depositary, in branches, and abroad, but also the total gold amount of 1.3 billion rubles.[29]

Timashev was not overly enthusiastic about giving a tour of the gold storage. He thought that inviting too many journalists would be interpreted as a sign of the government's anxiety over the lack of confidence. He also suggested not disclosing the sum of gold in the treasury's account, which did not belong to the Bank, so as "not to demonstrate all our [gold] stocks, the depletion of which is being closely observed."[30] This truncated publicity resulted in an awkward moment when one of the visitors, having observed the magnificent masses of gold, asked whether this gold was reserved only to serve as a collateral for the credit bills or whether it could be spent on the state's needs. Serguei Gan, the director of the department of the credit bills and gold reserve, evaded the question under the pretext that it was "beyond the sphere of his expertise." The liberal *Rus'* seized the opportunity to return to the question of whether a billion rubles in gold was a great deal of money or not. If it was only a collateral for the credit bills and remained untouched, it looked like a fortune. If, to the contrary, the government could use it for other means, this gold could be squandered very fast. In essence, this question repeated Wolf's argument that gold already pledged for credit rubles cannot serve as a guarantee of credibility on foreign loans.

The controversy around Wolf's articles continued for a few months. The ministry kept sending reports of the value of the gold kept in the State Bank, the impregnability of the vault's stone walls and iron doors, the number of guards protecting it—as if this could affect the credibility of a country caught in the flames of the revolution.[31] As soon as the debate began to die down, Rudolf Martin, an official of the German Imperial statistical office, subjected the Russian financial system to a devastating and humiliating critique. Martin's bestselling *The Future of Russia and Japan* appeared right when the representatives of the two countries met in Portsmouth to negotiate a peace agreement in the late summer of 1905, and suggested that "Russia was bankrupt beyond any possibility of redemption."[32] The book exposed the gold ruble reform as a masterful trick: the shine of gold was supposed to distract Russia's creditors from the financial instability and poverty of Russia's economy. Martin praised Witte's wit and the "financial technique" that allowed him to produce the illusion of solvency when in fact the war, the new loans, and the unfolding revolution were pushing Russia to the brink of financial collapse.[33] "I pay in gold, says the Russian state. We pay everything in gold, say the inhabitants of Russia." The illusory abundance of gold in the Bank, the treasury and people's pockets fooled both the creditors and the debtors themselves. The book drew comparisons between the situation in pre-revolutionary France and revolutionary Russia and compared Witte to Jacques Necker, finance minister for Louis XVI, with extra credit given to the Russian minister as a sly politician and financier. Martin's book appeared in translations and enjoyed immense popularity.[34] The government banned the import of Martin's book to Russia and organized a campaign to neutralize its influence in the European press, supplying reporters and correspondents with statistical data and templates for articles refuting Martin's insinuations.[35] It was not hard to prove that Martin had erred in his numbers; however, the very idea that the shine of gold concealed a mass of unresolved economic problems—most important, the extremely low productivity of the Russian economy—had appeared numerous times before. Martin just couched the poverty argument in the most sensational, paradoxical, and speculative manner.

The information war waged on Russian finances exposed the vulnerability of the system created by Witte's gold reform. Laying too much stress on the gold reserve exposed the weakness of the other, non-material guarantees of Russia's sustainability.[36] The *Rus'* correspondent who, among other journalists, had visited the gold vaults of the State Bank, highlighted the paradox in the most poignant way: the Russian State Bank had the largest gold deposit; however, European financiers did not believe in the stability of Russia's gold currency and even "treat it with a persistent . . . distrust." For example, the German Reichsbank's gold reserve was minuscule compared to the number of banknotes in circulation, but nobody ever doubted its credibility. "Our credit bills are more than fully backed by gold rubles, and, nevertheless, the existence of our gold currency is always doubted. . . . Where does this distrust come from?" This response once again evoked the old problem of the State Bank's lack of independence and the illegality of its activity. The Russian State Bank, unlike the semi-private Reichsbank, belonged entirely to the state and was perceived, especially abroad, "as the personal chancellery of the minister of finance." This would mean that the power of the minister of finance stood above the authority of the law that was supposed to regulate the bank's activity. The situation had to be reversed. "Less gold and more legality" was the recipe for improving the standing of Russian finances.[37]

Leaking Gold

The Russian Ministry of Finance's emphatic attempts to prove the colossal size of its gold reserve were all the more naïve because the reserve was indeed dwindling, and this was impossible to hide. In the first six months of war, the gold reserve lost 104 million rubles, but then the loan in Paris added 282 million rubles, and the total mass of gold even increased compared to the pre-war level.[38] The government had to limit the payments of gold and encourage the State Bank's clients to take credit bills of low denominations, which had not been seen in circulation since the beginning of the gold reform. Explaining the reasons for changing the State Bank's monetary policy, the minister of finance presented the limitation of the gold payments through the bank's offices as an "introduction of a complete freedom of monetary circulation; gold is no longer imposed on anyone."[39] After several years of the forceful imposition of gold and the withdrawal of small bills, the reappearance of paper rubles should have been seen as the government's response to society's "wishes and habit," but hardly anyone believed in this sudden benevolence. "The best monetary circulation is the one that corresponds with

the tastes and demands of the public,"[40] as it said in the draft of the minister's
report to the tsar on the state budget for 1905. Moreover, the government was
willing to support this "attitude of the public, based on its conviction of the
gold standard's stability."[41]

In 1905, the situation changed dramatically. In January 1904, the amount
of credit rubles in circulation had stood at 578.4 million; by January 1905, it
had risen to 853.7 million, and in January 1906, it had reached 1,205.7 million.
Concomitantly, from January 1904 to January 1905, the State Bank gold reserve
had increased, due to foreign loans, from 903 to 1,029.4 million; in January
1906, it fell to 919.7 million. Therefore, the paper-to-gold ratio dropped
from 1.56 to 0.76.[42] In other countries and under different circumstances, this
ratio would not have been a problem. But Russia did not have the luxury of
undermining its credibility due to the amount of state securities on the international market. Meanwhile, as the State Bank's governor Timashev observed,
gold leaked in all possible directions. The holders of Russian bonds tried to sell
their assets, demanding hard currency, and everyone preferred gold over credit
rubles. In the last months of 1905, especially after the Manifesto of October 17,
1905, which marked Russia's transition to a constitutional monarchy, people
rushed to withdraw their deposits from saving accounts, demanding payment
in gold and hoarding the coins that just a few years earlier had been so unwanted. "In the mornings, an anxious and menacing mob of a thousand people
would appear at several institutions," said the bank report.[43] Only repeated
cases of robbery could discourage the anxious public from their demands for
gold, while the bank, facing the collapse of the national transportation system,
was often simply unable to deliver money to its provincial offices, thereby
limiting exchange operations to the capital cities.[44] Despite the limitations
on the currency exchange, the sales of foreign currency between October 20
and December 8 exceeded 240 million rubles, sometimes reaching 2 million
rubles a day.[45] "Everyone who can, takes money and leaves the country. Dozens
of millions [of rubles] have been transferred abroad in one month only (by
the Grand Dukes, among others)," recorded a prominent Petersburg lawyer
Nikolai Tagantsev in his diary in November 1905.[46]

The gold panic reached it pinnacle when on December 2, 1905, five socialist
organizations issued the so-called Financial Manifesto, which encouraged the
already ongoing withdrawal of gold from banks and called on the populace to
demand gold in all state-paid wages and contracts in order to approach and
facilitate the collapse of the monarchy. Thus, radical revolutionaries arrived
at the same logic as the government, linking the regime's survival to the preservation of the gold standard that "had become worthless in comparison to

FIGURE 9.2 Caricature of bureaucrats fleeing the country with gold. A peasant at the border gate tells them to go but leave the gold behind. From *Voron.* 1905, no. 1.

the obligations of the state loans and the demands of trade." The Financial Manifesto, apparently drafted by Leon Trotsky, repeated almost verbatim the points that had been made by Lucien Wolf in *The Times* and summarized in Lenin's articles. It linked Russia's impending financial ruin to the unaccountability of a government that was borrowing money against its previous debts, to the falsity of the state budgets, and to the explanation of the delay in the convocation of the representative assembly by means of the "fear of popular control that could reveal in front of the entire world the government's financial insolvency." Several newspapers that dared to publish the Manifesto were immediately shut down by the government.

The revolution penetrated to the core of the money-making machine. In October 1905, the workers of the Expedition for the Production of State Papers went on strike, endangering the supply of new credit rubles. The strike came as a surprise, since the new management of the factory in the late 1890 had turned it into an exemplary enterprise run according to the most progressive principles of labor organizations. The factory's facilities included libraries, cafeterias, a children's day care center, a technical school, dorms, a hospital, summer camps for children, a brass band, church choir, tea house, and theater; workers were relatively well paid and received bonus payments from the factory's profit.[47] Still, the wave of printing-worker strikes in the city drew in the Expedition, threatening to leave the government without either paper or metallic money. "The danger will be aggravated especially if the moment comes to switch to paper-only circulation," stated one of the reports.[48] The poignancy of the situation was exacerbated as the leader of the workers' strike, Mikhail Ushakov, a member of the notorious workers organization run by the political police (*Okhranka*), had been appointed to the Expedition in 1903 by Witte's personal order.[49] As one of the Expedition's managers attested, Ushakov, relying on his "protection from above," essentially stopped working and switched to open propaganda among workers, gathering them in restrooms, corridors, and closets. In April 1905, he was fired for repeated failures to show up at work, but on November 11, 1905, the administration, in response to the strike demands, was forced to hire him back with compensation for the entire period of his dismissal.[50] Witte claims in his memoirs that during the revolution, Ushakov did not support the "anarchists"—that is to say, the Soviets (the Councils of the Workers' Deputies)—and stayed on the conservative side of the workers' movement.[51] Perhaps Witte wanted to use Ushakov to foil the insurgency inside the money-printing factory, but the situation spun out of control.[52] From the State Bank's perspective, it looked dramatic. The director of the credit ruble's department, Gan, urged Timashev to transfer from the Expedition to the State Bank all key operations that did not involve machines, employ women who were thought to be less susceptible to propaganda, and declare strikes at the Expedition illegal.[53] The State Bank was also impacted by the revolution. Bank offices and the transport of money had suffered from the repeated attempts at revolutionary "expropriations," and the administration had to employ 100 armed soldiers to protect the bank's vaults.[54]

FIGURE 9.3 The Department of Credit Rubles at the State Bank with women employees. From *Gosudarstvennyi bank: kratkiii ocherk deiatel'nosti za 1860-1910 gody*. St. Petersburg, 1910,

The paper ruble's gold backing hit rock bottom in December 1905, when the revolutionary movement culminated in an armed uprising in Moscow. The Committee of Finance, which had met several times in December to discuss measures for the preservation of the gold reserve, in particular "whether to continue the exchange of state credit rubles for gold or not," could not come to a firm decision and awaited the outcomes of the counter-insurgency measures. Besides, as Vladimir Kokovtsov recalled, it was almost impossible to tell how much gold was left in the State Bank's branches and regional treasury offices, since the railroad and postal service strikes had paralyzed the mechanisms of gathering financial information.[55]

Some members of the government argued that suspending the exchange would help keep the remaining gold.[56] However, the choice that the government faced in December 1905 was of a political rather than a financial nature. For the conservative establishment, the "moral costs" of suspending the ruble's convertibility and not surrendering to the revolutionary forces outweighed the financial rationale. However, the political constituent of the gold ruble question concerned not simply the issue of withstanding the pressure of the revolutionary propaganda. In an unpublished (and probably uncirculated) memo, Professor Illarion Kaufman pointed out that even though the gold currency had been introduced "against popular opinion," people became accustomed to it and came to regard it as their basic right: "The right to gold ... nowadays is among the most generally accepted concepts." Everyone is aware of this "right to gold, ... holds it firmly and insists on its inviolability." The revolution certainly contributed to the growth of the awareness of the gold ruble's status as a national treasure; therefore, "if the government gave ground to accusations of the destruction of this treasure, it would provoke criticism and condemnation that would only play into the hands of its mortal enemies."[57] Suspending the exchange to gold threatened to exacerbate the political crisis.

Anticipating the worst-case scenario, the new minister of finance, Ivan Shipov, who had replaced Kokovtsov after the constitutional reform and the formation of a new government headed by Russia's first prime minister, Serguei Witte, in October 1905, prepared the plan to suspend exchange operations. While considering the most appropriate form by which to announce the suspension, Shipov recalled that the last time the government had reverted to this measure was during the Crimean War. Back then, the suspension had been enacted through a series of the minister's orders, without a public announcement. "This way can hardly be followed in the present situation, since the circumstances have completely changed," he observed.[58] Therefore, Shipov drafted an imperial decree announcing the temporary suspension of the exchange and had Nicholas II sign it. One of the original versions of the decree contained a phrase that was later, quite wisely, deleted. Remarkably, it explained the need to suspend the exchange because it was necessary to "preserve in complete untouchability the realization of all commitments undertaken by the state in regard to its foreign loans."[59] Thus, contrary to what European observers (starting with Martin) predicted, even in the face of tremendous revolutionary upheaval, the government feared bankruptcy on foreign loans more than its default on domestic obligations. It seems that the government did not share the idea of the people's "right to gold" which Kaufman had underscored in his memo.

The suspension decree was never announced and put in practice. Nicholas II destroyed the signed copy in late 1907.[60] The government also did not approve and publicize the project of a new emission law that changed the ratio between gold and paper to a less strict 1:2, with a maximum of credit rubles in circulation established at 1.4 billion.[61] Fortunately, the former minister of finance, Vladimir Kokovtsov, came back from Paris with news of an advance loan of 100 million rubles. At the same time, the Russian army and police suppressed the major wave of the revolutionary rebellion. In early January 1906, taxes and payments started to trickle in, and the situation gradually improved. The ruble was saved with the help of foreign gold and bayonets as the price of Russia's political support for France's advances in Africa, which secured the loan floated in April 1906.[62] In total, from 1904 to 1906, Russia borrowed 1.092 billion rubles abroad; the sum exceeded the value of all the State Bank's gold and was, according to Witte, the largest international loan in history.[63] Of this sum, only a small portion (16 million) was physically delivered to Russia; most of it was spent on foreign payments (e.g., loans and exchange bills) and deposited in the Russian Treasury's accounts in foreign banks.[64]

The revolutionary crisis of the Russian currency had one more, rather unexpected consequence. It foiled the plan of Finland's monetary integration, which had been launched after the 1897 reform and would have required the extension of the State Bank's activity into Finland. Although the statement on the opening of a bank's branch in Helsinki emphasized the national neutrality of this institution, its activity was expected to have "political importance."[65] The State Bank's branch in Helsinki was meant to be fully independent of Finnish authorities and represent a counterpoint to the Bank of Finland. The branch opened its doors in August 1905 amid the revolutionary surge in Russia and the rise of an autonomous movement in Finland, but in February 1906, its director, Nikolai Vykovskii, suggested terminating its operations. Vykovskii, who had previously served in several other provincial branches, suddenly became the champion of Finnish autonomy and an ardent critic of the imperial government policy that had aimed to turn Finland "into something resembling Kaluga province." Vykovskii's reports urged the State Bank to retreat from Finland, which during the revolution had regained its autonomy and constitutional rights. Observing the popular mood, Vykovskii pointed out that the Finns considered both the establishment of the State Bank's branch in Helsinki, of which he was the director, and the policy of imposing Russian currency as detrimental to the Duchy's credit and monetary system. The discontent of the population, as Vykovskii pointed out, was quite understandable, since the Bank of Finland was "defined and checked by the representatives of the Finnish people," whereas the activity of the State Bank, a quintessentially bureaucratic institution, remained outside the sphere of such control.

The head of Russia's financial headquarters in Finland, instead of encroaching on Finland's autonomy, stated that Russia must follow its example and proclaim civil liberties and the inviolability of personal rights and property: "When the Russians finally receive the ability to use their constitutional rights, the Finns will have nothing to fear." Thus, the prerequisite for both the extension of the State Bank's activity into Finland and the financial

rapprochement between the empire and the Duchy of Finland was the political and financial reform in Russia, including the reform of the State Bank
modeled on the Bank of Finland. "It would be to the great advantage of our
institution if the State Bank were not subjugated to the Ministry of Finance
and the State Bank's activity were regulated by the State Duma. There would
be more trust in such an independent credit body in Finland," concluded
Vykovskii.[66]

The State Bank's branch in Helsinki was indeed closed twelve months after
its opening, but not out of respect for Finnish autonomy. The main reason
was financial rather than political. The branch, which served only the needs
of the Russian population, was a financial failure; it did not generate any income and only incurred significant losses. In addition, when the ruble became
de facto inconvertible, people started transferring money en masse to Finland
and converting it into Finnish markkas, exchanging the Finnish convertible
currency for foreign money and selling it back in Russia at a much higher
rate.[67] In other words, the State Bank's branch, instead of becoming an agent
of Russian influence in Finland, turned into the source of a massive drain of
gold. The government could not suspend the exchange of paper rubles for
gold-based markkas for fear of dropping the rate and the prestige of the imperial currency and therefore decided to close the branch, therefore abandoning
for good the plan of monetary unification.

After the Deluge

The financial crisis of 1905 simultaneously highlighted all the political, structural, and economic inconsistencies of the gold standard system created in
1897. Due to loans, the amount of gold did not decrease dramatically, but
the quantity of credit rubles swelled and destroyed the balance. The Russian
emission law of 1897, which required the highest proportion of gold to paper
money, did not specify exactly how many paper rubles could be issued in circulation. The law stated that the sum of paper rubles printed over the corresponding amount of gold must not exceed 300 million rubles; therefore, it
allowed the government to increase the volume of paper money while simultaneously filling the vaults (or, rather, foreign accounts) with borrowed gold.
In 1904–05, the government continued printing rubles, referring to the size
of its gold reserve, and when the reserve began to shrink, the government was
unable to control the situation.

The government therefore had set and publicly declared criteria of creditworthiness and financial legitimacy that it had a hard time observing.

Remarkably, when Kokovtsov in December 1905 toured European capitals searching for gold for the preservation of the exchange, his requests were met with bewilderment. Maurice Rouvier, the French head of the government and former minister of finance, declared that "France would not have acted like Russia, and on the day of the declaration of war would have suspended the exchange." A signed but not dated decree of suspension was always ready in the minister's lockbox. Emperor Wilhelm of Germany expressed his astonishment that Russia "cares so much about its monetary system when she has so many other problems."[68] The obsession with the ruble's exchangeability for gold created a vicious circle of obligation, a peculiar gold syndrome: it was a condition of Russia's credibility in the eyes of the foreign investors who gave Russia loans, yet the maintenance of the convertibility required additional loans and created new debts. This situation is not unknown in the history of finance: a similar paradox existed during the Napoleonic Wars, when Britain, a financially strong nation, abandoned the gold standard, borrowing heavily and generating inflation, while a financially weaker France followed more orthodox policies.[69] Russia, a newcomer to the world of the gold standard, could not afford even a temporary withdrawal and had to follow the gold orthodoxy faithfully.

Another issue, however, loomed large in the context of the anti-crisis measures. The Committee of Finance's and the ministry's reports on the amount of gold often mentioned how much of the total gold "belonged" to the State Bank and how much of it was owned by the Treasury. For instance, in mid-December, the State Bank's gold reserve consisted of 1 billion rubles out of 1.076 billion gold rubles in total, meaning that the Treasury possessed merely 76 million.[70] At the same time, the minister of finance listed various obligations in gold that the state had yet to meet (e.g., payments on foreign loans or short-term obligations of the State Treasury), and it followed that the State Bank's funds would be used to cover these expenses. Therefore, the question of whose gold was held in the vaults, asked by the *Rus'* reporter after the tour to the State Bank's deposit, was not idle, and it was not at all surprising that the reporter did not receive an answer. As Timashev admitted, "Our emission law is, of course, very strict compared to the West, but comparisons are hardly appropriate here." The lion's share of the gold, which, in theory, provided the convertibility of credit rubles, was "bound" by obligations on foreign loans. "It is impossible to separate the 'bound' gold [that is to say, the gold intended for payments] . . . from the gold that guarantees emissions [of credit rubles]."[71] Since the government prioritized those foreign obligations that were "absolutely impossible not to meet" over its domestic commitments, the preservation of the gold reserve depended on the government's credit activity.[72]

The absence of a separation between the State Bank and the State Treasury was a major divergence from the pre-reform principle that was repeatedly promulgated, for example, in the late eighteenth century, during Speransky's reform, or in the bureaucratic pseudo-financial constitution of 1881, which obliged the State Treasury to pay the State Bank its "debt" for credit rubles. The principle was reflected in the State Bank's accounting. The special section in the State Bank's balance sheet showed two graphs: "debit," which included gold and the treasury's obligations for credit rubles, and "credit," the amount of credit rubles in circulation. After 1897, when the treasury formally paid off all its debt (by devaluing the ruble), the separation was removed, and the State Bank's accounting merged all kinds of assets and obligations related to state credit rubles and the Bank's commercial operations and its operations with the treasury. Even at this moment, Petr Saburov warned Witte against mixing the accounts, which had left state credit rubles without a secure collateral, but Witte dismissed his warnings. In December 1905, the idea "to preserve a certain untouchable gold fund—similar to the one that had existed before the resumption of exchange in 1897" again surfaced in bureaucratic correspondence.[73] Someone (most likely Saburov) suggested allocating 400 million rubles from the remaining 941 million rubles in gold to the "untouchable" reserve fund and restoring separate accounts for the operations with credit rubles. The suggestion was not pursued further.

Thus, from the institutional point of view, the 1897 gold standard system proved to be even more vulnerable and unstable than the preceding model of 1881, which had rested on dutifully observed bureaucratic consensus and the separation of accounts. As critics of the reform project had claimed in 1895–96, Witte's system did not change anything in the government's power to dispose of the gold reserve. If the gold standard limited bureaucracy elsewhere, in Russia, it was just the opposite. The accumulation of the gold reserve and the adoption of the standard did not improve the credibility of the Russian currency. "The credibility of the Russian ruble had been probably lost irretrievably," wrote economist Pavel Migulin in 1906. The Russian ruble, despite its gold "content," was not equivalent to other gold-based currencies.

Migulin repeated what had been said many times and on different occasions: trust rests not on tangible collaterals but on institutions and rules. The state always preserves its sovereignty over the monetary system, but its power should be regulated by laws and restricted by the existence of independent banks of issue. "The independence of central banks . . . is provided by the parliamentary control of popular representatives, while the government's responsibility for the legality of its actions guarantees the untouchability and the inviolability of the banks' charters."[74] Migulin's articles and a brochure published in 1906 advocated the creation of a Russian Central Autonomous State Bank funded by state capital but independent of the executive power. Curiously, in the summer of 1905 and then again in 1906, newspapers reported rumors of ongoing negotiations between foreign investors and the Russian government regarding the State Bank's transformation into a joint-stock institution.[75] The ministry refuted this rumor, but the idea of a State Bank reform circulated widely. In 1906, Russia's central governmental apparatus and legislative system underwent a complete constitutional makeover, and the outdated nature of the State Bank's charter and bureaucratic organization became even more glaring. The expectation that the Russian state would retreat from the sphere of credit was widespread.[76]

After the constitutional reform of 1906 and the creation of the State Duma, Russia's first elected legislature, the State Bank's dependence on the ministry appeared in a different light. Even if the rejection of the participation of private money in the formation of the country's emission bank could be justified by the extreme scarcity of domestic capital, the refusal to offer the State Duma public control over the State Bank's activity looked unjustifiable. In light of the State Duma's extremely limited parliamentary rights in the sphere of finance, its inability to control the issuance of paper money and the gold reserve did not look surprising. The Duma could vote on the state budget; however, roughly 40% of state expenses (everything concerning the army, the navy, and the imperial court) were exempted from its consideration.[77] Furthermore, using legislative loopholes, the government could bypass the State Duma in voting on the budget as it could bypass it in all other legislative matters. In theory, the State Duma was supposed to approve state loans, but this arrangement did not help make the Ministry of Finance's activity any more transparent. Between 1906 and 1914, Russia did not conclude any new state foreign loans, and the State Duma had no pretext for intervening in the sphere of credit. As a result, the State Duma did not participate in issues of monetary policy. After a bizarre and rather senseless demarche of left-wing, mostly socialist, deputies of the Second Duma, who demanded the increase of the volume of paper money circulation and the remaking of 5- and 10-ruble coins into small change, the Duma did not initiate any legislative proposals in the sphere of monetary policy until the beginning of the First World War.[78]

In 1906–07, public debates over a "financial constitution" paralleled the debates over the political rights and the prerogative of Russia's first parliament.

Constitutional democrats argued that the Duma's "supreme control over the state's central issuing institution" would have offered even better guarantees of legality than the State Bank's privatization.[79] Only this institutional reform could turn Russian state paper money into real "banknotes." According to Leonid Yasnopolskii, a constitutional democrat, professor of financial law, and member of the First State Duma, "The financial constitution, similar to the political constitution, . . . consists in taking from the government the unlimited right of emission" and in "opposing" the government's power to make money to "the representation of the financial interests of the country" in the parliament.[80] Yasnopolskii concluded that a financial constitution had a greater chance at successful realization than a political one because it represented the interests of the "broad spectra of Russian society," which, regarding other questions, were usually divided along partisan interests.[81] The idea of using the financial rule of law to conduct political changes echoed early economic liberalism.

Ironically, around the same time that the constitutional democrats advanced their demands for a financial constitution, the initiative for exempting the State Bank from the Ministry of Finance's control came, quite unexpectedly, from Serguei Witte, by then a retired reformer preoccupied with the criticism of his successors and with his own attempts to return to power. After securing the crucial loan from French bankers and shortly before the opening of the First State Duma in April 1906, Witte was replaced as prime minister by conservative Ivan Goremykin. The once-omnipotent minister of finance and the author of Russia's new political order, Witte lost the last chance to return to government. Witte's minister of finance, Ivan Shipov, resigned, and Vladimir Kokovtsov once again took over the leadership of financial management. In early 1907, when the revolution was on the wane and state finances showed the first signs of recovery, Witte initiated a discussion about the current "abnormal" state of monetary circulation that, in his view, was inundated with paper money (credit rubles and treasury bonds, or the so-called series (*serii*)). Indeed, the volume of paper ruble circulation did not contract during 1906, although the critical point of disbalance between paper and gold had already been passed (1.194 billion credit rubles were matched by 1.183 billion rubles in gold). Witte blamed the Ministry of Finance and the State Bank for their currency policy, which consisted of indulging the government with paper rubles while keeping gold and not releasing it into circulation, and he even accused Kokovtsov of secretly preparing the suspension of convertibility.[82] The central point of Witte's memo was to accuse the treasury of "expropriating" the State Bank's gold for the government's needs:

To assume that the State Bank's gold, which had always served as the collateral for credit rubles, could also serve the needs of the State Treasury (for instance, for its foreign payments) is impossible. Otherwise, one would have to admit that the State Treasury, in order to meet its international commitments, may take the buildings on Nevsky Avenue, or any property that can be easily and conveniently appropriated. Only special sums designated in the state budget, and nothing else, can be used for the State Treasury's foreign payments; no other property, private or public, may serve this goal.

Accusing Kokovtsov of fraudulent policy, Witte unequivocally called the State Bank's gold "public property" that solely worked as collateral for credit rubles, and he compared the State Treasury's recurrence to it "expropriation."[83] Where did this confusion between "state" and "public" gold come from? According to Witte, it originated in the Ministry of Finance's administrative power over the State Bank and consequently its gold reserve. "Had the State Bank been set up independently . . . of any ministry. . . , it would be able to protect its gold."[84] Witte, who just ten years earlier had stood against any attempts to exempt the Bank from the ministry's control, suddenly started to advocate a diametrically opposite approach. In other words, he criticized the system that he himself had created. In a second memo, Witte bluntly admitted his fault:

> The State Bank is deprived of independence. Undeniably, this biggest flaw in the Bank's organization betrays a grave mistake that I made in 1897 during the currency reform. While leaving the Bank as a state institution, I should have granted it independence from the Ministry of Finance and placed it under the supervision of not only all relevant ministries (the supreme executive power) but also legislative power.

Had it been done then, the State Bank would not have found itself in such a critical situation in late 1905, when it was almost forced to suspend the exchange.[85]

Witte's conversion from inflationism to strict monetarism in 1895 was just one of many examples of his changing his mind. His about-face in 1907 was of course not of the same scale and importance, but it pointed to the volatility of Witte's and other bureaucrats' concepts regarding monetary policy. The rhetoric of "public" gold also betrayed Witte's new allegiances to the principles of constitutional monarchy that he had drafted in October 1905. A devoted monarchist and nationalist, he turned into the main advocate of constitutional principles in 1905; after his fall from power in 1906, he anxiously tried to find a place for himself under the new constitutional arrangements. Witte's initiative of 1907 could be interpreted within the context of his strife with the acting minister of finance, Kokovtsov. Suggestions concerning the liberation of the State Bank from the ministry's tutelage speak of Witte's attempts to earn the privilege to oversee the State Bank for the State Council, of which he was a member. It would be fair to say that his advocacy of the State Bank's autonomy, while betraying his personal bid for power, also showed an attempt to adapt the State Bank's status to the new political conditions.[86]

Witte's declaration had no serious consequences.[87] The State Bank continued to operate on its old administrative and legal foundations, while the question of whose gold lay in the State Bank's deposit and who had the upper hand in its disposal was also left in limbo. Indeed, the government treated the State Bank's gold as its own even though the political system of the monarchy underwent transformation after the revolution. The autocratic gold standard continued to exist in a constitutional state.

10

War and the End of the Gold Ruble

Fafner's Gold

"To travel from London to Antwerp, one has to obtain all kinds of various currencies—gold of different countries, paper notes and silver of different nationalities," wrote Vladimir Jabotinsky, a Zionist leader and a correspondent of *Russkie vedomosti*, in 1914. Feeling like an eighteenth-century traveler from Europe to India, Jabotinsky complained of the burden of motley coinage he was forced to carry, "hanging under my waistcoat in a suede bag, pulling my neck down."[1] Composer Sergei Prokofiev, a rising star of Russian music, described an even more arduous journey. On the way to Rome in February 1915, his companion, a Russian consul to Italy named Alekseev, boarded a train with two sealed boxes of gold for "the poor Serbs" (Russia's allies). "The consul had to constantly lug the boxes himself and sit with them like [the dragon] Fafner with his golden treasure," foregoing the chance to stretch his legs during train stops. Wagnerian metaphors were common at that time not only among musicians, and for good reason.[2] Gold in its tangible form became the most desired object, evoking parallels with the mystical or pre-modern world. As one Russian newspaper remarked, "It may seem that mankind has returned to the Middle Ages, when all efforts of the government were directed exclusively toward the accumulation of precious metals."[3] "If someone were to ask me now what my main impression is of the journey in Northern Europe during the war, I would have to say: civilization has suddenly disappeared. This is my main impression," reflected Jabotinsky.

The "civilization" that had suddenly disappeared with the outbreak of the disastrous war included, among other things, the public goods of the international monetary economy. The nineteenth-century reforms had universalized the rules of monetary circulation on the basis of the gold standard and eliminated meaningful distinctions between the material that money was made of and its nationality. Russia was fully incorporated into this process and benefited from the partial suspension of its monetary distinctiveness. In 1910 Russian economist Pavel Genzel suggested that European countries should modernize still further, adjusting their currencies to a single unit—the "golden gram"—and expressing the value of their money according to this international scale. Banks would then accept payments in different currencies, and anyone would be able to exchange ruble banknotes for gold, and vice versa, in the banks of England, France, or Italy.[4] On the eve of the First World War, the internationalization of capital had come so far that Genzel's idea hardly seemed outlandish. The war undid the effects of these changes, reinstating the hierarchy between metals and paper currency, and reemphasizing the national and political characteristics of money. The most curious transformation was that of gold, which commenced a feverish movement on the outbreak of the war. States, banks, and individuals were collecting, hoarding, sharing, and exchanging gold coins and bars. Gold was kept and carried in bags and boxes; it was loaded on train cars and on ships that traversed oceans. This fixation with the materiality of the gold standard, which prior to the war had been steadily transforming into an allegory of good finances rather than a strict principle, created a strange feeling of financial barbarism. Some economists reminded the public that this element was, after all, supposed to be the quintessence of the gold standard economy, but others began to doubt the rationality of "gold fetishism."

The first signs of the scramble for gold could be seen as early as 1911, when the Moroccan crisis and then the Balkan war touched off waves of anxiety. Germany began buying gold. That same year, part of Russia's gold reserve was relocated from St. Petersburg to Moscow and placed in the Great Kremlin Palace. The Ministry of the Imperial Court had to specially retrofit the part of the palace kitchen normally used to bake pastries and cakes during the royal family's visits to Moscow. After nearly a year of preparations, the move was made, in total secrecy, on March 31 and April 1, 1911, when 512,000 tons of gold left St. Petersburg in four trains of ten carriages each, accompanied by the director of the State Bank and a battalion of gendarmes.[5] When the Great War broke out, the rest of the gold reserve was relocated east and housed in the vaults of the newly constructed building of the State Bank branch in Kazan, rigged with a state-of-the-art alarm system. For the first time since the late 1850s, the storerooms of the State Bank in St. Petersburg stood empty.

In early 1914, the gold reserve of the Russian State Bank was the largest in Europe. Vladimir Kokovtsov, who served as minister of finance from 1906 to

January 1914, continued the policy of accumulating the yellow metal, a task facilitated by good harvests and industrial growth. However, the closure of the Dardanelles in 1913 disrupted Russia's grain trade, depriving it of its main source of gold (export furnished about 80% of Russia's gold income), and the State Bank began to actively purchase gold abroad. In April 1914, Western newspapers reported with astonishment Russia's unusually active participation in the "international scramble for the metal," when it absorbed a considerable amount of gold from South Africa offered on the London market. Russia's aggressive buying spree paralleled that of Germany and stirred sharp competition for gold among European powers.[6] "Russia . . . has been the strongest bidder in the competition and has paid unprecedented prices for its gold. Why Russia is doing so is something that is not known here," observed the *Wall Street Journal*. Analysts found Russia's "intent on getting gold regardless of cost" perplexing and "mysterious"; it seemed to signal both preparation for war and the influence of a "nationalist school in the Russian bureaucracy" that insisted on concentrating gold reserves in the country.[7] Streams of the yellow metal flowed into the vaults of the Russian State Bank from everywhere—South Africa, Russia's own gold fields in Siberia, and, of course, the United States. Gold bars were loaded onto trains that traversed the roughly 2,500 miles from the Pacific Coast to the subtreasury in New York City, where they were packed for further shipment—wrapped, to reduce abrasion, more delicately than if they had been cut glassware—and loaded onto steamers bound for Europe. When there were practically no bars left, gold coins, packed in five-gallon paint kegs, each containing $50,000, followed the same route across the Atlantic.[8] Just a few months later, this gold would flow, in far greater quantities, back to the United States.

Russia's pre-war efforts to accumulate gold mirrored the policy of Germany and France, but they also reflected the visions of financial stability that had been shaped by the late nineteenth-century policy of the gold standard. The architect of this policy, Sergei Witte, who until his death in early 1915 served as chairman of the Committee of Finance, defined gold currency as "the most important foundation of our financial-military preparedness."[9] The emphasis on the amount of gold the state held in its possession at any given moment conditioned both the principles and the biases of wartime financial policies in Russia and elsewhere. Along with efforts to adapt taxation to the new needs of the military economy, all belligerent countries competed for gold to mobilize domestic credit and raise loans abroad, a state of affairs eventually resulting in an unprecedented accumulation of gold resources in central banks. Although the world production of gold plummeted during the war, the amount of gold in governments' possession grew greatly. Russia, Europe's only gold-producing country, was also the continent's only country to slowly but steadily lose gold, both in absolute amounts and in the ratio of gold to paper money. In 1914, Russia's gold reserve, the largest in Europe, covered 101.8% of the paper money in circulation.[10] By September 1, 1917, the amount of paper money increased by a factor of 9.5, from 1.6 billion to 15.3 billion, whereas the gold reserve shrank, with coverage falling from 101.8% to just 8.4%.[11] To compare, in Germany, the amount of paper money in circulation increased by a factor of 3.2; its gold reserve doubled in size, but coverage fell from 52.5% to 26.8%. In England, the only country that did not fully suspend the exchange of banknotes, the amount of paper money grew 4.5-fold. In France, paper circulation increased by a factor of 3.3, while gold coverage fell from 71.3% to 26.6%. Judged from the standpoint of gold-based economies, Russia's war was a financial debacle.

Russia, the Allies, and the Traffic of Gold

On July 23, 1914, the Committee of Ministers suspended the ruble's exchange for gold. Had this not been done, as the minister of finance, Petr Bark, later explained, the reserve "would have been ransacked in a few days."[12] The decision to suspend exchange signified recognition of the unprecedented scale of the war.[13] By suspending exchange, the government closed only one of several valves, and leakage from the gold reserves continued. In November 1914, a new law imposed a ban on the export of gold and platinum in coins in the amount of more than 500 rubles. The measure proved too easy to circumvent by turning gold coins into crude jewelry, cigarette cases, boxes, and other trinkets that could be exported without restrictions. But the stream of gold carried in the pockets of travelers and smugglers was dwarfed by the outflow of gold resources used to purchase foreign munitions and supplies. The outbreak of the war revealed that Russia's domestic economy could not provide for the needs of national defense, and the War Ministry immediately requested enormous sums in gold or the equivalent of foreign currency to pay for imported military supplies and resources for the military industry. Speaking at the Duma financial committee's session in 1915, Petr Bark quoted the "terrifying numbers of money transferred abroad" in payments for Russia's orders: during the first year of the war, the government had to spend more than a billion rubles on import, compared to only 19 million rubles in 1910.[14] As American newspapers reported in October 1914, Russia was buying "everything from needles to locomotives."[15] Bark's attempts to curtail the demands for gold and foreign currency led to a bitter debate peppered with mutual accusations of unpatriotic behavior between him and the war minister, Vladimir Sukhomlinov.[16] The war once again revealed a tremendous gap between the shiny façade of gold-based finance and the development of industry: a country that exported grain and imported machines and technology became a hostage of the gold-seeking game unleashed by military hostilities.

The problem lay not only in the shortage of gold or foreign currency. The war closed the intangible financial borders between states, destroying the instruments of international cashless payment. France introduced a moratorium on deposit withdrawals and transfers from bank accounts, which affected Russia's foreign funds, and British banks also denied payments on Russian securities. Many deals for the purchase of American munitions did not go through because the Russian government was offering treasury bills that, as it was reported, "in a good many instances have been rejected by local banking institutions."[17] Both the deficit of foreign currency and the restoration of the mechanisms of transferring funds could only be fixed through foreign borrowing. Soon after the first shots were fired, Russia's minister of finance embarked on negotiations with the Allies regarding financial assistance in payments for military orders abroad.

As historians of Russia's financial relations with Great Britain and France during the First World War have shown, the Allies were trying to keep Russia fighting against the Central Powers and therefore supported it with credits.[18] However, they also wanted to ensure that the debts were paid. Russia's negotiations with Britain, the Allies' banker, often stumbled over the issue of sending gold to Britain or to North America as material collateral for virtual credits in foreign currency. When the issue of dispatching gold arose for the first time in the fall of 1914, the Russian minister of finance, Bark, called this arrangement unfair and referred to the insecurity of sending such a mass of gold during the war. There was also something odd and offensive in mortgaging money for money, since gold was a "monetary commodity" and Russia could exchange gold for any currency that it needed.[19] What is more, the gold sent to the Allies was taken from the State Bank's reserve that backed up paper credit rubles; therefore, every dispatch of gold in return for the loan weakened the ruble's standing. Eventually, the Russian government had to yield to the Allies' demands. As Alexander Krivoshein told the Council of Ministers, "As hard as it was to part with the gold, it would have been worse to keep the gold and remain without munitions."[20]

In October 1914, Russia dispatched the first portion of gold, in the amount of 75.3 million rubles (£8 million) in return for a loan of £12 million. Under the cover of night, the gold was loaded onto a British cruiser near Arkhangelsk on the White Sea. Despite all precautions, the British transport was spotted and attacked by German submarines but luckily reached its destination of Liverpool.[21] After this incident, all future deliveries of Russian gold followed a roundabout route: by train to Vladivostok and, from there, on Japanese ships to Vancouver. Russia's gold then swelled the Bank of England's reserve in Ottawa. Then it was delivered to the United States in payments for the Allies' orders. The question of gold shipments was raised again in late January (Old Style) or early February (New Style), 1915, when the Allies' ministers of finance met in Paris. Britain, represented by Chancellor of the Exchequer David Lloyd George, suggested the creation of a common gold fund to which Russia and France, whose gold reserves amounted to £150 million and £168 million, respectively, should contribute, in case the gold holdings of the Bank of England lost more than £10 million and dropped below £80 million.[22] France resisted the very principle of exchanging gold for credit.[23] Petr Bark also argued against Lloyd George's idea to consider "the gold reserves of all three banks of issue as a sort of common property."[24]

Bark's remark against pooling the gold resources of the Allies' central banks conveys the essence of the new attitude to gold as a "national treasure." Russia was not unique in this regard.[25] The French government and the Bank of France pursued a similar policy of gold austerity while heavily exploiting the rhetoric of financial nationalism. British economists and politicians, including a young employee of the Treasury Office, John Maynard Keynes, who participated in the financial negotiations among the Allies and drafted Britain's proposals, criticized the obsession of the European partners with the size of the gold reserve, which, "once specie payment has been suspended, [was] of very little importance." "Only the English have realized that the main use of gold reserves is to be *used*."[26] Keynes, however, understood well that Russia's reluctance to send gold was due to the domestic political issues and the sensitivity of Russian society to the size of its gold reserve. "The Russian authorities, in resisting so strongly the export of gold, seem to be thinking mainly of their published weekly returns. I think they attach an exaggerated importance to these [publications] and are probably influenced by erroneous ideas on the question of gold reserves," wrote Keynes in January 1915, when the Allies' ministries of finance were discussing credit arrangements. Keynes was right: the weekly publications of the State Bank's balances, which were perhaps excessively transparent during wartime, showed decreases in gold holdings.[27] Despite the secrecy that surrounded the shipments of gold to the Allies, these operations could not pass unnoticed, and the Russian newspapers' reports about the shrinkage of the gold reserve caused a public uproar.[28] As Keynes noted, in negotiating with Russia, one had to take into account "some psychological considerations," that is, the peculiar disposition of Russian authorities and their critics to the question of the reserve. Bark's critics attacked the minister not "for inflating the currency but . . . for anything that weakened the reserve."[29]

Bark was in the unenviable position of having to maneuver between the rigorous Allies, the recalcitrant Duma, and the anxious monarch. While trying to assure the tsar that the dispatches of gold did not affect the ruble, Bark was even more direct in speaking against the "gold fetishism" at the Committee of Finance: "One cannot postpone the purchase of shrapnel and rifles for the sake of an abstract principle."[30] Bark's declarations intended for newspapers and media, however, took a different tone. Russian society remained overly sensitive to the size of the reserve; therefore, sharing the details of the same loan arrangements with the representatives of major Petrograd and Moscow newspapers, the minister of finance declared that "the gold reserve of our State Bank . . . remains untouched. It is only possible that Russia will be lending gold to England in insignificant amounts. . . . There can be no conversation about the dispatch of gold." The wording of this claim suggested that England, rather than Russia, was a borrower. While declaring that no gold would depart from Russia, Bark added that the gold dispatched to England would be included in the State Bank's balances as part of the reserve backing up credit rubles.[31] So was Russia sending gold or not? Who was a borrower and who was a creditor?

From the point of view of Russia's creditors, gold served as a form of collateral and certainly not as a loan to England. As Keynes explained, "We want the gold as a safeguard against possible eventualities."[32] The difference was important: if gold was a collateral, then the request for gold betrayed Russia's low creditworthiness in the eyes of her creditors. If it was a loan, then the shipments were the result of England's need for gold. Both reasons likely played a role in the arrangements. Russia was not the party that dictated the conditions of credit transactions: the amount of gold in the State Bank's and the Treasury's possession, if it was converted to foreign currencies, was not enough to pay for all military supplies. But most important, the government could not simply afford to spend this gold because the reduction of the gold reserve depreciated the ruble even further. Thus, the shipments of gold represented the cost of credit which, in turn, reflected Russia's financial and political credibility in the eyes of its Allies. For its part, the British government had to deal with both domestic public opinion and the critics who insisted on the increase of the Bank of England's gold holdings and a stricter policy toward Britain's Allies.

The Battle for the Strong Ruble

Russia's financial diplomacy was deeply entangled with its domestic politics. While trying to procure funds for the payment of military orders abroad, the Ministry of Finance also had to manage Russia's increasingly volatile internal monetary system. About half of the military funds that were raised domestically, and about a third of all resources procured for military purposes, came from the printing press of the EZGB (Expedition for the Production of State Papers—Russia's money factory), which started to work with increased speed immediately after the declaration of war.[33] The steepest increase in the money supply occurred during the first months of war, especially after the suspension of state-controlled vodka sales on July 23, 1914, which had swept away about a quarter of the state's regular revenues. In total, in the last months of 1914 the Russian state budget lost 519 million rubles, showing the downfall of "ordinary" state revenues from 3,417 million rubles (1913) to 2,898 million rubles. Loans helped to bring in additional funds, but in the first months of war (July–December) Russia spent more than it had on the war with Japan, and the 1914 budget showed a deficit of 1,189 million rubles.[34] The same resolution of the Council of Ministers that had suspended the exchange also approved the emission of 1.2 billion credit rubles, raising the amount of credit rubles not covered by the gold reserve from 300 million to 1,500 million rubles.[35] The government borrowed money for its needs from the State Bank on the security of short-term treasury notes; the State Treasury therefore owed the Bank and, in principle, had to pay interest.[36] During the first months of war, Russia was spending 11.7 million rubles daily. A simple calculation suggested that the 1.2 billion extra paper rubles approved in July 1914 would last for only a few months. Russia was awash in paper money and yet constantly suffering from a deficit of cash.

A significant portion of the extra paper bills was absorbed by consumers: products that had usually been exported remained on the market, while the unavailability of credit increased the demand for cash.[37] In early spring of 1915, the volume of paper rubles started exerting pressure on the market, contributing to the rise in prices.[38] If the effect of inflation was delayed, the shortage of foreign currency became immediately noticeable. Industrialists, who depended on the supply of foreign machines and materials, as well as the importers of foreign goods, complained about the immense difficulties of procuring foreign cash. In the public perception, both the fall of the ruble's rate and the deficit of foreign currency, the so-called currency hunger, that enticed speculation and exacerbated inflation were strongly associated with the government's policy, or rather the lack of thereof. In October 1914, the head of the Moscow Stock Exchange Committee, Grigorii Krestovnikov, warned the government about the "colossal losses" that Russia had suffered due to the depreciation of its national currency.[39] One of several signals of the industrialists' discontent with the policy of non-interference, Krestovnikov's report demanded strong action on the part of the government for support of the ruble's rate.

What deserves attention is the industrialists' advocacy for the strong ruble and gold standard. As we have seen, in the 1880s and the 1890s, the Russian commercial community opposed the introduction of gold currency. Several years after the gold reform, businessmen did not want to return to the pre-gold epoch. In April 1915, the Congress of the Representatives of Stock Exchange Trade and of Agriculture voted on resolutions regarding measures for the preservation of the "untouchable" gold reserve and the stability of the ruble's rate.[40] The Congress voiced the industrialists' discontent about the dispatch of 75 million rubles of gold to England and spoke about both the "impermissibility" of such actions in the future and the necessity of preserving the balance between the emission of paper rubles and the gold backing that should not fall below a 1:3 ratio. Liberal economist Mikhail Fridman, commenting on the Congress's resolution, characterized it as "a symbolical and gratifying fact" that showed the resilience of "Russian merchants" to the agitation for the return to a paper-based economy.[41]

At the same time, the Congress's resolutions betrayed Russian industrialists' very peculiar understanding of the mechanisms of the gold standard, an understanding that, to be fair, had been imposed by the creators of Russia's monetary system. Merchants hoped that the government would help entrepreneurs overcome the crisis of currency exchange by floating special loans in Europe and offering the currency raised by the loans to private businesses at a fixed price.[42] The impudent request for cheap cash reflected the capitalists' expectation that the state must alleviate the detrimental effects of inflation. In the same vein, the Council of Congresses of the Representatives of Industry and Trade, Russia's main corporate organization of businessmen, blamed the government for its "apathetic" attitude to the rate of the ruble. "The state power must intervene in the process of defining the ruble's rate, and with a strong hand take measures toward the elimination of all causes that lead to the rate's fall and, conversely, toward the strengthening of factors that contravene this trend," declared the Council.[43] It urged the government to raise the production of gold, withdraw gold from circulation, prohibit the import of luxury goods, restrict tourism, regulate export, and float foreign loans. Interestingly, Russian business leaders did not welcome the state's growing intrusion in the sphere of production and entrepreneurship. In the imagination of Russian industrialists, "economic freedom" was absolutely compatible with the state's regulation of currency. Arguing for the "liberation of economic personality" and against the expansion of the "bureaucratic police state," industrialists saw the state's new major role in the design and implementation of the "general plan of the national economic program."[44] Thus, the state's role was to ensure the stability and convertibility of paper money while at the same time remaining outside the sphere of entrepreneurship.

While some businesses resisted planning and "regulation," others requested straightforward assistance. For example, gold mining had suddenly turned into a business of the highest state importance, and the government turned its attention to the needs of the producers. War mobilization swept away a substantial part of its manpower, and as a result of this and other factors, the production of gold dropped by a third. However, not even this gold stayed in the country. To encourage producers to deliver gold to state laboratories, in November 1915, the government introduced special 45% "premiums" for gold.[45] Nevertheless, the price of gold offered by private buyers and speculators was always much higher than the state rate, even with the premium.[46] Anxious to increase the inflow of gold, the government considered abolishing the free market of gold established in the aftermath of the monetary reform in 1901, that is to say, obliging all producers to deliver gold to the state. Ultimately, it decided against the state monopoly, fearing that it would stir illegal trade and diminish gold production. Instead, authorities tried to accelerate production by reducing taxes, freeing Russian mine workers from the military draft, and opening special credit lines.[47] In a sharp reversal from its pre-war policy of banning Chinese immigration, the government sanctioned the recruitment of Chinese workers for gold mines.[48] Economists warned that the "tempting simplicity" of fixing financial problems with the increase of gold mining was misleading, but the government saw no other way to replenish its reserve from within.[49]

The wartime demands by industrialists for government interference and the regulation of the ruble's rate often betrayed strong nationalist sentiments. Rumors of Chinese gold smugglers and German contrabandists were especially widespread. For ultra-nationalist journalists and politicians, the ruble once again turned into a symbol of national sovereignty and imperial prestige.

While nationalists resented the fluctuation of the ruble's ratio to the pound sterling, they were particularly sensitive to the Russian currency's fall vis-à-vis the Finnish markka, which they considered humiliating.[50] The reasons for the ruble's depreciation were rather simple: Russia's orders of goods from Finland contributed to the growing demand for markkas, while the demand for Russian currency in Finland remained low. The Committee of Finance judged that because the rate fluctuation resulted from a natural, though abnormal, imbalance of trade, it would not be a good idea to use administrative means to fix the rate. Instead, the Finance Committee planned to float a loan in Finland that would provide the Russian government with Finnish currency.[51] The nationalist press was simply outraged by this suggestion, accusing authorities of indifference to the fate of the ruble in Finland.[52] As they thought, instead of shamefully borrowing money from its own borderland, the government had to oblige the Bank of Finland to increase its issuance of markka and deliver those funds to Russian authorities.[53] It also had to "fix the rate by a decree of military authorities" and eventually eliminate Finnish monetary separateness altogether.[54]

The idea of saving the gold ruble united people of different political convictions. The gold ruble came to be seen as a bulwark of Russian autocratic sovereignty and, at the same time, a token of economic freedom and constitutionalism.[55] However, the seemingly unanimous support of the gold standard concealed a variety of attitudes and opinions. Even though the declaration Witte made shortly before his death regarding the "ruble's divorce from gold" sounded like a nightmare to most economists and politicians, very few of them imagined that the gold standard would remain the same when the war ended. "The experience of the first months of war would not pass without influencing the theory of money," wrote *Rech'* in early January 1915, allowing for the possibility of the post-bellum abandonment of the gold standard by several states. Many authors and politicians criticized a government that did not look beyond the preservation of the gold reserve, as if this were an end in itself: "They built the stock of gold, while the most urgent needs of the state were not met."[56] Russian society became accustomed to identifying the size of the gold reserve with prosperity, but the war showed that these optics were distorting: "It turned out that we had no railroads, no waterways, . . . no well-equipped harbors, no trade fleet . . . , but there was a brilliant budget bought through the increase of foreign debts."[57] The government misinterpreted the importance of the gold reserve, wrote Professor Kolomiitsev, observing that the size of the gold reserve is a "functional parameter" that helps balance the monetary market.[58]

As the war dragged on, doubts about the rationality of the gold standard system increased. "It is quite possible that after the war, all major states will reject the practice of the exchange for gold that was suspended during the war," wrote *Stock-Exchange Bulletin* in November 1916, suggesting that states would probably invent new, better means of supporting their currencies.[59] Ultimately, the ruble's fate depended on Russia's general economic condition, which, in turn, was a projection of her military successes. The monetary regime would get a boost from Russia's victories in the west and in the east: "Tsargrad [Constantinople] will support our paper money better than any gold reserve," wrote Ukrainian economist Mikhail (Mikhailo) Tugan-Baranovskii. [60] Tugan-Baranovskii became the most ardent critic of the pre-war ideal of the gold standard, which he described as the "falling idol" of European financial civilization. Projecting post-war financial development, he envisioned the emergence of a new model that would differ from the existing principles mostly by the degree of the state's involvement in the regulation of finances.[61]

How can economists' growing disillusionment with the gold standard be reconciled with the defense of the gold ruble? To be sure, there were two different registers of thinking about the gold standard, one economic and the other political. Economically, Witte's version of the gold standard was outdated and in need of revision. It is important to note that even the most energetic critics of the 1897 monetary system, including Pavel Migulin and Mikhail Tugan-Baranovskii, did not call for the elimination of the gold standard. In 1915–16, Russian economists, as well as their European counterparts, did not yet see an alternative to gold except for the autocratic system of paper money that had existed before the reform, which was associated with arbitrariness, secrecy, and corruption. In the Russian context, the gold standard was often still perceived as an antidote to the state's abuse of the money-printing privilege rather than an institution enabling new financial practices and possibilities. Similarly, Russian society perceived constitutionalism as a system that primarily aimed to restrict autocracy, while the role of the constitution in enabling the complex mechanisms of protecting rights and balancing powers was of secondary importance. The constitutional arrangements of the 1906 Fundamental Laws were seen as unsatisfactory, extremely restrictive, and very ungenerous in relation to the parliament, but society and politicians were nevertheless anxious to preserve even these modest acquisitions of the revolution and protect them from encroachments by the supreme power and executive authority. In the same vein, the liberal opposition appealed to Witte's laws when the government tried to circumvent the conditions established in

1897 by, for instance, increasing the emission cap without amending the law. Liberal politicians and economists also saw the government's uncontrolled manipulation of the gold reserve as endangering the ruble's future post-war restoration. As Leon Petrarzitsky declared at the State Duma's session, "The convertibility of credit rubles is a sort of financial constitution."[62] The defense of the gold ruble was equivalent to the protection of the limited space of the Duma's financial and political prerogatives during and after the war.

The government's opponents also actively used the idea of "saving the ruble" for their own goals of political and financial mobilization. Consider, for instance, the famous public campaign for domestic loans.[63] Emphasizing the political dimensions of financial mechanisms, economists urged the government to switch from the disproportional use of emission to credit. When the government issues paper notes, wrote Serguei Prokopovich, it "takes from the people's economy material resources that it needs, against the people's will, in a coercive way." The difference lay, then, in the absence of the people's consent and individual choice. While citizens might consider not buying state securities or even not paying taxes, they could not refuse accepting state-printed notes for the goods that they produced. In contrast to paper money, as Mikhail Fridman explained, "loans are a people's cause, as this war has become a people's war. The success of loans is the salvation from bankruptcy caused by the flood of paper money; it is a salvation from the foreign yoke."[64]

A public campaign in support of loans articulated the status of the national currency as a common good that should be protected with the help of loans. Echoing the ideas of the early nineteenth-century liberal Nikolai Mordvinov ("the ruble is the property of everyone"), Mikhail Bernatskii emphasized the role of credit operation to keep the Russian currency afloat: "The less successful are the loans, the more significant will be the destruction of Russia's monetary system, the lower falls the Russian ruble."[65] Participation in the public loan campaign was justified not only by the lofty goal of helping soldiers in trenches but also by the preservation of the gold reserve, which had been built "with so much labor and such significant sacrifices."[66] An advertisement for a loan, printed in large letters on the pages of *Rech*, bluntly declared the following: "Citizens, by participating in loans, you prevent both the fall of the currency's value and the growth of inflation."[67] Economists, public figures, and politicians, encouraging citizens to buy bonds, also advocated conscientious economic behavior and called for rational and patriotic spending practices. Domestic loans, along with the income tax introduced in 1916, came to be seen as quintessentially constitutional participatory financial instruments concomitant with the ideas of citizenship and, in the context of war, democratic patriotism.[68] In the context of public campaigns for loans and tax reform, the national currency came to be seen as the property of the political nation and the embodiment of popular sovereignty.

The government, while asking the Duma and media to support its efforts in popularizing the loans among peasants and urban middle classes, also grew increasingly concerned about the consequences of these campaigns and feared that liberals would try to sneak in their political messages. True, liberal politicians perceived an education in financial citizenship as an important component of political mobilization, drawing an analogy between purchasing a loan bond and casting a vote. Inculcating the idea of the ruble as a common good was a means of drafting supporters to the patriotic cause of national defense as well liberal reform. Seeing the government's inability to solve financial issues, liberals grasped the opportunity to take the cause of saving the ruble into their own hands. Alongside the media support for domestic loans, campaigns against luxury and unpatriotic spending were launched by public societies, calling on everyone, but especially women, to save money for a good cause.[69]

Financial Home Front

While the Russian army was fighting enemies on the battlefield or in Europe and the Caucasus, another battle was unfolding inside the country: the one between the government and the elected Duma for control over the gold reserve. With the outbreak of war, the parliaments of all European countries—the Allies as well as the Central Powers—experienced both a dramatic reduction of their prerogatives and the centralization of financial power. Historian Hew Strachan has observed the surprising ease with which France, "a fiercely republican country, could slough off the principles of parliamentary control" in the matters of war finances. The French parliament voluntarily entrusted the executive with the power to raise money by decree.[70] Furthermore, "Austria did not even consult its parliament between 1914 and 1916," while the German Reichstag was removed from the supervision of financial policy.[71] The limitation or elimination of parliamentary control was meant to ensure that financial agencies could effectively and rapidly meet the demands of the war economy. Against this backdrop, the claims of the Russian financial administration for the non-interference of representative institutions looked if not legitimate, then at least not so impertinent. In contrast to European legislatures, however, Russian representative institutions had had no access before 1914 to the issues of financial policy; the war offered the Duma the unique opportunity to participate in the discussion of monetary policy.

From the moment of their inception, Russian representative institutions had enjoyed only limited privileges in the sphere of budget and finance. What looked like an annoying restriction during peacetime evolved into a major political issue after the outbreak of the war, when the state budget was split into two very unequal parts. The State Duma was allowed to consider the tiniest part of the budget, that related to civil administration, while the giant share of state spending on the war remained under the government's exclusive control. However, legally speaking, the minister of finance could not singlehandedly change the law of 1897 that had established the norms of issuing paper money. Issuing credit rubles above the legal limit of 300 million rubles required legislative sanction, which could not be obtained without the State Duma's approval. Reluctant to seek the Duma's consent, the government often resorted to the infamous Article 87 of the Fundamental Laws, which allowed it to circumvent constitutional requirements and carry on its monetary policy without the Duma's intrusion, as it had done before 1914.[72] The Duma, for its part, was anxious to use the opportunity of the law's amendment hearings to discuss the government's overall monetary policy. As a result, the problem of the falling ruble grew into a problem of political cooperation and the relationships between government and society. The most surprising aspect of this contestation between government and parliament was that both agreed on the content of the policy, aimed at preserving the ruble and safeguarding the gold reserve. For the government and for the political opposition, it mattered how wartime measures were put into practice—who introduced taxes, approved loans, suspended or restored exchange, and approved the issuing of money.

Bark's reluctance to deal with the Duma was not accidental and did not simply betray his personal preference. The government's initial disrespect for constitutional arrangements can be found in its treatment of the gold reserve of autonomous Finland. The war did not have an immediate effect on Finland's currency or gold reserve, and in the first months after the declaration of war, Finland's monetary system was in even better shape than before. Nevertheless, after the suspension of the ruble's exchange and the evacuation of Russia's gold reserve, the Russian prime minister, Ivan Goremykin, very bluntly requested that the administration of the Duchy of Finland take similar measures (a draft of his message to Governor-General Zeyn even demanded the relocation of the Finnish gold reserve to Russia's interior or the Volga provinces).[73] The Finnish authorities did not object to the idea of suspending the exchange, which seemed inevitable, but the representatives of the Diet were adamant that this decision should emanate from the Finnish parliament, which controlled the Bank of Finland and the reserve. In contrast, most members of the administrative Senate, along with the general-governor, objected to the attempts of "Finnish constitutionalists" to expand the power of the parliament and claimed that the exchange should be suspended by the Senate's and the governor's administrative decision. However, when the news of this debate reached Petrograd, the imperial Council of Ministers decided that the preservation of Finland's gold was not Finland's business, and neither the Senate with the governor nor the Diet could consider this case. Thus, in January 1915, the Council of Ministers decided that the monarch had unilateral authority on the basis of the Swedish law of 1772 that endowed the king of Sweden with special prerogatives in the case of war. Although this legal precedent seemed sketchy, if not absurd, Nicholas II signed the law discontinuing the Finnish markka's exchange to gold on March 29/ April 11, 1915.[74]

The story of Finland's gold demonstrates that imperial authorities perceived monetary issues as the prerogatives of the crown. As Petr Bark asserted in 1915, "In Russia, the right of issue belongs to the sphere of royal mint privileges, similar to the minting of coins." Despite the fact that the State Bank administered the emission, "it always remains ... the exclusive and untransferable right of the Supreme authority, which is only being realized through the State Bank."[75] Still, to allow the Bank to print more credit rubles than was allowed by the law of 1897, the government had to formally amend it legislatively. In July 1915, Bark for the first time since the beginning of the war addressed the State Duma with a request to approve the emission of 1.2 billion paper rubles. By that time, the government had already increased to 2.5 billion, from the initial 300 million, the circulation of credit rubles not covered by gold.[76] Not surprisingly, the minister's demand resulted in a bitter debate about the political principles of the monetary regime during the war. The State Duma asked Bark why he had ignored the people's representatives in resolving the fate of the Russian currency. Nobody questioned the necessity of issuing more credit rubles into circulation, since the shortage of cash at the state's disposal seemed obvious to everyone. What became the main issue of the debate was the proper management of monetary policy with the due participation of various political forces.[77]

The State Duma rightly considered Bark's actions as the explicitly ignoring the legislature's authority.[78] For Duma politicians, it was a matter of principle: "The country is not afraid of big sacrifices, just tell us what they will be like."[79] They wanted to know the maximum thinkable amount of money that the government might need to print in the future. "Do you see the limit, or is it going to be limitless?" asked Andrey Shingarev, a constitutional democrat and one of the Duma's main speakers on financial issues; he also suggested that the government promise never to drop the gold coverage of paper rubles below 30%. But these appeals appeared pointless to Bark: "Can I tell you which credit operations I can carry out in Russia in a year? This is unthinkable, and no minister of finance can tell you that."[80] He also defended the government's right to increase the paper money supply when the need arose, and he refused to make any binding decisions.[81] The only concession that Bark made was a promise to consult the Duma the next time the government planned to increase the issue of paper money. In August 1915, the Duma approved the emission, but Bark did not keep his word. By that time, the Ministry of Finance had already embarked on another round of negotiations with the Allies, requesting a special credit "to support Russia's monetary system." Therefore, instead of dealing with the Duma and seeking its authorization for the issuance of credit rubles, Bark procured extra credits abroad that could be used in lieu of gold as a backup for paper money. Backing up the emission of paper rubles by the loan in convertible currency allowed Bark to expand the mass of paper rubles without the State Duma's approval.[82]

The arrangements of the new loan looked somewhat unusual, if not fraudulent. Russia promised to send gold in the amount of 400 million rubles (£40 million) to be used to pay for the Allies' orders in the United States. Britain opened a line of credit for the purchase of military supplies in the amount of £300 million and an additional, special loan of £200 million "to provide for our right of issue," that is, to back up the Russian credit rubles.[83] This part of the loan was a bookkeeping fiction, since it assumed no movement of funds, only the conditional allocation of money that was in Russia's accounts.[84] On this virtual foundation, as opposed to the ingots of gold in the Bank's vaults, Bark wanted to grant the new emission of paper rubles. Politically, it was a slap in the face to the Duma, which had thus far been relatively conciliatory in its approach to the Ministry of Finance and its policy.[85] Even though John Maynard Keynes could "fancy" a combination that would allow the substitution of virtual for real gold and keep the operation secret, Russian journalists and newspaper readers were too savvy not to notice it.[86] The operation was also, strictly speaking, illegal. Monetary laws permitted neither virtual gold nor the gold that Russia had mortgaged (or "loaned") and sent abroad to be counted in lieu of physical, material gold as a part of the reserve.[87] Oppositional economists excluded these sums of gold from the State Bank's balances, although the Bank continued counting this mortgaged gold as its own. As a result, the government and the economists operated with very different statistics on the state of Russian finance and, specifically, the ruble's gold coverage.[88] While the official numbers looked more or less optimistic, economists' estimates that did not include the credit line abroad or the mortgaged gold allowed the conclusion that Russia's monetary system was "almost entirely paper-based."[89] Indeed, by March 1, 1917, the virtual "gold reserve abroad" (2.141 billion rubles) exceeded the physical amount of gold in the State Bank (1.476 billion rubles) by a third. The difference was substantial, especially in relation to the amount of paper rubles released into circulation (9.975 billion): with foreign gold, the coverage constituted more than 36%, while without foreign gold, the gold coverage was less than 15%.

Bark's foreign loan maneuver did not eliminate the problem of seeking consensus with the Duma. The government quickly ran out of the cash issued through the British loan and the extension of the emission law, and in February 1916, Bark had to address the State Duma with another request to approve an increase in paper ruble circulation of 2 billion rubles. This time, Bark asked the Duma to grant him a blank check to change the emission limit when necessary and at his own discretion. Bark explained that such a model would allow the government to increase and decrease paper circulation without changing the law because frequent amendments had a detrimental influence on public opinion. In fact, Bark's counterpart in France enjoyed a similar privilege granted to him by the parliament when the war broke out. However, in Russia, the Duma had not gained legal control over monetary expansion until the war began, and it did not want to renounce it. Besides, the Duma had suffered a humiliating disregard of its financial authority, and it could not acquiesce to Bark's request. Not only did the Duma's committee object to the "right to the unlimited . . . issuance of credit rubles"; it also proposed a law "establishing a minimum size of the gold reserve backing the credit rubles." In its proposal, the committee designated 1.5 billion rubles of the gold reserve as an "untouchable" fund, that is, protected from being spent on military needs or payments abroad.[90] In other words, the Duma's deputies claimed that the gold reserve belonged to the people they represented, not to the government.

Bark was outraged. The principle of untouchability could jeopardize Russia's commitments to send gold to the Allies. A day before the State Duma session where the law would be discussed, Bark, who was attending another round of loan negotiation in London, sent a telegram to Petrograd asking that Andrey Shingarev, the committee's speaker on this issue, drop this clause, which could make a very bad impression on the Allies. If the Duma passed the law, he wrote, everything had to be done to prevent its approval by the State Council. If this could not be guaranteed, the chairman of the State Council must be asked not to include it on the agenda.[91] The Duma, however, passed the law with a minor change, reducing the "untouchable" sum from 1.5 billion to 1.4 billion, which reflected the actual size of the gold reserve at the time.[92] On June 17, 1916, three days after voting on the law, the Duma was dismissed for the summer recess, and the members of the State Council who were meant to consider the law on the inviolability of the gold reserve also went home.[93] On August 29, 1916, the government yet again reverted to Article 87 to sanction the issuance of 2 billion paper rubles,[94] and in September, it approved another agreement with Britain that committed Russia to send off gold for £20 million.[95]

Although he rejected the Duma's request to protect the remaining gold from its total disappearance, Bark communicated to the British side that dropping Russia's gold reserve below 1 billion rubles was "impermissible."[96] Remarkably, Andrey Shingarev, the Duma's main oppositional speaker on financial matters, shared Bark's stances on the question of the gold reserve. During his trip to Europe in April through June of 1916, he met with Reginald McKenna, chancellor of the exchequer, and with the French minister of finance, Alexandre Ribot, and expressed his bewilderment over Britain's request for gold, which undermined the stability of the monetary system and caused public discontent.[97] The Duma's decision to protect the remaining 1.4 billion in gold from the Allies or the government was therefore an attempt both to demonstrate the Duma's commitment to the preservation of the ruble and to make the insatiable demands of the Allies illegal. It was also an attempt to wrest the symbolic authority over the country's gold from the government. Yet, the Duma's attempt to establish control over monetary emission should not be viewed merely as a cynical exploitation of the ruble issue so as to increase the Duma's significance. Liberals considered the war a moment when government and opposition could and should cooperate. "As in the business of helping wounded soldiers, the state and the government rely on the large-scale mobilization of public organizations; in the questions of financial organization, they should seek the engagement of active public elements," wrote Vladimir Zheleznov.[98] The quest for public participation in the elaboration of financial policies echoed the mottoes of parallel campaigns for the mobilization of industry and hunger relief. As in the cases of the aforementioned initiatives, the Duma and the Ministry of Finance failed to find a middle ground. The critical lack of trust between state and society directly and indirectly affected the ruble's fate.

Harvesting Gold

Interactions between the state and the public over the issues of money and war were not limited to the debates in the Duma. Every financial reform or measure affected people's everyday economic practices, and the government, as a rule, showed little concern over the effect of its actions. The war transformed this relationship, making the state more dependent on its population than before. Because the government had to seek funds through domestic loans, it counted on people's patriotism while collecting increased taxes. The most remarkable and new aspect of this interaction was the government's attempts to extract gold from the public. Russian society had responded to Witte's policy of imposing gold without enthusiasm, if not hostility, and the Russian economy never reached the same level of saturation with gold as in England or France. The war changed the popular attitude toward gold overnight. The panic of the first days of the war immediately affected the availability of gold: gold coins, which only recently had been seen as awkward and undesirable, became the most sought-after monetary commodity. The only way to make people surrender their gold when the paper ruble turned inconvertible was to appeal to their patriotic feelings.

In designing the measures for extracting gold, Russia looked to the West. Statistics showed that at the time, all central banks increased their gold reserve, and, as simple calculation suggested, the gold was coming to the banks from people's pockets and hoards since the total amount of accumulated gold was significantly higher than the annual production of the gold mines.[99] Germany organized campaigns raising gold for war purposes, encouraging people to bring jewelry and other gold and even silver items to be melted into bars, which helped increase the Reichsbank's reserve by 1 billion marks, from 1.528 billion in July 1914 to 2.455 billion in July 1915.[100] Russian officials reported, with envy and amazement, that the German patriotic campaign to collect gold involved even schoolchildren, who received certain "privileges" for delivering gold coins to their teachers. Awards for donations in gold included free rides on airplanes and extra vacation time for soldiers. Ultimately, according to the report of the Russian commission on the accumulation of gold, Germany's government mandated that all gold coins in private possession be stamped and the circulation of unstamped coins outlawed.[101] The reaction to this campaign in Russia and elsewhere was mixed.[102] Russian-Jewish writer and journalist Lev Pasynkov (Leiba Pinch) described Germany's obsession with collecting gold, which drained the life-force out of people, with the "bronze disease," as a rare illness that turned a sick man's emaciated body reddish, with bronze undertones. The injection of metal into the veins of the economy was paralyzing the organism of the nation as the bronze disease transformed a person's body into a stiff and brittle statue.[103]

Germany was not the only power that started squeezing gold out of its population. France pursued a similar strategy, albeit with less coercion, mobilizing gold resources under the banner *"Pour la France, versez votre or: l'or combat pour la victoire."* When France opened special offices for the collection of gold, Bark made a similar proposal to the Committee of Finance. However, these measures could not be guaranteed a similar outcome, especially since Russia had been delayed in joining the gold-harvesting campaign and a significant portion of the gold had already been either hidden or taken away.[104] In an attempt to boost the gold-collecting operation, Bark suggested that the Duma launch a campaign to collect gold, in any amount or form, including jewelry. In its patriotic fervor, the Duma was ready to take energetic steps. Some Duma members suggested confiscating all gold objects from private owners and organizations. The only concern expressed in the debates was not over the legality of this measure but concern for the fate of historical and artistic objects that could be "squashed into bars" in the patriotic rush. The owners—private individuals or monasteries—were often unable to appreciate the value of things in their possession, such as old gold medals of historical value or gold utensils from church sacristies. To avoid the loss of valuable objects and advise people not to part with "ancestral jewels," the Duma commission suggested that items with artistic or emotional value to their owners be photographed, registered, and stored securely at the Bank with a commitment to return them after the war, while their weight would temporarily be counted against the gold reserve for the period of the war.[105]

The idea of a temporary gold fund perfectly illustrates the absurdity of the wartime obsession with the size of the gold reserve. This gold, taken conditionally from its owners, could not be used in payments for military supplies or state debts and was only supposed to improve the appearance of the State Bank's balance sheets. Collecting and storing personal gold items would probably lead to more problems than benefits. Therefore, when it came to its implementation, the project of the "temporary fund" disappeared. Instead, in August 1915, the State Duma addressed the Russian population with a plea to "bolster the State Bank gold fund" by selling or donating gold coins, medals, utensils, and items. "Ladies and Gentlemen, you have rings, bracelets, earrings and gold jewelry that you don't need; you've got a lot of gold trinkets, and it is your patriotic duty to deliver all this useless luxury to the state,"[106] declared Andrey Shingarev at the Duma session. Major newspapers republished the

Duma's call to bring in gold to replenish the State Bank's reserve. Nicholas II set a personal example by donating eight gold nuggets and a small bag of alluvial gold of about two pounds, valued at 1,200 rubles. The tsar's gold, melted into three bars, was placed in a special oak box with glass windows at the State Bank.[107]

Gold started to trickle in. Historian Mikhail Bogoslovskii, who was writing Peter the Great's biography, was among those patriotic citizens who responded to the request. He carried three gold coins to the bank "to increase the state gold reserve with this contribution."[108] Following the example of some celebrities who donated their gold jewelry, people sent wedding rings, medals, and other personal items, and newspapers reported on the patriotism of simple folk. The owner of a large horse-breeding farm donated eighteen gold medals that his horses had won at races, while the bishop of Perm invited women and girls who had received gold medals for their studies to donate them for war needs.[109] Suggestions were made to exchange gold wedding rings for metal rings with the inscription "For the Fatherland" or "1915," therefore comparing patriotic sentiments with the emotions associated with marriage and love. Others advised awarding donors with special chains and medallions with the motto "Must win!" (the title of a famous article by nationalist Mikhail Menshikov) or issuing special "patriotic" credit rubles indicating that these paper notes had been exchanged for gold.[110] Newspapers published the names of donors along with their touching letters.[111] The clergy of one the wealthiest parishes in the capital, the Kazan Cathedral, asked permission to donate their relics. Rumor had it that churches and monasteries were asked to compile their inventory of gold and silver church utensils; only the uncertain legal status of "monastic gold" held back the expropriation campaign.[112]

The government tried to invent new incentives for attracting gold. The State Bank encouraged its employees to motivate their clients to make payments in gold coins, offering a reward of 2% of the sum they managed to procure. They were also strictly instructed "not to release gold back into circulation."[113] Railroads offered the purchase of train tickets without having to queue up, which, under the circumstances of a catastrophic transportation crisis, was a significant privilege. Not surprisingly, these and similar other measures produced speculation and bribery, and instead of supporting the ruble's standing, they deepened the rift between "useful" gold money and not so useful "*kreditki*" (i.e., credit rubles).[114] The collection of gold often bordered on economic irrationality. Some items donated to the Bank, including a collection of historical coins, had a much higher market value than the gold they contained, so melting them into gold bars was senseless.[115] In any event, the results of this patriotic campaign were very modest. Between the beginning of the campaign on August 10, 1915, and its end on March 8, 1917, the State Bank received gold in the amount of 655,768 rubles, which included donations in the amount of 145,319 rubles and 510, 449 exchanged for credit rubles at par.[116] Mikhail Bernatskii called this outcome "pathetic" and lamented that the Russians revealed themselves as "not up to the occasion," failing to understand the importance of supporting the national currency in their own financial interest.[117] Along with the means to draw gold to the Bank, the government restricted its use for other purposes. It prohibited the use of gold for dentistry (except for surgery on wounded soldiers and officers), and in October 1916, it ordered the use of cheap metals to make its highest military awards, the crosses of St. George (it turned out that only in 1915, the production of medals (military and others) consumed 117 poods (1.8 tons) of gold). In this as in other cases, patriotism was meant to compensate for the lack of material benefits associated with the award.[118] It seems, however, that the patriotism of a few citizens was greatly outweighed by the frugality of others, especially when the calls to collect gold were complemented by a series of prohibitions, including a ban on the export of gold money. According to the official numbers, the amount of gold used by jewelers tripled during the war.[119] People tried to safeguard their savings by turning them into gold items that could be carried abroad. In response to the noticeable leak of gold as jewelry, customs officers were ordered to allow only those individuals carrying gold items across the border whose "social standing did not raise doubts whether this person might need these things during the journey." That is, an aristocrat would be permitted to wear gold jewelry, but a person of lower status might look like a smuggler.[120]

The government's hope to receive gold in exchange for credit rubles at the nominal value was fairly naïve, but the State Bank and the Ministry of Finance determined to preserve the pre-war equivalence between gold and paper. The only concession to the economic rationality of the population was the exchange of gold for foreign currency. However, the government bluntly rejected suggestions to pay for gold in credit rubles at its market rate, that is, beyond the nominal value, because this would mean officially recognizing the disparity between the gold ruble and the credit ruble. For the same reason, it also abandoned the idea of collecting customs duties in gold (the practice used from 1877 to 1899 to boost gold holding) or paying higher interest on deposits in gold coins.[121] The State Bank organized a campaign to purchase gold items mortgaged at pawnshops and credit offices, but other buyers almost always outbid the officials of the State Bank, who had been ordered to stick to a fixed price.[122] It seems that the government did not notice that gold had already ceased to be a method of payment equal to credit rubles and instead had become a commodity, and the term "gold ruble" became a misnomer. People brought their gold coins to pawnshops that accepted them as "gold in stacks."[123]

The gold-raising campaign rested on the assumption that there was a hefty amount of gold in private possession, both in coins and in gold items. Myths about Russian gold hoards circulated in Russia and abroad. "Russia is believed to have tens of thousands of hoarders of money. It is utterly impossible to guess at the amount of gold which the people of Russia have put into the ground or into the cellars of their homes," wrote the *Washington Post*.[124] Western commentators specifically emphasized the vast and mythical riches of the Orthodox Church. "Russia's holy gold fund" appeared in their imagination as "an almost inexhaustible hoard of wealth," and only the prevailing ignorance as to Russia's hidden resources could make someone believe that Russia was poor.[125] Moreover, Russian officials and journalists continued to popularize this idea. Monastic gold was listed among those "natural riches" of Russia that remained unexploited—a symbol of either a hidden reserve or a missed opportunity. "The value of the jewels and gold kept in Russian monasteries and ancient cathedrals is unknown. There are hundreds of rich monasteries in Russia, the wealth of which is known only unclearly. It is estimated that the Kievo-Pechersky monastery alone has more than 100 million rubles' worth of riches in its carefully guarded vaults," declared Joseph Dalinda, the editor of the Petrograd *Financial Newspaper* [*Finansovaia Gazeta*], in an interview that was supposed to dispel the myths of Russia's financial instability.[126]

At the same time, the publicly available data regarding the gold reserve holdings, combined with the amount of gold in circulation showed that even at the height of its gold accumulation there was still very little gold money in the country. "The largest aggregate holdings of gold, such as Russia, had also the smallest per capita holdings," wrote *The Globe*, showing that in per capita accumulation, Russia ($5.93) fell behind the United States ($19.48), the United Kingdom ($16.10), France ($30.30), Germany ($13.30), and even Austria-Hungary ($5.96), which, in sharp contrast to Witte's policy of saturating the economy with gold, introduced the standard but did not make its gold-based banknotes exchangeable for gold. While in other countries, the free gold in people's pockets and purses exceeded the holdings of the central banks, in Russia, the situation was reversed: the State Bank's possession of gold was three times higher than the amount of gold in circulation.[127]

According to Petr Bark, after the reform of 1897, the Russian State Bank released about 455 million rubles in gold, and approximately half of this amount had already left the country. In France, a "relatively small country," there were approximately 4 billion francs, or close to 1 billion rubles, in gold coins. In a single month after announcing the public campaign to collect gold, the Bank of France collected 277 million francs; in contrast, in the first six months of 1915, the Russian State Bank was able to purchase (i.e., "exchange for foreign currency") only 4 million rubles.[128] It was therefore clear that the policy of squeezing the public for gold could only result in the extraction of golden rings, medals, and snuffboxes possessed by the very thin strata of the upper and middle classes. As Mikhail Bernatskii concluded, because of the "unsatisfactory response" to the gold-raising campaign, "any further increase in the Bank's gold reserve during the war was entirely due to the current production of the Russian gold mines."[129]

Was it only people's poverty and lack of patriotism that caused the gold campaign to fail? Understanding the reasons for this failure requires examining the context in which the campaign unfolded. On the very same day that Shingarev, from the Duma's tribune, addressed the public with a call to bring in gold, people were storming the offices of the State Bank, demanding to exchange their credit rubles—not for gold but for silver and even copper coins. The "change famine," that is, the deficit of small change that had been noticeable since the beginning of the war, by August 1915 had grown into a real crisis exacerbated by the influx of refugees from the Western provinces occupied by the Germans.[130] Shops were unable to give change to customers, who, in their turn, had no coins to pay coachmen, tram conductors, and petty traders. Sometimes, customers took advantage of the shopkeepers by ordering *pirozhki* (little pies), eating them first and then offering a large bill in payment.[131] In Kharkiv, the waiters at Akzhitov's cafeteria asked customers to show their change before ordering lunch, and those who had nothing less than a ruble walked away hungry. The small-change hunger spread everywhere—Petrograd, Zhitomir, Rostov-on-Don, Kyiv, Riga.[132] On August 17, the State Bank's main office in Petrograd was forced to limit the exchange for coins in a move that almost caused a riot. The main calamities occurred, however, in the markets of different neighborhoods. When women came to buy food to feed their families and found most stores closed, they started crushing the stores and throwing goods on the floors. A few shopkeepers were beaten by infuriated housewives.[133] The "riot of female shoppers" [*buistvo pokupatelnits*] in Petrograd continued for two days. Police patrolled markets, and the military administration of Petrograd issued orders prohibiting hoarding and speculating with change, while the Ministry of Finance tried to explain that hoarding of token silver or copper coins made no sense because the price of metal was much lower than the nominal value of the coins.

Unable to find a rational explanation for the sudden surge of demand, the director of the St. Petersburg Mint described the events of August 17–18 as "bacchanalia." "Some sort of gregarious feeling spread among the broad masses of Petrograd's population," commented Baron P. V. Klebeck. Petr Bark went even further, characterizing people's behavior as "psychosis." To support this assessment, *Stock-Exchange Bulletin* interviewed eminent Russian psychiatrist Vladimir Bekhterev. Bekhterev agreed that, in tense times, "the public is susceptible to any kind of improbable excesses," and he supported Bark's diagnosis of the events as "mass psychosis." Perhaps it was psychosis, but ironically, it affected the same public that was expected to donate gold, and the calls in newspapers to donate appeared along with information pertaining to the fines for hoarding and the persecution of vendors who refused to give change to their customers.[134] Authorities contravened with reports that the mint was working day and night. The State Bank was inundated with complaints from governors, local banks, and railroads, and it received warnings of impending riots among workers who had not been paid due to the shortage of money. Nonetheless, the authorities continued to dismiss these complaints.[135] The administration preferred to think that the "change famine" was caused by rumors, or it blamed gullible peasants for burying coins in the ground.[136]

Strangely, while trying to satisfy the almost inexhaustible demand for metal, the Ministry of Finance did not consider the real reasons for the "mass psychosis": inflation increased the amount of paper money. While the influx of high-denomination bills (25–500 rubles) grew by 229%, low denominations increased by only 51.6% in volume, creating an imbalance.[137] Moreover, public anxiety over small change betrayed the public's lack of trust in the government. As Serguei Prokopovich noted, while hoarding token silver coins made no sense when the ruble's rate stood at 75%, doing so could become wise if the ruble fell to 25% of its pre-war gold value.[138] The small-change riot was stirred not only by a deficit of coins but also by persistent rumors of an imminent sudden fall of the ruble's value. At this time of anxiety and fear, the State Bank announced its readiness to accept gold as a donation or contribution "in exchange for credit rubles" at the nominal pre-war rate.[139]

Although still denying the problems that had caused the shortage of change, in September 1915, the government was forced to take extraordinary measures to alleviate the deficit. Instead of silver and copper coins, it released into circulation a new kind of "paper change": postage stamps with the portraits of tsar that had originally been designed in 1913 to celebrate the tercentenary of the Romanovs' rule. This strange choice was explained by the availability of templates and equipment at the Expedition for the Production of State Papers, where these machines had been idle since 1913.[140] The only adjustment made in the design was an inscription conveying that the stamps could circulate along with coins. The acceptance of the postage stamps, valued from 1 kopeck to 20 kopecks, was made mandatory. The government assured people that this measure was temporary; an eleven-year-old girl, Liuba Sluchevskaia, glued a stamp to the page of her diary with the comment, "Now instead of silver money, we have stamps like this. They are only for a while (a month)."[141] Yet the production of money stamps continued throughout the war and revolutionary period.[142] The inconvenience of using postage stamps was obvious, but the government resisted the idea of reissuing "paper change" in a size and form resembling credit rubles because, in the eyes of the public, it would eliminate the distinction between normal-sized credit rubles, which were backed by gold, and small paper-change money "without gold backing."[143] Despite the suspension of exchange and the total disappearance of all kinds of metal money, the government held firm in the belief that it could keep the ruble on the gold standard by regularly changing the emission law.[144]

Against the government's expectations, the introduction of stamps, which was supposed to alleviate the deficit of coins and pacify the angry population, produced even more discontent. People were confused as to whether they could still use stamps to mail letters and why other stamps, those that did not bear the images of the tsars, could not be used as money surrogates. Stamps were too small and thin for the coarse hands of peasants, who had to use matchboxes to keep them; coachmen, who carried no purses and usually kept coins in their pockets, did not accept stamps; fish vendors complained that thin stamps got wet and dirty in their hands.[145] Unlike credit rubles, the stamps were one-sided, so to see a stamp's denomination, one had to flip it printed side up. Newspapers joked that instead of circulating (in Russian, they were supposed to *"imet' khozhdenie,"* literally "walk"), stamps had a tendency to fly. People were advised to hold their breath while paying in stamps, since a light wind could blow them away while one was buying a newspaper or paying for a tram ride.[146] Puns were abundant, and of course the inconvenient coincidence that the word for "stamp," *marka,* sounded exactly like German "mark," invited nationalists to suggest that engineers at the EZGB, whose names were also coincidentally foreign, had conspired to issue the "marks."[147] When the *New Time* appeared with an article that unabashedly asked, "Who makes our *kreditki*?" and listed the names of the EZGB's key employees with

German-sounding names, Petr Bark was furious: "We fight our war with *kreditki* [credit rubles]. The trust in them is undermined?! What's next? What if they make a *pogrom* [i.e., destroy the Expedition]? Then what—the end of war? Did the enemy write this [article]? The Expedition for the Production of State Papers is the only mechanism to conduct the war."[148]

The EZGB, Russia's main money-making factory, certainly was not the only source of paper money during the war. Counterfeiting flourished, and

FIGURE 10.1 Stamp money: 10-kopeck stamp, 1915. Private collection.

the cheaply made stamps were also prone to forgery or imitation. According to N. I. Kardakov, German authorities had disseminated stamps identical to the original but bearing an inscription that paraphrased the inscription on the original stamps. Instead of "Circulate along with coins," they said "Circulate along with the plunder and deceit by the rulers" or "Circulate along with the bankruptcy of silver coinage."[149] Indeed, with the introduction of stamps, coins disappeared entirely. Ten months after Liuba Sluchevskaia glued a paper stamp to the page of her diary, she recorded: "Now we have gone so far that if one finds a silver coin, one keeps it as if it were gold, a rarity!"[150] With the issuance of the surrogate "paper change," the State Bank discontinued the exchange of credit rubles for silver and copper coins.[151]

All in all, the experiment with stamps, even if it was financially motivated, developed into a political disaster. Money surrogates with the tsar's portrait were soiled, complained about, and suspected to be of German origin, and they appeared at a moment when autocracy had suffered a tremendous decline in reputation. The unpopularity of the stamps was immediately reflected in the public's attitude toward the tsar, as if the rumors of treason in the imperial family were not enough for the desacralization of the monarchy.[152] The effect of the stamps' issuance on the ruble's rate was even more detrimental. As Mikhail Bernatskii observed, "Undoubtedly, their appearance and the bad impression they produced on the public contributed psychologically to the further depreciation of the ruble."[153] The stamps became one of the most unpopular measures of the wartime government, a tangible expression of crisis, and were used in revolutionary propaganda. In 1917, the printers of leaflets reproduced stamps with Nicholas II's portrait branded with a revolutionary Phrygian cap or an excerpt from the manifesto announcing Nicholas's abdication.[154]

In an attempt to quell the discontent over the disappearance of coins and the influx of stamps, the government sought a scapegoat to blame for the depreciation of the Russian ruble and the disappearance of metal money. In January 1916, the Department of Police issued the infamous circular that declared that Jews used the deficit of coins

with the goal of inciting general discontent in Russia, along with criminal propaganda in the army and in large industrial and factory centers of the Empire. . . . Because of the shortage of coins in circulation, Jews try to infuse people with distrust in Russian money, to depreciate it and therefore force bank depositors to withdraw their savings from state credit institutions and savings banks and to hoard metal coins as the only kind of money that has allegedly preserved value. As for the issuance of stamps, the Jews have persistently spread rumors that the Russian government is bankrupt and does not even have the metal to strike coins. At the same time, Jewish agents everywhere buy up silver and copper money at an abnormally high price.[155]

The circular was sent out to all governors and police authorities, confidentially, "for information." As the deputy director of the Police Department, Konstantin Kafafov, later explained, the entire text of the circular, based on "reliable news," had arrived at the Department from the High Command General Headquarters, and the Department itself had no clue as to the nature of this "news" and its sources.[156] Despite the confidentiality clause, the text of the circular became public, causing an uproar of the press and the liberal and socialist deputies of the State Duma. The issuance of the circular was rightfully assessed as a provocation and linked to the pogroms that took place in early 1916. As Paul Miliukov declared in his Duma speech, the government had put Jews "in front of a vengeful crowd, [saying]: here are the guilty ones, take them and give them short shrift, and leave us alone."[157] Andrey Shingarev echoed Miliukov's words, reminding the Duma that the rise of prices and the monetary problems for which the government was blaming the Jews resulted, at least partially, from the inflation of currency that the Duma itself had sanctioned.[158] Jewish deputies and the press urged the Duma to take the incident seriously. But internal disagreements among the members of the oppositional Progressive Bloc over tactics and the political inconvenience of putting the Jewish question at the top of Duma's agenda let the government off lightly, with a moderate interpellation address that was revoked after Kafafov's explanations.[159]

The story of the antisemitic circular is remarkable in many respects. A key episode in the anti-Jewish hysteria during the war, the circular revealed that the issue of money and metal had another important dimension: the traditional antisemitic connotation to "Jewish gold," in this case replaced with silver and copper. Jews were habitually accused of storing gold and selling it to Germans. In one such case, a prominent Jewish cotton trader and industrialist from Bukhara, Nikolai Poteliakhov, was arrested only because his firm held several thousand rubles in gold coins, allegedly brought from Moscow and intended for sale to the Germans.[160] Jews were certainly not the only target of nationalistic attack. Finns, who had allegedly depreciated the Russian ruble, and Chinese gold smugglers were also declared enemies of the ruble and scapegoated for its decay.[161] The "gold nationalism" of the international scramble for gold resources was complemented with imperial, ethnic financial nationalism. In addition, the government blamed Russian peasants for hoarding money and forcing the government to increase the print-run rubles and devalue the national currency. There was an element of unspeakable cynicism in the government's declarations that peasants who used to spend money on drinking, therefore indirectly paying their dues to the state, hid the money away after the prohibition of alcohol sales. Domestic loans, as a government circular announced, were meant to extract those mythical "billions" of "idle" rubles stored by the dark peasant masses.[162] The rhetoric of an inner enemy permeated this way of thinking, creating an atmosphere of distrust and hostility.

So, was the government's policy a complete failure? Financially, Bark and his ministry followed a set of more or less standard principles of war economics that rested on the combination of several financial instruments: taxes, credit regulation, loans, and emission. The belligerent countries borrowed financial models and decisions from each other, which resulted in a remarkable uniformity of policies among the key European participants in the conflict.[163] Although Russia performed worse than Germany and France, Russia's financial difficulties did not originate directly from Bark's missteps or errors. Rather, they reflected the specificity of Russia's financial organization and economic development established during the preceding decades. The government's critics described the most significant defect of this system as, first, the lack of economic planning, and second, the glaring gap between the fiction of good budgets and the full storage of the State Bank, on the one hand, and economic poverty and underdevelopment, on the other. The war brought disillusionment with the financial means of reflecting the state economy and society. It became apparent that the excessive straightforwardness of financial statistics—state budgets and Bank balances—was deceptive and in fact concealed the truth about the actual economic abilities of the state. The war therefore showed the fallacy of the government's premise of the primacy of finances over economy. In 1916, reflecting on the beginning of the war, the economist Bogopelov wrote that it had become obvious that the preparedness for war should not be measured in financial terms: "Until now [i.e., the First World War], people ... talked about financial strategic preparedness and were inclined to overestimate the importance of the medieval aphorism that the war needs money, money and more money. After the war, they will be talking about economic military preparedness."[164]

As was already clear in 1915, the war would not end due to the exhaustion of financial resources. Credit relations between the Allies seemed to provide an endless, although at times meager, source of financial support. The burden of war was tremendous, but compared to other belligerent armies, Russia invested more in human lives and much less in money than her Allies. This means that the effect of war on the economy was more structural than financial and more long-term than immediate. Russia's industry showed a slight increase of output during the first years of the war (1914 and 1915), but in 1916, the national income started its steep decline, falling below the pre-war landmark by nearly 20% in 1917. Agricultural production shrank visibly, creating problems with the food supply. Nevertheless, as historians Andrei Markevich and Mark Harrison have suggested, the decline of the GDP in Russia was below the average calculated for the continental powers (17% compared to the average of 23% for the European countries, excluding Greece and Great Britain).[165] Of course, since Russia's pre-war per capita GDP was one of the lowest in Europe, this drop hit poor people harder than elsewhere. The effect of the war on consumption was immediate and adverse, as the military state absorbed the lion's share of production, and the standard of living fell rapidly.[166]

If the verdict concerning the government's financial and economic policy was hard to render, there was no doubt that, politically and ideologically, the government's treatment of financial issues contributed to a total setback. The dispatches of gold abroad, the fall of the ruble's rate, and the ill-conceived campaigns to combat the shortage of change led to the demise of the government's authority and the deterioration of its relations with society. One of the most palpable effects of the war was that it drew the population and various political forces, including the Duma, into the politics of money. Loans and gold-raising public campaigns aimed to mobilize both peasants and urbanites for the support of the national currency, and liberal newspapers and politicians told their readers that the ruble was a public good and that its fate affected everyone's well-being. Even though these campaigns did not always reach their goals, people could see the immediate effect of financial decisions on their lives. The concern about national money ceased to be government's prerogative and responsibility, even though Minister of Finance Petr Bark continued to insist on monopolizing the rendering of Russia's gold and financial resources. The unfolding mass politics of finance in the context of the ongoing war and the disintegrating economy led to grave and unanticipated consequences that the new authorities were unable to handle.

Class Wars in a Paper Republic

On March 8, 1917, the minister of finance of the Provisional Government that had assumed power after the empire's collapse—thirty-year-old sugar magnate from Kyiv, Mikhail Tereshchenko—paid a surprise visit to the EZGB. The money factory had been on strike since February 27, jeopardizing the supply of money.[167] Yet Tereshchenko's gesture was unconventional. As *Rech'* reported, Tereshchenko's sudden appearance among workers "created a sensation." The minister delivered a "passionate speech" asking workers to resume their work, which was so essential "in the interest of the army."[168] Tereshchenko was the first minister to honor the Expedition with a visit, if not, as politician Vasilii Shulgin observed, the first minister to ever visit a factory on strike. This event, occurring at the end of the first week of the Provisional Government's existence, spoke volumes about the new authorities' goals and priorities; in contrast, during his three-month-long presence at the ministry, Tereshchenko had failed to hold an audience with the director of the treasury.[169]

Tereshchenko's unusual encounter with the workers carries double symbolism. Vasilii Shul'gin, who dedicated his editorial in *Kievlianin* to this episode, noted with optimism that the new minister demonstrated a "new style of relationship between power and population," observing that "in the workers' hands are the nerves of our life, down to the money-printing press."[170] In subsequent months, workers would further prove that statement, underscoring a previously unseen connection between labor and money. The state's physical, material dependence on workers' willingness to operate the printing machines, therefore, had political meaning. The *New Time* ran a short notice suggesting that before resuming the printing of credit rubles, the Expedition's workers had addressed the Executive Committee of the Soviet of Workers' Deputies, asking whether they should come back to work.[171] A week later, the government voted for a 50% increase of salaries for the Expedition's workers, along with other benefits.[172] The money factory became a symbol of the Provisional Government's short rule over the country's economy and finance, which came to be remembered mainly for the exponential curve in the mass of paper money.

The political regime that emerged from the ruins of autocracy in the last days of February and in early March 1917 defies one-word definition. The government, formed by former opposition politicians, the representatives of industry (like Tereshchenko), and the Duma's deputies, was reluctant to assume real power, fearing the lack of popular support from below, but it was burdened with the entirety of legislative and executive authority. Suffice to say that the Provisional Committee (a revolutionary organ that formed the Provisional Government on March 2) either failed, forgot, or did not care to make orders for the takeover of the State Bank, the Mint, and the EZGB; the only order that prescribed the transfer of finances into the hands of the new power came from the Petrograd Committee of Soldiers' and Workers' Deputies (Petrograd Soviet), an institution that had no formal power but enjoyed the support of workers and soldiers and bore no political responsibility for social disarray and economic failures. In a somewhat paradoxical gesture, the Petrograd Soviet instructed the Duma's Provisional Committee, over which it had no authority, to take measures to protect the State Bank, EZGB, the State Mint, and the State Treasury.[173] Common sense suggests that political dualism and uncertainty are bad for finance; add the strain of a prolonged war and the post-revolutionary chaos in governance, and financial disaster undoubtedly results. Managing finances in such a situation was a negative-sum game, but the government's inability to tackle the financial crisis resulted from objective causes that it could not control and for subjective reasons, namely, the government's sequence of poorly made financial decisions or, more often, its indecisiveness and inaction.

Perhaps the most uncomfortable feature of the Provisional Government's rule over finances was the almost immediate abandonment of the principles of the gold standard. Liberals and socialists, who had criticized the tsarist regime for both its abuse of the privileges of monetary emission and violation of the financial constitution, demonstrated even less self-restraint than their imperial predecessor. The imperial government had to formally ask the Duma's approval for the expansion of the paper currency, and when it occasionally failed to do so, this failure attracted the crushing censure of the parliament. After February, the Duma was gone. The Provisional Government, in Alexander Guchkov's words, "hung in the air, nothing above and nothing below it," creating the impression "of a seizure of power or imposture."[174] In the absence of any controlling authority, the Provisional Government held full authority over the State Bank (the promises of the State Bank reforms were not fulfilled) and was able to pour billions of rubles into circulation. On the first day of its existence, the government voted to expand monetary emission by 2 billion rubles, signaling that the state was in dire need of cash. During the eight months of its existence, the Provisional Government amended the monetary law five times and issued almost as many paper notes as did the imperial government during the more than thirty months since the outbreak of the war.[175] The staff of the EZGB grew from 750 to 8,000 people. As a socialist minister, Matvei Skobelev, attested, the Expedition represented the only enterprise that did not participate in the strike movement, and it was the only factory that increased productivity; this was not surprising, as the Expedition's workers enjoyed privileged status and tariffs due to the "special character of their work."[176] The government saw greater danger in not having enough cash than in inflating the monetary system with rubles that were losing their value. One particular statement made by the last minister of finance, Mikhail Bernatskii (Michael Bernatzky), is especially revealing. Explaining why the government in August 1917 reverted to issuing the notorious "*kerenki*"—Treasury notes printed from the templates of consular stamps in uncut sheets—Bernatskii observed that if the government had not done it, "the October Revolution would have become a September Revolution."[177]

The avalanche of paper money was indeed not a planned measure but rather signaled the government's inability to tackle the crisis and raise income through loans and taxes. The central element of the government's plan of financial recovery was the Liberty Loan, announced in late March 1917. Stakes were very high, and authorities made serious efforts to popularize this new financial measure as an act of revolutionary citizenship and patriotism. The government recruited artists and musicians to agitate for the loan, and decorated cars carrying orchestras drove around the cities during the "Loan Days" festival in August.[178] Despite all these efforts, the loan was a mixed success. It brought the government 3 billion rubles but could not prevent further monetary expansion and failed to extract excessive paper rubles from circulation.[179] Andrey Shingarev, who secured his appointment as the new minister of finance after Tereshchenko, blamed the Council of Workers' and Soldiers' Deputies for the loan's failure because it had reluctantly and ambiguously endorsed the loan with a five-week delay.[180] In fact, the population, wearied by war, simply could not respond to the state's call for sacrifice.

The loan's lack of success demonstrated that the government needed to seek support from the left in all its financial endeavors but simultaneously maintain a peaceful relationship with industrialists. The representatives of the Petrograd Council of Workers' and Soldiers' Deputies, along with the members of other public organizations, cooperatives, and peasant unions, were invited to sit on a committee to elaborate a financial plan.[181] The new coalition government of "socialists" and "capitalists," formed in May 1917, was also expected to be more attentive to the demands of "democracy." The economic commission of the Petrograd Council of Workers' and Soldiers' Deputies endorsed a program that called for a more active policy of "planned" economic regulation by the government. In the sphere of finance, it demanded the introduction of vigorous control over banks and the launch of a "compulsory loan" that would target wealthy classes.[182] Indeed, in mid-May 1917, the government admitted that it was considering "drastic measures to pump out money" from population.[183] On June 12, in a gesture that earned him the reputation of a converted socialist, the minister of finance, Andrey Shingarev, announced a steep increase in the income tax and the tax on wartime profit, along with a one-time levy on incomes exceeding 10,000 rubles: in total, the next tax could take up to 90% of earnings.

The tax reform was a radical but ill-conceived step, as the income tax had been introduced only in 1916, and Russian society was still unaccustomed to the principles of self-assessment.[184] Because normal taxes were collected in 50% to 70% of the levied amount, it was unrealistic to expect that people would comply with the new order.[185] Inaccurate calculation could result in the double taxation of an enterprise's profit, sometimes exceeding its actual revenues, while the businesses that had already accumulated impressive wealth during the first two years of the war would not be affected by this measure. The tax reform proved to be not only unpopular but also impossible to implement and was soon partially revoked under pressure from banks and the industrial elite. However, while the increase of taxes had little financial effect, it made a big rhetorical and political splash.[186] Among other things, the reform signaled the government's quest for transparency and obligation.[187] Ideally, the income tax was supposed to nurture citizenship, but in the strained atmosphere of economic crisis, it resulted in mutual denunciations and accusations among individuals as well as between competing social classes and political parties. Social democrats uncovered multiple loopholes used by capitalists to evade taxations, and liberals responded to the demands of high taxes for capitalists by reminding them that Russia had always been poor in capital and that the State Treasury could only sustain the pressure with the help of "the people's purse."[188] Interestingly, both the left and the right observed that the tax system had failed due to the collapse of the state and the absence of real authority.

The Provisional Government's financial policy was therefore becoming deeply enmeshed in the political contestation between classes. The Russian ruble had always appeared with various social undertones, but in the political climate of the inter-revolutionary era, all government attempts to safeguard the national currency were measured and assessed from the point of view of divided class interests. Because these attempts failed and the ruble continued its downfall, parties and politicians blamed their opponents for the currency's ruin and accused the government of being unable to balance class interests. Left-wing parties criticized the government for failing to extract resources from the wealthier classes, and the liberals blamed it for squandering the meager financial resources on salary increases, indulging workers' spending and promoting inflation. In these mutual accusations, the ruble was presented as the victim of either capitalists' irresponsibility or workers' greed.

"The revolution delivered a double blow to the country's finances: it increased the feeling of entitlement to the increase of salaries but failed to inculcate a sense of civic responsibility. The payment of taxes discontinued. Everyone demanded a raise," lamented the minister of finance, Shingarev.[189] In his view, the main source of financial distress was the increase of the costs of labor. "The new revolutionary regime costs . . . much more than the old order," declared Shingarev's successor in the cabinet, Nekrasov, a month later. "No other period of Russian history, no other tsarists' government was so prodigal . . . none of them was so generous in its spending as the government of revolutionary Russia."[190] Workers, Nekrasov said, paid back the government's generosity with ingratitude, demanding more and more money without raising the productivity of labor. The minister indirectly admitted, with some reservation, occasional mistakes in planning, but the burden of responsibility fell heavily on the population that did not pay taxes and wanted to live better. Nekrasov's rhetoric reflected the dominant thinking of industrialists who, like Pavel Riabushinskii, were outraged by the "predatory craving" of the masses.[191] The *Russian Bulletin* [*Russkie vedomosti*] explained "the flood of paper money" as originating from the growth of expenses that reflected the excessive demands of the working class: "If prior to the revolution, the increase of war expenditure was related to the . . . growth of profits, now the increase of expenses is related to the growth of wages."[192]

It might have seemed that these statements were backed up by numbers. The head of the Department of the State Treasury, Gavriil Dementiev, claimed that the steep increase in expenses, including military spending, had occurred due to the simultaneous increase of wages across all industries and occupations. Workers and postmen went on strikes, threatening to completely paralyze the already stagnating economy; teachers and railroad workers, clerks and servants also demanded raises. Demonstrating the tremendous increase of expenditures due to the rise of wages, Dementiev noted that, all of a sudden, the spending budget of the Department of Railroads grew from 2.818 billion to 3.330 billion rubles.[193] At the same time, a special commission, called to reconsider wages on railroads, revealed that 95% of railroad workers received a monthly salary of less than 100 rubles, which was below any meaningful level of subsistence.[194] Here and in other cases, the rhetoric of large numbers, used by the government and industrialists, was meant to shift the responsibility for the financial crisis from the government and the elites onto "democracy." Attributing financial chaos and the ruble's depreciation exclusively to the growing demands of the labor masses, in July 1917, Dementiev declared that "the [state] budget for 1917 does not exist," and the compilation of the 1918 budget seemed impossible.[195]

The most shocking number cited by Dementiev as an example of astronomical demands concerned the projected introduction of allowances for the newborn children of conscripted soldiers. As he contended, this measure could increase treasury spending on the allowances for soldiers' families from 3 to 11 billion rubles annually, which, compared to the total estimated military expenses of 26 billion rubles, looked absurdly high.[196] The numbers cited by Dementiev, unchecked and unaccompanied by other information, were subsequently repeated many times as proof of workers' and soldiers' greediness. Remarkably, these references never mentioned exactly how much the average family of a soldier, who was fighting in trenches instead of feeding his children, received from the state, nor did it mention how the allowance corresponded to the rising costs of living. The value of rations was indeed increasing in absolute numbers, but not due to the voracity of the soldiers' wives. Allowances paid in cash were prorated according to the local costs of produce; therefore, the growing value of allowances reflected both the effect of inflation and the rising number of conscripts and their dependents. In Petrograd, for example, the value of rations rose to 15 rubles monthly, compared to the average of 8 rubles in the rest of the country.[197] In total, by September 1917, Russia had conscripted almost 15 million soldiers, or 8% of its population, and the number of people receiving rations (i.e., members of soldiers' families) had grown to 36.5 million.[198] Compared to other countries, Russia spent much less on munitions, compensating its relative technical and material disadvantages with human fodder. As Serguei Prokopovich put it, "We, a poor country, fight in this war not with capital but with living force."[199] In 1914, the monthly allowance for the families of soldiers was as low as 4 rubles, allowing for relatively low expenditures on the human force. As the army grew, however, the costs for maintaining millions of soldiers increased. As historian Niall Ferguson has observed, in the epoch of the First World War, the state did not act as "if it owned material, companies or men (as the Soviet Union could in the Second World War): everything had to be paid for."[200] The revolution enhanced the notions of self-ownership and the entitlement to payment for military service. In other words, the only direct reason for the state's enormous expenses was war.

In the months leading up to the socialist revolution in October, both liberal and proletarian politicians and newspapers were engaged in a rhetorical battle for the ruble, discussing which class bore responsibility for the demise of the national currency. Unverified numbers regarding the fantastic salaries of workers trickled into official reports and the public speeches of ministers and officials and were later repeated in multiple memoirs, offering an easy explanation for the Provisional Government's financial misfortune. It would seem that soldiers' wives, laundresses, "simple *babas* without skills," and nurses in hospitals had contributed to the demise of Russian democracy and currency.[201] Vasilill Shul'gin was not sure how much it would cost to "satisfy the requests of railroad workers"—either 4 billion or 6 billion, but he was convinced that this "six billion in paper money paid to railroad employees will drop down our ruble even lower." Workers were therefore declared responsible for the rise of prices and the deficit of goods. Soon, Shulgin noted, there would be nothing to eat because peasants would not sell anything for the devalued rubles.[202] Another stereotypical accusation was addressed to the "dark masses" who held their paper rubles "gripped in fists," making the workers of the Expedition, mostly women who were "socially refined" and educated, work day and night printing millions of new ruble notes at the factory of money in Petrograd.[203]

Neither Shul'gin, nor Dementiev, nor other accusers of the working class tried to compare the actual growth of salaries with the growth of food prices, the rise of private profit, and the State Bank's emission activity. Such analysis would have revealed that monetary expansion—that is, the output of the EZGB, as well as the inflation that it produced—had grown in a proportion that many times exceeded the growth of wages.[204] Studies of factory workers in revolutionary Moscow and Petrograd confirm that the price rise ate away the benefits of increased wages.[205] By October 1917, the real wages, adjusted to the increase in the cost of living in Petrograd, constituted between 40% and 90% of the January 1917 level, which was already significantly lower than the pre-war level. The improvement of living conditions, which workers perceived as the main achievement of the February Revolution, was fading away, increasing frustration and political disillusionment.[206] Against this backdrop, the accusation that workers had caused the inflation and ruined the ruble might have sounded not just unfair but also offensive. Therefore, statistics and the methods of its presentation played an important role, and these numbers could be read differently. The ministers' lamentations about the costs of war, as the representative of the Menshevik fraction of the Social Democratic Party Nikolai Shukhanov recalled, "helped the Council [of Workers' and Soldiers' Deputies] win over the soldier masses . . in the question of war and peace."[207] Given the unpopularity of the war, which cost more than 50 million rubles daily, the government was seen as the main actor responsible for ruining finances.

The Mensheviks' stance regarding the question of workers' wages echoed the declarations of liberal ministers in the government. Using the high cost of labor as the main cause of inflation, socialist members of the coalition government made a case for the state's greater intrusion into the economy. Explaining the meaning of planned regulation to the attendees of the First All-Russia Congress of the Councils of Workers' and Soldiers' Deputies, the minister of labor, Menshevik Matvei Skobelev, admitted that regulation had to concern not only the "production" (i.e., the capitalists) but also the "interests and demands of individual classes of the population." According to Skobelev, the strike movement for increased wages "deprived state power of the possibility to regulate the wellbeing of the working class and coordinate its demands with the demands of other groups of democracy. . . . Only the state power can tell where the limits of the economic improvement of separate social classes are, in connection with the material wealth that the state can dispose at the moment."[208] Another socialist minister, Alexei Peshekhonov, seconded Skobelev by asserting that the main problem in restoring the economy was the intransigence of the labor masses. Peshekhonov, himself a member of the Petrograd Council of Workers' and Soldiers' Deputies, was adamant that "the masses," that is, workers and soldiers, should "understand, comprehend and feel" that they needed to be ready for "sacrifices," that one could not think about "improvement" and only wish for an "even and fair" distribution of available wealth. In other words, the government wanted workers to back off and let the problem of wages be solved at the state level. Otherwise, as socialist ministers believed, the increase of wages would accelerate the influx of paper money, and all hopes for improvement would be dashed by inflation.

Lenin responded to the Mensheviks' calls for a conciliatory policy with mockery. Interestingly, his main demand, voiced at the Congress of Soviets, may appear too simple and modest if not considered in the context of the rhetorical battle over the ruble. Lenin insisted on both the obligatory release of information about the wartime profit of enterprises, "those unheard-of profits reaching up to 500%–800%" and on public access to the financial reports of credit and industrial institutions.[209] This maneuver was meant not only to shift to the bourgeoisie full responsibility for the financial crisis that had hit workers so hard but also to prove that capitalists were avoiding the payment of taxes by hiding their profit under a veil of financial confidentiality. Fully immersed in the arguments about the causes of the ruble's fall, the Bolsheviks relied on financial statistics. Unlike the often groundless and obscure declarations about workers' demands for salaries, the articles of the Bolsheviks' *Pravda* cracked down on the obscure numbers of the joint-stock companies' reports and showed how industrialists had managed to double and triple their capital during the war.[210] Set against workers' meager salaries, the billions of rubles earned on the unpopular war looked astonishing. The position of the radical wing of social democrats who had refused to support the Provisional Government was clear: financial chaos and economic decay had originated solely through the "predation of capitalists." Therefore, what stood behind this seemingly modest request was the introduction of the de facto control over production, credit, and commerce and the expropriation of wartime profits.

What were the meaning and consequences of the rhetorical wars over the ruble in the inter-revolutionary period in terms of the political history of the Russian currency? First, these debates enhanced the class characteristics of money. The practice of designating the enemy of the ruble goes back to the late eighteenth century. During the war, the ruble's loss in value was blamed on national minorities (Jews, Finns, Germans, Chinese); after the February Revolution, blame was placed on social groups (workers, peasants, or industrialists).[211] A few months later, after the takeover of power, the leaders of the Bolsheviks reverted to the same rhetoric to shift the responsibility for the financial crisis of war communism onto the peasantry. The Bolsheviks used the old accusation against peasants of hoarding money and bringing down the ruble's rate to justify the policy of food requisitioning.

The second corollary of this process was a further transformation of the state's role in finance. After the February Revolution, debates about the gold standard and the gold reserve receded into the background. Very few people and newspapers paid attention to the dispatch of gold to England in July 1917, in fulfillment of Russia's pre-revolutionary arrangements.[212] The government's role, which had been seen as focused primarily on regulating the supply and demand of currency and watching over the gold reserve, appeared in a new light and included responsibilities that had always fallen outside of the state's purview, such as the regulation of wages. The state's intrusion into the economy grew incrementally during the war, and it increased dramatically after the fall of the monarchy. The government regulated the prices of most goods, and it declared all grain in the country to be the state's property; it nationalized leather and contemplated the introduction of several other kinds of state monopolies.[213] None of these measures directly affected labor relations. After the revolution and the currency crisis that followed, industrialists and the advocates for the working class called on the government to step in and regulate wages. Therefore, the Russian debates of 1917 about wages, prices and the fate of the ruble, while theoretically uninformed, revealed aspects of monetary policy that had been previously obscured by the obsession with the gold reserve.[214] The financial crisis of the period following the February Revolution suddenly brought to public attention the fact that labor policy, along with taxation, price management, and credit, had direct implications for the policy of monetary regulation. In other words, it demonstrated the social embeddedness of money.

The political consequences of this discovery were manifold. Workers, peasants, and industrialists, speaking through their representatives, demanded that the government tend to the new spheres of economic activities. Everyone talked about centralization and price control, the regulation of production and distribution, the control over people's earnings and spending. All these new roles required the creation of a new state apparatus and the increase of the government's authority, while the post-revolutionary state administration lay in ruins and the government was tragically losing its political support and legitimacy.[215] When the socialist minister Iraklii Tsereteli complained to the attendees of the Congress of the Councils of Workers' and Soldiers' Deputies that no government under the circumstances would be able to tame the economic crisis and that no political party would dare to voluntarily take power in the midst of chaos, Lenin famously shouted out that his party, that is, the Bolsheviks, would do it.[216]

The financial policy of the Provisional Government signified the end of the old liberal and imperial gold-standard era. The crisis of 1917 brought with it the realization that the gold standard, as it had existed in Russia, was a product of the old political system. It represented a means of bureaucratic self-restriction that also allowed Russia to play on the international monetary market and simultaneously maintain the centralized integrity of imperial financial space. The old state withered away, as did the principles of a fiscal constitution advocated by bureaucrats and liberal politicians. Parts of the former Russian Empire broke away and strove to create their own monetary systems, and the gold ruble lost its role as a symbol of imperial sovereignty and integrity. This transformation of the gold standard was not unique to Russia. Similar trajectories occurred in all belligerent countries, as the gold standard lost its sacrosanct status and people ceased to associate financial well-being with the size of the national gold reserve.[217] The ideal of a self-regulating, gold-based market system evaporated, as the government was expected take on the negative aspects of the financial crisis by regulating the impact of fluctuating monetary rates on the standard of living.

It seems that Russia faced these consequences of the war earlier than other countries. The disillusionment with the gold standard in Europe would not become apparent until a few years after the war. In Russia, however, the fall of autocracy, the tremendous decline in the standard of living, and, of course, the enormous expansion of paper money made the old ideals of the gold standard obsolete in 1917. Ironically, Mikhail Tugan-Baranovskii had predicted such a development in his articles in 1916, contending that after the war, the state would take into its hands the regulation of monetary mechanisms.[218] But in 1917, the Russian state fell apart, and the new government proved unable to fulfill the role that Tugan-Baranovskii had scripted for it. When the focus of attention shifted from the gold reserve to other means of securing material well-being through the regulation of prices, credit, wages, and employment, there was no effective political power or institution capable of doing it.

II

A Revolution That Did Not Happen

WHEN DID THE story of the imperial ruble end? On March 2, 1917, when Nicholas II signed the abdication, or on October 25, 1917, when the Provisional Government fell? Or perhaps on July 23, 1914, when the ruble was taken off the gold standard? None of these dates appears more accurate than the others. Even when the old state no longer existed and the two-headed eagles were replaced everywhere with red flags, the Orlov machines of the EZGB in Petrograd continued printing the banknotes of the Imperial State Bank, featuring tsarist regalia. For a few years after the coup, the Soviet economy continued to run on pre-revolutionary rubles despite their despised political symbolism. The survival of the old ruble revealed more than a lack of resources, a banal institutional inertia or psychological attachment. It hinged on the longevity of several key principles of state organization and was predicated on Lenin's plans for a political takeover. Between 1917 and 1922, Russian finances experienced a deep crisis, exceeded in desperation only by the dire situation in Weimar Germany. This was followed by an equally surprising revival that many observers of and participants in described as the restoration of the pre-war monetary order. In many ways, the revolution brought a repetition or a transfiguration of existing models (i.e., their reversal, but not their extinction). The resemblance between the tsarist and the Soviet empires was somewhat eclectically set off by the most bizarre financial experiments. But what does the analysis of continuity bring to the political history of the ruble?

Perhaps the most intriguing question regarding the transition is how and why money—which in Russia, unlike other countries, had always been purely a state institution—survived the annihilation of the old state. Money was an integral part of imperial organization, a token of autocratic (and then, briefly and faintly, republican) sovereignty. Most surprisingly, and contrary to Marx's predictions, money also became the anchor of Soviet power. This state-centered quality of the old system made it specifically usable and convenient for immediate appropriation. Lenin planned to build the credit-monetary system of the new state on the existing template, transforming some elements and upgrading others. All revolutionary rhetoric notwithstanding, revolutionary plans on the eve of the revolution and throughout the "transitional" period remained surprisingly conservative.[1] Despite the tectonic shifts in the forms of property and market relations, the revolution in money did not happen.

The patterns of governance through monetary policy that had been laid out in the nineteenth century hypertrophied under the new regime. At the same time, expert economists recruited by the revolutionary government continued their attempts to soften state centralism and introduce elements of fiscal legality, even when it looked like a totally hopeless business. The presence of these few trained officials in the Commissariat of Finance and the State (People's) Bank ensured the survival, albeit in a transformed shape, of some key general principles of monetary organization. Thus, while politicians speaking from the tribunes of multiple congresses and meetings made bold declarations and argued endlessly about the future of a moneyless society, state bureaucrats continued running finances the old way.

War communism was, certainly, a caesura, a short period when money was out of the state's control. The ruble was surpassed by myriad alternative kinds of money—goods, pieces of stamped paper, bread—and the government seriously considered its annihilation. Two visions of the ruble emerged at that time. Nationalization made the ruble into the main tool to manage industry (a quality it did not previously possess); the ruble also came to be seen as a weapon of class struggle—a way to extract wealth from the enemies of the regime, namely *kulaks* or peasants. Counterintuitively, both projects assumed the ruble's gradual disappearance, and both failed to reach this goal. Instead of getting rid of money, the government let it slip out of its hands. During the period of disarray and depreciation of money, money appeared in multiple new forms. The ruble space splintered into many dimensions: territorially (into hundreds of regional currencies), functionally (an "industrial ruble" of the nationalized economy differed from the ruble of the black market), materially (*kerenki, romanovki, penzenki*, and other kinds of state-printed money had different values), socially (a peasant's ruble differed from a worker's ruble), and politically. The dissolution of the ruble's domain signaled tremendous monetary chaos and the powerlessness of the state. At the same time, the pre-war imperial ruble, or rather its idea, turned out to be very resilient. It appeared even in the most bewildering financial projects of "labor money" and continued to live, independently of the state, in the practices of measurement and black-market deals. The ruble was also a valuable resource for trading with the population of former imperial territories that had broken away, therefore preserving ground for the post–civil war reconstruction of the imperial Soviet ruble domain.

The Takeover

Against almost complete uncertainty on the part of Russian and European Marxists about the future of money under socialism, Lenin was surprisingly confident in his program for post-revolutionary financial organization. Anticipating skepticism of the ability of the Bolshevik "to retain power" on the eve of the October 1917 coup, Lenin laid out the contours of the future state organization. His recipe was amazingly simple: the socialist state apparatus would comprise councils of workers, soldiers, and peasant deputies, plus the old tsarist banking system. Banks, therefore, were the only element in the imperial system left untouched, appropriated in their entirety by the socialist state. The rest of the state machine had to be mercilessly destroyed: "*Without the big banks, socialism could not be realized.* The big banks form the State machine we need for the realization of Socialism and which we take ready made from capitalism." Therefore, the Bolsheviks' task was merely "to chop off what capitalistically disfigures this otherwise excellent apparatus and to make it even *larger*, more democratic, more all-embracing. Quantity will pass over into quality. One State Bank as huge as possible with branches in every district, in every factory—this is already nine-tenths of the *Socialist* apparatus."[2]

Lenin's paragraphs about banks acting in lieu of the state apparatus, written in the early autumn of 1917, bear an eerie resemblance to early nineteenth-century liberal utopias. Nikolai Mordvinov, a prominent liberal of Alexander I's time, also imagined future society being transformed from within by the network of self-governed banks that were to control all aspects of economic and political life and essentially replace imperial bureaucracy. It is unlikely that Lenin read Mordvinov. His idea of a giant bank was inspired by the writings of European socialists, such as Henri de Saint-Simon, and the works of Marxist economists Rudolf Hilferding and Alexander Parvus, who advocated the use of banks during the transition to socialism.[3] However, pre-revolutionary debates between liberals, who for many decades had been trying to rescue the State Bank from the government's tutelage, and conservatives, who argued for even further centralization of the Russian banking system, most certainly played a role as well. As Lenin put it, a banking system "that

under capitalism is not wholly governmental" "will be completely governmental with us under Socialism" when the Bolsheviks "*take* it and set into
motion in one blow, by one decree."[4] Furthermore, although Lenin did not
fully appreciate it, the specificity of the Russian credit and monetary system,
with its super-centralized state-owned and state-governed bank, made the
takeover much easier. With the seizure of banks, Bolsheviks wanted to acquire simultaneously not only the mechanism of state accounting and control
but also the regulation of production and distribution. The first crucial step
consisted of establishing control over the flows of money; all banks had to be
merged into one central financial institution. Lenin envisioned this measure
to be as simple as the "unification of accounting" under the auspices of the
revolutionary-democratic state, a technical operation that would not affect
private property rights or even the structure of banks and their staff.[5] The
revolutionary government was supposed to simply absorb the existing credit
apparatus.

Seizing the State Bank was at the top of Lenin's to-do list for October 25,
1917, along with the takeover of the factory of money, the EZGB. However,
what had been planned as an immediate assault turned into a long siege. The
Bolshevik government established partial control over the Bank and its resources only on November 17, 1917, when the new government, the Council
of People's Commissars, finally received the first 5 million rubles from the
Bank. For more than three weeks, the revolutionary government existed
without money; it literally had no cash to buy paper and ink for its apparatus.[6] To be clear, during these first days, the government needed paper cash,
not gold. Although probably a fib, an anecdote about a "big chunk of gold"
that had been brought to Smolny (the government's headquarters) and left
forgotten on the floor until Lenin stumbled over it suggests nevertheless that
the depreciated paper money suddenly turned out to be in higher demand
than gold.[7] In any case, the State Bank's storage in Petrograd contained mostly
paper credit rubles because the gold reserve had been evacuated to Moscow
and Kazan.

The hitch in the takeover of the State Bank after the violent and momen-
tous overthrow of the Provisional Government might appear puzzling. The
revolutionaries wanted their financial actions to look both legal and financially accurate—hence the long negotiations with the banks' administration
and the attempts to refute all accusations of an illegal heist. Orders dispatched
from Smolny to the Bank during the tedious siege reflected an erratic mixture of coercion and revolutionary-bureaucratic legality. On October 30, five
days after the coup, Lenin issued a command to "open a current account in

the name of the Council of People's Commissars" at the Bank, provided the Council reported its spending to the Constituent Assembly. A week later, Lenin commanded the Bank to "grant, in the act of requisition, 10 million rubles" to the Council of People's Commissars, through a deposit to the government's current account, again with the promise to report to the Constituent Assembly.[8] When none of these actions brought results, the government resorted to other methods. One attempt, as many memoirists have recounted, ended in total embarrassment: when the representatives of the government, accompanied by armed troops and a military band, approached the building with rousing songs, they were shown the door.[9] There was also confusion regarding who was supposed to receive the money. The commissar of finance Viacheslav Menzhinskii (Wacław Mężyński) pointed to Lieutenant-colonel Muraviev, who commanded the troops, but Muraviev thought that it had been Menzhinskii's task. In any event, none of them had a proper document authorizing a withdrawal except for a certain request printed on a typewriter and not signed.[10] The State Bank's director, Ivan Shipov, and the Bank's board refused to give up any money because "according the Bank's charter, the Bank's means could not be diverted to the state's needs."[11]

The clumsy operation of the State Bank's takeover was one of the Bosheviks' major reputational lapses. It appeared that all those Saint-Simonian speculations about turning the bank into a machinery of economic governance ended with a crude heist, and the revolutionary leadership did not understand the difference between the treasury and the bank.[12] Perhaps the most unpleasant surprise was the soldiers' and workers' reaction to this event. The Bank's guards from the Semyonovskii regiment protested the takeover and declared that the attempt to seize "people's property" was illegal. Having received the news about the attempt at Bank's seizure, the Factory Committee at the EZGB voted a resolution "against the violent takeover of people's money by a group of people . . . who call themselves an authority without reason."[13] Apparently, the influence of Bolsheviks among soldiers and workers who sympathized with other socialist parties was weak, and the rhetoric of plunder of "people's money earned with people's labor, sweat and blood" did not add to the Bolsheviks' popularity.[14]

Meanwhile, the State Bank continued processing payments on the requests from the army and other institutions and private individuals, but it refused to recognize the legal status of the Bolsheviks government before its confirmation by the Constituent Assembly or, at least, the sanction of the new legislative authority, that is, the Central Executive Committee of the Congress of Soviets (VTsIK).[15] Arguably, during the weeks between the coup and the final seizure by the Bolshevik government, the Bank enjoyed unprecedented autonomy. When, finally, legal formalities were more or less complete, the government fired Shipov, appointed a new interim Bank director, and procured the keys to the Bank's storage rooms. However, nobody knew how to technically implement the order for the withdrawal of money.[16] The first allocation of money for the needs of the Soviet government on November 17, 1917, was arranged in the simplest way: Bolsheviks replaced the 5 million rubles taken from the cashier box with a copy of the decree. Sovnarkom's decree sanctioned this peculiar practice of bookkeeping ("putting the documents authorizing withdrawal in lieu of the money") as a temporary measure.[17] Two bags with 5 million in credit rubles were loaded onto a car and taken to Smolny, where they were placed in a wardrobe that served as the first Soviet "treasury."[18] Two days later, the official *Pravda* published a detailed "act" describing the exact contents of those bags (the quantity and denomination of banknotes) along with the acceptance report, which was supposed to legitimize this revolutionary and, therefore, illegal expropriation of money.[19]

This obsession, paradoxical for a revolutionary government, with a nonviolent transition in finances, appeared puzzling even to contemporaries. David Riazanov wondered why, instead of negotiating with the Bank, the government had not simply demanded withdrawal from the previous government's account in the State Treasury. Grigorii Sokol'nikov explained that the Bolsheviks cared how this event would be written about in history textbooks: "What would be the attitude of history to a proletarian state that receives money in *Fuchs* [i.e., wins accidentally] from the old budget and that does not dare to advance its demands to the State Bank?" Sokolnikov defended the tactics of the Soviet government that received its first money "according to the technique of the State Bank, but in a revolutionary way."[20] More likely, the Bolsheviks' reluctance to take the keys and the money at gunpoint betrayed their desire to leave the financial apparatus intact, which, in turn, belies their incompetence in financial issues. According to Nikolai Osinskii, who held the Bank director's seat for a few weeks in November and December 1917, none of the revolutionaries had even slight familiarity with the "technique of banking in general or the technique of the Russian State Bank."[21] Nikolai Osinskii recorded the experience of the first days at the State Bank: "We had in our hands an immense mechanism, with the working of which we were not familiar at all. In what form things should be done, where everything was located, what the main parts of the business apparatus were—everything was unknown to us. We entered the huge corridors of the bank as if we were entering a primeval forest."[22]

In November 1917, the government struck a deal with private banks that had agreed to continue servicing enterprises and institutions so they could pay workers their wages. However, eight days after the banks' reopening, the government broke the agreement and announced the nationalization of all private credit institutions. Contrary to the long and tedious siege of the State Bank, the seizure of private credit institutions on December 13, 1917, was swift and violent. Armed sailors arrested bank directors and took the keys from bank vaults and cash offices. The decision came from the top; even the key specialists at the Narkomfin (People's Commissariat of Finance) and the Supreme Council of the National Economy (VSNKh) were "stunned" by the news about this unprepared, impromptu action.[23] Private banks were turned into branches of the State Bank; money from the private banks' accounts was transferred to the State Bank, and all the commissars had to do was to change the signage on the former banks' entrances.[24] The government promised the inviolability of money in private accounts but restricted the withdrawal of funds to 250 rubles per week. Contrary to expectations, the nationalization of banks only exacerbated the crisis of the money supply. When cashless transfers of funds were stopped, the result was an immediate increase in the demand for cash.[25] With all their operations being disabled, the banks turned into empty buildings storing valuables and account books, while the State Bank, with most of its employees still on strike, was responsible for the management of all payments, transfers, and deposits for all nationalized and non-nationalized factories and institutions.[26]

The strike of the State Bank's employees, which lasted until March 1918, ruined Lenin's plan for taking over the old financial apparatus entirely and placing it in the service of the new state.[27] Bolshevik financiers had to create a new system from scratch—mixing old financial techniques with new political principles. True, the task was greatly simplified because in the situation of political and economic disarray, financial management was essentially reduced to two functions: printing money and distributing monetary notes.[28] Fortunately, the administration of the EZGB, which was also seized on the morning of the revolutionary day, collaborated with the authorities.[29] In the first nine weeks after the coup (October 25, 1917, through December 1917), the Bolshevik government printed 6.544 billion paper rubles, or 2.908 billion rubles per month, which exceeded the notoriously high emission of the Provisional Government (about 1.16 billion rubles monthly).[30] In an economy exhausted by war and political crisis as well as the destruction of state financial mechanisms, printing money represented the only source of state income. The EZGB worked day and night printing rubles from all available templates, compensating for the lack of banknotes with monetary surrogates—state securities, loan certificates, and coupons that circulated alongside and on a par with credit rubles.

The demand for money increased almost instantly after the revolution, as if the promise of its eventual extinction was a joke. The galloping inflation resulted only partially from the overprinting of money and the fall of the ruble's value. Prices rose faster than rubles could be printed, reflecting the acute deficit of goods, which was itself a consequence of the war and the collapse of industry. At the same time, the disproportionate growth of the state budget revealed a paradox: the state that lay in ruins nevertheless consumed more money than ever before. Most state expenses were the payment of state employees' salaries. By 1919, the early Soviet state, despite the loss of former imperial borderlands, employed three times more officials than its pre-revolutionary ancestor.[31] "The government, trying to replace private economy, takes on itself more and more grandiose tasks for the realization of which it has to employ [an] enormous staff of employees," wrote Mikhail Fridman, a former deputy minister of finance of the Provisional Government. The cost of the socialist project was unimaginable. The demands for money were heard everywhere. "The acute money hunger is obvious," admitted Grigorii Sokolnikov in early 1918. "The gnashing teeth of the administrative apparatus feverishly snap not only at credit rubles but any surrogate of financial 'food.'"[32] Desperate for money, regional and local authorities printed their own; unable to prevent monetary entropy, the government tried to regulate the process or at least keep track of the new kinds of substitutes.[33]

Thus, contrary to the expectation of die-hard revolutionaries, in the first months after the revolution, the elimination of money was out of question. Lenin felt that "during the transition from capitalist society to socialist society, it is absolutely impossible to dispense with money or to replace it within a short period of time." Instead of getting rid of the monetary economy, he emphasized the monopolization and control over the production and distribution of money with the help of a nationalized bank. Lenin called this policy "pulling out money" from the population.[34] Along with the distribution of goods via "consumption cooperatives" and communes, "the concentration of the entire number of monetary signs in the State Bank and its branches" would bring under control not only economic production but also consumption and eliminate the remnants of capitalist power.[35] Although the program of the compulsory extraction of cash was not fully implemented, other steps were taken to concentrate financial resources in the State Bank. In January 1918, the government established a state monopoly on trading gold, and the possession of gold in any form valued at more than 10 thousand rubles was prohibited. Under threat of confiscation and criminal prosecution, owners were asked to deliver their gold items to the State Bank and its branches.[36]

The revolution in finances consisted not of the annihilation of money or a change in its origin and nature. Revolutionaries took over the apparatus of making money and scaled it up, artificially inflating the state financial machinery. The State Bank thus turned into a gigantic super-centralized depository of all financial resources—individual, cooperative, public, and governmental. It was also becoming the only centralized source of funds for financing the entire nationalized industry. In his articles published in *Pravda* in December 1917, the newly appointed commissar of the State Bank, Georgii Piatakov, colorfully described the future model of the "People's Bank" with a network of branches "embracing all Russia," a "colossal centralized accounting center of public economy and a regulator of public production." All enterprises, "all participants of public production will be obliged to open current accounts at the People's Bank; therefore, all transactions will be taking place through and with assistance of the bank." The Bank would credit enterprises through cashless transactions, which would represent a "fiction," but a useful one, since it would be showing "the ongoing metabolism" of the economy. In this vision, the national economy appeared as a single giant household, or a human organism with the bank pumping fluids from one organ to another.[37]

Some elements of Piatakov's project were put into practice. First, the State Bank was renamed the People's Bank. More important, in January 1918, Piatakov forced from the Sovnarkom a decree that centralized the crediting of all enterprises at the Central Discount and Loan Committee of the State Bank (Uchetno-Ssudnyi Komitet), wresting the financing of the economy from VSNKh (The Supreme Council of National Economy)—the main organ for economic planning and the management of nationalized industry.[38] This was an important political move: the socialist Discount and Loan Committee was meant to become a successor of the imperial committee of the State Bank and a key organ for crediting industry and trade, only with a different set of people involved. Instead of sponsoring enterprises, the Discount and Loan Committee was supposed to issue funds on the basis of their creditworthiness. These two operations had different meanings. As Osinskii, who opposed Piatakov in this issue, pointed out, banks base their decisions to give money to enterprises on the assessed credibility of these enterprises, while the VSNKh would assess their "economic importance" to the socialist economy. Piatakov's rationale was the coordination of money flows and their rational allocation according to needs and economic efficiency.[39] Piatakov's views, despite being labeled "capitalist," prevailed at that moment, and the State Bank was entrusted with both the control of all currents of money nourishing the socialist economy and the remaining private enterprises. The Bank was supposed to issue credits; all state institutions and nationalized factories were mandated to keep their funds in its accounts; the payments between these institutions could be processed without cash by the transfer of funds. It is unclear whether this system was actually put into practice as intended, but it was indicative of a particular mode of thinking about the economy in this period that combined elements of commercialism and state control.[40] Starting in the spring of 1918, several different visions of the ruble and its future emerged simultaneously. This period through early autumn of 1918 came to be remembered for the striking polyphony of financial views and opinions.

Gukovskii's Interlude

Historians of the Russian Revolution seeking to understand what followed the first "heroic assault" in the fall and winter of 1917–1918 often turn to the foundational texts that promise to explain how the "economy of the transitional period" really worked. Sadly, these texts offer no clear picture, since the reality was complex and multidimensional. In the spring and summer of 1918, several plans for the arrangement of the banking and monetary systems emerged simultaneously from various expert committees, political groups, and governmental institutions. This variety of opinions betrayed uncertainty about the economic future of the regime during a temporal retreat sanctioned by Lenin under the banner of "state capitalism."[41] The first wave of industrial and financial nationalization was receding, but the plunder of money, gold, and resources did not bring prosperity. The ideas for getting out of this chaos went in two extremes: either persist in the revolutionary mode or take a step back. A multitude of compromise solutions dangled in the middle.

Disagreements between the proponents of various economic and financial plans are commonly interpreted as involving either the "left" or "right" wing of the Bolshevik party. The commissar of finance, Isidor Gukovskii, who replaced Menzhinski in March 1918 and held this position until August of the same year, is often described as right wing.[42] Gukovskii was against revolutionary excesses in financial policy inasmuch as the Soviet state was going to have one. He believed that a normal currency system should be based on gold, and since the rubles issued by the Soviet state promised convertibility, the government should start saving gold rather than giving it away to the

West.[43] Gukovskii did not hide his criticism of the clumsy nationalization of banks (even though he thought it was irreversible).[44] Speaking at the session of the All-Russian Central Executive Committee (VTsIK) in mid-April 1918, he admitted that nationalization had destroyed the existing credit system without creating a new one and caused a great deal of harm.[45] The criticism of bank nationalization certainly invited attack from the left, and Gukovskii's views were immediately cast as bourgeois. Even the policy of budget austerity, if one could refer to such a policy when the printing machines were working day and night, invited the accusation of counterrevolutionary retreat.[46] Indeed, Gukovskii suggested reducing expenses by lowering the salaries and wages for workers, introducing taxes, and observing budgetary discipline. The budget for the first part of 1918 was approved retroactively in June, and the second semi-annual budget for 1918 appeared in November. Both budgets showed enormous deficits (in total, 46 billion rubles of expenditures versus 15 billion rubles of income), but the very act of assembling them was a positive thing.[47] Most important among the steps toward normalization was the introduction of the "unity of state accounting," that is, the centralization of all government payments in the People's Bank and Treasury.[48]

On questions of monetary policy and bank organization, Gukovskii disagreed with Lenin. While calling for moderation in the policy of industrial nationalization, Lenin remained a hardliner in financial issues. Lenin's preliminary plan for monetary reform was primitive and radical. He wanted to make all citizens declare how much money they possessed and then exchange a certain limited number of old monetary signs for new Soviet currency, with the remaining funds above the quota being forfeited.[49] Gukovskii strongly opposed this plan as it contradicted Narkomfin's trend toward the normalization of monetary circulation and the restoration of people's trust in the state banking system.[50] Compulsion could not work in lieu of credibility and draw people's money into the State Bank. The denunciation of Russia's prerevolutionary loans and the principles of nationalization that imposed limits on withdrawing money from bank accounts had, along with other measures of financial nihilism, already negatively affected people's attitude toward Soviet financial institutions.[51]

Gukovskii also did not share Lenin's fascination with the idea of a Leviathan bank. Gukovskii's "theses on banking policy" (April 1918) started with a declaration of "not the monopolization but the nationalization of the banking apparatus" and condemned the tendency toward the hypercentralization of credit and money-making.[52] In response to Gukovskii's plan, Lenin drafted his own "theses" declaring that, in a socialist state, banks should transform into a "single apparatus of accounting and regulating the socialist economy in the entire country." This meant that the bank should work as an internal manager rather than an outside financial broker for economic agents. Gukovskii disagreed. In his view, socialist banks should function like banks in a capitalist economy, that is, as institutions of credit rather than the organs of financial governance.[53] Gukovskii's view of the monetary crisis was both radical, as he denied socialist dogma, and financially conservative, because he wanted to adhere to the old principles.

Does this plan sound like a "right" platform? It might. However, explaining Gukovskii's policy as right wing would be inaccurate for two reasons. First, in contrast to the "left communists," nobody cast themselves as "right," which was a pejorative term. The policy of "state capitalism" invited thoughts about the coexistence of the dictatorship of the proletariat with some elements of capitalist finances.[54] Second, and more important, many decisions in the financial sphere at the time were informed by the opinion of non-partisan experts who pursued the pragmatic goal of normalizing finances and retaining control over monetary processes. In the early Soviet state, financial policy often resulted from several trends: while the big issues continued to be debated at the top political level, rank-and-file officials and experts in the offices of financial agencies implemented a policy that consisted of a series of small but significant shifts, not always aligned with the main political line. Occasionally, these changes played more important roles than the political declarations of the commissar, which often remained unfulfilled.

Inviting experts to advise him on the policy of Narkomfin became Gukovskii's hallmark. A treasurer of the Petrograd party organization in 1917, Gukovskii had worked for several years as an accountant in the Baku city administration and then a manager of a private oil company. He had also been a member of the party practically since its inception. Gukovskii's role consisted of announcing the program of financial measures, but the key projects of financial decrees (on taxes, monetary emission, and others) were drafted by the deputy commissar, Dmitrii Bogolepov, the professor of financial law at Moscow university.[55] This was a common combination: a party figure in the political role of the agency's head, with an academic expert behind the scenes.[56] Perhaps the most interesting and remarkable episode of this collaboration was the invitation to several economists, managers, and directors of recently nationalized private banks to participate at the People's Bank in the work of a special commission chaired by a de facto Bank director, Alexander Spunde, in April and May 1918. Regarding methods to reform the Soviet credit system, experts outlined the principles of credit policy based on

two "inviolable" principles: earning back "the trust of the public" and, importantly, separating the function of issuing money from funding a nationalized
economy. In other words, one and the same bank should not be responsible
for printing money and distributing it among nationalized enterprises and
institutions.[57]

This principle of separation did not fit with Lenin's idea of a superbank, and
it was not fully put into practice. However, the Bank's experts and Narkomfin
managed to push through some changes that aimed at re-establishing the
Bank's relationship with the government and regulating the flood of newly
issued money. In 1918, when money printing served as the main source of state
income, this goal appeared as elusive as the immediate arrival of communism.
Nevertheless, experts nagged the government to take steps in this direction
and to legalize the terrifying mass of cash released into circulation.[58] How
could it be done? The pre-war imperial government could regulate the emission of credit rubles within the limits established by the law of 1897, while the
war-time regime allowed paper rubles to be issued above this limit through
amendments to the 1897 law. A small caveat to this war-time arrangement
preserved the appearance of legality: issuing rubles for the government's
needs was registered as the treasury's debt to the State Bank at the security of
the treasury's short-term bonds bearing 5% interest. Thus, the State Treasury
was supposed to pay interest to the bank on this debt. Arguably, this for-
mality could be interpreted as meaningless after the Bank's subjugation to the
Bolshevik government, but the staff and experts of the People's Bank insisted
on adhering to the old rule. The Soviet government, according to the experts'
report, remained the debtor of the People's Bank for the entire amount of
money printed above the legal threshold. Therefore, the Bank demanded
that the government issue bonds as the collateral of money printed after the
revolution or at least publicly recognize the Soviet government's debt to the
People's Bank.[59]

All financial technicalities aside, the heart of the issue was not simply the
question of financial bookkeeping or even the relationship between the Bank
and the government but, more generally, the government's credibility and accountability for the money that it printed, as well as its attitude toward the
obligations of its imperial and bourgeois-democratic predecessors. Despite
the imperial government's reluctance to allow for the autonomy of the State
Bank, Russian economists perceived the Bank as the agent of the state as a
whole (i.e., including the people), while the State Treasury represented the
government alone. Remarkably, this view of the relationship between the

Bank (i.e., the people) and the treasury (i.e., the government) was preserved after the revolutionary takeover.

Experts at the People's Bank and Narkomfin believed that the socialist state, inasmuch as it was going to have money, had to obey the general laws of a monetary economy. This meant that, in addition to recognizing its debt to the Bank, the Soviet government had to amend the emission law of 1897 and legalize the issuance of credit rubles.[60] Following experts' recommendations, Narkomfin asked to sanction the "extension of the State Bank's emission privileges" for 33.5 billion rubles from the norms established by "previous" (i.e., pre-revolutionary) legislation. In doing so, the government confirmed its succession to the old regime. That is, the same government that had canceled the entire Code of Laws and repudiated all foreign and most domestic loans admitted its responsibility for the mass of paper rubles issued before and after the revolution. In October 1918, Sovnarkom approved the law on emission and sanctioned the opening of an account at the People's Bank under the name "Loan to the Treasury," bearing 5% interest.[61] Ironically, the government hesitated to publish the decree on monetary emission, fearing bad publicity, but when it finally appeared in central *Izvestiia* in December 1918, the editor made a mistake, multiplying the sanctioned number by 1,000 (the newspaper mentioned 33,500 billion rubles).[62]

In this case, numbers did not matter as much as the principle of accountability. Explaining the meaning of the treasury's debt for paper money, the Narkomfin's preamble to the state budget of 1919 compared it to the gold backing of capitalist currency. In Soviet Russia, the state's debt rested on the "inexhaustible capacity for the exploitation of colossal riches hidden in the country's nature," which would form the "broad and unshakable foundation for all emissions of paper money . . . more robust and strong than this gold fetish that until now had been seen as the only regulating principle of the emission law and monetary circulation."[63] The emphasis in this passage should be placed not on the rejection of the gold standard but on the allegiance to the idea of paper money as "debt" secured by state socialist property. The notion of the treasury's debt to the Bank had been a red flag for nineteenth-century conservatives who saw in it the quintessence of Western liberal political economy. A few months later, in 1919, after the vector of monetary policy had changed, the new people's commissar of finance, Nikolai Krestinskii, tried to dissociate himself and his agency from this idea. He described the law on the treasury's debt to the People's Bank as a "sin," a tribute to the old principle of "dualism," that is, the separation of the government from the financially independent bank, that required covering the legal "hole" of the government's obligations.[64]

There was one more aspect of the issue of the treasury's debt for paper money. The dissolution of the Russian Empire in 1917 posed the problem of sharing the assets (including the gold reserve) and debts between the former metropole and the peripheries.[65] The Russian government was adamant that Ukraine, the biggest and the wealthiest former part of the Russian Empire, must accept its share of the treasury's debt for the credit rubles. The Ukrainian Central Rada's policy consisted of a combination of symbolic financial separatism with attempts at preserving economic integrity with Russia, such as renaming the Kyiv branch of the State Bank the Ukrainian State (Derzhavnyi) Bank while leaving its statute and structure unchanged, or introducing a national currency (karbovanets) that was nominally equivalent to the ruble.[66] When on April 22–25, 1918, the Russian committee, presided over by Karl Radek, met to discuss the principles of settling the economic and financial consequences of Ukraine's secession, it decided that even if "military and political union" with the Central Rada government was impossible, Soviet Russia and Ukraine should try to preserve common economic space, which included a tariff union, the unification of railroads, communication, and, importantly, a common currency. At the same time, the countries were to split assets and debts.[67] A few days later, the Rada government fell. Negotiations with the representatives of the new Ukrainian government of hetman Pavlo Skoropadskyi continued through the spring and summer of 1918. Meanwhile, it became clear that the initial idea of preserving financial connections between the countries was an illusion. Russian authorities anxiously watched how Ukraine was drifting away. In July 1918, Narkomfin's experts contended that since the creation of a new sovereign currency in Ukraine was unavoidable, efforts must be made to either postpone it or try to influence the reform process, so that the new unit would be tied to the ruble rather than the German mark. Even the idea of creating a Russo-Ukrainian monetary union "similar to the Latin Union" was floated in discussions. In any case, experts worried that Ukrainian monetary separatism could have "fatal consequences" for the Russian currency, ejecting "a sea of Russian rubles" into the foreign market and ruining the ruble's rate.[68]

Negotiations around the problem of imperial inheritance stumbled over the question of the principles of separating debts and properties. Russia was interested in shifting a significant part of its liabilities onto Ukraine, including the liabilities for credit rubles, while claiming its share in the value of industrial factories and other immovables.[69] Ukraine, while agreeing to accept one-fifth of Russia's debt, including the debt for credit rubles, laid claim to her share of Russia's natural riches—"northern forests" and mines, the value

FIGURE 11.1 100 Karbovantsiv, Ukrainian People's Republic, 1917. Courtesy of Division of Work and Industry, National Museum of American History, Smithsonian Institution.

of which could not only cancel out Ukraine's debt but also leave Russia indebted.[70] Debates over the financial consequences of imperial dissolution evoked an array of theoretical and political problems, including the history of Ukraine's absorption by the Muscovite state (was it a union or an annexation?), the nature of Ukrainian liberation (why should Ukraine redeem its freedom like the former serfs who had paid for their emancipation?), and the nature of the state's power in its relation to resources (what is more important for its definition—territoriality or citizenship?).[71] The negotiations also redefined the connection between state debt, including the debt of paper money, and the wealth that secured these liabilities. Trying to limit Ukraine's claims to the assets of the former empire, members of the Soviet committee suggested the reconsideration of the formula of the "entirety of state wealth," which had been printed on the imperial credit rubles and then had reappeared, in slightly rephrased form, on Soviet notes. As the committee reckoned, this notion should include not only the property of the state but "most importantly, the labor force of the state's entire population and its paying capacity."[72] This was a new and somewhat paradoxical twist on the idea of the state's responsibility for paper money: the creditor, that is, the population, was at the same time a subject and an object of the debt, whose ability to pay taxes and produce value was mortgaged in the process of issuing paper money.

Negotiations over debts and properties did not reach a positive resolution, and after Ukraine's loss of independence, the issue of debt settlement became obsolete. However, it was an important episode in the early history of Soviet financial policy. Despite the declared denunciation of debts in January 1918, Soviet financial authorities counted the significant share of imperial liabilities, including the credit rubles, among the debts of the new state.[73]

Thus, economic chaos and poverty notwithstanding, the Soviet financial administration exhibited less financial nihilism than it might seem during the first year of its existence. "Old experts" at the Bank and the Commissariat of Finance spoke against the most drastic changes in the financial system. The political uncertainty of spring–summer 1918 also enabled a theoretical retreat to the ideas of restoring the ruble and normalizing financial mechanisms. The stance of Gukovskii and his advisers turned out to be positioned midway between the left communists—(most prominently, Yurii Larin and Nikolai Bukharin), who characterized Gukovskii's policy as the betrayal of the revolution and insisted on the immediate elimination of money—and liberal economists—who in March 1918 still considered it possible to recommend the return to private trade- and industry-oriented currency.[74] Liberals were, apparently, inspired by a temporary suspension of nationalization and hoped that private industry and credit could exist in parallel to the Bolshevik state and economy; their agenda had no chance at realization. As for left radicalism, despite his disagreements with Gukovskii, Lenin supported the commissar of finance in counterbalance to the left dissenters, who represented a greater political threat. Gukovskii's policy did not entirely fit Lenin's concept of "state capitalism" as an intermediary stage between capitalism and socialism. Defining this strange hybrid, Lenin emphasized "state" and the transformative power of state-owned economic institutions over the remnants of the private-capitalist economy. Gukovskii, it seemed, emphasized the capitalist features of the state economy (e.g., credit, gold-based currency). Left communists denied both elements, warning about the dangers of excessive state centralism, the revival of capitalism, and the delay of socialist changes. The termination of the short-lived policy of state capitalism also predetermined Gukovskii's fall. By the end of summer, his political position became extremely weak, he was bullied and ignored, and in August 1918, he resigned.[75] Soon after his departure, Bogolepov left the commissariat and returned to his academic career.

By that time, civil war was fully under way, and set against news from the front lines, the plans for financial restoration may sound somewhat fantastical. Two facts suffice to illustrate the political and economic conditions of the summer of 1918. First, the EZGB, which in February–March 1918 had been evacuated from Petrograd to Penza (more than 800 miles southeast), nearly fell into the hands of the Czechoslovak Legion in June. Lenin, via his personal secretary Nikolai Gorbunov, discussed with the Expedition's management the possibility of destroying the pumps of the money printing machines and templates lest they be seized by the enemy.[76] Had this happened, the government would have been left with almost no possibility of producing any kind of money for a long period, which would likely have led to total political and economic collapse. The main danger, however, came from within.[77] Authorities discovered a plot involving local militia to seize the Expedition and negotiate with potential new powers; the local population—workers and peasants—was unfriendly; and, when authorities ordered the relocation of the Expedition westward to Moscow, the Expedition's workers tried to stop the train, demanding three months' payment in advance (Trotsky gave the order to meet their demands).[78] In the end, the Expedition with its equipment was successfully relocated; however, against the backdrop of the chaotic move of the state's only money-printing enterprise chased by the anti-Bolshevik forces and by discontented workers, any discussions about monetary normalization must have seemed absurd. What's more, two months later, the Bolsheviks lost most of Russia's remaining gold reserve, which had been moved for safekeeping to Kazan, to the People's Army of Komuch. The Bolsheviks' evacuation commission rescued only 100 boxes of gold, worth 6 million rubles; more than 1 million pounds of gold, equivalent to more than 645 million rubles, were gone (they would be partially recovered in March 1920).[79] The gold was transported to Samara, to Ufa, and finally, to Siberia, where it became the treasury of Admiral Kolchak's counterrevolutionary government in Omsk.[80] The Soviet republic was under siege, its government controlling only a fraction of Russia's former territory. The civil war de facto negated the plans for financial reconstruction.

The Rise and Fall of the Leviathan Bank

In light of such intense historical revolutionary changes, people who had lived through the revolution often felt tempted to reflect and interpret recent events. In June 1920, a group of economists at Narkomfin's expert think tank—the Institute of Economic Research—met to discuss the "history" of Soviet monetary policy. Analyzing the swift changes in finances since October 1917, they debated when, how, and why the Soviet government had made a sharp turn from a compromised policy of financial restoration in 1918 to the thoroughgoing destruction of the monetary system. Were the reasons for such sudden change ideological, political, economic, or personal? On the one hand, as Semyon Fal'kner explained, ideology mattered. Until mid-1918, moderate ideas enjoyed full support in the government, but then the equilibrium began to shift: "a known group was pushing the Commissariat of Finance toward weakening the role of money in Russia's economy." However, most decisive was the economic factor, namely, the nationalization of industry that was launched with full speed after June 1918: "The demand for money from the industrial management of the VSNKh exceeded the amount of resources that were available: this endless need for cash encouraged people to push for the elimination of the role of money in Russia toward the transition to the moneyless system of payment." All in all, as Fal'kner and others agreed, the disequilibrium between the economy's demands and the state of finances triggered the leap from the compromised financial policy of early state capitalism to a moneyless economy.[81] The meaning of this transition was more complex than it may seem, and there was no unanimity about how it could be accomplished.

According to the economists, the fate of the ruble in 1919–20 depended on the choice of methods of financing nationalized industry. Why was it so? The nationalization of industry immediately increased the demand for cash: private, non-nationalized factories did not require state support and, in theory, could be taxed, while state-owned, that is, nationalized, enterprises that had been put on the state payroll brought very little or no income and consumed a large amount of funds. Nationalization created new social obligations (payment to workers) and produced enormous bureaucratic machinery that included *sovnarkhozy* (councils of national economy), commissariats, and other institutions to manage industry. As a result, nationalization accelerated the tempo of monetary emission. The outpouring of money eventually got out of control, producing inflation and triggering ideas about getting rid of money altogether. At the same time, since governing and financing industry came to be seen as almost identical to ruling the country, different institutions began competing for the upper hand in this process. One claimant for the central role in financial and economic governance was the People's Bank (and Narkomfin); another was the Supreme Council of National Economy (VSNKh), which wanted to establish control over all administrative institutions and even aspired to legislative authority.[82] Ironically, participants in this competition for control over monetary flows asserted that their ultimate goal was the elimination of money.

Tensions between these two institutions could be, in principle, reduced to banal intragovernmental strife, but the scenario of bureaucratic competition betrayed a particular view of the economy and its relations to politics and finance. In imperial Russia, the Ministry of Finance extended its influence over all spheres of the country's economy and beyond.[83] The Ministry of Industry and Trade, created in 1905, played a secondary, even auxiliary, role. In other words, making money was a way of governing the imperial economy that remained predominantly private. The nationalization of industry after the revolution reversed this order. In a socialist economy, the state is at once a main producer and a main consumer; therefore, the role of finance as an institution facilitating the exchange was vanishing.[84] As the opening article of the first issue of Narkomfin's weekly journal, the *News of the People's Commissariat of Finance*, admitted, the commissariat's employees worked toward self-annihilation.

Despite frequent declarations about the future without finance, the new head of Narkomfin, Nikolai Krestinskii, and his subordinates did not think it would happen soon. During the transitional period to a money-free economy, the role of the financial administration and, specifically, the People's Bank, was supposed to remain central, albeit in a transformed way.[85] Therefore, Narkomfin and the People's Bank favored a gradual transition to the moneyless order through internalizing all state payments and concentrating all transactions within the People's Bank in a cashless form.[86] This vision corresponded somewhat with Lenin's initial idea of a "Leviathan bank," a mega-structure controlling all spheres of the economy and society.[87]

It seemed logical that if everything belonged to the state, then institutions and enterprises could easily bypass the use of cash. In January 1919, Sovnarkom's decree introduced a new cashless system of financial transactions between state institutions and nationalized enterprises.[88] There was nothing particularly new or even particularly socialist in this order. To the contrary, in pre-war capitalist countries, cash was rarely used in transactions between economic agents.[89] Nevertheless, Soviet propagandists presented it as an important step toward a socialist moneyless future. In the new system of exchange, the People's Bank was becoming the only institution distributing financial means and therefore executing the financial plan.[90] The Bank ceased to be a credit institution in the purest sense of the term, turning into a giant "accounting mechanism of the socialist economy, a colossal central bookkeeping office of the entire economy."

The Bank's transformation necessitated drastic changes to its organization. As Lenin had planned it in 1918, the Bank absorbed almost all other financial institutions. First was the Credit Chancellery (which, among other things, controlled the distribution of foreign currencies) and the administration of the EZGB. Next, the Central State Treasury was merged with the Bank and converted into a Department of Budget. In June 1919, a new department for "financing nationalized industry and the operations in national economy" was established.[91] This positioned the Bank to oversee all stages in the money-making process: printing money, budget planning, distribution, spending, and collection. The People's Bank, with its extensive network of branches reaching through all aspects of economic and administrative activity, was meant to act as an instrument of financial and, possibly, political power.[92]

Merging the functions of making (printing) and distributing money went against the theoretical principles advocated by the Bank's experts in 1918, but it conformed to the new vision of the Bank's role in the economy. In May 1919, the government passed a law that allowed the People's Bank to issue money "within the limits of the real need of the national economy in cash," that is to say, without limits.[93] This law marked another major departure from the 1918 policy. The bank that claimed to play a key role in financing industry was also in a position to provide it with money. Even this combination, which violated all principles of political economy, revealed an interesting iteration of an old doctrine that argued that a bank should issue banknotes in the amount corresponding to the demands of the national economy (in a market economy, this demand is represented through a discount operation). The major departure from this doctrine was the complete internalization of financial operations: the People's Bank and nationalized enterprises represented one giant firm, in contrast to a free-market space where credit institutions, traders, and producers interact. Nevertheless, financial authorities still found it possible to justify financial centralization as a necessity to stabilize currency, and they argued that the Bank should run the accounting of all state resources, both financial and material.

The new rationale of the Bank's organization betrayed an interesting mix of old "bourgeois" principles and new doctrine. The Bank's role was to ensure that the emission of paper rubles did not exceed the entirety of the state's wealth, which served as "material collateral" of the emission. For this purpose, the Bank planned to compile a comprehensive financial and material "balance sheet" of the state's entire wealth, evaluated not only in rubles but also in foreign currencies.[94] In this proposal, the early Soviet mania for counting and calculating reached its extreme; however, the idea of counting the republic's wealth as collateral for its paper money certainly showed the resilience of thinking about paper money as the state's credit obligation issued at the security of its wealth.

After the nationalization of factories, their products, and their resources, the size of the state domain grew tremendously, and the calculation of the republic's wealth represented a formidable, if not completely utopian, task.

Nevertheless, it is remarkable that the Bank claimed this role in order to maintain the equilibrium of money and economy. The idea of guaranteeing the creditworthiness of money also made its way into the design of Soviet "accounting notes," the first original paper money of the Soviet state, printed in 1919. Ironically, the phrase "guaranteed by the entirety of the republic's wealth," which appeared on Soviet rubles in 1919, reproduced the wording invented for Nicholas I's rubles in 1843.[95] This phrase also reappeared, in a grotesque form, on regional and surrogate money issued by local banks and institutions. For example, Soviet authorities in the Semirechie region in Central Asia backed their emission by opium stored at the State Bank's branch in Vernyi. One may argue that the proletarian state could easily bypass this detail, assuming that the trust in Soviet money should not be propped up by senseless promises, all the more so because the resources of the Soviet republic were not redeemable.[96] What, in theory, could the state sell, and to whom? Theoretical and political inconsistences notwithstanding, Soviet money appropriated the "bourgeois" principles of monetary circulation.

The newly reorganized People's Bank with its centralized financial governance and control over nationalized industry and finance, did not meet with unanimous enthusiasm. If in Piatakov's view the eradication of money was associated with the Bank's growing presence in the economy, others thought that the Bank would be a spare part. "The People's Bank will die at the moment when the socialist order has been completed," predicted one letter written to the *Life of Economy* [*Ekonomicheskaia Zhizn'*] newspaper in response to Piatakov's report outlining the banking system for financing industry. Russia was moving toward a moneyless economy, and the Bank's role seemed redundant. In the opinion of Soviet managers, transactions through the Bank created an unnecessary circuit. For example, a factory that needed metal for production had to ask for funds for the purchase of metal, "go to the bank to pay for it," and then bring the receipt to another unit in the *sovnarkhozy* system, instead of just receiving metal for free. This practice of paying for state resources needed for the production of state-owned goods seemed excessive, even if transfers were cashless. "If the budget shows metal or fuel, the Sovnarkhoz should supply metal or fuel."[97] The system of cashless payments did not eliminate the use of money. Even though these transactions did not involve cash, they still represented monetary transactions, that is, the transfer of rubles, rather than the movement of tons of steel or coal.[98]

Soviet managers thought that attempts by the People's Bank's to control the distribution of funds through its accounting system was annoying and backward. Vlas Chubar, a member of VSNKh's presidium, observed with indignation that the Bank dared not release cast iron, very much needed for a factory, because it was unpaid, or the Bank delayed the issuance of money because of some kind of a debt on the factory's account. "There are cases when railroads do not release cargos without payment for transportation, when factories do not deliver goods without payment by their customers— state institutions." Chubar felt that these situations betrayed the Bank's allegiance to the old "private-capitalist methods" and that they needed to be "neutralized," that is to say, state-owned enterprises should be able to receive funds and goods according not to their financial means and performance but to their needs.[99]

The attempts to eradicate the system of controlled financial transactions made visible both a common frustration with the inability to create something radically new and the reemergence of the old forms of law and economic activity, even under the veil of the Soviet order. The persistence of the old bourgeois economic rules was revealed in the language of contracting relations that involved charging fees for services and goods, concluding contracts, and disputing their fulfillment. The old notions of "debt," "income," and "profit," which implied the existence of autonomous wills and interests expressed in monetary units, needed to disappear along with financial institutions so as to free space for the direct management of the nationalized economy, without the Bank's mediation.[100]

There was an alternative solution: building a parallel structure for the management of the nationalized economy, one that would eliminate its dependence on the People's Bank and Narkomfin. The leadership of VSNKh entertained this idea. As early as in September 1918, the head of VSNKh, Rykov, spoke of a special bank for industry as an "ideal solution" for the problem of financing—an organization "analogous to the Commissariat of Finance but focused on the industrial and economic life of the country."[101] In 1919, VSNKh discussed the plan of introducing a special currency for industry that would exist in parallel to the depreciated ruble and shield industry from the detrimental influence of inflation. In any iteration, VSNKh's projects of a special bank and special money certainly demoted the People's Bank to the level of an auxiliary structure.[102] The leadership of VSNKh, with its swelling administrative apparatus, pushed forward the program of centralization, creating a gigantic parallel institution for the management of industry that was meant to include finances.[103]

Thus, in the wake of transforming the Bank into a financial superstructure, it was already doomed to obsolence.[104] An unsigned memo, "On Financial Policy," bluntly accused the financial agencies' leadership of delaying the transition to a moneyless economy and material budget. Financial authorities, according to the memo's authors, "artificially exaggerated the role of money, increasing its circulation and curtailing the tendencies toward its annihilation." The institutions of finance and control received an unduly large role in financing industry but ignored the "essence of the economic plan" by prioritizing financial objectives.[105] The only way to correct this system was to abolish the model of bank-based financing and accounting; instead, all enterprises were supposed to receive funds directly from the treasury and deliver their products, free of charge, to other enterprises or state institutions.

The People's Bank was finally abolished by the government decree of January 19, 1920. Functions that were related to state incomes and expenses were handed over to the "Budget-Accounting Administration" of Narkomfin. Everything concerning the financial management of industry passed to the parallel structure of the VSNKh,[106] while the role of the guardian of Russia's gold reserve was later entrusted to Gokhran, a new institution that accumulated valuables confiscated from private owners.

How did the abolition of People's Bank affect the fate of the ruble? The Bank's disappearance was a major change in the management of the Soviet economy, as the intention had been for the entire order of the financing economy to be transformed. The practices of acquiring goods through purchase from other state institutions transformed into a system of direct material "supply," and salaries were meant to be replaced by payments in kind.[107] However, as we will see, the dream of moneyless exchange among industrial enterprises was not realized. The share of operations "in kind" remained relatively small, and the claim that the abolition of the Bank would approach a moneyless future was an empty promise. Narkomfin explained that the transition to material budgets and a money-free economy was unfeasible due to the simple fact that the material resources that were supposed to circulate instead of money simply did not exist. Russian producers, which were able to deliver 10%–30% of their pre-war output, did not make enough goods to satisfy each other's demands and the needs of workers: "The state is not able to give a laboring man, in payment for his work, an equivalent amount of material values, and, therefore, until that moment, it must pay for labor in other equivalents, i.e., monetary signs, that will give him an opportunity to purchase on the free market those goods that the state cannot give to laborers," stated an anonymous memo written by someone at the commissariat of finance.[108] Such honest assessments of the state of the economy and the methods of management sounded like a note of dissent and were hardly ever released or circulated. In any case, the abolition of the People's Bank was a political

decision meant to demonstrate the seriousness of declarations about the extinction of money. The meaning of the Bank's disappearance was not limited
to the sphere of industry. The decree on the Bank's abolition also repealed the
law that established a "debt" relationship between the State Treasury and the
Bank and therefore annulled the government's debt for paper money issued
above the legal threshold. The state was no longer accountable to its citizens,
bearing no liability for billions of rubles released into circulation.[109]

The absorption of the People's Bank was a symptom of larger changes
taking place in the Soviet state, part of the transformation of the role of
money and finance and its relation to the Soviet economy. The future communist order was imagined as the network of organs distributing goods according to a plan, and what in 1918 had appeared a bold fantasy of radical
left communists was becoming reality: money was losing its functions and
role in society. The Bank "failed to defend its role as the 'chief accountant'
as the accounting of distribution acquired 'natural,' 'material forms,'" wrote
Grigorii Sokolnikov in 1922 about this period. "The Bank was dying. They
buried it, and—since consciousness is determined by being—the known
theory hammered an appropriate ideological nail into its coffin."[110] The
role of other institutions running state finance was also declining, both at
the local level, where the officials of financial organs were often bullied by
party and administrative authorities, and at the center. As Sokolnikov stated
in 1922, during war communism, "Narkomfin . . . was liquidated by almost
90%."[111]

Socialist Money and the Problem of Accounting

On paper, everything might have looked very simple: factories, working under
the centralized leadership of authorities, exchanged materials without the use
of money. In practice, the distribution of things involved more effort, people,
and resources than the regular exchange based on monetary transactions.
It required more order too, and, remarkably, despite extinguishing monetary transactions in some spheres, the government needed to find other
mechanisms for measuring resources. In other words, it needed money, albeit
of a new and different kind. Most suggestions for the new kind of socialist
currency recommended measuring the value of things and resources through
human labor—the only abundant resource in Russia.

Historians have often dismissed Soviet "labor money" projects as exotic
manifestations of socialist utopianism. However, these projects revealed
several important features of early Soviet thinking about money and the

functioning of a planned economy. They betrayed the intense preoccupation of Soviet economists and managers with measuring and accounting, and they showed that socialist money was not very socialist in nature and in fact represented an iteration of nominalist currency. Most projects originated from an idea that a socialist economy cannot dispense with the notion of value and "live without any assessments."[112] Looking for an alternative to bourgeois forms of currency, Stanislav Strumilin, an economist and one of the first theoreticians of the planned economy, suggested replacing the old ruble with a *tred*—a unit equivalent to "the value of goods produced by one worker of the first (i.e., basic) professional category making 100% of the planned norm." *Treds* were meant to assess the productivity of workers and industrial units as well as the "social usefulness" of "goods" (things and services); another unit, the *dov*, equivalent to 2,000 calories of food, was meant to measure the demands of producers.[113] Interestingly, Strumilin admitted the technical impossibility of using smaller units for a more subtle assessment of labor-based value, such as those based on an hourly rate, due to the simple fact that among Russians, watches and clocks were still a rarity.

Strumilin's "labor unit," like many other similar projects of the kind, assumed "the creation of a new system of exchange instead of the monetary one."[114] However, strictly speaking, this system departed from Marx's original dictum about the annihilation of exchange. In a society without a division of labor, the distinction between "my" and "your" labor could not exist, and everyone could give according to one's abilities and receive according to one's needs. Besides, Marx's utopia assumed an unimaginable freedom of labor not constrained by rigid capitalist specialization. In contrast, Strumilin's model could only function under the conditions of "labor mobilization" established during "war communism": workers were bound to their workplace as serfs. Thus, the labor value of things in fact originated from the forced labor of proletarians converted by the state into monetary units.

Why was this theory not revolutionary enough? Transforming the idea of gold-based currency, Strumilin's theory displaced the emphasis without significantly changing its meaning. In "bourgeois" monetary theory, it was not the inherent value of gold that gave the units of money its value but the human and material resources spent on its production. In other words, gold was a representation of the value of labor and resources that helped balance the market value of various goods. Strumilin's concept simply omitted gold from this equation, preserving the logic of representation and exchange. In other words, labor currency was a compromise that offered a poor alternative to the capitalist monetary order. Economist Zakharii Katsenelenbaum was against such a compromise: the Soviet state should either stick to the old system and restore it or else annihilate money altogether. While he obviously preferred the first option, he felt that if and when socialism became a reality, socialist society would dispense of any "measures of value." Instead, it would require the elaboration of more subtle and sophisticated, but not monetary, mechanisms for the control of production.[115]

In the same vein, Alexander Chaianov, a young economist who distinguished himself with his work on the economics of peasant households, remarked that labor currency "only changed the external form of representing economic phenomena," leaving untouched the main elements of capitalist economy and accounting.[116] Strumilin's *tred*, despite its radical appearance, looked more like the old currency renamed than the elimination or the transformation of the money's essence. While describing the approximate value of one *tred*, Strumilin mentioned that it would be almost equivalent to one pre-war gold ruble.[117] Therefore, the new monetary order would not have altered the machinery of calculating prices and other major economic criteria. Chaianov called for more radical changes, namely, the transition to accounting without units of value. According to this logic, and in contrast to labor currency that was focused on the productive abilities of individuals and enterprises, economic agents just needed to record and control their spending of resources—material (things) and labor, in appropriate units (tons, hours, miles, etc.).[118] The judgment of profitability and economic efficiency would move up to the level of entire industries and provinces, whose balances could show the relative productivity of different units working under similar economic circumstances.

In other words, Chaianov advocated replacing money with things, rather than another version of state-made units. Despite the fact that Chaianov's plan was more Marxist, it was not seriously considered, while Strumilin's project earned Sovnarkom's approval as a draft of a state decree. In any case, while Chaianov and Strumilin vehemently debated theoretical issues of socialist money, the spontaneous transition to "material accounting" (Chaianov's style) was already under way.[119] Since the ruble was no longer deemed to be reliable (what could one do with a balance sheet if the same horse costs 30,000 rubles in January and 300,000 in December?), accountants switched to its more robust alternatives.[120] Economists suddenly became preoccupied with the development of "warehouse management," writing the balances of steel, textiles, chairs, nails, and other things. Most remarkable in this regard was the experience of Petrograd *Chrezuchet* (literally, "extraordinary accounting"): its accountants rejected traditional bookkeeping in favor of their newly developed model of a "subject-and-function card."[121] But even in an economy based on things and barter, the ghost of money was not fading away. Things were still swapped for other goods on the basis of some sort of calculations of their relative values, often expressed in common units such as pre-war gold rubles or sacks of grain. By avoiding state-imposed units and practices of accounting, economic agents were avoiding the purview of the state.

The Machine Gun of Class War

One of the paradoxes of war communism was that, despite the extreme centralization of financial, economic, and political power, the state was gradually losing its ability to control the economy. While the government was looking for ways toward a moneyless future, money was slipping from its hands and assuming its independent existence or, rather existences.

The main reason for this was an enormous increase in emission. In 1918, the Soviet government issued 33.7 billion rubles; in 1919, it was 164.4 billion rubles. In 1920, the flywheel of emission produced 943.6 billion rubles, and in the first six months of 1921, 1,178.6 billion rubles were issued. These numbers did not include various local emissions. From July 1, 1918, to January 1, 1921, the monetary mass increased from 43.260 billion rubles to 1,168.597 billion rubles.[122] As the mass of paper rubles grew exponentially, the state, which produced these notes, seemed unable to restrain this growth or to contain the ruble's depreciation.[123] In reality, the expression "value of the ruble" became a misnomer because the ruble turned into a very vague category that included dozens of various types of currencies. Material equivalents, as well as multiple surrogate bonds, notes, and marks, dissolved the state's monopoly on the production of money, challenging the government's sovereignty and ruining the financial integrity of the state. Surrogate notes were like impostors, claiming the ruble's identity or pretending to be its doppelgängers. As economist Leonid Iurovskii observed, the problem was not even in the astounding number of various monetary signs (over 2,000) but in the emergence of parallel emission systems which, while preserving the same name, had their own rate and stood as foreign currencies in relation to the ruble, both politically and economically.[124] Regional and local money was also complemented by the phenomenon of "the ruble abroad"—Russian currency that circulated in Russia's former borderlands, which the government had no way to regulate. But that was not all. Even rubles issued by the central authority circulated with different values. First, the value of the cashless ruble (in internal state transactions) was not equal to the value of the real ruble, that is, of cash used for purchases on the free market. Second, even material rubles differed in price. Above all stood *romanovki*, credit rubles issued by the tsarist government before the February revolution (the Bolshevik government continued to print these rubles secretly until 1922).[125] The value of *romanovki* also depended on the denomination: high-denomination banknotes cost a thousand times more than their nominal value in Soviet rubles, and they served as a means of saving, that is, they played the role of the gold coins that had disappeared. Next came the Provisional government's *kerenki* and the Duma's rubles (*dumskie*), which were often used in daily transactions, while Soviet rubles (*piatakovki*) and accounting notes (*raschetnye znaki*) were at the bottom of the hierarchy of rubles.[126] In June 1920, the Mobilization Department of the General Staff complained that it could not procure horses for the army. Forced to use Soviet money, it could not compete with other organizations and institutions that paid in the rubles of tsarist and Provisional governments, that "cost several times more than the monetary signs of the Soviet republic." Food procurement agencies also begged to be sent *kerenki*, since it was impossible to buy anything with the new rubles.[127]

Pretending that the meteoric rise of emission had been planned in advance, economists portrayed the catastrophic fall of Russian currency as a natural and even positive phenomenon. Working within this paradigm, economist Semyon Fal'kner coined the term "emission economy" (*emissionnoe khoziaistvo*) and explained its mechanisms by comparing French revolutionary assignats with Russian rubles. An emission economy is based on the state's monopoly on the production of money that must be strictly enforced in all private and public transactions. The state converts emission into its main source of income instead of taxes and uses it to "exchange for real wealth." Thus, in a system based on taxation, the government collects income by withdrawing money, but in the emission economy, it makes its living by issuing money in an unlimited amount, which inevitably leads to the depreciation of currency.[128] However, in Fal'kner's view, depreciation was just a normal mechanism of "compensation" for the value of exempted goods. Fal'kner suggested assessing the stability of an emission economy not by the stability of the rate but the "stability of the depreciation rate," meaning that the value of currency had to fall at a certain consistent pace.[129] The government's task was to maintain the stability of this depreciation, periodically denominate money, control prices, and ensure state monopoly over the issuance of money.

Analyzing the experience of French assignats and the reasons for their failure, Fal'kner concluded that the system could collapse only if the government loosened its monopoly or permitted the circulation of metal money along with its paper currency. As long as the government persisted in enforcing the compulsory use of paper notes and prohibited the circulation of coins, its currency would continue to provide stable income.[130] Thus, Fal'kner's theory of the emission economy, despite its very controversial conclusions and bizarre optimism, expressed the new mode of thinking about money as a political weapon of the proletarian state that justified state compulsion and centralization. Emission came to be seen as a normal way of "extracting" wealth, as a revolutionary alternative to taxes and a form of financial nationalization.[131]

Evgenii Preobrazhenskii, a Bolshevik economist, developed this idea into a more coherent political concept. He famously dedicated his book *Paper Money in the Epoch of Proletarian Dictatorship* to the printing press, "the machine gun of the Narkomfin" that "fired on the bourgeois regime . . . by turning the laws of monetary circulation . . . into the weapons of its destruction and the source of financing the revolution." Elaborating on the concept of revolutionary money, Preobrazhenskii even claimed that, in each country where the proletariat takes power, it will have to resort to the printing press.[132] One may wonder what sort of wealth the Soviet state sought to extract with the help of its paper ruble. Who were the class enemies targeted by the emission? Preobrazhenskii explained that monetary emission was a form of tax that initially targeted those who hoarded money, that is, traders and peasants. It was also a means of extracting real value—grain and agricultural produce—from the countryside. However, exactly at this point, namely, the procurement of food supply, that the ruble proved to be an ineffective means of "extraction." The more the devaluation of the ruble progressed, the less willing rural producers were to sell to the state what remained in their granaries. The future of the ruble came to be tied to the vital question of bread and, more generally, social and economic relations between the Soviet proletarian state and the peasantry.

The fluctuation of the ruble's rate and its negative consequences were often attributed to the economic behavior of classes or social groups and estates. During the First World War, peasants became the target of government policies aimed at procuring food for the army and the city. After the experiment with fixed prices had ended, the tsarist government switched to food requisitioning, followed by the introduction of a grain monopoly.[133] Peasants were commonly believed to be hoarding money, forcing the state to increase monetary emission, and hiding grain, thus pushing the urban population to the brink of starvation. The revolutionary crisis of food supply exacerbated the prejudices against the peasantry. In December 1917, Yurii Larin unequivocally described the relationship between peasants and workers as a "de facto dictatorship of the peasantry, even if in a form of the proletariat's dictatorship." The proletariat had yielded to the peasants' demands on all accounts, and the peasants paid them back with ingratitude by continuing to hoard money and grain.[134]

One way to resolve the problem of the food supply was to offer peasants something that they valued, such as manufactured goods. In the spring of 1918, the government introduced a system of institutionalized barter: a certain portion of manufactured goods (e.g., textiles, shoes, matches, soap, agricultural tools) was seized by the Commissariat of Food Supply, which could swap these goods for foodstuffs.[135] The strategy of procuring grain through voluntary or even involuntary exchange never fully materialized because food procurement detachments resorted to requisitioning in spring–summer 1918 on the basis of arbitrarily defined "surpluses." However, starting in January 1919, they switched to the even more brutal armed requisitioning of foodstuff.

The policy of food requisitioning, therefore, changed the ruble's political meaning. Peasants' grain was not taken for free. However, they were not offered manufactured goods in exchange but were paid in depreciated rubles at a fixed price that was many times lower than the market price of produce and was not prorated according to the rate of inflation. Lenin cynically called rubles the "certificate of loan" from the peasantry to the proletarian state, thereby recognizing the injustice of exchange. One of the rationales for this unjust "loan" was the widespread opinion that peasants were responsible for the "deluge" of monetary signs. As Yurii Larin declared, without explaining the source of his numbers, three-fourths of the 230 billion rubles printed by the tsarist, Provisional, and Soviet governments disappeared into the pockets and hoards of peasants in the countryside, who did not pay taxes and did not contribute anything to the state. In Larin's view, while peasants were interested in inflation, workers needed stable prices because the rise of their salaries could not catch up with the growth rate of prices. Larin saw the only solution in the "naturalization of the state budget," that is, the elimination of money.[136]

At the same time, food requisitioning contradicted the theory of the emission economy, spurring the rate of inflation and jeopardizing the government's ability to receive income from the emission.[137] Evgenii Preobrazhenskii complained that Narkomprod (People's Commissariat of Food Supply) started competing with Narkomfin in "seizing real values," and the profitability of emission plummeted.[138] Although requisitions could not deliver as much as was hoped, they nevertheless dropped the ruble's purchasing power, necessitating further emission of rubles and reducing the government's revenues from it. It may have seemed that the only solution to this crisis was the elimination of money. Indeed, broken ties between city and country-side were often cited as the main argument for the transition to a moneyless economy.

If the discussion of industrial nationalization and its consequences for the ruble's future are compared to the development of policy in the countryside, it becomes clear that in both cases, the idea of eliminating money came from the de facto inability of the government to regulate the processes of exchange. In industry, the system of accounting and exchange, which expanded immediately after the nationalization, stagnated, and the government was also unable to establish a relationship between the city and the grain-producing village. In a way, the proclamation of the transition to material exchange was an attempt to regain authority over economic processes that had gotten out of hand. The irony was that, while eliminating the ruble in transactions that involved the state, the government was pushing it into the sphere of shadow market exchanges and losing the ability to control the monetary economy.

Several measures undertaken by the government in 1919–20 seemed to make sense: the gradual elimination of payments for state services (mail, telephone, telegraph services, transportation) was followed by the expansion of payments in kind to workers and state employees. Many decisions that aligned with the ideology of a money-free society were in fact made out of necessity or convenience. For instance, after the nationalization of industry, the share of free postal correspondence between state institutions grew from 33% (in 1915) to 90%, and it made no sense to collect money for the remaining 10% of correspondence that brought very little income (the government declared that it wanted to increase literacy by encouraging people to write letters).[139] The series of laws that expanded the sphere of "free" services culminated in the elimination of payments for housing and utilities in Moscow and Petrograd from December 1920 to January 1921. These decisions were often made out of the desire to reduce the volume of paper money, eliminate the costs of collecting fees that often exceeded the return, and lower financial pressure on workers and state employees.[140]

The naturalization of wages also represented a natural response to the shortages of foodstuffs, the deficit in the labor force, and the tremendous decline in workers' productivity.[141] All of these factors had led to the introduction of labor duty and the bonding of workers to their workplace. The distribution of goods instead of salaries corresponded to the distribution of

a workforce that had replaced voluntary hire, as the elimination of the free
market of material capital was concomitant with the delegalization of the free
market of the workforce. One of the most deceptive features of war communism was that it looked like a coherent system in which all the main elements
(money, industry, foodstuff, and labor) were tightly interconnected. The nationalization of industry led to the elimination of money, distribution of food,
and the nationalization of the labor force. This was a logic of entropy: the
decay of production caused financial collapse and the crisis of human capital.

What prevented the catastrophe was the existence of the last remnants of
a market—the "black," that is, illegal market of goods that the government
unsuccessfully tried to eradicate along with the elimination of the currency.
In this area, the ruble, out of reach of the state, still had firm standing. The
country owed the survival of its ruling proletarian class to the clandestine
activity of "speculators"—peasants and other "bag-men" (*mechochniki*) who
carried bread in bags and even suitcases to the markets of starving cities.[142]
Wages in goods certainly alleviated the problem of deficit and chronic
hunger, but they could not meet all the demands of workers who still spent
up to 90% of their cash salaries buying things on the black market. The crucial role of free trade was not understood at the time. To the contrary, Soviet
economists saw the market, along with the problem of the labor force, as the
main obstacle to the transition to a moneyless economy, and they argued for
the immediate and complete naturalization of salaries.

As a contemporary economist observed, since these remaining payments
in cash "consumed billions of rubles from the state budget, breaching the
system of moneyless circulation, the practical meaning of this system [was]
significantly decreased."[143] However, it was not only the workers who resorted
to the free market. State factories unable or reluctant to procure materials
and supplies from other nationalized enterprises had to turn to the market
as well. Ironically, among those enterprises that turned to private producers
was Goznak (the former EZGB), because state-owned contractors could not
provide it with materials necessary for the production of paper notes.[144] The
system of cashless transactions between factories that was expected to con-
stitute half of their revenues and up to one-third of their expenses in 1919,
and even more in 1920, in reality stagnated. To explain, Narkomfin gave
"objective" reasons, such as the scarcity of materials, and subjective ones, including psychological factors such as the unsurmountable stubbornness of
the contractors, "petty bourgeois" individuals who preferred cash to banking
transactions.[145] Managers, in turn, complained that the existence of two
ways of purchasing goods—through cashless transactions within the state

system and through cash on the market—brought about two different kinds of rubles. Which ruble should be used for calculating the budgets of Soviet enterprises if the virtual ruble of cashless payments was not equal to the real ruble of the market?[146]

Thus, despite the optimistic declarations of authorities, the Soviet war-time system of money-free exchange was very far from complete. Instead, it just increased the multiplication of money, adding the mechanisms of material exchange to the existent chaos of Soviet monetary system. Politicians dutifully repeated the mantra of a money-free society. However, political declarations did not always align with real policy. When speaking to Western journalists in April 1919, Lenin allegedly declared the "deliberate intention" to "debauch the currency" in order to exterminate the spirit of capitalism (J. M. Keynes picked up the phrase and used it in his famous *The Economic Consequences of the Peace (1919)*).[147] But in December 1919, when Yurii Larin tried to include the discussion of the elimination of money in the agenda of the VII Congress of Soviets, Lenin cut him short. Eliminating money was neither possible nor, in fact, desirable.

Historians have debated whether the words about the elimination of money were merely rhetorical and were not supposed to be put into action. Most historians claim that the elimination of payments for state services and the naturalization of wages were forced choices, dictated by the almost complete loss of the ruble's value and the desire to reduce the influx of paper money.[148] Others see in these steps earnest attempts to establish a planned economic system of distribution and supply that would have worked had the government fixed the problem of the peasant economy and normalized the exchange between the city and countryside.[149] Perhaps the main question of the debate is simply misplaced. Whether the Bolsheviks tried or did not try to bring about a money-free economy is irrelevant. What matters is that, despite all the efforts of the communist leaders and economists, their policies and the vision of a future order remained within the same paradigm of a monetary economy.[150] While economists and practitioners tried to find new measures of value that would replace the fallen currency, they did not notice that the new equivalents—labor, money, and things—were just other iterations of currency.

In 1920, the future of the ruble remained unclear. In April, the government asked the experts of the Institute of Economic Research whether money should exist under socialism. Mikhail Fridman opened the discussion with the assurance that "there was yet no conclusive decision on this question in the ruling circles."[151] The Institute's experts almost unanimously spoke in favor of retaining the ruble for the sake of rationality and freedom. One argument in favor of the ruble stood out in the debate. Vladimir Zheleznov argued that the existence of money was not linked to the form of social relations or the abolition of private economic transactions. Money was the only "language" expressing social needs, a mechanism that connected an individual with the collective, forming the "compromise between personal freedom and social organization." Zheleznov cited Dostoevsky's famous words from *The House of the Dead* about money, the "coined liberty" of prisoners in a Siberian *ostrog* that helped people preserve their individual freedom even in settings that exclude any possibility of it. "Of course, one could think of a society in which for some reason it would be desirable to eradicate even the last snippets of freedom that the authority of pre-reform Russia had left to the *katorga* prisoners," concluded Zheleznov. But even in such a society, there would remain a notion of its own economic interest, and for the sake of this interest, society needs money.[152]

Remembering the Tsarist Ruble

Zheleznov's emphasis on freedom echoed the Aristotelian view of money as the weft of social fabric—an approach propagated by several generations of Russian liberals. Yet Dostoevsky's ode to money can also be interpreted in a different way: it points out the resilience of money that reappears under almost any circumstances, in any collective, despite prohibitions and constraints. The dissolution of the state financial system in Russia during the civil war did not mean that money withered away. Instead, it slipped out of the government's hands, and the state could no longer control monetary processes or benefit from them financially; as Preobrazhenskii remarked, the ruble had turned into "a bad scoop." The most poignant description of this situation can be found in Arkadii Averchenko's stories, including his grotesque *The Crash of the Dromaderov Family*, in which money was being produced in each household, with husband and wife determining the emission and the children stamping pieces of paper with their family logo.[153] If money was a symbol of sovereignty, the monetary entropy of war communism meant the dissolution of state power and the erosion of sovereignty.

Therefore, when in spring 1921 the government once again reversed its course and launched the "new economic policy" (NEP), it hardly planned to fully embrace liberal financial principles allowing for the freedom of society and the government's financial accountability. The ruble's restoration under the banner of NEP was dictated by the goals of reviving economic productivity, which had fallen to 13% of the pre-war period, and of increasing state revenues and rebuilding an imperial currency domain that had disintegrated during the revolution and the civil war. It was also meant to return the ruble to the sphere of state control. The flourishing markets and relatively free domestic trade that became the symbol of the NEP should not distract from the fact that these phenomena were the means and by-products of the policy of reconstructing the state, its finances, and a nationalized economy.

The process of monetary reform was not abrupt. By carefully lifting one after another restriction and prohibition on monetary exchanges and restoring monetary forms of payments for goods and state services, the government was rolling out the fabric of economic relations that had shriveled up during the war, restoring economic ties between the countryside and the cities. The notorious food requisitions were replaced with taxes, and citizens were allowed to keep money in any amount, not fearing the expropriation of extras. They were also required to pay for public transport and housing. The introduction (and re-introduction) of taxes allowed the government to increase the tax share in state incomes. Factories received permission to use cash to buy products outside the network of state agencies, and distribution was gradually replaced with trade transactions, although payment between state-owned enterprises remained virtual. The reanimation of monetary transactions and the revival of the market did not result in the ruble's full and immediate recovery; inflation continued to accelerate with meteoric speed, rendering rubles unusable.[154] Instead of rubles, individuals and enterprises employed a variety of equivalents creating bewildering and incongruous categorizations of objects. For example, two kerchiefs equaled one pound of butter, one pound of soap—two pounds of millet, one pair of men's boots -one cartload of hay, three women's combs—four *poods* of hay.[155]

If individual traders could conduct their transactions in pounds of butter or loaves of bread, the government had to find a more stable and universal unit. Most shocking, perhaps, was that the state budget of 1922 was calculated not in Soviet money but in tsarist pre-war gold rubles that in November 1921 were deemed equivalent to 60,000 Soviet rubles (by March 1922, the gold ruble's rate had risen to 200,000 rubles).[156] The ratio between pre-war and post-war currencies was allegedly established through the calculations of price indexes for major commodities, regardless of the fact that pre-war prices reflected a different economic and social reality and demands.[157] After a few months, the practice of counting in tsarist rubles was abandoned. But if the financial meaning of using the tsarist ruble as a temporary virtual unit in Soviet accounting remained questionable and contested, its ideological value turned out to be significant. The reemergence of Witte's gold currency as an ideal form of measuring things, or, as Evgenii Preobrazhenskii described it, the "remembrance" of the pre-war gold ruble, enhanced the retrospective flare of the NEP and linked the financial reforms of 1921–24 to the experience of the 1890s–1900s. "Old" experts, including a former tsarist minister (N. Kutler), deputy ministers, and bankers, were invited to participate in the preparation of the reform, and they enthusiastically drafted the projects of establishing the gold standard. The symbolism of reconstruction was very common, and although the monetary reform of 1921–24 ended the story of the material imperial ruble (starting in 1922, *romanovki* and *kerenki* were gradually exchanged and exempted from circulation), the imperial gold ruble left a significant imprint on the principles of the new monetary system.

The revival of the gold ideal in the midst of poverty and crisis may have seemed surprising, especially because World War I had been a pivotal moment in world finances to show that the gold standard had probably not been an ideal monetary mechanism, especially for countries with weak finances. Maintaining the gold standard was extremely costly, and having slipped from it, European powers did not rush back: England restored the gold standard in 1925, France in 1928. Why was Soviet Russia, the country most devastated by war, the first to take steps toward its restoration, albeit in a very peculiar form? One explanation comes from the retrospective utopia of pre-war prosperity. This illusion was not unique to Russia; in early 1920s Europe, gold was not a symbol of a bright and unknown future but the object of nostalgia for stability and peace.[158] A second explanation comes from the comparison with Witte's arguments in favor of the reform. Lenin, like Witte, considered the gold standard to be a ticket to the club of economically civilized nations. The pre-revolutionary Russian government had used the size of its gold reserve as an argument for its creditworthiness, compensating for the lack of trust in the government.[159] In 1922, as in 1897, Russia needed foreign loans and normal economic relations with the world, and restoring the gold reserve was the key condition to achieving both. However, in 1895, when Witte started the preparation for the reform, he had at his disposal an impressive amount of gold amassed by his predecessors. In contrast, by 1922, Russia's gold reserve, which included 409 million recovered from Kolchak in 1920, had almost disappeared. Between 1918 and 1920, the reserve lost 407 million gold rubles, in 1921 another 321 million were gone, and in 1922 the government spent 134 million gold rubles—with only 34 million earned in 1921–22.[160] The Bolshevik government paid in gold for coal, cotton, metal, machines for agriculture and industry, aircraft, and foodstuffs. It also funded left-wing parties and organizations in Europe.[161] In February 1922, Sokolnikov reported to Lenin that the government had at its disposal 217.9 million rubles in gold, plus valuables in silver, platinum, and foreign currency for 33.5 million rubles; however, about 144 million, including 115 million of gold, had been already pledged for state payments abroad.[162] In response to that need in gold, in March 1922 Lenin urged the government to intensify plundering the coffers of the Orthodox church, hoping to amass "several hundred million gold rubles (and perhaps even several billion)," which could help Russia defend its position during the Genoa conference in 1922.[163] Religious objects, revered for centuries by Orthodox believers, were melted into gold bricks and poured into Soviet Russia's growing gold reserve to serve as a token of Russia's solvency.[164]

The Genoa conference was held in spring 1922 with the goal of discussing post-war reconstruction, including the problem of Russian debt and the new monetary order. Lenin instructed the delegation of Soviet diplomats to advocate the restoration of gold currency. He also told them to study J. M. Keynes's *Economic Consequences of the Peace*; indeed, Georgii Chicherin, head of the delegation, was reported by the English press to be diligently reading Keynes.[165] Pleased and intrigued, Keynes met with Chicherin on April 13, 1922, and on April 15, his article in the *Manchester Guardian* declared that "the Russian financial phoenix may rise from the ashes of the rouble."[166] Keynes's article "Financial System of the Bolsheviks," based on materials he received from Chicherin and Preobrazhenskii, praised the Soviet government's efforts to balance budgets and called its project of monetary reform "formidable."[167] The Genoa Conference, which advised that all countries return to the gold standard, did not solve the "Russian debt problem." Russia refused to recognize its debts under the conditions offered and failed to procure a loan for its monetary reform. Yet the tide was turning, and financial stabilization on the basis of gold played an important role in this process. Financial reputation and creditworthiness were among the most important aspects of the reform. Lenin most aptly expressed the rationale for putting up with gold by citing the Russian proverb "Who keeps company with the wolf shall learn how to howl." He asked Soviet citizens to tolerate gold until the arrival of socialism, when the Soviets would recast all this gold into street toilet bowls.[168] In the meantime, if the Soviet Union wanted to trade with the capitalist world, it had to accept the rules of good finance.

There was no hesitation about deciding that Russia should adopt gold as the foundation for its monetary system, but no one could figure out how to do it.[169] In many respects this Soviet monetary reform resembled the situation of the 1890s: a group of academic experts, persistent in their doctrinarism, elaborated the design of a reform that reflected the key principles of liberal monetary organization. This proposal for creating a Soviet gold-based currency assumed that transactions in gold would be legalized, and the country would have an independent joint-stock bank for issuing money. In contrast to this approach, the head of Narkomfin, Nikolai Krestinskii, thought the bank should not be a separate institution but become the Bank Department of the People's Commissariat of Finance.[170] The final version represented a compromise between the two views: the State Bank reestablished in October 1921 as a major credit institution was placed under the full control of the Commissariat of Finance, while the Bank's capital was created through a grant from the State Treasury. In 1922, the Bank received the right to issue a new kind of money, the *chervonetz*, equivalent in value to 10 pre-war gold rubles with 25% backing in gold. The *chervonetz* had no explicitly stated nominal value in rubles. Its worth was indicated in grams of gold, which opened the possibility of regulating the *chervonetz*'s standing vis-à-vis Soviet paper rubles and foreign currencies.[171] For two years, the old rubles, which were scornfully named *sovznaki*, circulated along with the stable *chervontzy*, underscoring the advantages of the gold-based currency.[172] The transitional system of "parallel circulation" marked by a gradual spread of the *chervonetz* and the further demise of the *sovznak*, represented perhaps the most distinctive and original part of the reform. In 1924, the old *sovznak* ceased to exist. Instead, the State Treasury started issuing subsidiary treasury notes of 1, 3, and 5 "gold rubles" and small silver change coins, which people welcomed with enthusiasm. Therefore, the reform set up two kinds of money: "treasury" notes, nominated in gold rubles and backed up by the property of the state, and "banknotes," nominated in *chervonetz* and backed up by gold.[173] The distinction—meaningless and hardly understood by anyone—continued until 1991. People soon forgot about the initial "gold" origin of the *chervonetz*, and the word became a nickname for 10-ruble bills.[174]

Monetary reform was a radical and, in many ways, very original and effective resolution to a financial crisis. As the Institute of Economic Research's experts admitted, the task of converting the chaos of war-communism money into a more stable system was partially eased by the deep impoverishment of the economy.[175] In March 1922, the entire volume of money in circulation, all those trillions of rubles, was worth only around 30 million gold pre-war rubles, compared to more than 2 billion gold rubles before the war. The extremely modest size, by pre-war standards, of the gold reserve was sufficient to redeem this mass and to back up new currency by gold. Interestingly, Keynes

FIGURE 11.2 One *chervonetz* banknote, 1922. Private collection.

noted, "In some ways so complete a collapse will help her; for the old money is wiped out, and no one in Russia will put off devaluation in the vain hope of a return to the pre-war value." In other words, because the Soviet state essentially denounced its obligations for the enormous mass of depreciated rubles, it could start from scratch—a luxury that other European states could not afford.[176]

So, in what ways did this reform re-create the Russian pre-revolutionary gold standard, which differed so drastically from other models of the nineteenth century?[177] Soviet and imperial systems were certainly characterized by the centrality of the state. Despite the proclaimed liberalization of the credit system, which allowed for the creation of local private and cooperative credit institutions, the Soviet State Bank preserved its domineering role and, in a certain sense, its monopoly on the market.[178] The State Bank ran credit operations and, at the same time, served as the main cashier and accountant of the government, handling all operations concerning the state budget and the distribution of funds. In 1921, experts hoped that the State Bank would stay away from the production of money and that a new, independent, and private bank for issuing money would be set up alongside it—because one and the same institution could not make money and simultaneously both finance the government and credit state-owned enterprises.[179] However, with the creation of the *chervonetz*, the State Bank developed in the opposite direction of the experts' vision. As Lev Eliasson from the Institute of Economic Research observed, "The State Bank inherited the original sin of its predecessor: its state character. The old state bank [i.e., the imperial State Bank] was not a bank of issue in the sense that this institution had acquired . . . in European countries." In fact, the State Bank represented the "emission department of the state." The new State Bank, however, enjoyed even less autonomy, covering the emission activity of the Narkomfin.[180] The Bank's director, Aaron Sheinman, was also resentful of the State Bank's dependent status and named the pressure by Narkomfin as the main danger to the newly created system. The commissariat, as Sheinman attested, tended to turn the Bank and the State Treasury into its "vest pockets."[181]

Therefore, if, as many die-hard liberal economists believed, pre-revolutionary gold rubles could not in a proper sense be called banknotes (since the State Bank was a branch of the central government), the Soviet *chervonetz* was even less deserving of this name. Sheinman complained that "our banking emission . . . bears the character of a treasury emission," both in its form and its purpose; it lacked the "credit" character that characterized bank activity because long-term loans to state-owned enterprises in most cases represented subsidies rather than credits.[182] This meant that the monetary system, based on a distinction between the State Bank and the State Treasury, made little sense because both were government-controlled institutions and played similar roles.[183] The *chervonetz* was deemed a better kind of paper money than treasury notes, and it was quoted on exchange markets and represented, seemingly, tangible gold. However, as Yurovskii put it, its value had been "made up," grown on the basis of the depreciated *sovznak*. After the *sovznak*'s disappearance, the government, including Narkomfin, the State Bank and the political police (OGPU), continued investing much effort and capital into maintaining its rate and reputation.[184]

Neither the *chervonetz* nor the treasury rubles were convertible to gold, and although the *chervonetz* featured a promise of exchange for gold "upon government decree," this decree never followed. Apparently, the government did not even plan to open the exchange. As Grigorii Sokolnikov explained, "We have squeezed out gold as a means of payment from domestic circulation. It does not circulate. This was one of the tasks of our financial policy for which we had fought mercilessly." Therefore, "if a certain Ivanov comes to State Bank, pulls out a chervonetz and says that we have to change it and give him gold," he will get nothing because "we do not have to do it." Instead, Ivanov can go to the stock exchange and buy gold there, because Ivanov is probably either a smuggler or a counterrevolutionary, and he wants to buy "a little gold mug with the tsar's portrait."[185] In other words, a Soviet citizen did not need gold and had no reason to demand the exchange. Reality, however, differed from this ideal: in the mid-1920s, the sale of gold to individuals through the state-controlled stock exchange was steadily growing. Moreover, in 1925–26 the State Bank minted and sold to the population tsarist gold coins in the amount of 25.1 million rubles in order to maintain the standing of the *chervonetz*. Sold only as commodities, these coins were used for savings and could not circulate.[186] The government was clearly exploiting the popularity of Nicholas II's gold coins to strengthen the rate of its new currency.

At the same time, the government embarked on a vigorous policy of amassing gold, domestically as well as internationally. The key element of this strategy was the export of grain and raw materials (timber, oil) that became possible with the general economic improvement in Europe.[187] Grigorii Sokolnikov, supported by most of the Politburo, was adamant that the success of monetary reform depended on the abolition of the government's monopoly on foreign trade. However, Lenin overruled his suggestion, and the state retained a full monopoly on import and export operations.[188]

Thus, Soviet Russia's first hard currency emerged under very peculiar conditions: in addition to foreign trade, the government controlled all operations with foreign currency and regulated domestic trade, while the bank had no ability to affect monetary circulation through the usual means. These conditions endowed the government with unlimited power to manipulate the *chervonetz*'s rate and establish it independently of the currency's purchasing ability.[189] The Soviet state firmly held all the mechanisms and levers of monetary regulation. Although the government emphasized the "goldenness" of its currency, it represented a peculiar, even oxymoronic model of a planned gold standard. As economist Victor Novozhilov explained it in 1928, "The Soviet monetary system is not and has never been gold currency in a pure sense of the word. Moreover, the essential peculiarity of 'classic' monometallism, its self-regulation, is considered a virtue from the point of view of liberalism but does not correspond to the principles of Soviet organization. Therefore, under our conditions, gold currency can hardly exist."[190]

Monetary reform was also a powerful means of financial centralization in the nascent structure of the Soviet Union—a quasi-federative state created in 1922 through the annexation of the Russian Empire's former borderlands. The first attempts at monetary unification were made as early as in 1918–19, but these efforts remained mostly futile until the end of the war. The most important exception was the absorption of Ukraine into the ruble zone. In 1918, the Hetmanate government took several steps toward the expulsion of rubles from the Ukrainian currency system.[191] However, the plan of a fully independent currency ran into insurmountable difficulties, mainly the impossibility of designing and producing a sufficient amount of paper notes.[192] After the fall of the Hetmanate regime, the new government, the Directorate, commissioned the printing of new *hryvna* notes in Germany, but the Ukrainian government's defeat by Soviet forces ended the project of a separate Ukrainian monetary system.[193]

In 1920, the government annulled the money of White (anti-Bolshevik) governments. That same year, it decreed the exchange of Turkestan's *turkbon* for Soviet money.[194] However, further centralization required political moves and, most important, the normalization of the currency.[195] With the beginning of the New Economic Policy, the ruble's standing in national republics and borderlands declined sharply, while trade was increasingly conducted in silver and gold coins and foreign or regional currencies. In 1922, having considered introducing the ruble in Transcaucasia, the government had to postpone the reform, due to the tremendous fall of the ruble's value in relation to local currencies (the Russian ruble cost 1/20 of the Georgian ruble).[196] Moscow had to recognize that "to force Transcaucasian republics to share the sad fate of the Russian ruble ... would be utterly senseless and in many respects detrimental not only to Transcaucasia but also to the RSFSR [Russian Soviet Federative Socialist Republic]."[197] With a free Batumi harbor, which served as a center of regional commerce, and an independent emission bank issuing convertible currency, Georgia and the two Transcaucasian republics that had clung to it economically enjoyed full financial sustainability. Thus, instead of forcefully introducing the ruble, the government opted for transitional steps: the unification of currencies in Armenia, Georgia, and Azerbaijan on the basis of Georgian money, and, most important, the liquidation of financial autonomy.[198] The abolition of autonomy shook the balance between Transcaucasian currency and the Russian ruble, and the introduction of the *chervonetz* delivered the decisive blow. In January 1924, the *chervonetz* cost 465 million Transcaucasian rubles, and in April 1924, the emission of Transcaucasian currency was discontinued.[199] A similar scenario was pursued in the Far East, where the Japanese yen essentially became the main regional currency, and the population preferred old tsarist money and various coins to the devaluated *sovznak*. The prohibition against using the yen was introduced at the same time the *chervonetz* started to penetrate the economy of the region, and in February 1924, the gold ruble was proclaimed the main monetary unit in the Far East.[200]

So, what was the Soviet gold ruble, or what did it represent? The gold standard had evolved historically as a peculiar hybrid—a public institution that rested on private economic power and international cooperation. It represented a mechanism of commitment that indirectly forced the issuing institutions to maintain a rational monetary policy and protect the economy from the government's excessive demands for cash. Of course, the practice of monetary policy often differed from the ideal: central banks enjoyed various degrees of independence and state involvement, and they sometimes compensated for the state character of funds and the absence of shareholders in their management by strict parliamentary control. However, the key elements of the political system behind the gold standard were constitutionalism, political representation, and the transparency of financial policy, while the size of the gold reserve played a secondary role. The Russian gold standard of 1897 emerged under different conditions: the immense gold reserve compensated for the lack of a constitution and served as an additional guarantor of the government's financial, if not political, accountability. Undoubtedly, the post-war gold standard differed from its original form and allowed for greater state intervention.[201] But, what looked like interventionism compared to the pre-war arrangements in Europe was, by the standards of pre-war Russia, a norm.[202] The efforts of the Soviet government to popularize the "gold chervonetz" and to amass a large quantity of the yellow metal were meant to showcase the state's grandeur and increase the state's credibility. This obsession with the size of the gold reserve later evolved into a true mania.[203]

The Soviet version of hard currency, a hypertrophied variant of Witte's state-centered gold standard, allowed no possibility of enforcing the balance between paper money and its backing through public control, and it hinged on a very flimsy legal foundation.[204] As such, it inherited many vulnerabilities of the pre-war model. If Witte's gold standard was tailored to his immortality or at least his indefinite presence as the minister of finance, the fate of the *chervonetz* depended on the ability of the People's Commissar of Finance Sokolnikov to sustain the attacks of other commissariats and planning institutions. (No wonder the *chervonetz*'s demise started soon after Sokolnikov's departure.)[205] This was a far cry from the ideas of economists such as one of the key authors of the reform, Vladimir Tarnovskii, who argued that the stability of a monetary system can be achieved only if the bank that emits money remains independent of executive authority.[206] The liberal ideal remained in the realm of utopian dreams because the NEP was not about liberalism.

Epilogue

THE RUBLE THAT CANNOT BE SPENT

ARKADY AND BORIS Strugatsky's science fiction novel *Monday Starts on Saturday* (1965) begins with the story of a young computer engineer, Alexander Privalov. One day, traveling rather aimlessly in his old Zhiguli, he finds himself in a town named Solovetz. Strange things start happening to Privalov immediately after his arrival: the world around him looks modern but is packed with objects that come from Russian folktales—a flying carpet, a magic tablecloth, and a house on chicken legs that belongs to the old sorceress, Baba Yaga. But the most surprising is the discovery of an unusual 5-kopeck coin. It looks like a regular *piatak,* save for one detail: in the inscription "5 kopecks 1961," the "6" is obscured by a shallow dent. Whenever Privalov exchanges it to pay for a newspaper, a glass of soda, or a box of matches, he discovers it again in the pocket of his jeans. Perplexed, Privalov decides to run an "experiment" and comes to the following conclusion:

> What we were dealing with was a so-called "unchangeable" 5-copeck piece [*nerazmennyi piatak,*] in action. In itself, the fact of unchangeability did not interest me very much. What astounded me most of all was the possibility of the extraspatial displacement of a physical body. It was absolutely clear to me that the mysterious transference of the coin from the seller to the buyer represented a clear case of the notorious "zero-transport," well known to lovers of science fiction . . . The possibilities in prospect were dazzling.[1]

Privalov's amusement does not last very long. A savvy salesperson promptly reports him to the police, and Privalov is apprehended. The police report states that citizen Privalov "had come into possession of a working model of an unchangeable 5-kopeck piece of type State Standard 718-62, of which [he] had made improper use." In other words, what he held in his pocket was not a magic tool but a product of Soviet engineering. Reprimanded for his ignorance and dishonesty, Privalov has to reimburse the state for the losses inflicted on it and surrender the "working model of an unexchangeable 5-kopeck piece to the duty officer."

The Strugatskys' seemingly benign anecdote, which reminded Soviet readers of the monetary reform of 1961, allowed for interpretations that highlighted the improbable nature of Russian money. In the story, the Soviet state creates and patents a way of making money that can reproduce itself by magic or "extraspatial displacement." The irony is hidden even in the quality of the unchangeability, or inconvertibility, of the coin: the Soviet ruble, as everyone knew, had an officially fixed, permanent rate to foreign currencies, but it could be exchanged for neither dollars, nor francs, nor anything else. The unexchangeable Soviet ruble was nicknamed "wooden," assuming its peculiar indigenous quality that was untranslatable into Western monetary values.

Like the other "miracles" of Soviet modernity portrayed by the Strugatskys, the 5-kopeck coin has a prototype in folklore: the unexchangeable ruble of Russian traditional fairytales. To procure an unexchangeable ruble, one had to tie up a black cat with a rope soaked in resin and sell it at a market; other tales recommended leaving a 1-ruble bill in a bathhouse, wiping a black cat with it, and saying spells during a church service. Most scenarios included a feline, but sometimes it could be swapped for a fried goose. In any incarnation, these stories betray popular dreams of prosperity and a life free from arduous toil, which remained unattainable for many laboring people before and after the Revolution. Unsurprisingly, populists came to use the metaphor of the unexchangeable ruble in class terms: for the wealthy classes, the unexchangeable ruble meant an inherited estate or a well-paid job in a government office, while peasants eked out an income from their meager plots of land, while dreaming of a more secure source of income.

Despite their differences in meaning, the unexchangeable rubles—the real ones (Soviet and imperial) and their magic counterparts—shared a common quality: the mystique of their inception. In the fairytales, the unexchangeable ruble came from the devil, whereas in the world of the Russian imperial and Soviet economies, portrayed in a grotesque form by the Strugatskys, it was the state that played the role of the magician. The ruble's origin had to be shrouded in secrecy, and the public was not privy to this secret. The ruble's unexchangeability was a manifestation of its indigenous and untranslatable character, even though it contradicted the main premise of money, the enabling economic exchange. To play its role as economic mediator, money cannot be infinite and reproduce itself—a quality that was strikingly absent in Russian finance for prolonged periods of time. Perhaps because of this peculiarity, the ruble became a common character in folktales, stories, novels, and plays.

Demystifying Soviet Rubles

Many Western experts and observers were strangely enthralled by the oddities of Russian money—an oxymoron deprived of "moneyness."[2] Soviet money contradicted the elemental principles of finance, yet it continued to operate, and the Soviet economy remained, strictly speaking, a "monetary economy." The role of money in the USSR differed from all known Western models, although many of the ruble's features resembled, albeit in a hypertrophied form, the traits of its imperial predecessor. In 1926, amid growing difficulties of maintaining *chervonetz*'s value and the falling size of the gold reserve, the government pulled down the financial iron curtain; it prohibited free operations with gold and foreign currencies and banned the export of Soviet banknotes. In 1928 the short reprieve of the NEP came to a close and, with it, ended the period of the "dictatorship of finance" in economic governance characterized by the efforts to maintain the stability of currency.[3] The political role of the People's Commissariat of Finance and the State Bank noticeably decreased (almost all leaders and top managers of these two institutions, including V. Obolenskii, G. Piatakov, N. Krestinskii, G. Sokolnikov, N. Briukhanov, G. Grinko, V. Chubar', L. Yurovskii, and others, were arrested and executed during the Great Terror of 1937–38). The so-called credit reform of the early 1930s turned the ruble back into a subsidiary tool of the command planned economy.[4] The State Bank automatically transferred money to the accounts of state-owned enterprises on the production of goods prescribed by the plan, which was itself a product of the Politburo's political decisions. The capital exchange between Soviet enterprises was made cashless, splitting the monetary system into two disconnected circuits: the virtual rubles of the industrial economy could not be converted into the physical rubles that people received in wages and spent for consumer goods.[5] The prices of products, as well as all financial needs of the economy, including the volume of cash, were determined from above. As economist Alfred Zauberman eloquently put it, "Within the sphere of production the ruble ceased to serve as a vehicle for the transfer of purchasing power and became an index-unit for efficiency control. In the realm of consumption, the ruble had to serve as a sort of a generalized "ration-card" in a classless society living almost entirely on wage-type incomes."[6] In practice, however, the system did not work according to its design, and the disruptions in its implementation triggered the development of an entire sub-system of informal economy that included surrogate money, perverted market mechanisms of bribes and informal exchanges, and pseudo-commercial credit.[7]

Did the demise of the ruble's economic importance mean that money ceased to play a central role in state and society? To the contrary, the ostensible demonetization of the economy only exacerbated the politicization of money and strengthened its role as a means of governance. The Russian imperial state also had an overwhelming presence in the economy: it monopolized the issuance of money and eliminated public control over its monetary policies. However, the imperial state did not replace or embrace the market. In other words, people, except for bureaucrats, did not get money out of the state's hands, and they spent it on services outside the state's purview. In contrast, the Soviet state, with a few exceptions, was both the sole employer and the main provider of goods and services. Rubles paid in wages by state enterprises and institutions returned to the state in payment for these goods and services, as well as taxes and obligations. Therefore, money embodied the most crucial political and financial link between the government and Soviet citizens, an expression of the state's demands on an individual.

Consider, for instance, the monetary reform of 1947 that was meant to extract from circulation billions of extra rubles issued during the Second World War. Reminiscent of Lenin's early Soviet ideas of monetary confiscations, which even in the context of war communism appeared too radical, the 1947 reform withdrew and exchanged old banknotes for the new ones at the rate of 10:1, without a corresponding recalculation of salaries and prices.[8] The predatory rate and conditions of the exchange were designed in such a way that the reform robbed millions of people of their savings, freed the government from financial obligations (domestic state bonds were devalued), and gave it leeway to issue paper money. Announcing the reform, the government openly declared that it represented the "last sacrifice" that the citizens had to make for the country's well-being, as if the taxes extracted from the Soviet people during the war were not heavy enough.[9] Soviet economists discussed other ways of improving credit mechanisms and transforming the mechanisms of emission, but all these ideas were declared "unwanted."[10] The exchange of 1947 was a political reform that used rubles as a weapon of class struggle, although the class enemy was not clearly identified; it was a demonstration of power and a way to increase control over the population. To sweeten the pill, the government combined the exchange of money with the abolition of rationing, followed by a series of price cuts on consumer goods that partially reduced the gap between the pre-war and post-war costs of living.[11] The Soviet government may have tried to improve citizens' well-being, but the policy of devaluing savings and reducing centrally defined prices of goods represented the quintessence of the Soviet concept of prosperity. People's well-being was a subject of state discretion and could not be a matter of individual choice.

Diplomacy and international trade represented another dimension of the ruble's political existence. The 1947 reform also served as a pretext for severing the ruble's ties to the US dollar, which after the Bretton-Woods agreement of 1944 had replaced gold as the main anchor of the international monetary system. In February 1950, the USSR introduced a new gold standard, conspicuously independent of the gold-dollar ratio: the Soviet ruble, which since 1937 had been pegged to the US dollar, switched to gold, and the dollar's value vis-à-vis the ruble was lowered by 32.5 percent.[12] The post-war financial reconstruction in Europe took several years, and most currencies restored full convertibility only in the mid-1950s. Therefore, the Soviet revival of the ideology of the gold standard was purely a propagandistic bid for turning the ruble into a new world currency. As one Soviet economist declared, "Placing the ruble on the gold basis means that the ruble is the only currency in the world with a hard, gold content."[13]

Despite its "gold" foundation, the inconvertible ruble, unlike American dollar and other competitors, remained cut off from the world markets. In 1952, Serguei Mikhalkov, a famous children's writer and the author of the Soviet anthem's lyrics, wrote a fictional dialogue in verse between "Ruble and Dollar." The Ruble acknowledges that the Dollar can travel everywhere, but wherever it goes, it brings "poverty and death." In contrast to the Dollar, the Ruble does not know the world, but it is the "people's money." Yet this financial nationalism, worthy of comparison with the nineteenth-century conservative theories, did not align with economic and political realities. Like Lenin before him, Stalin fetishized gold but not for the pure symbolism of the metal. Instead, for a technologically and industrially backward country, gold and foreign currency were the means of procuring machines, equipment, and resources for industry.[14] That is why the Soviets obsessively counted and accumulated the yellow metal and convertible foreign currencies through various means—export, expropriation, and the sale of luxury and deficit objects to Soviet citizens and foreigners. The main burden of the Soviet gold rush fell on the prisoners of the Gulag camps who worked and died in the inhuman conditions of the Eastern Siberian gold mines. The size and value of the gold reserve was a state secret, and no one, except Stalin and a few trusted officials, knew its exact size.[15] Ironically, Western experts and intelligence agencies shared this obsession with Soviet gold and closely monitored the output of the Soviet gold industry. Fears that the Soviet government could make the ruble fully convertible to gold and bring down the US dollar ran rampant. As one author remarked, convertible rubles could become "a monetary sputnik."[16] These stories about the mythical Soviet gold created an aura of mystique and exoticism around Soviet currency.

The reality was both more banal and more complex. The idea of creating a sustainable socialist currency—like the Fichtean money of the "closed commercial state"—did not work. The USSR needed access to international markets, but, as economist Franklyn Holzman showed, the overvaluation of the "gold" ruble led to a paradoxical situation in which the Soviets were exporting goods at prices that were substantially below domestic prices. Asserting the prestige of the ostensibly strong ruble came at a price of substantial nominal loss, and the country that tried to expand its foreign trade had to adjust the standing of its currency.[17] At the same time, devaluing the ruble in relation to foreign currencies without causing public embarrassment also seemed impossible.[18] To solve this problem, in May 1960 the government announced the blanket denomination of all banknotes at the rate of 10:1, to which the Strugatskys' story of an unexchangeable 5 kopecks coin alluded. The 1961 reform that was presented to the population as a technical measure concealed an attempt to correct the ruble-to-dollar ratio; after the reform, the dollar cost 90 kopecks instead of 40 kopecks, as it was supposed to.[19] At the same time, the designated ruble's gold content increased from 0.22187 to 0.987412 gram and appeared higher than after Witte's gold reform of 1897. Although the reform devalued the ruble, it seemed to have gained in value and weight, and propaganda celebrated the change as a victory over the dollar that, as the Soviet press reported, was in free fall.[20] Counterintuitively, with the declarations of the dollar's decline, the government drastically increased the penalty for possessing foreign currency. In July 1961, the Supreme Court of the Russian Federation, at Khrushchev's prompting, reconsidered the case of three men who had been accused of speculation with foreign money and gold coins. The three prisoners—guilty only of trading one currency for others—were executed.[21]

The quintessence of the Soviet attitude to money was that political ideology prevailed over economic rationality and people's interests. Even economically pragmatic decisions, such as the adjustment of rate, did not ultimately change or challenge higher political objectives. Individual rights were never considered a central focus of Soviet monetary policy, and public declarations about people's prosperity could not fool anyone. After the ill-fated reform of 1947 and until the regime's fall in 1991, rumors about monetary reforms appeared with regularity, people rushed to empty (or fill) their bank deposits, and shoppers rushed to stores trying to convert their rubles into rugs, pianos, jewelry, boots, or coats before the money was devalued or superseded. The famous writer Kornei Chukovsky, observing another "monetary panic" in June 1953, noted with sarcasm: "How strong is people's trust to its government if it is so afraid of a scam!"[22] The announcement of a planned denomination in May 1960 was also met with disbelief. "The government never engages in philanthropy. There must be a scam here," recorded a diarist.[23] Sudden changes in financial policy exacerbated deep and persistent distrust. In 1956, Khrushchev suspended widely celebrated annual price cuts, and in 1962, the government announced a 30%–35% rise in the prices of meat, dairy products, and eggs. Along with silent, creeping discontent, this sudden increase in prices produced the workers' rebellion in Novocherkassk, followed by the massacre that killed dozens, a trial, and executions.

The so-called monetary reforms of 1947 and 1961, which were not accompanied by structural improvements in the economy, show clearly that Soviet money was, first and foremost, a political institution, the instrument of governance, propaganda and Cold War diplomacy. Its nature and existence were predicated on the stability of Soviet power. Therefore, when the foundational elements of the Soviet regime began to sway in the late 1980s, the principles of the Soviet monetary order also started unraveling. Mikhail Gorbachev's attempts at political liberalization overlapped with an economic crisis that was triggered by the fall of oil prices and exacerbated by the ill-conceived economic reforms. Encouraged by the promises of freedom, people started demanding the state's accountability and public control over monetary policy.

As controls over the movement of people and capital were relaxed and some private economic activity was permitted, the situation of the late 1980s slightly resembled the aftermath of the Crimean debacle and the beginning of the Great Reforms when Russia started opening itself to the West. In the 1980s, as in the late 1850s, reforms were initiated from above, and the restoration of the ruble—both in financial and moral terms—turned into a symbol of Perestroika. In June 1987, Gorbachev brought up the issue of "strengthening and raising the reputation of the ruble" at the Plenum of the Central Committee of the Communist Party, and the party leadership embraced the idea of convertible Soviet currency. The ruble's convertibility appeared at first to be a recipe for transforming old Soviet institutions without a major overhaul, a means of repairing the socialist system with some elements of the market.[24] Skeptical experts asserted that convertibility should not be a remedy for but a consequence of structural reforms—the dissolution of the command-administrative system and planned economy.[25] Economists called for the "free[ing of] the monetary relations from administrative constraints" and ensuring the independence of the State Bank.[26] Meanwhile, the country was flooded with paper rubles, the old system of production and distribution fell apart, and goods disappeared from stores. The decay of the ruble's purchasing power was steep and fast, much like the war communism disaster. Enterprises, freed from many obligations and control, switched to barter and foreign currency. The Soviet ruble was literally becoming unexchangeable because it could not be used to buy even the most fundamental things—food, clothing, medications. People started sending letters to central newspapers and the Communist Party organizations demanding that the state intervene.[27] "Why can't the government just declare our ruble convertible?" asked a pensioner from Irkustk.[28] As one journalist observed, the very word convertibility (*konvertiruemost'*) "caused euphoria among citizens. Many people deem it to be a panacea for our economy." For many, it stood simply for the accessibility of goods—in contrast to the unexchangeable ruble that could not be spent and didn't buy anything.[29]

In August 1989, the Institute of Economics of the USSR Academy of Sciences announced a competition for the best proposal for restoring the ruble's convertibility. The competition drew 600 participants from twenty-three countries, and the selection committee included, among others, Nobel Prize laureate Wassily Leontief and an American expert on the Soviet economy, Ed A. Hewett, an adviser to President George H. W. Bush.[30] The monetary reform of 1921–24 and the creation of parallel currencies with a gradual elimination of the old rubles was often cited by the competition's participants as an example of successful restoration. The competition jury ultimately decided that the model of parallel currency from the early 1920s would not work in the 1990s, but the idea of putting the ruble on gold or, quite literally, the reintroduction of the *chervonetz* acquired significant popularity as a viable alternative to full convertibility. Meanwhile, the Soviet gold reserve was dwindling. According to the leader of the reform team, economist Egor Gaidar, between 1989 and 1991, the government sold more than 1,000 tons of gold, and the size of the gold reserve fell below 300 tons.[31] This outflow of gold produced myths about "the party's gold" that was allegedly carried away and stored in the secret accounts of the Communist Party functionaries in Western banks.

The reforms of the late 1980s–early 1990s are usually seen as a radical break with the past. Yet the novelties of the late Soviet and early post-Soviet transformations throw into sharp relief important features of Russian monetary and political history. For instance, the imperial and early Soviet government repeatedly tried to fix the monetary system without changing the institutional and political foundations of the economy, and these attempts backfired. Similarly, the late Soviet government's efforts to strengthen the ruble without reforming crucial elements of the command-administrative system, such as the principles of price formation, came to naught.[32] Another persistent feature of Russian financial history was that people always bore the costs of monetary reforms. The reformist governments of the early 1990s did not alter this practice. In January 1991, a few months before the collapse of the Soviet Union, the government annulled the banknotes of the largest denomination (citizens had three days to exchange a limited number of these banknotes, but the state did its utmost to eliminate this possibility). Thousands of Soviet citizens who kept their meager savings at home fell victim to this cynical, treacherous, and humiliating measure that allegedly targeted the "mafia" but affected everyone. In 1993, when the Soviet Union had already collapsed, the government of the Russian Federation, faced with an uncontrollable influx of rubles from the former Soviet republics, decided to exchange all Soviet banknotes issued between 1961 and 1992 for the new Russian money. This exchange, confiscatory in nature and reminiscent of the 1947 reform, once again wiped out people's savings. As the prime minister Victor Chernomyrdin half-jokingly recognized, "We wanted the best, but it turned out as always." Chernomyrdin's phrase went viral and came to symbolize the persistence of old patterns in government policy that prioritized state interests over the needs of the impoverished population.

The Soviet ruble, an element of the planned economy, was also a symbol of imperial dominance and centralization, and its demise accelerated the Soviet Union's dissolution. Economic entropy was so profound that the union was doomed economically long before it formally ceased to exist. When the Soviet Union disintegrated in 1991, the newly independent states that emerged celebrated their sovereignty by introducing their own national currencies.[33] Running from the ruble meant not only that the new states escaped the legacy of oppression and insulated their national economies from the ruble's crisis but it also symbolized their transition to the new principles of monetary policies and institutional organization, such as the independence of the central bank. In early 1992, the new government of the Russian Federation eliminated the last pillars of the command planned economy and let the free market define the prices of goods. Between 1992 and 1994, inflation went down from 2,250 percent to 224 percent, and the government stood on the path to financial reconstruction.[34] The state was slowly regaining control over its monetary system.

Never fully convertible but relatively reputable and scaffolded by high gas and oil prices, the Russian ruble became the tool for building another empire in the late 1990s–2000s. It absorbed the costs of two wars in Chechnya, the attacks against Georgia, and the annexation of Crimea and Eastern Ukraine. In early 2022, when the Russian troops invaded Ukraine, Russian money was banned from foreign banks and stock exchanges and denied the privilege of convertibility. The unexchangeable ruble turned again into the symbol of Russian authoritarianism and autarky.

———

The ruble's 200-year history may appear like none other. But for all its idiosyncrasies, it represents the common problems of the historical development of money in its most acute, concentrated form, highlighting the qualities of currencies that in other economies often appear muted. The parallel persistence of certain political forms and financial policies indicates the extent of the dependency between monetary institutions, the systems of governance, and the modes of political existence. The ruble's story shows that money does not simply reflect an existing (or imagined) social and political order but creates it; it is not a consequence or an attribute but an integral and constitutive part of any regime—authoritarian, liberal, or democratic.

The government's use of the ruble as a means of governance and oppression should not obscure the existence of liberal, constitutional, and democratic views and ideas about money in Russia. In these discourses, a monetary note appeared not simply as a means of obtaining goods or services but as a proxy for citizenship and as a mandate for rights. European philosophers had discovered the connection between citizenship and currency before Russian thinkers did, but because people in Russia enjoyed limited civic rights and the currency was faltering, this connection seemed more obvious than anywhere else. Therefore, any conversation about the ruble was always more than talk about money. Like the mythical unexchangeable ruble that signified dramatically different things to many people and yet persisted in the cultural and economic imagination for centuries, the actual Russian currency was the subject of constant discussion among a wide range of voices. This book tries to recover these stories, projects, and visions and show how the Russians perceived their past and present and projected the future while thinking in monetary categories. The biography of the ruble, in other words, is a history of the Russian state, written in the language of money.

Appendix

Table A.1 The Ruble Assignat, 1769–1839: Issuance and Rate

Year	Rubles assignat issued	Rubles assignat withdrawn	Total value of paper money in circulation (in rubles assignat)	The value of silver ruble in ruble assignat
1769	2,619,975		2,619,975	1.01
1770	3,758,799		6,378,675	1.01
1771	4,291,325		10,670,000	1.02
1772	3,378,225		14,048,225	1.03
1773	3,796,500		17,855,725	1.02
1774	2,155,275		20,000,000	1.00
1775	1,500,000		21,500,000	1.01
1776	2,000,000		23,500,000	1.01
1777			23,500,000	1.01
1778			23,500,000	1.01
1779	500,000		24,000,000	1.01
1780	500,000		24,500,000	1.01
1781	5,500,500		30,000,000	1.01
1782	7,000,000		37,000,000	1.01
1783	3,101,100		40,101,100	1.01
1784	2,414,750		42,515,850	1.02
1785	2,794,575		45,310,425	1.02
1786	862,525		46,172,950	1.02
1787	53,827,050		100,000,000	1.03
1788			100,000,000	1.08
1789			100,000,000	1.09
1790	7,000,000		107,000,000	1.15
1791	6,000,000		113,000,000	1.23
1792	3,000,000		116,000,000	1.26

(*continued*)

Table A.1 Continued

Year	Rubles assignat issued	Rubles assignat withdrawn	Total value of paper money in circulation (in rubles assignat)	The value of silver ruble in ruble assignat
1793	4,000,000		120,000,000	1.35
1794	30,000,000		150,000,000	1.41
1795			150,000,000	1.46
1796	7,703,640		157,703,640	1.42
1797	53,595,600	628,785	210,670,455	1.26
1798		88,850	210,581,605	1.37
1799		581,605	210,000,000	1.51
1800	2,689,335		212,689,335	1.53
1801	8,799,000		221,488,335	1.51
1802	8,976,090		230,464,425	1.38
1803	19,555,755	20,180	250,000,000	1.25
1804	10,658,550		260,658,550	1.26
1805	31,540,560		292,199,110	1.30
1806	27,040,850		319,239,960	1.34
1807	63,089,545		382,329,505	1.49
1808	95,039,075		477,368,580	1.87
1809	55,832,720		533,201,300	2.25
1810	46,172,580		579,373,880	3.24
1811	7,020,520	5,000,000	581,395,400	3.94
1812	64,500,000		645,894,400	3.88
1813	103,440,000		749,334,400	3.97
1814	48,791,500		798,125,900	3.96
1815	30,197,800	2,500,000	825,823,700	4.21
1816	5,600,000		831,423,700	4.04
1817	4,576,300		836,000,000	3.84
1818		38,023,875	797,976,125	3.79
1819	1,578,500	80,229,030	719,325,595	3.72
1820	1,461,055	35,614,105	685,172,545	3.74
1821		37,242,410	651,685,100	3.78
1822		44,968,230	606,776,870	3.75
1823		10,940,560	595,776,310	3.73
1824			595,776,310	3.74
1825			595,776,310	3.72
1826			595,776,310	3.72
1827			595,776,310	3.73

Table A.1 Continued

Year	Rubles assignat issued	Rubles assignat withdrawn	Total value of paper money in circulation (in rubles assignat)	The value of silver ruble in ruble assignat
1828			595,776,310	3.71
1829			595,776,310	3.69
1830			595,776,310	3.69
1831			595,776,310	3.72
1832			595,776,310	3.66
1833			595,776,310	3.61
1834			595,776,310	3.59
1835			595,776,310	3.58
1836			595,776,310	3.57
1837			595,776,310	3.55
1838			595,776,310	3.54
1839			595,776,310	3.50

Source: A.E. Denisov, Bumazhnye denezhnye znaki Rossii, t.1, Moskva: Numizmaticheskaia literatura, 2002, 32,35,38.

Table A.2 Monetary System after the "Silver Standard" Reform

Year	Assignats in circulation, million silver rubles	Deposit certificates, million silver rubles	Credit rubles, million silver rubles	Total	Metal reserve, million silver rubles	Paper ruble's value in silver ruble
1840	170.22	24.17	-	194.39	24.17	1.0145
1841	170.22	36.95	-	207.17	36.95	1.0044
1842	170.22	43.79	-	214.01	43.79	0.9783
1843	160.67	31.49	30.3	222.47	35.92	0.9748
1844	93.08	17.81	121.80	232.62	59.40	0.9890
1845	55.12	8.59	189.42	253.12	86.81	0.9846
1846	34.92	4.38	226.17	265.47	101.29	0.9922
1847	18.85	1.94	289.58	310.37	117.90	0.9868
1848	4.32	0.28	306.63	311.24	117.08	0.9520
1849	1.62	-	300.32	301.94	107.33	0.9617
1850	0.62	-	301.58	302.20	108.23	0.9925
1851	0.41	-	303.80	304.21	111.32	0.9837
1852	-	-	311.28	311.28	123.71	0.9949
1853	-	-	333.44	333.44	131.48	1.04
1854	-	-	356.34	356.34	123.17	0.9426
1855	-	-	511.1	511.1	138.00	0.9344
1856	-	-	689.2	689.2	146.6	0.9826
1857	-	-	735.3	735.3	141.5	0.9595
1858	-	-	644.6	644.6	110.8	0.9330
1859	-	-	638.2	638.2	97.7	0.9113
1860	-	-	713.0	713.0	92.9	0.9265

Source: I.I. Kaufman, *Statisticheskii vremennik Rossiiskoi Imperii.* Ser.5, vyp.15. *Statistika gosudarstvennykh finansov Rossii v 1862–84 godakh.* St. Petersburg, 1886, pp. 46–47.

Table A.3 Credit Rubles Issuance, Metal Reserve, and the State Treasury's Debt to the State Bank, 1860–1910

Year (by January 1)	Credit rubles in circulation, million silver rubles	State Bank reserve, gold.	State Bank reserve, silver	State Treasury's debt to the State Bank	Credit ruble's value in "metal" rub.
1861	712.976	81.743	52.100	602.8	0.8724
1862	713.596	71.888	52.662	609.8	0.9012
1863	691.104	81.540	43.323	583.9	0.9483
1864	636.526	64.851	31.425	559.39	0.8355
1865	664.075	71.557	13.306	572.4	0.8165
1866	661.565	78.091	10.751	567.2	0.7602
1867	697.244	78.264	15.650	566.3	0.8456
1868	674.914	89.896	19.699	594.1	0.8420
1869	702.806	188.618	29.348	530.8	0.7943
1870	694.388	201.163	21.658	513.4	0.7729
1871	694.098	205.211	8.190	506.5	0.8338
1872	752.034	236.213	6.380	511.2	0.8490
1873	748.301	285.287	10.239	474.6	0.8400
1874	773.989	296.018	25.285	480.66	0.8699
1875	763.936	309.603	31.995	468.04	0.8612
1876	751.639	310.122	30.728	467.37	0.8091
1877	766.881	186.528	29.012	561.6	0.6745
1878	1,014.422	203.764	18.806	805.7	0.6366
1879	1,152.511	229.857	11.996	959.1	0.6309
1880	1,129.922	276.110	4.739	815.3	0.6537
1881	1.085.051	298.408	2.507	839.9	0.6572
1882	1,028.114	271.432	2.696	795.98	0.6302
1883	973.182	264.420	2.514	752.48	0.6180
1884	959.279	298.382	2.910	695.88	0.6316
1885	899.761	303.374	3.949	694.38	0.633
1886	906.655	366.524	6.196	674.03	0.589
1887	941.024	381.967	7.268	669.93	0.557
1888	971.181	389.894	7.366	654.32	0.595
1889	973.145	429.917	6.136	585.85	0.659
1890	928.426	475.185	6.192	575.63	0.726
1891	907.416	575.794	7.099	583.38	0.668
1892	1,054.805	642.158	6.217	569.81	0.620
1893	1,074.081	851.838	6.290	453.35	0.653

(*continued*)

Appendix

Table A.3 Continued

Year (by January 1)	Credit rubles in circulation, million silver rubles	State Bank reserve, gold.	State Bank reserve, silver	State Treasury's debt to the State Bank	Credit ruble's value in "metal" rub.
1894	1,071.868	894.841	5.442	322.83	0.66
1895	1,047.681	911.563	6.708	320.11	0.66
1896	1,055.305	963.780	8.306	246.15	0.66
1897	1,067.901	1,095.471	16.821	197.64	1*
1898	901.026	1,184,614	39.550	175.00	-
1899	661.839	1.007.979	46.622	100.00	-
1900	491.163	843.035	57.073	50.00	-
1901	554.979	737.394	64.889	-	-
1902	542.409	709.452	72.739	-	-
1903	553.547	769.166	72.271	-	-
1904	578.433	906.060	76.028	-	-
1905	853.713	1,031,567	79,854	-	-
1906	1,207.485	926.500	32.891	-	-
1907	1,194.556	1,190.614	47.062	-	-
1908	1,154.705	1,169.117	54.437	-	-
1909	1,087.134	1,220.056	69.545	-	-
1910	1,173.785	1,414.592	70.355	-	-

* Monetary reform of 1897: gold ruble established as legal tender.

Source: columns 1-5 – *Gosudarstvennyi Bank. Kratkii ocherk deiatelnosti za 1860–1910 gg.* St. Petersburg, 1910, pp. 138–139; column 6 – Denisov, Bumazhnye den'gi, t.3, 10,14,17.

Table A.4 Credit Rubles Issuance, Gold Reserve, and the State Bank's
Right of Issue

Year (by January 1)	Gold reserve, million rubles (domestic and abroad)	Credit rubles issued (million rubles)	State Bank's right of issue (by January 1, million rubles)
1911	1,450	1,234	516
1912	1,436	1,326	410
1913	1,556	1,495	361
1914	1,695	1,664	330
1915	1,733	2,946	285
1916	2,260	5,616	143
1917	3,617	9,103	1,013

Source: Gosudarstvennyi Bank, Otchet. Za 1910, p. VII, za 1912, p. VI, za 1916, p. 9.

Table A.5 Monthly Emissions of Paper Money (Pre-reform Money, all kinds and denominations, in millions of rubles), 1917–1923

YEAR	1917	1918	1919	1920	1921	1922	1923
January	348.7	1,913.3	4,200.3	35,216.1	130,232.0	12,238,965.00	633,677,519.33
February	431.8	1,455.8	3,822.9	32,831.7	189,394.0	18,756,143.20	607,389,981.24
March	1,123.6	2,956.3	5,836.1	47,599.3	198,460.6	32,645,722.70	1,246,161,174.38
April	476	4,290.6	5,864.5	47,044.4	230,568.3	48,328,256.40	1,594,142,568.02
May	738.5	2,477.2	11,429.9	62,962.2	205,040.5	84,243,130.20	974,422,268.09
June	874.8	2,968.5	8,550.8	61,146.9	224,871.8	106,198,658.80	1,981,104,524.48
July	1,080	2,683	11,319.3	68,888.0	460,932.6	154,843,557.80	3,424,195,960.99
August	1,286.6	2,279.1	13,857.8	70,641.8	702,577.5	221,348,047.60	4,399,814,476.72
September	1,954.4	2,851.5	21,993.7	93,811.9	1,018,753.7	155,345,142.39	12,898,315,593.84
October	1,999.5	2,700.2	21,907.3	117,608.3	1,950,285.2	244,002,600.90	39,190,451,298.64
November	5,717.6	3,074.9	22,343.5	132,870.8	3,365,481.8	383,729,848.99	46,720,269,657.07
December	2,355.2	3,955.6	32,562.9	172,960.3	7,694,037.2	515,245,147.67	109,972,964,537.87
Total	18,386.7	33,676	163,689.0	943,581.7	16,370,635.2	1,976,925,221.65	223,642,909,560.67

Source: Nashe denezhnoe obrashchenie. Sbornik materialov po istorii denezhnogo obrashcheniia, 1914–1924, edited by L. N. Yurovskii. Moskva: Fin izd-vo NKF SSSR, 1926, 152.

Table A.6 Gold Reserve of the Leading Central Banks (in metric tons)

	Russia	United Kingdom	France	Germany (incl. war fund, 1875–1913)	United States	Italy
1870	160	161	217	-	107	30.8
1875	230	154	337	43	87	26
1880	195	170	242	81	208	22
1885	195	141	344	99	371	142
1890	312	166	370	186	442	133
1895	695	305	460	252	169	132
1900	661	198	544	211	602	115
1905	654	199	836	267	1149	285
1910	954	223	952	240	1660	350
1913	1233	248	1030	437	2293	355
1915	1250	585	1457	876	2568	397
1920	-	864	1622	391	3679	307
1925	141	1045	1201	432	5998	498
1930	375	1080	3160	794	6358	420
1935	7,456	1464	3907	56	8998	240

Source: Timothy Green, *Central Bank Gold Reserves: An Historical Perspective since 1845* (London: World Gold Council, 1999).

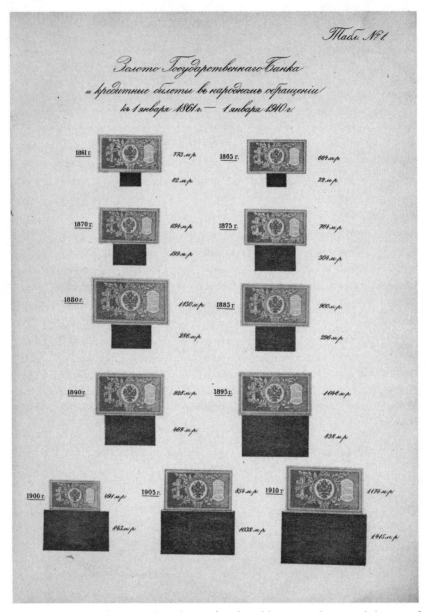

FIGURE A.1 Ratio between the volume of credit rubles in circulation and the size of the State Bank's gold reserve. From *Gosudarstvennyi bank: kratkiii ocherk deiatel'nosti za 1860–1910 gody*. St. Petersburg, 1910.

FIGURE A.2 Annual gold production, 1822–1922.

Notes

INTRODUCTION

1. The adventure of coins portrayed as individuals was a popular genre of eighteenth-century European literature. Rebecca L. Spang, "Money, Art, and Representation: The Look and Sound of Money," in *A Cultural History of Money in the Age of Enlightenment*, edited by Christine Desan (London: Bloomsbury Academic, 2021), 121.

2. Nigel Dodd, *The Social Life of Money* (Princeton: Princeton University Press, 2016), ix. Felix Martin uses the biographical metaphor in the title of his book, although he does not attach to it the same meaning. Felix Martin, *Money: The Unauthorised Biography* (London: Bodley Head, 2013).

3. Viviana Zelizer was first to question the fungibility of money, showing the variety of social, cultural, and gender connotations ascribed to money. Viviana A. Zelizer, *The Social Meaning of Money* (New York: Basic Books, 1994), and the collection of essays titled *Money Talks: Explaining How Money Really Works*, edited by Nina Bandelj, Frederick F. Wherry, and Viviana A. Zelizer (Princeton: Princeton University Press, 2017). See also six volumes in the series *A Cultural History of Money*, general editor Bill Maurer (London: Bloomsbury Academic, 2019).

4. Ian Hacking, "Making Up People," in *Reconstructing individualism*, edited by P. Heller, M. Sosna, and D. Wellbery (Stanford, CA: Stanford University Press, 1986), 222–236.

5. For the constitutional approach to money, see Christine Desan, "The Constitutional Approach to Money," in *Money Talks: Explaining How Money Really Works*, edited by Nina Bandelj, Frederick F. Wherry, and Viviana A. Zelizer (Princeton: Princeton University Press, 2017), 110; Christine Desan, *Making Money: Coin, Currency, and the Coming of Capitalism* (Oxford: Oxford University Press, 2014); and most recently, Stefan Eich, *The Currency of Politics: The Political Theory of Money from Aristotle to Keynes* (Princeton: Princeton University Press, 2022). Yanni Kotsonis has made a similar argument about the fiscal system that reflects and enables political changes in *States of Obligation: Taxes and Citizenship in the Russian Empire and Early Soviet Republic* (Toronto: University of Toronto Press, 2014).

6. John Maynard Keynes, "Indian Currency and Finance [1913]," in *The Collected Writings of John Maynard Keynes*, vol. 1 (Cambridge: Cambridge University Press, 1978), 11,14, 21.
7. Eich, *The Currency of Politics*, 7.
8. Most important, see Desan, *Making Money*, 38. This is also the main argument in David Graber, *Debt: The First 5,000 Years* (Brooklyn, NY: Melville House, 2010). The debate about the origin of money echoes the discussion on the origin of property. As Carol Rose has shown, modern property did not grow naturally, but was imposed by the state from above. Carol M Rose, "Property as the Keystone Right?" *Notre Dame Law Review* 71, no. 3 (1996).
9. Michel Foucault famously compared the epistemological foundation of political economy and linguistics. "In fact, the concepts of money, price, value, circulation, and market were not regarded, in the seventeenth and eighteenth centuries, in terms of a shadowy future, but as part of a rigorous and general epistemological arrangement.... The analysis of wealth is to political economy what general grammar is to philology and what natural history is to biology." *The Order of Things: An Archaeology of the Human Sciences* (New York: Routledge, 2002), 182.
10. Karl Mannheim, "Conservative Thought," *From Karl Mannheim*, with an introduction and edited by K. H. Wolff (New York: Oxford University Press, 1971).
11. James C. Scott, *Weapons of the Weak: Everyday Forms of Peasant Resistance* (New Haven, CT: Yale University Press, 1985).

CHAPTER 1

1. For a detailed description, see A. E. Denisov, *Bumazhnye denezhnye znaki Rossii, 1769–1917* (Moskva: Numizmaticheskaia literatura), 2002, ch.1, 54–55.
2. The linguistic awkwardness of his phrase (in Russian: *Liubov' k otechestvu deistvuet k pol'ze onogo*) suggests that it might have been borrowed and translated from another language. Although I could not find a source, the sound of this phrase in Latin, *amor patriae illae prodest*, may indicate its possible origin. It is also possible that the authors invented this Roman phrase and translated it into Russian. Many thanks to Yelena Baraz for helping me to decode this phrase.
3. Jacob Emery, "Species of Legitimacy: The Rhetoric of Succession around Russian Coins," *Slavic Review* 75, no.1 (Spring 2016): 2–3, 15–21.
4. One of the reasons for the reform, according to I. G. Spasskii and A. S.Melnikova, was the annexation of Ukraine and the necessity for aligning Moscow's monetary system with the Polish standards. A. S. Melnikova, *Russkie monety on Ivana Groznogo do Petra Pervogo* (Moskva: Finansy i Statistika, 1989), 199.
5. A. I. Iukht, *Russkie den'gi ot Petra Velikogo do Aleksandra I* (Moskva: Finansy i Statistika, 1994), 16. As Iukht demonstrates, between 1698 and 1711, during the first and most intensive part of the Northern war, the government minted silver coins for 20.8 million rubles and earned on this operation 6.1 million rubles, that is,

29.3% of the total value of coins. After 1711, the net profit of silver coinage slightly decreased to 26.2% (Iukht, *Russkie den'gi ot Petra*, 21–22).

6. P. A. Shtorkh, "Materialy dlia istorii denezhnykh znakov v Rossii," *Zhurnal Ministerstva Narodnogo Prosveshcheniia*, ch. 137, no. 3, 1868, 781.

7. Shcherbatov finished his translation of Law's treatise in March 1720, two months before the crash of Law's system, and sent it to Peter I. The Russian translation (*Den'gi i kupechestvo. Rassuzhdeno s predlogami k prisovokupleniu v narod deneg chrez gospodina Ivana Liuausa, nyne upravitelia korolevskomu banku v Parizhe*) was never published. The circumstances of Law's endeavor and the consequences of the crash were well known in Russia from the dispatches of a Russian agent in France. On the translation of Law's treatise: T. D. Korkina, "Traktat Dzhona Lo 'Den'gii kupechestvo': Istoriia russkogo perevoda 1720 i tekstologicheskii analiz spiskov," *Acta Linguistica Petropolitana. Trudy instituta lingvisticheskikh issledovanii*, 2020, vol. 16.3. On John Law's ideas in Russia, see D. N. Kopelev, "Dzon Lo, frantsuzskie kolonial'nye proekty epokhi Regentstva i Petr Velikii," in *Prirodnoe i kul'turnoe nasledie: mezhdistsiplinarnye issledovaniia, sokhranenie i razvitie* (St. Petersburg: RGPU im.A.I.Gertsena, 2017); S. M. Troitskii, ""Sistema" Dzhona Lo i ee russkie posledovateli," in *Franko-Russkie ekonomicheskie sviaz*, edited by Fernand Braudel (Moskva, Paris: Nauka, 1970). Konstantin Arseniev lamented that if John Law had come to Russia, Peter I would have used his ideas in a much more productive way than the unfortunate Regent Philippe, Duke of Orleans. K. Arseniev, "Istoriko-statisticheskoe obozrenie monetnogo dela v Rossii," *Zapiski Russkogo Geograficheskogo Obshchestva*, kn.1–2, 1846, 68.

8. Ivan Pososhkov, *The Book of Poverty and Wealth*, edited and translated by A. P. Vlasto and L.R. Lewitter (Stanford, CA: Stanford University Press, 1987), 376. Pososhkov died in February 1726 in prison.

9. A. V. Bugrov suggests that the Copper Bank (1758–63) was the antecedent of the Assignat Bank. A. V. Bugrov, *Kazennye Banki v Rossii 1754–1860* (Moskva: Tsentralnyi Bank RF, 2017), 129.

10. Georgii Mikhailovich [Romanov], *Monety tsarstvovania imperatritsy Ekateriny II*, vol. 1 (St. Petersburg, 1894), VI. A similar pattern existed in Sweden during the seventeenth century. The so-called copper notes represented "the nucleus of paper money" that "subsequently paved the way to an early experiment with a fiat-currency system." Nils Herger, "An Empirical Assessment of the Swedish Bullionist Controversy," *Scandinavian Journal of Economics* 122, no. 3, 2020, 911–936. A.V. Bugrov has emphasized the importance of the Swedish model for the early projects of paper money and banks: Bugrov, *Kazennye banki v Rossii*, 68, 72, 133–134.

11. Iukht, *Russkie den'gi*, 254.

12. PSZ I, vol.18, December 29, 1768, no. 13219.

13. Searching for a new storage of copper coins, Shuvalov invited architects to inspect the palaces of dignitaries in St. Petersburg. As the architects reported, only Kyril Razumovskii's palace (Anichkov palace) had storage rooms large enough to

keep a part of the reserve. (Andreiu Shuvalovu ot arkhitektorov Ivana Gerarda i Aleksandra Vista, November 14, 1774. RGADA, f.19, op.1, d. 419, ch.1, ch.2, 271).

14. Andrei Shuvalov, Zapiska k dokladu (1783), RGADA, f.19, op.1, d.419, ch.3, 123.

15. Untitled memo [1772], RGADA, f.19, op.1, d.419, ch.1, 670b-68; on the same subject "O ostanovlenii otpuska assignatsii v kazennye mesta" (1773)—RGADA, f.19, op.1, d.419, ch.1, 70 ob.

16. P. P. Migulin, *Russkii gosudarstvennyi kredit*, vol. 1, Khar'kiv, 1899, 2, 4

17. The Nakaz of Catherine the Great (The Macartney-Dukes text), in *The Nakaz of Catherine the Great. Collected Texts*, edited by William E. Butler and Vladimir Tomsinov (Clark, NJ: Lawbook Exchange, 2009), 485.

18. Uchrezhdenia Sanktpeterburgskomu i Moskovskomu bankam dlia vymena gosudarstvennykh assignatsii. PSZ 1, vol. 18, no. 13219. December 29, 1768.

19. *AGS*, Tom1, *Sovet v tsarstvovanie imperatritsy Ekateriny II*, St. Petersburg, 1869, 516–517, May 27, May 31, June 7, 1770. There was yet one more aspect to the debate: Shuvalov suggested that the Assignat Banks should be allowed to accept deposits, provide credit, discount promissory notes, and transfer capital between banks and their branches. In other words, emitting assignats had to be linked to the issuing of credit and commercial activity at home and abroad—a vision that likened Russian paper money to the banknotes of European banks. "Mnenie o uchrezhennykh bankakh dlia vymena gosudarstvennykh assignatsii," RGADA, f.19, op.1. 419, 53–65 ob.

20. Thomas Kaiser, "Money, Despotism, and Public Opinion in Early Eighteenth-century France: John Law and the Debate on Royal Credit," *Journal of Modern History* 63 (March 1991): 5

21. In the early nineteenth century, several Russian liberal economists wrote about John Law's theories and experiments and blamed the royal authority for the failure of Law's beautiful plan (Mikhail Orlov wrote about the "genius" and "greatness" of Peter I who had not lost belief in Law's ideas and continued his correspondence with him even after Law's fall). "Iz neizdannogo sochineniia Mikhaila Fedorovicha Orlova (ob uchrezhedenii vol'nogo banka v Moskve)," *Russkii Arkhiv*, 1874, kn.1, no.6, 1578–79.

22. David Bien, "Old Regime Origins of Democratic Liberty," in *The French Idea of Freedom: The Old Regime and the Declaration of Rights of 1789* (Stanford, CA: Stanford University Press, 1994), 23–71.

23. P. G. M. Dickson, *The Financial Revolution: A Study in the Development of Public Credit* (London: Macmillan, 1967). John Brewer seconded Dickson's account while also underscoring the role of taxation and the development of administrative apparatus. John Brewer, *The Sinews of Power: War, Money, and the English State, 1688–1783* (Cambridge: Cambridge University Press, 1983). North and Weingast theorized the dependence between "constitutions and commitment" in Douglass North and Barry Weingast, "Constitutions and Commitment: The Evolution of Institutions Governing Public Choice in 17th-century England, " *Journal of*

Economic History 49, no. 4 (1989): 803–832. See also the development of this idea in David Stasavage, *Public Debt and the Birth of the Democratic State, France and Great Britain, 1688–1789* (Cambridge: Cambridge University Press, 2003).

24. Peter Bernholz, "Political Parties and Paper Money Inflation in Sweden during the 18th Century," *Kyklos* 54 (2001), fasc.2/3, 207–212; Herger, "An Empirical Assessment of the Swedish Bullionist Controversy." Herger emphasizes that the political debates on the issues of inflation "fell into the Age of Liberty (1720–1772)" when "the Riksdag, rather than the monarchy, was at the centre of political power," 917. In the Habsburg Empire, the Estates turned into "a major financier of the dynastic state." William D. Godsy, *The Sinews of Habsburg Power: Lower Austria in a Fiscal-Military State* (Oxford: Oxford University Press, 2018), 25.

25. Reglament Sankt-Peterburgskomu i Moskovskomu bankam dlia vymena gosudarstvennykh assignatsii. RGADA, f.19, op.1, d.419 ch.3, 346–347.

26. Shuvalov, undated letter to Alexander Bezborodko, RGADA, f.19, op.1, d.421, ch.2., Zapiski ot grafa Andreia Petrovicha Shuvalova po Assignatsionnomu Banku," 1786, 201.

27. Charles-Louis de Secondat baron de Montesquieu, *The Spirit of Laws*. Cambridge Texts in the History of Political Thought (Cambridge: Cambridge University Press, 1989), bk. 22, ch. 2, 399.

28. Montesquieu referred to Elizabeth's prosecution of Jews, Montesquieu, *The Spirit of Laws*. bk. 22, ch.14, 416–417

29. N. Grigorovich, *Kantzler Kniaz' Aleksandr Andreevich Bezborodko v sviazi s sobytiiami ego vremeni*, t.1 (St .Petersburg, 1879), 87.

30. A. Shuvalov, "Zapiska k dokladu," 1783, RGADA, f.19, op.1, d.419, ch.3. 122 ob.

31. Shuvalov, who wrote his memo in Russian, used the expression "*avoir un compte au banque*" that he could have drawn from the famous *L'Encyclopedie*. The article on "*banque*" explains the meaning of this term. *L'Encyclopedie ou Dictionnaire raisonné des sciences, des arts et des métiers,* vol .2, p. 60, accessed via *Édition Numérique Collaborative et Critique de l'Encyclopédie ou Dictionnaire raisonné des sciences, des arts et des métiers (1751–1772)*, http://enccre.academie-sciences.fr/encyclopedie/.

32. This last suggestion could be inspired either by the example of the Bank of Amsterdam, which issued *bank florins*, or banknotes widely used in commercial transactions, or the banknotes of the Bank of England. The Bank of Amsterdam also resembles Russian Assignat banks in keeping a substantial hoard of coins as a collateral for paper notes. See Stephen Quinn and William Roberds, "A Policy Framework for the Bank of Amsterdam, 1736–1791," *Journal of Economic History* 79, no. 3 (September 2019).

33. For more details of this reform project, see V. V. Morozan, *Istoriia bankovskogo dela v Rossii, vtoraia polovina XVIII—pervaia polovina XIX veka* (St. Petersburg: Kriga, 2004), 76–84.

34. AGS, t.1, 546.

35. For more on this aspect of the reform, see Boris Ananich et al., *Kredit i banki v Rossii do nachala XX veka. Sankt-Peterburg i Moskva* (St.Petersburg: Izd-vo S.-Peterburgskogo universiteta, 2005), 93–99. Remarkably, despite declarations, cities did not receive as much in funding as they were supposed to; instead, the treasury spent more than 6 million rubles of the amount intended for cities to cover gaps in the state budget. P. A. Nikolskii, *Bumazhnye den'gi v Rossii*, Kazan', 1892, 177.

36. A. Viazemskii, "Mnenie o proekte Andreia Petrovicha Shuvalova po povodu uchrezhdeniia novogo zaemnogo banka, ob uvelichenii chisla gosudarstvennykh assignatsii i o platezhe gosudarstvennogo dolga v bankovye kontory," May 29 1786, OR RNB, F.484, op.1, d. 47, 4–70b.

37. A. Shuvalov, Zapiska k vsepoddanneishemu dokladu [1789] RGADA, f.19, op.1, d.421, ch.8, 320.

38. Louis de Jaucourt's article on money in *L'Encyclopedie* is built around the polemics with Jean Boizard and John Locke who had claimed that the value of money originates from "public authority." On the contrary, as *L'Encyclopedie* suggested, money's worth depended either on the value of its matter or the "circumstances of commerce" (Le chevalier de Jaucourt, "Monnaie," *L'Enclyclopedie*, vol. 10 (1765), 644). On this debate see also Thomas Luckett, "Imaginary Currency and Real Guillotines: The Intellectual Origins of the Financial Terror in France," *Historical Reflections/Réflexions Historique* 31, no. 1 (Spring 2005): 119–122. *Mnenie ob uchrezhdennykh bankakh dlia vymena gosudarstvennykh assignatsii* (1769) refers to the *L'Encyclopedie* article (*RGADA*, f.19, op.1, d.419, ch.1, 65). On a similar discussion in Sweden that predated the famous bullionist debate in the early nineteenth century, see Robert Eagly, "Monetary Policy and Politics in mid-Eighteenth Century Sweden," *Journal of Economic History* 29, no. 4 (December 1969): 739–757.

39. *Proekt pozemelnogo imushchestvennogo banka* (b.m., b.g.) 8. L. V. Khodskii, *Pozemel'nyi kredit v Rossii i otnoshenie ego k krestianskomu zemlevladeniiu* (Moskva, 1882), 73. According to V. V. Morozan, the Assignat Bank delivered 5 million rubles to the Noble Bank. Morozan, *Istoriia bankovskogo dela v Rossii, vtoraia polovina XVIII—pervaia polovina XIX v.*, 36.

40. N. Grigorovich, *Kantzler Kniaz' Aleksandr Andreevich Bezborodko v sviazi s sobytiiami ego vremeni*, t.1 (St. Petersburg, 1879), 169.

41. PSZ 1, vol.22, No.16407, June 28, 1786.

42. Vlasii Sudeikin, *Operatsii Gosudarstvennogo banka* (St. Petersburg, 1888), 55.

43. Zapiska o trebuemykh na budushchii 1791 gold mednykh den'gakh. *RGADA*, f.19, op.1, d.421 ch.9, 1140b.

44. Arcadius Kahan, *The Plow, the Hammer, and the Knout. An Economic History of Eighteenth-century Russia* (Chicago: University of Chicago Press, 1985), 337. For state revenues and expenditures, see "Gosudarstvennye dokhody i rashkhody v tsarstvovanie Ekateriny II," *Sbornik RIO*, vol. V, VI, 1870.

45. "Chem bolee verit' obshchestvu, tem bolee doverie ego priobretaetsia. Dobroe delo i blagie namereniia ne trebuut zaves." *AGS*, t.1, 551.

46. Sekretnoe mnenie grafa Bezborodko otnositelno nuzhd gosudarstvennykh v den'gakh. 1794; a letter to A. A. Bezborodko in RGADA, f.19, op.1, d.47, 3, 18.

47. Ivan Novikov, *Kliuch k vykladkam kursov ili nyne izobretennyi samyi kratchaishii sposob verno vykladyvat' aglinskoi i gollandskoi kurs* (Mosvka, 1794), 1.

48. N. N. Firsov, *Pravitel'stvo i obshchestvo v ikh otnosheniiakh k vneshnei torgovle Rossii v tsarstvovaniie imperatritsy Ekateriny II*, Kazan', 1902, 103

49. Firsov, *Pravitel'stvo i obshchestvo*, 115.

50. Arcadius Kahan, "The Costs of 'Westernization' in Russia: The Gentry and the Economy in the Eighteenth Century," *Slavic Review* 25. no. 1 (March 1966): 40–66.

51. Firsov, *Pravitel'stvo i obshchestvo*, 129.

52. Firsov, *Pravitel'stvo i obshchestvo*, 139.

53. N. K. Brzheskii. *Gosudarstvennye dolgi Rossii* (St. Petersburg, 1884), tables 3, 4.

54. These assignats represented almost half of the net profit from the projected devaluation of copper money: immediately after Catherine's death, Paul suspended her unrealized plan of debasing copper coins. *AGS*, t.2, Tsarstvovanie Imperatora Pavla, St. Petersburg, 1888, 28; Iukht, *Russkie den'gi*, 223.

55. AGS, t.2, December 4, 1796, 30.

56. I. I. Kaufman, *Iz istorii bumazhnykh deneg v Rossii* (St. Petersburg, 1909), 19.

57. David Graeber, *The Debt: The First 5,000 years* (Brooklyn: Melville House, 2011), 339.

58. "Kopiia s podlinnoi ruki kantslera kniazia Bezborodko," *RGADA*, f.19, op.1, d.173, l.10b.

59. Michael Kwass, *Privilege and the Politics of Taxations in Eighteenth-century France* (Cambridge: Cambridge University Press, 2000),, 12.

CHAPTER 2

1. I. S. Shikanova, "Novye materialy o denezhnykh znakakh Rossiisko-Amerikanskoi Kompanii," in *Rossiia + Amerika = 200. K iubileiu Rossiisko-Amerikanskoi kompanii, 1799–1999* (Moskva: Gos. Ist. Muzei, 1999), 51; *Russkaia Amerika v "zapiskakh" Kirilla Khlebnikova: Novo-Arkhangel' sk* (Moskva: Nauka, 1985), 240–243.

2. On the Russian system of economic exploitation and labor conscription in Russian America, see A. V. Grinev, *Aliaska pod krylom dvuglavogo orla (rossiiskaia kolonizatsiia Novogo Sveta v kontekste otechestvennoi i mirovoi istori,* (Moskva: Akademia, 2016), 193–197; Sonja Luehrmann, "Russian Colonialism and the Asiatic Mode of Production: (Post-)Soviet Ethnography Goes to Alaska," *Slavic Review* 64, no. 4 (Winter 2005): 851–871.

3. N. S. Mordvinov, "Proekt Trudopooshchritelnogo Banka," *Arkhiv Grafov Mordvinovykh*, vol. 3, 148. Interestigly, Mordvinov's idea of money based on labor predated the ideas of cooperative movement in England and even Robert Owen's project of labor notes. On Owen's labor notes, see Mary Poovey, *Genres of the*

Credit Economy: Mediating Value in Eighteenth- and Nineteenth-Century Britain (Chicago: University of Chicago Press, 2008), 210–211.

4. Michael Speransky, "O korennykh zakonakh gosudarstva," in M. M. Speranskii, *Izbrannoe* (Moskva: ROSSPEN, 2010), 195.

5. Fedor Virst, *Rassuzhdeniia o nekotorykh predmetakh zakonodatelstva i upravleniia finansami i kommertsiei Rossiiskoi Imperii* (St. Petersburg: Imperatorskaia tip, 1807), 41. Fedor Virst (Ferdinand Würst), a German economist in Russian service, wrote one of the most comprehensive treatises on Russian finances to that date (it was an extended edition of his German book that came out in 1805). On Würst's influence, see Ludwig Heinrich v. Jacob, *Denkwurdigkeiten aus meinem Leben* (Halle an der Saale: Universitätsverlag Halle-Wittenberg, UVHW, 2011).

6. E. I. Lamanskii, *Istoricheskii ocherk denezhnogo obrashcheniia v Rossii* (St. Petersburg, 1854), 149, 151.

7. V. I. Semevskii, "Padenie Speranskogo," *Otechestvennaia voina i russkoe obshchestvo*, vol. 2 (Moskva, 1911), 232. Russia's annual military spending grew from 41 million rubles in 1804, to 160 million in 1812 and to 278 million rubles in 1815. *Ministerstvo Finansov, 1802–1902* (St. Petersburg, 1902), 616–617, 620–621.

8. It suffices to illustrate the economic reality of double values with one random example: an instruction to provincial post offices issued in 1807 suggested that when someone sent gold or silver rubles to an addressee without indicating the rubles' rate to assignats, then, if the money were lost or disappeared, the Post Department would pay back the insured sum in copper or assignats (that is to say, one-third or one-fourth of the original value). If, however, a sender indicated the rate she would receive the original sum in hard currency or in assignats according to the indicated rate. The cost of risk was commensurate to the cost of the insurance premium: in the first case, one could pay it in assignats, while in the second, the insurance fee was due in silver, gold, or in assignats according to the rate. *Instruktsiia gubernskomy pochtmeisteru* (St. Petersburg, 1807), 16.

9. Alexei Vasiliev (1802–1807), Fedor Golubtsov (1807–1810), and Dmitrii Guryev (1810–1823).

10. M. M. Speranskii, "Proekt ulozheniia gosudarstvennykh zakonov v Rossiiskoi Imperii," "Kratkoe nachertanie gosudarstvennogo obrazovaniia," "Obshchee obozrenie vsekh obrazovanii i raspredelenie ikh po vremenam," all in M.M. Speranskii, *Izbrannoe* (Moskva, ROSSPEN, 2010).

11. Historians often consider the two parts of Speransky's plan in isolation: the analysis of Speransky's constitutionalism rarely includes his plans for monetary reform, while the assessments of his monetary ideas overlook the political meaning of Speransky's initiative. In both cases, an important component of Speransky's plan gets lost, and the radicalism of his suggestions is not fully appreciated. Not surprisingly, there has been no consensus in the assessment of Speransky's reformism. Bringing the two elements of Speransky's plan together highlights the true scale of this transformation. See Marc Raeff for an assessment of Speransky as a conservative

reformer (Marc Raeff, *Michael Speransky: A Statesman of Russia* [The Hague: M. Nijhoff, 1969]); David Christian and John Gooding have criticized Raeff's view and emphasized the centrality of liberalism in his thought (David Christian, "The Political Ideals of Michael Speransky," *Slavonic and East European Review* 54, no. 2 (April 1976): 192–213; John Gooding, "The Liberalism of Michael Speransky," *Slavonic and East European Review* 64, no. 3 (July 1986): 401–424

12. As Speransky noted, the government should have no relation to the bank other than being one of its investors. M. M. Speransky, "Plan finansov," *Sbornik Imperatorskogo Russkogo Istoricheskogo Obshchestva*, vol. 45 (St. Petersburg, 1885), 63–67.

13. See, for instance, Nikolai Turgenev's 1810 dissertation, "Rassuzhdenie o bankakh i o bumazhnykh den'gakh kak sledstvii osnovaniia sikh pervykh, 1810 [On banks and paper money, as the consequence of the foundation of the former.]*—OR IRLI RAN (Pushkinskii Dom)*, f.309, d.2061, 25, 27, 33. See also his treatise on the theory of taxes that includes large excerpts from this dissertation. N. I. Turgenev, *Opyt teorii nalogov* (St. Petersburg, 1818), 344. Interestingly, one of the examples of the harm caused by the government's arbitrary involvement in financial matters was the story of the "good [slavnyi] [John] Law." Turgenev exonerated the Law system that had enjoyed popular trust until 1719, when the crown "seized" the bank and turned it into a royal institution.

14. See his "Obshchee obozrenie vsekh preobrazovanii i raspredelenie ikh po vremenam" ("General Overview of All Reforms and Their Chronological Layout"), in M.M. Speransky, *Izbrannoe* (Moskva: ROSSPEN, 2010), 376–381.

15. A. V. Predtechenskii, *Ocherki obshchestvenno-politicheskoi istorii Rossii v pervoi chetverti XIX veka* (Moskva, Leningrad: Izd-vo Akademii Nauk SSSR, 1957), 258–259.

16. Simon Sherratt, *Credit and Power: The Paradox at the Heart of the British National Debt* (Abingdon, Oxfordshire; Routledge, 2021), 19–53.

17. Jean-Marie Thiveaud, "1814: La Banque de France au défi de son indépendance. La question cruciale de la confiance," *Revue d'économie financière* 22 (Automne 1992): 233–248.

18. Mordvinov emphasized that he followed the model of the Bank of England. While his project resembles the Bank of England principle of private capital, it is nevertheless very original. "Vnutrennii dolg i Volnyi Rossiiskii Bank" (September 1809), *Arkhiv Grafov Mordvinovykh*, vol. 3 (St. Petersburg, 1903), 647–648.

19. "Vnutrennii dolg i Vol'nyi Rossiiskii Bank," 662–663.

20. "Vnutrennii dolg i Vol'nyi Rossiiskii Bank," 662–663.

21. In 1816 the tsar approved the publication of Mordvinov's plan. See A. A. Arakcheev's letter to Mordvinov: RGIA, f.994, op.2, d.238, l.1.

22. "Izlishestvo bumazhnoi monety," *Arkhiv Grafov Mordvinovykh*, vol.4 (St. Petersburg, 1903), 633.

23. Jacobs, a member of Speransky's team, had a very low opinion of Mordvinov's expertise in finance: "Admiral Mordvinov, an old man who knew nothing at all about

economics and finance, but still had the gift of chatting about everything." Jacob, *Denkwurdigkeiten aus meinem Leben*, 221.

24. Jacob mentioned that Alexander I had read his work on assignats and approved the *Financial Plan*. Jacob, for instance, received the Order of Anne second degree and a brilliant ring as a reward for his participation in this work. Jacob, *Denkwurdigkeiten aus meinem Leben*, 224.

25. PSZ 1, vol. 31, no. 24064. Metallic money was supposed to gradually spread in circulation at the expense of paper assignats. To this end, the Ministry of Finance suggested declaring the freedom of silver and gold mining. Anyone could bring silver or gold to the state laboratories or the Mint and either receive a corresponding amount in coins or simply watch their silver or gold being melted and minted. These measures encouraged the production of metals while the treasury benefited from the mining tax paid in "product" (i.e., gold or silver). The acceptance of gold and silver from "free" sellers did not bring immediate results because of the overall very low production. However, after the discovery of rich deposits of gold in Siberia in the 1820s, the influx of gold increased manifold, owing to the regime of free mining established in 1812. "O merakh k ispolneniiu Vysochaishego manifesta o monetnoi sisteme," *RGIA*, f.1152, op.1, 1810, d.114, ll.55–60. *AGS*, vol. 4, *Tsarstvovanie imperatora Aleksandra I*. (St. Petersburg, 1881), 632–634; PSZ 1 32, no. 25119 (May 28, 1812). "O predostavlenii prava vsem rossiiskim poddannym otyskivat' i razrabatyvat' zolotye i serebrianye rudy, s platezhom v kaznu podati."

26. "Zapiska Rumiantseva ob istreblenii assignatsii dlia vosstanovleniia kredita," RGADA, f.19, op.1, d.64, 2.

27. PSZ 1, vol. 31, No .24244; PSZ 1, vol. 31, no. 24116.

28. Rebecca Spang, *Stuff and Money in the Time of the French Revolution* (Cambridge, MA: Harvard University Press, 2015), 71.

29. It is also possible that Speransky counted on the later realization of the Silver Bank project and the introduction of two parallel kinds of money: banknotes, issued by an independent private bank and backed up by bullion reserve and bills of exchange, and assignats, issued by the government and backed up by taxes or state properties. For the analysis of these two models, see the works of Speransky's advisor Friedrich Würst (F. G. Virst). F. G. Virst, *Ob uchrezhdenii Assignatsionnogo i Zaemnogo banka dlia spospeshestvovaniia narodnomu bogatstvu, izdano st.sovetnikom i redaktorom po kommertsii v Komissii sostavleniia zakonov F.G. Virstom* (St. Petersburg, 1808), 14, and *Rassuzhdenie o nekotorykh predmetakh zakonodatelstva i upravleniia finansami i kommertsiei Rossiiskoi imperii*, (St. Petersburg, 1807), 370.

30. M. M. Speransky, "Plan finansov," in *Sbornik Imperatorskogo Russkogo Istoricheskogo Obshchestva*, vol. 45 (St. Petersburg, 1885), 59.

31. Speransky, "Plan finansov," 38.

32. "Mnenie admirala Mordvinova o vrednykh posledstviiakh dlia kazny i chastnykh imushchestv ot oshibochnykh mer upravleniia gosudarstvennym kaznacheistvom,"

Chtenia v Imperatorskom Obshchestve Istorii i Drevnostei Rossiiskikh (Moskva, 1859), kn.4, 60.

33. Speransky, "O dukhe pravitelstva," in *Izbrannoe*, 297, 201. See also the Manifesto of February 2, 1810, expressing this idea. PSZ 1, vol. 31, no. 24116.

34. P. P. Migulin, *Russkii Gosudarstvennyi Kredit*, vol. 1 (Khar'kiv, 1899), 47. From 1809 to 1810 tax income increased from 52 to 82 million rubles, but the most substantial was the increase of salt duties—from 8 to 14 million rubles. Due to the introduction of protectionist tariffs in 1810 and the end of the embargo regime, state income from customs also increased: from 8 million rubles in 1809 to 11 million in 1810, 15 million in 1811, 19 million in 1812 and 31 million rubles in 1813. *Ministerstvo Finansov, 1802–1902* (St. Petersburg, 1902), 616.

35. Speransky, "Plan finansov," 40–41; N. I. Turgenev, *Opyt teorii nalogov* (St. Petersburg, 1818), 312.

36. Elena Korchmina, "Peer Pressure: The Puzzle of Aristocrats' Tax Compliance in Early Nineteenth-century Moscow," *Economic History Review*, October 20, 2021, 10, 1–22.

37. On Guryev's resistance, see Jacob, *Denkwurdigkeiten aus meinem Leben*, 224.

38. Alexei Vasiliev, Zapiska o znachenii assignatsii v denezhnoi sisteme Rossii, OR RNB, f.484, d.22, l.3–4.

39. One small detail indicates the addressee of this part of the "Memoir." As a book that exemplified the liberal trend, Karamzin chose the work of Johann Georg Busch. Alexander I apparently read Busch's works. His tutor, a Swiss republican Frédéric-César de La Harpe, recommended to him Busch's treatises on money and banks in 1795. (*Imperator Aleksandr I i Frederik-Sezar Lagarp: pis'ma, dokumenty* [Moskva: ROSSPEN, 2014], 161). Among other things, Busch's *Abhandlung von dem Geldumlauf in anhaltender Rücksicht auf die Staatswirtschaft und Handlung* (1780) advocated the convertibility of paper money. Keith Tribe, "'Staatswirtschaft,' 'Staatswissenschaft,' and 'Nationaloekonomie': German Economic Discourse in the Time of Goethe," in *Goethe and Money: The Writer and Modern Economics*, edited by Vera Hierholzer and Sandra Richter (Frankfurt: Freies Deutsches Hochstift, 2012), 96

40. Karamzin's hypothesis about the existence of leather money in Rus originated from the names of the money—"kuny" (from *kunitsa*—marten), "mordki" (from *morda*—muzzle), bely (from *belki*—squirrels). For a detailed analysis of the leather money problem, see N. P. Bauer, *Istoriia drevnerusskikh denezhnykh system, IX v.–1535* (Moskva: Russkoe Slovo, 2014), 6–20; V. L. Yanin, *Denezhno-vesovye sistemy domongol'skoi Rusi i ocherki istorii denezhnoi sistemy srednevekovogo Novgoroda* (Moskva: Yazyki slavianskikh kultur, 2009), 20–26 Yanin suggests that coins and furs (but not leather assignats) circulated in parallel.

41. N. M. Karamzin, *Istoria gosudarstva rossiiskogo*, 4th ed. (first edition—1816–17) (St. Petersburg, 1834), vol. 5, 387. Ironically, Karamzin was the only person who claimed to have seen leather money—in the Aleksandrovskii monastery (Karamzin, *Istoria*,

vol. 1, endnotes, 143). Many authors referred to Karamzin's testimony. However, when P. S. Kazansky visited the monastery, he could not find the "sac of leather money" mentioned by Karamzin. P. S . Kazanskii, "Dopolneniia k issledovaniiu o drevnei russkoi monetnoi sisteme," in *Zapiski Imperatorskogo Arkheologicheskogo Obshchestva*, vol.6 (St. Petersburg, 1853), 486.

42. N. M. Karamzin, *Karamzin's Memoir on Ancient and Modern Russia: A Translation and Analysis*, edited by Richard Pipes (Ann Arbor: University of Michigan Press, 2005), 171.

43. Speransky closely followed Napoleon's policy of fixing France's monetary system: one of his assistants, Wurst, included the translation of the Bank of France's charter (1800) into his polemical brochure on money that ended with a rhetorical question "Wouldn't it be desirable for us to have an institution similar to this bank, when the value of our money is subjected to such strong fluctuation.?" F. G. Virst [Wurst], *Ob uchrezhdenii Assignatsionnogo i Zaemnogo banka dlia spospeshestvovaniia narodnomu bogatstvu, s prisovokupleniem statutov Frantsuzskogo banka* (St. Petersburg: Imperatorskaia Akademiia Nauk, 1808), 55

44. Karamzin, *Karamzin's Memoir*, 172.

45. Karamzin, *Karamzin's Memoir*, 174.

46. Cara Camcastle, *More Moderate Side of Joseph de Maistre: Views on Political Liberty and Political Economy* (Montreal: McGill-Queen University Press, 2005), 93.

47. Camcastle, *More Moderate Side of Joseph de Maistre*, 99.

48. J. G. Fichte, *The Closed Commercial State*, trans. Anthony Curtis Adler (Albany: State University of New York Press, 2012), 173. On Fichte's political philosophy of money, see Stefan Eich, *The Political Theory of Money from Aristotle to Keynes* (Princeton: Princeton University Press, 2022), 93–102.

49. Fichte, *The Closed Commercial State*, 174.

50. Fichte, *The Closed Commercial State*, 180.

51. According to Richard Gray, this vision of money went against the Enlightenment semiotic theory "where a firm, empirically comprehensible relationship exists between the signifier and the signified" and that "substance is supposed to vouchsafe the nominal value of the coin, countering symbolic fluctuations with the stable content of the gold or silver itself." Richard T. Gray, "Economic Romanticism: Monetary Nationalism in Johann Fichte and Adam Müller," in *Money Matters: Economics and the German Cultural Imagination, 1770–1850* (Seattle: University of Washington Press, 2008), 89.

52. Gray positions *The Closed Commercial State* between Fichte's earlier writings on epistemology (*On the Concept of the Science of Knowledge*, 1794) and his later famous *Addresses to the German Nation* (1808), tying together Fichte's transcendental philosophy, his theory of money, and political nationalism.

53. On the connection between linguistic epistemology and monetary theory in John Locke's writings, see Eich, *The Currency of Politics*, 63–67. On common epistemological foundation of monetary theory and language in European thought,

see Michel Foucault, *The Order of Things. An Archaeology of the Human Sciences* (New York: Routledge, 2002), ch.6.

54. On Alexander Shishkov and his circle, see Mark Altshuller, *Beseda liubitelei russkogo slova. U istokov russkogo slavianofilstva* (Moskva: NLO, 2007).

55. Y. Lotman and B. Uspenskii, "Spory o iazyke nachala XIX veka kak fakt russkoi kul'tury," in *Istoriia i tipologiia russkoi kul'tury* (St. Petersburg: Iskusstvo-SPb, 2002), 450. See also B. A. Uspenskii, "Yazykovaia programma karamzinistov: zapadnoevropeiskie istoki," in *Vokrug Trediakovskogo. Trudy po istorii russkogo iazyka i russkoi kul'tury* (Moskva: Indrik, 2008), 23–79.

56. Quoted from V. M. Zhivov, *Yazyk i kul'tura v Rossii XVIII veka* (Moskva: Shkola "Iazyki russkoi kul'tury," 1996), 442. "O bogatstve iazyka," in N. M. Karamzin, *Izbrannye sochineniia v dvukh tomakh*. T.2 (Moskva: Khudozh. lit-ra, 1964), 142.

57. Gray, "Economic Romanticism," 99.

58. Adam Mueller's main treatise on money (*Versuche einer neuen Theorie des Geldes*) was published in 1816, so it is unlikely that he could have influenced Karamzin.

59. Mordvinov, "O bankakh na serebrianom osnovanii" (March 1812) *Arkhiv Grafov Mordvinovykh*, vol.4, p. 611–618, RGIA, f.1152 (Soed. Dep. Zakonov v Gos Ekonomii), op.1, 1812, d.44. Newspapers listed grain prices in the western provinces only in silver rubles; in all other provinces they were listed in assignat. See, for example, "Vedomost' o prodazhnykh tsenakh na khleb," *Severnaia Pochta*, May 4, 1812.

60. "O rasshirenii kruga obrashcheniia assignatsii," RGIA, f.1152 (Obshchee sobranie), op.1, 1812, d.2; "Ob ustanovlenii kursa assignatsii na serebro" f.1152, op.1, 1812, d.21.

61. In 1814–15, he argued against the existence of a separate currency in Poland: "Vsepoddanneishii doklad ministra finansov Gurieva," November 8, 1814, g. RGIA, f.560, op.10, d. 69, 7–90b.; "Voprosy, po kotorym nado dogovorit'sia s Tsarstvom Polskim, chtoby perenesti liniu tamozhen na vneshnie granitsy Tsarstva," *Vneshniaia Politika Rossii XIX i nachala XX veka. Sbornik dokumentov*, ser.2, vol.1, 415–416.

62. V. I. Semevskii, "Padenie Speranskogo," *Otechestvennaia voina i russkoe obshchestvo*, vol. 2, 232, 245.

63. Jacob, *Denkwurdigkeiten aus meinem Leben*, 220.

64. According to general M. A. Barclay de Tolly's report to the tsar (1815), the military campaigns of 1812–13 cost 157 million rubles. This sum apparently did not include the enormous costs of post-war reconstruction and the repayment of debts accumulated during the war. K. V. Sivkov, "Finansy Rossii posle voin s Napoleonom," *Otechestvennaia Voina i Russkoe Obshchestvo*, vol. 7, 125. Other estimates were as much as four times higher than this number, up to 650 million rubles. For a detailed analysis, see Sivkov, "Finansy Rossii posle voin s Napoleonom," 127.

65. "Reskript Aleksandra I poslu v Londone Kh.A. Livenu," 20 ianvaria 1813, *Vneshniaia Politika Rossii XIX i nachala XX veka. Sbornik dokumentov*, ser.1, vol.7, 36–37. See also "Sekretnyi ofitsialnye svedemiia o polozhenii nashikh finansov v 1813 i ob

izyskanii sredstv k prodolzheniiu voennykh deistvii v chuzhikh kraiakh," *Sbornik istoricheskikh materialov izvlechennykh iz Arkhiva sobstvennoi EIV kantseliarii,* Vyp.1 (St. Petersburg, 1876), 45–91; "Zapiska ministra finansov o gosudarstvennykh dokhodakh i raskhodakh na 1814 g ot 31 oktiabria 1813 g," *Sbornik istoricheskikh materialov izvlechennykh iz Arkhiva sobstvennoi EIV kantseliarii,* Vyp.3 (St. Petersburg, 1890), 330.

66. See more in Liudmila Marnei, *D. A. Guryev i finansovaia politika Rossii v nachale XIX veka* (Moskva: Indrik, 2009), 194–195; *Vneshniaia Politika Rossii XIX i nachala XX veka. Sbornik dokumentov,* ser.1, vol.7, 23, 296, 579, 784. This was not the only project of federative money. Alexander Bugrov describes an early project of a European monetary system (*système fédérative de finance et de commerce*) written by Nikolai Novosiltsev. This project assumed the issuance of banknotes accepted in custom payment throughout Europe. A.V. Bugrov, *Kazennye banki v Rossii, 1754–1860* (Moskva: Tsentralnyi Bank RF, 2017), 347–353.

67. Nadezhda Durova told a heartbreaking story of how she gave a poor beggar an assignat bill while she had coins in her purse and could not forgive herself for greediness because she knew that the beggar would not be able to redeem the bill. Later she found out that two coins were accidentally wrapped inside the useless assignat. Nadezhda Durova, *The Cavalry Maiden: Journals of a Russian Officer in the Napoleonic Wars,* translation, introduction, and notes by Mary Fleming Zirin (Bloomington: Indiana University Press, 1988, 195–196.

68. AVPRI, f.133, op.468, 1814, d.5283, 7–15, 24–34.

69. Draft of the report, June 1813. As the report suggested, in June 1813 the army again did not receive its money for salaries due in January in the sum of 18 million rubles (RGVIA, f.103, op.208a, d.31 sv.28, 163). In response, Guryev suggested that to preserve the assignats' rate, soldiers should be paid half their salary at that time and the rest when they returned to Russia so they would spend the money inside the country. Guryev to Barklay De Tolly, June 24, 1813 (RGVIA, f.103, op.208a, d.31 sv.28, 196). See RGVIA, f.103, op.208a, d.31 sv.28 for other requests for the transfers of money for the provision of Russian troops abroad.

70. AVPRI, F.133, op.468, 1814, d.5283, 7–15, 24–34.

71. *Zhizn' i voennye deianiia general-feldmarshala svetleishego kniazia Mikhaila Larionovich Golenishcheva-Kutuzova Smolenskogo* (St. Petersburg, 1813–14), 91.

72. "Zapad na Severe. September 1813. Dnevniki N.I. Turgeneva," *Arkhiv bratiev Turgenevykh* (St. Petersburg, 1911), t.2, 259 (emphasis in the original).

73. Alexander Pushkin, *Eugene Onegin,* trans. Stanley Mitchell (London: Penguin Classics, 2008), 10.

74. While questioning the premises of Western monetary theory, politically, Nikolai Turgenev continued to profess liberal ideas. His project of issuing special "auxiliary assignats" to compensate people impoverished by war suggested that all troubles in financial matters originated from a wrong assumption that money "is the tool in the hands of the government" and, as such, is guaranteed by the state's

immovable property. In fact, however, paper money was the "means of circulation" that depends "solely on popular economy, and not on the wealth of the government."- "Zapad na Severe. September 1813. Dnevniki N.I. Turgeneva," 259.

75. "L'État n'est autre chose que l'idividu qui le composent; ces individus et l'État sont absolument la meme chose; c'est donc comme ci je disait je me paye mes dettes." Ideés sur les finances, 1816, in "O finansakh voobshche. Iz bumag grafa Andreia Kirillovicha Razumovskogo," RGADA, f.19, op.1, d.433, ll.10–13.

76. "Vsepoddanneishii doklad ob okonchanii i rezultatakh raboty Komiteta dlia rassmotreniia plana d'Ivernois ob umensheniii gosudarstvennykh assignatsii," OR RNB, f.484, op.1, d.106, L.4–10. This was a project proposed by a Swiss economist Francis d'Ivernois. To repair the financial status of Russian paper money, the project suggested exempting 60% of assignats from circulation by converting them into state loans with 5% interest while devaluing the remaining 40% of the assignats. More on this project in Marnei, *D.A. Guryev*, 161–164.

77. Marnei, *D. A. Guryev*, 161–164.

78. "Zapiska grafa V. P. Kochubeiia o polozhenii Imperii i o merakh k prekrashcheniiu besporiadkov i vvedenii luchshego ustroistva v raznye otrasli, pravitelstvo sostavliaiushchie, December 1814," in *Bumagi Komiteta uchrezhdennogo vysochaishim reskriptom 6 dekabria 1826 goda. Sbornik IRIO*, vol. 90 (St. Petersburg, 1894).

79. On the rhetoric of peasants' backwardness see Yanni Kotsonis, *Making Peasants Backward: Agricultural Cooperatives and the Agrarian Question in Russia, 1861–1914* (Houndmills, UK: Macmillan, 1999).

80. Kaufman, *Bumazhnye den'gi Avstrii*, 13.

81. "Vsepoddanneishchii doklad," March 20, 1818. RGIA, f.583, op.4, d. 219, 153–157.

82. By exchanging assignats to silver at a current rate, the government admitted the de facto devaluation of the ruble, although it did not announce this publicly. Kaufman, *Bumazhnye den'gi Avstrii*, 13; M. I. Bogolepov, *Bumazhnye den'gi* (Petrograd, 1922), 79.

83. N. I. Turgenev, *Rossiia i russkie* (Moskva: OGI, 2001), 324. Turgenev explained the absurdity of the government's action as a consequence of its isolation and unwillingness to listen to the opinion of public experts; he even discussed such measures in the government's collective consultative institutions. "Public opinion could not be expressed in the press; perhaps, the State Council could have stopped the Emperor, if the tsar had remained faithful to the spirit that had led to the creation of that institution, and if he had allowed the Council to fulfill its primary duty and subject the minister's project to scrupulous examination." None of this happened: Guryev submitted his monetary plan directly to the tsar, and the Council could only vote the law after it had been already approved by the monarch.

84. M. I. Tugan-Baranovskii, *Bumazhnye den'gi i metall* (Petrograd, 1917), 94.

85. N. P. Demidov, *O bumazhnykh den'gakh* (St. Petersburg, 1829), 28.

86. P. A. Viazemskii, *Zapisnye knizhki (1813–1848)* (Moskva: Akademiia nauk, 1963), 26-27; first publication—"Moskovskii telegraf," ch.12, 1826, otd.2. 39–41.
87. Viazemskii, *Zapisnye knizhki*, 26–27; emphasis in the original.
88. Later, Viazemskii served at the Ministry of Finance and was the director of the Credit Bank in the 1830s and 1840s. On his literary work, political views, and bureaucratic career, see P. V. Alulshin, *P.A. Viazemskii, Vlast' i obshchestvo v doreformennoi Rossi* (Moskva: Pamiatniki istoricheskoi mysli, 2001).
89. On money and language: Marc Shell, *The Economy of Literature* (Baltimore: Johns Hopkins University Press, 1978); Eich, *The Currency of Politics*, 63–67.

CHAPTER 3

1. On the early production of platinum, see P. G. Sobolevskii, *Izvestie o platinovom proizvodstve v Rossii* (St. Petersburg, 1834).
2. A.S-ii, "Alexander von Humboldt v Rossii i poslednie ego trudy," *Vestnik Evropy*. 6 (1871): 6.
3. E. Kankrin's letter to A.Humboldt, August 15, 1827, *Perepiska Aleksandra Gumbol' dta s uchenymi i gosudarstvennymi deiateliami Rossii* (Moskva, Izd-vo Akademii nauk SSSR, 1962), 38–39.
4. A. Humboldt's letter to E. Kankrin, November 19, 1827, *Perepiska Aleksandra Gumbol'dta*, 47.
5. A. Humboldt's letter to E. Kankrin, November 19, 1827, *Perepiska Aleksandra Gumbol'dta*, 48.
6. PSZ 2, vol. 3, no. 1987; the decree issued on July 26, 1829, prescribed accepting platinum coins on the same conditions as silver and gold; vol. 4 no. 3038
7. Kankrin's letter to Humboldt, *Perepiska Aleksandra Gumbol'dta*, 63, 65.
8. O sravnitelnoi tsene platiny s inostrannoi, i o sdelannykh rasporiazheniiakh otnosiltelno vvoza onoi iz-za granitsy i o ne prieme ee na Monetnyi Dvor. *RGIA*, f. 37, op. 2, d.112.
9. Gosudarstvennyi Sovet, *O vosstanovlenii chekanki platinovoi monety* (St. Petersburg, 1861), 2.
10. Humboldt wrote to Kankrin in 1838 asking him to explain the "disappearance of the most part of platinum coins (it seems, you have spent on it about 800 poods of platinum?)." Humboldt's letter to Kankrin, *Perepiska Aleksandra Gumbol'dta*, 137.
11. "Vnutrennie izvestiia," *Kommercheskaia gazeta*, May 7, 1846, no. 53, 209.
12. Another attempt to introduce platinum coins was made in the late 1850s, when monetary reform was again an emergency while the country lacked silver and gold. That time, the law on issuing platinum coins was prepared and approved by the State Council but never put into practice. "O prodazhe platiny," RGIA, f.583, op.4, d.258; Gosudarstvennyi Sovet, *O vosstanovlenii chekanki platinovoi monety* (St. Petersburg, 1861).

13. On Kankrin's cameralism, see Chris Monday, "Kameralizm kak istochnik nauchnogo apparata Kankrina," in E. F. Kankrin, *Mirovoe bogatstvo i natsionalnaia ekonomika* (Moskva: Delo, 2018), 59–81.

14. Georg Cankrin, *Weltreichtum, Nationalreichtum und Staatswirtschaft; oder, Versuch neuer ansichten der politischen Oekonomie* (München: K. Thienemann, 1821), 68–69.

15. Kankrin's memo was a response to Dmitrii Guryev's new plan of monetary reform that he submitted shortly after his dismissal. Surprisingly, Guriev's project of 1823 reproduced almost verbatim the ideas of Speransky's earlier plan of 1810–12. It suggested a gradual replacement of assignats with coins and banknotes convertible to silver and issued by a newly established Russian State Bank. The adoption of the silver standard was the centerpiece of the new plan aimed at drawing Russia closer to those countries "where the representative signs of coins preserve their unchangeable value." Gur'ev, "Ob okonchatelnykh merakh Finansivogo plana 1817"(August 14, 1823), *RGIA*, f.560, op.22, d.24, 56-124. See also L. P. Marnei, *D.A. Guryev i finansovaia politika Rossii v nachale XIX veka* (Moskva: Indrik, 2009), 173–180. Kankrin's memo debunked Guryev's proposal and criticized his policy of reducing the number of assignats. (See the memo of the Committee of Finance: *RGIA*, f.560, op.22, d.24, L.24-45. The memo was signed by Kankrin, prince Alexei Kurakin, and count Alexei Arakcheev.)

16. E. F. Kankrin, "O budushchei kreditnoi sisteme, osoblivo o assignatsiiakh," December 16, 1823, RGIA, f.560, op.22, d.24, l. 13

17. E. F. Kankrin, "O budushchei kreditnoi sisteme, osoblivo o assignatsiiakh," December 16, 1823, RGIA, f.560, op.22, d.24, 14–18 ob. Wootz is steel alloy, the recipe for which had been lost and then rediscovered. Clearly, we can see here the influence of Kankrin's father, who was a mining engineer.

18. The connection between Kankrin's and Uvarov's stances may not be accidental: in the early 1820s, as a young bureaucrat, Uvarov "made himself a friend of the Kankrin family" and probably even owed his career growth to the minister of finance. S. S. Uvarov, *Izbrannye trudy* (Moksva: ROSSPEN, 2010), 15. Uvarov shared Kankrin's skepticism of the late eighteenth and early nineteenth centuries in respect to "political economy," that is, its liberal trend. See his essay "O narodonaselenii," in his *Izbrannye Trudy*, 287–293.

19. "To allow the existence of leather tokens and branded scraps that circulated in place of coins in various provinces of ancient Russia, means to admit the existence of state credit in such a period and under such circumstances when human mind could neither produce, nor even conceive this fruit of civilized collectivity and civil organization." "O kozhanykh dengakh," in M. T. Kachenovskii, *Dva rassuzhdeniia o kozhanykh dengakh i o Russkoi Pravde* (Moskva: Universitetskaia tipografiia, 1849), 20. See Kachenovskii's other works on leather money: "Nechto dlia drevnei numizmatiki," *Vestnik Evropy* 91, no. 1 (1817): 44–51; "O bel'iikh lobkakh i kun'ikh mordkakh," *Vestnik Evropy* 160, no. 13 (1828): 17–48; "O

kozhanykh den'gakh," *Uchenye zapiski Moskovskogo universiteta*, ch. 8, c. 333–370; ch. 8, c. 3–34; "O starinnykh nazvaniiakh v Rossii deneg metallicheskikh v smysle khodiachei monety," *Vestnik Evropy*, 1827, ch. 154, nos.14–16; ch. 155, no.18, 20; ch. 156, nos. 21–23.

20. For other opinions about leather money, see [Stanislav de Chodoire, baron], *Obozreniie russkikh deneg i inostrannykh monet upotrebliavshchikhsia v Rossii s drevnikh vremen. Sochinenie Barona Stanislava de Shoduara* (St. Petersburg: EZGB, 1837), part 1, p. 7; S. M. Soloviev, *Istoriia Rossii s drevneishikh vremen*, vol. 1 (3) (St. Petersburg: Obshchestvennaia Polza, 1894; 1st ed. 1854), 716; V. N. Leshkov, *Russkii narod i gosudarstvo. Istoriia russogo obshchestvennogo prava do XVIII veka* (Moskva: Universitetskaia tipografiia, 1858), 176–177. The leather money debate had an interesting continuation: Heinrich Storch in his famous *Cours d'économie politique* published in 1815, interpreted the case of Russian leather money as an example of ancient *monnaies de confiance* that predated the appearance of other fiat money—copper and paper. In 1859 Karl Marx, in his *Contribution to the Critique of Political Economy*, quoted Storch's account, presenting Russian leather tokens as a unique case of early fiat money, and a predecessor to paper notes: "Russia affords a striking example of a spontaneously evolved token of value. At a time when hides and furs served as money in that country, the contradiction between the perishable and unwieldy material and its function as a medium of circulation led to the custom of substituting small pieces of stamped leather for it; these pieces thus became money orders payable in hides and furs." Karl Marx, *Contribution to the Critique of Political Economy*, https://www.marxists.org/archive/marx/works/download/Marx_Contribution_to_the_Critique_of_Political_Economy.pdf. I. G. Spasskii, "Ocherki po istorii russkoi numizmatiki," *Trudy Gosudarstvennogo Istoricheskogo Muzeia*, vyp. 25 (Numizmaticheskii sbornik, ch.1 (Moskva, 1955), 104–105.

21. For a more detailed analysis of epistemological debates, see Ekaterina Pravilova, "Truth, Facts, and Authenticity in Russian Imperial Jurisprudence and Historiography," *Kritika: Explorations in Russian and Eurasian History* 21, no. 1 (Winter 2020): 7–39

22. Georg Cankrin, *Weltreichtum, Nationalreichtum und Staatswirtschaft; oder, Versuch neuer ansichten der politischen Oekonomie* (München, K. Thienemann, 1821), 217. A recent Russian edition: E. F. Kankrin, *Mirovoe bogatstvo i natsionalnaia ekonomika* (Moskva: Delo, 2018), 287.

23. E. F. Kankrin, *Graf Kankrin i ego ocherki politicheskoi ekonomii i finansii* (St. Petersburg, 1894), 124. Original edition: Georg Cankrin, *Die Oekonomie der menschlichen Gesellschaften und das Finanzwesen. Von einem ehemaligen Finanzminister* (Stuttgart: E. Schweizerbart, 1845), 146. See also in S. Ya. Borovoi, *Kredit i banki Rossii* (Moskva: Gosfinizdat, 1958),, 163.

24. On Kankrin's attitude to the idea of crediting industry, see Walter M. Pintner, "Government and Industry during the Ministry of Count Kankrin, 1823–1844," *Slavic Review* 23, no. 1 (March 1964): 45–62.

25. "O vypuske IV razriadov (serii) biletov Gosudarstvennogo Kaznacheistva," RGIA, f.1152, op.2, 1834, d.1, 7; see, for example, the Committee of Finance's approval of a loan for Alexei Ermolov's campaign in Persia: RGIA, f.565, op.2, d.162, l.199–200.

26. "O vypuske IV razriadov (serii) biletov Gosudarstvennogo Kaznacheistva," RGIA, f.1152, op.2, 1834, d.1, 8. In October 1833, the Loan (*Zaemnyi*) and the Commercial Banks held together about 26.6 million rubles, while the deposit trust banks (*sokhrannye kazny*) accumulated no more than 15 million rubles.

27. Kankrin reported to the State Council that in Moscow, foreign coins outnumbered Russian coins by four. V. T. Sudeikin, *Vosstanovlenie v Rossii metallicheskogo obrashcheniia (1839–1843). Istoricheskii ocherk* (Moskva, 1891), 24.

28. Sudeikin, *Vosstanovlenie v Rossii*, 21, 22; Kaufman, *Iz istorii bumazhnykh deneg v Rossii.* St.Petersburg, 1909, 58–64.

29. Kaufman mentioned that in the archive of the Credit Chancellery he came across a massive folder with correspondence on the subject, "The prohibition to accept in state revenues payments in silver and gold coins." Kaufman, *Iz istorii*, 48.

30. "Poet-igrok, o Beverlei-Goratsii, Proigryval ty kuchki assigtatsii, i serebro, nasledie ottsov." A. S. Pushkin, "Poet-Igrok, o Beverlei-Goratsii," A. S. Pushkin, *Polnoe Sobranie Sochinenii v 16 tomakh* (Moskva, Leningrad: Izd-vo AN SSSR, 1949), t.3, kn.2, 155

31. N. V. Gogol, "Mertvye Dushi," tom pervyi, in *Polnoe sobranie sochinenii v 14 tomakh* (Moskva, Leningrad, Izd-vo AN SSSR, 1951), v. 6, 136.

32. N. V. Gogol, "Nos," in *Polnoe sobranie sochinenii v 14 tomakh* (Moskva, Leningrad, Izd-vo AN SSSR, 1951), v. 3, 63. Alexander Pushkin was the editor of the "Contemporary" that published Gogol's story, and only because of his personal request, made to the censor A. L. Krylov, was Gogol able to keep this fragment, at the expense of others. *Polnoe sobranie sochinenii v 14 tomakh* (Moskva, Leningrad, Izd-vo AN SSSR, 1951), v. 3, 654.

33. N. V. Gogol, "Portret," in *Polnoe sobranie sochinenii v 14 tomakh* (Moskva, Leningrad, Izd-vo AN SSSR, 1951), v. 3, 110. Pushkin's bookseller also offered to convert the poet's "little leaves" with verses into the "bunch of cash assignats." A. S. Pushkin, "Razgovor knigoprodavtsa s poetom," in *Polnoe sobranie sochinenii v 16 tomakh* (Moskva, Leningrad: Izd-vo AN SSSR, 1949 t.3, kn.1, 1947, 324.

34. Jillian Porter, *Economies of Feeling: Russian Literature under Nicholas I* (Evanston, IL: Northwestern University Press, 2017; Russell Scott Valentino, "What's a Person Worth: Character and Commerce in Dostoevskii's Double," *American Contributions to the 13th International Congress of Slavists, Ljubljana, August 2003*, edited by Robert Maguire. and Alan Timberlake, vol. 2, 203–212 (Slavica Publishers: Bloomington, 2003.

35. Gogol, "Zapisnaia knizhka," *Polnoe sobranie sochinenii v 14 tomakh* (Moskva, Leningrad, Izd-vo AN SSSR, 1951), v. 7, 354

36. E. P. Pertsov, *Iskusstvo brat' vziatki: rukopis naidennaia v bumagakh Tiazhalkina, umershego tituliarnogo sovetnika* [*The art of bribe taking. Manuscript found in the papers of Tiazhalkin, a deceased titular councilor*] (St. Petersburg, 1830), 29–31.

37. Astolphe Marquis de Custine, *Rossiia v 1839 godu (osnovnoi tom)* (St. Petersburg: Kriga, 2008), 564

38. "Vekselnye i denezhnye kursy na 3 ianvaria," *Kommercheskaia gazeta*, 5 ianvaria 1839, 8.

39. R. I. Sementkovskii, *E. F. Kankrin: Ego zhizn' i gosudarstvennaia deiatelnost'* (St. Petersburg, 1893), 73.

40. For a useful explanation, see P. A. Ostroukhov, "Iz istorii denezhnogo obrashcheniia (Prostonarodnye lazhi i torgovlia den'gami na Nizhegorodskoi iarmarke)," *Zapiski Russkogo nauchno-issledovatelskogo ob'edineniia v Prage*. Tom XI (XVI) (Praha, 1941),

41. "Vnutrennie izvestiia," *Kommercheskaia gazeta*, January 3, 1839, no.1, 2.

42. "Moskva. 2 ianvaria," *Kommercheskaia gazeta,* January 26, 1839, no.11. P. Veretennikov, "Razlichie poniatii o denezhnom lazhe," *Kommercheskaia gazeta*, May 23, 1839, no.61, 258.

43. See the examples of budget calculation that included *lazh* on assignats in Akinf Zhukov, *Nachal'nye osnovaniia russkogo sel'skogo khoziastva* (Moskva, 1837), 239–244.

44. "Vnutrennie izvestiia. St. Petersburg, 29 marta," *Kommercheskaia gazeta*, March 29, 1839, nos. 37–38, 145; also in RGIA, f.651, op.1, d.238, 3; "Vnutrennie izvestiia. St. Petersburg, 10 aprelia," *Kommercheskaia gazeta*, April 11, 1839, no. 43, 165.

45. See the lists of merchants who joined the campaign: *Kommercheskaia gazeta*, April 13, 1829, no. 44; April 18, 1839, no. 46; April 22, 1839, no .48; April 25, 1839, no. 49; April 27, 1839, no. 50; April 29, 1839, no. 51; May 6, 1839, no. 54; May 16, 1839, no. 58. On the prohibition of using *lazh* at the exhibition of manufactured goods, see "Ob'iavlenie ot Ministerstva Finansov," *Kommercheskaia gazeta*, April 1, 1839, no. 39.

46. P. Morozov, whose article criticizing "lazh" appeared in the *Agricultural Newspaper* and then was reprinted by the *Commercial Newspaper*, called the "coin ruble" "an imaginary, arbitrary unit." P. Morozov, "O lazhe na den'gi, suchchestvuiushchem vo vnutrennikh guberniiakh Rossii," *Kommercheskaia gazeta*, March 21, 1839, no.34, 133.

47. K. I. Fisher, *Zapiski senatora* (Moskva: Zakharov, 2008), 135. The government attempted to prohibit the practice of double counting, which, predictably, brought no results. On the elaboration of prohibition, see Zhurnal Komiteta finansov, September 28 1834, OR RNB, f.484, d.81.

48. Sudeikin, *Vosstanovlenie v Rossii*, 49.

49. PSZ 2, vol. 14, no. 12497.

50. As Kankrin's biographer claimed, most people did not pay attention to this aspect of the operation: if in the 1810s and 1820s the fall of the national currency still appeared abnormal, in the 1830s and 1840s "people accustomed to it, and the recognition of the treasury's insolvency could not shock anybody." Sementkovskii, *E. F. Kankrin*, 76.

51. V .A. Kokorev, *Ekonomicheskie provaly* (Moskva: Kontseptual, 2013) (initial publication 1887). On July 2, 1839, Mariia, daughter of Nicholas I, married Maximilian Herzog von Leuchtenberg.

52. "Zapiski grafa Aleksandra Ivanovicha Ribopiera," *Russkii Arkhiv*, 1877, kn.2, vyp.5, 11.

53. Astolphe Marquis de Custine, *Rossiia v 1839 godu (osnovnoi tom)*, 564–565.

54. A. V. Nikitenko, *Dnevnik*, vol. 1, 213, cited by Vera Milchina, Alexander Ospovat, *Kommentarii k knige Astolfa de Kustina "Rossiia v 1839 godu"* (St. Petersburg: Kriga, 2008), 935–936.

55. Sementkovskii, *E. F. Kankrin*, 78.

56. Nikolai Mordvinov, Admiral Alexei Greyg, and Petr Kiselev also submitted projects of reforms that differed in their radicalism, ideology, and thoroughness.

57. Historians suggest that Kankrin's plan was based on Speransky's recommendations outlined in a memo "on monetary circulation" that he wrote in the 1830s. A. V. Bugrov, *Kazennye banki v Rossii, 1754–1860* (Moskva: Tsentralnyi Bank RF, 2017), 246; Dubianskii, "E.A. Kankrin—zhizn' i deiatelnost'," in E. F. Kankrin, *Mirovoe bogatstvo i natsionalnaia ekonomika* (Moskva: Delo, 2018, 38). Speransky repeated his old idea of replacing assignats with banknotes, but he did not specify the institutional arrangements for the bank reform. (M. M. Speransky, *Zapiska o monetnom obrashchenii grafa Speranskogo s zamechaniiami grafa Kankrin*a [St. Petersburg, 1895]). Kankrin used only the contours of Speransky's plan, including the intermediary stage with the deposit certificates, but he rejected the idea of introducing banknotes. He also used Speransky's moral authority to promote his plan.

58. 595,776,310 rubles assignat equaled 170,221,802 rubles in silver. "Proekt predstavleniia v Gosudarstvennyi Sovet ob obmene assignatsii" (January 1843), RGIA, f.560, op.22, d.108, ll.3–4.

59. Kankrin planned to take 6.5 million from the reserve sums of the Commission for the State Debts and borrow 4 million either from treasury banks (i.e., from the deposit accounts of the banks' clients) or the military fund.

60. Nicholas I's memo: RGIA, f.560, op.22, d.108, ll.12–14.

61. A. Chernyshev's memo: RGIA, f.560, op.22, d.108, l.45

62. RGIA, f.560, op.22, d.101, ll. 134; 276 (on speculation).

63. Drucki-Lubecki referred to the changes of the amount of copper coins minted of one *pood* of metal (from 16 to 24 and 36 rubles and then back to 16). All these changes happened gradually, which suggested that the government could also change the weight of the silver ruble and the value of certificates, since the deposit certificates did not indicate their silver content.

64. RGIA, f.560, op.22, d.101, l.132.

65. RGIA, f.560, op.22, d.101, l.69 ob (request for personal audience), l.73. December 1839.

66. "Osnovnoi Ustav Pol'skogo Banka," January 17(29) 1828 (parallel texts in Russian and Polish), *Sbornik administrativnykh postanovlenii Tsarstva Polskogo. Vedomstvo Finansov. Tom X. Polskii Bank* (Warsaw: Tip Goldmana, 1867).

67. Henryk Radziszewski, *Bank Polski* (Poznan: Ostoja, 1919), 18. The Sejm was summoned only four times during Nicholas's reign; therefore, the Bank's charter was issued by the tsar's decree.

68. RGIA, f.560, op.22, d.101, ll.115, 116.

69. "Delo sekretnogo komiteta sobiravshegosia v ianvare, fevrale i marte 1841 goda v vysochaishem prisutstvii," RGIA, f. 560, op. 22, d. 547, l. 2–3.

70. "Delo sekretnogo komiteta sobiravshegosia v ianvare, fevrale i marte 1841 goda v vysochaishem prisutstvii," RGIA, f. 560, op. 22, d. 547, l.19.

71. It probably wasn't a coincidence that in September 1840 the *Commercial Newspaper* published an article about the Bank of Poland (reprinted from another edition— *Biblioteka znanii*) that was quite different from the newspaper's customary content. "Polskii Bank," *Kommercheskaia gazeta*, September 3, 1840, no.106, 424–425; September 5, 1840, no.107, 428–429.

72. M. A. Korf, "Nikolai I v soveshchatelnykh sobraniiakh," *Sbornik IRIO*, 98 (1896):147.

73. For instance, the minister of the navy, Alexander Menshikov, wrote about the establishment of a bank of issue as the only way to strengthen the credibility of credit rubles because the government simply did not possess enough means to create a fund sufficient to maintain the value of paper representatives. Even if no one doubted the government's honesty, people might question the government's solvency; therefore, the success of the operation was possible "only with the assistance of such a helper" as the special bank that could attract private funds. Menshikov, as well as Drucki-Lubecki, referred to the example of "other European states where all state papers that enjoy trust were based on bank credit." RGIA, f.560, op.22, d. 108, ll.173–176

74. M. A. Korf, "Nikolai I v soveshchatelnykh sobraniiakh," *Sbornik IRIO*, 98 (1896): 186.

75. RGIA, f.560, op.2 2, d. 547, l. 19.

76. In addition to that, the treasury was supposed to contribute 7 million rubles from the defense fund.

77. RGIA, f.560, op. 22, d. 108, l.33 ob.

78. Sementkovskii, *E. F. Kankrin*, 206.

79. See PSZ 1, vol. 31, February 2, 1810, no. 24116; PSZ 1, vol. 34, April 16, 1817, no. 26791.

80. Korf, "Nikolai I v soveshchatelnykh sobraniiakh," 196, 198, 203. Alfred Schmidt, *Das russische Geldwesen 1823–1844* quoted in I. N. Bozherianov, *Graf Egor Frantsevich Kankrin, ego zhizn', literaturnye trudy i dvadtsatiletniaia deiatel'nost' upravlenia Ministerstvom Finansov* (St. Petersburg, 1897), 193. in refs

81. Sudeikin, *Vosstanovleniie metallicheskogo obrashcheniia v Rossii*, 58, 60.

82. "Ustav Ekspeditsii Gosudarstvennykh Kreditnykh Biletov," PSZ 2, vol. 18, June 1, 1843, no.16904.

83. Sementkovskii, *E. F. Kankrin*, 78. The reserve repository had been built on a fast schedule: Nicholas ordered construction to begin in 1843 and to be completed by December 1844.

84. "Vnutrennie izvestiia. St. Petersburg, Dekabria 4," *Kommercheskaia gazeta*, December 5, 1844, no. 144, 573; "Vnutrennie izvestiia. St. Petersburg, Dekabria 15," *Kommercheskaia gazeta*, December 16, 1844, no.149, 593–594.

85. I. I. Kaufman, "Zolotoi rubl' v Rossii i emissionnaia operatsiia Gosudarstvennogo Banka," TsGIA SPB, f.2098, op.1, d.58, l.61.

86. Kaufman described Russia's idea of the reserve as "indigenous, not borrowed from anywhere." Kaufman, "Zolotoi rubl' v Rossii i emissionnaia operatsiia Gosudarstvennogo Banka," TsGIA SPB, f.2098, op.1, d.58, l.28.

87. "Angliiskii Bank," *Kommercheskaia gazeta*, June 3, 1844, no. 65, 258–259.

88. Walter Bagehot, *Lombard Street. A Description of the Money Market* (London, 1882), 23, 35

89. Fake assignats continued to circulate even though the locals knew about their origin. The authorities were so struck by the quality of fake assignats and the ingenuity of the engraver, illiterate peasant Mayorov, that instead of punishing him with hard labor, they sent him to work at the Lapidary factory in Ekaterinburg. O delateliakh fal'shivykh assignatsii v Bogorodskom uezde, GARF, 109, 4 eksp, op. 185, 1845, d. 107, ll.3 ob, 62–63 ob., 104, 136.

90. P. P. Migulin, *Nasha bankovaia politika* (Kharkiv, 1914), 50.

91. S. F. Khrolenok, *Zolotopromyshlennost' Sibiri (1832–1917): Istoriko-ekonomicheskii ocherk* (Irkutsk: Izd-vo Irkutskogo universiteta, 1999), 27. See also V. V. Danilevskii, *Russkoe zoloto. Istoriia otkrytiia i dobychi do serediny XIX v* (Moskva: Gos nauchno-tekhn. Izd-vo, 1959).

92. The state considered gold mined by private entrepreneurs as its own. For instance, the new rules on gold mining obliged the gold producers to combat theft in their private gold mines. The gold expropriated from "spoilers" was confiscated by the state without compensation to the owners of mines in retribution for their negligence. "O sostavlenii postanovlenii o pokhititeliakh zolota, a takzhe pravil o prieme zolota ot volnoprinositelei na Monetnyi Dvor," RGIA, f.37, op.2, d.59.

93. Khrolenok, *Zolotopromyshlennost' Sibiri*, 43–44. In 1849, the mining duty was again reconsidered: the new flexible scale ranged from 5% to 35% of produced gold, depending on the profitability of enterprises. Khrolenok, *Zolotopromyshlennost' Sibiri*, 45.

94. "Otchet ministra finansov za desiat' let, 1823-1833," RGIA, f.560, op.22, d.70, l.271-273. "O prieme v kaznu serebrianoi i platinovoi monety na vsiakuiu summu," PSZ 2, vol.6, no.4241. Only in 1833 did the government, responding to the demands of the people, allow them to bring gold coins to the state offices.

95. L. N. Yasnopolskii, "Gosudarstvennyi Bank," in *Voprosy gosudarstvennogo khoziaistva i buidzhetnogo prava* (St. Petersburg, 1907), 237. For budgetary statistics, see I. I. Kaufman, *Statistika gosudarstvennykh finansov v 1862–1884 godakh. Statisticheskii vremennik Rossiiskoi Imperii* (St. Petersburg, 1886), 39.

96. RGIA, f.563, op.2, d.21, L.9. The "treasury bonds" (bilety Gosudarstvennogo Kaznacheistva, or "serii"), each worth 250 rubles assignat and bearing 4.32%

interest, were redeemable within four years and accepted in all state payments. Between 1831 and 1847, the government issued "series" for 100 million rubles. Thus, Kankrin's treasury bonds, initially intended as an extraordinary resource "in case a European war erupts," turned into a permanent substitute for "bad" assignats (and then credit rubles) and a means to raise funds for wars, railroad construction, and current budgetary needs without making a lot of fuss. Treasury bonds continued to be issued until 1917. RGIA, f.1152, op.2, 1834, d.1, l.8–10; see also f.563, op.2, d.62. As I. I. Kaufman's data show, the government was actively using these bonds between 1852 and 1884; it reduced their amount substantially in the 1890s and resumed the massive emission of "series" in 1905–1906 during the crises of the Russo-Japanese war and the revolution. See Kaufman's memo to the State Bank's Council (1907), TsGIA SPb, F.2098, op.1, d.57, ll. 2–3.

97. It increased from 207,490,954 to 462,269,415 rubles. This sum included "debts registered in the State Book of Debts" (previous loans), loans from state credit institutions, Treasury bonds, and new foreign loans. P. P. Migulin, *Gosudarstvennyi Kredit*, vol.1, 126.

98. RGIA, f.37, op.18, d.92, ll.90b–100b.

99. "O prieme assignatsii Pol'skogo banka," RGIA, f.562, op.2, d.63. ll.1–8.

100. "O priniatii mer k vosstanovleniiu doveriia k gosudarstvennym kreditnym biletam po zapadnym guberniiam," RGIA, F.565, op.13, d.849, ll.17, 21–22, 360b.

101. "Zapiska o finansovykh oborotakh Tsartstva Polskogo i raschetakh onogo s Kaznacheistvom Imperii, sostavlena sov Starynkevichem," RGIA, f.869, op.1, d.611, l.87 ob.

102. "Zapiska o finansovykh oborotakh Tsartstva Polskogo," RGIA, f.869, op.1, d.611, ll.85–86.

103. RGIA, f.583, op.4, d.252, l.141, 151; f.583, op.4, d.258, ll.35–-361.

104. RGIA, f.583, op.2, d. 262, ll.47–55.

105. See report on relocating the remaining 9 million rubles from the depositary at the Peter and Paul Fortress to the Expedition of Credit Rubles. August 14, 1854, RGIA, f.583, op.4, d.252, l.277.

106. O rassmotrenii v Komitete finansov voprosa o vyvoze zolotoi monety za granitsu. 26 fevralia 1854, RGIA, f.583, op.4, d. 252, ll. 109–110, 138.

107. RGIA, f.565, op.4, d.14000, ll. 56–560b.

108. Vsepoddanneishii doklad, October 18, 1857, RGIA, f.583, op.4, d.258.

109. P.A. Nikolski, *Bumazhnye den'gi v Rossii* (Kazan', 1892), 329

110. Zapiska komissii dlia obsuzheniia mer k luchshemu ustroistvu bankovoi i denezhnoi sistemy, RGIA, f.940, op.1, d.14, l.37; "O merakh uluchshenia bankovoi i denezhnoi sistemy," 9 Iulia 1859, RGIA, f.563, op.1, d.9, 19-190b.

111. RGIA, F.583, op.4, d. 242, l.277.

112. I. I. Kaufman, "Zolotoi rubl' i emissionnaia operatsiia Gosudarstvennogo Banka," TsGIA SPB, f.2098, op.1, d.58, ll.17–18.

113. The absence of an official declaration later led to academic debates about the "end" of convertibility. See: Spravka o vremeni priostanovleniia razmena kreditnykh biletov na zvonkuiu monetu. RGIA, f.583 op.3, d.1017, 3.

114. See the report on the dispatch of police forces to the Expedition: RGIA, f.579, op.1, d.1411. O prisylke politsii k vorotam Ekspeditsii (kreditnykh biletov) po sluchaiu stecheniia publiki. See also Kniazhevich's report about the "crowds of people storming the Expedition and demanding gold": RGIA, f.583, op.4, d.262, l.73.

CHAPTER 4

1. "Storm in the Baltic," *The Times*, October 9, 1860; "The Late Gales in the North," *Morning Chronicle*, October 5, 1860.

2. American Banknote Company to Knyazhevich, St. Petersburg, December 18, 1860, *TsGIA* SPb, f.1458, op.2, d.426, l.69.

3. Ministerstvo Finansov–Upravliaiushchemu tipograficheskim otdeleniem EZGB Vinbergu, December 6, 1859, *TsGIA* SPb, f.1458, op.2, d.426, l.3.

4. A. A. Bogdanov, *Den'gi, kotorykh ne bylo. Iz istorii proektirovaniia bumazhnykh deneg v Rossii* (St. Petersburg: Goznak, 2020), 37.

5. O predlozhenii upolmomochennogo amerikanskoi kompanii Bankovskie bilety Guddelia izgotovliat' kreditnye bilety usovershenstvovannym sidrograficheskim sposobom, June 3, 1859, RGIA, f.583, op.4, d.263, ll.44–47. On this collaboration, see also A. V. Alyokhov, "Amerika–Rossiia: kreditnye bilety 1866 goda," *Numizmaticheskii almanakh* 1 (2001): 2.

6. Alyokhov, "Amerika," no. 1, 35.

7. Reutern–Upravliaiushchemu EZGB, September 13, 1863, TsGIA SPb, f.1458, op.2, d.426, 140. See also for the sources of portraits (paintings in museums and collections) TsGIA SPb, f.1458, op.2, d.426, l.142 ob.

8. "O zamene nyneshnikh kreditnykh biletov," RGIA, f.563, op.2, d.172, l.90b–100b.

9. "O novom ustroistve EZGB, December 9, 1860," RGIA, f.1152, op.5, 1860g., d.414, l.14–15, 18, 20.

10. In 1849, the Committee of Finance voted to decline the offer of a loan in gold referring, to the inconvenience of accepting gold under the regime of the silver standard. Komitet finansov, "Po predlozheniiu bankirov v Berline Mendelsona i Syna otkryt' zaem na zolotuiu valiutu," September 16, 1849; *Izvlechenie iz podlinnykh del Komiteta finansov* (St. Petersburg, 1895); RGIA, pechatnaia zapiska 1155, 3.

11. See one of these proposals: Yu. Gagemeister, "O zamene serebrianogo rublia zolotym," January 20, 1859, RGIA, f.560. op.2. d.111.

12. Nikolai Printz, *Podgotovitelye mery k vosstanovleniiu zvonkoi monety* (St. Petersburg, 1887), 7–10; VU mnenie Gos soveta 27 fevralia 1861 . . . ob otmene zapreshcheniia na vyvoz za granitsu kreditnykh biletov, PSZ 2, vol. 36, no.36699.

13. G. Kamenskii, "Ponizhenie kursa na London na S.Peterburgskoi birzhe," *Vestnik Promyshlennosti* (1859): 1, 2.

14. Jonathan Levy eloquently defined capitalism through the centrality of investment, as opposed to physical assets and labor. Jonathan Levy, *Ages of American Capitalism. A History of the United States* (New York: Random House, 2021), xiv–xv.

15. "Obozrenie promyshlennosti i torglovli," *Vestnik promyshlennosti,* (1858): 237.

16. M. N. Katkov, *Sobranie peredovykh statei Moskovskikh Vedomostei* (hereafter—*SPS*) za 1864 (Moskva 1897), 396 (no.142, June 26 1864)

17. *SPS* za 1864, 538 (no. 194, September 3, 1864).

18. Official declarations say that the operation began in 1857. However, the first attempts to raise the rate through the transfer of rubles were made in March 1854. See report of minister of finance, March 12, 1854, in RGIA, f.583, op.4, d.252.

19. Yu. A. Gagemeister, *Znachenie denezhnykh znakov v Rossii* (Moskva, 1864), 54.

20. "O razmennom kapitale," October 18, 1857, RGIA, f.583, op.4, d.258.

21. I. V. [Ivan Vernadsky], "Veksel'nyi kurs i torgovyi balans," *Ekonomicheskii Ukazatel'* 16 (April 16–28, 1860): 289–291; *SPS* za 1863, 692 (no. 254, November 20, 1863).x

22. Russians who applied and received passports for international travels could also exchange a limited sum of credit rubles for gold at nominal value, even if the ruble's real market value was far below the nominal one. According to Kniazhevich, these traveling Russians were responsible for carrying up to 20 million rubles out of the country annually. RGIA, f.563, op.2, d.134, l.30.

23. Igor Khristoforov, unpublished paper. Khristoforov has described two groups of experts who defined the contours of financial policy: the representatives of the older generation of scholars and bureaucrats, such as Ludwik Tęgoborski (1793–1857), Grigorii Nebolsin (1811–1896), and economist Yulii Gagemeister (1806–1878), and a group of younger economists that included the future minister of finance, Mikhail Reutern (1820–1890), Nikolai Miliutin (1818–1872), Evgenii Lamanskii (1825–1902), Vladimir Bezobrazov (1828–1889), Nikolai Bunge (1823–1895), and Fedor Terner (1828–1906).

24. V-skii, "Politiko-ekonomicheskoe znachenie nekotorykh obshchestvennykh faktov. Schetnaia edinitsa," *Ekonomicheskii Ukazatel'* 26 (1858): 582–583.

25. F. G. Terner, *Vospominania zhizni* (St. Petersburg, 1910), 164.

26. Yu. A. Gagemeister, *O kredite* (St. Petersburg, 1858), 116.

27. V. Dubenskii, *Chto takoe den'gi?* (Moskva, 1859), 9, 27.

28. E. Lamanskii, "Gosudarsvtennye chetyrekhprotsentnye, nepreryvnodokhodnye bilety (29 marta 1859)," *Ekonomicheskii Ukazatel'* (1859): 322.

29. Lamanskii, "Gosudarsvtennye chetyrekhprotsentnye," 322.

30. Memoires sur nos finances présentée à S. M. L'Empereur et envoyée à Nice au Grand Duc Constantine par le conseiller privé Tęgoborski en Fevrier 1857, RGIA, f.1044, op.1, d.148 l.11, 13.

31. For a detailed and thorough explanation of this move, see Steven Hoch, "The Banking Crisis, Peasant Reform, and Economic Development in Russia, 1857–1861," *American Historical Review* 96, no. 3 (June 1991): 795–820.

32. On this episode, see Alfred Rieber, *The Imperial Russian Project. Autocratic Politics, Economic Development, and Social Fragmentation* (Toronto: University of Toronto Press, 2017, 190–191.

33. O merakh uluchsheniia bankovskoi i denezhnoi sistemy, July 10, 1859, RGIA, f.563, op.1, d.9, 30b.–4.

34. Guryev suggested simply suspending all payments from the state banks in credit rubles and forcing the banks' clients to take other treasury promissory notes instead. In essence, it was a camouflaged bankruptcy for the sake of keeping the paper ruble afloat. As he wrote, "The problem of assignats [i.e., credit rubles] is more important than the bank problem." Zapiska Guryeva, *RGIA*, f.940, op.1, d.13, l.1–14.

35. E. I. Lamanskii, "Vklady v bankakh ili bilety nepreryvnogo dokhoda?" *Russkii Vestnik* 20 (1859): 232. On this operation and Lamanskii's critique, see also Terner, *Vospominania zhizni*, 143–145.

36. "Zapiska komissii dlia obsuzhdeniia mer k luchshemu ustroistvu bankovoi i denezhnoi sistemy, RGIA, f.940, op.1, d.14, l.4

37. E. I. Lamanskii, "Gosudarsvtennye chetyrekhprotsentnye, nepreryvnodokhodnye bilety," *Ekonomicheskii Ukazatel'* (1859): 324.

38. E. I. Lamanskii, *Vospominania 1840–1890* (Penza: Zemstvo, 1995), 50–52.

39. "O reforme Kommercheskogo banka," RGIA, f. 940, op.1, d.14, ll.48–55.

40. S. V. Pakhman, *O zadachakh predstoiashchei reformy aktsionernogo zakonodatelstva* (Kharkov, 1861), 24, 25.

41. Pakhman, *O zadachakh predstoiashchei reformy*, 147.

42. Zakliuchenie ministra finansov, RGIA, f. 940, op.1, d.14, ll. 59–60. P. P. Migulin, *Nasha bankovaia politika*, 70.

43. Zhurnaly Soveta Gosudarstvennogo Banka ob osnovaniiakh preobrazovaniia Gosudarstvennogo Banka, RGIA, f.587, op.60, d.20, ll. 4–5.

44. The State Bank's Charter of May 31, 1860, *PSZ 2*, vols. 3 5, no. 35847.

45. *Kredit i banki v Rossii do nachala XX veka. Sankt-Peterburg i Moskva.* (St. Petersburg: Izd-vo S.-Peterburgskogo universiteta, 2005),199.

46. Lamanskii, *Vospominania*, 75

47. I.I. Kaufman, *Kreditnye bilety, ikh upadok i vosstanovlenie* (St.Petersburg, 1888), 144; Lamanskii, *Vospominania*, 56.

48. Kaufman, *Iz istorii bumazhnykh deneg v Rossii.* (St.Petersburg, 1909), 168.

49. V. G. Chernukha, *Vnutrenniaia politika tsarizma s serediny 50-kh do nachala 80-kh gg. XIX v.* (Leningrad: Izd-vo AN SSSR, 1978), 25.

50. Chernukha, *Vnutrenniaia politika tsarizma*, 34.

51. RGIA, f.563, op.2, d.155, l. 43–45 ob., May 5, 1862.

52. "Russkii gosudarstvennyi dolg," *Russkii Vestnik*, 20 (1860): 203.

53. "O zakliuchenii zaima na 15 millionov funtov sterlingov" April 14, 1862, RGIA, f.563, op.2, d.155.
54. "Ob otpuske na Sankt-Petersburgskii Monetnyi Dvor zolotykh slitkov, dostavlennykh ot Rotshilda," RGIA, f.587, op.43, d.38a.
55. A. A. Golovachev, *Desiat' let reform, 1861–1871* (St. Petersburg, 1872), 38. For more on the 1863 attempt at restoring the convertibility, see Pavel Lizunov, "Regulirovanie denezhnogo obrashcheniia. Vypusk vnutrennikh vyigryshnykh zaimov 1864 i 1866 g.," in *Gosudarsvtennyi Bank Rossiiskoi Imperi*, edited by Yu. A. Petrov and S. V. Tatarinov (Moskva, Tsentralnyi Bank Rossii, 2010), vol. 1.
56. Lamanskii, *Vospominania*, 79.
57. *SPS* za 1863, 651 (no. 240, November 4, 1863).
58. Perhaps coincidentally, or maybe anticipating the impending failure of the exchange, in September 1863 the Committee of Finances voted to change the credit ruble's design and to eliminate the texts of paragraphs 3 and 4 printed on the reverse side of the credit bills that stipulated the conditions of the credit rubles exchange. These paragraphs were eliminated because there was insufficient gold in the exchange fund to meet the conditions. Nevertheless, the first two paragraphs—the declaration of convertibility to silver or gold (instead of imprecise "metallic currency") pledged by the "entirety of the state"—continued to be published even though Russian credit rubles remained inconvertible until 1897. Komitet finansov, "O zamene nyneshnikh obraztsov gosudarstvennykh kreditnykh biletov novymi," September 5, 1863, in *Izvlechenie iz podlinnykh del Komiteta finansov* (St. Petersburg, 1895), RGIA, p.z.1155, 7.
59. After the reform of 1839–43, the gold half-imperial coin of 5 rubles cost 5 rubles, 15 kopeks.
60. P. Migulin, *Regulirovanie bumazhnoi valiuty v Rossii* (Kharkov, 1896), 13.
61. Kaufman, "Zoloti rubl' v Rossii," TsGIA SPb, f.2098, op.1, d.58, l.20.
62. V. P. Bezobrazov, "O nekotorykh iavleniiakh denezhnogo obrashcheniia v Rossii," *Russkii Vestnik*, November 1863, 376–416 (although the article appeared in a November issue, according to the censorship record, it was published in December, that is, after the suspension of the exchange). See also a separate edition under the same title (Moscow: tip. Katkova, 1863).
63. A. A. Golovachev, "Ob'asnenie po povodu otvetov na voprosy ob operatsiiakh Gosudarstvennogo Banka," *Vestnik Evropy* 2 (March 1874): 373; Migulin, *Regulirovanie*, 1.3.
64. Abram Zak to Dmitrii Solskii, RGIA, f.694, op.2, d.84, l.3.
65. Abram Zak to Dmitrii Solskii, RGIA, f.694, op.2, d.84, l.3.
66. A. A. Golovachev, *Desiat' let reform, 1861–1871* (St. Petersburg, 1872), 15.
67. Golovachev, *Desiat' let reform*, 22.
68. The government displayed its preoccupation with the symbolism of good financial housekeeping as it publicly burned the excess 60 million paper rubles on May 24, 1858; this was witnessed by more than thirty guests, including the representatives

of the commercial world and foreigners. "O sozhzhenii kreditnykh biletov," RGIA, f.583, op.4, d.260, 225–228.

69. I. I. Kaufman, *Iz istorii bumazhnykh deneg v Rossii* (St. Petersburg, 1909), 179,

70. M. Kh. Reitern, "Zapiska, predstavlennaia vel.kniaziu Konstantinu Nukolaevichu d.st.s. Reiternom v 1857 godu," *Reka Vremen, kniga piataia. Gosudar', gosudarstvo, gosudarstvennaia sluzhba* (Moskva: Ellis Lak, 1996), 182.

71. Pavel Lizunov, "Regulirovanie denezhnogo obrashcheniia," 175; Terner, *Vospominaniia zhizni*, 206.

72. Lamanskii, *Vospominania*, 71,

73. Gagemeister, *Znacheniie denezhnykh znakov v Rossii*, 6.

74. Gagemeister, *Znacheniie denezhnykh znakov v Rossii*, 6.

75. Reutern, [O merakh po uluchsheniu finansovogo i ekonomicheskogo polozhenia gosudarstva], 154. Reutern nevertheless warned against abusing people's trust and squeezing monetary resources out of the country with the means of state-issued bonds. "The string is overstretched, and by stretching it further we won't achieve our goal but subject the state to a serious threat."

76. Explaining the peculiarity of the Russian financial system to a certain (unknown) foreign correspondent, Reutern remarked: "By the method of their emission, they are closer to paper money than banknotes." He concluded that "in fact, no bank of issue actually exists in Russia," AVPRI, F.133, op.469, d.48, l.52.

77. "Memoires sur nor finances presentee a S. M. L'Empereur et envoyeé a Nice au Grand Duc Constantine par le conseiller prive Tęgoborski en Fevrier 1857," RGIA, f.1044, op.1, d. 148, l.80b–9.

78. See Katkov's articles on financial publicity: *SPS za 1869*, 597 (no. 203, September 17, 1869); *SPS za 1870*, 61–62 (no. 21, January 26, 1870).

79. For the details and the various schemes of the speculative operation, see Pavel Lizunov, "Neudachnoe nachalo 'novoi ery' russkikh finansov," in *Stranitsy russkoi istorii. Problemy, sobytiia, liudi. Sbornik statei v chest' B.V. Ananicha* (St. Petersburg, 2003),100–106.

80. On this episode, see Terner, *Vospominania zhizni*, 186.

81. Terner, *Vospominania zhizni*, 203.

82. The article in question must have been the one published in *Moskovskie Vedomosti* on May 23, 1863, no.111.

83. *SPS za 1863* (no. 240, 241, November 4, November 5, 1863).

84. Valuev's letter to Katkov, November 11, 1863, OR RGB, f.120, papka 19, no.1, l.11.

85. Valuev's letter to Katkov, December 26, 1863. OR RGB, f.120, papka 19, no.1, l.14.

86. Louis Wolowski, "Les finances de la Russie," *Revue de deux mondes* no.2 (1864): 431–452.

87. Nikolai Ogarev, *Finansovye spory* (London: Truebner, 1864).

88. See the collection of responses to Wolowski's article and his response to them in a separate publication: Wolowski, *Les finances de la Russie* (1864).

89. *SPS* za 1864, 167 (no. 64, March 19, 1864); *Birzhevye Vedomosti*, November 5, 1863; *Birzhevye Vedomosti*, November 26, 1863.

90. *SPS* za 1864, 506 (no. 182, August 18, 1864).

91. *Birzhevye Vedomosti*, November 30, 1863.

92. Editorial, *Sankt-Peterburgskie Vedomosti*, September 18, 1865. no. 243.

93. "Svoboda bankov i zolotaia valiuta," *Birzhevye Vedomosti*. 1865, no.174.

94. Editorial, *Severnaia Pochta*, September 16, 1865, no.199.

95. Editorial, *Sankt-Peterburgskie Vedomosti*, September 18, 1865.

96. *SPS* za 1865, 597 (no. 208, September 23, 1865).

97. "Svoboda bankov i zolotaia valiuta," *Birzhevye Vedomosti*, 1865, no.174.

98. "Vysochaishee postanovlenie on 8 noiabria 1865 goda o metallicheskoi monete kak edistvenno zakonno deistvitelnoi v Finlandii," in *Materialy po voprosu o denezhnom obrashchenii v Velikom Kniazhestve Finlandskom* (St. Petersburg: Gos tipografiia, 1900), 26–27.

99. Ob ob'iavlenii serebrianoi monety edinstvennym platezhnym sredstvom v Finlandii. Committee of Finance, 19 dekabria 1864, RGIA, f.563, op.1, d.14, 12–140b.

100. Ob ob'iavlenii serebrianoi monety edinstvennym platezhnym sredstvom v Finlandii. Committee of Finance, 19 dekabria 1864, RGIA, f.563, op.1, d.14, 39 ob.

101. Vysochaishee postanovlenie ot 9 dekabria 1867 goda kasatel'no upravleniia i zavedyvaniia Finliandskim bankom. RGIA f.563, op.1, d.14, 34–39. For a detailed treatment of the reform in Finland, see Antti Kuusterä and Juha Tarkka, *Bank of Finland, 200 Years. I. Imperial Cashier to Central Bank* (Suomen Pankki—Bank of Finland and Otava Publishing, 2011), 226–249.

102. Khronika, Vnutrennee obozrenie. *Vestnik Evropy* 2 (March 1874): 337, 357.

103. K. A. Skal'kovskii, *Nashi gosudarstvennye i obshchestvennye deiateli* (St. Petersburg, 1891), 531.

104. *SPS* za 1867, 314–319 (no.134, June 19, 1867). There were rumors, though, that Katkov had learned about the emissions from one of the ministry's officials, Alexander Korsak, who subsequently lost his position. K. A. Skalkovskii, *Vospominania molodosti (po moriu zhiteiskomu)* (St. Petersburg, 1906), 285.

105. *SPS* za 1869, 58–60 (no. 19, January 23, 1869), See also *SPS* za 1867, 698 (no. 254, November 18, 1867; no. 268, December 7, 1867).

106. Thomas C. Owen, "The Moscow Merchants and the Public Press," 1858–1868," *Jahrbücher für Geschichte Osteuropas*, vol. 23 (1975), h.1, 26–38.

107. V. A. Kokorev, *Ekonomicheskie provaly po vospomianiia s 1837 goda* (Moskva, 2002), 73, 127. Kokorev was writing about the economic "failure" that began in 1856 with the arrival of "They."

108. Kokorev, *Ekonomicheskie provaly*, 77.

109. "Even if every state credit bill were backed up by a corresponding amount of coins in the [Peter and Paul] fortress's storage, we would still be feeling the shortage of the means of payment, because, due to the overbalance of import over export,

we would still have to pay interests for foreign loans in gold and silver. . . . All these huge sums of money paid to foreigners are lost for us forever." "Obozrenie promyshlennosti i torgovli," *Vestnik Promyshlennosti*, April, 1861. Similar point: Moskovskii kupets, "Torgovyi krizis i nuzhdy nashego denezhnogo rynka," *Vestnik Promyshlennosti*, June, 1861, 310–311

110. I. Shill, *O kreditnykh biletakh* (St. Petersburg: Tipografia Bezobrazova, 1866), 26.

111. A. Shipov, *O sredstvakh k ustraneniiu nashikh ekonomicheskikh i finansovyckh zatrudnenii* (St. Petersburg, 1866). 23-25.

112. I. Shil, "O kreditnykh biletakh," *Torgovyi sbornik*, April 30 1866, no. 18, 147.

113. M. Stepanov, *Vnutrennii gosudarstvennyi kredit* (St. Petersburg, 1866), 6, 43

114. V. A. Panaev, "Dengi–tovar" [1861], in *Finansovye i ekonomicheskie voprosy* (St. Petersburg, 1878), 113.

115. M. P. Pogodin, "K N.N." [December 1856], *Utro. Literaturnyi i politicheskii sbornik* (Moskva, 1866).

116. Pogodin, "Zapiska dlia razvlechenia A. M. v doroge" [September 1861], *Utro. Literaturnyi i politicheskii sbornik* (Moskva, 1866), 282.

117. Pogodin, "K M.M." [April 1862], *Utro. Literaturnyi i politicheskii sbornik* (Moskva, 1866), 287–288.

118. Pogodin, "Pismo k Kobdenu," *Utro. Literaturnyi i politicheskii sbornik* (Moskva, 1866), 288–289.

119. N. P., "Novoe osnovanie denezhnoi sistemy," *Torgovyi Sbornik*, no. 34, August 21, 1865. The author suggested linking one ruble to 1/100,000 of one railroad's *versta*; one *versta* equals approximately 0.7 miles.

120. Thomas C. Owen, *Dilemmas of Russian Capitalism: Fedor Chizhov and Corporate Enterprise in the Railroad Age* (Cambridge, MA: Harvard University Press, 2005), 95, 98.

121. GARF, f.109, op.154, 3 eksp, 1869, d.92, ll.100–101.

122. GARF, f.95, op.1, d.329.

123. Raport adjutanta namestnika v Tsarstve Polskom Goldmana, GARF, f.109,op.40,1865, d.23, ch.21, l.38–380b.

124. GARF, f.109, op.154, 3 eksp, 1869, d.92; f.109, op.152, 3 eksp, 1867, d.138; f.109, op.40, 1865, d.23, ch.21, 16–16 ob; O fabrike falshivykh kreditnykh biletov okrytoi v oktiabre 1867 g v derevne Sent-Andresse bliz Gavra. f.95, op.1, d. 417, 3-60b; f.95. op.1, d.329.

125. Agenturnye doneseniia, GARF, f.109, op.3a, d.2918, l.9; f.109, op.3a, d. 2920, l.19, 22–23.

126. RGIA, f.560, op.12, d. 476, ll.32–34.

127. GARF, f.109, op.42, 1 eksp, d.12, ch.12, l. 52, 78.

128. Zapiska nachalnika Sankt-Peterburgskoi sysknoi politsii, "Po delu o poddelyvateliakh i sbytchikakh falshivykh biletov kreditnykh i gos. Kaznacheistva," RGIA, 1282, op.2, d.70, l. 9.

129. Nachalnik Moskovskogo gubernskogo zhandarmskogo upravleniia, November 6, 1868. RGIA, 1282, op.2, d.70, l.52.
130. General-major Sem-ii, report.—RGIA, 1282, op.2, d.70, l. 61–62; GARF, f.109, op.223/85,d.33, l.169.
131. Zapiska nachalnika Sankt-Peterburgskoi sysknoi politsii, "Po delu o poddelyvateliakh i sbytchikakh falshivykh biletov kreditnykh i gos. Kaznacheistva," RGIA, 1282, op.2, d.70.–
132. Putilin's report: RGIA, f.560, op.33, d.299, ll.105–108; Reutern's report about Putilin's activity in Moscow and the arrests of other groups of counterfeiters, not related to Guslitsy: RGIA, f.583 op.4, d.276, ll. 9–10. For these operations, Putilin was awarded the order of Anna, 2nd degree. See also Putilin's fictionalized memoir: M. V. Shevliakov, "Na rozyske," Po rasskazam byvshego nachalnikia Sankt-Peterburgskoi sysknoi politsii I. D. Putilina, in Ivan Putilin, *Russkii Sherlock Holmes: Zapiski nachalnika Sankt-Peterburgskogo syska* (Moskva: Eksmo-Press, 2001), 334–337.
133. GARF, f.109, op.42, 1 eksp, d.12, ch.12, l. 98.
134. Officer Linev reported in January 1870 about counterfeiting in ten villages of the Bogorodskii district and one village of the Egorievskii district. False bills were distributed via taverns and small shops. RGIA, f.560, op.33, d.299, l.103.
135. Different numbers of the total sum of stolen blanks was provided: RGIA, f.583, op.4, d.276, ll.179, 205–206, and GARF, f.109, op.43, 1 eksp, 1868, d.15, ch.12. In 1868, the Expedition hired an officer to spy on the factory workers: RGIA, f.560, op.33, 294.
136. *Sudebnyi Vestnik*, 1868, n. 44–47; *Po povodu protsessa o pokhishchenii kreditnoi bumagi iz Ekspeditsii Zagotovleniia Gosudarstvennykh Bumag* (brochure) in GARF, f.109, op.43, 1 eksp, 1868, d.15; Kantseliariia po sekretnoi chasti Ministerstva finansov—Ministerstvo Vnutrennikh Del, January 30, 1866, RGIA, f.560, op.33, d.260, ll. 9–10.
137. Kopiia s otosheniia Kostromskogo gubernatora Rudzekevicha v Ministerstvo Vnutrennikh Del, March 30, 1864, RGIA, f.560, op.33, d.225, ll. 2–3.
138. Komissiia o merakh protiv delatelei i perevoditelei falshivykh kreditnykh biletov, RGIA, f.560, op.12, d.476, ll.14–18.
139. In 1872, the sensational arrest of Polish noblewoman Josephina Dobrowolska, who carried bundles of fake credit bills under her hoop-skirt, revealed the network of the production and transfer of counterfeit money from Europe run by princess Maria Ogińska. "O zaderzhanii na st. Verzhbolovo dvorianki Josefiny Dobrovolskoi s falshivymi kreditnymi biletami, i o proizvodstve sledstviia," RGIA, f.560, op.33, d.339; "Zapiska o vvoze v Rossiiu falshivykh kreditnykh biletov polskimi zhenshchinami," August 1, 1872, GARF, f.678, op.1, d.641.
140. "Po otnosheniiu Varshavsogo gen-gubernatora i prokurora Varshavskoi sudebnoi palaty o priniatii mer k povsemestmomu presledovaniiu poddelyvatelei i perevoditelei russkikh gosudarstvennykh bumag za granitsei," RGIA, f.560, op.33,

d.403; "Po perepiske s Kalishskim gubernatorom," RGIA, f.560, op.33, d.423. see also: RGIA, f.560, op.33., d. 424, d. 425.

141. Komissiia o merakh protiv delatelei i perevoditelei falshivykh kreditnykh biletov, RGIA, f.560, op.12, d.476, ll.29-290b, 44 ob.

142. O vospreshchenii chastnym litsam i obshchestvam vypuska denezhnykh znakov, RGIA, f.1149, op,7, 1868, d.57, l.49.

143. O vospreshchenii chastnym litsam i obshchestvam vypuska denezhnykh znakov, RGIA, f.1149, op,7, 1868, d.57, l.70.

144. O vospreshchenii chastnym litsam i obshchestvam vypuska denezhnykh znakov, RGIA, f.1405, op.65, d.3521, 6-7, 30 ob.

145. O vospreshchenii chastnym litsam i obshchestvam vypuska denezhnykh znakov, RGIA, f.1149, op.7, 1868, d.57, l. 32.

146. O vospreshchenii chastnym litsam i obshchestvam vypuska denezhnykh znakov, RGIA, f.1405, op.65, d.3521, 6-7, l.25; F.1149, op.7, 1868, d.57, ll.99,100.

147. Historians indicate that there were several "emissions" of Maltsov's money: in 1862–54, 1866, 1867–69, 1870–77, and 1878–82. L. I. Zakharova, Yu.T. Trifankov, V. V. Dziuban, and N. G. Fedkin, *S.I. Mal'tsov: Sotsialnaia initsiativa v promyshlennom regione vo vtoroi polovine XIX veka* (Briansk: BGTU, 2014), 113; A. A. Bauer, "Mal'tsovskie denezhnye surrogaty, " in *S .I. Mal'tsov i istoriia razvitiia maltsovskogo promyshlennogo raoina* (Briansk: BGTU, 1998), 62–68.

148. A. A. Makushev, *Predprinimatelskaia deiatelnost' Maltsovykh vo vtoroi polovine XVII–nachale XX veka: industrial'noe nasledie* (Saransk: Mordovskoe knizhnoe izd-vo, 2006).

149. Ob uchrezhdenii Komissii dlia rassledovanii poddelki i rasprostraneniia falshivykh kreditnykh biletov, 1867, RGIA, f. 1282, op.2, d.70, l.2–3.

CHAPTER 5

1. V. A. Shishanov, ""Kostry iz assignatsii" ili pervye meropriiatiia Pavla I v otnoshenii bumazhnykh deneg," in *Dengi v rossiiskoi istorii. Sbornik materialov*, edited by Andrei Bogdanov (St. Petersburg: Goznak, 2019), 152.

2. RGIA, f.583, op.4, d. 293, l. 393.

3. Ob izmenenii sposoba unichtozheniia braka kreditnykh biletov i drugikh bumag, *TsGIA SPb*, f.1458, op.2, d. 627.

4. O sposobe pogasheniia kreditnykh biletov, RGIA, 587, op.33, d.353, 18, 22–27. The construction of a new building for chemical reprocessing of old or defective credit bills (similar to the technology used by the Bank of France) was approved in 1914 but the building was never completed. Ob iz'atii vetkhikh kreditnykh biletov, RGIA, f.587, op.43, d.808.

5. M. V. Khodiakov, "Iz'atie iz denezhnogo obrashcheniia i unichtozhenie kreditnykh biletov v Sankt-Peterburge v nachale XX veka," *Trudy Istoricheskogo fakulteta Sankt-Peterburgskogo universiteta* (St. Petersburg, 2010), 295–305.

6. On crying babushkas: V. A. Lebedev, *Bumazhnye den'gi* (St. Petersburg, 1889), 62.

7. "Zapiska M. Kh. Reuterna, predstavlennaia E.I.V. v Livadii 3-go oktiabria 1876 g," in *M. Kh. Reutern*, edited by A. N. Kulomzin and V .G. Reutern-Nolkeln, 166 (St. Petersburg, 1910).

8. "Prebyvanie M.Kh. Reuterna v Livadii v Oktiabre 1876 g," in *M.Kh. Reutern*, edited by A. N. Kulomzin and V. G. Reutern-Nolkeln, 159 (St. Petersburg, 1910).

9. "O vzimanii tamozhennykh poshlin zolotom," RGIA, f.564, op.2, d.232, l.2.

10. RGIA, f.563, op.2, d.233, l.50b, April 1877.

11. Sevket Pamuk, *A Monetary History of the Ottoman Empire* (New York: Cambridge University Press, 2000), 214-215; Roderic H. Davison, "The First Ottoman Experiment with Paper Money," in *Essays in Ottoman and Turkish History, 1774– 1923* (Austin: University of Texas Press, 1990), 60–72. For an interesting discussion on the bankruptcy of the Ottoman state and the relatively wealthy status of its population, see "Zametka po povodu nastoiashchei voiny," *Slovo*, January 1878, 84. The Russian press extensively discussed Ottoman financial policy and its bankruptcy. See, for instance, "Finansovyi krizis v Turtsii," in *Gertsogovinskoe vosstanie i vostochnyi vopros* (St. Petersburg, 1876), 59–63; "Politicheskaia i obshchestvennaia khronika," *Delo*, no.1, 1876, 104–130; "Inostrannoe obozrenie. Turetskie finansy," *Vestnik Evropy*, September, 1875, 388–392; A. Felkner, *Slavianskaia bor'ba. Istoricheskii ocherk vosstaniia balkanskikh slavian* (St. Petersburg, 1877), 53–61.

12. Anatole Leroy-Beaulieu, "L'empire des tsars et les russes: III. Les finances. II. Les dépenses, la dette et le papier-monnaie," *Revue de Deux Mondes*, January 1877, 153.

13. RGIA, f.563, op.2, d.233, l.60b. See also the Committee of Finance's pessimistic observation on the financial perspectives of war. RGIA, f.563, op.2, d.233, l.15 ob.

14. *M.Kh. Reutern*, edited by A. N. Kulomzin and V. G. Reutern-Nolkeln, 176.

15. *Gosudarstvennyi Bank. Kratkii ocherk deiatelnosti za 1860-1910 g.* St. Petersburg, 1910. 138-139. The Committee of Finance had slightly different numbers: 229 million rubles in gold in 1875 (compared to 59 million in 1867), which corresponded to 797 million credit rubles in circulation in 1875 (compared to 652 million in 1867) . RGIA, f.563, op.2, d.229, l.60b. The inconsistency in numbers could result from different times and methods of calculation (for instance, including or not including gold-based securities in the gold reserve, counting or not short-term obligations in the mass of "paper rubles.")

16. I. I. Kaufman, Zolotoi rubl' v Rossii, TsGIA SPB, f.2098, op.1, d.58, 45.

17. A. E. Denisov, "Gosudarstvennye bumazhnye denezhnye znaki 1840–1896," 108– 109, in *Bumazhnue denezhnye znaki Rossii, 1769–1917* (Moskva: Numizmaticheskaia literatura, 2003).

18. According to the new law, custom duties could be collected in various Russian "gold" securities (such as the bonds of Russian foreign loans and the bonds issued by the Commission of the State Debt), currencies of foreign countries that had already adopted the gold standard, receipts issued by the Mint to the producers, and, of course, gold. The payers could also receive "custom duties certificates" in

exchange for any "gold" securities or currencies, but only at the State Bank office in St. Petersburg. And only in this central office could merchants submit foreign bills of exchange for an examination of a special committee (similar to the Discount Committee) that then accepted (or rejected) them for custom certificates. In 1877, custom duties brought in 15.9 million rubles in gold. RGIA, f.583, op.4, d.287, 488.

19. D. A. Obolenskii, *Zapiski kniazia Dmitriia Aleksandrovicha Obolenskogo, 1855–1879* (St. Petersburg: Nestor-Istoriia, 2005), 407.

20. See the polemics around Golos's article: "Vnutrennee obozrenie. 1 Avgusta 1877," *Vestnik Evropy*, 741.

21. A. N. Engelgard, *Iz derevni. 12 pisem, 1872–1887* (St. Petersburg: Nauka, 1999), 218. (Pis'mo shestoe. First publication—*Otechestvennye Zapiski,* 1878, no.3)

22. I. Kaufman, *Statistika gosudarstvennykh finansov Rossii v 1862–84 godakh. Statisticheskii vremennik Rossiiskoi Imperii* (St. Petersburg, 1886), 17.

23. According to the State Bank's report quoted in SPS za 1878, 486. (no.284, November 6, 1878).

24. For a more detailed account of the financial outcomes of war, see V. L. Stepanov, "Tsena pobedy: Russko-Turetskaia voina i ekonomika Rossii," *Rossiiskaia Istoriia* 6 (2015): 99–119. A. I. Bukovetskii, "Svobodnaia nalichnost' i zolotoi zapas," *Monopolii i inostrannyi capital v Rossii* (Leningrad: Izd-vo AN SSSR, 1962), 366.

25. "Exchange," *Encyclopedia Britannica*, vol. 8 (Chicago, 1895), 794.

26. "Exchange," *Encyclopedia Britannica*, vol. 8 (Chicago, 1895), 794..

27. *Golos*, no. 255, 1879; Kievlianin no.127, 1879.

28. SPS za 1878, 28 (no.12 B, January 12, 1878); SPS za 1878, 535 (no. 305, November 29, 1878).

29. SPS za 1878, 518-20, 535, 537 (November 18, 1878, no. 2 95; November 29, 1878, no. 305).

30. SPS za 1878 (November 29, 1878, no. 305), 537.

31. He claimed the treasury did not make use of this money. SPS za 1880, 51–52 (January 25, 1880, no. 25)

32. Kaime—temporary state notes issued in 1876 and retired in 1880. SPS za 1879, 578 (November 9, 1879, no. 287).

33. SPS za 1879, 29, (January 15, 1879, no.1 3).

34. The Ottoman Public Debt Administration (ODPA) included the representatives of France, Germany, Austria, Italy, Britain, and Holland. On the role of this institution in the peripheralization of the Ottoman economy, see Murat Birdal, *The Political Economy of Ottoman Public Debt: Insolvency and European Financial Control in the Late Nineteenth Century* (London: I. B. Tauris, 2010); Christopher Clay, *Gold for the Sultan: Western Bankers and Ottoman Finance 1856-1881: A Contribution to Ottoman and to International Financial History* (London: I. B. Tauris, 2000).

35. B. M. [P. A. Valuev,] *Ekonomicheskie i finansovye zametki* (St. Petersburg, 1881) (originally published in *Otgoloski*, 1880), 169–170.

36. B. M. [P. A. Valuev], *Ekonomicheskie i finansovye zametki*, 173.

37. Kaufman, "Bumazhno-denezhnye," 358. N. Ya. Danilevskii, "Neskolko myslei po povodu nizkogo kursa nashikh bumazhnykh deneg i nekotorykh drugikh ekonomicheskikh iavlenii i voprosov," in *O nizkom kurse nashikh deneg* (St. Petersburg, 1885), 1. Originally published in *Russkii Vestnik*, 1882, no. 8.

38. "Ob uplate dolga Gosudarstvennogo Kaznacheistva Gosudarstvennomu Banku," RGIA, f.563, op.2, d.244. Witte asserted that he had seen the draft of the decree handwritten by Nikolai Bunge, Abaza's deputy minister. "Protokoly zasedanii Soedinennykh Departamentov Gosudarstvennoi Ekonomii, Zakonov i Grazhdanskikh i Dukhovnykh Del po delu ob ispravlenii denezhnogo obrashcheniia," RGIA, f.1152, op.12, 1897, d.78a, ll.778–779.

39. SPS za 1881, 21 (January 9, 1881, no.10). Katkov's newspaper accused the ministry of faking the reform that had put the burden of payment on the Russian people: the treasury's debt to the State Bank required additional domestic loans because the treasury did not have money for repayment. On the loan for the payment of the treasury's debt, see Bunge's memo: "Ob uplate dolga Gosudarstvennogo Kaznacheistva Gosudarstvennomu Banku," RGIA, f.563, op.2, d.244, L.90b.

40. *PSZ* III, vol.1, January 1, 1881, no.61730.

41. P.A. Valuev, *Dnevnik, 1877-1884,* (Petrograd, 1919), 136. A record was made after the meeting of the Committee of ministers that approved the decree.

42. S predstavleniem novykh risunkov gosudarstvennykh kreditnykh biletov 1,3,5,10 i 100 rub dostoinstva, RGIA, f.583, op.4, d. 292, ll.41–42.

43. Katkov explained the ruble's fall as a reaction to Jewish pogroms instigated by revolutionaries. SPS za 1881, 235 (May 15 1881, no. 134).

44. His first boss was Samuel Greig, replaced by Abaza in October 1880. On Bunge's career trajectory, see V. L. Stepanov, *N.Kh. Bunge: Sud'ba reformatora* (Moskva: ROSSPEN, 1998), 110–127.

45. SPS za 1881, 311 (June 30, 1881, no.180), Katkov's newspaper, reported the rumor that the reform of the State Bank, along with the withdrawal of 380 million rubles and the restoration of convertibility to gold with a help of a foreign loan, had already been done. SPS za 1880, 384 (July 14, 1880, no. 194); SPS za 1880, 477 (September 1880, no.253), In fact, Bunge thought that the state of the Russian economy would not allow such a reform. N. Kh. Bunge, "Zametka o nastoiashchem polozhenii nashei denezhnoi sistemy i sredstvakh k ee uluchsheniiu," *Sbornik gosudarstvennykh znanii* 8 (1880): 87–127. Bunge wrote about the reform of the State Bank in his brochure published in 1878, just two years before his appointment, but in 1880 and 1881 he refrained from advancing this idea. See N. Kh. Bunge, *O vosstanovlenii postoiannoi denezhnoi edinitsy v Rossii* (Kyiv, 1878), 60–61. x

46. Five days after accessing the throne, the tsar asked the minister of finance, Abaza, to "simplify" his memos. E. A. Peretz, *Dnevnik* (Moskva: Gos.izd-vo, 1927), 29–30.

47. V. P. Meshcherskii, *Pis'ma k imperatoru Aleksandru III, 1881–1894* (Moskva: NLO, 2018), 302, April 17, 1886. Meshcherskii often embellished his letters with anecdotal conversations with real or imagined people: for example, when a certain

tea trader, Kuznetsov, was asked what needed to be done to improve economic conditions, he allegedly said, "To raise agriculture, to improve the conditions of noble landowning, to support factories in Russia . . . and not to be stingy with the issuance of credit rubles. This is our, domestic, state cause, and not a foreign one." Meshcherskii, *Pisma*, 88, November 25, 1884.

48. Meshcherskii, *Pis'ma*, 57, 61, 142, April 23,1885.

49. Meshcherskii, *Pisma*, 234–235, 244, 363.

50. Meshcherskii, *Pis'ma*, 303, April 17, 1886.

51. B. V. Ananich and R. Sh. Ganelin, "I.A. Vyshnegradskii i S.Yu. Witte— korrespondenty *Moscovskikh vedomostei,*" *Problemy obschestvennoi mysli i ehkonomicheskaya politika Rossii XIX–XX vekov: Sbornik statei* (Leningrad: Nauka, 1972), S. 13–20, 14.

52. George E. Snow and N. Kh. Bunge, "The Years 1881–1894 in Russia: A Memorandum Found in the Papers of N. Kh. Bunge. A Translation and Commentary," *Transactions of the American Philosophical Society*, New Series 71, no. 6 (1981): 47.

53. Ananich and Ganelin, "I.A. Vyshnegradskii i S.Yu," 12. In 1882, a rumor spread that he had been offered a position on the State Council and rejected it; to complete the legislative chamber's humiliation, Katkov repudiated it as flattering but fake news.

54. Komitet finansov, "O somneniiakh, vozbuzhdaiushchikhsia po povodu valiuty nekotorykh nashikh zaimov," *Izvlechenie iz podlinnykh del Komiteta finansov* (St. Petersburg, 1895), RGIA, Library, pechatnaia zapiska no. 1155, 9.

55. Po voprosu o dozvolenii sovershat' sdelki na zoloto, RGIA, f.563, op.2, d.235.

56. RGIA, f.563, op.2, d.250, ll.15–150b. See Bunge's proposal, the Committee of Finance's minutes, and Nebolsin's memo in *Materialy po denezhnoi reforme 1895–1897*. Pod red. A. I. Bukovetskogo. Vyp.1 (Petrograd: In-t Ekonomicheskikh Issledovani,i 1922), 49–88. On the discussion of this measure and the opposition to it: A. A. Polovtsov, *Dnevnik gosudarstvennogo sekretaria*, v.1 (Moskva: Nauka, 1966), 70; [Staryi professor], *Zamechatel'naia epokha v istorii russkikh finansov* (St. Petersburg, 1895), 16.

57. Delo o prodazhe zolota v Arkhangelskoi, Odesskoi, Onezhskoi, Rostovskoi i Khar'kovskoi kontorakh, RGIA, f.588, op.3, d.545, l. 1–2.

58. See similar requests from the Rostov branch: RGIA, f.588, op.3, d.545, l. 513–515, 575. Speculators and commissioners charged high fees for delivering gold coins and "gold" securities, while the offices of the State Bank added only 1–2 kopecks extra to the rate of "half-imperials" quoted by the St. Petersburg stock exchange (until 1885, a half-imperial gold coin bore an inscription "5 Rubles" while its official legal value was 5 rubles 15 kopecks, and the stock exchange value fluctuated around 8 rubles 20 kopecks).

59. See several documents in the collection of the St. Petersburg branch of the State Bank: RGIA, f.588, op.3. In 1887 the Ministry of Finance was ordered to supply custom offices with gold. Importers were invited to buy gold for credit rubles, but then they had to pay custom duties on the same gold coins. Therefore, the "custom

gold" stayed in local custom offices as an asset for exchanges. "Novye meropriiatiia," *Ekonomicheskii zhurnal*, 1887, 11–12, 133–134

60. "O predstavlenii slepkov portretov Ego Imperatorskogo Velichestva gravirovannykh medalierami Alekseevym, Grilikhesom, Shteimanov i dr dlia rublei novogo obraztsa," September 23, 1885. In Georgii Mikhailovich, vel kn. *Russkie monety 1881–1890* (St. Petersburg, 1891), 42.

61. Georgii Mikhailovich, vel kn. *Russkie monety 1881–1890*, vol. 2.

62. Ministerstvo finansov, Proekt Monetnogo ustava, September 20, 1885, in Georgii Mikhailovich, vel kn. *Russkie monety 1881–1890*, vol. 2., 34.

63. P.P. Migulin, *Reforma denezhnogo obrashcheniia v Rossii i promyshlennyi krizis, 1893-1902* (Kharkiv, 1902) 6, 9.

64. Several times Bunge suggested suspending further payments of the treasury's debt to the State Bank. In total, between 1881 and 1885, the treasury paid the Bank 250 million rubles: 150 million rubles in cash and 100 million in state securities. On the payments of treasury's debts, see RGIA, f.563, op.2, d. 256; f.563, op.2, d.259, f.563, op.2, d.265.

65. Valuev, *Dnevnik, 1877–1884*, 216.

66. On the negative effect of not fulfilling the promises, see I .I. Kaufman, *Serebrianyi rubl' ot ego vozniknoveniia do kontsa XIX veka* (St. Petersburg, 1910), 227.

67. Kaufman, "Bumazhno-denezhnye proekty i ekstraordinarnye finansy," *Sbornik gosudarstvennykh znanii*, t.7 (St. Petersburg, 1879), 347–348. See Katkov's response to Kaufman's essay: SPS za 1879, 384 (July 28, 1879, no. 193).

68. N. Kh. Bunge, *Zametka o nastoiashchem polozhenii nashei denezhnoi sistemy i sredstvakh k ee uluchsheniiu* (St. Petersburg, 1880),, 90–91.

69. L. V. Khodskii, *Pozemel'nyi kredit v Rossii i otnoshenie ego k krestianskomu zemlevladeniiu* (Moskva, 1882), 73.

70. N. Eroshsevskii, *K voprosu o pozemel'nom kredite* (Odessa, 1881), 21; N. A. Proskuriakova, *Zemel'nye banki Rossiiskioi Imperii* (Moskva: ROSSPEN, 2002), 57.

71. P. A. Shtorkh, *O nyneshnem sostoianii pozemel'nogo kredita v Rossii. Sistema zakladnykh listo* (St. Petersburg, 1867).

72. *Ob osnovnom pozemel'nom kredite* (St. Petersburg, 1865) (Originally— *Aktsioner*, 1860, no.15.); similar plan—I. Shill', *Predpolozheniia ob uchrezhdenii russkogo gosudarstvennogo ili zemskogo zaemnogo banka* (St. Petersburg, 1861), *Prenia v Moskovskom gubernskom zemskom sobranii po voprosu o pozemel'nykh bankakh* (Moskva, 1866), "Obzor voprosov podvergavshikhsia rassmotreniu v Moskovskom ocherednom gubernskom zemskov sobranii," *Sovremennaia letopis'* no. 5 (1868): 14.

73. To assist land banks in procuring credit, the government approved the creation of a Russian Central Land Bank solely for purchasing the "paper" bonds of local land banks and issuing "gold" bonds on its behalf under the government's guarante. The fear of the ruble's fall and a threat of being enslaved by foreign capitalists were often seen as the main obstacles. See, for instance, count A. P. Shuvalov's objection

to the idea of "metallic" bonds: A. P. Shuvalov, *Metallicheskii rubl' i pozemel'nye banki* (St. Petersburg, 1866).

74. P. M-ev, *Zolotoi bank i ego sud'ba. Episod iz istorii nashego pozemel'nogo kredita* (St. Petersburg, 1890).

75. *Doklad soedinennogo prisutstviia pravleniia i finansovo-organizatsionnoi komissii obshchemu sobraniiu chlenov Obshchestva Vzaimnogo Pozelemnogo Kredita 26 ianvaria 1886 goda O merakh k oblegcheniiu polozheniia zaemshchikov Obshchestva po metallichesskim ikh zaimam* [1886].

76. Selskii zhitel', "K predstoiashchemu obshchemu sobraniiu Obshchestva Vzaimnogo Pozemel'nogo Kredita," *Moskovskie Vedomosti*, February 6, 1888.

77. V. Okhotnikov, *Finansovye Besedy (Grazhdanin, 1885–1886)* (St. Petersburg, 1887), 116–117. Originally *Grazhdanin*, February 16, 1886.

78. Okhotnikov, *Finansovye Besedy*.

79. In a fictional letter allegedly addressed to the editor of *The Citizen* that Meshcherskii shared with the tsar, a certain "smart Russian man" wrote about establishing a State Mortgage Bank with the right to issue interest-bearing bills of high denominations (100, 1,000, and 10,000 rubles) and to offer loans on the security of land property. These state notes "backed up by real estate" were meant ultimately to replace the 100-rubles state credit bills in the total amount of "around 200 million rubles" (Meshcherskii, *Pis'ma*, 121–124, December 27, 1884). The idea of inventing an alternative to the gold standard of the West appeared in various forms. See, for instance, V. A. Belinskii, *Chto takoe bumazhnye den'gi i myslim li finansovyi krizis v Rossii* (Kharkiv, 1877); [Anonymous], *Proekt pozemel'nogo imushchestvennogo banka* (b.m., b.g.).

80. Ministerstvo finansov, Ob uchrezhdenii Gosudarstvennogo Zemel'nogo Banka, February 22, 1885, 98, RGIA, f.1152, op.10, 1885, d.281.

81. I. V. Andriyashev, *K voprosu o gosudarstvenom pozemel'nom kredite v Rossii (Po povodu Dvorianskogo banka)* (Kiev, 1885),, 7.

82. D. I. Richter, *Gosudarstvennye zemel'nye banki v Rossii i ikh dal'neishaia sudba* (Petrograd, 1917), 4.

83. RGIA, f.626, op.1, d.110, Perepiska Pravlenia Banka s Obshchestvom vzaimnogo pozelemnogo kredita i russkimi i inostrannymi bankami i bankirskimi domami ob uchastii ikh v konversii 5% zakladnykh listov. 1887.

84. Stepanov, *N. Kh. Bunge*, 188–191.

85. A. I. Chuprov, "Russkaia ekonomicheskaia zhizn' v 1886 godu," *Iuridicheskii Vestnik* 24 (1887): 310. Similar assertion was made by the French newspaper *Economiste*. Quoted in I. Kolesov, *Pochemu sem' let mirnogo vremeni ne prinesli nikakogo uluchsheniia v nashikh finansakh* (St. Petersburg, 1887), 116. Kolesov blamed the State Land Bank for Nobility for draining the State Bank's resources and thereby causing it to issue extra credit rubles in 1888. I. Kolesov, "Neudavshaiasia kreditnaia operatsiia," *Ekonomicheskii zhurnal* 10 (1888): 59. N. Kh. Vessel' also pointed out the influence of the State Land Bank for Nobility's credit policy on the issuance

of credit rubles: N. Kh. Vessel', *Otchego Gosudarstvennyi Bank ne uprochil kreditnoi denezhnoi sistemy i kak ee uprochit?* (St. Peterbusrg, 1893), 11, 12.

86. A. V. Bugrov, "Gosudarstvennyi bank Rossiiiskoi imperii: iz istorii melioratsionnogo kredita," *Den'gi i Kredi* 1 (2014): 63–68.

87. "Nebyvalaia polemika," *Ekonomicheskii Zhurnal* 8 (1886).

88. Anan'ich and Ganelin, "I. A. Vyshnegradskii i S.Yu. Vitte"; Stepanov, *Bunge*, 227–240;

89. In a brochure authored by a deputy ober-procurator of the Holy Synod, N. P. Smirnov, instigated by an arch-conservative Synod procurator, Konstantin Pobedonostsev, and intended for a narrow circle of courtiers and the emperor himself, Bunge was unequivocally accused of assaulting autocracy. N. P. Smirnov, *Sovremennoe sostoianie nashikh finansov, prichiny upadka ikh i sredstva k uluchsheniiu nashego gosudarstvennogo khoziaistva* (St. Petersburg, 1885). (Pobedonostsev, however, denied his role in the appearance of Smirnov's brochure. Pobedonostsev—Alexander III, January 25, 1886.—*Pis'ma Pobedonostseva k Aleksandru III*, vol .2 [Moscow: Tsentrarkhiv, 1926], 96–99). Bunge's response: N. Kh. Bunge, *Zamechania ministra finansov na zapisku tainogo sovetnika Smirnova ozaglavlennuiu Sovremennoe sostoianie nashikh finansov, prichiny upadka ikh i sredstva k uluchsheniu nashego gosudarstvennogo khoziaistva* (St. Petersburg, 1886); for his rebuttal of constitutionalism, see p. 71,

90. *Vsepoddanneishii doklad ministra finansov po gosudarstvennoi rospisi dokhodov i raskhodov na 1886 g* (St. Petersburg, 1887), 15.

91. In 1887, the exchange fund was increased by 40 million gold rubles—"Predstavlenie ministra finansov d.t.s. Vyshnegradskogo ot 12 ianvaria 1888 g.," *Materialy po denezhnoi reforme 1895-97 gg.* (Petrograd: NKF, In-t Ekonomicheskikh Issledovanii, 1922), 94.

92. Izvlechenie iz Zhurnala Komiteta Finansov 28 iunia 1887 i.—RGIA, biblioteka. PZ n.1146.

93. Olga Crisp, "Russian Financial Policy and the Gold Standard at the End of the Nineteenth Century," *Economic History Review*, new series, 6, no. 2 (1953): 162–164. To compare: Bunge managed to increase the gold reserve by 125 million rubles. Kaufman, *Serebrianyi Rubl'*, 233.

94. B. C. Endelman, *Le monometallisme-or en Russie: histoire de la réforme monétaire et de la circulation fiduciaire russe depuis 1897: étude historique et économique* (Berne: Impr. A. Tanner, 1917), 106.

95. "Predstavlenie ministra finansov," 94–95.

96. *The Moscow Bulletins* rushed to fully exculpate Vyshnegradskii, who had been brought to the office by the late editor and owner of the *Moscow Bulletins*, by describing this measure as the previous minister's legacy. *Moskovskie Vedomosti*, February 7, 1888. See also *Birzhevye Vedomosti*, February 11, 1888; "Tretia popytka," *Novoe Vremia*, February 8, 1888.

97. Vyshnegradskii's memo to the tsar, February 12, 1888, RGIA, f.583, op.4, d.298, l. 11.

98. "Rubl'—171!" *Birzhevye Vedomosti*, February 9, 1888. (The title alluded to the rate of 100 rubles equal to 171 German marks, while the average rate for this year was about 220 marks).

99. N. A. Naidenov, *Vospomimaniia o vidennom, slyshannom i ispytannom* (Moskva: Izd.dom Tonchu, 2007), 166, 186, 188, 241.

100. Naidenov, *Vospomimaniia o vidennom*, 252.

101. Vladimir Bezobrazov, "Voprosy dnia. Nashi bumazhnye dengi," *Nabliudatel'* 3 (1888): 362.

102. [Ministerstvo Finansov. Osobennaia kantseliariia po kreditnoi chasti], *O vosstanovlenii obrashcheniia zvonkoi monety*. 1888 [b.g., b.m.] 103, 137. Similar argument—Ratkov-Rozhnov: "simple folk do not know about the rate" [Ministerstvo Finansov], *O vosstanovlenii*, 84.

103. [Ministerstvo Finansov], *O vosstanovlenii obrashcheniia zvonkoi monety*, 152. Similar statement—Ratkov-Rozhnov, [Ministerstvo Finansov], *O vosstanovlenii obrashcheniia zvonkoi monety*, 115, 153.

104. [Ministerstvo Finansov], *O vosstanovlenii obrashcheniia zvonkoi monety*, 122. On Wogau and Co, see Yu. A. Petrov, "Nemetskie predprinimateli v dorevoliutsionnoi Moskve: torgovyi dom "Vogau i Ko," *Ekonomicheskaia Istoriia, Ezhegodnik 2000* (Moskva: ROSSPEN, 2001).

105. [Ministerstvo Finansov], *O vosstanovlenii obrashcheniia zvonkoi monety*, 97.

106. [Ministerstvo Finansov], *O vosstanovlenii obrashcheniia zvonkoi monety*, 137. Similar argument—I. N. Shcherbakov, *O vosstanovlenii obrashcheniia zvonkoi monety*, 103.

107. V. P. Kardashev, "Fondovye birzhi v Rossii," *Bankovaia Entsiklopediia. T.2. Birzha. Istoriia i sovremennaia organizatsiia fondovykh birzh* (St. Petersburg, 1916), 191.

108. "O sposobe vychisleniia srednego kursa," in F. F. Kolaiko, *Spravochnaia kniga S.-Peterburgskogo birzhevogo kupechestva* (St. Petersburg, 1889), 104.

109. V. Sudeikin, *Birzha i birzhevye operatsii* (St. Petersburg, 1892), 20.

110. Sudeikin, *Birzha i birzhevye operatsii*, 21.

111. *Kredit i banki v Rossii do nachala XX veka. Sankt-Peterburg i Moskva*, (St.Petersburg: Izd-vo S.-Peterburgskogo universiteta, 2005), 273.

112. *Kredit i banki v Rossii*, 348.

113. P. V. Lizunov, *Sankt-Peterburgskaia birzha i rossiiskii rynok tsennykh bumag* (St. Petersburg: Blitz, 2004), 240.

114. On regional, national, and confessional stratification of Russia's commercial elite, see Alfred Rieber, *Merchants and Entrepreneurs in Imperial Russia* (Chapel Hill: University of North Carolina Press, 1982)

115. *Kredit i banki v Rossii*, 339.

116. V. I. Kovalevskii, "Vospominaniia," *Russkoe proshloe* 2 (1991): 32.

117. [Ministerstvo Finansov], *O vosstanovlenii obrashcheniia zvonkoi monety*, 135.

118. [Ministerstvo Finansov], *O vosstanovlenii obrashcheniia zvonkoi monety*, 111, 144.

119. [Ministerstvo Finansov], *O vosstanovlenii obrashcheniia zvonkoi monety*, 145.

120. [Ministerstvo Finansov], *O vosstanovlenii obrashcheniia zvonkoi monety*, 144.

121. [Ministerstvo Finansov], *O vosstanovlenii obrashcheniia zvonkoi monety*, 108.

122. [Ministerstvo Finansov], *O vosstanovlenii obrashcheniia zvonkoi monety*, 143.

123. Jeffrey Frieden, *Currency Politics. The Political Economy of Exchange Rate Policy* (Princeton: Princeton University Press, 2015), 9. Marc Flandreau cautions against the simplistic classification of the pro- and anti-gold camps. He has observed that in France during the gold-bimetallism debate of the 1860s–1870s, the positions did not always coincide with the agrarian versus business and bankers communities. In fact, French bankers spoke in favor of bimetallism. Marc Flandreau, "The French Crime 1873: An Essay on the Emergence of the International Gold Standard, 1870–1880," *Journal of Economic History* 56, no. 4 (December 1996): 877.

124. L. E. Shepelev, Introduction to "21 dekabria 1886." Zapiska I. A. Vyshnegradskogo Aleksandru III, "Ob izmenenii finansovogo upravlenia," in *Sud'by Rossii. Doklady i zapiski gosudarstvennykh deiatelei imperatoram o problemakh ekonomicheskogo razvitiia strany* (St. Petersburg: Liki Rossii, 1999), 275.

125. P. Kh. Shvanebach, *Denezhnoe preobrazovanie i narodnoe khoziaistvo* (St. Petersburg, 1901), 4.

126. B. C. Endelman, *Le Monometallisme-Or en Russie: Histoire de la Reforme Monetaire et de la Circulation Fiduciaire Russe Depuis 1897: Etude Historique et Economique* (Berne: Impr. A. Tanner, 1917), 106–107

127. See numbers in P.Kh. Shvanebakh, *Denezhnoe preobrazovanie i narodnoe khoziaistvo* (St. Petersburg, 1901), 23.

128. For the analysis of the government's policy of building the stock of gold and numbers, see Endelman, *Le Monometallisme-Or en Russie*, 98–107

129. *Journal de St. Pétersbourg* 18, no. 30 (Octobre 1892): 1.

130. Eteocle Lorini, *La reforme monétaire de la Russie* (Paris: V. Giard & E. Briere, 1898), 78-79.

CHAPTER 6

1. Michael D. Bordo and Anna J. Schwartz, "The Operation of the Specie Standard: Evidence for Core and Peripheral Countries, 1880–1990," in *Currency Convertibility: The Gold Standard and Beyond*, edited by Jorge Braga de Macedo, Barry Eichengreen, and Jaime Reis (New York: Routledge, 1996), 14,16. Barry Eichengreen and Marc Flandreau, "The Geography of the Gold Standard," in *Currency Convertibility: The Gold Standard and Beyond*, edited by Jorge Braga de Macedo, Barry Eichengreen, and Jaime Reis (New York: Routledge, 1996), 113–143. On the gold standard peripheries, see Pablo Martin Aceña and Jaime Rei, eds., *Monetary Standards in the Periphery: Paper, Silver, and Gold, 1854–1933* (New York: St. Martin's Press, 2000); Anders Ögren and Lars Fredrik Øksendal, eds., *The Gold Standard Peripheries: Monetary Policy, Adjustment and Flexibility in a Global Setting* (New York: Palgrave Macmillan, 2012).

2. For the discussion on consistent patterns and contingencies, see Barry Eichengreen and Marc Flandreau, "The Geography of the Gold Standard," and Angela Redish, "Comment," in *Currency Convertibility: The Gold Standard and Beyond*, edited by Jorge Braga de Macedo, Barry Eichengreen, and Jaime Reis (New York: Routledge, 1996), 147.

3. K. P. Pobedonostsev–Alexander III, December 3, 1886, *Pis'ma Pobedonostseva k Aleksandru III* (Moscow: Tsentrarkhiv, 1926), vol.2, 123.

4. Lamanskii blamed the State Bank for withholding paper money that it had received in "debt" payments from the State Treasury—E. I. Lamanskii, *Sdelki na zolotuiu valiutu kak sredstvo k uluchsheniiu bumazhnogo denezhnogo obrashcheniia* (St. Petersburg, 1895).

5. George F. Kennan, *The Decline of Bismarck's European Order: Franco-Russian Relations, 1875–1890* (Princeton: Princeton University Press, 1980), 342–343.

6. N. Novoselskii, *Birzhevaia spekuliatsiia, naznachaiushchaia kurs nashego kreditnogo rublia* (St. Petersburg, 1885), 16.

7. Pavel Lizunov, "Birzhevaia spekuliatsiia na kurse kreditnogo rublia i mery protivodeistviia ei Ministerstva finansov," *Trudy Istoricheskogo fakulteta Sankt-Peterburgskogo universiteta* 5 (2011): 151.

8. Vlasii Sudeikin, *Birzha i birzhevye operatsii* (St.Petersburg, 1892), 86. IN REF

9. N. Novoselskii, *Birzhevaia spekuliatsiia, naznachaiushchaia kurs nashego kreditnogo rublia* (St. Petersburg, 1885), 6. in ref

10. Rostislav Sementkovskii, *Nash vekselnyi kurs (prichiny ego neustoichivosti)* (St. Petersburg, 1892), 11–12. Sementkovskii claimed that the influence of speculation on the rate had been very overestimated.

11. K.P. Pobedonostsev—Alexander III, February 11, 1888. *Pis'ma Pobedonostseva*, vol. 2, 173–174. Shubinsky later became famous as a right-wing politician.

12. This opinion was expressed even earlier: see *Birzha i spekuliatsiia* (St. Petersburg, 1878), 49.

13. Quoted from Lizunov, "Birzhevaia spekuliatsiia na kurse kreditnogo rublia i mery protivodeistviia ei Ministerstva finansov," 153–154.

14. S. M. Shekhter, *Novye tablitsy dlia opredeleniia veksel'nykh kursov na Angliiu, Frantsiiu, Belgiiu, Italiiu i Gollandiiu, a takzhe i kursov tamozhennykh kuponov* (Odessa, 1889), ii. The St. Petersburg Stock Exchange also rescheduled its regular meetings for the definition of the rate before the opening of the Berlin Stock Exchange. This gesture was supposed to demonstrate liberation from German influence.

15. See correspondence between the Ministries of Foreign Affairs and Finance and the agent (Veselitskii-Bozhidarovich), GARF, f.543, op.1, d.294 and F.543, op.1, d.294(a). The Ministry of Finance also subsidized another edition (*Allgemeiner Reichs-Correspondenz*).

16. In 1888, the Ministry of Finance bought 40 million credit rubles on the bourses of Berlin and St. Petersburg at the cost of 22 million rubles in gold. The operation was extremely risky, and Vyshnegradskii's correspondence with the State Bank's

director Alexei Tsimsen conveys the minister's anxiety. Selling too much gold for the purchase of paper rubles threatened to exhaust the gold reserve, yet suspending the operation could drop the rate of the ruble even further and lead to a tremendous increase in the amount of the government's payment for foreign obligations in gold, RGIA, f.587, op.56, d. 696, O pokupke na Peterburgskoi i Berlinskoi birzhakh kreditnykh biletov i tratt, 19–21, 55–56; S. K. Lebedev, *S.-Peterburgskii Mezhdunarodnyi Kommercheskii Bank vo vtoroi polovine XIX veka: evropeiskie i russkie sviazi* (St. Petersburg: ROSSPEN, 2003), 173. Two years later, the rate started to grow steeply. The ruble's fast growth was as detrimental as its sudden fall: since the domestic prices of grain could not adjust quickly to the falling prices of gold currency, the ruble's rise threatened to deprive Russian export-oriented agriculture of profit. The government was forced to sell gold to bring the paper ruble's rate from 0.75 gold rubles down to 0.62 gold rubles.

17. Shvanebakh, *Denezhnoe preobrazovanie i narodnoe khoziaistvo* (St. Petersburg, 1901), 50–51.

18. V. L. Stepanov, "I.A. Vyshnegradskii i Vitte. Partnery i konkurenty," *Rossiiskaia istoriia* 6 (2014): 39–60.

19. "Po voprosu o spekuliatsii s kreditnym rublem," January 8, 1893; "O vospreshchenii sdelok na raznost' po pokupke i prodazhe zolotoi valiuty, tratt, i t.p. tsennostei, napisannykh na zolotuiu valiutu," May 1, 1893; "O vremennykh merakh k usileniiu nadzora za birzhami," May 1, 1893, all inS. Iu. Vitte, *Sobranie sochinenii i dokumental'nykh materialov*, T.3, kn.1 (Moskva: Nauka, 2006).

20. O vremennykh merakh po usileniiu kontrolia za birzhami, RGIA, f.1405, op.542, 1893, d.90. See also Lizunov, "Birzhevaia spekuliatsiia na kurse kreditnogo rublia i mery protivodeistviia ei Ministerstva finansov," "Ob izmenenii pravil o nadzore za proizvodstvom kreditnymi uchrezhdeniiami i drugimi bankirskimi zavedeniiami operatsii na zolotuiu valiutu," November 30, 1894, RGIA, f.1287, op. 9, d.3450, and Vitte, *Sobranie*, v.3., kn.1. See also Serguei Beliaev, "Politika S.Iu. Vitte v oblasti kredita i bankovskoi sistemy Rossii," in Vitte, *Sobranie*, vol. 3, kn.3, 47.

21. A. A. Polovtsov, *Dnevnik, 1893–1909* (St. Petersburg: Aleteia, 2014), 102, November 19, 1894.

22. "Po voprosu ob uchete vyvoza za granitsu kreditnykh biletov i privoza ikh ottuda v Imperiiu, a takzhe ob oblozhenii sikh biletov tamozhennoi poshlinoi," RGIA, f.563, op.2, d.324. On this campaign; see also Olga Dragan, "Gosudarstvennyi Bank i mery po stabilizatsii kursa rublia nakanune denezhnoi reformy 1897 g," in *Rossiia i Mir v kontse XIX—pervoi polovine XX v. Sbornik k 85-letiiu Borisa Vasil'evicha Anan'icha* (St. Petersburg: Liki Rossii, 2017).

23. "O prodlenii deistviia zakona ob oblozhenii kreditnykh biletov tamozhennoi poshlinoi," November 20, 1893, RGIA, f.1152, op.11, 1893, d. 436.

24. Po voprosu ob uchete vyvoza za granitsu kreditnykh biletov i privoza ikh ottuda v Imperiiu, a takzhe ob oblozhenii sikh biletov tamozhennoi poshlinoi, RGIA, f.563, op.2, d.324., 2–3.

25. Petr Brok's comment on the margin of the report: RGIA, f.587, op.56, d.1628, l.31. Contrary to the widespread opinion about greedy bankers from St. Petersburg speculating on national currency, most violators caught for the "illegal" transfer of money were lower and middle-class traders. Smuggled money was subjected to a 25% confiscation rate, and the State Bank closed the violators' accounts, often pushing them to the brink of bankruptcy.

26. In addition to being illegal, these measures negatively affected normal operations with bills of exchange and restricted the ability of banks to provide credit to their clients in Russia and Europe—Lebedev, *S-Peterburgskii mezhdunarodnyi kommercheskii bank*, 175.

27. Migulin, *Reforma denezhnogo obrashcheniia i krizis*, 43–44. N. Fan-Jung, "La réforme de la circulation monétaire en Russie," *Revue d'économie politique* 12, no.12 (1898): 956.

28. Textbooks on international finance mentioned Witte as the "bear squeeze" inventor. See, for instance, Brendan Brown, *Money Hard and Soft: On the International Currency Market* (New York: Wiley, 1978),, 114.

29. "Na etoi spekuliatsii on sovsem pomeshalsia," A.A. Polovtsov, *Dnevnik, 1893–1909* (St. Petersburg: Aleteia, 2014), 105. (November 23, 1894).

30. See the materials of the "confidential" investigation compiled by Witte, RGIA, f.583, op.5, d.145. This file includes copies of Vyshnegradskii's correspondence with Abaza, Raffalovich's handwritten testimony, a few documents from Rafalovich's books, and Witte's report. According to the report, Abaza had destroyed all evidence. It is striking, however, that the file contains no testimony or explanation received from Abaza himself.

31. Witte told this story in his memoir. As Witte recalled, when Bunge discussed the report about Abaza's speculations with the tsar, he tried to exculpate his former boss by pointing out that Abaza's actions went hand in hand with the Ministry of Finance's policy of restraining the ruble's sudden rise. Had it been the opposite, it would have meant that Abaza was speculating against the state's interests (the tsar perceived this explanation as a joke). S.Yu. Vitte, *Vospominaniia*, v.1 (Moskva, Izdvo sotsinalno-ekon. lit-ry, 1960).

32. According to Vladimir Kovalevskii, in his student years, Witte worked as a tutor in the Raffalovich family in Odessa and therefore knew Alexander Raffalovich well. V. I. Kovalevskii, "Iz vospominanii o grafe Sergee Iliueviche Vitte" *Russkoe proshloe* 2 (1991): 82.

33. RGIA, f.626, op.1, d.51, ll.9-11 (in French).

34. As Rothstein claimed, the operations with bills of exchange that affected the ruble's rate were inherently tied to other credit operations, and restriction of the possibility to transfer funds (bills of exchange) to Europe that targeted speculators affected the banks' ability to fulfill their credit commitments. On that aspect of Rothstein's letter, see Serguei Lebedev, *Sankt-Peterburgskii Mezhdunarodnyi Bank*, 175–178.

35. RGIA, f.626, op.1, d.51, l.18.

36. "Soobshchenie Ministerstva finansov o kurse kreditnogo rublia na 1896 god," *Birzhevye Vedomosti*, December 13, 1895, front page.

37. Serguei Beliaev, "Politika S.Iu. Vitte v oblasti kredita i bankovskoi sistemy Rossii," in Vitte, Sobranie sochinenii, T. 3, kn.3, p. 50.

38. O. V. Dragan, *Reforma Gosudarstvennogo Banka: tseli, proekty, resultaty. Konets 80kh - vtoraia polovina 90kh gg. XIX veka.* Dissertatsia na soiskanie stepeni kand ist. nauk, (St. Petersburg: Sankt-Peterburgskii Institut Istorii RAN) 2008.

39. See, for example, Alexander Glukhovskoi's report *The Passage of the Amu-Darya's Waters along Its Old Riverbed to the Caspian Sea, and the Formation of a Non-stop Route from the Borders of Afghanistan via Amu-Darya, the Caspian Sea, Volga, and the Mariinskii Canal System to St. Petersburg and the Baltic Sea* (A. I. Glukhovskoi, *Propusk vod r. Amu-Darii po staromu ee ruslu v Kaspiiskoe more i obrazovanie nepreryvnogo vodnogo Amu-Dariisko-Kaspiiskogo puti ot granits Afganistana po Amu-Darie, Kaspiiu, Volge, i Mariiskoi sisteme do Peterburga i Baltiiskogo moria* (St. Petersburg, 1893)). On these plans, see Ekaterina Pravilova, "River of Empire: Geopolitics, Irrigation, and the Amu Darya in the Late 19th Century," in *Cahiers d'Asie Central* 17–18 (2009): 255–287. On the use of paper money for this construction: Ya. I. Yankevich, *O podniatii kursa kreditnogo rublia* (St. Petersburg, 1884).

40. Ya. I. Yankevich, *O podniatii kursa*; N. Ya. Danilevskii, "Neskolko myslei po povodu nizkogo kursa nashikh bumazhnykh deneg i nekotorykh drugikh ekonomicheskikh iavlenii i voprosov," in *O nizkom kurse nashikh deneg* (St. Petersburg, 1885), 76. Originally published in *Russkii vestnik*, 1882, no.8.

41. V. P. Vasiliev, *Assignatsii-den'gi* (St. Petersburg, 1887), esp. 26–33. The earlier version of this article appeared in V. P. Vasiliev, *Tri voprosa* (1878) and as newspaper articles in *Grazhdanin* in 1877.

42. N. A. Shavrov, *Russkii put' v Zakavkazie* (St. Petersburg, 1883), 7,8, 27; N. A. Shavrov, "O referate barona A.V. Kaulbarsa," in *Materialy dlia razresheniia voprosa o povorote Amu-Darii v Kaspiiskoe more* (Tiflis, 1887), 6,7. (Same idea in Nikolai Notovich, *Gde doroga v Indiiu?* [Where is the route to India?] [Moskva, 1889], 32.) Shavrov's publications on the development of borderlands: *Put' v Tsentral'nuiu Aziiu po napravleniiu, ukazannomu Petrom Velikim* (St. Petersburg, 1871); *Proekt glavnoi linii Sibirskoi zheleznoi dorogi* (St. Petersburg, 1873); *O razvitii Severa Rossii* (St. Petersburg, 1884), and many others.

43. Editorial, *Russkoe Delo*, 1888, no.3.

44. A. Ya. Antonovich, *Teoriia bumazhno-denezhnogo obrashchenia i gosudarstvennye kreditnye bilety* (Kyiv, 1883), 102–3.

45. Antonovich, *Teoriia bumazhno-denezhnogo obrashchenia*, 251.

46. Antonovich, *Teoriia bumazhno-denezhnogo obrashchenia*, 256; Danilevskii, *O nizkom kurse nashikh deneg*, 174.

47. On the financial aspect of railroad construction in Russia, see A. P. Pogrebinskii, "Stroitelstvo zheleznykh dorog i finansovaia politika tsarisma (60–90 e gody

XIX veka);' *Istoricheskie zapiski* 47 (1954): 149–180. On the debates on the Trans-Siberian railroad, Steven Marks, *Road to Power: The Trans-Siberian Railroad and the Colonization of Asian Russia, 1850–1917* (Ithaca, NY: Cornell University Press, 1991), chs. 6–8.

48. A. N. Kulomzin, *Perezhitoe. Vospominania* (Moskva: ROSSPEN, 2016), 409.

49. Vsepoddanneiishii doklad ministra finansov, "O sposobakh sooruzheniia Velikogo Sibirskogo zheleznodorozhnogo puti," November 6, 1892, *RGIA*, f.560, op.27, d.6, l.23–24 ob.

50. Dragan, "Gosudarstvennyi bank." "O sposobakh sooruzheniia Velikogo Sibirskogo zheleznodorozhnogo puti," 25.

51. I. V. Lukoianov, "S.F. Sharapov i S.Yu.Vitte," *Otechestvennaia istoriia i istoricheskaia mysl' Rossii XIX—XX vekov* (St. Petersburg: Nestor-Istoriia, 2006), 338; Sharapov's articles: *Russkoe obozrenie* 1893, August, September, November, December. On Siberian money, see the November issue, 272–274. After Witte's and Sharapov's break-up and the minister's sharp reversal from inflationism to monetarism, Sharapov revised his articles into a brochure that criticized Witte's policy, removing, however, the passages about the railroad money.

52. RGIA, f.694, op.2, d.67, l.10.

53. In 1888 and again in 1891, Vyshnegradskii received the tsar's approval for temporary issuance of credit rubles under the condition that each new paper ruble would be matched by one ruble in gold added to the exchange fund. This required inviting the members of the auditing committee, representatives of the St. Petersburg Stock Exchange, and foreign guests to observe the relocation of gold ingots and coins from one depot of the State Bank to another. "O vremennom vypuske kreditnykh biletov na 75 millionov rublei," RGIA, f.563, op.10, d. 310. On the operation of transferring gold, see "O vremennom vypuske kreditnykh biletov pod obespechenie zolota na osnovanii vys. Ukaza 28 iiulia 1891 g.," RGIA, f.587, op.43, d. 242. In total, 150 million rubles were issued on the conditions of a one-to-one paper-gold ratio. In principle, Vyshnegradskii's measures did not violate the law 1881 while they allowed for greater flexibility of financial administration. "O vremennom vypuske kreditnykh biletov na 75 millionov rublei," February–March 1892, RGIA, f.563, op.2, d.310.

54. He suggested yet another issuance of paper rubles to be backed by gold at the current exchange rate of 1:1.5 instead of 1:1. "O vypuske kreditnykh biletov (1893)," RGIA, f.563, op.2, d. 326, l.14.

55. "O vypuske kreditnykh biletov (1893)," RGIA, f.563, op.2, d. 326, l.32.

56. On the State Bank reform of 1894, see Olga Dragan, "Reforma Gosudarstvennnogo Banka 1892–1894: evropeiskii opyt i rossiiskaia praktika," *Ekonomicheskaia istoriia. Ezhegodnik, 2005* (Moskva: ROSSPEN, 2005), 237–256, and O. V. Dragan, *Reforma Gosudarstvennnogo Banka: tseli, proekty, rezultaty.*

57. Zhurnaly Vysochaishe Uchrezhdennoi Komissii po peresmotru ustava Gosudarstvennogo Banka (January 1893), RGIA, pechatnaia zapiska no. 1481, ll. 11, 19.

58. "O neobkhodimosti i zadachakh reformy Gosudarstvennogo Banka," RGIA, pechatnaia zapiska no. 1481, 51.

59. Kulomzin, *Perezhitoe,* 490.

60. Dokladnaia zapiska N.Kh. Bunge, D.M. Sol'skomu o vypuske novykh kreditnykh biletov, February 1893, RGIA, f.694, op.2, d. 67, ll. 2,3,8, 80b.,12.

61. Olga Dragan, "Reforma Gosudarstvennnogo Banka 1892–1894," 251.

62. See Bunge's preface in Dzh .Gorn, *Zhon Lo. Opyt issledovaniia po istorii finansov,* Per. Ivana Shipova (St. Petersburg, 1895), vols. 5, 6, 10, 14, 19–20. V. Bunge's preface is dated June 1894.

63. See *Katalog knizhnogo sobraniia S.Yu.Vitte. Rekonstruktsiia,* in Vitte, *Sobranie sochinenii,* v.5, 7.

64. See a copy of Antonovich's pitiful letter to Witte in which he asked for a dismissal pay of 200,000 rubles (instead of 10,000 that Witte had offered) and hoped that Witte would let him go quietly. "It is not my fault that I turned out to be useless, but this is the life itself with its nonsense and anxiety. I tried to do my best and worked hard," RGIA, f.1622, op.1, d. 397, l.1; see also Kulomzin, *Perezhitoe.* 490–491, 501.

65. *Vestnik finansov, promyshlennosti, i torglovl* 10 (March 5, 1895): 569–570.

66. Meshcherskii to Witte, RGIA, f.1622, op.1, d.448, ll. 1–9.

67. Sharapov to Mikhail Mikhailovich [Andronnikov], RGIA, f.1622, op.1, d.487, 30b., 4 ob.

68. Vitte, S.Yu. Vitte, *Vospominaniia,* vol.2 (Moskva, Izd-vo sotsinalno-ekon. lit-ry, 1960): 88.

69. Protokoly zasedanii Soedinennykh Departamentov Gosudarstvennoi Ekonomii, Zakonov i Grazhdanskikh i Dukhovnykh Del po delu ob ispravlenii denezhnogo obrashcheniia, RGIA, f.1152, op.12, 1897, d.78a, l.780.

70. O padenii tsen na serebro, July 6, 1893, RGIA, f.583, op.4, d.306, ll.1–3.

71. Zhurnal Komiteta finansov po voprosu, "Ob izmenenii sposoba rascheta kazny s serebropromushlennikami za dobyvaemoe imi serebro," April 4, 1894, Vitte, *Sobranie sochinenii,* t.3, kn.1, 361–364; O padenii tsen na serebro. July 6, 1893, RGIA, f.583, op.4, d.3066 ll. 1–10; O priniatii nekotorykh mer vsledstvie obestseneniia serebra, RGIA, f.583, op.4, d.306, l. 30.

72. O pokupke za granitsei serebra i chekanke na inostrannykh monetnykh dvorakh rossiiskoi serebrianoi polnotsennoi monety, RGIA, f.583, op.4, d.308, ll.244–246. Starting from 1896 copper coins (lowest denominations) were made in England, RGIA, f.583, op.4, d.311, l.168.

73. Among bimetallists was Alphonse Rothschild, who participated in the placement of Russian bonds in France. Alfred Rothschild, from the English line of the banker dynasty and a director of the Bank of England, was a strong opponent of bimetallism. See his speeches at the International Monetary Conference in Bruxelles in 1892. *Conférence Monétaire Internationale,* 1892, *Procès-verbaux* (Bruxelles, 1892). Witte also mentioned, among bimetallists who tried to convince Russia to choose this standard, President Emile Loubet: Vitte, *Vospominaniia,* vol.2, 90.

74. I was not able to locate Méline's original memo that Raffalovich mentioned in his report "Quelques rémarque sur le problème monétaire par M. Méline," RGIA, f.560, op.22, d.285, l. 117. See also two memos printed in St. Petersburg by publisher Kirshbaum, apparently in a very limited number of copies. None of the state libraries in Russia or elsewhere has the copies of these memos except for the Library of the Ministry of Finance of the Russian Federation that has inherited the collection of the Academic Committee of the imperial Ministry of Finance. *La question monétaire. Le mémoire de M. Méline. La situation générale et les intérêts de la Russie* (St. Petersburg: tip. V. Kirshbauma, no publication date). *Note complémentaire sur la question monétaire* (St. Petersburg: tip. V. Kirshbauma, no publication date).

    On French proposals, see also Joseph Waller, "La naissance du rouble-or," *Cahiers du monde russe et soviétique* 20, nos. 3–4 (Julliet–Decembre 1979: 292–293; Vitte, *Vospominaniia*, vol. 2, 91. On French bimetallism, see Marc Flandreau, *The Glitter of Gold: France, Bimetallism, and the Emergence of the International Gold Standard, 1848–1873* (Oxford: Oxford University Press, 2004).

75. Raffalovich, an economist and journalist, had long been involved in the debates on monetary politics. In 1892, he represented Russia at the International Monetary Conference in Brussels. Unlike Prince Urusov, the official ambassador to the conferences who was incompetent in these matters and kept silent, Raffalovich played a very active role in the debates on bimetallism and defended the status quo. *Conférence Monétaire Internationale, 1892* Procès-verbaux (Bruxelles, 1892). Raffalovich spoke as a private individual since the government's position was declared neutral.

76. RGIA, f.560, op.22, d.285, ll.119, 125. This report, like most of Raffalovich's dispatches, was written in French.

77. RGIA, f.560, op.22, d.285, ll.119, 134.

78. RGIA, f.560, op.22, d.285, ll.119, 118.

79. RGIA, f.560, op.22, d.285, ll.119, 137.

80. RGIA, f.560, op.22, d.285, ll.119, 127.

81. In contrast to Europe, bimetallism did not gain popularity in Russia. As Chapter 7 will show, the anti-gold campaign in Russia was run under the banner of "no standard" rather than a double standard of gold and silver or just in favor of silver. For the defense of bimetallism, see, for instance, L. A. Raffalovich, "Lazh na serebro i khlebnye tseny," *Sankt-Peterburskie Vedomosti*, November 25, 1896; L. A. Raffalovich, "Serebro," *Novoe Vremia*, March 27, 1895; L. A. Raffalovich, "Bimetallism i Evropa," *Birzhevye Vedomosti*, February 19, 1896; L. A. Raffalovich, "K voprosu ob osushchestvlenii zolotogo standarta v Rossii," *Birzhevye Vedomosti*, February 17, 1896; L. A. Raffalovich, *Serebrianaia agitatsiia* (St. Petersburg, 1897). I. P. Sokalskii, *Reforma na ocheredi* (Kharkov, 1895). The ministry conducted a very aggressive campaign against international bimetallism in its official weekly magazine, *Herald of Finance*, but it looked more like a justification of its choice than a response to opponents.

82. A. Guriev, *Reforma denezhnogo obrashcheniia*, ch.1, vyp.1(St. Petersburg, 1896), 278.
83. Nikodim Kondakov, *Russkie Klady. Issledovanie drevnostei velikokniazheskogo perioda* (St. Petersburg, 1896).

CHAPTER 7

1. On the power of narratives in creating Witte's image, see Francis W. Wcislo, *Tales of Imperial Russia: The Life and Times of Sergei Witte, 1849–1915* (Oxford: Oxford University Press, 2011).
2. For a detailed critical analysis of Witte's memoir, see B. V. Anan´ich and R. Sh. Ganelin, *S. Iu. Vitte—Memuarist* (St. Petersburg: SPbF IRI RAN, 1994).
3. I .F. Gindin, "S.Iu. Vitte kak gosudarstvennyi deiatel," *Serguei Iulievich Vitte— gosudarstvennyi deiatel, reformator, economist (k stopiatidesiteletiiu so dnia rozhdeniia)* (Moskva: In-t Ekonomiki, 1999), 83–84.
4. On the personnel of the Ministry of Finance: B. V. Anan'ich and R. Sh. Ganelin, *Serguei Iulievich Vitte i ego vremia* (St. Petersburg: Dmitrii Bulanin, 1999).
5. N. A. Veliaminov, "Vstrechi i znakomstva," in *S. Yu.Vitte (Gosudarstvennye deiateli Rossii glazami sovremennikov)*, edited by I. V. Lukoianov (St. Petersburg, 2018), 143–144. Von Laue called Witte "one of the giants in the succession from Peter to Lenin." Theodore von Laue, *Sergei Witte and the Industrialization of Russia* (New York: Atheneum 1969), 36.
6. Laue, *Sergei Witte*, 144.
7. Marc Flandreau, "The French Crime of 1873: An Essay on the Emergence of the International Gold Standard, 1870–1880," *Journal of Economic History* 56, no.4 (December1996).
8. Milton Friedman, "The Crime of 1873," *Journal of Political Economy* 98, no. 6 (December, 1990): 1159–1194
9. "67 vmesto 100 rublei," *Novoe Vremia*, March 14, 1895.
10. For example, in February 1895 Witte sought Suvorin's assistance in foiling the campaign launched by Ilya Tsion (or, as he spelled his name in French, Elie de Cyon)—a former agent of the Ministry of Finance in Paris and the author of a pamphlet criticizing Witte's monetary initiatives. Elie de Cyon, *M. Witte et les Finances Russes d'apres des Documents Officiels et Inedits (Paris, 1895)* (Witte, letter to Suvorin, February 15, 1895, RGALI, f.459, op.1, d.719, 23–24).
11. V. A. Lebedev, "Reforma denezhnogo obrashcheniia," *Schetovodstvo*, 1896, n.10, 150.
12. RGALI, f.459, op.1, d.719. Witte to Suvorin, March 7, 1895. Wahl was dismissed in December 1895.
13. "Zoloto ili serebro?" (pis'mo v redaktsiiu) *Novoe Vremia*, March 16, 1895.
14. "Zoloto ili serebro?"
15. "Malen'kie pis'ma," *Novoe Vremia*, March 20, 1895, in A. V. Suvorin, *V ozhidanii veka XX: malen´kie pis´ma 1889-1903 gg* (Moskva: Algoritm, 2005).
16. Witte to Suvorin, March 20, 1895, RGALI, f.459, op.1, d.719, l.30.

17. *Birzhevye vedomosti, Sankt-Peterburgskie vedomosti, Russkie vedomosti, Moskovskie vedomosti*, quoted from M. V. Melenkov, "Sudba zolotogo rublia. Spory mezhdu storonnikami i protivnikami denezhnoi reformy S.Iu. Vitte, 1895–1897 gg," *Novyi istoricheskii vestnik* 23, no. 1 (2010): 14.

18. A. V. Suvorin, "Malen'kie pis'ma," March 31, 1895, in *V ozhidanii veka XX*, 495–497.

19. "Serebro. Pis'mo v redaktsiiu," *Novoe Vremia*, March 17, 1895.

20. Witte to Suvorin, RGALI, f.459, op.1, d.719, ll. 32–34.

21. Among several publications against the legalization of gold, see L. Slonimskii's articles in the *Herald of Europe*: L. Z. Slonimskii, "Denezhnye nedoumeniia," *Vestnik Evropy*, June 1895; L. Z. Slonimskii, "Finansovye zadachi. Zoloto ili serebro," *Vestnik Evropy*, July 1895. In February 1895, Witte's proposal to legalize gold was approved by the Committee of Finance, yet when the State Council gathered on April 6, 1895, to discuss the issue, the presiding head of the departments' meeting, Dmitrii Sol'skii, noted that "after the unanimous decision of the Committee of Finance, there appeared in journals and public opinion such an opposition to this measure, the members of the committee should no longer consider themselves bound by their [earlier] opinions." As Alexander Polovtsov, who recorded the incident, remarked, Solskii's declaration was "met with silence," and the State Council approved the reform. A. A. Polovtsov, *Dnevnik, 1893–1909*, 141; Predstavlenie v Gosudarstvennyi Sovet, "O prieme zolotoi monety po kursu vo vse kazennye platezhi," in Vitte, *Sobranie sochinenii*, v. 3. p.1, 82–103; Zhurnal Soedinennykh Departmamentov Gosudarstvennoi Ekonomii, Zakonov i Grazhdanskikh i Dukhovnykh Del Gosudarstvennogo Soveta, April 6, 1895, in *Materialy po denezhnoi reforme 1895–1897*, 36–39, 97–102.

22. Suvorin to Witte, April 7, 1895, RGALI, f.459, op.1, d.185, 5. Grand Duke Constantine (better known under his pen name K. R. (Konstantin Romanov) was a writer and an academic with liberal views. He was appointed a member of the Committee of Finance in March 1895

23. Witte to Suvorin, December 17, 1895, RGALI, f.459, op.1, d.719, ll.52–53.

24. Witte wrote to Suvorin on December 29, 1895: "I am very grateful for your compliance with my request not to escalate the currency issue." However, the minister did not keep his earlier promises to allow the *New Time* to publish the speech. Instead, he only let Suvorin read it and use the speech's content without mentioning the source. Witte to Suvorin, RGALI, f.459, op.1, d.719, l.51.

25. "Rech, proiznesennaia ministrom finansov v Obshchem sobranii Gosudarstvennogo Sovera 28 dekabria 1895 goda," in Vitte, *Sobranie sochinenii*, vol. 3, pt. 1, 105–107.

26. G. N. A. [A. Guryev], "Po povodu denezhnoi reformy," *Novoe Vremia*, March 15, 1896; *Denezhnaia reforma. Svod mnenii i otzyvov* (St. Petersburg, 1896), 1.

27. "V uchenom obshchestve," *Novoe Vremia*, March 21, 1896. See the transcripts of the debates at the Free Economic Society: *Reforma denezhnogo obrashcheniia v Rossii: Doklady i preniia v III Otdelenii Imperatorskogo Vol' nogo ekonomicheskogo obshchestva. Stenograficheskii otchet* (St. Petersburg, 1896).

28. *Birzhevye Vedomosti*, April 11, 1896.

29. Vitte, *Vospominaniia*, vol. 2, 93.

30. G. N. A. [A. Guryev], "Po povodu denezhnoi reformy," *Novoe Vremia*, March 15, 1896.

31. Zapiska N. P. Nepenina o denezhnoi reforme v Rossii, 17 iulia 1896, RGIA, f.1566, op.1, d.382b, l.1.

32. Stanislav Propper recalled using this argument in his conversation with Witte in 1896. Stanislav Propper, *Was nicht in die Zeitung kam. Erinnerungen des Chefredakteurs der "Birschewyja Wedomosti"* (Frankfurt am Main: Frankfurter Societäts-Dr., 1929), 222–224

33. I. F. Tsion, *Kuda vremenshchik Vitte vedet Rossiiu?* (Paris, 1896), 42, 45–46.

34. Nefinansist, "Spravedlivost' i deval'vatsiia," *Novosti i Birzhevaia Gazeta*, February 24, 1896.

35. G. N. A. [A. Guryev], "Po povodu denezhnoi reformy," *Novoe Vremia*, March 22, 1896. Witte and Guryev argued that raising the ruble's rate would destabilize prices and credit and would greatly disadvantage debtors who had borrowed money in paper rubles (including the State Treasury), increasing their debts by 50%. Witte also charged a group of lawyers with the task of defining "the legal and moral foundations" of the reform: the expert commission formulated a convincing argument for why the phrase printed on credit rubles did not oblige the government to exchange credit rubles for gold at parity. Experts argued that relations between the government and people, that is, the bearers of credit rubles, belonged to the sphere of public rather than civil law. Therefore, the obligation to pay in metal for paper bills should not be interpreted as a contract. "Zhurnal Komissii v.u. 6 oktiabria dlia razrabotki s iuridicheskoi storony voprosa o tom, kakoi monetoi, soglasno deistvuiushchim zakonopolozheniiam, russkoe pravitelstvo obiazano oplachivat' gosudarstvennye kreditnye bilety," Dekabr' 1895, Vitte, *Sobranie sochinenii*, t.3, kn.2., 172.

36. Sharapov in *Reforma denezhnogo obrashcheniia v Rossii: Doklady i preniia*, 81–82.

37. N. Polenov, "Po voprosu ob uderzhanii zapasov zolota," *Denezhnaia Reforma. Svod mnenii i otzyvov*, 54–55.

38. K. F. Golovin, "Nakanune denezhnoi reformy", *Denezhnaia Reforma. Svod mnenii i otzyvov*, 72

39. F. Romer, "Provintsiia i denezhnaia reforma, 2," *Sankt-Peterburgskie vedomosti*, April 3, 1896.

40. *Denezhnaia reforma. Svod mnenii*, 301. Very similar to that: I. Bortkevich, *O denezhnoi reforme, proektiruemoi Ministerstvom Finansov* (St. Petersburg, 1896).

41. G. N. A. [A. Guryev], "Po povodu denezhnoi reform," *Novoe Vremia*, March 27, 1896.

42. *Reforma denezhnogo obrashcheniia v Rossi: Doklady i preniia*, 98.

43. S. F. Sharapov, "Bumazhnyi rubl'," in *Bumazhnyi rubl' i drugie raboty* (Moskva: Rodnaia strana, 2017), 39.

44. Golovin, "Eshche po povodu denezhnoi reformy," April 23, 1896. During the transition period, the old gold coins with the denomination of 5 rubles valuing 7.5 rubles and the new coins with the denomination of 10 rubles and the same value (10 rubles) were supposed to circulate in parallel. The whole system was incomprehensible for simple folk. "V zashchitu denezhnoi reformy," *Sankt-Peterburgskie vedomosti*, April 16, 1896.

45. I. A. Saburov, letter to P. A. Saburov, October 1, 1896, RGIA, f.1044, op.1, d.430, l. 62; Suvorin, Malenkie pis'ma, *Novoe Vremia*, April 10, 1896, *V ozhidanii veka XX*, 560.

46. In France, the bills of exchange matured on average in twenty-four days, in Germany—thirty to sixty days, while in Russia—180 days, with a maximum term of twelve months, Ministerstvo finansov. *Ob ispravlenii denezhnogo obrashcheniia*. March 14, 1896, [no publication date or place], 72.

47. RGIA, f.356, op.2, d.357, l.70b. Three members of the Committee of Finance wondered whether the reform should include another revision of the State Bank's charter. Witte responded that he was in favor of the reform, but he could come back to it later, RGIA, f.356, op.2, d.357, 70b–8.

48. M. V. Bernatskii, *Russkii gosudarstvennyi bank kak uchrezhdenie emissionnoe* (St. Petersburg, 1912), 43, Stanislas Skarzynski, *Essai sur un Banque de Russie* (Paris: Guillaumin,1901), 54–55, 58; H. Saulgeot, *Deux types de banque d'Empire*: Allemagne, Russie (Paris, A. Rousseau, 1905), 131.

49. Skarzynski, *Essai sur une Banque de Russie*, 49.

50. Saulgeot, *Deux types de banque d'Empire*, 50.

51. *Reforma denezhnogo obrashcheniia v Rossii: Doklady i preniia*, 185; Khodskii also suggested "a fundamental transformation of the State bank in the sense of its independence from the Ministry of Finance, *Reforma denezhnogo obrashcheniia v Rossii: Doklady i preniia* , 54; editorial in *Novosti i Birzhevaia Gazeta*, February 18, 1896.

52. *Reforma denezhnogo obrashcheniia v Rossii: Doklady i preniia*, 74–75.

53. *Reforma denezhnogo obrashcheniia v Rossii: Doklady i preniia*, 85; "Samostoiatel'nost' emissionnogo banka," *Novosti i Birhzevaia Gazeta*, May 2, 1896.

54. *Reforma denezhnogo obrashcheniia v Rossii: Doklady i preniia*, 107.

55. *Reforma denezhnogo obrashcheniia v Rossii: Doklady i preniia* , 213.

56. Pikhno–Witte, March 22 [1896?], RGIA, f.560, op.22, d.189, 460b–47.

57. A. N. Guryev, *Reforma deleznhogo obrashcheiia*, Ch.2, vyp.1 (St. Petersburg, 1896), 498.

58. Guryev, *Reforma deleznhogo obrashcheiia: Doklady i preniia*, 535.

59. Guryev, *Reforma deleznhogo obrashcheiia: Doklady i preniia,* v.2, vyp.1, 538, 539.

60. Suvorin to Witte, March 24, 1896, RGIA, f.560, op.22, d.189, ll. 49–50.

61. *Ob ispravlenii denezhnogo obrashcheniia*, 77.

62. Pikhno to Witte, March 22, 1896, RGIA, f.560, op.22, d.189, l.48.

63. G.N.A.[A. Guryev], "Po povodu nyneshnei reformy," *Novoe Vremia*, March 15, 1896.

64. *Reforma denezhnogo obrashcheniia v Rossii: Doklady i preniia*, 123, 229.

65. S. Sharapov, "Bumazhnyi rubl'," in *Bumazhnyi rubl' i drugie raboty*, 45.

66. Gofshteter, "Vopros o denezhoi reforme v Imperatorskom Volnom Ekonomicheskom Obshchestve," *Sankt-Peterburgskie Vedomosti*, April 9, 1896.

67. On that movement, see I.P. Sokal'skii, *Reforma na ocheredi* (Kharkiv, 1895)

68. *Reforma denezhnogo obrashcheniia v Rossii: Doklady i preniia*, 212.

69. Suvorin, Malenkie pis'ma, November 16, 1899, *V ozhidanii veka XX*, 725.

70. See especially the collection of speeches and articles by Georgii Butmi: G. V. Butmi, *K voprosu o denezhnoi reforme (soobrazheniia sel'skogo khoziaina)* (Odessa, 1897); see also Sharapov's speech at the Free Economic Society meeting: *Reforma denezhnogo obrashcheniia v Rossii: Doklady i preniia*, 169. At the ministry's request, P. A. Shostak calculated the effects of the falls and rises of the ruble's rate, concluding that although "cheap" ruble allowed exporters to sell grain in Europe with certain profit, these gains were immediately neutralized because the massive influx of Russian grain usually lowered prices. P. A. Shostak, *K voprosu o vliianii kursa kreditnogo rublia na khlebnye tseny* (St. Petersburg, 1896).

71. I. Hofshtetter, "Vopros o denezhnoi reforme v Imperatorskom Volnom Ekonomicheskom Obshchestve," *Sankt-Peterburgskie Vedomosti*, April 9, 1896.

72. A. I. Bukovetskii, "Kratkii obzor prepodavaniia finansovoi nauki i finansovogo prava v Peterburgskom (Petrogradskom) universitete v XIX—pervoi chetverti XX veka," *Vestnik Sankt-Peterburgskogo universiteta*, Ser. 5. Ekonomika, 1993, vyp. 1, 17–22; see also biographical essays about Khodskii and Yarotskii in O. Ansberg, Yu. Bazulin, S. Belozerov, et al., *Ocherki po istorii finansovoi nauki: Sankt-Peterburgskii universitet* (Moskva: Proekt, 2009), 443–478, 479–489.

73. *Reforma denezhnogo obrashcheniia v Rossii: Doklady i preniia*, 31.

74. See also his critique of Antonovich and the idea of "productive money" in his textbook on political economy: L. Khodskii, *Osnovy gosudarstvennogo khoziaistva. Posobie po finansovoi nauke* (St. Petersburg, 1894), 441.

75. *Reforma denezhnogo obrashcheniia v Rossii: Doklady i preniia*, 153.

76. Gamma, "Zolotoe obrashchenie," *Birzhevye vedomosti*, March 26, 1896.

77. Struve's speech at the Free Economic Society, *Reforma denezhnogo obrashcheniia v Rossii: Doklady i preniia*, 35.

78. L. V. Khodskii, *Osnovy gosudarstvennogo khoziaistva. Posobie po finansovoi nauke* (St. Petersburg, 1891), 19

79. *Reforma denezhnogo obrashcheniia v Rossii: Doklady i preniia*, 150.

80. Gretchen Ritter, *Goldbugs and Greenbacks. The Antimonopoly Tradition and the Politics of Finance in America, 1865-1896* (Cambridge: Cambridge Unikversity Press, 1997), 2, 73, 152–207.

81. L. Z. Slonimskii, "Eshche o denezhnoi reforme," *Vestnik Evropy*, 1897, June, 781, 782.

82. *Reforma denezhnogo obrashcheniia v Rossii: Doklady i preniia*, 209, 241. Apparently, the French term referred to "*enquêtes parlamentaires*" that appeared in France during the Juliette Monarchy. Another prototype widely used in Russian politics was the Blue books of the British parliament.

83. Stanislav Propper, the editor of the *Stock Exchange Bulletins*, dedicated an entire chapter of his memoirs to his interactions with Witte during the preparation of the gold reform and his participation in the public campaign. Stanislav Propper, *Was nicht in die Zeitung kam,* 222–224. According another memoirist, Propper owed to Witte the expansion of his edition. Ieronim Yasinskii, *Roman moei zhizni. Kniga vospominanii.* (Leningrad: Gos. izdatelstvo, 1926), 278.

84. Witte to Suvorin, RGALI, f.459, op.1, d.719, l.57.

85. RGALI, f.459, op.1, d.719, l.620b.

86. Suvorin, Malen'kie pis'ma, April 10, 1896, *V ozhidanii XX veka*, 560–562.

87. A. S. Suvorin, *Dnevnik* (Moskva: Nezavisimaia Gazeta, 2000), 214.

88. Suvorin, *Dnevnik*, 215. According to Suvorin, Nicholas II read excerpts from the Free Economic Society's protocols. Suvorin, *Dnevnik*, 221.

89. Suvorin, *Dnevnik,* 221.

90. Geiden to A. S. Ermolov (minister of agriculture), January 17, 1897, RGIA, f.398, op.63, d. 2022.

91. RGIA, f.398, op.63, d. 2022, 65.

92. K. M. Staniukovich, "Pis'ma znatnogo inostrantsa," *Sobranie sochinenii*, vol.11 (1898), 440–441.

93. See "Soobrazheniia chlena Gosudarstvennogo Soveta D. G. Von Derviza po voprosu ob ispravlenii denezhnogo obrashcheniia," March 27, 1896, in Vitte, *Sobranie sochinenii*, v.3, kn.2.; P. Saburov, "O denezhnoi reforme," Vitte, *Sobranie sochinenii*, v.3, kn.2.

94. Vitte, *Vospominaniia*, v.2, 95–96

95. Suvorin, *Dnevnik*, October 24, 1896, 262.

96. A. A. Polovtsov, *Dnevnik*, 190.

97. PSZ 3, vol. 17, no.13611, January 3, 1897.

98. A. A. Polovtsov, *Dnevnik*, 191.

99. Suvorin, *Dnevnik*, 276, January 5, 1897.

100. Protokol zasedaniia Soedinennykh Departamentom Gosudarstvennoi Ekonomii, Zakonov, Grazhdanskikh i Dukhovnykh Del February 27, 1897, in Vitte, *Sobranie sochinenii*, vol.3, kn.2. 453.

101. Vitte, *Sobranie sochinenii*, vol.3, kn.2., 457.

102. Copy of the telegram to the French government, April 5, 1897, RGIA, f.560, op.22, d.185, l.167.

103. "Finances Russes," in RGIA, f.560, op.22, d.185, l. 170; also reprinted in *L'Economiste Europeen,* RGIA, f.560, op.22, d.185, ll. 188–191. Théry's article, reprinted in other newspapers, started a campaign that involved most major French periodicals, so that Witte's agent in France, Raffalovich, suggested requesting the French

government to put an end to it. Witte, however, was not very worried by the demarche: other European newspapers praised the reform as a major step toward the normalization of Russian finances, RGIA, f.560, op.22, d.185, l.180, l. 176.

104. Vladimir Meshcherskii naively interpreted the withdrawal of the reform from the State Council as Witte's retreat and praised his respect of the law and legal propriety, June 8, 1897— V. P. Meshcherskii, *Dnevnik kniazia V. P. Meshcherskogo za mai, iiun', iul', avgust 1897 g* (St. Petersburg, 1897), 70–72.

105. The edict passed without even the Committee of Finance's deliberation (the formal reason was that most of the committee's members were still on vacation). Ob ustanovlenii soglasovannogo s Imennym Vysochaishim ukazom 3 ianvaria 1897 g tverdogo osnovaniia vypuska gosudarstvennykh kreditnykh biletov v obrashchenie, August 29, 1897, RGIA, f.583, op.4, d.310, l.101–107.

106. PSZ 3, vol. 17, 14504, August 29, 1897.

107. "Finansovaia khronika," *Vestnik finansov, promyshlennosti i torgovli*. September 14, 1897, 435.

108. Ob ustanovlenii pravil po vypusku i iz'iatiiu kreditnykh biletov pod obespechenie zolotom na osnovanii Vys. Ukaza 29 Avgusta 1897, RGIA, f.587, op.43, d.313, 13.

109. F. A. Iurgens, *Vospominaniia o Evgenii Ivanoviche Lamanskom v sviazi s deiatel'nostiu Gosudarstvennogo Banka* (St. Petersburg, 1901), 33–37. Extra-legal loans from the State Bank had existed since the 1870s, but the sum of these loans spiked between 1898 and 1902. As of 1900, the Bank had issued loans for 40 million rubles; in 1901, this sum rose to 65 million and in 1902 to 100 million rubles. L. N. Yasnopolskii, "Gosudarstvennyi Bank," *Voprosy gosudarvennogo khoziaistva i buidzhetnogo prava* (St. Petersburg, 1907), 262. See also the report of State Controller that shows even higher sums of extra-legal credits: Zakliuchenie gos. kontrolera po otchetu Gos Banka za 1900, RGIA, f.588, op.5, d.10, l.24.

110. I. F. Gindin, "Neustavnye ssudy Gosudarstvennogo Banka i ekonomicheskaia politika tsarskogo pravitelstva," *Istoricheskie Zapiski* 35 (1950): 103; I. Kh. Ozerov, "Gosudarstvennyi bank i vneustavnye ssudy," *Russkoe Slovo* 22 (1906); Yasnopolskii, "Gosudarstvennyi Bank," 262.

111. Ob otchetakh Gosudarstvennogo Banka za 1894-1897 gg., RGIA, f.1044, op.1, d.221, l.16 ob.

112. Despite the secrecy in which these loans had been shrouded, the State Controller managed to discern the number of illegal loans from the State Bank's accounting books; he brought these numbers to the State Council's attention, demanding that in future, such subsidies be considered by a supreme collegiate state institution. Zakliuchenie Gosudarstvennogo Kontrolera po otchetu Gosudarstvennogo Banka za 1900 g., RGIA, f.588, op.5, d.10, l. 24 ob. See Witte's response to the State Council's inquiry and the State Controller complaints in: Ob otchetakh Gosudarstvennogo Banka za 1894-1897 gg." RGIA, f.1044, op.1, d.221, 7-90b. The rules of the revision of the State Bank emission activity by State Controller are in RGIA, f.587, op.33, d.368.

113. The change was noticeable in the minute details and practices of everyday life— for example, the Bank's balance sheets, which were usually delivered promptly to the Public Library on Nevsky Avenue, were delayed by several months. Iurgens, *Vospominania*, 46.

114. Vitte, *Vospominaniia*, vol. 3, 113–114.

115. Ivan Saburov to Petr Saburov, October 1, 1896, RGIA, f.1044, op.1, d.430, l. 61.

CHAPTER 8

1. John Maynard Keynes, *Indian Currency and Finance* [1913] in *The Collected Writings of John Maynard Keynes*, vol.1 (Cambridge: Cambridge University Press, 1978, 21, 14, 11.

2. Mark Metzler, *Lever of Empire: The International Gold Standard and the Crisis of Liberalism in Prewar Japan* (Berkeley: University of California Press, 2006), 36.

3. Adolph Wagner, one of the main speakers of *Kathedersocialisten*, who had previously taught in the Russian Empire and written about the reform of the Russian ruble, believed in bimetallism. However, in his expert opinion on Russia's transition to gold, he emphasized the importance of making the "mass of population, the so-called 'small people,' peasants etc." use "real coins." "O proekte reformy dlia vosstanovleniia russkoi valiuty," otzyv d-ra Vagnera, October 25, 1896, in *Vitte, Sobranie sochinenii*, v.3, kn.2, 569, 571. Wagner solicited a hefty reward for his services. See his correspondence with Arthur Raffalovich, the Ministry of Finance's agent in France: RGIA, f.560, op.22, d.285, ll.83–101.

4. As Witte suggested, there should be no more than 3 rubles of silver rubles per capita; and the maximum amount of payment in silver was established at 50 rubles. See "Zapiska v Komitet finansov, 'Ob osnovaniiakh obrashcheniia vysokoprobnoi serebrianoi monety i o proizvodstve vsekh raschetov na rubli v 1/15 imperiala,' January 12 1898," in S. Iu. Vitte, *Sobranie sochinenii i documentalnykh materialov* (Moskva: Nauka, 2006). v.3, kn.1, 502–524.

5. P. P. Migulin, *Reforma denezhnogo obrashcheniia* (Kharkiv, 1902), 148.

6. RGIA, f.587, op.56, d.295, 87, 89.

7. See the report of the Kyiv branch in RGIA, f.587, op.56, d.295, l.92

8. Report of the Rostov on Don branch in RGIA, f.587, op.56, d.295, 109. See also RGIA, F.588, op.3, d. 539.

9. RGIA, f.587, op.56, d.295. The State Bank's response to the report from Rostov-on-Don, ibid., l.99.

10. RGIA, f.587, op.56, d.295, l. 118

11. "Nakanune reformy," *Birzhevye vedomosti*, August 4, 1895.

12. Instruction to the heads of State Bank's branches, "O vypuske v obrashchenie zolotoi i serebrianoi monety," 11 iiulia 1895, RGIA, f.588, op.3, d.539, l.44.

13. Nefinansist, "Spravedlivost' i deval'vatsiia," *Novosti i Birzhevaia Gazeta*, February 24, 1896, no.54. In addition to popular discontent with the imposition of gold, the

ministry was blamed for a sudden fall of stocks: the deficit of cash money prompted people to sell bonds and other securities, which lowered their price. The situation appeared so bad that the ministry had to address the public and explain that they had fallen victim to stock exchange speculators, their own gullibility, and the paper standard that caused the disappearance of money. "Bezdenezhie i spekuliatsiia," *Vestnik finansov*, October 8, 1895, no.41, ll.153–156.

14. O prekrashchenii vypuska v obrashchenie kreditnykh biletov rublevogo i trekhrublevogo dostoinstva i ob ikh zamene zvonkoi monetoi, RGIA, f.587, op.33, d.355, l.2; O sposobakh uregulirovaniia denezhnogo obrashcheniia, RGIA, f.587, op.33, d.356, l.18.

15. M .G. Nikolaev, "Koshelek 'na udachu,' K istorii odnogo iz novopriobretennykh eksponatov muzeino-ekspozitsionnogo fonda Banka Rossii," *Den'gi i Kredit*, 2017, no. 5, 73–77.

16. In 1899, the government made yet another change in the coinage of gold money, discontinuing the production of the 7.5-ruble and 15-ruble coins sanctioned in 1897 and reintroducing gold coins with old denominations of 5 and 10 rubles but with a new, reduced weight: these newly minted gold coins were meant to replace the 5- and 10-ruble bills.

17. See the secret instruction of October 23, 1899, put together on the basis of this plan: RGIA, f.587, op.33, d.356, l.55; Ob usilenii vypuska v obrashchenie kreditnykh biletov krupnykh kupiur, RGIA, f.587, op.43, d.427, ll.7, 11. This policy was changed in 1904–5 during the financial crisis caused by the war when the State Bank resumed printing 5-, 10- and then even 3-ruble bills.

18. O neobkhodimosti vyrabotki plana deistvii, RGIA, f.587, op.33, d.356, ll.27, 290b.

19. O prekrashchenii vypuska v obrashchenie kreditnykh biletov rublievogo i trekhrublevogo dostoinstva i ob ikh zamene zvonkoi monetoi, RGIA, f.587, op.33, d.355, ll.62–620b, 64; O zamene v narodnom obrashchenii kreditnykh biletov melkikh dostoinstv bankovym serebrom, RGIA, f.587, op.56, d.598, ll.4 ob, 6, 9, 27, 29, 36, 65.

20. See instructions on the enforcement of the distribution of silver of October 2, 1899; April 19, 1900; and May 10, 1900: *Sbornik tsirkuliarov Ministerstva finansov kazennym palatam, kaznacheistvam i podatnym inspektoram za 1898–1901 gg.* (Kyiv, 1902), 4–77. In 1896–97, the State Bank ordered its correspondent banks in Europe to dispatch silver coins in significant quantities and commissioned the production of silver coins in Europe. See RGIA, f.588, op.3. d.1851.

21. O meropriatiiakh po snabzheniiu naseleniia serebrom, October 1899, RGIA, f.587, op.33, d.358, ll.36, 174.

22. See the directive (tsirkuliar) of October 23, 1899, in RGIA, f.587, op.33, d.7.

23. RGIA, f.587, op.33, d.7.

24. A. Aleksandrova, *Rasskazy o zolote* (St. Petersburg, 1900), 64; B. C. Endelman, *Monometallism-or en Russie* (Berne, 1917), 103–4.

25. Ob ustanovlenii perevozki kassami Ministerstva Finansov zolotoi i serebrianoi monety po zheleznym dorogam, RGIA, f.587, op.43, d.299.

26. *Instruktsiia dlia pochtovo-telegrafnykh i pochtovykh uchrezhdenii, opredeliaiushchaia poriadok i usloviia priema deneg dlia perevoda po pochte i po telegrafu* (Kharkiv, 1896); *Pochtovo-telegrafnaia statistika za 1899 god* (St. Petersburg, 1900), III.
27. Ob obrazovanii raspredelitenykh tsentrov po snabzheniiu bankovykh uchrezhdenii monetoi (1899), RGIA, f.587, op.33, d.359.
28. Po raznym voprosam voznikaiushchim pri otsylke zolotoi i serebrianoi monety v provintsialnye uchrezhdeniia Gos Banka i za granitsu, RGIA, f.588, op.2, d.41, ll.5, 6, 16, 21, 24, 53, 60.
29. RGIA, f.588, op.2, d.41, 64, 66. "Gruz zolota," *Sankt-Peterburgskaia Gazeta*, 1897, no.299.
30. Professor Iarotskii mentioned that the closures of Nevsky Avenue due to the movement of gold in March 1896 gave ground for speculations about the coinage of new money. *Reforma denezhnago obrashcheniia v Rossii; doklady i preniia v III Otdelenii Imperatorskago Vol' nago ekonomicheskago obshchestva. Stenograficheskii otchet*, 85.
31. RGIA, f.588, op.2. d.41, ll.780b.; RGIA, f.583, op.3, d.884.
32. Migulin, *Russkii gosudarstvennyi kredit*, vol.3, 1060. k
33. O vydache v ssudu Germanskomu Imperskomu Banku zolota na summu do 250 mill.marok, September 8, 1899, RGIA, f.583, op.4, d.312, ll.116–119. As Migulin wrote, the president of the Imperial Bank declined the offer. Migulin, *Reforma denezhnogo obrashcheniia*, 244. k
34. Zapiska sostavlennaia v Ministerstve finansov o sovremennom sostoianii denezhnogo rynka. November 11, 1899, RGIA, f.1044, op.1, d.214, ll.2-20b, 5.
35. Proekt doklada Komiteta finansov Nikolaiu II, 1899, ibid, f.1044, op.1, d.213, l. 1 ob.-3.
36. Migulin, *Reforma denezhnogo obrashcheniia i krizis,*, 253.
37. Witte to Suvorin, RGALI, f.459, op.1, d.719, l. 58.
38. Vsepoddanneiishii doklad ministra finansov o gosudarstvennoi rospisi dokhoddov i raskhodov na 1899, *Vestnik Finansov,* 1899, n.1, 7.
39. Vsepoddanneiishii doklad ministra finansov o gosudarstvennoi rospisi dokhoddov i raskhodov na 1900, *Vestnik Finansov*, 1900, n.1, 8.
40. See the summary of the committee's and individual speakers' statements regarding the currency question in D. I. Nikiforov, *Svod trudov mestnykh komitetov po 49 guberniam Evropeiskoi Rossii. Denezhnoe obrashchenie* (St. Petersburg, 1903).
41. *Trudy mestnykh komitetov o nyzhdakh selskokhoziastvennoi promyshlennosti.* Mogilevskaia guberniia, (St. Petersburg, 1903), 60.
42. *Trudy mestnykh komitetov o nyzhdakh selskokhoziastvennoi promyshlennosti.* Tulskaia guberniia, 362; *Trudy mestnykh komitetov o nyzhdakh selskokhoziastvennoi promyshlennosti.* Mogilevskaia guberniia (St. Petersburg, 1903), 160.
43. *Trudy mestnykh komitetov o nyzhdakh selskokhoziastvennoi promyshlennosti.* Smolenskaia guberniia (St. Petersburg, 1903), 88, 140.
44. *Trudy mestnykh komitetov o nyzhdakh selskokhoziastvennoi promyshlennosti.* Vladimirskaia guberniia, 114; *Trudy mestnykh komitetov o nyzhdakh*

selskokhoziastvennoi promyshlennosti. Kievskaia guberniia (St. Petersburg, 1903), 721.

45. *Trudy mestnykh komitetov o nyzhdakh selskokhoziastvennoi promyshlennosti.* Smolenskaia guberniia (St. Petersburg, 1903), 148.

46. *Trudy mestnykh komitetov o nyzhdakh selskokhoziastvennoi promyshlennosti.* Simbirskaia guberniia (St. Petersburg, 1903), 175. Their opponents predicted that if Russia abandoned the gold standard, it would go bankrupt; furthermore, given the extent of Russia's indebtedness in Europe, the European governments would have to intervene and declare war on Russia to protect the financial interests of their citizens. *Trudy mestnykh komitetov o nyzhdakh selskokhoziastvennoi promyshlennosti.* Tverskaia guberniia (St. Petersburg, 1903), 40.

47. Haim Barkai, "The Macro-Economics of Tsarist Russia in the Industrialization Era: Monetary Development, the Balance of Payments and the Gold Standard," *Journal of Economic History* 33 (June 1973), 338–371; Arcadius Kahan, "Government Policies and the Industrialization of Russia," *Journal of Economic History* 27 (December 1967), 460–477. For the survey of historiography (up to 1976) and the critique of Barkai's and Kahan's statements, see Paul Gregory, "Russian Monetary Policy and Industrialization, 1861–1913," *Journal of Economic History* 36 (December 1976): 836–871. For a critical assessment of the reform, see also "Dvizhenie Zolotogo Zapasa v Rossii v kontse XIX—nachale XX v," in *Istoria Ministerstva Finansov Rossii V chetyrekh tomakh*, edited by A. L. Kudrin, vol.1, 167–168 (Moskva: Infra-M, 2003).

48. Theodore von Laue, *Sergei Witte and the Industrialization of Russia* (New York: Atheneum 1969), 145.

49. Paul Gregory, "Russian Monetary Policy and Industrialization," 848.

50. Olga Crisp, "Russian Financial Policy and the Gold Standard at the End of the Nineteenth Century," *Economic History Review*, new series, 6, no. 2 (1953): 168.

51. Michael D. Bordo and Hugh Rockoff, "The Gold Standard as a 'Good Housekeeping Seal of Approval,'" Papers Presented at the Fifty-Fifth Annual Meeting of the Economic History Association, *Journal of Economic History*. 56, no. 2 (June 1996): 389–428

52. *Protokoly sionskikh mudretsov (po tekstu Nilusa). Vsemirnyi tainyi zagovor* (Berlin, 1922), 72, 116.

53. "Vsepoddanneishii doklad ministra finansov ot 26 noiabria 1898 goda o vvedenii v Velikov Kniazhestve Finliandskom odnoobraznoi s ostal'noi Imperiiei monetnoi sistemy," in *Materialy po vorposu o denezhnom obrashchenii v Velikov Kniazhestve Finliandskom* (St. Petersburg, 1900) 243–248.

54. Ob iz'atii iz obrasheniia sredneaziatskoi tuzemnoi monety, RGIA, f.563, op.2, d.292; Ob obmene monety khanstv, prilegaiushchikh k raionu deistviia Tashkentskogo otdelenia Gos Banka, 1875, RGIA, f.587, op.33, d.141, ll. 28–31.

55. O vvedenii v Bukharskom khanstve rossiiskoi denezhnoi sistemy, December 31, 1899, RGIA, f.563, op.2, d.397, l.3.

56. Khod razvitiia monetnogo voprosa v Bukhare, AVPRI, f.147, op.485, d.254, l.15.

57. RGIA, f.588, op.3, d.432, l. 2–3.

58. Lessar (political agent in Bukhara) to Vrevskii, general governor of Turkestan, August 2, 1894, AVPRI, f.147, op.485, d.254, l. 86ob.–87.

59. In 1899, the emir deposited 1 million rubles bearing 3.5 % interest at the Bukhara branch of the State Bank in the name of his son. The operation was kept in strict secret because "the Muslim laws prohibited lending money on interest."—Delo o vklade emirom bukharskim 1,000,000 rublei v Bukharskoe otdelenie Gosudarstvennogo Banka, AVPRI, f.147, op.485, 1899, d.271; O vkladakh bukharskogo emira, RGIA, f. 587, op.56, d.1662, l.7. In 1901 and 1902, the emir made two more deposits of approximately 9 million rubles.

60. RGIA, f.588, op.3, d.433, l.46.

61. RGIA, f.588, op.3, d.433, 139 ob., 140 ob.

62. "Pis'mo iz Bukhary," *Russkie Vedomosti*, September 12 1897, AVPRI, f.147, op.485, d.254, l.122.

63. "K voprosu o bukharskoi tenge," *Promyshlennaia Gazeta*, September 23, 1897, no.207, RGIA, f.588, op.3, d.433.

64. Po voprosu o bukharskoi tenge, RGIA, f.588, op.3, d.433, August 14, 1897, 139.

65. Lessar to the Ministry of Foreign Affairs, November 28, 1893, AVPRI, f.147, op.485, d.254, ll.47–52.

66. Zhurnal Soveshchaniia po torgovle s aziatskimi gosudarstvami, February 4 and March 4, 1894, AVPRI, f.147, op.485, d.254, l.70 ob.

67. AVPRI, f.147, op.485, d.254, 70 ob. Reference to Kh. M. Fren, *Monety khanov ulusa Dzhuchieva ili Zolotoi Ordy s monetami inykh mukhammedanskikh dinastii v pribavlenii* (St. Petersburg, 1823); Kh. M. Fren, "Katalog monet dzhuchidov ili khanov Zolotoi Ordy," *Zapiski ANO*, t.2, St. Petersburg, 1850.

68. Komitet finansov, April 3, 1900, RGIA, f.563, op.2, d.397. This plan was elaborated in 1894–98 by a special committee "on the trade with Asian states" chaired by Dmitrii Kobeko.

69. Vrevsky to the minister of finance, November 18, 1898, AVPRI, f.147, op.485, d.254, 233. The Ministry of Foreign Affairs insisted on the plan that demonstrated more respect for the emir's "autonomy": allowing the emir to fix the rate by his own decree and opening the exchange for rubles at the State Bank, from the emir's personal account where all available amounts of tenga would be deposited. AVPRI, f.147, op.485, d.254, 285 ob, 313 ob.

70. Soobrazheniia d.t.s. Ternera po voprosu o vvedenii rossiiskoi denezhnoi sistemy v Bukharskom khanstve, RGIA F.563, op.2, d.397.

71. Turkestan general governor to the minister of finance, December 31, 1897, p. 9, RGIA F.563, op.2, d.397. The same opinion was expressed by the "political agent" in Bukhara Ignatiev.

72. The emir could resume the coinage of *tenga*; however, these new coins, after their acceptance for state payments, were also meant to be delivered to the State

Bank and gradually exempted. In 1904 the coinage of silver money was supposed to be permanently discontinued. See RGIA F.563, op.2, d.397. O priniatii
na schet Gosudarstvennogo Kaznacheistva chasti ubytkov on perechekanki
nakhodiashcheisia v Gosudarstvennom Banke istertoi bukharskoi tengi January 31,
1903, RGIA, f.583, op.4, d.316, l.16–18.

73. Twenty million tenga coins were handed immediately to the State Bank. The
emir also received the right to strike 25 million coins that had to be delivered to
the Bank. After that emission, the emir lost his right to issue money forever. The
Russian government had the right to mint tenga on the emir's mint from "Russian
silver" if economic conditions necessitated another influx of silver currency.

74. The government claimed that the stabilization of the tenga's rate "cost" 5.3 million
rubles.

75. Po voprosu ob okhrane vyezdnoi razmennoi kassy, September 28, 1901, RGIA,
f.588, op.3, d.436, ll. 73-74, 119.

76. RGIA, f.588, op.3, d.436, 58 ob.

77. Eteocle Lorini, *La réforme monétaire de la Russie* (Paris: V. Giard & E. Briere, 1898,
96–97. At the time Lorini was writing, the reform was not yet completed.

78. A. F. Gubarevich-Radobylskii, *Ekonomicheskii ocherk Bukhary i Tunisa* St.
(Petersburg, 1905),, 160.

79. Dmitrii Logofet, who traveled in the region between 1904 and 1911, confirmed that
even after the suspension of the *tenga*'s coinage, local and foreign coins continued to
circulate along with the rubles, and the project of monetary unification remained
unfinished. D. N. Logofet, *Bukharskoe khanstvo pod rossiiskim protektoratom* (St.
Petersburg, 1911), vol. 2, 69–73.

80. RGIA, f.588, op.3438, 8, 20–22: Pleske's telegram to the head of the State Bank
branch in Bukhara, January 16, 1903.

81. Sobolevskii, head of the Bukhara branch of the State Bank, April 17, 1909, RGIA,
f.588, op.3, d. 439, 13 ob.

82. Sobolevskii, head of the Bukhara branch of the State Bank, April 17, 1909, RGIA,
f.588, op.3, d. 439, 13 ob.

83. See reports on the monetary situation in this province in 1912, AVPRI, f.147,
op.485, d.255, l.266-274.

84. Kopiia s otnoshevniia rossiikogo imperatorskogo agentstva v Bukhare na imia
turkestanskogo general-gubernatora, April 22 1912, AVPRI, f.147, op.485, d.255,
274 ob.

85. "Persidskie krany v Zakaspiiskom krae," *Kavkaz*, May 6, 1901, RGIA, f.588,
op.3, d.21.

86. O splave na Sankt-Peterburgskom monetnom dvore bukharskoi stertoi tengi v
osobye slitki dlia razmennoi operatsii v Manchzhurii, RGIA, f.588, op.3, d. 444.

87. N. Poppe, "Denezhnoe obrashchenie v Severnoi Manchzhurii," *Sbornik konsulskikh
donesenii, 1904* (St. Petersburg, 1904), 312; A. Dombrovskii and V. Voroshilov,
Manchzuriia (St. Petersburg, 1904), 196.

88. Alexei Ivanovskii, who traveled in Manchuria in the 1890s, noticed that some of these coins in bundles were minted as early as in the seventh century, and these were not even considered numismatic rarities. Ivanovskii, "Mednaia moneta v Man'chzhurii," *Zapiski Vostochnogo Otdelenia RAO*, v.7, 1893, 301–307. There were also paper bonds issued by private bankers, trade houses, and even hotels in lieu of these bundles, but they circulated only locally and were very susceptible to counterfeiting. Dombrovskii and Voroshilov, *Manchzuriia*, 197.

89. Poppe, "Denezhnoe obrashchenie v Severnoi Manchzhurii," 313

90. RGIA, f.560, op.28, d.34, 3–7, Report of Mukden's governor (Tsian-Tsiun). For a detailed analysis, see Chia Yin Hsu, "The "Color" of Money: The Ruble, Competing Currencies, and Conceptions of Citizenship in Manchuria and the Russian Far East, 1890s–1920s," *Russian Review* 73 (January 2014), 87–93.

91. See the protocol of the special meeting of the Board and the Revision committee of the Eastern Chinese Railroad society, Zhurnal Osobogo soveshchaniiia Pravleniia i revizionnogo Komiteta Obshchestva KVZhD po voprosu o monete, naibolee pregodnoi dlia rasplat v Manchzhurii, 18 okriabria 1897, RGIA, f.323, op.1, d.1109. Ya. G. Alekseev argued for the introduction of rubles. Witte remarked on the margin: "No. This would mean introducing gold"—RGIA, f.323, op.1, d.1109, l.70 ob. Witte insisted on keeping "silver in ingots" as the main means of payment.

92. RGIA, f.323, op.1, d.1110, l.130.

93. GARF, f.543, op.1, d.204, V.N. Kokovtsov, Zamechania na zapisku Golovina o sposobakh pokrytiia voennykh raskhodov s naimen'shim obremeneniem Gosud. Kaznacheistva, 3.

94. Boris Demchinskii, *Rossiia v Man'chzhurii*, (St. Petersburg, 1908), 99.

95. B. L. Putnam Weale, "Manchu and Muscovite," quoted from *Report on the Introduction of the gold-exchange standard into China, the Philippine Islands, Panama, and other Silver-Using Countries, and on the Stability of Exchange. Submitted to the Secretary of State, October 22, 1904 by the US Commission on International Exchange. Hugh H. Hanna, Charles A. Conant, Jeremiah W. Jenks* (Washington, DC: Government Printing Office, 1904), 278–282.

96. Jeremiah W. Jenks, *Considerations on a New Monetary System for China* (Ithaka: U.S. Commission On International Exchange, 1904), 11-12; *Stability of international exchange. Report on the introduction of the gold-exchange standard into China and other silver-using countries, submitted to the Secretary of State, October 1, 1903 by the US Commission on International Exchange. Hugh H. Hanna, Charles A. Conant, Jeremiah W. Jenks* (Washington, DC: Government Printing Office, 1903). 11–12, 15

97. *Stability of International Exchange*, 30.

98. According to the commission's report, Russia's representatives declared that "the American plan would have our approval if it were so amended as to mean a national silver currency issued on Government account, which should be given as soon as practicable a fixed parity with gold," *Stability of International Exchange*, 31.

99. O priezde v Sankt-Peterburg komissarov Pravitelstva Soedinennykh Shtatov Severnoi Ameriki dlia peregovorov ob ustanovlenii bolee ustoichivoi tseny serebra, June 27, 1903, RGIA, f.583, op.4, d.316, l.91. Russia, as the commission's report suggested, was the only country that protested against adopting the uniform ratio of silver to gold (1:32) "to be established in the Orient," *Stability of International Exchange*, 105.

100. V. N. Kokovtsov, Zamechania na zapisku Golovina o sposobakh pokrytiia voennykh raskhodov s naimen'shim obremeneniem Gosud. Kaznacheistva, GARF, f.543, op.1, d.293, 1–4.

101. "Zapiska Kokovtsova v komitet finansov ot 17 marta 1904 g," in *Russkie finansy i evropeiskaia birzha v 1904–1906 gg.* (Moscow, Leningrad: Tsentrarkhiv, 1926), 51–52, 60.

102. O sostavlenii vsepoddanneishego doklada m-ra finansov o gosudarstvennoi rospisi na 1905 g., RGIA, f.560, op.26, d.505, 380b.

103. *Russko-iaponskaia voina 1904–1905 gg. T.VII. Tyl deistvuiushchei armii* (St. Petersburg, 1910), ch.1, 391. According to the minister's report, the "silver reserve fund" in Manchuria was worth 12 million rubles: part of it had been taken as war booty from "Chinese fortresses and cities," O sostavlenii vsepod. doklada m-ra finansov o gosudarstvennoi rospisi na 1905 g. RGIA, f.560, op.26, d.505, 37 ob.

104. RGIA, f.323, op.1, d.1110, l.169.

105. Normally, silver came from London, but British silver grew too expensive. Poppe, "Denezhnoe obrashchenie," 317.

106. G. D. Dementiev, *Vo chto oboshlas' nashemu gosudarstvennomu kaznacheistvu voina s Iaponiei* (Petrograd, 1917).

107. Metzler, *Lever of Empire*, 40–42.

108. Russia's experience was quoted by foreign experts as the example of a persistent colonial monetary policy. See references to Russia's policy in Bukhara: *Stability of International Exchange*, 14; *Gold Standard in International Trade. Report on the Introduction of the Gold-exchange Standard*, 91, 192.

109. Of the value of commitments, see Michael D. Bordo and Finn E. Kydland, *The Gold Standard as a Rule*, NBER working paper series, No. 3367 (Cambridge, MA: National Bureau of Economic Research, 1990).

110. B. V. Anan'ich and R. Sh. Ganelin, *Serguei Iulievich Vitte i ego vremia* (St. Petersburg: Dmitry Bulanin, 1999), 88.

111. L. Yasnopolskii and L. Feldzer, "Predislovie," *Bankovaia entsiklopediia. T.2. Birzha* (Kyiv, 1916).

112. Milton Friedman, "Real and Pseudo Gold Standards," *Journal of Law & Economics* 4 (October 1961): 66–79.

113. For a similar idea about the political permissive factor of the gold standard, see Leland Yeager, "The Image of the Gold Standard," in *A Retrospective on the Classical Gold Standard, 1821–1931*, edited by Michael D. Bordro and Anna J. Schwartz (Chicago: University of Chicago Press, 1984), 665.

CHAPTER 9

1. "V tsarstve zolota," *Peterburgskaia Gazeta*, March 19, 1905, 2.

2. Al. Ivanovich, "V zolotykh kladovykh," *Novoe Vremia*, March 19, 1905.

3. Ironically, Witte assisted China in obtaining the loan to pay the indemnity.

4. Mark Metzler, *The Lever of Empire: The International Gold Standard and the Crisis of Liberalism in Prewar Japan* (Berkeley: University of California, 2006), 3. The rhetoric of the reform memorandum written by Count Matsukata Masayoshi, minister of state for finance, shows many similarities between Russia and Japan. In both cases the emphasis was on balancing the amount of paper money and gold, and on joining the "golden" club of other nations. Japan, unlike Russia, reformed its bank of issue: it copied the bank's organization from the Bank of Belgium that "stood highest" in "the perfectness of organization and the well-regulated condition of business management." The government became "the Bank's shareholder to the amount of one half the entire capital of the bank"; the other part of capital was available for private shareholders in Japan, Matsukata Masayoshi, *Report of the Adoption of the Gold Standard in Japan* (Tokyo: Government Press, 1899), 65–68.

5. See, especially, A. A. Guryev, *Reforma denezhnogo obrashcheniia* (St. Petersburg, 1896), ch.i., vyp.i, 206–241; M. I. Bogolepov, *Finansy, pravitel'stvo i obshchestvennye interesy* (St. Petersburg, 1907), 250–251; Bukovetskii, "Svobodnaia nalichnost' i zolotoi zapas," 366.

6. GARF, f.543, op.i, d.279a, O znachenii denezhnoi reformy dlia sosredotocheniia sredstv v sluchae chrezvychainykh sobytii, April 1900.

7. Many European observers noted the difference in the size of the gold reserve. See, for example, Karl Helfferich's book on the financial aspect of the Russo-Japanese War published in 1904 and translated (in October 1904) into French: *Die Finanzielle Seite des russisch-japanischen Krieges* (Bonn: Marine-Rundschau: Zeitschrift für Seewesen, 1904); cited from second edition (1906) *Das Geld im russisch-japanischen Kriege* (Berlin: E. S. Mittler und Sohn, 1906), 67, 69, 70. Helfferich refers to a number of publications in France and Germany, all favorably assessing Russia's financial shape. Russian authorities also watched the development of the gold reform in Japan. A report of the Ministry of Foreign Affairs points out the scarcity of gold: Vypiska iz otcheta Iaponskogo Min. Finansov o zolotoi valiute v Iaponii, AVPRI, f. 138, op. 467, 1900, 185.

8. Raphaël-Georges Lévy, "Finances de guerre: Russie et Japon," *Revue de Deux Mondes* 22, no.i (Juillet 1904): 127.

9. "Zapiska Kokovtsova v Komitet finansov," *Russkie finansy i evropeiskaia birzha v 1904-1906 gg.* (Moskva, Leningrad: Tsentrarkhiv, 1926), 42–43.

10. P.P. Migulin, *O finansovoi gotovnosti k voine*, (Kharkiv,, 1904), 7.

11. "Zapiska Kokovtsova," 59. V. N. Kokovtsov, *Iz moego proshlogo. Vospominaniia* (Moskva: Nauka, 1992), kn.i, 40–42.

12. Zhurnal komiteta finansov utverzhdennyi 27 Marta 1904, g. *Russkie finansy i evropeiskaia birzha*, 66.

13. A. I. Putilov to A. G. Rafalovitch, *Russkie finansy i evropeiskaia birzha*, 86.

14. O sostavlenii vsepoddanneishego doklada m-ra finansov o gosudarstvennoi rospisi na 1905 g., RGIA, f. 560, op.26, d. 505, 30 ob.

15. Boris V. Ananich, "Russian Military Expenditures in the Russo-Japanese War, 1904–5," in *The Russo-Japanese War in Global Perspective: World War Zero*, edited by John W. Steinberg et al., 452–454 (Leiden: Brill, 2005). In addition to this loan in Paris, Russia floated two more loans in Berlin in 1905 and four domestic loans in the total sum of 1.2 billion rubles.

16. Edward S. Miller, "Japan's Other Victory: Overseas Financing of the Russo-Japanese War," in *The Russo-Japanese War in Global Perspective: World War Zero*, edited by John W. Steinberg et al. (Leiden: Brill, 2005), 274.

17. Jennifer Siegel, *For Peace and Money: French and British Finance in the Service of Tsars and Commissars* (Oxford: Oxford University Press, 2014), 50–85.

18. Russian Finance, *The Times*, October 12, 1904, no. 37523.

19. Among his sources of Serguei Sharapov, Petr Butmi, and Petr Shvanebakh. Lucien Wolf was a champion of Jews' rights in Europe and Russia, and he repeatedly wrote about Russian atrocities against the Jews. It is therefore surprising that he chose Serguei Sharapov, a known anti-Semite, as a point of reference.

20. "Is Russia Solvent?" *The Times*, March 11, 1905, 10. The article appeared along with Leo Tolstoy's essay "The Crisis in Russia" and information about the battle of Mukden—one of Russia's military disasters.

21. "Is Russia Solvent?" *The Times*, March 12, 1905, 3.

22. Henry Norman, "The Gold Reserve of Russia," *World's Work*, May 1904, 4920.

23. The editor's commentary on Wolf's article, *The Times*, March 14, 1905.

24. Copy of Kokovtsov's letter "to the editor of *The Times*," RGIA, f.560, op.22, d.291, l.5.

25. "French Capital in Russia (from our own correspondent)," *The Times*, March 15, 1905.

26. V. I. Lenin, "Evropeiskii capital i samodezhavie," in *Polnoe sobranie sochinenii*, t.9, (Moskva: Politizdat, 1967), 376, first publication *Vperiod*, April 4 (March 23) 1905.

27. RGIA, f.560, op. 22, d.291, 13. Telegram from *The Times* to Kokovtsov. *The Times*, however, published, without comments, a note with the numbers concerning the size of the gold reserve and an official communique rebuking "the statement regarding Russia's gold reserve contained in a letter from Mr. Lucien Wolf." "Russia's Gold Reserve," *The Times*, March 18, 1905; "The Russian Gold Reserve," April 3, 1905. *The Times* also published Petr Shvanebakh's letter protesting the misinterpretation of numbers and judgements provided in his earlier book quoted by Wolf. "The Russian Gold Reserve," *The Times*, April 4, 1905. The same issue featured a letter to the editor from Charles Littmann, stating that the gold standard regime is

not maintained in Russia because, despite the ruble's convertibility, the export of gold is severely restrained.

28. *Daily Express* wanted to "obtain the invitation," declined by *The Times*. However, the government's agent Routchkowsky (Ruchkovskii) advised against it, pointing out that this was a newspaper "secondary, without influence." The *Daily Mirror* volunteered to send a photographer: RGIA, f.560, op.22, d.291, 14-23. See also "Perepiska s ministrov finansov ob osmotre zolotykh kladovyckh banka predstaviteliami pechati i gazetnye vyrezki," RGIA, f.587, op.56, d.34, ll. 3–12.

29. Kokovtsov's letter to Timashev, RGIA, f.587, op.56, d.34, l.19.

30. RGIA, f.587, op.56, d.34, l.21-21a.

31. RGIA, f.560, op.22, d.291. See also the polemics between Sir Howard Vincent and Lucien Wolf on the matter of the Russian gold reserve: *The Times*, April 29, May 25, May 27, 1905.

32. A summary of Martin's book is in "Rudolf Martin on Russia's Financial Conditions," *New York Times*, June 24, 1906. Many thanks to Harold James for pointing out this article.

33. Rudolf Martin, *Die Zukunft Russlands und Japans. Die deutchen Milliarden in Gefahr* (Subtitle on the original edition's cover: *Soll Deutchland die Zeche bezahlen*) (Berlin: Heymann, 1905), 69.

34. M. Fridman, "Neizbezhno li bankrotstvo Rossii?" *Rech'*, June 18, 1906, no. 103.

35. In September 1905, the Ministry of Finance sent these materials to the representatives of the German press: Karl Rene in Berlin and Oscar Leman in Meinz; RGIA, f.560, op.26, d.506, l.5. In August 1906, Kokovtsov discussed with banker Ernst von Mendelssohn-Bartholdy (Berlin) the publication of a popular brochure based on the materials sent to him by the minister. The brochure was supposed to be published anonymously under the title *"Von dem Russen!"* (Ibid, 91–94). See also another anti-Martin pamphlet *"The Prophet of Our Time,"* in RGIA, f.560, op.26, d.507. In 1906, Martin published a new edition of the same book focused only on Russia. See the Ministry of Finance's documents related to the attempts at neutralizing the influence of these publications: RGIA, f.560, op.26, d.610. After the suspension of censorship restrictions, two editions of Martin's book appeared in Russian under the title *Budushchnost' Rossii i Iaponii*, trans by I. Novik (Moska: Sytin, 1906); transl by M. S. Zakovich and S. B. Veinberg (Moska: Sytin, 1907).

36. As *The Times'* correspondent pointed out, "Russian credit both at home and abroad is based entirely on the presence of a large gold reserve, and the Government is sparing no effort to keep the gold in the country. But the moment it begins to flow out national credit will collapse"; "The Financial Strain in Russia," *The Times*, August 5, 1904.

37. "Zolotoi milliard" [The Golden Billion], *Rus'*, April 2, 1905.

38. O sostavlenii vsepoddanneishego doklada m-ra finansov o gosudarstvennoi rospisi na 1905 g., RGIA, f.560, op.26, d.505, l.31.

39. O sostavlenii vsepoddanneishego doklada m-ra finansov o gosudarstvennoi rospisi na 1905 g., RGIA, f.560, op.26, d.505, 7 ob.

40. O sostavlenii vsepoddanneishego doklada m-ra finansov o gosudarstvennoi rospisi na 1905 g., RGIA, f.560, op.26, d.505, 7 ob.

41. Witte noted on the margin of the draft report that it was not the conviction that mattered but the "actual gold backing," and the report was corrected accordingly: O sostavlenii vsepoddanneishego doklada m-ra finansov o gosudarstvennoi rospisi na 1905 g., RGIA, f.560, op.26, d.505, 7 ob., 299. See the final version of the report: "Vsepoddanneishii doklad Ministra FInansov o gosudarstvennoi rospisi dokhodov i raskhodov na 1905 god i obshchaia gosudarstvennaia rospis' dokhodov i raskhodov na 1905 god," *Vestnik Finansov, Promyshlennosti i Torgovli*, 1905, no.1, 7.

42. "Zapiska predsedatelia pravleniia Gosudarstvennogo banka S.I. Timasheva o denezhnom obrashchenii v Rossii v 1904–1907 gg., 12 Fevralia 1907," in "Denezhnoe obrashchenie i finansovoe polozhenie Rossii (1904–1907)," *Istoricheskii Arkhiv*, 1956, no. 3, 116.

43. "Polozhenie Gosudarstvennogo Banka i denezhnogo obrashcheniia s oktiabria 1905 po aprel 1906 (April 1906)," TsGIA SPb, f.2098, op.1, d.54, l.21 ob.

44. S. I. Timashev, Avtobiograficheskie zapiski, in A. L. Vychugzhanin, *S.I. Timashev: zhizn' i deiatelnost'* (Triumen': Slovo, 2006), 217–218. As the official memo suggested, more than 70 million rubles in gold were dispatched from St. Petersburg to regional offices for exchange. In December 1905 the State Bank changed its policy and started retracting gold from provinces to St. Petersburg. "Polozhenie Gosudarstvennogo Banka i denezhnogo obrashcheniia s oktiabria 1905 po aprel 1906" (April 1906), TsGIA SPb, F.2098, op.1, d.54, l.23 ob, 25 ob.

45. "Dokladnaia zapiska Komiteta finansov Nikolaiu II o katastroficheskom finansovom sostoianii strany i merakh sokhraneniia zolotogo zapasa, December 14, 1905," *Istoricheskie Zapiski* 2 (1955): 127.

46. N. S. Tagantsev, *Perezhitoe* (Petrograd, 1919), 68.

47. O peresmotre polozhenia ob EZGB, TsGIA SPb, f.1258, op.2, d.904, l. 9–10.

48. Serguei Gan's reports to the Bank's director Timashev, RGIA, f.587, op.56, d.703, 190–212.

49. Delo domovoi kontory EZGB Ushakova Mikhaila Andreevicha, RGIA, f.1682, op.1, d.55; O rabochem Ushakove F.1682, op.1, d.57 (Witte's letter recommending Ushakov's appointment in which Witte attested that he was a "reliable worker"). On Ushakov's leadership in the strike: O rabochem Ushakove, RGIA, f. 1682, op.1, d.109, 14.

50. RGIA, f.1682, op.1, d.55, l.5.

51. Witte also claimed that Ushakov had played a key role in persuading Grand Duke Nikolai Nikolaevich of the necessity of granting the constitution. The Grand Duke then convinced the tsar to sign the Manifesto of October 17, 1905. S.Yu. Vitte, *Vospominaniia*, vol.3 (Moskva: Izd-vo sotsialno-ekonomicheskoi literatury, 1960),

44, 53. Mikhail Ushakov, "Vospominaniia o besede s velikim kniazem" *Krasnyi Arkhiv*, 1923, 4, 413–417.

52. See reports about revolutionary incidents that leaked to the press: O raznykh proisshestviakh, TsGIA SPb, f. 1458, op.2, d.468, O dostavlenii v Osvedomitel'noe biuro svedenii, TsGIA SPb, f.1458, op.2, d.941. The Expedition's administration had to purchase revolvers and hand them out to the employees of cash offices and storage facilities. O priniatii mer dlia okhrany denezhnykh summ . . . i o pokupke revol'verov. TsGIA SPb, f.1458, op.2, d.428.

53. See Gan's reports: RGIA, f.587, op.56, d.703, ll.193–212.

54. Perepiska upravliaiushchego Gos. Bankom s glavnokomanduiushchim okruga o postanovke okhrany banka, RGIA, f. 587, op.56, d.347.

55. Kokovtsov, *Iz moego proshlogo*, 109.

56. Petr Saburov advocated this view in the Committee of Finance; however, economist Illarian Kaufman pointed out that it was simply too late. He thought that suspension could only help as a precautionary measure, not a measure of last resort. Besides, the gold standard represented a bridge between Russia and the world, and if gold was carried away in the political hysteria that gripped Russian wealthy society, it could come back only if this bridge stayed intact. Terminating the exchange meant losing this gold forever. Untitled memo, November 21–28, 1905, TsGIA SPB, f.2098, op.1, d.56.

57. TsGIA SPB, f.2098, op.1, d.56, l.13

58. Predlozheniia ministra finansov I. P. Shipova o merakh sokhraneniia zolotogo zapasa Rossii"—*Istoricheskii Akhiv* 1955, no.2, 137.

59. RGIA, f.560, op.26, d.38, l. 85.

60. B. V. Ananich, "Finansovyi krizis tsarizma 1904–1905 gg.," *Trudy Leningradskogo Otdelenia Instituta Istorii AN SSSR*, vol.8, Leningrad, 1967, 308.

61. Ananich, "Finansovyi krizis tsarizma 1904–1905 gg.," 314.

62. Siegel, *For Peace and Money*, 77–85; Boris Ananich, *Rossiia i mezhdunarodnyi kapital, 1897–1914. Ocherki istorii finansovykh otnoshenii* (Leningrad: Izd-vo AN SSSR, 1970), 149–177.

63. Vitte, *Vospominaniia*, vol.3, 249.

64. "Zapiska predsedatelia pravleniia Gosudarstvennogo Banka S.I. Timasheva o denezhnom obrashchenii v Rossii v 1904–1907 ii, 12 fevralia 1907," *Istoricheskii Arkhiv*, 1956, no.3, 101–103.

65. Draft of the report on the opening of the State Bank's branch in Helsinki (1903): RGIA, f.588, op.3, d.427, 810b. Witte quarreled with the general governor of Finland, Viacheslav Plehve, about the procedures of appointing the branch's director, the importance of financial expertise over political reliability, and, in general, the priority of economic goals over the policy of russification. "Ob otkrytii otdeleniia Gos Banka v Gelsingforse." RGIA, f.588, op.3, d.427, 44, 45–47, 51, 62, 65–66, 68, 73–74, 81.

66. See Vykovskii's reports to the State Bank, RGIA, f.588, op.3, d.427, l.139–148.

67. Minister of finance (Shipov) to general-governor N. N. Gerard - RGIA, f.588, op.3, d.427, ll. 169–170. In 1911 the discussion about opening the State Bank's branch in Finland was resumed. The government decided to start with Vyborg—the city closest to the Russian border, RGIA, f.1276, op.18, d.365, f.587, op.56, d.1685.

68. Kokovtsov, *Iz moego proshlogo*, 115, 119.

69. Michael D. Bordo and Eugene N. White, "A Tale of Two Currencies: British and French Finance during the Napoleonic Wars," *Journal of Economic History* 51, no.2 (June 1991): 303.

70. RGIA, f.560, op.26, d.38, l.43.

71. RGIA, f.587, op.33, d.23, 7.

72. "Predlozhenia ministra finansov I. P. Shipova o merakh po sokhraneniiu zolotogo zapasa strany," *Istoricheskie zapiski* 2 (1955): 137.

73. RGIA, f.560, op.26, d.38, l.10 ob.

74. P. P. Migulin, *Russkii Tsentralnyi Avtonomnyi Gosudarstvennyi Bank* (Kharkov, 1906), 13. See also Petr Saburov's (incomplete) response to Migulin's project: "Zamechaniia P.A. Saburova na brochuru Migulina Russkii Avtonomnyi Tsentralnyi Emissionnyi Bank," RGIA, f.1044, op.1, d.285.

75. Migulin, *Russkii Tsentralnyi*, 11; "La semaine financière," *Le Temps*, August 27, 1906.

76. Stanislav Skarzhinskii, "Gosudarstvennyi ili aktsionernyi bank?" *Slovo*, September 6, 1905.

77. *Voprosy gosudarstvennogo khoziaistva i buidzhetnogo prava* (St. Petersburg, 1907), 14.

78. O preobrazovanii denezhnoi sistemy v interesakh uspeshnogo razvitiia narodnogo khoziaistva, RGIA, f.1278, op.1-Sozyv 2, d.1201.

79. See Yasnopolskii's chapter on the State Bank in a collection published by Petr Dolgorukov and Ivan Petrunkevich, two prominent members of the constitutional-democratic party, and focused on the financial aspect of the constitutional regime in Russia. The authors reiterated their demands to strengthen the public's and the Duma's control over finances and grant the State Bank autonomy from the Ministry of Finances; L. Yasnopolskii, "Gosudarstvennyi Bank," in *Voprosy gosudarstvennogo khoziaistva i buidzhetnogo prava*, edited by P. D. Dolgorukov and I. I. Petrunkevich (St. Petersburg, 1907).

80. Yasnopolskii, "Gosudarstvennyi Bank," 254.

81. Yasnopolskii, "Gosudarstvennyi Bank," 282.

82. See also Witte's critique of Kokovtsov's monetary policy in his memoirs: Vitte, *Vospominaniia*, vol. 2, 401.

83. Witte, March 3, 1907, RGIA, f.587, op.56, d.1670, ll.163–178.

84. Witte, March 3, 1907, RGIA, f.587, op.56, d.1670, ll.163–178.

85. Witte, zapiska April 3, 1907, RGIA, f.587, op.56, d.1670, ll.110–117.

86. In January 1906, Professor Illarion Kaufman wrote a long note to Witte "on the undesirability of converting the State Bank into a joint-stock [bank]" in which he focused on the financial aspect of that idea. The conversion would have required tripling the size of the Bank's capital. It was unlikely that in the circumstances the

bank would be able to generate sufficient dividend income to satisfy its potential shareholders. See "Zapiska dlia Vitte o nezhelatelnosti prevrashcheniia Gosud. Banka v aktsionernyi," TsGIA SPb, f.2098, op.1. d.52. It is possible that Witte considered reforming the State Bank without changing the nature of the bank's capital and governance.

87. In 1908, the government put an end to the discussion of the State Bank's independence by entrusting the reform to the Bank's administration. Not surprisingly, the Bank's council reluctantly considered the problems of its own violations of the charter and the strengthening of the external control of its activity. It also categorically spoke against the idea of introducing private stock capital and separating the bank from the government. Zhurnal Soveta Gosudarstvennogo Banka ob osnovaniiakh preobrazovaniia Gosudarstvennogo Banka, RGIA, f.587, op.60, d. 20, 7–8.

CHAPTER 10

1. V. Zhabotinskii, "Cherez Angliiu," *Russkie Vedomosti*, September 20, 1914. Also quoted in M.I. Bogolepov, "Voina i den'gi," *Vorposy mirovoi voiny* (Petrograd, 1915), 399.
2. S. V. Prokofiev, *Dnevnik, 1907–1918* (Paris: SPRKFV, 2002), 543 (record for February 1 and 3, 1915).
3. "Zolotye zapasy soiuznykh gosudarstv," *Birzhevye Vedomosti*, February 8 1915, 14658.
4. Pavel Genzel', "Zolotoi gramm, kak osnova mezhdunarodnoi valiuty," *Russkie Vedomosti*, July 14, 1910.
5. On the arrangement of space in the Great Kremlin Palace, see RGIA, f. 472, op.50, d. 1684 and RGIA, f. 482, op.6, d.222; on the relocation itself and the protective measures: RGIA, f.587, op.56, d. 158.
6. "Russia's Demand for Gold due to Political Affairs," *Wall Street Journal*, April 24, 1914, 8.
   "Paris Exchange Threatens Gold Movement to That Center," *Wall Street Journal*, April 9, 1914.
   "Great European Banks Are Competing Sharply for Gold," *Wall Street Journal*, March 31, 1914.
7. L. J. Burnes, "Flow of Gold Abroad Analyzed," The Annalist, *Wall Street Journal*, June 20, 1914; "Keen Competition for Gold in London Market," *Wall Street Journal*, May 19, 1914; "Foreign Exchanges' High Point in over Four Years," *Wall Street Journal*, May 13, 1914; "London Perplexed at American Markets," *The Globe*, May 11, 1914, 8. As *The Globe* reported, between January and early May, the Russian State Bank added 7 million pound sterling to its gold reserve.
8. "The Outgoing of Gold," *Los Angeles Times*, July 7, 1914; " 'Holland' writes of Recent Record Exportation of Gold to Europe," *Washington Post*, July 2, 1914.
9. A. L. Sidorov, *Finansovoe polozhenie Rossii v gody pervoi mirovoi voiny* (Moskva: Akademia Nauk SSSR, 1960), 103.

10. For detailed financial statistics, see S. G. Beliaev, *Bark i finansovaia politika Rossii 1914–1917* (St. Peterburg: Izd-vo Sankt-Petersburgskogo Un-ta, 2002), 575. This sum, taken from the annual reports of the State Bank, included the so-called gold abroad, that is, virtual gold in securities deposited in European banks. Many Russian economists and politicians objected to counting "foreign gold" as part of the gold reserve. Without this gold, prewar gold coverage constituted 90%.

11. Z. S. Katzenelenbaum, *Voina i Finansovo-Ekonomicheskoe Polozhenie Rossii* (Moskva, 1917), 41.

12. *Stenograficheskii otchet zasedanii soedinennykh komissii biudzhentoi i finansovoi 4,5 i 6 avgusta 1915 po rassmotreniiu zakonoproektov o rasshirenii predostavlennogo Gosudarstvennomu banku prava vypuska gosudastvennykh kreditnykh biletov. Gosudarstvennaia Duma. Chetvertyi sozyv, sessiia 4. Prilozheniia k stenograficheskim ontchetam n.26 i 38* (Petrograd, 1915), 14. Critics of the government still observed that its week-long hesitation cost 1.6 million gold rubles that had been withdrawn between July 16 and July 23, 1914. I. A. Mikhailov, *Voina i nashe denezhnoe obrashchenie. Fakty i tsifry* (Petrograd, 1916), 5.

13. The suspension of exchange immediately affected the ruble's standing vis-à-vis other currencies: from the pre-war gold-based ratio of £10 for 94 rubles, 57 kopeck, the rate grew up to 130 rubles in September 1914 and then stabilized at 110–120 rubles throughout 1915. The ruble's rate kept fluctuating, reflecting economic conditions as well as the military successes of the Russian army and diplomatic conditions

14. In 1910 Russia paid 19 million rubles for imported gold, in 1911—47 million, 1912—175 million, 1913—165 million. *Stenograficheskii otchet zasedanii soedinennykh komissii biudzhentoi i finansovoi 4,5 i 6 avgusta 1915 po rassmotreniiu zakonoproektov o rasshirenii predostavlennogo Gosudarstvennomu banku prava vypuska gosudastvennykh kreditnykh biletov. Gosudarstvennaia Duma. Chetvertyi sozyv, sessiia 4. Prilozheniia k stenograficheskim ontchetam n.26 i 38*, 59.

15. "Allies Buy War Munitions Here," *New York Tribune*, October 23, 1914.

16. The Council of Ministers prohibited the import of food supplies and goods that Russia usually exported (dried and salted meat and other produce). Osobyi zhurnal Soveta Ministrov August 23, 1914, in *Osobye zhurnaly Soveta Ministrov Rossiiskoi Imperii, 1909–1917. "1914"* (Moskva: ROSSPEN, 2006), 313; RGIA, f. 1276, op.10, d.248, ll. 1–72.

17. "Allies Buy War Munitions Here," *New York Tribune*, October 23, 1914. Grand Duke Andrei Vladimirovich complained on the pages of his diary about the problems of munitions: "[They] bought rifles in America, but something happened with the payment. The Americans wanted to be paid in gold, and we wanted to pay with promissory notes. Our financial agent in America protested the payments in promissory notes saying that the appearance of our promissory notes on the US stock exchanges may negatively affect the rate." "Voennyi dnevnik velikogo kniazia Andreia Vladimirovicha Romanova," *Oktiabr'*, 1998, no. 4, https://magazines.

gorky.media/october/1998/4/voennyj-dnevnik-velikogo-knyazya-andreya-vla dimirovicha-romanova.html.

18. Sergei Beliaev, *P. L. Bark i finansovaia politika Rossii 1914–1917* (St. Peterburg: Izd-vo Sankt-Petersburgskogo Un-ta, 2002); Jennifer Siegel, *For Peace and Money: French and British Money in the Service of Tsars and Commissars* (New York : Oxford University Press, 2014), 125–167,

19. Petr Bark, *Vospominaniia poslednego ministra finansov Rossiiskoi Imperii* (Moskva: Kuchkovo pole, 2017), vol.1, 313, 308. This was not exactly true: the government could not simply pay for all military orders in gold bars from the State Bank's reserve, and the amount of money borrowed in cash or credit exceeded the nominal value of pawned gold.

20. Krivoshein also added that one of the roles of the gold reserve was to serve as a military fund. This last observation was legally incorrect, but it was widely shared, and Bark had nothing to say against this argument. Bark, Petr Bark, *Vospominaniia poslednego ministra finansov Rossiiskoi Imperii* , vol.1, 315, September 25, 1914.

21. Sidorov, *Finansovoe polozhenie*, 231.

22. Vincent Barnett suggests that John Maynard Keynes, who in early 1915 joined the Treasury and actively participated in the preparation of financial agreements, drafted this plan. Vincent Barnett, "Calling Up the Reserves: Keynes, Tugan-Baranovsky and Russian War Finance," *Europe-Asia Studies* 53, no. 1(2001): 153.

23. Siegel, *For Peace and Money*, 143.

24. Bark's report on the financial conference of the Allies in Paris, January 20–23, 1915. "Finansovye soveshchaniia soiuznikov vo vremia voiny. Soveshchanie trekh ministrov v Parizhe 20-23 ianvaria 1915 g.," *Krasnyi Arkhiv*, 1924, vol. 5, 53. x

25. On "monetary nationalism," see Hew Strachan, *The First World War* (Oxford: Oxford University Press, 2001), vol.1, 819, quoting Marcello de Cecco, *The international gold standard : money and* empire (New York : St. Martin's Press, 1984), Stephen Gross argues that despite the demonetization of gold in Germany, it played an important symbolic role as a mechanism of mobilization and commitment. Stephen Gross, "Confidence and Gold: German War Finance 1914–1918," *Central European History* 42 (2009): 226.

26. J. M. Keynes, "Is It Important for Russia, from Her Point of View, to Keep All Her Gold?" in J. M. Keynes, *The Collected Writings*, vol. 16, *Activities 1914–1919: The Treasury and Versailles* (Cambridge: Cambridge University Press, 2013), 49,72.

27. Ivan Shipov, State Bank's director, at the meeting of the Economic Council of Provisional Government, later said that the State Bank's balances were "too frank. At least among belligerent countries such frankness is uncommon." *Stenograficheskii otchet zasedaniia Ekonomicheskogo Soveta pri Vremennom Pravitelstve*, August 3, 1917 (Petrograd, 1917), 8.

28. *Torgovo-Promyshlennaia Gazeta*, October 28, 1914; RGIA, f.1276, op.10, d.248, 53; Siegel, *For Peace and Money*, 139.

29. Keynes, from "Note on the Finance of Russia," *The Collected Writings*, vol. 16, 130–131.
30. Finansovye soveshchaniia soiuznikov vo vremia voiny (doklady ministra finansov P. L. Barka). O finansovykh soglasheniiakh, zakliuchennykh s angliiskim i frantsuzskim ministrami finansov i s upravliaiushchim angliiskim bankom (October 9, 1915). Bark's report to the tsar, *Krasnyi Arkhiv*, 1924, no. 5, 66; A. Iakhontov, "Tiazhelye dni," 88–89, quoted in Bark, *Vospominaniia*, vol. 2, 99.
31. "U ministra finansov," *Birzhevye vedomosti*, October 2, 1915, no.15123, 1; "Chto privez P. L. Bark?" *Birzhevye vedomosti*, October 2, 1915, no.15123, 3.
32. Keynes, "Russia," in *The Collected Writings*, vol. 16, 68,
33. Sidorov, *Finansovoe polozhenie*, 149.
34. G. D. Dement'ev, *Gosudarstvennye dokhody i raskhody Rossii i polozhenie Gosudarstvennogo Kaznacheistva za vremia voiny s Germaniei i Avstro-Vengriei do 1917 goda* (Petrograd, 1917), 8–9, 12. In 1913, the monopoly on spirits provided 27.9% of state income. Dement'ev, *Gosudarstvennye dokhody* 5. According to Dement'ev, the cost of the Russo-Japanese War (without post-war financial settlements) constituted 2,112 million rubles. Military expenses in 1914 only claimed 2,540 million rubles. Dementiev, *Gosudarstvennye dokhody*, 4, 12,
35. The resolution on the suspension of exchange: "Osobyi zhurnal Soveta ministrov 23 iulia 1914 goda o priostanovlenii razmena gosudarstvennykh kreditnykh biletov na zolotuiu monetu," *Osobye zhurnaly Soveta Ministrov Rossiiskoi Imperii, 1909–1917gg.* "1914," (Moskva, 2006), 221. Not all newly printed credit rubles were intended for the government's needs: part of the cash went to support various private banks that were expected, in their turn, to credit industry.
36. State Bank's balances reflected these assets, so one could trace how much the government borrowed from the Bank and spent on defense. Government borrowings were indicated as the amount of treasury obligations discounted by the bank. See, for instance, how *Russkie Vedomosti* interpreted the State Bank's balance: "Moskva, 11 Marta" [editorial], *Russkie Vedomosti*, 1915, no. 57. See also Paul Apostol, "Credit Operations," in Alexander M. Michelson, Paul Apostol, and Michael Bernatzky, *Russian Public Finance during the War* (New Haven: Yale University Press, 1928), 282–285.
37. Michael Bernatzky, "Monetary policy," in *Russian Public Finance during the War*, 372.
38. Mikhail Tugan-Baranovskii explained the phenomenon of the delayed effect of inflation in a series of articles on the problem of the value of money published in *Vestnik Finansov* in 1916. See, especially, *Vestnik Finansov* 1916, no.18, 211–213. See a similar view in V. N. Tverdokhlebov, "Bumazhnye den'gi i tovarnye tseny," *Vestnik Finansov* 1917, no. 4 142–144. For the analysis of prices, see Z. Katsenelenbaum, "Voina i russkii rubl'," in *Trudy Komissii po izucheniiu sovremennoi dorogovizny*, Vyp.3 (Moskva, 1915). Petr Struve claimed, however, that the growth of domestic prices was caused by the problem of transport and, quite paradoxically, by the improvement

of peasants' financial well-being after the prohibition of alcohol. See "Rasshirenie emissionnogo prava Gosudarstvennogo Banka," *Birzhevye vedomosti*, March 11, 1915.

39. Krestovnikov asked the government to introduce special mechanisms that would allow industrialists and the merchants who were importing goods to get foreign currency at a "more or less normal rate." Zapiska predsedatelia Moskovskogo birzhevogo komiteta G. A. Krestovnikova, October 10, 1914, *RGIA*, f.563, op.2, d.,528, 127–131.

40. "S'ezd predstavitelei birzhevoi torglovli i selskogo khoziaistva," *Birzhevye vedomosti*, April 7, 1915.

41. M. I. Fridman, "Russkoe kupechestvo o zolotoi valiute," *Birzhevye vedomosti*, April 9, 1915. See also the Council of Congress's memo based on these resolutions: "O valiutnom voprose v otnoshenii k tovarnym tsenam i vneshnei torgovle Rossii," *Sovet s'ezdov predstavitelei birzhevoi torglovli i sel'skogo khoziaistva. Otchet za 1915 god.* Petrograd, 1916, ll. 56–64.

42. Fridman, "Russkoe kupechestvo o zolotoi valiute." As a matter of fact, in June 1915 the Credit Chancellery tried to establish the "maximum" price of foreign currency and obliged banks to offer currency for the same price: it managed to lower the rate for 1–2 days, after which the rate sprang back. Katsenelenbaum, "Voina i russkii rubl'," *Trudy Komissii po izucheniu sovremennoi dorogovizny*, 23. In an effort to control the market of foreign currency, the government established strict rules and norms for distributing foreign money among importers and industrial enterprises via a special unit at the Ministry of Finance. This measure did perhaps restrain abrupt, "jumping" fluctuations of the rate caused by speculation, but it did not resolve the problem. Materialy ob usstanovlenii kontrolia nad soversheniem operatsii s inostrannoi valiutoi i o raspredelenii inostrannoi valiuty mezhdu chastnymi firmami, RGIA, F.583, op.16, d.148; Vypiska po voprosu o kurse russkoi denezhnoi edinitsy na zagranichnom rynke, RGIA, f. 560, op. 26, d. 767.

43. See the council's address to the State Duma and the Ministry of Trade and Industry (dated July 23, 1915). Dokladnye zapiski tovarishcha predsedatelia Soveta ministru finansov o neokhodimykh merakh dlia prekrashcheniia padeniia kursa rublia, RGIA, f.32, op.2, d.86, l.1.

44. Doklad Soveta S'ezdov o merakh i razvitiiu proizvoditelnykh sil Rossii, 4–5.

45. M. Bernatskii, "Premii na zoloto," *Finansovaia gazeta*, December 3, 1915.

46. Perepiska i drugie materialy po voprosu ob uvelichenii zolotogo zapasa gosudarstva, otmene svobodnogo obrashcheniia zolota i organizatsii ego skupki v tseliakh bor'by s otlivom zolota za granitsu, RGIA, f.49, op.1, d.131; Protokoly i zhurnaly Osobogo mezhduvedomstvennogo soveshchaniia dlia obsuzhdeniia voprosa o priniatii mer k usileniiu dobychi zolota v Imperii, RGIA, f.49, op.1, d.127; "Skupka i otpravka zolota v Kitai," *Novoe Vremia*, September 6, 1916, 3.

47. "Kak protekaet dobycha zolota?" *Birzhevye Vedomosti*, August 15, 1915, 3.

48. Lewis H. Siegelbaum, "Another 'Yellow Peril': Chinese Migrants in the Russian Far East and the Russian Reaction before 1917," *Modern Asian Studies* 12,

no. 2 (1978): 326. In 1910–13, Chinese workers formed 80–87% of the labor force in the gold mining industry. O dopuske kitaiskikh rabochikh na zolotye promysly Priamuria, RGIA, f.49, op.1, d.14, 149.

49. "Moskva 11 dekabria" [Editorial] *Russkie Vedomosti*, December 12, 1915, no.285; for criticism of the government's obsession with gold mining, see P. P. Genzel', "Russkii rubl'," *Finansovaia Gazeta*, August 5, 1915; Migulin, "Zolotopromyshlennost' i nashi zolotopromyshlenniki," *Novyi Ekonomist* 28 (1916): 3.

50. Lektor, "Kto ponizhaet russkii rubl' v Finliandii", *Novoe Vremia*, July 31, 1915. By January 1916, the ruble's rate fell from 2.5 markka for 1 ruble in 1914 to 2.16 markka.

51. Ob uchete v Finlandskom banke kratkosrochnykh obiazatelstv Gos kaznacheistva, RGIA, f.563, op.2, d.502, 37–38.

52. V. Za-k, Rubl' i finliandskaia marka, *Novoe Vremia*, September 29, 1916.

53. M. M-mov, "Kurs rublia v Finliandii," *Novoe Vremia*, January 17, 1916; Lector, "Voennye raskhody Findliandii I mezhdunarodnaia otsenka russko-finliadskoi valiuty," *Novoe Vremia*, February 3, 1916,; R., "Zaem v Finliandii," *Novoe Vremia*, February 4,; A. Rezvoi, "Kto zhe v Imperii ustanavlivaet kurs russkogo rublia?" *Novoe Vremia*, April 26, 1916,; M. M-M-mov, "Rubl' v Finliandii," *Novoe Vremia*, June 28, 1916. In fact, many institutions in Finland—railroads, post offices, and customs—had to accept rubles at nominal value, which caused significant losses on the differences of rate. See Ob obiazatelnom prieme russkikh deneg pri razlichnykh platezhakh v Finliandii, RGIA, f.1276, op.14, d.202.

54. "Rubl' v Finliandii," *Novoe Vremia*, August 31, 1915; "Vosstanovlenie kursa rublia v Finliandii," *Novoe Vremia*, September 24, 1915. *Novoe Vremia* was literally obsessed with this topic and dedicated dozens of articles to the problem of the ruble's rate in Finland.

55. One episode from the political debates on monetary issues is characteristic: when in April 1915 the Ministry of Finance briefly considered issuing treasury money, a move that would require a partial withdrawal from the principles of the monetary reform of 1897, the public—liberal as well as conservative—turned against it. The project, penned by economist Pavel Migulin, replaced credit rubles of small denominations with treasury notes without gold coverage (England and Germany also resorted to this method). Migulin justified this operation by the need to protect the ruble from depreciation: by issuing inconvertible treasury notes, the government could free gold resources earmarked (theoretically) for the exchange of convertible credit rubles up to 1 billion rubles and therefore drastically improve the appearance of the paper to gold ratio. The project was unanimously rejected by all experts and evoked a very critical, even adverse, response in the press. *O vypuske osobykh kaznacheiskikh denezhnykh znakov, ne vkhodiashchikh v sostav obespechivaemykh zolotom gosudarstvennykh kreditnykh biletov* [1915]. "Finansovye buffonady," *Novoe Vremia*, April 15, 1915. Pavel Migulin, "Rubl' zolotoi i rubl' bumazhnyi," *Novyi Ekonomist*, 1915, no. 9, 3–5; "Bumazhnye den'gi," *Novyi Ekonomist*, 1915, no. 15, 3–6.

56. V. I. Karpov speaking at the session of the State Council, quoted in "V Gosudarstvennom Sovete," *Novoe Vremia*, August 4, 1915, no. 14152.

57. S. Aleksandrov, "Padenie kursa rublia," *Golos Moskvy*, January 18, 1915.

58. Prof. N. P. Kolomiitsov, "Zolotoi fond i spros na den'gi," *Utro Rossii*, July 1, 1915.

59. "Zolotoi fond," *Birzhevye Vedomosti*, November 19, 1916.

60. M. Tugan-Baranovskii, "Rasshirenie emissionnogo prava Gosudarstvennogo Banka," *Rech'*, March 13, 1915.

61. In 1915–16, Tugan-Baranovskii published numerous articles in *Rech* and *Novyi Ekonomist* on the future of the monetary system. His major work, *Paper Money and Metal (Bumazhnye den'gi i metal* (Petrograd, 1917)), that summarizes his monetary ideas, appeared in 1917.

62. Quoted in Tugan-Baranovskii, *Bumazhnye den'gi i metal*, 157.

63. Strakhov, "Vnutrennie zaimy v Rossii v Pervuiu Mirovuiu Voinu," *Voprosy Istorii* 9 (2003): 29–32. The government announced its first military loan in October 1914, which was soon followed by another credit operation in March 1915. However, these first two loans were not public and targeted mostly banks and big capital. In addition, the government issued short-term 5% treasury bonds that did not even land on the public market until 1916 and were taken over exclusively by the State Bank and private credit institutions. In contrast, the third loan, announced in October 1915, as well as the fourth, fifth, and sixth loans that followed in 1915 and 1916, aimed to involve all social strata and therefore required the popularization of this financial initiative.

64. M. Friedman, "Rol zaimov v finansirovanii voiny" (December 1916), in *Voennye Zaimy. Sbornik statei po obshchei redaktsiiei M.I. Tugan-Baranovskogo* (Petrograd, 1917), 141. The share of loans in covering military expenses was this: 1914–16%, 1915–25%, 1916–33%, 1917–18%; A. Shisha, "Voina i finansy," *Vestnik finansov* 12 (1928): 113.

65. Bernatskii's words, "The ruble is the property of the wealthy and the poor alike," are quoted in *Rech'*, May 5, 1916. M. Bernatskii, "Denezhnoe obrashchenie i zaimy," *Voennye Zaimy. Sbornik statei* (Petrograd, 1917), 102.

66. "Milliardnyi zaem," *Birzhevye Vedomosti*, April 19, 1915.

67. *Rech'*, March 16, 1916.

68. On income tax and its political meaning: Yanni Kotsonis, *States of Obligation: Taxes and Citizenship in the Russian Empire and Early Soviet Republic.* (Toronto : University of Toronto Press, 2014)

69. A. A. Bublikov, "Shal'nye den'gi," *Birzhevye Vedomosti*, October 24, 1916; "Patrioticheskii dolg," *Rech'*, March 27, 1916. See also the advertisement in *Novoe Vremia* that called women to relinquish the urge to "satisfy her whims." *Novoe Vremia*, December 11, 1916.

70. Strachan, *The First World War*, 856; Martin Horn, *Britain, France, and the Financing of the First World War* (Montreal: McGill-Queen's University Press, 2002, 32.

71. Hew Strachan, *The First World War*, 853, 862.

72. Article 87 of the Fundamental Laws allowed the government to issue laws in administrative order when the State Duma was not in session and after that seek the Duma's post-factum formal approval. Since the schedule of the Duma's work depended entirely on the tsar, the government could procure the tsar's support, dismiss the chamber, and enact the laws without the Duma's participation.

73. O poriadke khraneniia zolotogo fonda v Finliandii, RGIA, f.1276, op.18, d.535, 1, 3-30b.

74. O vremennom prekrashenii obmena na zoloto biletov Finliandskogo banka, RGIA, f.1276, op.18, op.550, 1–43. Finland, in contrast to the Russian Empire, used the New Style (Gregorian) calendar, hence the differences in dates.

75. *O vypuske osobykh kaznacheiskikh denezhnykh znakov, ne vkhodiashchikh v sostav obespechivaemykh zolotom gosudarstvennykh kreditnykh biletov* [Petrograd, 1915], 18.

76. The Duma approved post-factum the first increase in July 1914. In March 1915 the government used art. 87 to raise the amount of paper rubles not covered by gold to 2.5 billion rubles. Ob uvelichenii emissionnogo prava Gos Banka, RGIA, f.563, op.2, d.517.

77. See for instance, Andrey Shingarev's explanation for why Bark's extension of the emission law was necessary from a financial point of view but was politically irrational: A. Shingarev, "Rasshirenie emissionnogo prava Gosudarstvennogo Banka," *Rech'*, March 18, 1915.

78. *Stenograficheskii otchet zasedanii soedinennykh komissii biudzhentoi i finansovoi 4,5 i 6 avgusta 1915 po rassmotreniiu zakonoproektov o rasshirenii predostavlennogo Gosudarstvennomu banku prava vypuska gosudastvennykh kreditnykh biletov. Gosudarstvennaia Duma. Chetvertyi sozyv, sessiia 4. Prilozheniia k stenograficheskim ontchetam n.26 i 38* (Petrograd, 1915), 15–16.

79. *Stenograficheskii otchet zasedanii,* 10

80. *Stenograficheskii otchet* zasedanii, 11.

81. *Stenograficheskii otchet zasedanii,* 111, 117, 120.

82. The Duma opposition was outraged by Bark's betrayal. See Pokazania A. I. Shingareva, 21 avgusta 1917. P. E. Shchegolev, ed., *Padenie tsarskogo rezhima. Stenograficheskie otchety doprosov i pokazanii, dannykh v 1917 godu v Chrezvychanoi sledstvennoi komissii Vremennogo pravitelstva* (Moskva, Leningrad, 1927), t.7, 117–118f.

83. RGIA, f.1276, op.10, d.248, 191; *Osobyi zhurnal Soveta Ministrov,* October 2, 1915, in *Osobye zhurnaly Soveta Ministrov Rossiiskoi Imperii, 1909–1917. 1915* (Moskva: ROSSPEN, 2008), 412.

84. Sidorov, *Finansovoe polozhenie,* 273.

85. See the assessment of the Duma's contribution to financial policy: "Ekonomicheskaia nedelia," *Birzhevye Vedomosti*, September 7, 1915, 6.

86. J. M. Keynes, "Russia," January 30, 1915, in *Collected Writings,* vol. 16, 68. Harvey Fisk also believed that this "arrangement, which was pure camouflage, in bank parlance 'kiting' . . . was not perceived by the public at large." "This was one of the

financial secrets of the war, which only came to light after the fall of the Czarist government." Harvey Fisk, *The Inter-Ally Debts. An Analysis of War and Post-war Public Finance, 1914–1923* (New-York: Bankers Trust Company, 1924), 138. Fisk, obviously, underestimated the abilities of the Russian "public" to crack this secret.

87. For the interpretation of Bark's step as a violation of the law on emission: Finansist, "Vorposy emissii," *Rech'*, October 16, 1915. The practice of counting foreign funds as part of the gold reserve that had dated back to pre-war years, always raised significant criticism. For the amount of gold abroad, see *Otchet Gosudarstvennogo Banka za 1905* (St. Petersburg, 1906), 16; *Otchet Gosudarstvennogo Banka za 1906* (St. Petersburg, 1907), 16; *Otchet Gosudarstvennogo Banka za 1907* (St. Petersburg, 1908), 16. For data for 1909–1913 see *Otchet Gosudarstvennogo Banka za 1913* (St. Petersburg, 1914), 9. See also the Ministry of Finance's official response to criticism in a brochure, *Russkii zolotoi zapas za granitsei* (St. Petersburg, 1913).

88. Bernatskii, "Denezhnoe obrashchenie i zaimy," 85.

89. Bernatskii, "Denezhnoe obrashchenie i zaimy," 85.

90. Gosudarstvennaia Duma Chetvertyi Sozyv. Soedinennye komissii finansovaia i biudzhetnaia. Doklad po zakonoproektu o rasshirenii predostavlennogo Gosudarstvennomu Banku prava vypuska gosudarstvennykh kredinykh biletov, in *Prilozheniia k stenograficheskim otchetam Gosudarstvennoi Dumy. Chetvertyi Sozyv. Sessiia IV.* Vypusk V. N.330 (Petrograd, 1916), 6, 13.

91. Perevod shifrovannoi telegrammy ministra finansov otpravlennoi iz Londona 16/29 iiunia 1916, RGIA, f.1276, op.10, d.248, l.207.

92. *Gosudarstvennaia Duma. Chetvertyi Sozyv. Stenograficheskie otchety. 1916. Sessia 4* (Petrograd, 1916), stlb.5593.

93. Shingarev interpreted this move as an "artificial disruption" of the legislative process. A. Shingarev, "Emissionnyi vopros," *Rech'*, June 28, 1916.

94. O rasshirenii emissionnogo prava Gos. Banka, RGIA, f.1276, op.12, d.574.

95. The agreement was signed on October 14, 1916.

96. RGIA, f.563, op.2, d.541, l.6.

97. "If people find out that the gold is disappearing and that the papers [i.e., paper money] are increasing in number, it is going to be dangerous," said Shingarev in his conversation with Ribot, suggesting that it was in the Allies' interest to help Russia maintain "the integrity of public mood." "Mezhdunarodnoe finansovoe polozhenie tsarskoi Rossii vo vremia mirovoi voiny (doklad A.I. Shingareva v Voenno-morkoi komissii Gosudarstvennoi Duma 20 Iunia 1916g.)," *Krasnyi Arkhiv* 64 (1934): 10.

98. V. Zheleznov, "K preobrazovaniiu russkoi finansovoi sistemy," *Russkie Vedomosti*, August 17, 1914.

99. The *New York Tribune* wrote about the "Mystery of Europe's Gold Reserve," showing that by August 1916 the net increase of gold in central banks' coffers amounted to $238,000,000. "Where did the balance of the $238,000,000 come from?" The main source of gold in non-gold producing countries was its own population. "Mystery of Europe's Gold Reserve," *New York Tribune*, August 10, 1916.

100. See Reichsbank's balance sheet reproduced in Stephen Gross, "Confidence and Gold: German War Finance, 1914–1918," *Central European History* 42 (2009): 234.

101. Zhurnal soveshchaniia po voprosu o privlechenii zolotoi monety v pravitelstvennyi kassy, May 26, 1915, RGIA, f.1276, op.11, d.291. With these and other measures, Germany managed to increase its pre-war gold reserve from 1,356 million marks to 2,378 million marks (in May 1915), RGIA, f.563, op.2. d.517, 2 ob.

102. As the *Manchester Guardian* noted, emphasizing the coerciveness of government's actions, "every kind of moral pressure was brought to bear to induce people to send gold to the bank." "The Hunt for Gold," *Manchester Guardian*, July 31, 1915.

103. Lev Pasynkov, "Bronzovaia bolezn'," *Birzhevye Vedomosti*, January 7, 1915.

104. S. N. Prokopovich, *Voina i naroldnoe khoziaistvo* (Moskva, 1917), 100.

105. Gosudarstvennaia Duma, Chetvertyi sozyv, sessiia IV, *Stenograficheskii otchet zasedanii soedinennykh komissii biudzhetnoi i finansovoi 4,5 i 6 avgusta 1915 po rassmotreniiu zakonoproektov o rasshirenii predostavlennogo Gosudarstvennomu banku prava vypuska gosudastvennykh kreditnykh biletov. Prilozheniia k stenograficheskim otchetam n.26 i 38* (Petrograd, 1915), 89–90, 91, 103–104.

106. Gosudarstvennaia Duma, Chetvertyi Sozyv, Sessiia IV, *Stenograficheskie otchety, 1915* (Petrograd, 1915), 907–908; "Rasshirenie emissionnogo prava Gos. Banka," *Birzhevye Vedomosti*, August 19, 1915, 5.

107. RGIA, f.587, op. 33, d. 440, 24.

108. M. M. Bogoslovskii, *Dnevniki 1913–1919* (Moskva: Vremia, 2011), 83, 162.

109. Obmen zolota na den'gi. *Birzhevye Vedomosti,* August 15, 1915, no.15026, 1; "Sbor zolota," *Birzhevye Vedomosti*, September 29, 1915, 3; Iskatel' zolota, "Eshche zolotye medali," *Novoe Vremia*, April 25, 1916.

110. S [M. Menshikov], "Dolzhny pobedit'," *Novoe Vremia*, March 14, 1915.

111. "Zolotaia medal' dlia usileniia sredstv kazny," *Birzhevye Vedomosti*, September 30, 1915, no. 15119, 3.

112. "O monastyrskom zolote," *Birzhevye Vedomosti*, August 23, 1915, no. 15044, 2; "Privlechenie monastyrei k uchastiiu v voennykh raskhodakh," *Birzhevye Vedomosti*, August 25, 1915, 15047, 4. More on the church's role in "collecting gold": "Sobiranie zolota," *Birzhevye Vedomosti*, September 12, 1915, no15083, 5.

113. RGIA, f.587, op.33, d.430.

114. Gennadii Oz-ii, "Eshche o zolote," *Rech'*, November 11, 1915; "Kustarnoe zolotoe obrashchenie," *Russkie Vedomosti*, October 1, 1915, no. 224.

115. P. Migulin, "Zolotoi fetish," *Novyi Ekonomist*, 1915, no.50, 6.

116. Spravki po operatsii priema zolota v dar i obmen, RGIA, f.588, op.3, d.653, 157.

117. Mikhail Bernatskii quoted in *Finansovaia gazeta*, November 28, 1915.

118. O zamene zolota i serebra upotrebliaemykh pri izgotovlenii medalei i ordenskikh znakov bolee deshevymi metallami, RGIA, f.1276, op.12, d.499. .

119. *Stenograficheskii otchet zasedaniia Ekonomicheskogo soveta pri Vremennom pravitelstve*, August 3, 1917, no. 6 (Petrograd, 1917), 16.

120. O rasprostranenii deistvuiushchego vospreshcheniia vyvozit' za granitsu zolotuiu monetu i zoloto v syrom vide i slitkakh takzhe i na zoloto i platinu v vide razlichnykh izdelii, June, 1915, RGIA, f.1276, op.12, d.427.

121. O privlechenii zolota v kaznu, RGIA, f.1276, op.11, d.291, 11, 18, 22, 39-43 ob; O merakh privlecheniia zolota v kaznu i borby s otlivom ego za granitsu, RGIA, f.1276, op.12, d.260, 2–11; "Vopros o zolote v komitete finansov," *Birzhevye Vedomosti*, January 17, 1915, no. 14617.

122. Ob operatsii pokupki zolota ssudnymi kaznami za schet Gos Banka, RGIA, f.588, op.3, d.578, 25–29.

123. "Nedostatok razmennoi monety", *Birzhevye Vedomosti*, September 14, 1915, no. 15087, 5.

124. "Vast Treasures in Hidden Hoards," *Washington Post*, August 16, 1914.

125. "Russia's Holy Gold Fund: An Almost Inexhaustible Hoard of Wealth," *Los Angeles Times*, September 17, 1915.

126. The article with Dalinda's interview was written by Ivan Narodny, a famous literary swindler. Ivan Narodny, "Tells of Russia's Untouched Wealth," *New York Tribune*, March 19, 1916.

127. "How World's Gold Store Is Distributed: An Interesting Comparison of Per Capita Holdings," *The Globe*, November 17, 1914. Indeed, in December 1914, the value of the gold reserve (1,553 million rubles) was three times higher than the value of gold coins in circulation (460 million). If we consider the Russian population at roughly 166 million, then without the reserve, there were 2.7 rubles of gold per capita; with the reserve, this number increases to 12.12 rubles, *Statisticheskii sbornik za 1913–1917*. Vyp.2. (Moskva, 1922), 92, 98.

128. Gosudarstvennaia Duma. Chetvertyi Sozyv. Sessia IV. *Stenograficheskii otchet zasedanii soedinennykh komissii biudzhetnoi i finansovoi 4,5 i 6 avgusta 1915 g.,* 89; Gosudarstvennaia Duma, Chetvertyi Sozyv, Sessia IV, *Stenograficheskie otchety,* 1915 (Petrograd, 1915), 924.

129. Michael Bernatzky, "Monetary Policy," 371.

130. On the influence of the refugees' crisis, see Prokopovich, *Voina i narodnoe khoziaistvo*, 102.

131. Nedostatok razmennoi monety, *Rech'*, August 18, 1915, no. 226.

132. Nedostatok razmennoi monety, *Birzhevye Vedomosti,* August 23, 1915, no. 15043; *Birzhevye Vedomosti,* August 16, 1915, no. 15029; *Birzhevye Vedomosti,* September 14, 1915, no. 15087.

133. "Iz-za razmennoi monety," "Nedostatok melkoi razmennoi monety," "Razgrom bazara," *Novoe Vremia* August 18, 1910 no. 14166, 5; "Iz-za razmennykh deneg," *Novoe Vremia,* August 19, 1915, no. 14167.

134. "Razmennyi golod," *Birzhevye Vedomosti*, August 18, 1915, 3; "Razmennyi golod," *Birzhevye Vedomosti,* August 19, 1915, 4; "O razmennoi monete," *BV* (evening edition), August 19, 1915. See also Onegin, "Malen'kii felieton. Numizmaty," *Birzhevye Vedomosti*, August 20, 1915, no. 15037.

135. During the first year of war, the Petrograd Mint produced coins for 30 million rubles, which was ten times more than the average of previous years, and the Ministry of Finance claimed that the shortage of coins could not take place, RGIA, f.587, op.33, d.442, 33; O zatrudneniiakh isputyvaemykh vsledstvie nedostatka serebrianoi i mednoi monety, RGIA, f.587, op.33, d,443, 28, 51.

136. There was a grain of truth in stories about peasants' hoards: archaeologists have observed an increase, in comparison to the pre-war period, of a number of treasure troves dated to the period of the First World War. A. Veksler and A. Melnikova, *Rossiiskaia istoriia v moskovskikh kladakh* (Moskva: Zhiraf, 1999), 180.

137. Prokopovich, *Voina i narodnoe khoziaistvo*, 103–104.

138. Prokopovich, *Voina i narodnoe khoziaistvo*, 106.

139. "V Gosudarstvennom Banke," *Birzhevye Vedomosti*, August 22, 1915, 3.

140. Interview with the director of Petrograd branch of the State Bank I.I. Nazimov, "Marki vmesto razmennykh deneg," *Birzhevye Vedomosti*, October 3, 1915, 3.

141. Liubov' Martynova (Sluchevskaia), *Dnevnik*, October 24, 1915, https://prozhito.org/note/244227.

142. In 1915, the government released 48.8 million rubles, in 1916 its amount doubled, and in 1917 the circulation of stamps reached 213.5 million rubles. *Nashe denezhnoe obrashchenie 1914–1925: Sbornik materialov*, edited by L.N. Iurovskii (Moskva: Finansovoe izdatel'stvo NKF SSSR, 1926), 82–83.

143. "Novye bumazhnye den'gi," *Birzhevye Vedomosti*, October 4, 1915, 5.

144. On November 13, 1915, the Committee of Finance approved the issuance of treasury exchange notes of the same denominations as stamps, but ultimately these notes were not released into circulation, "Razmennye kaznacheiskie znaki," *Vestnik Finansov* 49 (1915): 344.

145. Doneseniia upravliaiushchikh mestnykh otdelenii kontor i kaznacheistv Otdelu kreditnykh biletov Banka o reaktsii naseleniia na vvedemie v obrashchenie razmennykh marok v sviazi s otsutstviem serebrianoi monety, RGIA, f.587, op.60, d.91; O vypuske v obrashchenie razmennykh marok i kaznacheiskikh znakov, RGIA, f. 587, op.33, d.447, 41.

146. "Marki vmesto razmennykh deneg," *Birzhevye Vedomosti*, October 1, 1915, 4; A. Rennikov, "Malen'kii felieton. Izobretateli," *Novoe Vremia*, October 2, 1915

147. A. Rennikov, "Malen'kii felieton. Izobretateli," *Novoe Vremia*, October 2, 1915.

148. "Kto delaet nashi kreditki?" *Novoe Vremia*, October 13, 1915; Iakhontov, "Bumagi Iakhontova," 291, quoted in P. L. Bark, *Vospominaniia*, vol. 2, 121.

149. I. D. Ditiatovskii, "Malen'kie svideteli velikoi smuty," *Al'manakh Obshchestva ROI*, kn.3 (Moskva, 2017), 308; original source—N. I. Kardakov, "Russkie marki-den'gi germanskogo izgotovleniia," *Rossika* 46–47 (1955).

150. Dnevnik Liubovi Sluchevskoi (Martynovoi), August 20 , 1916, https://prozhito.org/note/244285; on the circulation of silver coins see I. A. Mikhailov, *Voina i nashi denezhnoe obrashchenie*, 36–37.

151. "Novye bumazhnye den'gi," *Birzhevye Vedomosti*, October 4, 1915, 5. According to Mikhail Bernatskii [Bernatzky], the coins struck in 1916 and 1917 "never came into circulation except in a few districts and by their issue to the Russian troops in Persia." Bernatzky, "Monetary Policy," 384.

152. B. I. Kolonitskii, "The Desacralization of the Monarchy: Rumours and the Downfall of the Romanov," in *Interpreting the Russian Revolution: The Language and Symbols of 1917* (New Haven: Yale University Press, 1999).

153. Bernatzky, "Monetary Policy," 383.

154. I. D. Ditiatovskii, "Malen'kie svideteli velikoi smuty," *Almanakh Obshchestva ROI*, kn.3 (Moskva, 2017), 309–310.

155. Quoted from Rafail Ganelin, "Gosudarstvennaia Duma i antisemitskie tsirkuliary 1915–1916 gg.," *Vestnik Evreiskogo Universiteta v Moskve* 3, no. 10 (1995): 6.

156. Dopros K. D. Kafafova, *Padenie tsarskogo regima*, T.2 (Leningrad, 1925), 135.

157. Gosudarstvennaia Duma, Chetvertyi sozyv, *Stenograficheskie otchet,*. Sessiia 4, 1916, zasedaniia 17–37, Petrograd, 1916, 1312.

158. Gosudarstvennaia Duma, Chetvertyi sozyv, 3039.

159. For the details of this story, see Rafail Ganelin, "Gosudarstvennaia Duma i antisemitskie tsirkuliary 1915–1916 gg.," *Vestnik Evreiskogo Universiteta v Moskve* 3, no. 10 (1995): 4–37; Victor Kelner, "Politicheskoe biuro pri evreiiskikh deputatakh IV Gosudarstvennoi Dumy," *Peterburgskii Istoricheskii Zhurnal* 1 (2015): 83–89.

160. "Skupshchiki zolota dlia Germanii," *Novoe Vremia*, August 7, 1916, 6. Poteliakhov was later released.

161. The *New Time* routinely published articles about Chinese and German smugglers of gold. See, for instance, "Kitaitsy-zolotokhishchniki," *Novoe Vremia*, October 4, 1915, no. 14213; "Skupka zolota," *Novoe Vremia*, January 14, 1915, no. 13952; "Zoloto," *Novoe Vremia*, July 6, 1915; "Skupshchiki zolota dlia Germanii," *Novoe Vremia*, August 7, 1916.

162. About the circular: "Podpiska na voennyi zaem," *Birzhevye Vedomosti*, October 26, 1916.

163. On the uniformity of financial policies, see Niall Ferguson, *The Pity of War: Explaining World War I* (New York: Basic Books, 2001, 322–324).

164. Mikhail Bogolepov, *O putiakh budushchego. K voprosu ob ekonomicheskom plane* (Petrograd, 1916), 15. Same point is made in P. P. Migulin, "Voina i den'gi," *Novyi Ekonomist* 34 (1915): 2.

165. Andrei Markevich and Mark Harrison, "Great War, Civil War, and Recovery: Russia's National Income, 1913–1928," *Journal of Economic History* 71, no.3 (September 2011), 690.

166. Peter Gattrell and Mark Harrison, "The Russian and Soviet Economies in Two World Wars: A Comparative View," *Economic History Review,* New Series, 46, no. 3 (August 1993): 430–432, 438, 440; Markevich and Harrison, "Great War, Civil War, and Recovery," 682–683, 685.

167. On the EZGB strike: M. Lemke to I. Shipov, March 30, 1917, TsGA SPb, f.1255, op.1, d.205, 23.
168. "Ministr finansov na mitinge rabochikh," *Rech'*, March 8, 1917.
169. "Ministr finansov na sobranii rabochikh" (two articles about this event in the same issue), *Rech'*, March 8, 1917; V. I. Starstev, *Vnutrenniaia Politika Vremennogo Pravitelstva Pervogo Sozyva* (Leningrad: Nauka, 1980), 133; on the Treasury— A. A. Bublikov, *Russkaia Revoliutsiia (ee nachalo, arest tsaria, perspektivy)* (Moskva: Gos.publichnaia istoricheskaia biblioteka, 2018), 54.
170. V. V. Shul'gin, "Peredovaia statia 10 marta 1917," in Shul'gin, *Rossiia v 1917 godu. Izbrannye raboty* (Moskva: Posev, 2020); original publication: "Kiev, 10 marta," in *Kievlianin*, March 10, 1917.
171. "Kreditnye bilety," *Novoe Vremia*, March 9, 1917. There is no Executive Committee documentation of this request
172. *Zhurnaly zasedanii Vremennogo pravitelstva, Mart-Oktiabr' 1917,* vol. 1 (Moskva: ROSSPEN, 2001), 92 (March 14, 1917)
173. Postanovlenie Ispolkoma Petrogradskogo Soveta Rabochikh deputatov [February 28], O. A. Shaskova, ed., *Fevral'skaia revoliutsiia 1917 goda. Sbornik dokumentov i materialov* (Moskva: Rossiiskii Gos Gumanitarnyi Universitet, 1996), 85. Why the Provisional Committee failed to do it in the first place remains unknown. It is unclear who was responsible for bringing the State Bank under the new authority—who gave the order to bring armored cars to the bank's building and dismiss the regiment that had been guarding the institution to protect it from being looted. Apparently, in the absence of such an order, the person who acted on behalf of the Provisional Committee was an enthusiastic imposter. For a detailed account of events, see A. B. Nikolaev, *Dumskaia Revoliutsiia. 27 fevralia—3 marta 1917*, vol. 1 (St. Petersburg: Izdatel'stvo RGPU im. A. I. Gertsena, 2017), 382–385. The person who claimed responsibility for taking over the Bank was A. I. Merkulov.
174. *Aleksandr Ivanovich Guchkov rasskazyvaet. Vospominaniia Predsedatelia Gosudarstvennoi dumy i voennogo ministra Vremennogo pravitel'stva* (Moskva: Voprosy Istorii, 1993), 122.
175. Bernatzky, "Monetary Policy," 397. On July 16, 1914, that is, after the first amendment of the monetary law, there were 1.633 billion rubles in circulation; on March 1, 1917, the number was 9.949 billion; by October 23, 1917, the amount money increased to 18.917 billion rubles.
176. On the increase of the Expedition's staff: "Nashi gosudarstvennye finansy," *Russkie Vedomosti*, September 29, 1917; Skobelev's speech at the First All-Russian Congress of Soviets, *Pervyi Vserossiiskii s'ezd Sovetov Rabochikh i Soldatskikh Deputatov* (Moskva: Gos. Izd-vo, 1930), vol.1, 227. Also see the Provisional Government's decision regarding benefits to the Expedition's workers and special tariffs: *Zhurnaly Zasedanii Vremennogo Pravitel'stva* 2 (June 10, 1917): 236.

177. Quoted from: M. V. Khodiakov, "Kerenki" i ikh izgotovlenie v Petrograde v 1917 godu, in *Istoria, Universitet, Istorik* (St. Petersburg, 2014), 122. On the issuance of "kerenki" also see Bernatzky, "Monetary Policy," 386–388.

178. "Dni zaima svobody," *Novoe Vremia*, July 28, 1917, 2.

179. P. V. Volobuev, *Ekonomicheskaia politika Vremennogo pravitelstva* (Moskva: AN SSSR, 1962), 342–343.

180. "S'ezd partii kadetov: Finansovoe polozhenie," *Russkie Vedomosti*, July 26, 1917. Social-democrats considered the vote on the loan as a vote on confidence in the Provisional government. "Vopros o zaime v Sovete Rabochikh i Krestianskikh Deputatov," *Novoe Vremia*, May 6, 1917, 4.

181. "Beseda s ministrom finansov," *Utro Rossii*, March 12, 1917.; "Beseda s ministrom finansov," *Russkie Vedomosti*, April 15. 1917; "Ministr finansov, Beseda s zhurnalistami," *Utro Rossii* April 15, 1917.

182. N. N.Sukhanov, *Zapiski o revoliutsii*, t.2, kn.3–4 (Moskva: Politizdat, 1991), 214-216. Resolution of the Executive Committee of May 16, 1917.

183. "Finansovyi krisis," *Utro Rossii*, May 17, 1917.

184. As Kulisher observed, Russia came to the income tax "too late." I. M. Kulisher, "Finansovyi krizis i sudba podokhodnogo naloga," *Utro Rossii*, July 7, 1917.

185. Nekrasov on the results of tax collection: the percentage of underpayment varied from 11 to 69. *Ekonomicheskoe polozhenie Rossii Nakanune Velikoi Oktiabr'skoi Sotsialisticheskoi Revoliutsii* (Moskv: Institut istorii SSSR, 1957), ch. 2, 416.

186. The treasury expected to receive about 500 million rubles in income tax compared to 150–200 previously calculated before the reform, plus 80 million rubles of a non-recurrent tax and 100 million rubles in a tax on wartime "super-profi," Volobuev, *Ekonomicheskaia Politika*, 325.

187. Kotsonis, *States of Obligation*, 179–198.

188. V. Stein, "Finansovaia demagogiia," *Rech'*, July 29, 1917, 2.

189. "S'ezd partii kadetov. Fnansovoe polozhenie," *Russkie Vedomosti*, July 26, 1917.

190. Doklad ministra finansov N. V. Nekrasova v Gosudarstvennom soveshchanii o sostoianii finansov August 12, 1917—*Ekonomicheskoe polozhenie Rossii nakanune Velikoi Oktiabr'skoi Sotsialistichekoi Revoliutsii*, ch.2, 411–419.

191. *Vtoroi Vserossiiskii promyshlennyi s'ezd v Moksve 3–5 avgusta 1917. Stenograficheskii otchet o pervom plenarnom zasedanii s'ezda* (Moskva, Tip. T-va Riabushinskikh, 1917), 3.

192. Editorial, *Russkie Vedomosti*, August 1, 1917, quoted from *The Russian Provisional Government 1917. Documents Selected and Edited by Robert Paul Browder and Alexander F. Kerensky* (Stanford, CA: Stanford University Press, 1961), vol. 2, 509.

193. *Stenograficheskii otchet zasedaniia Ekonomicheskogo soveta pri Vremennom praviltelstve*, July 31, 1917, No. 5 (Petrograd, 1917), 1.

194. N. N. Sukhanov, *Zapiski o Revoliutsii*, t.2. kn.3–4, 228.

195. *Stenograficheskii otchet zasedaniia Ekonomicheskogo soveta pri Vremennom praviltelstve,* July 26, 1917, No. 4 (Petrograd, 1917), 31.

196. *Stenograficheskii otchet zasedaniia Ekonomicheskogo,* July 31, 1917. No. 5 (Petrograd, 1917), 8

197. Grudina A. D., "Organizatsiia materialnoi podderzhki semei riadovogo sostava Pervoi mirovoi voiny i ee vliianie na razvitie protestnykh nastroenii v Petrograde," *Nauchnyi Dialog* 7 (2018): 242.

198. *Rossiia v mirovoi voine 1914–1918 (v tsifrakh)* (Moskva, Tsentralnoe statisticheskoe upravlenie, 1925), 4, 49.

199. Prokopovich, *Voina i narodnoe khoziaistvo,* 74. On the material versus human asset: Gattrell and Harrison, "The Russian and Soviet Economies in Two World Wars," 431. On the growing value of allowance: Peter Gattrell, *Russia's First World War. A Social and Economic History* (Harlow, UK: Pearson Educational Limited, 2005), 136.

200. Ferguson, *The Pity of War,* 318.

201. See, for instance, A. A. Bublikov, *Russkaia revoliutsiia (ee nachalo, arest tsaria, perspektivy). Vpechatleniia i mysli ochevidtsa i uchastnika* (Moskva: GPIB, 2018), 85–90; Anton Denikin, *Ocherki russkoi smuty. Krushenie vlasti i armii. Fevral-sentiabr 1917* (Moskva: Nauka, 1991), 224.

202. Shul'gin, "Peredovaia statia 26 sentiabria 1917 g.," in Shul'gin, *Rossiia v 1917 godu,* 469–471, originally "Kiev. 25-go sentiabria," *Kievlianin,* September 26, 1917. See also his articles of May 24, September 28, in *Rossiia v 1917 godu,* 351–353, 472–474. The financial assistance to railroad workers was meant to be a distribution of wartime bonuses of less than 100 rubles in areas with the highest cost of living. William Rosenberg, "The Democratization of Russia's Railroads in 1917," *American Historical Review* 86. no. 5 (December 1981): 996.

203. S. Radaev, "Fabrika deneg," *Rech',* June 13, 1917, 2.

204. Diane Koenker, *Moscow Workers and the 1917 Revolution* (Princeton: Princeton University Press, 1981), 117–119, 130–131.

205. As S. A. Smith observed, "To keep abreast of inflation, workers had to at least double their monthly earnings, and by no means all of them managed to do so." S. A. Smith, *Red Petrograd: Revolution in the Factories* (Cambridge: Cambridge University Press, 1983), 70. S. G. Strumilin, *Zarabotnaia plata i proizvoditelnost' truda v russkoi promyshlennosti za 1913–1922 gg.* (Moskva: Voprosy truda, 1923). 12, 74. Also see the statistics of "real wages in industry" in Peter Gattrell, *Russia's First World War: A Social and Economic History* (Hoboken, NJ: Taylor and Francis, 2014), 69.

206. Smith, *Red Petrograd,* 117, 119.

207. Sukhanov, *Zapiski o revolutsii,* t.2, kn.3–4, 31.

208. June 4, 1917, *Pervyi Vserossiiskii s'ezd sovetov rabochikh i soldatskikh deputatov,* vol. 1, 92.

209. *Pervyi Vserossiiskii s'ezd sovetov rabochikh,* 70.

210. N. Lenin, "Pochemu nuzhen control nad proizvodstvom," *Pravda*, July 8, 1917, no.91, 3-4 (251–252); "Doklad Bukovetskogo o sostoianii finansov," *Rabochii Put'* 43 (1917): 9.

211. Finland was the sole exception. Russian newspapers and the government anxiously watched the fall of Russian ruble vis-à-vis the Finnish markka, which used to cost two-thirds of the ruble and rose to parity. The Russian government had to ask Finland for a loan to cover its expenses in markkas, but Finland declined the request. As *Novaia Zhizn'* observed, the Finns rightly demanded that Russia put at their disposal and on their territory post serves, telegraphs, state offices, and treasury lands in return for the money. "Konflikt s Finlandiei," *Novaia Zhizn'*, June 24, 1917, no.57, 1; see also: "Vopros o russkom zaime v Finliandii," *Novaia Zhizn'*, July 8, 1917, no. 69, 1. The *New Time* traditionally expressed its anti-Finnish position, accusing Finns of dropping the ruble's rate. *Novoe Vremia*, May 17, 1917, no. 14779, 5; "Rubl' za marku," *Novoe Vremia*, June 21, 1917, no. 14808, 4.

212. The *New Time* mentioned a 187-million ruble decrease of the State Bank's gold holding due to the dispatch of gold: "Polozhenie zolotoi nalichnosti," *Novoe Vremia*, July 20, 1917, no. 14831.

213. Economists saw this process as a series of interconnected measures: for instance, if the state appropriates the functions of "a financial capitalist," it has to take the responsibility of supplying capital and raw resources to the producers. A. Shatov, "Denezhnyi rynok i gosudarstvo," *Novaia Zhizn'*, June 3, 1917, no. 39, 1. The problem of state intrusion into financial and economic activity remained central throughout the inter-revolutionary period. For an example of a critique of the state's growing interference, see Finansist, "Predely gosudarstvennogo vmeshatel'stva," *Novoe Vremia*, June 17, 1917, no. 14805, 3.

214. As an example of analysis arguing for the state regulation of wages, see I. S. Voitinskii, *Minimal'naia zarabotnaia plata* (Petrograd, 1917). The pre-Keynesian political economy, counting Keynes's era from his 1923 *Tract on Monetary Reform*, traditionally overlooked any connection between money and labor.

215. As economist Serguei Prokopovich observed, "The regulation of public economic life, the regulation of the circulation of goods assume the existence of an appropriate apparatus, and here we faced difficulties": the lack of centralized power in the capital, and the lack of public initiative on the local level. *Gosudarstvennoe Soveshchanie. Stenograficheskii otchet* (Moskva: Gos.izd-vo 1930), 22.

216. *Pervyi Vserossiiskii S'ezd Sovetov*, vol. 1, 65.

217. As Melchior Palyi observed, "The stability of price levels and of employment hit closer to home than the gold standard and the budgetary balance, directly affecting . . . people's aspiration for a better life." Melchior Palyi, *The Twilight of Gold, 1914–1936* (Chicago: H. Regnery, 1972), 52–53.

218. M. I. Tugan-Baranovskii, *Bumazhnye Den'gi i Metall*, 1917. Tugan-Baranovskii's ideas remarkably preempted the ideas of Keynes's *Tract on Monetary Reform* that also postulated that after the war, there was "no escape from the 'managed' currency."

CHAPTER 11

1. Rebecca Spang makes similar argument about financial conservatism of lawmakers in Revolutionary France: Rebecca L. Spang, *Stuff and Money in the Time of the French Revolution* (Cambridge, MA: Harvard University Press, 2015), 58.

2. V. I. Lenin, "Uderzhat li Bolsheviki gosudarstvennuiu vlast'?" *Polnoe sobranie sochinenii*, vol. 34, 307, quoted from V. Lenin, *Will the Bolsheviks Maintain Power?* (London: Labour Publishing, 1922), 47–48. Emphasis in the original.

3. On Parvus's and R. Hilferding's influence on Lenin, see George Garvy, "The Origins of Lenin's Views on the Role of Banks in the Socialist Transformation of Society," *History of Political Economy* 4, no. 1 (1972). Many thanks to Friedrich Asschenfeldt for pointing out this article.

4. Lenin, *Will the Bolsheviks Maintain Power?*, 48.

5. V. I. Lenin, "Groziashchaia katastrofa i kak s nei borot'sia" (September 1917), in Lenin, *Polnoe sobranie sochinenii*, izd. 5-e (Moskva: Gos. Izd-vo polit. lit, 1962), nt. 34, 161–167.

6. Vospominaniia ob Oktiabr'skom perevorote, *Proletarskaia revolitsiia* 10 (1922): 62.

7. Z. V. Atlas, *Sotsialisticheskaia denezhnaia sistema* (Moskva: Finansy, 1969), 63, 66.

8. Sovnarkom–Gosudarstvennyi bank, October 30 1917. Signed by Lenin and Menzhinskii (copy), GARF, f. 130, op.1, d.26, 58a; Sovnarkom–Gosudarstvennyi bank, November 6, 1917. Signed by Lenin, Trotsky, Lunacharskii, Menzhinskii, Bonch-Bruevich, and Gorbunov (copy), GARF, f. 130, op.1, d.26, 54.

9. David Riazanov nicknamed the participants of this event "our drummer-bankers" [*nashi barabannye finansisty*]. Riazanov's speech at the First Congress of people's councils of national economy: *Trudy I Vserossiiskogo S'ezda Sovetov Narodnogo Khoziaistva, 25 maia—4 iunia 1918* (Moskva: VSNKh, 1918), 150. On this event, see also *Russkaia revoliutsiia glazami petrogradskogo chinovnika. Dnevnik 1917–1918*, edited and annotated by Jens Petter Nielsen and Boris Weil (Oslo: Reprosentralen Universitetet i Oslo, 1986), 24; N. Osinskii, "Kak my ovladevali Gosudarstvennym Bankom," *Ekonomicheskaia Zhizn'* 1, November 6, 1918.; A. Shliapnikov, "K Oktiabriu," *Proletarskaia revoliutsiia* 10 (1922): 41; According to Trotsky, a similar "operation" (i.e., with an orchestra) in Moscow, turned out to be successful. "Vospominania ob Oktiabr'skom perevorote," 63. "Sobytiia v Gos. Banke v dni Okriabr'skoi revoliutsii," *Krasnaia letopis'*, 6 (1923): 335. There are different versions of who led the troops on this day—Menzhinsky, Trotsky, or Spiridonov. Apparently, nobody wanted to acknowledge participation in this parade.

10. "V Gosud. Banke," *Novaia Zhizn'*, November 8, 1917, no. 175; "Doklad o Gosudarstvennom Banke," *Novaia Zhizn'*, November 9, 1917, no. 176.

11. Obolenskii, "Kak my ovladevali Gosudarstvennym bankom"; A. M. Gindin, *Kak bolsheviki ovladeli Gosudarstvennym Bankom* (Moskva: Gosfinizdat, 1961), 24, 29, 30, 37, 45; *Russkaia revoliutsiia glazami*, 25.

12. "Gosudarstvennyi Bank i komissar Menzhinskii," *Novaia Zhizn'*, November 15, 1917, no. 181.

13. Protokoly sobraniia rabochikh deputatov Ekspeditsii Zagotovleniia Gosudarstvennykh Bumag. November 8, 1917, TsGA SPb. F.1255, op.1, d. 1085, ll. 95–96.

14. "Zabastovka v Gosudarstvennom Banke," *Nasha Rech'*, November 16, 1917.

15. *Russkaia revoliutsiia glazami petrogradskogo chinovnika*, 28. This request made no sense to the Bolsheviks who denied the separation of powers. According to Yakov Sverdlov, *Sovnarkom* (the Council of People's Commisars) was meant to combine "legislative, executive, and administrative powers." E. G. Gimpel'son, *Sovetskie upravlentsy, 1917–1920* (Moskva: Institut Istorii RAN, 1998), 14. Historians suggest that while it rejected the requests of the Bolshevik government, the Bank conspiratorially directed some funds to the counter-revolutionary "provisional government." At the same, according to Trotsky, the Department of Treasury did not go on strike and cooperated with the government, submitting requests for payments. Trotsky, "Vospominania ob Oktiabr'skom perevorote," 64. Sovnarkom's archival file reflects the Bank's payments made only after November 14, 1917, GARF, f. 130, op.1, d.26, 40, 64.

16. Shipov was fired on November 11, 1917. The act documenting the procurement of the eight keys for Bank's storages on November 15, 1917: GARF, f. 130, op.1, d.26, 36; the request to issue money, in cash, to the secretary of the Council of People's Commissars, November 17, 1917, GARF, f. 130, op.1, d.26, 44.
    Another anecdotal story concerned the appointment of the Bank's first director Stanislav Pestkovskii, who held this position for three days. Pestkovskii's role was purely decorative, and his appointment was an improvisation of the People's Commissar of Finance Menzhinskii, who wanted to fire stubborn Shipov and put someone else in his place. As Stephen Kotkin wittily observed, the appointment had an absurdist quality that characterized the performative style of the new authority. (Stephen Kotkin, *Stalin: The Paradoxes of Power, 1878–1928* [New York: Penguin Books, 2014], 230). Famously, the People's Commissariat of Finance occupied a corner in one room of Smolny and was literally represented by a couch on which Commissar Menzhinskii took naps. Gindin, *Kak Bolsheviki ovladeli Gosudarstvennym bankom*, 16; S. Pestkovsky, "Ob oktiabrskikh dniakh v Pitere," *Proletarskaia revoliutsiia* 10 (1922): 99–101.

17. O vremennom poriadke proizvodstva uplaty po dokumentam Petrogradskoi kontoroi Banka. Dekret SNK ot 30(17) noiabria 1917—*Denezhnoe obrashchenie i kreditnaia Sistema Soiuza SSR za 20 let. Sbornik vazhneishihk zakonodatelnykh materialov za 1917–1937g* (Moskva: Gosfinisdat, 1939).

18. M. I. Iroshnikov, Sozdanie sovetskogo gosudarstvennogo apparata. Sovet narodykh komissarov n narodnye komissariaty (Leningrad: Nauka, 1967), 89; N. Gorbunov, "Kak sozdavalsia rabochii apparat Sovnarkoma," *Vospominaniia o Vladimire Il'yche Lenine* 3 (1961): 191.

19. Gindin, *Kak bolsheviki*, 60; "Akt ob osmotre meshkov s den'gami, pribyvshikh iz Gosudarstvennogo Banka v rasporiazhenie Soveta Narodnykh Komissarov," *Pravda*, November 19, 1917, no. 194.

20. Sokol'nikov's speech at the First Congress of people's councils of national economy: *Trudy I Vserossiiskogo S'ezda Sovetov Narodnogo Khoziaistva, 25 maia–4 iunia 1918*, 174.

21. Obolenskii, "Kak my ovladevali Gosudarstvennym bankom." In December 1917, Lenin telegrammed Waclaw Worowski, the party representative in Stockholm, asking him to send over "three accountants with high expertise to work on the bank reform. Knowledge of Russian language is not necessary," Telegramma V. V. Vorovskomu, in *Istoriia Gosudarstvennogo Banka SSSR v dokumentakh* (Moskva: Finansy, 1971), 49. Some bank employees who went on strike were "forcefully brought" to the workplace, according to the decision of the Revolutionary-Military Committee. Iroshnikov, *Sozdanie sovetskogo tsentralnogo gosudarstvennogo apparata*, 198n.

22. Obolenskii replaced Pestovsky as a director of the State Bank on November 13, 1917.

23. Riazanov called it a *Red-Army-zation* instead of nationalization. See Riazanov's speech at the First Congress of people's councils of national economy: *Trudy I Vserossiiskogo S'ezda Sovetov Narodnogo Khoziaistva, 25 maia–4 iunia 1918*, 105; Dmitrii Bogolepov, who worked at the People's Commissariat of Finance, also noted that the decision to nationalize private banks and divert all their financial resources to the State Bank, came as a surprise to those few specialists who worked at the commissariat. D. P. Bogolepov, "Finansovoe stroitel'stvo v pervye gody Oktiabr'skoi revoliutsii," *Proletarskaia Revoliutsiia* 4 (1925): 166; On the event: A. Gindin, *Kak bol'sheviki natsionalizirovali chastnye banki (fakty i dokumenty posleoktiabr'skikh dnei v Petrograde)* (Moskva: Gosfinizdat, 1962), 29–30.

24. See, for instance, the list of People's Bank's branches in Petrograd, with addresses mostly on the Nevsky avenue, indicating which of the former private banks they occupied: "Spisok otdelenii Narodnogo Banka v Petrograde," in *RSFSR. 1-e Otdelenie Narodnogo Banka, Petrograd: Instruktsii, tsirkuliary i prikazy, N.1* (Petrograd: Tip "Fridrich Kan," 1918). Otchet o rabotakh pervogo Vserossiiskogo s'ezda predstavitelei finansovykh otdelov Oblastnykh, gubernskikh i uezdnykh S.R i Kr. D., sozvannyi po initsiative Otdela mestnogo khoziaistva Nar. KVD (Moskva: tip. "Fasol," 1918), 9, 12.

25. Non-Bolshevik newspapers repeatedly pointed out that the destruction of private banks, while it delivered quick cash, deprived the Bolshevik government of the sources of capital. See ibid.; B. Avilov, "Dekret o bankakh," *Novaia Zhizn'*, December 30, 1918, no. 204; Z. Katzenelenbaum, "Likvidatsiia Bankov," *Russkie Vedomosti*, December 21, 1917, no. 272; "O polozhenii bankov," *Russkie Vedomosti*, November 12, 1917, no. 248.

26. On banks as "empty buildings": B. Avilov, "Den'gi i tseny," *Novaia Zhizn'*, February 6, 1918, no. 17. Moisei Larsons described how angry workers demanding the

payment of salaries and threatening to loot and destroy the bank, laid siege to the office of the Bank's commissar. M. Ya. Larsons, *V sovetskom labirinte. Epizody i siluety* (Paris: Strela, 1932), 18–19.

27. Unable to force them to work, the new Soviet management of the bank tried to "squeeze out" from them information about the banking operations. M. Ya. Larsons, *Na sovetskoi sluzhbe: Zapiski spetsa* (Paris: La Source, 1930), 31–34.

28. Income from taxes would continue to dwindle: if in 1918 taxes were still expected to bring up to 76% of state income (this number was very exaggerated and reflected expectations, rather than actual results), by 1920 their share fell to 0.3%. *Gosudarsvtennyi Bank SSSR: Kratkii ocherk k sorokaletiiu Oktiabria* (Moskva: Gosfinizdat, 1957), 134.

29. See the memoir of Mikhail Lemke, the director of the Expedition for the Production of State Papers: M. K. Lemke, ""Oni proderzhatsia ne bolshe 5–7 dnei" (po dnevniku)," *Nemerknushchie gody. Ocherki i vospomimaniia o Krasnom Petrograde* (Leningrad, 1957), 273–278.

30. M. I. Fridman, *Gosudarstvennoe khoziaistvo i denezhnoe obrashchenie v Rossii, 1913–1919* (Moskva: Sovet Vserossiïskikh kooperativnykh s'ezdov, 1919), 19, 29.

31. *Rospis' obshchegosudarstvennykh dokhodov i raskhodov Rossiiskoi Sotsialisticheskoi Federativnoi Sovetskoi Respubliki na ianvar'-iiun' 1919 goda s ob'asnitelnoi zapiskoi Narodnogo Komissara Finansov.* (Petrograd: 4-a gos tip, 1919), 57.

32. G. Ya. Sokol'nikov, "Denezhnyi krisis," *Narodnoe khoziastvo* 2 (1918): 3–4.

33. On local monetary surrogates, see M. V. Khodiakov, *Den'gi Revoliutsii i Grazhdanskoi voiny* (St. Petersburg: St. Petersburgskii Gosudarstvennyi Universitet, 2018), 53–55.

34. V. I. Lenin, "Nabrosok programmy ekonomicheskikh meropriatii," December 1917; Lenin, *Polnoe sobranie sochinenii*, t.35, 124. According to this plan, all money had to be deposited in the State Bank and no one could withdraw more than 125 rubles weekly; funds above the 500 rubles limit should be confiscated.

35. Variant stat'i "Ocherednye zadachi sovetskoi vlasti," V. I. Lenin, *Polnoe sobranie sochinenii,* t. 36, 134–136; Chernovoi nabrosok proekta programmy (VII ekstrennyi s'ezd RKP(b), V. I. Lenin, *Polnoe sobranie sochinenii,* t. 36, 74–75l.

36. "O natsionalizatsii bankov," Dekret VTsIK on 27(14) dekabria 1917; "O revizii stalnykh iashchikov (seifov) v bankakh" Postanovlenie TsIK ot 27 (14) dekabria 1917; "Ob utverzhdenii sektsii blagorodnykh metallov VSNKh i ob ustanovlenii kazennoi monopolii torgovli zolotom i platinoi" Postanovlenie VSNKh on 12 ianvaria 1918, in *Denezhnoe obrashchenie i kreditnaia Sistema Soiuza SSR za 20 let. Sbornik vazhneishihk zakonodatelnyh materialov za 1917-1937g,*(Moskva: Gosfinizdat, 1939), 2–7

37. P. Kievsky [G. Piatakov], "Proletariat i banki," *Pravda,* December 25, 1917, no. 212.

38. The committee included the representatives of governmental institutions, trade unions, the councils of workers, soldiers, and peasant deputies as well as industrialists whose businesses had not yet been taken over. "Ob uchrezhdenii Tsentralnogo

uchetno-ssudnogo komiteta," Dekret SNK, in *Denezhnoe obrashchenie i kreditnaia Sistema Soiuza SSR,* 8–9. ok

39. *Protokoly Prezidiuma Vyschego Soveta Narodnogo Khoziastva, Dekabr' 1917–1918. Sb. dokumentov* (Moskva: Nauka, 1991); Protokol no.17, 24 ianvaria 1918, 44–49.

40. The editors of *Ekonomicheskaia Zhizn'* observed, however, that the decree on the reorganization of the State Bank's Council was hardly put into practice. "Bankovskaia politika sovetskoi vlasti," *Ekonomicheskaia Zhizn', Prilozhenie za 1919,* no. 2, 25.

41. For more on state capitalism of 1918, see Stephen F. Cohen, *Bukharin and the Bolshevik Revolution: A Political Biography, 1888–1938* (Oxford: Oxford University Press, 1971), 69–78; E. H. Carr, *The Bolshevik Revolution 1917–1923,* vol. 2 (New York: W. W. Norton) , 1985, 88–100.

42. E. H. Carr wrote about Gukovskii's "rigid and unimaginative purism" that "ranged him with the extreme Right of the party"; E. H. Carr, *The Bolshevik Revolution,* vol. 2, 246. For a different assessment, see Dmitrii Bogolepov and Solomon Lozovskii in *Protokoly zasedanii Vserossiiskogo Tsentralnogo Ispolnitelnogo Komiteta 4-go sozyva (stenograficheskii otchet)* (Moskva: Gos. Izd-vo, 1920), 133, 135. Dmitrii Bogolepov, who served at the financial commissariat until early 1919, characterized Gukovskii's administration of finances as a short intermission, some sort of a pre-image of the post-1921 "new economic policy." D. P. Bogolepov, "Vospominaniia o Lenine," in *O Lenine. Vospominaniia. Kn.4. Pod red. i s predisl. N. L. Meshcheriakova* (Moskva: Gos. izd-vo,1925, C.), 116–121; Bogolepov, "Finansovoe stroitelstvo," 173. In 1922, the new commissar of finance, Grigorii Sokol'nikov, described the "new economic policy" as a return to the policy of 1918. G. Ya. Sokol'nikov, "Gosudarstvennyi capitalism i novaia finansovaia politika," in G. Ya. Sokol'nikov, *Novaia finansovaia politika: na puti k tverdoi valiute* (Moskva: Nauka, 1991), 56.

43. Getting rid of gold was Grigorii Sokol'nikov's idea: he believed that the West would not return to the gold standard. See Gukovskii's speech at the First Congress of people's councils of national economy: *Trudy I Vserossiiskogo S'ezda Sovetov Narodnogo Khoziaistva, 25 maia—4 iunia 1918,* 129–143.

44. *Trudy I Vserossiiskogo S'ezda Sovetov Narodnogo Khoziaistva, 25 maia—4 iunia 1918,* 129–143.

45. Gukovskii's report was published in *Pravda,* April 17, 19, 1918, nos. 74 and 75. The record of his speech, more extensive but truncated, also appeared in *Protokoly zasedanii Vserossiiskogo Tsentralnogo Ispolnitelnogo Komiteta 4-go sozyva (stenograficheskii otchet)* (Moskva: Gos. Izd-vo, 1920), 112–117. Some reference to his words (apparently, not recorded) are scattered throughout other delegates' responses to his speech and debates.

46. See Bukharin's speech at the VTsIK session: *Protokoly zasedanii Vserossiiskogo Tsentralnogo Ispolnitelnogo Komiteta 4-go sozyva (stenograficheskii otchet)* (Moskva: Gos. Izd-vo, 1920); see also Grigorii Sokol'nikov's very critical article: "Revolutionnye finansy v svete burzhuaznoi kritiki," *Pravda,* 1918, no.77. E. G. Gimpel'son, *"Voennyi Kommunizm": Politika, Praktika, Ideologiia* (Moskva: Mysl',

1973), 31–32. Also, see an article criticizing Gukovskii's policy in the main journal of left communists "Kommunist": Afanasii Lomov, "Programma finansovykh reform komissara Gukovskogo," *Kommunist* 2 (1918): 20–22. Lomov scorned Gukovskii and Bogolepov for their frugal budgetary policy and the "rationality" of the Narkomfin's actions. To Gukovskii's disadvantage, some "bourgeois" economists, including the former minister of finance Mikhail Bernatskii, favorably assessed his actions, thereby adding fuel to the fire.

47. Fridman, *Gosudarstvennoe khoziaistvo i denezhnoe obrashchenie.* 22. Only the first semi-annual budget for 1918 was published: *Obshchaia rospis' gosudarstvennykh dokhodov i rashkhodov Rossiiskoi Respubliki na ianvar'-iiun' 1918 goda* (Moskva: Izd. VTsIK, 1918). The work on the 1918 budget had begun much earlier, and it was assumed that the Constituent Assembly would approve it. N. A. Razmanova, "Dmitrii Petrovich Bogolepov v Narkomfine v 1917–1918 godakh," *Vestnik Finansovoi Akademii,* 2001, no. 2, 69.

48. "O sobliudenii edinstva kassy." Dekret SNK 2 Maya 1918, *Istoriia Gosudarstvennogo Banka SSSR v dokumentakh,* 61; E. N. Sokolov, *Denezhnaia i biudzhetnaia politika Sovetskoi respubliki* (Riazan': Riazanskii universitet im. S. A. Yesenina, 2012), 32–33.

49. He insisted on the "compulsory" opening of checking accounts that was essentially equivalent to a hidden expropriation of funds, grouping the population into cooperatives of consumers for the distribution of goods. V. I. Lenin, "Osnovnye polozheniia khoziaistvennoi i v osobennosti bankovoi politiki" [April 1918], *Leninskii sbornik,* 21 (Moskva: Gosizdat, 1933), 160. See also Lenin's speech at the First All-Russia Congress of the representatives of financial departments of the regional and local councils of deputies (May 17–21, 1918): *Otchet o raborakh pervogo Vserossiiskogo s'ezda predstavitelei finansovykh otdelov oblastnykh, gubernsikh i uezdnykh S.R. i Kr D* (Moskva: tip. "Fasol'," 1918), 21–26, and in Lenin, *Polnoe sobranie sochinenii,* vol. 36, 350–355. As Larin recalled, when Lenin mentioned his plan in public, the rate of the ruble on foreign markets, already very low, plummeted to a new extreme. Yu. Larin, "U kolybeli," *Narodnoe Khoziaistvo* 11 (1918): 21.

50. Gukovskii summarized some of these principles in the report to VTsIK: *Protokoly zasedanii Vserossiiskogo Tsentralnogo Ispolnitelnogo Komiteta 4-go sozyva (stenograficheskii otchet)* (Moskva: Gos. Izd-vo, 1920); see also, Bogolepov, "Finansovoe stroitelstvo," 173–174. The plan of absorbing money could not work because people did not want to bring their money to the Soviet bank: before the war, there were 1.6 billion rubles in circulation and 5 billion rubles in bank accounts; "now we have 30 billion rubles in circulation, but in saving and direct deposit accounts there is less than 10 billion rubles."

51. *Protokoly zasedanii Vserossiiskogo Tsentralnogo Ispolnitel'nogo Komiteta 4-go sozyva (stenograficheskii otchet)* (Moskva: Gos. Izd-vo, 1920), 112–117.

52. A. M. Gindin, *Kak bolsheviki natsionalizirovali chastnye banki,* Moskva: Gosfinizdat, 1962, 118.

53. V. I. Lenin, "Tezisy o bankovoi politike," in Lenin, *Polnoe sobranie sochinenii*, t.36, 220. See also Aleksandr Spunde's letter to Lenin on this matter written on March 14, 1918, in *"Samo proshedshee kak ono bylo . . .", Perepiska Anny Kravchenko i Aleksandra Spunde* (Moskva: Izd-vo polit.literatury, 1990), 42–43. Lenin's concept of bank's organization was based, in Andrea Granziosi's words, on "the centralist program of reducing society to one large firm." Andrea Graziosi, "G. L. Piatakov (1890–1937): A Mirror of Soviet History," *Harvard Ukrainian Studies* 16, no. 1–2 (June 1992): 155.

54. Alexander Spunde, who called himself a "left communist," stood behind initiatives that were later cast as "right," for instance, the invitation of former bankers to advise on the reform of the State Bank. On Spunde's left communism: M. G. Nikolaev, "Bankir voleiu partii: stranitsy biografii A.P. Spunde (1892–1962)," *Ezhegodnik Ekonomicheskaia Istoriia 2019* (Moskva: Rosspen, 2020), 191.

55. Bogolepov had come to the commissariat in November 1917 on Lenin's invitation. N. A. Razmanova mentioned that Gukovskii was often ill, and Bogolepov de facto managed the commissariat. Razmanova, "Dmitrii Petrovich Bogolepov v Narkomfine v 1917–1918 godakh," 69. Bogolepov led the preparation of the state budget; he also prepared the law that legalized the issuing of new rubles. Iroshnikov, *Sozdanie sovetskogo tsentralnogo gosudarstvennogo apparata*, 126.

56. On Gukovsky, see *Vse ministry finansov Rossii, 1802–2004* (Moskva: REO, 2004), 287–294. Accusations of unprofessionalism were common, although Dmitrii Bogolepov, who worked under Gukovskii, admired him and praised his program. Bogolepov, "Finansovoe stroitelstvo." Similarly, in the People's Bank, deputy-director Alexander Spunde replaced the absentee nominal director Georgii Piatakov. On Alexander Spunde, see M. G. Nikolaev, "Bankir voleiu partii: stranitsy biografii A. P. Spunde, 18921–962," 184–216.
    In 1918–19 (the strike of the bank's employees was over by that time), the People's Commissariat of Finance and People's Bank were staffed well, with no shortage of employees with university degrees. (As an example, see the list of employees at the Bank's key department on the financing industry: "Spiski sotrudnikov otdela po finansirovaniiu natsionalizirovannoi promyshlennosti," RGAE, f.2324, op.9, d.43.)

57. A. M. Gindin, *Kak bol'sheviki natsionalizirovali chastnye banki* (Moskva: Gosfinizdat, 1962), 112–117. See also short reports about the commission's meetings in *Novaia Zhizn'*: "Soveshchanie of bankakh," *Novaia Zhizn'*, April 11 and April 12,1918. For analysis of the principle of separating the issuing of money from the funding industry: Lurie, "Iz istorii ideologii i zakonodatelstva o denezhnom obrashchenii RSFSR," doklad 3 iunia 1920, in *Trudy sektsii po voprosam denezhnogo obrashcheniia i kredita pod pred. M.I. Fridmana i V. Ya. Zheleznova. Denezhnoe obrashcheniie i kredit. Denezhnoe obrashchenie v Rossii i za granitsei v gody voiny i revoliutsii (1914–1921* (Petrograd: 1922), 447.

58. Two files contain various materials of this issue, including memos from a "technical adviser" (his name is undecipherable) who strongly insisted on

the legalization of issuing money: "Delo o poriadke kreditovaniia kazny Narodnym Bankom i o peresmotre postanovleniia dekreta 21 ianvaria 1918 o kratkosrochnykh obiazatelstvakh Gos. Kaznacheistva," RGAE, f. 2324, op.1, d. 66; "Delo o raschirenii emissionnogo prava Narodnogo banka," RGAE, f.2324, op.1, d.178.

59. In January 1918, the government's decree repudiating domestic debts, converted the 5% bonds into interest-free paper money equal to the credit rubles, therefore changing the nature of the collateral.

60. Russia's gold reserve constituted 1.1 billion rubles, plus 2.5 billion rubles mortgaged abroad. Previous laws had sanctioned the issuing of 16.5 billion rubles, therefore 21.5 billion were released in circulation above the legal limit. In nine months since the October Revolution 1917, the Soviet government had printed 22.7 billion rubles in addition to 18.9 billion rubles that had been released by the tsarist and the Provisional governments—41.6 billion rubles in total. Of this sum, according to Narkomfin's calculations, 21.5 billion were issued above the legislatively approved limit. Narkomfin estimated that the economy would need 12 billion rubles for the next five months (these calculations were far too modest)

61. *Izvestiia*, November 5, 1918, no. 242, 4.

62. *Izvestiia*, December 7, 1918, no. 268, 3. The experts at the People's Bank continued insisting to the government that the unpublished law had no meaning because what mattered for the population as well as for the "Western financial market" was not the astronomically high numbers of credit rubles (they were already known) but the recognition of that debt by the government. Narodnyi Bank—Upravlenie delami SNK, RGAE, F.2324, op.1, 1918, d.178, l.72; Glavnomu komissaru uplavliaiushchemu Naroldnym Bankom. Tekhnicheskii sovetnik, November 11, 1918, RGAE, F.2324, op.1, 1918, d.178, l.690b-70.

63. *Rospis'... na ianvar'-iun' 1919*, 25.

64. *Trudy Vserossiiskogo s'ezda zaveduiushchikh finotdelami. Plenarnye zasedaniia* (Moskva: Redatsionno-izdatelskaia kollegiiia NKF, 1919), 77–78.

65. On the allocation of debts between Russia and Ukraine, see Materialy po rassmotreniu voprosa o vvedenii na Ukraine samostoiatelnoi denezhnoi sistemy, RGAE, f.7733, op.1, d.128, 60b (July 1, 1918); O neobkhodimosti konsolidatsii v dolg kazny chisliashchikhsia na schete zolota Banka za granitsei 1891.5 m.r. velikobritanskikh kreditov, August 6, 1918, RGAE, f.2324, op.1, d.14, 25–26; Krestinskii, Piatakov to the SNK, October 29, 1918, "O kratkosrochnykh obiazatelstvakh," RGAE f. 2324, op.1, d. 66, l.53–56; Materialy po russko-ukrainskim mirnym peregovoram o razdele gosudarstvennykh imushchestv. GARF, f. R-546, op.1, d.3, d.4.

66. Pavlo Hai-Nyzhnyk, *Finansova polityka uriadu Ukraïn'skoi Derzhavi Get'mana Pavla Skoropads'kogo (29 kvitnia—14 grudnia 1918 r)* (Kyiv, 2001), 32, 34, 51; L. M. Nemanov, *Finansovaia politika Ukrainy 7 noiabria 1917—4 fevralia 1919* (Moskva: Koop. izd-vo, 1919), 33, 34.

67. Zhurnal soveshchaniia chlenov delegatsii i drugikh lits 23, 24, 25 aprelia 1918 in Materialy po russko-ukrainskim mirnym peregovoram o razdele gosudarstvennykh imushchestv, GARF, f. R-546, op.1, d.3, 1–7.

68. Experts who floated the ideas of creating a Russo-Ukrainian monetary union "similar to the Latin Union" even thought about inviting the Ukrainian representatives to sit on the board of Russia's People's Bank. Materialy po rassmotreniiu voprosa o vvedenii na Ukraine samostoiatelnoi denezhnoi sistemy. Spravka; "O samostoiatelnoi denezhnoi sisteme na Ukraine," RGAE, f.7733, op.1., d.128; on "Latin union," see N. D. Silin, "O nashei denezhnoi politike v sluchae sozdaniia Ukrainskoi denezhnoi sistemy," ibid, 32–33; July–August 1918. S. Zaks (Gladnev) criticized these plans as not taking into account that Ukraine's independence was a "fait accompli" and that the two countries were on the way to developing very different economic and financial system. Zaks (Gladnev), Otzyv na Proekt doklada Osobogo otdela po finansovym voprosam, stoiashchim v sviazi s osushchestvleniem Brestskogo dogovora, August 28, 1918, RGAE f.7733, op.1, d.128, 3–40.

69. There was a debate about which principle should be used in defining each country's share—the calculation by territory, the size of population, or its share in tax income. Zhurnal zasedanii 23 i 30 iunia i 3 iiulia Soveshchaniia iz predstavitelei uchrezhdenii Narodnogo Komissariata finansov po rassmotreniiu prislannykh i Kieva materialov, otnosiashchikhsia k russko-ukrainskim mirnym peregovoram, in Materialy po russko-ukrainskim mirnym peregovoram o razdele gosudarstvennykh imushchestv, GARF, f. R-546, op.1, d.3, 45–47). Christian Rakovskii worried that the Russian delegation had miscalculated and Ukraine's claims for properties would be too high (*"my mozhem progadat"*) Materialy po russko-ukrainskim mirnym peregovoram, GARF, f. R-546, op.1, d.4, 47). Ukraine initially insisted on one third of debts and assets, which were supposed to include natural resources (Spravka, , GARF, f. R-546, op.1, d.4, 99). Finally, Ukraine's share was settled at 20% of liabilities and properties.

70. Chetvertoe zasedaniie finansovo-raschetnoi komissii, August 7, 1918, *Materialy po russko-ukrainskim mirnym peregovoram,* GARF, f. R-546, op.1, d.4, 51–52.

71. 6-e zasedaniie finansovo-raschetnoi komissii, August 14, 1918, GARF, f. R-546, op.1, d.4, 130–132.

72. Zhurnal soveshchaniia pri Osobom otdele po finansovym voprosam stoiashchim v sviazi s osushchestvleniem Brestskogo dogovora, July 23, 1918, in *Materialy po russko-ukrainskim mirnym peregovoram*, GARF, f. R-546, op.1, d.4, 39.

73. The representatives of the Credit Chancellery in the committee on Russian-Ukrainian financial negotiations could not say for sure which part of the debt was canceled by the Decree of January 21, 1918, or how many credit rubles had been issued. They estimated that in January 1918, the debt equaled about 60 billion rubles, but by late June–early July, it had risen to 74 billion., Zhurnal zasedanii 23 i 30 iiunia in Materialy po russko-ukrainskim mirnym peregovoram, GARF, f. R-546, op.1, d.3, 44–45.

74. The idea was to have two parallel currencies—state banknotes of the People's Bank for transactions within the nationalized economy and governance, and commercial money, issued by private joint-stock banks. Curiously, VSNKH also entertained similar plans. This model of parallel money was later used in the monetary reform of 1921–24. See A. E. Lomeier, "Vneshniaia torgovlia, kredinyi rubl', i proekt chastnoi denezhnoi edinitsy," and A. N. Za. "Reforma denezhnogo obrashcheniia i Gosudarstvennyi Bank," in *Voprosy denezhnogo obrashcheniia. Tsentral'nyi Narodno-Promyshlennyi Komitet. Otdel Vneshnei Torgovli. Doklady M.V. Bernatskogo, A.N. Gurieva, A.N. Zaka, V.S. Ziva, N.I. Lodyzhenskogo, A.E. Lomeiera, F.A. Menkova i ikh obsuzhdenie* (Petrograd, 1918).

75. Bogolepov, *Finansovoe stroitel'stvo*, 174.

76. Rasgovor Gorbunova s Minkinym i Kolokutskim, 18 iiunia v 9 chas.vechera, GARF, f.130, op.2, d.230, l.164 and following. During the conversation, Gorbunov periodically went to "talk to Lenin."

77. Gorbunov: "Opasnost' mne kazhetsia ne snaruzhi, a iznutri" (transcript of telephone conversation with Minkin), GARF, f.130, op.2, d.230, l. 190 and after.

78. See plans for evaluation and transcripts of phone conversations between Gorbunov and Minkin on June 20 and 21, 1918, Minkin's telegram to Lenin from Penza, GARF, f. 130, op.2, d.230.

79. See the report of Nikolai Kazanovskii ("zaveduiushchii poezdom s zolotym zapasom") about the recovery of the gold reserve (May 28, 1920). The total value of recovered treasures was 409,624,870 rubles (236 million rubles in gold had been spent or sold). RGAE, 7733, op.1, d.1346, 24–28.

80. For the most complete account of the gold's fate, see Oleg Budnitskii, *Den'gi russkoi emigratsii: Kolchakovskoe zoloto, 1918–1957* (Moskva: NLO, 2008).

81. Discussion on Lourie's report "Iz istorii ideologii i zakonodatelstva o denezhnom obrashchenii" on June 4, 1920, in RGAE, f.7733, op.1, d.6267 Zhurnaly i protokoly zasedanii komissii po voprosam denezhnogo obrashcheniia. The June 28, 1918, decree sanctioned the nationalization of the most important spheres of industry. "Poriadok finansirovaniia natsionalizirovannoi promyshlennosti," *Izvestiia NKF*, No.1–2, 1919 (September 1, 1919), 4–5. According to Gimpel'son, by the end of 1918, 3,338, or 35% of the enterprises in Central Russia had been nationalized. E. G. Gimpel'son, *"Voennyi Kommunism,"* 42.

82. On the "incorrect line" of Rykov and Miliutin, as well as their attempts to elevate VSNKh to the level of central government (Sovnarkom), see F. Samokhvalov, *Sovety narodnogo khoziaistva v 1917–1932 gg.* (Moskva: Nauka, 1964), 59–62. Stephen Cohen observed that VSNKh was the creation of the group of "young Muscovites"—Nikolai Bukharin, Nikolai Osinskii, Vladimir Smirnov, and Georgii Lomov—who formed the nucleus of the "left opposition." Cohen, *Bukharin and the Bolshevik Revolution*, 62. For a detailed analysis of VSNKh's activity, see Silvana Malle, *The Economic Organization of War Communism, 1918–1921*, ch. 5, "Industrial Administration" (New York: Cambridge University Press, 1985),"

83. Early Soviet historian Mikhail Pokrovskii compared Witte's Ministry of Finance to VSNKh. Theodore von Laue, *Sergei Witte and the Industrialization of Russia* (New York: Atheneum, 1969), 164.

84. About the "state as a main consumer," see L. Ivan, "Gosudarsvennyi uchet narodnogo khoziastva i znachenie v nem gosudarstvennogo schetovodstva," *Izvestiia NKF*, no. 7 (1919), 3.

85. L. L. Obolenskii, "Nashi zadachi," *Izvestiia Narodnogo Komissariata Finansov* 1–2 (September 1, 1919): 1.

86. Leonid Iurovskii commented on that idea: "During the epoch of war communism, the opinion that the system of transactions through the bank serves as a transitional step toward money-less accounting . . . was very widespread," Leonid Iurovskii, *Denezhnaia politika Sovetskoi vlasti (1917–1927)* (Moskva: Ekonomika, 2008), 99 (initial publication—1928).

87. N. V. Valentinov (Vol'skii), *Novaia ekonomicheskaia politika i krizis partii posle smerti Lenina* (Moskva: Sovremennik, 1991), 36–37, quoted in M. G. Nikolaev, "Bankir voleiu partii: stranitsy biografii A. P. Spunde (1892-1962)," 191.

88. "O Raschetnykh Operatsiiakh," Dekret SNK, January 23, 1919, in *Istoriia Gosudarstvennogo banka v dokumentakh*, 76–77. x

89. Cashless transactions had been introduced in Russia in the 1890s by Serguei Witte as a means of reducing the demand for paper money. Narkomfin claimed that the Soviet model made a big step toward the reconstruction of the Soviet budget. However, the biggest novelty was the prohibition of buying supplies from private contractors on the market if these goods could be obtained from Soviet nationalized enterprises in a cashless manner. See *Rospis' obshchegosudarstvennykh dokhodov i raskhodov RSFSR na ianvar'—iiun' 1919 goda s obiasnitelnoi zapiskoi NKF*, 29.

90. As the Bank's commissar Georguii Piatakov explained, after the creation of industrial "centers" (glavki—that is, departments that managed entire spheres of industries; for instance, Center-Textile [Tsentrtekstil'], Center-Nail [Glavgvozd']), Center-Soap, etc.), the People's Bank lost contact with the enterprises and instead credited these new organs, which then distributed funds among factories at their own discretion. One of the consequences of this system was the "colossal rise of the need in cash, and, consequently, the endless dizzying growth of the new issues of monetary signs." The very essence of the mechanism was supposed to change; instead of "credits" to factories' "current accounts" that allowed for a free use of funds by account holders, Piatakov suggested strict distribution of financial resources according to the budgets compiled by the sectoral councils of people's industry (SNKh, or *sovnarkhozy*). G. Piatakov, "O finansirovanii natsionalizirovannoi promyshlennosti," *Ekonomicheskaia Zhizn'*, November 17, 1918, no. 9.

91. Dekret SNK or 31 oktiabria 1918 o sliianii kaznacheistv s uchrezhdeniiami Narodnogo Banka, in *Sbornik dekretov i rasporiazhenii po finansam*, vol.1: 1917-19

(Petrograd: Narkomfin, 1919), 41; Postanovlenie NKF ot 28 dekabria 1918 no.268 ob uprazdnenii Osobennoi Kantseliarii po Kreditnoi chasti, in *Sbornik dekretov i rasporiazhenii po finansam*, 46; Prikaz NK po narodnomu banku RSFSR ot 3 ianvaria 1919 goda o raspredelenii del b. Osobennoi Kantseliarii po Kreditnoi chasti, in *Sbornik dekretov i rasporiazhenii po finansam*; Prikaz NFK po Narodnomu Banku RSPRS ot 3 ianvaria 1919 ob uchrezhdenii Otdela mezhdunarodnykh raschetov, in *Sbornik dekretov i rasporiazhenii po finansam*, and other orders on the Bank's new structure, in *Sbornik dekretov i rasporiazhenii po finansam*, 47–49, 51. Spravka o preobrazovanii tsentralnogo upravleniia Narbanka. October 1, 1919, in *Istoriia Gosudarsvennogo banka SSSR v dokumentakh*, 86,

92. E. N. Sokolov, *Denezhnaia i biudzhetnaia politika Sovetskoi respubliki v 1917–nachale 1921 g.*, 46.

93. Dekret SNK ot 15 Maia 1919 o vypuske v obrashchenie novykh kreditnykh biletov obraztsa 1918, in *Sbornik dekretov i rasporiazhenii po finansam*, vol.1, 10–11. This decision coincided with the issue of a new series of credit rubles, in addition to the old rubles that continued to circulate. The new rubles were printed from old templates made by the Provisional government, with a crownless two-headed eagle and featuring the signature of G. Piatakov (hence their nickname "piatakovki," or else known as "penzenki" because they were printed in Penza). As Krestinskii admitted, "Except for Piatakov's signature, there was nothing communist in this money." *Trudy Vserossiiskogo s'ezda zaveduiushchikh finotdelami. Plenarnye zasedaniia* (Moskva: Pedaktsionno-izdatelskaia kollegiia NFK, 1919), 28. Besides, they were also released in the name of a "non-existent bank" (the imperial State bank that had already been renamed) and referred to the exchange to gold that was also non-existent.

94. This draws on a memo published in the official organ of Narkomfin and signed by "V": V., "Raboty po sozdaniiu gosudarstvennogo balansa," *Izvestiia NKF*, no. 8 (October 25, 1919), 3–4. Interestingly, the memo also put forward a theoretical justification, explaining that during the transitional period, the national economy and the state still represented two different entities, which would merge under socialism. Until then, though, it was important to keep strict control over the balance of the state's obligations and its means.

95. The first Soviet money of the "1918 issue" was in fact released in circulation in May 1919. Khodiakov, *Den'gi revoliutsii*, 59–60. In October 1919, the government's decree approved the release of a new type of credit ruble with the phrase about the guarantees by the republic's wealth. Interestingly, instead of this phrase, one of the variants of the inscription mentioned the gold content of one ruble (17,424 shares of gold). Unsigned draft, GARF, f. 130, op.2, d.230, 99.

96. On the emergence of this principle after the French Revolution, see Rebecca Spang, *Stuff and Money*, 69–84.

97. Veinberg, speaking at the Second Congress of *sovnarkhozy*. *Trudy II Vserossiiskogo s'ezda Sovetov Narodnogo Khoziaistva (19 dekabria—27 dekabria 1918 g.* (Moskva: VSNKh, 1918), 273.

98. Sotsial'naia revoliutsiia i finansy. Sbornik k III congressu kommunisticheskogo internatsionala (Moskva: Narkomfin, 1921), 111. NKF separated funds that circulated among soviet enterprises into a special category in the state budget: "oborotnye" (circulating) funds.

99. V. Ya. Chubar', "Voprosy finansirovaniia na II Vserossiiskom s'ezde Sovetov Narodnogo Khoziiaistva," *Narodnoe Khoziiaistvo* 2 (1919): 22.

100. There were two competing proposals for the law on the mechanisms for funding nationalized industry: VSNKh's project put financial administration under its control; the commissariat of finance, trying to protect its (and the Bank's) autonomy, submitted a "counter-project." See *Ekonomicheskaia Zhizn'*, February 27, 1919, no. 45; G. Dementiev, "Predstoiashchaia reforma nashego gos. biudzheta," *Ekonomicheskaia Zhizn'*, March 9, 1919, no. 53. For a detailed discussion of the principles of financing industry, see Evgenii Sokolov's *Denezhnaia i biudzhetnaia politika Sovetskoi respubliki*, 47–57, and Malle, *The Economic Organization of War Communism, 1918–1921*, 234–248.

101. A. I. Rykov, Doklad po organizatsionnomu voprosu na Plenume 20 sentiabria 1918, in A. I. Rykov, *Izbrannye proizvedeniia* (Moskva: Ekonomia, 1990), 75. See also N. N. Osinskii, "Organy proletarskoi diktatury v ekonomicheskoi oblasti," in N. N. Osinskii, *Stroitel'stvo sotsializma: Obshchie zadachi. Organizatsiia proizvodstva* (Moskva: "Kommunist," 1918), 62, 68–69.

102. See also the resolution of the Second Congress of *sovnarkhozy* in December 1918: Trudy II Vserossiiskogo s'ezda Sovetov Narodnogo Khoziaistva (19 dekabria—27 dekabria, 1918 g.) (Moskva: VSNKh, 1918); V. Ya. Chubar', "Voprosy finansirovaniia na II Vserossiiskom s'ezde Sovetov Narodnogo Khoziaistva," *Narodnoe Khoziaistvo* 12 (1919): 21.

103. In this policy, VSNKh also competed with other commissariats and even the central government. See Rykov's speeches in 1918: Doklad Prezidiuma VSNKh na plenume VSNKh (14 sentiabria 1918); Rykov, Doklad po organizatsionnomu voprosu na Plenume 20 sentiabria 1918, in A. I. Rykov, *Izbrannye proizvedeniia* (Moskva: Ekonomia, 1990), 55–57, 67, 75.

104. The principles of the Bank's absorption were described, for instance, in D. Trakhtenberg's article in January 1919. Trakhtenberg, "K reorganizatsii Narodnogo Banka," *Ekonomicheskaia Zhizn'*, no. 20 (January 29, 1919). Izvestiia NKF announced the plan of the Bank's absorption in mid-September 1919. "Reorganizatsiia finansovykh organov Respubliki," *Izvestiia NKF*, no. 3–4 (September 15, 1919), 16–17. This announcement appeared along with a delayed publication of the decree on the Treasury's absorption into the Bank. "Reorganizatsiia finansovykh organov Respubliki", *Izvestiia NKF*, no. 3–4 (September 15, 1919), 27.

105. Unsigned memo, "Finansovaia politika," RGAE, f.2324, op.9, d.58, l.51. The memo (probably a copy) has the names of addressees: Serguei Chutskaev, deputy commissar of finances, and Dmitrii Spasskii, director of the People's Bank's department on the financing of nationalized industry, and the date when it was sent to them (January 23 and 24, 1920).

106. *VSNKH, Finansovo-Schetnyi Otdel. Ego zadachi i deiiatelnost'* (Moskva: VSNKh, 1919), 9.

107. See, for instance, the description of the system of "*metallosnabzhenie*" (metal-supply) in Gal', "O polozhenii metallosnabzheniia," *Narodnoe khoziaistvo* 9–10 (1919): 3-4. It did not mean, though, that government agencies and enterprises did not need money. The demand for money only rose, but in the absence of the Bank, monetary signs were distributed by a special Commission (Osobaia mezhvedomstvennaia komissiia po raspredeleniiu denehznykh znakov). Iurovskii, *Denezhnaia politika Sovetskoi vlasti*, 112. The emphasis on "distribution" or "supply" suggested that money turned into another kind of goods.

108. Memo without author and date. RGAE, f.2324, op.9, d.58, 57–60. The memo also asserted that VSNKh had failed to create a system of economic planning and coordination between industries (each factory had its own plan based on pre-war unrealistic calculations). Lev Kritzman described the state of the economy under war communism as "the anarchy of proletarian-natural economy," L. Kritzman, *Geroicheskii period velikoi russkoi revolutsii (opyt analiza t.n. "voennogo kommunizma")* (Moskva: Gos. izd-vo, 1926), 114–115.

109. Ob uprazdenii Narodnogo Banka, Dekret SNK, January 19, 1920, *Istoriia Gosudarstvennogo Banka SSSR v dokumentakh*, 88.

110. Sokol'nikov, "*Gosudarstvennyi kapitalizm i novaia finansovaia politika,*" 57.

111. Sokol'nikov, Doklad na X Vserossiiskom s'ezde Sovetov 25 dekabria 1922 g, in G. Ya. Sokol'nikov, *Novaia finansovaia politika: na puti k tverdoi valiute*, 104.

112. Strumilin, *Problemy trudovogo ucheta*, 202.

113. Strumilin, *Problemy trudovogo ucheta*, 217. See also Strumilin, "Trudovoi ekvivalent," *Ekonomicheskaia Zhizn'*, July 31, 1920, no. 167.

114. Rozentuk, "Sozdanie novoi sistemy obmena vzamen denezhnoi," *Izvestiia VSNKh* 6 (1918), no. 6. See the overview of other ideas of labor money in Iurovskii, *Denezhnaia politika sovetskoi vlasti*, 133–175.

115. Zakharii Katsnelenbaum, "Problema deneg i otsenki v sotsializme" (July 2, 1920), in *K teorii deneg i ucheta* (Moskva [no publisher], 1922), 33, 34, 43, 54.

116. A. Chaianov, *Metody bezdenezhnogo ucheta khoziaistvennykh predpriatii. Trudy Vysshego Seminaria s-kh ekonomii i politiki pri Petrovskoi S-Kh Akademii* (Moska: Gos. Izd-vo, 1921) (written in October 1920), 39–40.

117. Moreover, the first price-current of goods and services in *treds* was supposed to be based on pre-war prices in imperial rubles (the Council of Labor and Defense had to convert these prices into new units on the basis of certain "coefficients," presumably based on inflation). See Sovnarkom's proposed decree: Proekt

Polozheniia o trudovoi edinitse ucheta v gosudarstvennom khoziaistve, in *Denezhnoe obrashchenie i kredit. Denezhnoe obrashchenie v Rossii i za granitsei v gody voiny i revoliutsii (1914–1921),* 421.

118. A. Chaianov, *Metody bezdenezhnogo ucheta khoziaistvennykh predpriatii. Trudy Vysshego Seminaria s-kh ekonomii i politiki pri Petrovskoi S-Kh Akademii* (Moskva: Gos. Izd-vo, 1921).

119. See Strumilin and Chaianov's discussion in *Ekonomicheskaia zhizn':* Strumilin, Trudovoi ekvivalent, *Ekonomicheskaia Zhizn',* July 31, 1920, no. 167; Chaianov, "Problema khoziastvennogo ucheta v sotsialisticheskom gosudarstve," *Ekonomicheskaia Zhizn',* October 16, 1920, no. 231; Strumilin, "Problema trudovogo ucheta," *Ekonomicheskaia Zhizn',* October 23, 1920, no. 237; Chaianov, "Substantsiia tsennosti i sistema trudovykh ekvivalentov," *Ekonomicheskaia Zhizn',* November 4, 1920, no. 247; Varga, "Ischislenie stoimosti proizvodstva v bezdenezhnom khoziaistve," *Ekonomicheskaia Zhizn',* November 18, 1920, no. 259.

120. A. Chaianov, "Poniatie vygodnosti sotsialisticheskogo khoziaistva (opyt postroeniia bezdenezhnogo ucheta sovetskikh khoziaistv," in *Metody bezdenezhnogo ucheta khoziaistvennykh predpriiatii* (Moskva: Gos. Izd-vo, 1921), 5

121. P. Amosov and A. Savich, *Problema materialnogo ucheta v sotsialisticheskom khoziaistve* (Petrograd: Petrogradskii SNKh, 1921); A. Izmailov, *Materialnyi uchet* (Moskva: [n.p.], 1921). In this experiment we can clearly see the influence of "scientific management." On the role of accounting in the economy of war communism, see Anne O'Donnell, *Taking Stock: Power and Possession in Revolutionary Russia* (forthcoming)

122. Gimpel'son, *Voennyi kommunizm*, 102.

123. The ruble's value was falling but not as fast as the state increased the volume of paper money: the depreciation of the ruble's value expressed in the growth rate of prices many times exceeded the tempo of emission. In total, from November 1917 to July 1921, the money supply increased 119 times, while average prices grew by a factor of 7,911. *Nashe denezhnoe obrashchenie 1914–1925*, 13, 15.

124. Iurovskii, *Denezhnaia politika Sovetskoi vlasti*, 213.

125. Khodiakov, *Den'gi revoliutsii i Grazhdanskoi voiny*, 79–96

126. In early 1920, a tsarist banknote of 500 rubles cost 8,000 rubles in Soviet money; a 100 ruble Romanov banknote went for 1,500 rubles in Soviet notes. The Duma's money cost six times more than their nominal value, *kerenki*—three times more than the equal sum in Soviet rubles. By October, the price of Romanov's money increased even further: 1,000 rubles in two 500 rubles banknotes were valued at 60–75 thousand Soviet rubles. Khodiakov, *Den'gi revoliutsii i Grazhdanskoi voiny*, 94.

127. Mobilizatsionnoe upravlenie Vserossiiskogo Glavnogo Shtaba—Narkomfin, August 10, 1920, RGAE, f.7733, op.1, d.187, 153. Kaluzhskii finotdel—Narkomfin, August 20, 1920, RGAE, f.7733, op.1, d.187, 173. See the polemics about the causes of the stratification of money: V. Kopp, "Nashe denezhnoe obrashchenie

i ego reformy. "Khoroshie" i "plokhie" den'gi. Sud'ba kerenki," *Ekonomicheskaia Zhizn'*, May 6, 1919; S. A. Fal'kner, "Prichiny rassloeniia denezhnoi massy," *Ekonomicheskaia Zhizn'*, May 13, 1919.

128. Historically, it represented the third type of financial state organization after the seignorial state, which derived income from the crown's property, and the tax state. S. A. Fal'kner, *Problemy teorii i praktiki emissionnogo khoziastva* (Moskva: Ekonomicheskaia Zhizn', 1924), 40. Fal'kner claimed that the emission of assignats covered 80% of the French revolutionary state's expenditures.

129. S. A. Fal'kner, *Bumazhnye den'gi Frantsuzskoi revoliutsii* (Moskva: VSNKh, 1919) (the book was written in late 1916–early 1917 and then completed during 1918), 280.

130. See also the review of Fal'kner's book: *Izvestiia NKF* 2, no. 18 (1919): 11–12. In 1917–1922 there was an unusual surge of academic interest in French revolutionary assignats. However, most historians disagreed with Fal'kner's assessments. See, for instance, N. I. Kareev, "Bumazhnye den'gi Frantsuzskoi revoliutsii," *Niva* 49 (1918), no. 33, 526–528; A. I. Smirnov, *Krizis denezhnoi sistemy Frantsuzskoi revoliutsii* (Petrograd: Pravo, 1921).

131. Grigorii Sokol'nikov retrospectively described the emission of the war communism as "the expropriation of monetary capital." "Through emission, the Revolution expropriated a sum whose value in monetary equivalent was no lesser that the value of factories, plants, lands, etc." Doklad v Sotsialisticheskoi Akademii 22 noiabria 1923 g., in G. Ya. Sokol'nikov, *Novaia finansovaia politika: na puti k tverdoi valiute*, 164.

132. E. A. Preobrazhenskii, "Bumazhnye den'gi v epokhu proletarskoi diktatury," in E. A. Preobrazhenskii, *Arkhivnye dokumenty i materialy, 1886–1920* (Moskva: Glavrkhiv, 2006), 621.

133. A good example of urban folks' indignation about "peasant girls" who buy calico, soap, metal jewelry, mirrors, candies, Christmas decoration, and "even" sometimes parfums and silk, quoted in D. Kuzovkov, *Osnovnye momenty raspada i vosstanovlenia denezhnoi sistemy* (Moskva: Izd-vo Kommunisticheskoi Akademii, 1925), 39.

134. Yu. Larin, "O sotsialnom soderzhanii posleoktiabr'skoi diktatury" (December 27, 1917), in *Krestiane i rabochie v russkoi revoliutisii* (Petrograd: Izd-e Petrogradskogo Soveta Rab I Krasnoarmeiskikh Deputatov, 1919), 4–5.

135. According to A. Iuriev, this system, introduced in April 1918, failed, and in May 1918, VTsIK switched to a more rigorous model of exchange: a greater share of industrial goods was transferred to Narkomprod, while the exchange became "mandatory" (A. Iuriev, "Gosudarstvennaia tovaroobmennaia sistema," *Narodnoe khoziaistvo* 11–12 (1919): 16–17. In September 1918, Alexei Rykov, head of VSNKh, declared that the only way to feed starving workers was to monopolize manufactured goods and exchange them for grain and produce on the basis of fixed prices. Rykov's speech at Plenum VSNKh in September 1918. Plenum VSNKH, 14–23

sentiabria 1918 r (stenograficheskii otchet) (Moskva: VSNKh, 1918), 13–14, 17. In November 1918, Narkomprod was granted the right to *seize* manufactured goods for the exchange. Iuriev, "Gosudarstvennaia tovaroobmennaia sistema," 17.

136. Yu. Larin, "Sekret denezhnogo potoka (k s'ezdu Sovnarkhozov), *Ekonomicheskaia Zhizn'*, January 22, 1920. Preobrazhenskii disagreed: peasants' hoards, if they existed, were devalued by the fall of the ruble; therefore, peasants were more interested in spending money on purchasing industrial goods rather than hoarding. The decline of industrial production, and, consequently, the fall of the ruble's value, hurt peasants instead of enriching them.

137. E.N. Sokolov, *Denezhnaia i biudzhetnaia politika Sovetskoi respubliki v 1917–nachale 1921 g.*, 74.

138. Later, Preobrazhenskii calculated the relative change of state income from requisitioning and emission (he used pre-war gold rubles for calculation): if in 1918/1919 food requisitioning brought 127 million rubles compared to 523 million received from emission, in 1920–21, the value of goods received from requisitioning constituted 480 million, while the income from emission dropped to 186 million. Preobrazhenskii, "Voprosy finansovoi politiki [1921]," in *Den'gi i mirovoi capitalism (issledovaniia, nauchno-populiarnye raboty 1921–1931)* (Moskva: Glavarkhiv, 2011), 7. Zakharii Atlas's calculation shows that in 1919 the income from emission dropped by 58% compared to 1918, and in 1920, by 77%. Z. V. Atlas, *Sotsialisticheskaia denezhnaia sistema* (Moskva: Finansy, 1969), 106.

139. "K dekretu o besplatnoi peresylke pisem," *Ekonomicheskaia Zhizn'*, December 18, 1918, no. 35.

140. Gimpel'son, "*Voennyi Kommunizm*," 119–131.

141. The argument for the elimination of money and the transition to natural payment: A. Goltsman, *Regulirovanie i naturalizatsiia zarabotnoi platy* (Moskva, 1918); L. V. Borisova, *Trudovye otnosheniia v Sovetskoi Rossii (1918–1924)* (Moskva: Sobranie, 2006); E. G. Gimpel'son, *Sovetskii rabochii klass, 1918–1920* (Moskva: Nauka, 1974), 128–183. As Gimpel'son noted, by 1920, the monetary salary of Moscow workers had risen (since 1913) by 400 times, while prices increased by 20,000 times. Thus, the introduction of "rationing" and payments in goods was a necessity. Gimpel'son, "*Voennyi Kommunizm*," 152.

142. A. Yu. Davydov, *Meshochniki i diktatura v Rossii, 1917–1921* (St. Petersburg: Aleteiia, 2007), 98, 101, 115, 134.

143. V. Kopp, "Nashe denezhnoe obrashchenie i ego reformy," *Ekonomicheskaia Zhizn'*, May 9, 1919, no. 93.

144. Yu. M. Goland, *Diskussii ob ekonomicheskoi politike v gody denezhnoi reformy 1921–1924* (Moskva: Ekonomika, 2006), 10-11.

145. "Bezdenezhnye raschety," *Izvestsia NKF* 10–11 (June 16, 1920). In July 1920, another decree ultimately prohibited the purchase of goods outside the system of distribution without special permission.

146. "'Volnyi rynok' i dekret 23 ianvaria 1919," *Ekonomicheskaia Zhizn'*, 1919, no. 264

147. Michael V. White and Kurt Schuler, "Retrospectives: Who Said 'Debauch the Currency': Keynes or Lenin?" *Journal of Economic Perspectives* 23, no. 2 (2009); White and Schuler point out that J. M. Keynes read Lenin's interviews in the Daily *Chronicle* and the *New York Times* in which the Bolshevik leader allegedly spoke about "debauching" currency. However, the authenticity of the interviews has not been proven. I'm grateful to Harold James for letting me know about this source.

148. Gimpel'son, "*Voennyi Kommunizm*," 142. For the discussion of literature and historiographical debates, see Silvana Malle. *The Economic Organization of War Communism 1918–1921*, 1–28.

149. Yu. P. Bokarev, "Rubl' v epokhu voin i revoliutsii," in *Russkii rubl.' Dva veka istorii,* (Moskva: Progress-Akademiia, 1994).

150. Katherine Verdery has made a similar argument about "socialist property" as not an absence of property but a different kind of property. Katherine Verdery, "After Socialism," in *A Companion to the Anthropology of Politics,* edited by Joan Vincent and David Nugent (Malden, MA: Blackwell, 2004), 21–36.

151. Zhurnaly i protokoly zasedanii sektsii Komissii po voprosam denezhnogo obrashcheniia, April 30, 1920, RGAE, f.7733, op.1, d.6267.

152. V. Ya. Zheleznov, "Rol' deneg v tovaroobmene," *K teorii deneg i ucheta* (Moskva, no publisher, 1922), 8.

153. A. Averchenko, "Krakh sem'i Dromaderovykh," in A. T. Averchenko, *Rasskazy i fel'etony* (Moskva: Direkt-Media, 2015), 548–551.

154. From July 1921 to December 1922, the mass of money grew by 1,000 times—that is, ten times faster than previously—although after the introduction of monetary taxes the share of emission in state revenues steeply declined. *Nashe denezhnoe obrashchenie 1914–1925*, 19.

155. Veisberg, *Den'gi i tseny*, 110–110. See also calculations for "what is worth of one day of a plumber's works in flour currency?" V. N. Dmitriev, *Rastsenka rabochei sily i glavneishikh stroitelnykh rabot s pereuchetom tsen dovoennogo vremeni na muchnye rubli i sovetskie denezhnye znaki* (Petrograd: no publisher, 1922), 34.
Depending on the specificity of the regional economies, various commodities (firewood, milk, potatoes, salt) came to play the role of currency, but the most ubiquitous and, as economists suggested, most justified was the "flour" or the "bread" ruble. The devastating famine of 1921 made the idea of a "bread fund" as opposed to the gold reserve of the past, sound more vital and, at the same time, more challenging. M. S. Cherniak, *Problema volnogo rynka i volnykh rynochnykh tsen* (Kursk, 1922). In April 1922, Pavel Haensel wrote a proposal for a "bread currency," i.e., to pay workers in special interest-bearing bonds that they could redeem for bread. "Proekt platezhnykh obiazatelstv Narkomfina, vyrazhennykh v khlebnoi valiute," RGAE, f.7733, op.1, d.6896, 145–146.

156. As experts remarked, the rate of the pre-war ruble was artificially lowered and did not reflect its drop in purchasing ability. Therefore, this attempt to find an "ideal

counting unit" failed, RGAE, f.7733, op.1, d.6355, 11. For the explanation of how it worked: N. Derevenko, "Eshche po voprosu o dovoennykh rubliakh," *Vestnik Finansov*, 1922, no. 5, 51–54.

157. Nikolai Kutler, a former minister in Witte's government who actively participated in the preparation of Soviet monetary reform, described the return to the ghostly tsarist currency as a witty but entirely fictitious invention. Protokol soveshchania v NKF 2 marta 1922, *Denezhnaia reforma 1921–24 gg.: sozdanie tverdoi valiuty. Dokumenty i materialy* (Moskva: ROSSPEN, 2008), 161.

158. Carole Frank, *The Genoa Conference: European Diplomacy, 1921–22* (Chapel Hill: University of North Carolina Press, 1984), 235.

159. Grigorii Sokol'nikov, explaining the importance of gold, complained that there was nothing else to offer, and no person could represent Russia: "When we were fighting against Poles, we could put forward [general] Brusilov," Doklad Sokol'nikova, RGASPI, f.670, op.1, d.19, l.56.

160. Raskhod zolota i ego postuplenie na 1918–1922 gody (po 1 oktiabria 1922 goda), July 7, 1922, RGASPI, f.670, op.1. d.36, 118–121.

161. L. V. Sapogovskaia, "Zoloto v politike Rossii (1917–1921), *Voprosy Istorii*, 2004, no.6.

162. Sokol'nikov's note to Lenin's secretary Fotieva with a request to pass this information to Lenin, RGASPI, f.670, op.1, d.36, l.7.

163. Lenin, Pis'mo V. M. Molotovu dlia chlenov Politbuiro TsK RKPb, March 19, 1922, in *V. I. Lenin: Neizvestnye dokumenty, 1892–1922* (Moskva: ROSSPEN, 2017), 517. Lenin's cynicism is shocking: he insisted that the expropriations be speeded up while the peasants were broken down by famine and were less likely to protest. It is also obvious from this letter that the church gold was meant not for the procurement of food to alleviate famine, as propaganda asserted, but for "industrial construction" and defending Russia's position in Genoa.

164. Along with this new method of acquiring gold, the government also tried to increase the production of gold, which had fallen from 4,056 *poods* in 1914 to 84 *poods* in 1921. By 1925–26, the gold mining industry had restored 50 to 60% of its capacity (about 2,000 poods a year). Grigorii Sokol'nikov, "Nakoplenie zolota i dobycha zheltogo metalla," *Ekonomicheskaia Zhizn'*, September 24, 1926, no. 220 (2339).

165. Lenin, "Proekt direktivy zamestiteliu predsedatelia i vsem chlenam Genuezskoi delegatsii," February 1, 1922, *Polnoe sobranie sochinenii*, vol. 44, 375; Stephen White, *The Origins of the Détente: The Genoa Conference and Soviet-Western Relations, 1921–1922* (New York: Cambridge University Press, 1985), 120.

166. J. M. Keynes, "The Finance Experts at Genoa," in *The Collected Writings of John Maynard Keynes*, vol.17 (Cambridge: Cambridge University Press, 2013), 378, 381.

167. "Who knows but that Russia may not give us a final surprise by being the first of the European belligerents to stabilize her money?" J. M. Keynes, "The Financial System of the Bolsheviks" (April 26, 1922), in *The Collected Writings of John*

Maynard Keynes, vol. 17, 407. Another article in the *Manchester Guardian* (May 1, 1922) provided a detailed analysis of the plans for monetary reform: "The Russian Rouble and the Basis of Future Trade," *The Collected Writings of John Maynard Keynes*, vol. 17, 411–420. Soviet newspapers proudly popularized J. M. Keynes's endorsement of Russia's financial successes: "Prof. Keynes o russkoi valiute," *Izvestiia*, May 20, 1922, no. 111.

168. Lenin, "O znachenii zolota teper' i posle polnoi pobedy sotsializma," November 6–7, 1921, in Lenin, *Polnoe sobranie sochinenii* (Moskva: In-t Marksizma-Leninizma, 1960), t.44, 226.

169. For a detailed analysis of the reform's preparation, see Yu. Goland, *Diskussii ob ekonomicheskoi politike*.

170. K. S. Yadryshnikov, "Vosstanovlenie Gosudarstvennogo Banka RSFSR v 1921 g. (pravovoi aspekt)," *Aktual'nye problemy rossiiskogo prava* 3 (2009): 103.

171. One of the earliest proposals for new Soviet "banknotes" introduced a new measure of the gold *grivna* instead of the ruble (one "banknote" was equivalent to ten grivnas). This name was abandoned—probably because it was reminiscent of the Ukrainian currency from the short period of Ukraine's independence. "Tezisy o bankbiletakh," RGASPI, f.670, op.1, d.25, 34.

172. Ironically, the inscription "guaranteed by the entire wealth of the republic" printed on the gold rubles did not guarantee the value of the *sozvnaki*, while the *chervonetz's* slogan "guaranteed by the gold reserve of the State Bank," which was legally smaller than the entirety of the republic's wealth, vouched for its full value.

173. This model wasn't the Soviet government's invention. England and Germany issued treasury notes during the First World War; in 1915, the Russian government also considered introducing treasury notes to create the visibility of an increased gold backing for the ruble. The idea belonged to Pavel Migulin. *O vypuske osobykh kaznacheiskikh denezhnykh znakov, ne vkhodiashchikh v sostav obespechivaemykh zolotom gosudarstvennykh kreditnykh biletov* [1915] See infra, ch.10, note 55. Discussions about parallel systems of money continued in 1918–1920.

174. The idea of merging the two systems was discussed in the context of monetary reforms in 1947 and 1961. Both times the government decided against it. Apparently, it did not want to give the impression that the new money would not be backed by gold.

175. Zakliuchenie po voprosu i regulirovanii denezhnogo obrashcheniia Rossii Soveta finansovoi sektsii i komissii po voprosam denezhnogo obrashcheniia Instituta Ekonomicheskikh Issledovani NKF, June 12, 1921, RGAE, f. 7733, op.1, 6909, 41.

176. J. M. Keynes, "The Financial System of the Bolsheviks," *The Collected Writings of John Maynard Keynes*, vol. 17, 407.

177. To make it clear: the reforms of 1895–97 and 1921–24 pursued similar purposes through different scenarios. Witte's "devaluation" was not an option because the ruble's value decreased not by one-third but by one million times. Nevertheless, it was often mentioned in the debates. See, for instance, "Izvlechenie iz tezisov,

predstavlennykh pravleniiu Gosbanka komissiei prof. A. A. Manuilova, Z. S. Katsenelenbauma, and L. B. Kafengauza," in *Denezhnaia Reforma 1921–24 gg.: sozdanie tverdoi valiuty. Dokumenty i materialy* (Moskva: ROSSPEN, 2008), 121. In 1922 the Institute of Economic Studies published a collection of documents on the preparation of Witte's reform: A. I. Bukovetskii, ed., *Materialy po denezhnoi reforme 1895–1897 gg.* (Moskva: Institut ekonomicheskikh issledovanii, 1922).

178. There was an idea to insert the word "*monopol'nyi*" (monopoly) in the first article of the Bank's Statute. Krestinskii's speech at the 4th session of All-Russian Central Executive Committee, October 7, 1921. *I-IV Sessii Vserossiiskogo Tsentral'nogo Ispolnitel'nogo Komiteta VIII sozyva. Stenograficheskii otchet* (Moskva: VTsIK, 1922), 377. See VTsIK's resolution concerning the creation of the State Bank on the basis of "state-credit monopoly" (gosudarstvenno-bankovskoi monopolii). Rezoliutsiia IV Sessii VTsIK October 6, 1921, *I-IV Sessii Vserossiiskogo Tsentral'nogo Ispolnitel'nogo Komiteta VIII sozyva. Stenograficheskii otchet*, Prilozhenie, 36; and Polozhenie o Gosudarstvennom Banke (October 13, 1921) –*Sbornik dekretov i rasporiazhenii po finansam*, vol. 4, 26–27.

In the mid-1920s, the State Bank's monopoly was significantly diluted by the influx of other credit institutions (banks specialized in crediting branches of industry (*otraslevye banki*), credit cooperatives, and communal banks). The State Bank often was the main shareholder in the capital of these banks and controlled their activity. According to official statistics, in 1923, out of 614 credit institutions, 252, or 41%, belonged to the State Bank networks, and by 1926, the State Bank held 488 out of 1,815 institutions (27%). Its share of credit operations in the national economy constituted 66% in 1923 and fell to 48% in 1926. In the late 1920s, the tendency reversed, and the presence of autonomous credit institutions began to dwindle. Gosbank v kreditnoi sisteme SSSR, Table 1.1.2 in *Po stranitsam arkhivnykh fondov Tsentral'nogo Banka Rossiiskoi Federatsii. Vyp.9. Balansy Gosudarstvennogo Banka SSSR (1922-1990 gg)* (Moskva: TsB RF, 2010), 9.

179. Several memos written by experts at the Narkomfin's Institute of Economic Research argued for the establishment of a private joint-stock emission bank. For instance, L. S. Eliasson, "Sistema parallel'nykh valiut kak blizhaishchii etap k uporiadocheniiu denezhnogo obrashcheniia" (March 1922), RGAE f.7733, op.1, d.6901, 1–3; "O sozdanii nariadu s sushchestvuiushchei edinitsei novoi— bolee ustoichivogo kharaktera," RGAE, F.7733, op.1, d.6893, l.117; S. V. Voronin, "Vneshnii kurs rublia v poslednie gody," RGAE, f.7733, op.1, d.6911, 180; Doklad V. V. Tarnovskogo, iiun' 1921, in *Denezhnaia reforma 1921–24 gg.: sozdanie tverdoi valiuty. Dokumenty i materialy* (Moskva: ROSSPEN, 2008), 50; Tezisy k zapiske V.V. Tarnovskogo, 7 fevralia 1922 g., *in Denezhnaia reforma 1921–24 gg*, 97–98.

180. Eliasson even thought that calling this institution a bank would be a misnomer, since banks are supposed to operate with the capital of economic agents and individuals, while the State Bank that had received its capital from the government and was predominantly working with the government's funds did not have

this quality. According to Eliasson, only 5% of funds on deposit accounts belonged to private individuals. L. S. Eliasson, "Gosudarstvennyi Bank i ego politika," doklad (November 10, 1922), RGAE, f.7733, op.1, d.6901, 126. According to N. G. Tumanov, "the bank emission is in fact regulated by NKF, and it is obvious that it will continue to be regulated by it." Stenogramma soveshchania v NKF SSSR, ianvar' 1924, *Denezhnaia reforma 1921–1924: sozdanie tverdoi valiuty*, 484.

181. *Denezhnaia reforma 1921–1924: sozdanie tverdoi valiuty*, 302; Stenogramma soveshchania v NKF SSSR, ianvar' 1924, *Denezhnaia reforma 1921–1924: sozdanie tverdoi valiuty*, 480.

182. "Banknote emission as it stands today is not credit emission because it serves... to cover the budget deficit of industry." Stenogramma soveshchania v NKF SSSR, Ianvar' 1924, 470, 479.

183. L.S. Eliason, "Dekret 11 noiabria o vypuske bankovykh biletov," *Vestnik Finansov*, 1922, no. 38, 27–28.

184. Yurovskii, *Denezhnaia politika*, 306–330, 319, Yurii Goland, "Currency regulation," 1254–1255. OGPU initiated a campaign against foreign currency "speculators" and conducted it with such vigor that it undermined Narkomfin's efforts of regulating the *chervonetz*'s rate. David Woodruff, *Money Unmade. Barter and the Fate of Russian Capitalism* (Ithaca, NY: Cornell University Press), 1999, 29–30.

185. A record of Sokol'nikov's speech, no date, RGASPI, f.670, op.1, d.21, 46. One of the earliest instances of introducing "banknotes" declared that the date of opening the exchange "should not be later than one year after opening the exchange for gold by the German State Bank." No explanation was given for choosing financial reconstruction in Germany as a landmark for the Soviet reform. [Sokol'nikov], Proekt punktov o vypuske banknot, RGASPI, f.670, op.1, d.25, 72. All experts, except for Leonid Yurovskii, argued for allowing a free circulation of gold in coins. Pavel Haensel also pointed out that the state's policy of pulling out gold from private possessions should change: instead of confiscation and expropriation, the government should use market mechanisms. P. Haensel, Ob obrazovanii zolotogo fonda i poriadke skupki zolotykh veshei, RGAE, f.7733, op.1, d.427.

186. Yurii Goland, "Valutnoe regulirovanie"; Osokina, *Zoloto dlia industrializatsii*, 34–35. In March 1926, operations with foreign currency and gold were prohibited, Osokina, *Zoloto*, 36.

187. Oscar Sanchez-Sibony, "Global Money and Bolshevik Authority: The NEP as the First Socialist Project," *Slavic Review* 78, no. 3 (2019). In July 1922, Sokol'nikov outlined a plan of export operation that was supposed to bring in 250 million gold rubles, including 100 million from the export of grain, 40 million from timber, and 35 million from oil. "O zolotom reserve," RGASPI, f. 670 op. 1, d. 19, l.78.

188. All experts also spoke in favor of abolishing Vneshtorg's monopoly. See, for instance, Zapiska no.18 P. P. Genzelia, "O kredite i kreditnoi politike v sovremennykh usloviiakh RSFSR," RGAE, f. 7733, op.1, d.6302, 72–74.

Goldberg, Vneshniaia politika i regulirovanie valiutnogo rynka (1923), RGAE, f.7733, op.1, d.6907, 138. Also, Alskii, Nadlezhashchaia organizatsiia zavedyvaniia nashim valiutnym fondom, April 1921, RGAE, f.7733, op.1. d.378, 6–14. Valiuta i Vneshtorg, RGAE, f.7733, op.1, d.6907, 16–18. According to Yurii Goland, by January 1925, the State Bank's assets reached 344.3 million rubles, of which 180.8 million were in gold; 253.6 million rubles in the State Bank's holdings backed up the *chervonetz's* issue with 42.6% (that is to say, above the 25% threshold). Yurii Goland, "Currency Regulation in the NEP Period," 1259.

189. Yurovskii also indicated the possibility of dual rates—one for foreign trade, another for the domestic market. Yurovskii, *Denezhnaia politika Sovetskoi vlasti*, 379–380.

190. V. V. Novozhilov, Kharakteristika nashei denezhnoi sistemy, December 29, 1928, RGAE, f.7733, op.1, d.6909, 105.

191. Among the advocates of drastic separation was the ex-minister of finance in the Rada government, economist Mikhailo Tugan-Baranovskii, who warned that Russia's financial catastrophe would inevitably draw in Ukraine. M. Tugan-Baranovskii, "Neodkladna sprava," *Nova Rada* 133 (1918), no. 133.

192. On the fabrication of Ukrainian money in Germany and its transportation to Ukraine, see Pavlo Hai-Nyzhnyk, "Dostavka dlia uriadu Direktori Ukrainskikh groshei s Nimetchiny i zagibel' Vitovskogo (1919)," in *Gurzhivski historichni chitannia. Sbornik nauchnikh pratz* (Cherkasy, 2009), 290–294. Eighteen flights between Germany and Ukraine delivered 1.242 billion hryvna. One airplane crashed; another had to make an emergency landing in the territory of Romania, and the money (300 million hryvna) was seized.

193. Z. Katsenelbaum, speaking at the session of the Institute of Economic Research, IEI, Zhurnaly i protokoly zasedanii komissii po voprosam den. obrashcheniia, RGAE, f.7733, op.1, d. 6267, 20.

194. Materialy o provedenii denezhnoi reformy v Turkestanskoi respublike, RGAE, f.7733, op.1, d.427. The rate of exchange was 10 *turkbon* = 1 *sovznak*. Interestingly, the instruction brochure for propagandists ("agitators") described how to explain why ten turkbon were worth only one ruble: the "Moscow" money could buy the products of Moscow manufacture and industrial goods (assuming that Turkestan's raw cotton was much less valuable). Ibid, 46.

195. During 1921, the government signed a series of "union treaties" with Soviet republics, and each of them was accompanied by a financial agreement that regulated budgetary rights of the republics and the Union.

196. In 1922, the ruble was valued at one-sixth to one-seventh of Georgian currency and stood on a par with bons in Armenia and Azerbaijan. On negotiations and agreement, see S. Kistenev, "Finansovoe soglashenie s zakavkazskimi respublikami," *Vestnik Finansov*, 1922, no. 12, 9–15; on the ruble's fall: Chalkhshian, "Dizazhio sovrublia v Zakavkazie," *Vestnik Finansov*, 1922, no. 17, 24–26. On the unification of three Transcaucasian currencies and the Decree of January 10, 1923, see

Zakavkazskii finansovo-statisticheskii sbornik, 1918–1923 (Tiflis, no publisher, 1924), ch.1, 73–76.

197. "Spravka Narkomfina ob istorii finansovykh otnoshenii s zakavkazskimi respublikami i khode podgotovki denezhnoireformy," in *Ekonomicheskie otnosheniia Rossii s budushchimi soiuznymi respublikami 1917–1922: Dokumenty i materialy* (Moskva: Vostochnaia literatura, 1996), 263.

Narkomfin explained the embarrassing fall of the Soviet ruble by Georgia's favorable economic conditions: the "privileged" position of the Batumi harbor that enjoyed the "freedom of private trade with the outer world" and its isolation from Russia. Georgia's financial well-being came at the cost of "economic and financial isolation from other parts of the RSFSR, . . . the sacrifice of our ruble, economic and monetary hegemony of Constantinople's market, and finally, privileging the local population . . . to the detriment of the treasury and at the expense of a Russian consumer." Doklad sotrudnika Narkomfina RSFSR, A. G. Orlova, "Finansovoe i ekonomicheskoe ob'edinenie Zakavkazskoi federatsii s RSFSR," *Ekonomicheskie otnosheniia*, 297; L. Moiseev, "K finansovomu ob'edineniiu s Zakavkaziem," *Vestnik Finansov*, 1922, no. 28, 27–30; "Finansovo-ekonomicheskoe polozhenie Yugo-Vostoka Rossii," *Vestnik Finansov*, 1922, no. 30, 56.

198. Transcaucasia was integrated into Russia's custom and budgetary system. A. Orlov, "Finansovoe i ekonomicheskoe ob'edinenie Zakavkazkoi Federatsii s RSFSR," *Vestnik Finansov*, 1922, no. 38, 34–40. "The unification of currencies in all-federal scale represents not a politico-financial problem, but rather a strictly political one," wrote R. Goldenberg in July 1922. R. G. Golderberg, "K voprosu ob unifikatsii russkoi denezhnoi sistemy," July 1922, RGAE, f.7733, op.1, d.6355, 101.

199. As the local statistical bureau reported, "The introduction of chervonetz started to exert pressure on the value of *zakdenznak* [Transcaucasian monetary sign]," and its value plummeted. *Zakavkazskii finansovo-statisticheskii sbornik, 1918–1923*, ch.1 (Tiflis: 1924), 89–90.

200. More on the reform in the Far East region: A. I. Pogrebetskii, *Denezhnoe obrashchenie i denezhnye znaki Dalnego Vostoka za period voiny i revoliutsii (1914–1924)* (Kharbin: Obshchestvo izucheniia Manchzhurskogo kraia, 1924); Chia Yin Hsu, The "Color" of Money: The Ruble, Competing Currencies, and Conceptions of Citizenship in Manchuria and the Russian Far East, 1890s-1920s, *Russian Review* 73, no. 1 (January 2014): 83–110.

201. David M. Woodruff, "The Politburo on Gold, Industrialization, and the International Economy, 1925-1926," *The Lost Politburo Transcripts: From Collective Rule to Stalin's Dictatorship* (New Haven, CT: Yale University Press, 2008), 218.

202. Compare to Laura Engelstein's analysis of the applicability of Michel Foucault's theory to Russia: was the soft, but expansive, power of a liberal state such a horrible thing for autocratic Russia with the underdeveloped practices of governance?

Laura Engelstein, "Combined Underdevelopment: Discipline and the Law in Imperial and Soviet Russia," *American Historical Review* 98, no. 2 (1993).

203. Elena Osokina, *Zoloto dlia industrializatsii: Torgsin* (Moskva: ROSSPEN, 2009), 83.

204. Soviet "emission law" was reduced to a brief and unsubstantial instruction to the State Bank. A project of the Monetary Code (*Denezhnyi Ustav SSSR*) elaborated at the Institute was never approved. Victor Shtein, "Emissionnyi zakon Gosudarstvennogo Banka," RGAE, f.7733, op1., d.6355, 175. The project of the Monetary Code: Denezhnyi Ustav SSSR. Proekt. RGAE, f.7733, op.1, d.6270.

205. For a very detailed explanation of how it happened, see Yurii Goland, "Currency Regulation in the NEP Period," *Europe-Asia Studies*46, no. 8 (2007).

206. V. Doklad V. Tarnovskogo, Iiun' 1921, in *Denezhnaia reforma 1921–24 gg.: sozdanie tverdoi valiuty. Dokumenty i materialy* (Moskva: ROSSPEN, 2008), 50. Elsewhere he stated bluntly that "state power should surrender its emission privileges." Tezisy k zapiske Tarnovskogo, *Denezhnaia reforma 1921–24 gg.: sozdanie tverdoi valiuty*, 98.

EPILOGUE

1. Arkady Strugatsky and Boris Strugatsky, *Monday Starts on Saturday*, trans. Andrew Bromfield (London: Gateway, 2016), 41.

2. Gregory Grossman, "Gold and the Sword: Money in the Soviet Command Economy," *Industrialization in Two System:. Essays in Honor of Alexander Gerschenkron*, edited by Henry Rosovsky (New York: Wiley, 1966), 215.

3. R. W. Davies and O. Khlevniuk, "Gosplan," in *Decision-making in the Stalinist Command Economy, 1932–37*, edited by E. A. Rees (New York: St. Martin's Press, 1997, 37).

4. On this reform and the multiplicity of money in the Soviet planned economy: David Woodruff, *Money Unmade: Barter and the Fate of Russian Capitalism* (Ithaca, NY: Cornell University Press, 1991), 21–55.

5. Paul Gregory and Aleksei Tikhonov, "Central Planning and Unintended Consequences: Creating the Soviet Financial System, 1930–1939," *Journal of Economic History* 60, no. 4 (December 2000); 1017; Woodruff, *Money Unmade*, 21–55.

6. Alfred Zauberman, "Gold in Soviet Economic Theory and Policies," *American Economic Review* 41, no. 5 (December 1951): 881.

7. Gregory and Tikhonov, "Central Planning and Unintended Consequences"; Oleg V. Khlevniuk, " 'Tolkachi.' Parallel´nye stimuly v stalinskoi ekonomicheskoi sisteme 1930-e–1950-e gody," *Cahiers du monde russe* 59, no. 2–3 (2018).

8. Savings accounts under 3,000 rubles were not affected by devaluation, but savings over 3,000 were subjected to different rates of devaluation depending on the total sum of the deposit. For a detailed analysis of the reform, its preparation, and outcomes, see Igor Chudnov, *Denezhnaia refoma 1947 goda* (Moskva: ROSSPEN,

2018). Similar confiscatory reform was conducted in East Germany in 1957. Jonathan R. Zatlin, *The Currency of Socialism* (New York: Cambridge University Press, 2007), 42–47.

9. For the analysis of the financial burden imposed on the population in 1941–45 see Oleg Khlevniuk, "Finansiruia voinu. Formirovamie gosudarsvennogo biudzheta SSSR v 1941–1945 gg.," *Rossiiskaia Istoriia* 3 (2020): 21–35.

10. A. G. Zverev, *Zapiski ministra* (Moskva: Politizdat, 1973), 182.

11. Kristy Ironside, *A Full-value Ruble: The Promise of Prosperity in the Postwar Soviet Union* (Cambridge, MA: Harvard University Press, 2021).

12. Arthur Nussbaum, "The Legal Status of Gold," *American Journal of Comparative Law* 3, no. 3 (Summer 1954), 362. The ruble was pegged to the US dollar from 1937 to 1950 at the rate of 1 USD = 5.3 RUB. The new rate established in 1950 was 1 USD = 4 RUB.

13. Quoted from Zauberman, "Gold in Soviet Economic Theory and Policies," 885, 887.

14. Zauberman, "Gold in Soviet Economic Theory and Policies," 9–11

15. L. V. Sapogovskaia, "Zolotye resursy SSSR v voenno-ekonomicheskom protivostoianii 1939-1945 godov (postanovka problemy)," *Voprosy Istori* 4, no. 5 (2005): 5.

16. Oscar L. Altman, "Russian Gold and the Ruble," Staff Papers (International Monetary Fund) vol. 7, no.3 (April 1960,): 416. More on "myths": Seigfried G. Schoppe and Michel Vale, "Changes in the Function of Gold within the Soviet Foreign Trade System since 1945–46," *Soviet and Eastern European Foreign Trade* 15, no. 3 (Fall 1979): 60–95.

17. Franklyn D. Holzman, "The Ruble Exchange Rate and Soviet Foreign Trade Pricing Policies, 1929–1961," *American Economic Review* 58, no. 4 (September 1968): 809, 815–816.

18. Predlozheniia V. S. Gerashchenko, "O provedenii denezhnoi reformy," June 5, 1958, *Po stranitsam arkhivnykh fondov Tsentralnogo Banka Rossiiskoi Federatsii. Vyp.15. Iz neopublikovannogo. Voprosy denezhnogo obrashenia. Vedomstvennye materialy* (Moskva: Tsentralnyi Bank RF, 2014): 91.

19. In 1961, as earlier in 1947, the final word in determining the ruble/dollar ratio belonged to the ruler: as V. K. Sitnin attested, Soviet statisticians suggested 1:1 parity, but Khrushchev insisted that the dollar should be cheaper than the ruble. V. K. Sitnin, *Sobytiia i liudi: Zapiski finansista* (Moskva: Luch, 1993), 17.

20. "Vesomyi Rubl," "Prestizh dollara padaet," *Izvestiia*, November 17, 1960.

21. Anna Ivanova, Magaziny "Beriozka," *Paradoksy potrebleniia v pozdnem SSSR* (Moskva: NLO, 2018), 30; Yu. Feofanov, "Firma terpit krakh," *Izvestiia*, May 19, 1961.

22. Kornei Chukovskii, *Dnevnik. 1936–1969, Sobranie sochinenii*, vol.13 (Moskva: Terra, 2007), 149.

23. Leonid Lipkin, [unpublished diary], https://prozhito.org/person/5382. Many other personal sources published by project "Prozhito" (a collection of diaries and memoirs) document people's attitude toward monetary reforms.

24. One of the first steps toward convertibility was the transition to "partial convertibility" in relations with the COMECON countries. O. Shelkov, "Po kursu tverdogo rublia," *Pravda*, August 28, 1989.

25. "Iz pochty AiF," *Argumenty i Fakty*, February 3, 1990, no.5. For opposite opinion (first convertibility, then reforms), see interview with the director of the Central Economico-Mathematical Institute of the Academy of Sciences. Ya. Petrakov: "Mnenie spetsialista. Vernut' rubliu byluiu slavu," *Argumenty i Fakty*, September 30, 1989, no. 39.

26. O. Rogova and L. Moiseeva, "Denezhnaia sistema: Mekhanizm i napravlenie stabilizatsii," *Voprosy Ekonomik* 7 (1990); 75, 77.

27. V. Perlamutrov, "Ekonomicheskie besedy: Kanaly infliatsii," *Argumenty i Fakty*, June 11, 1988, no. 24.

28. See other letters and responses from economist Yu. Konstantinov in "Byt' rubliu konvertiruemym," *Pravda*, August 8, 1988, no. 221.

29. T. Alekseev, "Kak rubliu stat' valiutoi," *Delovoi Mir*, June 10, 1991.

30. "O Mezhdunarodnom konkurse na luchshuiu rabotu po konvertiruemosti rublia," *Voprosy Ekonomiki* 9 (1990): 3–68; B. Milner, "Kak konvertirovat' rubl'," *Argumenty i Fakty*, June 23, 1990, no.25.

31. Egor Gaidar, *Dni porazhenii i pobed* (Moskva: Alpina, 2014), 134–135.

32. O. Rogova and L. Moiseeva, "Denezhnaia sistema: mechanism i napravleniia stabilizatsii," 75.

33. See more in Patrick Conway, *Currency Proliferation: The Monetary Legacy of the Soviet Union* (Princeton, NJ: International Finance Section, Dept. of Economics, Princeton University, 1995).

34. Stephen Kotkin, *Armageddon Averted: The Soviet Collapse, 1970–2000*. New York: Oxford University Press, 2001, 124.

Bibliography

ARCHIVES

AVPRI—Arkhiv Vneshnei Politiki Rossiiskoi Imperii
GARF—Gosudarstvennyi Arkhiv Rossiiskoi Federatsii
OR IRLI RAN—Otdel Rukopisei Instituta Russkoi Literatury Rossiiskoi Akademii Nauk (Pushkinskii Dom)
OR RGB—Otdel Rukopisei Rossiiskoi Gosudarstvennoi Biblioteki
OR RNB—Otdel Rukopisei Rossiiskoi Natsionalnoi Biblioteki
RGADA—Rossiiskii Gosudarstvennyi Arkhiv Drevnikh Aktov
RGALI—Rossiiskii Gosudarstvennyi Arkhiv Literatury i Iskusstva
RGASPI—Rossiiskii Gosudarstvennyi Arkhiv Sotsialno-Politicheskoi Istorii
RGIA—Rossiiskii Gosudarstvennyi Istoricheskii Arkhiv
RGVIA—Rossiiskii Gosudarstvennyi Voenno-Istoricheskii Arkhiv
TsGA SPb—Tsentralnyi Gosudarstvennyi Arkhiv g. Sankt-Peterburga
TsGIA SPB—Tsentralnyi Gosudarstvennyi Istoricheskii Arkhiv g. Sankt-Peterburga

NEWSPAPERS

Argumenty i Fakty
Birzhevye Vvedomosti.
Ekonomicheskaia Zhizn'
Finansovaia Gazeta
Golos Moskvy
Kommercheskaia Ggazeta.
Los Angeles Times
Moskovskie Vvedomosti
Nasha Rech'
The New York Times
The New York Tribune
Novaia Zhizn'
Novoe Vremia
Novosti i Birzhevaia Gazeta

Novyi Ekonomist
Pravda
Promyshlennaia Ggazeta
Rech'.
Rus'
Russkie Vvedomosti.
Sankt-Peterburgskie Vvedomosti.
Severnaia Ppochta.
Slovo
The Globe
The Times (London)
Utro Rossii
The Wall Street Journal
The Washington Post

PRIMARY SOURCES

AGS—*Arkhiv Gosudarstvennogo Soveta.* T.1–4. St. Petersburg, 1869.

PSZ—*Polnoe Sobranie Zakonov Rossiiskoi Imperii.* I—1649–1825; II—1825–1881; III—1881–1913.

SPS—Katkov, M. N. *Sobranie peredovykh statei Moskovskikh Vedomostei.* vols.1–25 (1863–1887). Moskva, 1897–1898.

Amosov, P., and A. Savich. *Problema materialnogo ucheta v sotsialisticheskom khoziaistve.* Petrograd: Petrogradskii SNKh, 1921.

[Andrei Vladimirovich [Romanov], vel.kn.]. "Voennyi dnevnik velikogo kniazia Andreia Vladimirovicha Romanova." *Oktiabr',* 1998, no.4.

Andriyashev, I. V. *K voprosu o gosudarstvenom pozemel'nom kredite v Rossii (Po povodu Dvorianskogo banka).* Kyiv, 1885.

[Anonymous]. *Proekt pozemel'nogo imushchestvennogo banka* (b.m., b.g.).

Antonovich, A.Ya. *Teoriia bumazhno-denezhnogo obrashchenia i gosudarstvennye kreditnye bilety.* Kyiv, 1883.

Arkhiv Grafov Mordvinovykh. T. 1–4. St. Petersburg, 1901–1903.

Arseniev, K. K. "Istoriko-statisticheskoe obozrenie monetnogo dela v Rossii." *Zapiski Russkogo Geograficheskogo Obshchestva,* kn.1–2, 1846.

Averchenko, A. T. "Krakh sem'i Dromaderovykh," in A. T. Averchenko, *Rasskazy i felietony.* Moskva: Direkt-Media, 2015.

Bagehot, Walter. *Lombard Street. A Description of the Money Market.* London, 1882.

Bark, P. L. *Vospominaniia poslednego ministra finansov Rossiiskoi Imperii.* vols. 1,2. Moskva: Kuchkovo pole, 2017.

Belinskii, V. A. *Chto takoe bumazhnye dengi?* Kharkiv, 1879.

Bernatskii, M. V. *Russkii gosudarstvennyi bank kak uchrezhdenie emissionnoe.* St. Petersburg, 1912.

Bezobrazov, V. P. "O nekotorykh iavleniiakh denezhnogo obrashcheniia v Rossii." *Russkii vestnik*, November 1863.

Bezobrazov, V. P. "Voprosy dnia. Nashi bumazhnye den'gi." *Nabliudatel'*, 1888, no.3.

Birzha i spekuliatsiia. St. Petersburg, 1878.

Bogolepov, D. P. "Finansovoe stroitelstvo v pervye gody Oktiabr'skoi revoliutsii." *Proletarskaia Revoliutsiia*, 1925, no.4.

Bogolepov, D. P. "Vospominaniia o Lenine." *O Lenine. Vospominaniia*. Kn.4. Pod red. i s predisl. N. L. Meshcheriakova, Moskva: Gos. izd-vo, 1925.

Bogolepov, M. I. *Bumazhnye den'gi*. Petrograd: Koop izd-vo, 1922.

Bogolepov, M. I. *Finansy, pravitel'stvo i obshchestvennye interesy*. St. Petersburg, 1907.

Bogolepov, M. I. *O putiakh budushchego*. Petrograd, 1916.

Bogolepov, M. P. "Voina i den'gi." *Vorposy mirovoi voiny*. Petrograd, 1915.

Bogoslovskii M. M. *Dnevniki 1913–1919*. Moskva: Vremia, 2011.

Bortkevich, I. *O denezhnoi reforme, proektiruemoi Ministerstvom Finansov*. St. Petersburg, 1896.

Brzheskii, N. K. *Gosudarstvennye dolgi Rossii*. St. Petersburg, 1884.

Bublikov, A. A. *Russkaia Revoliutsiia (ee nachalo, arest tsaria, perspektivy)*. Moskva: Gos. Publichnaia Istoricheskaia Biblioteka, 2018.

Bunge, N. Kh. *Zamechania ministra finansov na zapisku tainogo sovetnika Smirnova ozaglavlennuiu Sovremennoe sostoianie nashikh finansov, prichiny upadka ikh i sredstva k uluchsheniu nashego gosudarstvennogo khoziaistva*. St. Petersburg, 1886.

Bunge, N. Kh. *O vosstanovlenii postoiannoi denezhnoi edinitsy v Rossii*. Kyiv, 1878.

Bunge, N. Kh. *Vsepoddanneishii doklad ministra finansov po gosudarstvennoi rospisi dokhodov i raskhodov na 1886 god*. St. Petersburg, 1887.

Bunge, N. Kh. *Zametka o nastoiashchem polozhenii nashei denezhnoi sistemy i sredstvakh k ee uluchsheniiu*. St. Petersburg, 1880.

Butmi, G. V. *K voprosu o denezhnoi reforme (soobrazheniia sel'skogo khoziaina)*. Odessa, 1897.

Chaianov, A. V. *Metody bezdenezhnogo ucheta khoziaistvennykh predpriatii. Trudy Vysshego Seminaria s-kh ekonomii i politiki pri Petrovskoi S-Kh Akademii*. Moskva: Gos. Izd-vo, 1921.

Chalkhshian, "Dizazhio sovrublia v Zakavkazie." *Vestnik Finansov*, 1922, no.17.

Cherniak, M. S. *Problema vol'nogo rynka i vol'nykh rynochnykh tsen*. Kursk, [no publisher], 1922.

Chodoire, Baron, Stanislav de. *Obozreniie russkikh deneg i inostrannykh monet upotrebliavshchikhsia v Rossii s drevnikh vremen. Sochinenie Barona Stanislava de Shoduara*. St. Petersburg, 1837.

Chubar', V. Ya. "Voprosy finansirovaniia na II Vserossiiskom s'ezde Sovetov Narodnogo Khoziaistva." *Narodnoe Khoziaistvo*, 1919, no.1–2.

Chukovskii, K. I. *Dnevnik. 1936–1969. Sobranie sochineni,*. vol. 13. Moskva: Terra, 2007.

Chuprov, A. I. "Russkaia ekonomicheskaia zhizn' v 1886 godu." *Iuridicheskii Vestnik*, 1887, vol. 24.

Conférence Monétaire Internationale, 1892. *Procès-verbaux*. Bruxelles, 1892.

Custine, Astolphe marquis de. *Rossiia v 1839 godu*. St. Petersburg: Kriga, 2008.

Danilevskii, N. Ya. "Neskolko myslei po povodu nizkogo kursa nashikh bumazhnykh deneg i nekotorykh drugikh ekonomicheskikh iavlenii i voprosov." *O nizkom kurse nashikh deneg*. St. Petersburg, 1885.

Danilevskii, V. V. *Russkoe zoloto. Istoriia otkrytiia i dobychi do serediny XIX v.* Moskva: Gos nauchno-tekhn. Izd-vo, 1959.

Demchinskii, B. N. *Rossiia v Manchzhurii*. St. Petersburg, 1908.

Dementiev, G. D. *Gosudarstvennye dokhody i raskhody Rossii i polozhenie gosudarstvennogo kaznacheistvo za vremia voiny s Germaniei i Avstro-Vengriei do 1917 goda*. Petrograd, 1917

Dementiev, G. D. *Vo chto oboshlas' nashemu gosudarstvennomu kaznacheistvu voina s Iaponiei*. Petrograd, 1917.

Demidov, N. P. *O bumazhnykh den'gakh*. St. Petersburg, 1829.

Denezhnaia reforma 1921–24 gg.: sozdanie tverdoi valiuty. Dokumenty i materialy. Moskva: ROSSPEN, 2008.

Denezhnaia reforma. Svod mnenii i otzyvov. St. Petersburg, 1896

"Denezhnoe obrashchenie i finansovoe polozhenie Rossii (1904–1907)." *Istoricheskii Arkhiv*, 1956, no.3.

Denezhnoe obrashchenie i kredit. Denezhnoe obrashchenie v Rossii i za granitsei v gody voiny i revoliutsii (1914–1921). Moskva: Narkomfin, 1922.

Denezhnoe obrashchenie i kreditnaia Sistema Soiuza SSR za 20 let. Sbornik vazhneishikh zakonodatelnykh materialov za 1917–1937g. Moskva: Gosfinisdat, 1939.

Denikin, A. I. *Ocherki russkoi smuty. Krushenie vlasti i armii. Fevral-sentiabr 1917*. Moskva: Nauka, 1991.

Derevenko, N. "Eshche po voprosu o dovoennykh rubliakh." *Vestnik finansov* 5 (1922).

Dmitriev, V. N. *Rastsenka rabochei sily i glavneishikh stroitelnykh rabot s pereuchetom tsen dovoennogo vremeni na muchnye rubli i sovetskie denezhnye znaki*. Petrograd: [no publisher], 1922.

Doklad soedinennogo prisutstviia pravleniia i finansovo-organizatsionnoi komissii obshchemu sobraniiu chlenov Obshchestva Vzaimnogo Pozelemnogo Kredita 26 ianvaria 1886 goda O merakh k oblegcheniiu polozheniia zaemshchikov Obshchestva po metallichesskim ikh zaimam [1886].

"Dokladnaia zapiska Komiteta finansov Nikolaiu II o katastroficheskom finansovom sostoianii strany i merakh sokhraneniia zolotogo zapasa. December 14, 1905." *Istoricheskie Zapiski* 2 (1955).

Dombrovskii, A., and V. Voroshilov. *Manchzuriia*. St. Petersburg, 1904.

"Dopros K. D. Kafafova." *Padenie tsarskogo regima*. T.2. Leningrad: Gos. izd-vo, 1925.

Dubenskii, V. *Chto takoe den'gi?* Moskva, 1859.

Durova, Nadezhda. *The Cavalry Maiden: Journals of a Russian Officer in the Napoleonic Wars*. Translation, introduction, and notes by Mary Fleming Zirin. Bloomington: Indiana University Press, 1988.

"Dvizhenie zolotogo zapasa v Rossii v kontse XIX—nachale XX v." *Istoria Ministerstva Finansov Rossii v chetyrekh tomakh*, edited by A.L. Kudrin, vol.1. Moskva: Infra-M, 2003.

Ekonomicheskie otnosheniia Rossii s budushchimi soiuznymi respublikami 1917–1922: Dokumenty i materialy. Moskva: Vostochnaia literatura, 1996.

Ekonomicheskoe polozhenie Rossii Nakanune Velikoi Oktiabr'skoi Sotsialisticheskoi Revoliutsii. ch.2. Moskva: Institut istorii SSSR, 1957.

L'Encyclopedie ou Dictionnaire raisonné des sciences, des arts et des métiers, vol. 2, accessed via *Édition Numérique Collaborative et Critique de l'Encyclopédie ou Dictionnaire raisonné des sciences, des arts et des métiers (1751–1772)*, http://enccre.academie-scien ces.fr/encyclopedie/.

Endelman, B. C. *Le monometallisme-or en Russie: histoire de la réforme monétaire et de la circulation fiduciaire russe depuis 1897: étude historique et économique*. Berne: Impr. A. Tanner, 1917

Engelgard. A. N. *Iz derevni. 12 pisem, 1872–1887*. St. Petersburg: Nauka, 1999.

Eroshsevskii, N. *K voprosu o pozemel'nom kredite*. Odessa, 1881.

"Exchange," *Encyclopedia Britannica*, vol. 8. Chicago, 1895.

Fal'kner, S. A. *Bumazhnye den'gi Frantsuzskoi revoliutsii*. Moskva: VSNKh, 1919.

Fal'kner, S. A. *Problemy teorii i praktiki emissionnogo khoziastva*. Moskva: Ekonomicheskaia zhizn', 1924.

Fel'kner, A. *Slavianskaia borba. Istoricheskii ocherk vosstaniia balkanskikh slavian*. St. Petersburg, 1877.

Fevral'skaia revoliutsiia 1917 goda. Sbornik dokumentov i materialov. Moskva: Rossiiskii Gos. Gumanitarnyi Universitet, 1996.

Fichte, J. G. *The Closed Commercial State*, trans. Anthony Curtis Adler. New York: State University of New York Press, 2012.

"Finansovye soveshchaniia soiuznikov vo vremia voiny. Soveshchanie trekh ministrov v Parizhe 20-23 ianvaria 1915 g." *Krasnyi Arkhiv* 5 (1924).

"Finansovyi krizis v Turtsii." In *Gertsogovinskoe vosstanie i vostochnyi vopros*. St. Petersburg, 1876.

Firsov, N. N. *Pravitel'stvo i obshchestvo v ikh otnosheniiakh k vneshnei torgovle Rossii v tsarstvovaniie imperatritsy Ekateriny II*. Kazan', 1902

Fisher, K. I. *Zapiski senatora*. Moskva: Zakharov, 2008.

Fren, Kh. M. "Katalog monet dzhuchidov ili khanov Zolotoi Ordy." *Zapiski ANO*, t.2. St. Petersburg, 1850.

Fren, Kh. M. *Monety khanov ulusa Dzhuchieva ili Zolotoi Ordy s monetami inykh mukhammedaskikh dinastii v pribavlenii*. St. Petersburg, 1823.

Fridman, M. I. "Rol' zaimov v finansirovanii voiny." *Voennye Zaimy. Sbornik statei po obshchei redaktsiiei M.I. Tugan-Baranovskogo*. Petrograd, 1917.

Fridman, M. I. "Voina i gosudarstvennoe khoziaistvo Rossii." *Voprosy Mirovoi Voiny*. Petrograd, 1915.

Fridman, M. I. *Gosudarstvennoe khoziaistvo i denezhnoe obrashchenie v Rossii, 1913–1919*. Moskva: Sovet Vserossiiskikh kooperativnykh s'ezdov, 1919.

Gagemeister, Yu. A. *O kredite*. St. Petersburg, 1858.

Gagemeister, Yu. A. *Znachenie denezhnykh znakov v Rossii*. Moskva, 1864.

Gaidar, E.T. *Dni porazhenii i pobed*. Moskva: Alpina, 2014.

Gal'. "O polozhenii metallosnabzheniia." *Narodnoe khoziaistvo*, no. 9–10, 1919.

Ganelin, R. Sh. "Gosudarstvennaia Duma i antisemitskie tsirkuliary 1915–1916 gg." *Vestnik Evreiskogo Universiteta v Moskve* 3, no. 10 (1995).

Georgii Mikhailovich, [Romanov], vel kn. *Russkie monety 1881–1890*. St. Petersburg, 1891.

Georgii Mikhailovich[Romanov], vel.kn. *Monety tsarstvovania imperatritsy Ekateriny II*, vol.1. St. Petersburg, 1894.

Glukhovskoi, A. I. *Propusk vod r. Amu-Darii po staromu ee ruslu v Kaspiiskoe more i obrazovanie nepreryvnogo vodnogo Amu-Dariisko-Kaspiiskogo puti ot granits Afganistana po Amu-Darie, Kaspiiu, Volge, i Mariiskoi sisteme do Peterburga i Baltiiskogo moria*. St. Petersburg, 1893.

Gogol, N. V. "Mertvye Dushi." *Polnoe sobranie sochinenii v 14 tomakh*. Moskva: Izd-vo AN SSSR, 1951, vol. 6.

Gogol, N. V. "Nos." *Polnoe sobranie sochinenii v 14 tomakh*. vol. 3. Moskva: Izd-vo AN SSSR, 1951.

Gogol, N. V. "Portret." *Polnoe sobranie sochinenii v 14 tomakh,* vol. 3 Moskva: Izd-vo AN SSSR, 1951.

Golovachev, A. A. *Desiat' let reform, 1861–1871*. St. Petersburg, 1872.

Golovachev, A. A. "Ob'asnenie po povodu otvetov na voprosy ob operatsiiakh Gosudarstvennogo Banka." *Vestnik Evropy* 2 (March 1874).

Goltsman, A. *Regulirovanie i naturalizatsiia zarabotnoi platy*. Moskva, 1918.

Gorbunov N. "Kak sozdavalsia rabochii apparat Sovnarkoma." *Vospominaniia o Vladimire Il'yche Lenine*, vol.3, Moskva: Gospolitzidat, 1961.

Gorn, Dzh. *Zhon Lo. Opyt issledovaniia po istorii finansov*. Per. Ivana Shipova. St. Petersburg, 1895.

Gosudarstvennaia Duma Chetvertyi Sozyv. Sessia IV. Soedinennye komissii finansovaia i biudzhetnaia. "Doklad po zakonoproektu o rasshirenii predostavlennogo Gosudarstvennomu Banku prava vypuska gosudarstvennykh kredinykh biletov." In *Prilozheniia k stenograficheskim otchetam Gosudarstvennoi Dumy*. Vypusk V, no.330. Petrograd, 1916.

Gosudarstvennaia Duma. Chetvertyi sozyv, sessiia IV. "Stenograficheskii otchet zasedanii soedinennykh komissii biudzhentoi i finansovoi 4,5 i 6 avgusta 1915 po rassmotreniiu zakonoproektov o rasshirenii predostavlennogo Gosudarstvennomu banku prava vypuska gosudastvennykh kreditnykh biletov." *Prilozheniia k stenograficheskim ontchetam n.26 i 38.* Petrograd, 1915.

Gosudarstvennaia Duma. Chetvertyi Sozyv. Sessia IV. *Stenograficheskie otchety. 1916.* Petrograd, 1916.

Gosudarstvennoe Soveshchanie. Stenograficheskii otchet. Leningrad: Gosizdatel'stvo, 1930.

Gosudarstvennye dokhody i rashkhody v tsarstvovanie Ekateriny II." *Sbornik RIO,* vol.V, VI. 1870.

Gosudarstvennyi Bank. *Otchet Gosudarstvennogo Banka za 1905.* St. Petersburg, 1906.

Gosudarstvennyi Bank. *Otchet Gosudarstvennogo Banka za 1906.* St. Petersburg, 1907.

Gosudarstvennyi Bank. *Otchet Gosudarstvennogo Banka za 1907.* St. Petersburg, 1908.

Gosudarstvennyi Bank. *Otchet Gosudarstvennogo Banka za 1913.* St. Petersburg, 1914.

Gosudarstvennyi Sovet. *O vosstanovlenii chekanki platinovoi monety.* St. Petersburg, 1861.

Gosudarstvennyi Bank. Kratkii ocherk deiatelnosti za 1860-1910 g. St. Petersburg, 1910.

Gosudarstvennyi Bank SSSR. Kratkii ocherk k sorokaletiiu Oktiabria. Moskva: Gosfinizdat, 1957.

Grigorovich, N. *Kantzler Kniaz' Aleksandr Andreevich Bezborodko v sviazi s sobytiiami ego vremeni,* t.1. St. Petersburg, 1879.

Gubarevich-Radobylskii, A. F. *Ekonomicheskii ocherk Bukhary i Tunisa.* St. Petersburg, 1905.

Guchkov, A. I. *Aleksandr Ivanovich Guchkov rasskazyvaet. Vospominaniia Predsedatelia Gosudarstvennoi dumy i voennogo ministra Vremennogo pravitel'stva.* Moskva: Vosprosy Istorii, 1993

Guriev, A. N. *Reforma denezhnogo obrashcheniia.* St. Petersburg, 1896.

Helfferich, Karl. *Das Geld im russisch-japanischen Kriege.* Berlin: E. S. Mittler und Sohn, 1906.

Helfferich, Karl. *Die Finanzielle Seite des russisch-japanischen Krieges.* Bonn: Marine-Rundschau: Zeitschrift für Seewesen, 1904.

Humboldt, Alexander von. *Perepiska Aleksandra Gumbol'dta s uchenymi i gosudarstvennymi deiateliami Rossii.* Moskva: Izd-vo Akademii nauk SSSR, 1962.

I–IV Sessii Vserossiiskogo Tsentralnogo Ispolnitelnogo Komiteta VIII sozyva. Stenograficheskii otchet. Moskva, VTsIK, 1922.

Imperator Aleksandr I i Frederik-Sezar Lagarp: pis'ma, dokumenty. Moskva: ROSSPEN, 2014.

"Inostrannoe obozrenie. Turetskie finansy." *Vestnik Evropy,* 1875, September.

Instruktsiia dlia pochtovo-telegrafnykh i pochtovykh uchrezhdenii, opredeliaiushchaia poriadok i usloviia priema deneg dlia perevoda po pochte i po telegrafu. Kharkiv, 1896.

Instruktsiia gubernskomy pochtmeisteru. St. Petersburg, 1807.

Istoriia Gosudarstvennogo Banka SSSR v dokumentakh. Moskva: Finansy, 1971.

Iurgens, F. A., *Vospominaniia o Evgenii Ivanoviche Lamanskom v sviazi s deiatel'nostiu Gosudarstvennogo Banka.* St. Petersburg, 1901.

Iur'ev, A. "Gosudarstvennaia tovaroobmennaia sistema." *Narodnoe khoziaistvo*, 1919, no.11–12.

Iurovskii, L. N. *Denezhnaia politika Sovetskoi vlasti (1917–1927)*. Moskva: Ekonomika, 2008.

Ivanovskii, A. O. "Mednaia moneta v Man'chzhurii." *Zapiski Vostochnogo Otdelenia RAO*, vol.7, 1893.

Izmailov, A. *Material'nyi uchet*. Moskva: [n.p.] 1921.

Izvlechenie iz podlinnykh del Komiteta finansov. St. Petersburg, 1895.

Jacob, Ludwig Heinrich von. *Denkwurdigkeiten aus meinem Leben*. Halle an der Saale: Universitätsverlag Halle-Wittenberg, UVHW, 2011.

Jenks, Jeremiah W. *Considerations on a New Monetary System for China*. Ithaca, NY: Andrus and Church (US Commission on International Exchange), 1904.

Kachenovskii M. T. "Nechto dlia drevnei numizmatiki." *Vestnik Evropy* 91, no. 1 (1817).

Kachenovskii, M. T. "O bel'iikh lobkakh i kun'ikh mordkakh." *Vestnik Evropy* 160, no. 13 (1828).

Kachenovskii, M. T. "O kozhanykh den'gakh," *Uchenye zapiski Moskovskogo universiteta*, ch. 7, no.9, ch. 8.no.10 (1835)

Kachenovskii, M. T. "O starinnykh nazvaniiakh v Rossii deneg metallicheskikh v smysle khodiachei monety." *Vestnik Evropy* 154, nos.14–16; 155, nos. 18, 20; 156, nos. 21–23 (1827).

Kachenovskii, M. T. *Dva rassuzhdeniia o kozhanykh den'gakh i o Russkoi Pravde*. Moskva: Universitetskaia tipografiia, 1849.

Kamenskii, G. P. "Ponizhenie kursa na London na S. Peterburgskoi birzhe." *Vestnik Promyshlennosti* 1 (1859), "Nauki."

Kankrin, E. F.[Cankrin, Georg] *Die oekonomie der menschlichen gesellschaften und das finanzwesen: Von einem ehemaligen finanzminister*. Stuttgart: E. Schweizerbart, 1845.

Kankrin, E. F. [Cankrin, Georg]. *Weltreichtum, Nationalreichtum und Staatswirtschaft; oder, Versuch neuer ansichten der politischen Oekonomie*. München, K. Thienemann, 1821.

Kankrin, E. F. *Graf Kankrin i ego ocherki politicheskoi ekonomii i finansii*. St. Petersburg, 1894,

Kankrin, E. F. *Mirovoe bogatstvo i natsionalnaia ekonomika*. Moskva: Delo, 2018.

Karamzin, N. M. "O bogatstve iazyka." In N. M. Karamzin, *Izbrannye sochineniia v dvukh tomakh*. T.2. Moskva: Khudozh. lit-ra, 1964.

Karamzin, N. M. *Istoria gosudarstva rossiiskogo*, 4th ed. St. Petersburg, 1834, vol. 5.

Karamzin, N. M. *Karamzin's Memoir on Ancient and Modern Russia: A Translation and Analysis*, edited by Richard Pipes. Ann Arbor: University of Michigan Press, 2005.

Kardashev, V. P. "Fondovye birzhi v Rossii." *Bankovaia Entsiklopediia*. T.2. *Birzha. Istoriia i sovremennaia organizatsiia fondovykh birzh*. St. Petersburg, 1916.

Kareev, N. I. "Bumazhnye den'gi Frantsuzskoi revoliutsii." *Niva* 49, no.33 (1918).

Katalog knizhnogo sobraniia S.Yu.Vitte. Rekonstruktsiia [Vitte S.Yu.] *Sobranie sochinenii i dokumentalnykh materialov v 5 tomakh*. Moskva: Nauka, 2007, vol. 5.

Katsenelenbaum, Z. S. "Voina i russkii rubl." *Trudy Komissii po izucheniiu sovremennoi dorogovizny.* Vyp.3. Moskva, 1915.

Katsnelenbaum, Z. S. "Problema deneg i otsenki v sotsializme." *K teorii deneg i ucheta,* Moskva, [no publisher], 1922.

Katzenelenbaum, Z. S. *Voina i finansovo-ekonomicheskoe polozhenie Rossii.* Moskva, 1917.

Kaufman, I. I. "Bumazhno-denezhnye proekty i ekstraordinarnye finansy." *Sbornik gosudarstvennykh znanii,* t.7. St. Petersburg, 1879.

Kaufman, I. I. *Bumazhnye dengi Avstrii, 1762–1911.* St. Petersburg, 1913.

Kaufman, I. I. *Iz istorii bumazhnykh deneg v Rossii.* St. Petersburg, 1909.

Kaufman, I. I., *Serebrianyi rubl' ot ego vozniknoveniia do kontsa XIX veka.* St. Petersburg, 1910.

Kaufman, I. I., *Statistika gosudarstvennykh finansov Rossii v 1862–84 godakh. Statisticheskii vremennik Rossiiskoi Imperii.* St. Petersburg, 1886.

Kazanskii, P. S. "Dopolneniia k issledovaniiu o drevnei russkoi monetnoi sisteme." *Zapiski Imperatorskogo Arkheologicheskogo Obshchestva,* vol.6. St. Petersburg, 1853.

Keynes, J. M. "Russia," January 30, 1915. In *The Collected Writings of John Maynard Keynes,* vol. 16. Cambridge: Cambridge University Press, 2013.

Keynes, J. M. "The Finance Experts at Genoa." In *The Collected Writings of John Maynard Keynes,* vol. 17. Cambridge: Cambridge University Press, 2013.

Keynes, J. M. "The Financial System of the Bolsheviks." In *The Collected Writings of John Maynard Keynes,* vol.17. Cambridge: Cambridge University Press, 2013.

Keynes, J. M. "Indian Currency and Finance [1913]." In *The Collected Writings of John Maynard Keynes,* vol. 1. Cambridge: Cambridge University Press, 2013.

Khodskii, L. V. *Pozemelnyi kredit v Rossii i otnoshenie ego k krestianskomu zemlevladeniiu.* Moskva, 1882.

Kistenev, S. "Finansovoe soglashenie s zakavkazskimi respublikami." *Vestnik Finansov,* 1922, no. 12.

Kochubei V. P. "Zapiska grafa V.P. Kochubeiia o polozhenii Imperii i o merakh k prekrashcheniiu besporiadkov i vvedenii luchshego ustroistva v raznye otrasli, pravitelstvo sostavliaiushchie." *Bumagi Komiteta uchrezhdennogo vysochaishim reskriptom 6 dekabria 1826 goda. Sbornik IRIO,* vol. 90. St. Petersburg, 1894.

Kokorev, V. A. *Ekonomicheskie provaly.* Moskva: Kontseptual, 2013.

Kokovtsov, V. N. *Iz moego proshlogo. Vospominaniia,* vols. 1,2. Moskva: Nauka, 1992.

Kolesov, I. N. "Neudavshaiasia kreditnaia operatsiia." *Ekonomicheskii zhurnal,* 1888, no.10.

Kolesov, I. N. *Pochemu sem' let mirnogo vremeni ne prinesli nikakogo uluchsheniia v nashikh finansakh.* St. Petersburg, 1887.

Kondakov, N. P. *Russkie Klady. Issledovanie drevnostei velikokniazheskogo perioda.* St. Petersburg, 1896.

Korf, M. A. "Nikolai I v soveshchatel'nykh sobraniiakh." *Sbornik IRIO,* vol. 98. (1896).

Kovalevskii, V. I. "Iz vospominanii o grafe Sergee Iliueviche Vitte." *Russkoe proshloe* 2 (1991).

Kritzman, L. N. *Geroicheskii period velikoi russkoi revolutsii (opyt analiza t.n. "voennogo kommunizma")*. Moskva: Gos. izd-vo, 1926.

Kulomzin, A. N. *Perezhitoe. Vospominania*. Moskva: ROSSPEN, 2016.

Kuzovkov, D. V. *Osnovnye momenty raspada i vosstanovlenia denezhnoi sistemy*. Moskva: Izd-vo Kommunisticheskoi Akademii, 1925.

L., Ivan. "Gosudarsvennyi uchet narodnogo khoziastva i znachenie v nem gosudarstvennogo schetovodstva." *Izvestiia NKF*, no. 7, 1919.

Lamanskii, E. I. "Gosudarstvennye chetyrekhprotsentnye, nepreryvnodokhodnye bilety." *Ekonomicheskii Ukazatel'*, no. 118, 1859.

Lamanskii, E. I. "Vklady v bankakh ili bilety nepreryvnogo dokhoda?" *Russkii Vestnik* 20 (1859).

Lamanskii, E. I. *Istoricheskii ocherk denezhnogo obrashcheniia v Rossii*. St. Petersburg, 1854.

Lamanskii, E. I. *Vospominania 1840-1890*. Penza: Zemstvo, 1995.

Lamanskii, E. I. *Sdelki na zolotuiu valiutu kak sredstvo k uluchsheniiu bumazhnogo denezhnogo obrashcheniia*. St. Petersburg, 1895.

Larin, Yu. "O sotsialnom soderzhanii posleoktiabr'skoi diktatury" (December 27, 1917). In *Krestiane i rabochie v russkoi revoliutisii*. Petrograd: Izd-e Petrogradskogo Soveta Rab i Krasnoarmeiskikh Deputatov, 1919.

Larin, Yu. "U kolybeli." *Narodnoe Khoziaistvo* 11 (1918).

Larsons, M. Ya. *Na sovetskoi sluzhbe. Zapiski spetsa*. Paris: La Source, 1930.

Larsons, M. Ya. *V sovetskom labirinte. Epizody i siluety*. Paris: Strela, 1932.

Lebedev, V. A. "Reforma denezhnogo obrashcheniia." *Schetovodstvo*, 1896, n.10.

Lebedev, V. A. *Bumazhnye den'gi*. St. Petersburg, 1889.

Lemke, M. K. ""Oni proderzhatsia ne bolshe 5-7 dnei" (po dnevniku)." *Nemerknushchie gody. Ocherki i vospomimaniia o Krasnom Petrograde*. Leningrad: Sovetskii pisatel', 1957.

Lenin, V. I. "Nabrosok programmy ekonomicheskikh meropriatii." December 1917. In V. I. Lenin, *Polnoe sobranie sochinenii*, t.35 Moskva: In-t Marksizma-Leninizma, 1962.

Lenin, V. I. "O znachenii zolota teper' i posle polnoi pobedy sotsializma." In V. I. Lenin, *Polnoe sobranie sochinenii*, t.44, Moskva: In-t Marksizma-Leninizma, 1964.

Lenin, V. I. "Osnovnye polozheniia khoziaistvennoi i v osobennosti bankovoi politiki" [April 1918], *Leninskii sbornik*, 21. Moskva: Gosizdat, 1933.

Lenin, V. I. "Proekt direktivy zamestiteliu predsedatelia i vsem chlenam Genuezskoi delegatsii." In V. I. Lenin, *Polnoe Sobranie Sochinenii*, vol. 44. Moskva: In-t Marksizma-Leninizma, 1964.

Lenin, V. I. "Tezisy o bankovoi politike." In V. I. Lenin, *Polnoe Sobranie Sochinenii*, t.36. Moskva: In-t Marksizma-Leninizma, 1962.

Lenin, V. I. "Evropeiskii capital i samodezhavie." In V. I. Lenin, *Polnoe sobranie sochinenii*, vol. 9. Moskva: In-t Marksizma-Leninizma, 1960.

Lenin, V. I. Chernovoi nabrosok proekta programmy (VII ekstrennyi s'ezd RKP(b. In V. I. Lenin, *Polnoe sobranie sochinenii,* t. 36. Moskva: In-t Marksizma-Leninizma, 1962.

Lenin, V. I. *V. I. Lenin:Neizvestnye dokumenty, 1892–1922.* Moskva: ROSSPEN, 2017.

Lenin, V. I. Variant statii "Ocherednye zadachi sovetskoi vlasti." In V. I. Lenin, *Polnoe sobranie sochinenii,* t. 36. Moskva: In-t Marksizma-Leninizma, 1962.

Lenin, V. I. *Will the Bolsheviks Maintain Power?* London: Labour Publishing, 1922.

Leroy-Beaulieu, Anatole. "L'empire des tsars et les russes: III. Les finances. II. Les dépenses, la dette et le papier-monnaie." *Revue de Deux Mondes,* January 1877.

Leshkov, V. N. *Russkii narod i gosudarstvo. Istoriia russogo obshchestvennogo prava do XVIII veka.* Moskva: Universitetskaia tipografiia, 1858.

Lévy, Raphaël-Georges. "Finances de guerre: Russie et Japon." *Revue de Deux Mondes,* vol. 22, no.1 (Juillet 1904).

Lipkin, Leonid [Dnevnik]. https://prozhito.org/person/5382.

Logofet, D. N. *Bukharskoe khanstvo pod rossiiskim protektoratom,* vol. 2. St. Petersburg, 1911.

Lomeier, A. E. "Vneshniaia torgovlia, kredinyi rubl', i proekt chastnoi denezhnoi edinitsy," and A. N. Za., "Reforma denezhnogo obrashcheniia i Gosudarstvennyi Bank." In *Voprosy denezhnogo obrashcheniia. Tsentral'nyi Narodno-Promyshlennyi Komitet. Otdel Vneshnei Torgovli. Doklady M.V. Bernatskogo, A.N. Gurieva, A.N. Zaka, V.S. Ziva, N.I. Lodyzhenskogo, A.E. Lomeiera, F.A. Menkova i ikh obsuzhdenie.* Petrograd: *Tsentral'nyi Narodno-Promyshlennyi Komitet,* 1918.

Lomov, Afanasii. "Programma finansovykh reform komissara Gukovskogo." *Kommunist* 2 (1918).

Lorini, Eteocle. *La réforme monétaire de la Russie.* Paris: V. Giard & E. Briere, 1898.

Lurie. "Iz istorii ideologii i zakonodatelstva o denezhnom obrashchenii RSFSR." *Trudy sektsii po voprosam denezhnogo obrashcheniia i kredita pod pred. M.I. Fridmana i V. Ya. Zheleznova. Denezhnoe obrashcheniie i kredit. Denezhnoe obrashchenie v Rossii i za granitsei v gody voiny i revoliutsii (1914–1921.* Petrograd: Narkomfin, 1922.

M-ev, P. *Zolotoi bank i ego sudba. Episod iz istorii nashego pozemel'nogo kredita.* St. Petersburg, 1890.

Martin, Rudolf. *Die Zukunft Russlands und Japans. Die deutchen Milliarden in Gefahr.* Berlin, Heymann, 1905.

Marx, Karl. *Contribution to the Critique of Political Economy,* https://www.marxists. org/archive/marx/works/download/Marx_Contribution_to_the_Critique_of_ Political_Economy.pdf.

Masayoshi, Matsukata. *Report of the Adoption of the Gold Standard in Japan.* Tokyo: Government Press, 1899.

Materialy po denezhnoi reforme 1895–97 gg. Petrograd: NKF, In-t Ekonomicheskikh Issledovanii, 1922.

[Méline, Jules.] *La question monétaire. Le mémoire de M. Méline. La situation générale et les intérêts de la Russie.* St. Petersburg: tipografiia V. Kirshbauma, no publ. date.

Men'kov, F. A. *Sdelki na zolotuiu valiutu.* Petrograd, 1916.

Meshcherskii, V. P. *Dnevnik kniazia V. P. Meshcherskogo za mai, iiun', iul', avgust 1897 g.* St. Petersburg, 1897.

Meshcherskii, V. P. *Pisma k imperatoru Aleksandru III, 1881–1894.* Moskva: NLO, 2018.

"Mezhdunarodnoe finansovoe polozhenie tsarskoi Rossii vo vremia mirovoi voiny (doklad A.I. Shingareva v Voenno-morkoi komissii Gosudarstvennoi Duma 20 Iunia 1916g.)," *Krasnyi Arkhiv*, 1934, vol. 64.

Migulin, P. P. *Regulirovanie bumazhnoi valiuty v Rossii.* Kharkiv, 1896.

Migulin, P. P. "Bumazhnye den'gi." *Novyi Ekonomist* 15 (1915).

Migulin, P. P. "Rubl' zolotoi i rubl' bumazhnyi." *Novyi Ekonomist* 9 (1915).

Migulin, P. P. "Zolotopromyshlennost' i nashi zolotopromyshlenniki." *Novyi Ekonomist* 28 (1916).

Migulin, P. P. *Nasha bankovaia politika.* Khar'kiv, 1914.

Migulin, P. P. *Russkii gosudarstvennyi kredit.* Khar'kiv, 1899.

Migulin, P. P. *Russkii Tsentralnyi Avtonomnyi Gosudarstvennyi Bank.* Khar'kiv, 1906.

Mikhailov, I. A. *Voina i nashe denezhnoe obrashchenie. Fakty i tsifry.* Petrograd, 1916.

Ministerstvo Finansov, 1802–1902. St. Petersburg, 1902.

Ministerstvo finansov. *Ob ispravlenii denezhnogo obrashcheniia.* March 14, 1896 [no publication date or place].

Ministerstvo Finansov. Osobennaia kantseliariia po kreditnoi chasti. *O vosstanovlenii obrashcheniia zvonkoi monety.* 1888 [[no publisher]].

Montesquieu, Charles-Louis de Secondat baron de. *The Spirit of Laws* (Cambridge Texts in the History of Political Thought). Cambridge: Cambridge University Press, 1989.

Mordvinov, N. S. "Izlishestvo bumazhnoi monety." *Arkhiv Grafov Mordvinovykh*, vol. 4. St. Petersburg, 1902.

Mordvinov, N. S. "Mnenie admirala Mordvinova o vrednykh posledstviiakh dlia kazny i chastnykh imushchestv ot oshibochnykh mer upravleniia gosudarstvennym kaznachestvom." *Chtenia v Imperatorskom Obshchestve Istorii i Drevnostei Rossiiskikh*, 1859, kn. 4.

Mordvinov, N. S. "Vnutrennii dolg i Volnyi Rossiiskii Bank" (September 1809). *Arkhiv Grafov Mordvinovykh*, vol.3. St. Petersburg, 1902.

Morozov, P. "O lazhe na den'gi, suchchestvuiushchem vo vnutrennikh guberniiakh Rossii." *Kommercheskaia gazeta* 34 (March 21, 1839).

N. P. "Novoe osnovanie denezhnoi sistemy." *Torgovyi Sbornik* 34 (1865).

Naidenov, N. A. *Vospomimaniia o vidennom, slyshannom i ispytannom.* Moskva: Izd. dom Tonchu, 2007.

Nashe denezhnoe obrashchenie 1914–1925. Sbornik materialov, edited by L. N. Iurovskii. Moskva: Finansovoe izdatel'stvo NKF SSSR, 1926.

Nebyvalaia polemika." *Ekonomicheskii Zhurnal* 8 (1886).

Nikolskii, P. A. *Bumazhnye den'gi v Rossii.* Kazan', 1892.

Note complémentaire sur la question monétaire, St. Petersburg, tipografiia V. Kirshbauma, no publication date.

Notovich, N. A. *Gde doroga v Indiiu?* Moskva, 1889.

Novikov, Ivan. *Kliuch k vykladkam kursov ili nyne izobretennyi samyi kratchaishii sposob verno vykladyvat' aglinskoi i gollandskoi kurs.* Moskva, 1794.

Novoselskii, N. A. *Birzhevaia spekuliatsiia, naznachaiushchaia kurs nashego kreditnogo rublia.* St. Petersburg, 1885.

"Novye meropriiatiia." *Ekonomicheskii zhurnal* 11–12 (1887).

"O sposobe vychisleniia srednego kursa." F. F. Kolaiko, *Spravochnaia kniga S.-Peterburgskogo birzhevogo kupechestva.* St. Petersburg, 1889.

"O valiutnom voprose v otnoshenii k tovarnym tsenam i vneshnei torgovle Rossii." In *Sovet s'ezdov predstavitelei birzhevoi torglovli i sel'skogo khoziaistva. Otchet za 1915 god.* Petrograd, 1916.

O vypuske osobykh kaznacheiskikh denezhnykh znakov, ne vkhodiashchikh v sostav obespechivaemykh zolotom gosudarstvennykh kreditnykh biletov [1915].

Ob osnovnom pozemel'nom kredite. St. Petersburg, 1865.

Obolenskii, D. A. *Zapiski kniazia Dmitriia Aleksandrovicha Obolenskogo, 1855–1879.* St. Petersburg: Nestor-Istoriia, 2005.

Obolenskii, L. L. "Nashi zadachi." *Izvestiia Narodnogo Komissariata Finansov 1–2* (1919)

"Obozrenie promyshlennosti i torglovli." *Vestnik promyshlennosti* 2 (1858).

Obshchaia rospis' gosudarstvennykh dokhodov i rashkhodov Rossiiskoi Respubliki na ianvar'-iiun' 1918 goda. Moskva: Izd. VTsIK, 1918.

"Obzor voprosov podvergavshikhsia rassmotreniu v Moskovskom ocherednom gubernskom zemskov sobranii." *Sovremennaia letopis'* 5 (1868).

Ogarev, N. P. *Finansovye spory.* London: Truebner, 1864.

Okhotnikov, V. N. *Finansovye besedy (Grazhdanin, 1885–1886).* St. Petersburg, 1887.

Orlov, A. "Finansovoe i ekonomicheskoe ob'edinenie Zakavkazskoi Federatsii s RSFSR." *Vestnik Finansov* 38 (1922).

Orlov, M. F. "Iz neizdannogo sochineniia Mikhaila Fedorovicha Orlova (ob uchrezhedenii volnogo banka v Moskve)." *Russkii Arkhiv*, 1874, kn.1, no.6.

Osinskii, N. N. "Kak my ovladevali Gosudarstvennym Bankom." *Ekonomicheskaia Zhizn'* (November 6, 1918).

Osinskii, N. N. "Organy proletarskoi diktatury v ekonomicheskoi oblasti." *Stroitel'stvo sotsializma. Obshchie zadachi. Organizatsiia proizvodstva.* Moskva: "Kommunist," 1918.

Osnovnoi Ustav Pol'skogo Banka. 1828. *Sbornik administrativnykh postanovlenii Tsarstva Polskogo. Vedomstvo Finansov. Tom X. Polskii Bank.* Warsaw, 1867.

Osobye zhurnaly Soveta Ministrov Rossiiskoi Imperii, 1909–1917. "1914," Moskva: ROSSPEN, 2006.

Osobye zhurnaly Soveta Ministrov Rossiiskoi Imperii, 1909–1917, "1915," Moskva: ROSSPEN, 2008.

"Osobyi zhurnal Soveta ministrov 23 iulia 1914 goda o priostanovlenii razmena gosudarstvennykh kreditnykh biletov na zolotuiu monetu," *Osobye zhurnaly Soveta Ministrov Rossiiskoi Imperii, 1909–1917gg. "1914."* Moskva: ROSSPEN, 2006.

Ostroukhov, P. A. "Iz istorii denezhnogo obrashcheniia (Prostonarodnye lazhi i torgovlia den'gami na Nizhegorodskoi iarmarke)." *Zapiski Russkogo nauchno-issledovatelskogo ob'edineniia v Prage.* Tom 11 (16). Praha, 1941.

Otchet o raborakh pervogo Vserossiiskogo s'ezda predstavitelei finansovykh otdelov oblastnykh, gubernsikh i uezdnykh soldatskikh, rabochikh i krestianskikh deputatov. Moskva: tip. "Fasol," 1918.

Ozerov, I. Kh. "Gosudarstvennyi bank i vneustavnye ssudy." *Russkoe Slovo* 227 (1906).

Padenie tsarskogo rezhima. Stenograficheskie otchety doprosov i pokazanii, dannykh v 1917 godu v Chrezvychainoi sledstvennoi komissii Vremennogo pravitel'stva. Leningrad: Gos.Izd-vo, 1927, t.7.

Pakhman, S. V. *O zadachakh predstoiashchei reformy aktsionernogo zakonodatel'stva.* Kharkiv, 1861.

Panaev, V. A. "Den'gi—tovar." *Finansovye i ekonomicheskie voprosy.* St. Petersburg, 1878.

Peretz, E. A. *Dnevnik gosudarstvennogo sekretaria.* Moskva, Leningrad: Gos.izd-vo, 1927.

Pertsov, E. P. *Iskusstvo brat' vziatki: rukopis' naidennaia v bumagakh Tiazhalkina, umershego tituliarnogo sovetnika.* St. Petersburg, 1830.

Pervyi Vserossiiskii s'ezd Sovetov Rabochikh i Soldatskikh Deputatov. Moskva: Gos. Izd-vo, 1930.

Pestkovsky, S. "Ob oktiabrskikh dniakh v Pitere." *Proletarskaia revoliutsiia* 1922, no.10.

Pis'ma Pobedonostseva k Aleksandru III. Moskva: Tsentrarkhiv, 1926.

Plenum VSNKH, 14–23 sentiabria 1918 z (stenograficheskii otchet). Moskva: VSNKh, 1918.

Po stranitsam arkhivnykh fondov Tsentralnogo Banka Rossiiskoi Federatsii. Vyp.9. Balansy Gosudarstvennogo Banka SSSR (1922–1990 gg). Moskva: TsB RF, 2010.

Po stranitsam arkhivnykh fondov Tsentralnogo Banka Rossiiskoi Federatsii. Vyp.15. Iz neopublikovannogo. Voprosy denezhnogo obrashenia (1919-1982). Vedomstvennye materialy. Moskva: TsB RF, 2014.

Pochtovo-telegrafnaia statistika za 1899 god. St. Petersburg, 1900.

Pogodin, M. P. *Utro. Literaturnyi i politicheskii sbornik.* Moskva, 1866.

"Politicheskaia i obshchestvennaia khronika." *Delo* 1 (1876).

Polovtsov, A. A. *Dnevnik gosudarstvennogo sekretaria.* Moskva: Nauka, 1966.

Polovtsov, A. A. *Dnevnik, 1893–1909.* St. Petersburg: Aleteia, 2014.

Poppe, N. "Denezhnoe obrashchenie v Severnoi Manchzhurii." *Sbornik konsulskikh donesenii, 1904.* St. Petersburg, 1904.

Pososhkov, Ivan. *The Book of Poverty and Wealth*, edited and translated by A. P. Vlasto and L. R. Lewitter. Stanford, CA: Stanford University Press, 1987.

"Prebyvanie M.Kh. Reuterna v Livadii v Oktiabre 1876 g.," A. N. Kulomzin, V. G. Reutern-Nolkeln, *M.Kh. Reutern.* St. Petersburg, 1910.

Prenia v Moskovskom gubernskom zemskom sobranii po voprosu o pozemel'nykh bankakh. Moskva, 1866.

Preobrazhenskii, E. A. "Bumazhnye den'gi v epokhu proletarskoi diktatury." In E. A. Preobrazhenskii, *Arkhivnye dokumenty i materialy, 1886–1920*. Moskva: Glavrkhiv, 2006

Preobrazhenskii, E. A. "Voprosy finansovoi politiki [1921]." E. A. Preobrazhenskii, *Den'gi i mirovoi capitalism (issledovaniia, nauchno-populiarnye raboty 1921–1931)*, Moskva: Glavarkhiv, 2011.

Printz, N. *Podgotovitel'nye mery k vosstanovleniiu zvonkoi monety*. St. Petersburg, 1887.

Proekt pozemel'nogo imushchestvennogo banka [no publication date].

Prokofiev, S. V. *Dnevnik, 1907–1918*. Paris: SPRKFV, 2002.

Prokopovich, S. N. *Voina i narodnoe khoziaistvo*. Moskva, 1917.

Propper, Stanislav. *Was nicht in die Zeitung kam. Erinnerungen des Chefredakteurs der "Birschewyja Wedomosti."* Frankfurt am Main: Frankfurter Societäts-Dr., 1929.

Protokoly Prezidiuma Vyschego Soveta Narodnogo Khoziastva, Dekabr' 1917–1918. Sb. dokumentov. Moskva: Nauka, 1991.

Protokoly sionskikh mudretsov (po tekstu Nilusa). Vsemirnyi tainyi zagovor. Berlin, 1922.

Protokoly zasedanii Vserossiiskogo Tsentral'nogo Ispolnitelnogo Komiteta 4-go sozyva (stenograficheskii otchet). Moskva: Gos. Izd-vo, 1920.

Pushkin, A. S. "Poet-Igrok, o Beverlei-Goratsii," *Polnoe Sobranie Sochinenii v 16 tomakh* Moskva, Leningrad: AN SSSR, 1949 t.3, kn.2

Pushkin, A. S. "Razgovor knigoprodavtsa s poetom." *Polnoe sobranie sochinenii v 16 tomakh*, t.3, kn.1, Moskva: AN SSSR, 1947.

Pushkin, A. S. *Eugene Onegin*, translated by Stanley Mitchell. London: Penguin Classics, 2008.

Raffalovich, L. A. *Serebrianaia agitatsiia*. St. Petersburg, 1897.

Reforma denezhnogo obrashcheniia v Rossii; doklady i preniia v III Otdelenii Imperatorskogo Vol' nogo ekonomicheskogo obshchestva. Stenograficheskii otchet. St. Petersburg, 1896.

Reutern, M. Kh. "Zapiska M.Kh. Reuterna, predstavlennaia E.I.V. v Livadii 3-go oktiabria 1876 g." A. N. Kulomzin and V. G. Reutern-Nolkeln, *M. Kh. Reutern*. St. Petersburg, 1910.

Reutern, M. Kh. "Zapiska, predstavlennaia vel.kniaziu Konstantinu Nukolaevichu d.st.s. Reuternom v 1857 godu." *Reka Vremen, kniga piataia. Gosudar', gosudarstvo, gosudarstvennaia sluzhba*. Moskva: Ellis Lak, 1996.

Report on the Introduction of the gold-exchange standard into China, the Philippine Islands, Panama, and Other Silver-Using Countries, and on the Stability of Exchange. Submitted to the Secretary of State, October 22, 1904 by the US Commission on International Exchange. Hugh H. Hanna, Charles A. Conant, Jeremiah W. Jenks. Washington, DC: Government Printing Office, 1904.

Ribopier, A. I. "Zapiski grafa Aleksandra Ivanovicha Ribopiera." *Russkii Arkhiv*, 1877, kn.2, vyp.5.

Richter, D. I. *Gosudarstvennye zemel'nye banki v Rossii i ikh dal'neishaia sudba*. Petrograd, 1917.

Rospis' obshchegosudarstvennykh dokhodov i raskhodov Rossiiskoi Sotsialisticheskoi Federativnoi Sovetskoi Respubliki na ianvar'-iiun' 1919 goda s ob'asnitelnoi zapiskoi Narodnogo Komissara Finansov. Petrograd: 4-a gos tip, 1919.

Rossiia v mirovoi voine 1914–1918 (v tsifrakh). Moskva: Tsentr. Statisticheskoe upravlenie, 1925.

RSFSR. 1-e Otdelenie Narodnogo Banka, Petrograd. Instruktsii, tsirkuliary i prikazy, N.1. Petrograd: Tip. "Fridrich Kan," 1918.

Russkaia Amerika v "zapiskakh" Kirilla Khlebnikova: Novo-Arkhangel'sk. Moskva: Nauka, 1985.

Russkaia revoliutsiia glazami petrogradskogo chinovnika. Dnevnik 1917–1918, edited and annotated by Jens Petter Nielsen and Boris Weil. Oslo: [Reprosentralen Universitetet i Oslo], 1986.

Russkie finansy i evropeiskaia birzha v 1904–1906 gg. Moskva: Tsentrarkhiv, 1926.

"Russkii gosudarstvennyi dolg," *Russkii Vestnik.* 1860, vol.20.

Russkii zolotoi zapas za granitsei. St. Petersburg, 1913.

Russko-iaponskaia voina 1904–1905 gg. T.VII. Tyl deistvuiushchei armii, ch.1. St. Petersburg, 1910.

Rykov A. I. *Izbrannye proizvedeniia.* Moskva: Ekonomia, 1990.

S-ii, A. "Alexandr Gumbol'dt v Rossii i poslednie ego trudy." *Vestnik Evropy,* vol. 6, 1871.

"Samo proshedshee kak ono bylo . . .", Perepiska Anny Kravchenko i Aleksandra Spunde. Moskva: Izd-vo polit. literatury, 1990.

Saulgeot, H. *Deux types de banque d'Empire.* Paris: A. Rousseau 1905.

Sbornik tsirkuliarov Ministerstva finansov kazennym palatam, kaznacheistvam i podatnym inspektoram za 1898–1901 gg. Kyiv, 1902.

"Sekretnyie ofitsial'nye svedeniia o polozhenii nashikh finansov v 1813 i ob izyskanii sredstv k prodolzheniiu voennykh deistvii v chuzhikh kraiakh." *Sbornik istoricheskikh materialov izvlechennykh iz Arkhiva sobstvennoi EIV kantseliarii.* Vyp.1. St. Petersburg, 1876.

Sementkovskii, R. I. *Nash veksel'nyi kurs (prichiny ego neustoichivosti).* St. Petersburg, 1892.

Sharapov, S. F. "Bumazhnyi rubl'." *Bumazhnyi rubl' i drugie raboty.* Moskva: Rodnaia strana, 2017.

Shavrov N. A. *O razvitii Severa Rossii.* St. Petersburg, 1884.

Shavrov N. A. *Put' v Tsentral'nuiu Aziiu po napravleniiu, ukazannomu Petrom Velikim.* St. Petersburg, 1871.

Shavrov, N. A. "O referate barona A. V. Kaulbarsa." *Materialy dlia razresheniia voprosa o povorote Amu-Darii v Kaspiiskoe more.* Tiflis, 1887.

Shavrov, N. A. *Proekt glavnoi linii Sibirskoi zheleznoi dorogi.* St. Petersburg, 1873.

Shavrov, N. A. *Russkii put' v Zakavkazie.* St. Petersburg. 1883.

Shekhter, S. M. *Novye tablitsy dlia opredeleniia veksel'nykh kursov na Angliiu, Frantsiiu, Belgiiu, Italiiu i Gollandiiu, a takzhu i kursov tamozhennykh kuponov.* Odessa, 1889.

Shill, I. *O kreditnykh biletakh.* St. Petersburg: Tipografia Bezobrazova, 1866.

Shill, I. *Predpolozheniia ob uchrezhdenii russkogo gosudarstvennogo ili zemskogo zaemnogo banka*, St. Petersburg, 1861.

Shipov, A. *O sredstvakh k ustraneniiu nashikh ekonomicheskikh i finansovyckh zatrudnenii*. St. Petersburg, 1866.

Shipov, I. V. "Predlozhenia ministra finansov I. P. Shipova o merakh po sokhraneniiu zolotogo zapasa strany." *Istoricheskie zapiski* 2 (1955).

Shisha, A. "Voina i finansy." *Vestnik finansov* 12 (1928).

Shostak, P. A. *K voprosu o vliianii kursa kreditnogo rublia na khlebnye tseny*, St. Petersburg, 1896.

Shtorkh, P. A. *O nyneshnem sostoianii pozemel'nogo kredita v Rossii. Sistema zakladnykh listov*. St.Petersburg, 1867.

Shuvalov, A. P. *Metallicheskii rubl' i pozemel'nye banki*. St. Petersburg, 1866.

Shvanebach, P. Kh. *Denezhnoe preobrazovanie i narodnoe khoziaistvo*. St. Petersburg, 1901.

Sitnin, V. K. *Sobytiia i liudi. Zapiski finansista*. Moskva: Luch, 1993.

Skalkovskii, K. A. *Nashi gosudarstvennye i obshchestvennye deiateli*. St. Petersburg, 1891.

Skalkovskii, K. A. *Vospominania molodosti (po moriu zhiteiskomu)*. St. Petersburg, 1906.

Skarzynski, Stanislas. *Essai sur une Banque de Russie*. Paris: Guillaumin, 1901.

Slonimskii, L. Z. "Denezhnye nedoumeniia." *Vestnik Evropy*, June 1895.

Slonimskii, L. Z. "Finansovye zadachi. Zoloto ili serebro," *Vestnik Evropy*, July 1895.

Sluchevskaia (Martynova) Liubov'. *Dnevnik*. https://prozhito.org/note/244285.

Smirnov, A. I., *Krizis denezhnoi sistemy Frantsuzskoi revoliutsii*. Petrograd: Pravo, 1921.

Snow, George E. "N. Kh. Bunge, "The Years 1881–1894 in Russia: A Memorandum Found in the Papers of N. Kh. Bunge. A Translation and Commentary." *Transactions of the American Philosophical Society*, New Ser., 71, no. 6 (1981).

Sobolevskii, P. G. *Izvestie o platinovom proizvodstve v Rossii*. St. Petersburg, 1834.

Sokalskii, I. P. *Reforma na ocheredi*. Kharkiv, 1895.

Sokolnikov, G. Ya. "Denezhnyi krisis." *Narodnoe khoziastvo* 2 (1918).

Sokolnikov, G. Ya. "Gosudarstvennyi capitalism i novaia finansovaia politika." G. Ya. Sokolnikov, *Novaia finansovaia politika: na puti k tverdoi valiute*. Moskva: Nauka, 1991.

Soloviev, S. M. *Istoriia Rossii s drevneishikh vremen*, vol. 1 (3). St. Petersburg: Obshchestvennaia Pol'za, 1894.

Sotsial'naia revoliutsiia i finansy. Sbornik k III congressu kommunisticheskogo internatsionala. Moskva: NKF, 1921.

Speranskii, M. M. *Izbrannoe*. Moskva, ROSSPEN, 2010.

Speranskii, M. M. "Plan finansov," *Sbornik Imperatorskogo Russkogo Istoricheskogo Obshchestva*, vol. 45. St. Petersburg, 1885.

Speranskii, M. M. *Zapiska o monetnom obrashchenii grafa Speranskogo s zamechaniiami grafa Kankrina*. St. Petersburg, 1895.

Stability of international exchange. Report on the introduction of the gold-exchange standard into China and other silver-using countries, submitted to the Secretary of State, October 1, 1903 by the US Commission on International Exchange. Hugh

H. Hanna, Charles A. Conant, Jeremiah W. Jenks. Washington, DC: Government Printing Office, 1903.

Staniukovich, K. M. "Pis'ma znatnogo inostrantsa." *Sobranie sochinenii*, vol.11. Moskva, 1898.

Staryi professor. *Zamechatel'naia epokha v istorii russkikh finansov.* St. Petersburg, 1895.

Stenograficheskie otchety zasedanii Ekonomicheskogo soveta pri Vremennov praviltelstve [Petrograd, 1917].

Stepanov, M. *Vnutrennii gosudarstvennyi kredit.* St. Petersburg, 1866.

Storch [Shtorkh], Heinrich Friedrich von. "Materialy dlia istorii denezhnykh znakov v Rossii," *Zhurnal Ministerstva Narodnogo Prosveshcheniia*, 1868, ch. 137, no. 3.

Strugatsky, Arkady, and Boris Strugatsky. *Monday Starts on Saturday*, translated by Andrew Bromfield. London: Gateway, 2016.

Strumilin, S. G. *Zarabotnaia plata i proizvoditel'nost' truda v russkoi promyshlennosti za 1913–1922 gg.* Moskva: Voprosy truda, 1923.

Sudeikin, V. T. *Birzha i birzhevye operatsii.* St. Petersburg, 1892.

Sudeikin, V. T. *Operatsii Gosudarstvennogo banka.* St. Petersburg, 1888.

Sudeikin, V. T. *Vosstanovlenie v Rossii metallicheskogo obrashcheniia (1839–1843).* *Istoricheskii ocherk.* Moskva, 1891.

Sukhanov, N. N. *Zapiski i revoliutsii.* t.2, kn.3-4. Moskva: Politizdat, 1991.

Suvorin, A. V. *V ozhidanii veka XX. Malen'kie pis'ma 1889–1903 gg.* Moskva: Algoritm, 2005.

Svod trudov mestnykh komitetov po 49 guberniam Evropeiskoi Rossii. Denezhnoe obrashchenie St. Petersburg, 1903.

Tagantsev, N. S. *Perezhitoe.* Petrograd, 1919.

Terner, F. G. *Vospominania zhizni.* St. Petersburg, 1910.

The Lost Politburo Transcripts: From Collective Rule to Stalin's Dictatorship, edited by Paul R. Gregory and Norman Naimark. New Haven: Yale University Press, 2008.

"The Nakaz of Catherine the Great" (The Macartney-Dukes text). In *The Nakaz of Catherine the Great. Collected Texts*, edited by William E. Butler and Vladimir Tomsinov. Clark, NJ: Lawbook Exchange, 2009.

The Russian Provisional Government 1917. Documents selected and edited by Robert Paul Browder and Alexander F. Kerensky, vol. 2. Stanford, CA: Stanford University Press, 1961.

Timashev, S. I. "Zapiska predsedatelia pravleniia Gosudarstvennogo Banka S.I. Timasheva o denezhnom obrashchenii v Rossii v 1904–1907 ii. 12 fevralia 1907." *Istoricheskii Arkhiv*, 1956, no.3.

Timashev, S. I. Avtobiograficheskie zapiski, in A. L. Vychugzhanin, *S. I. Timashev: zhizn' i deiatelnost'.* Triumen': Slovo, 2006.

Trudy I Vserossiiskogo S'ezda Sovetov Narodnogo Khoziaistva, 25 maia—4 iunia 1918. Moskva: VSNKh, 1918.

Trudy II Vserossiiskogo s'ezda Sovetov Narodnogo Khoziaistva, 19 dekabria–27 dekabria 1918 g. Moskva: VSNKh, 1918.

Trudy mestnykh komitetov o nyzhdakh selskokhoziastvennoi promyshlennosti. Mogilevskaia guberniia, St. Petersburg, 1903.

Trudy mestnykh komitetov o nyzhdakh selskokhoziastvennoi promyshlennosti. Tulskaia guberniia, St. Petersburg, 1903

Trudy mestnykh komitetov o nyzhdakh selskokhoziastvennoi promyshlennosti. Smolenskaia guberniia, St. Petersburg, 1903.

Trudy mestnykh komitetov o nyzhdakh selskokhoziastvennoi promyshlennosti. Vladimirskaia guberniia, St. Petersburg, 1903.

Trudy mestnykh komitetov o nyzhdakh selskokhoziastvennoi promyshlennosti. Kievskaia guberniia, St. Petersburg, 1903.

Trudy mestnykh komitetov o nyzhdakh selskokhoziastvennoi promyshlennosti. Simbirskaia guberniia, St. Petersburg, 1903.

Trudy mestnykh komitetov o nyzhdakh selskokhoziastvennoi promyshlennosti. Tverskaia guberniia, St. Petersburg, 1903.

Trudy Vserossiiskogo s'ezda zaveduiushchikh finotdelami. Plenarnye zasedaniia, Moskva: NKF, 1919.

Tsion, I. F. (Elie de Cyon). *M.Witte et les finances russes d'apres des documents officiels et inedits.* Paris, 1895.

Tsion, I. F. *Kuda vremenshchik Vitte vedet Rossiiu?* Paris, 1896.

Tugan-Baranovskii, M. I., *Bumazhnye dengi i metall.* Petrograd, 1917.

Turgenev, N. I. "Zapad na Severe. September 1813. Dnevniki N.I. Turgeneva." *Arkhiv bratiev Turgenevykh.* St. Petersburg, 1911, t.2.

Turgenev, N. I. *Opyt teorii nalogov.* St. Petersburg, 1818.

Turgenev, N. I. *Rossiia i russkie.* Moskva: OGI, 2001.

Tverdokhlebov, V. N. "Bumazhnye dengi i tovarnye tseny." *Vestnik Finansov,* no.4, 1917.

Ushakov, M. A. "Vospominaniia o besede s velikim kniazem." *Krasnyi Arkhiv,* 1923, no.4.

Uvarov, S. S. *Izbrannye trudy.* Moksva: ROSSPEN, 2010.

V-skii, I. "Politiko-ekonomicheskoe znachenie nekotorykh obshchestvennykh faktov. "Schetnaia edinitsa." *Ekonomicheskii Ukazatel'.* 1858, no. 26.

V. "Raboty po sozdaniiu gosudarstvennogo balansa." *Izvestiia NKF,* no.8, 1919

Valentinov (Volskii), N. V. *Novaia ekonomicheskaia politika i krizis partii posle smerti Lenina.* Moskva: Sovremennik, 1991.

Valuev, P. A. *Dnevnik, 1877–1884.* Petrograd, 1919.

Valuev, P. A. *Ekonomicheskie i finansovye zametki.* St. Petersburg, 1881.

Vasiliev, V. P. *Assignatsii-den'gi.* St. Petersburg, 1887.

Veisberg, R. E. *Den'gi i tseny (podpolnyi rynok v period "voennogo kommunizma").* Moskva: Izd-vo Gosplana, 1925.

Veliaminov, N. A. "Vstrechi i znakomstva." *S.Yu. Vitte (Gosudarstvennye deiateli Rossii glazami sovremennikov),* edited by I.V. Lukoianov. St. Petersburg: Pushkinskii fond, 2018.

Vernadsky, I. "Veksel'nyi kurs i torgovyi balans." *Ekonomicheskii Ukazatel',* 16 (1860).

Bibliography

Vessel', N. Kh. *Otchego Gosudarstvennyi Bank ne uprochil kreditnoi denezhnoi sistemy i kak ee uprochit'?* St. Petersburg, 1893.

Viazemskii, P. A. *Zapisnye knizhki (1813–1848).* Moskva: AN SSSR, 1963.

Virst [Wurst], F. G. *Ob uchrezhdenii Assignatsionnogo i Zaemnogo banka dlia spospeshestvovaniia narodnomu khoziaistvu, izdano st.sovetnikom i redaktorom po kommertsii v Komissii sostavleniia zakonov F.G. Virstom.* St. Petersburg, 1808.

Virst [Wurst], F. G. *Rassuzhdenie o nekotorykh predmetakh zakonodatel'stva i upravleniia finansami i kommertsiei Rossiiskoi imperii,* 1807.

Vitte, S. Iu. *Sobranie sochinenii i dokumentalnykh materialov,* vols. 1–5. Moskva: Nauka, 2006.

Vitte, S. Yu. "Vsepoddanneiishii doklad ministra finansov o gosudarstvennoi rospisi dokhodov i raskhodov na 1899 god." *Vestnik Finansov* 1 (1899).

Vitte, S. Yu. "Vsepoddanneiishii doklad ministra finansov o gosudarstvennoi rospisi dokhoddov i raskhodov na 1900 god." *Vestnik Finansov* 1 (1900).

Vitte, S. Yu. "Vsepoddanneishii doklad ministra finansov ot 26 noiabria 1898 goda o vvedenii v VKF odnoobraznoi s ostalnoi Imperiiei monetnoi sistemy." *Materialy po vorposu o denezhnom obrashchenii v Velikov Kniazhestve Finliandskom.* St. Petersburg, 1900.

Voitinskii, I. S. *Minimal'naia zarabotnaia plata.* Petrograd, 1917.

Voprosy gosudarstvennogo khoziaistva i buidzhetnogo prava. St. Petersburg, 1907.

"Vospominaniia ob Oktiabr'skom perevorote." *Proletarskaia revolitsiia* 19 (1922).

VSNKH. Finansovo-Schetnyi Otdel. Ego zadachi i deiiatelnost'. Moskva: VSNKh, 1919.

Vtoroi Vserossiiskii promyshlennyi s'ezd v Moksve 3–5 avgusta 1917. Stenograficheskii otchet o pervom plenarnom zasedanii s'ezda. Moskva: Tip. T-va Riabushinskikh, 1917.

Vyshnegradskii, I. A. "Zapiska I.A. Vyshnegradskogo Aleksandru III "Ob izmenenii finansovogo upravlenia." In *Sud'by Rossii. Doklady i zapiski gosudarstvennykh deiatelei imperatoram o problemakh ekonomicheskogo razvitiia strany.* St. Petersburg: Liki Rossii, 1999.

"Vysochaishee postanovlenie on 8 noiabria 1865 goda o metallicheskoi monete kak edistvenno zakonno deistvitelnoi v Finlandii." *Materialy po voprosu o denezhnom obrashchenii v Velikom Kniazhestve Finliandskom,* St. Petersburg, 1900.

Wolowski, Louis. "Les finances de la Russie." *Revue de Deux Mondes* 2 (1864).

Yankevich, Ya. I. *O podniatii kursa kreditnogo rublia.* St. Petersburg, 1884.

Yasinskii, Ieronim. *Roman moei zhizni. Kniga vospominanii.* Leningrad: Gos. izdatelstvo, 1926.

Yasnopolskii, L. N. "Gosudarstvennyi Bank." In *Voprosy gosudarstvennogo khoziaistva i biudzhetnogo prava,* edited by P. D. Dolgorukov and I. I. Petrunkevich. St. Petersburg, 1907.

Zakavkazskii finansovo-statisticheskii sbornik, 1918–1923, ch.1. Tiflis: [no publisher], 1924.

"Zametka po povodu nastoiashchei voiny." *Slovo,* January 1878.

"Zapiska ministra finansov o gosudarstvennykh dokhodakh i raskhodakh na 1814 g ot 31 oktiabria 1813 g." *Sbornik istoricheskikh materialov izvlechennykh iz Arkhiva sobstvennoi EIV kantseliarii.* Vyp.1 St. Petersburg, 1876; Vyp.3. St. Petersburg, 1890.

Zheleznov, V. Ya. "Rol' deneg v tovaroobmene." *K teorii deneg i ucheta.* Moskva: [no publisher], 1922.

Zhizn' i voennye deianiia general-feldmarshala svetleishego kniazia Mikhaila Larionovicha Golenishcheva-Kutuzova Smolenskogo. St. Petersburg, 1813–14.

Zhukov, Akinf. *Nachalnye osnovaniia russkogo selskogo khoziastva.* Moskva, 1837.

Zhurnaly zasedanii Vremennogo pravitelstva, Mart-Oktiabr' 1917, vol. 1. Moskva: ROSSPEN, 2001.

Zverev, A. G. *Zapiski ministra.* Moskva: Politizdat, 1973.

SECONDARY SOURCES

A Cultural History of Money. Bill Maurer, general editor. London: Bloomsbury Academic, 2019.

Altman, Oscar L. "Russian Gold and the Ruble," *Staff Papers* (International Monetary Fund), April, 1960, vol.7, no.3.

Alulshin P. V. *P. A. Viazemskii, Vlast i obshchestvo v doreformennoi Rossii.* Moskva: Pamiatniki istoricheskoi mysli. 2001.

Alyokhov, A. V. "Amerika—Rossiia: kreditnye bilety 1866 goda," *Numizmaticheskii almanakh* 1 (2001).

Anan'ich, B. V. "Finansovyi krizis tsarizma 1904–1905 gg." *Trudy Leningradskogo Otdelenia Instituta Istorii AN SSSR*, vol. 8. Leningrad, Nauka, 1967.

Anan'ich, B. V. "Russian Military Expenditures in the Russo-Japanese War, 1904-5." In *The Russo-Japanese War in Global Perspective: World War Zero*, edited by John W. Steinberg et al. Leiden: Brill, 2005

Anan'ich, B. V. *Rossiia i mezhdunarodnyi kapital, 1897–1914. Ocherki istorii finansovykh otnosheni.* Leningrad: Izd-vo AN SSSR, 1970.

Anan'ich, B. V. and Ganelin, R. Sh. *S. Iu. Vitte—memuarist.* St. Petersburg: SPbF IRI RAN, 1994.

Anan'ich, B. V. and Ganelin, R. Sh. "I. A. Vyshnegradskii i S. Yu. Witte—korrespondenty "Moskovskikh vedomostei"." *Problemy obschestvennoi mysli i ehkonomicheskaya politika Rossii XIX-XX vekov: Sbornik statei*, Leningrad: Nauka, 1972.

Anan'ich, B. V., and Ganelin., R. Sh., *Serguei Iulievich Vitte i ego vremia.* St. Petersburg: Dmitry Bulanin, 1999.

Ansberg, O., Yu. Bazulin, S. Belozerov, et al. *Ocherki po istorii finansovoi nauki: Sankt-Peterburgskii universitet.* Moskva: Proekt, 2009.

Al'tshuller, M. G. *Beseda liubitelei russkogo slova. U istokov russkogo slavianofil'stva.* Moskva: NLO, 2007.

Atlas, Z. V. *Sotsialisticheskaia denezhnaia sistema.* Moskva: Finansy, 1969.

Bandelj, Nina, Frederick F. Wherry, and Viviana A. Zelizer, eds. *Money Talks: Explaining How Money Really Works*. Princeton: Princeton University Press, 2017.

Barkai, Haim. "The Macro-Economics of Tsarist Russia in the Industrialization Era: Monetary Development, the Balance of Payments and the Gold Standard." *Journal of Economic History* 33 (June 1973).

Barnett, Vincent. "Calling Up the Reserves: Keynes, Tugan-Baranovsky, and Russian War Finance." *Europe-Asia Studies* 53, no. 1 (2001).

Bauer, A. A. "Mal'tsovskie denezhnye surrogaty." *S.I. Mal'tsov i istoriia razvitiia mal'tsovskogo promyshlennogo raoina*. Briansk: BGTU, 1998.

Bauer, N. P. *Istoriia drevnerusskikh denezhnykh system, IX v.–1535*. Moskva: Russkoe Slovo, 2014.

Beliaev, S. G. *Bark i finansovaia politika Rossii 1914–1917*. St. Petersburg: Izd-vo Sankt-Petersburgskogo Un-ta, 2002.

Beliaev, S. G., "Politika S.Iu. Vitte v oblasti kredita i bankovskoi sistemy Rossii." S. Yu.Vitte, *Sobranie sochinenii i dokumentalnykh materialov v piati tomakh*. T. 3, kn.3. Moskva: Nauka, 2006.

Bernatzky, Michael. "Monetary Policy." In *Russian Public Finance during the War*. New Haven: Yale University Press, 1928.

Bernholz, Peter. "Political Parties and Paper Money Inflation in Sweden during the 18th Century." *Kyklos* 54, 2001, fasc.2/3.

Bien, David. "Old Regime Origins of Democratic Liberty." In *The French Idea of Freedom: The Old Regime and the Declaration of Rights of 1789*. Stanford, CA: Stanford University Press, 1994.

Birdal, Murat. *The Political Economy of Ottoman Public Debt. Insolvency and European Financial Control in the Late Nineteenth Century*. London: I. B. Tauris, 2010.

Bogdanov, A. A. *Den'gi, kotorykh ne bylo. Iz istorii proektirovaniia bumazhnykh deneg v Rossii*. St. Petersburg: Goznak, 2020.

Bokarev, Yu. P. "Rubl' v epokhu voin i revoliutsii." *Russkii rubl'. Dva veka istorii, XIX–XX v*. Moskva: Progress-Akademiia, 1994.

Bordo, Michael D., and Eugene N. White. "A Tale of Two Currencies: British and French Finance during the Napoleonic Wars." *Journal of Economic History* 51, no.2 (June 1991).

Bordo, Michael D., and Anna J Schwartz. "The Operation of the Specie Standard: Evidence for Core and Peripheral Countries, 1880-1990." *Currency Convertibility: The Gold Standard and Beyond*, edited by Jorge Braga de Macedo, Barry Eichengreen, and Jaime Reis. New York: Routledge, 1996.

Bordo, Michael D., and Anna J. Schwartz, eds. *A Retrospective on the Classical Gold Standard, 1821–1931*. Chicago: University of Chicago Press, 1984.

Bordo, Michael D., and Finn E. Kydland. *The Gold Standard as a Rule*. NBER working paper series. No. 3367. Cambridge, MA: National Bureau of Economic Research, 1990.

Bordo, Michael D., and Hugh Rockoff. "The Gold Standard as a 'Good Housekeeping Seal of Approval.'" *Journal of Economic History* 56, no. 2. Papers Presented at the Fifty-Fifth Annual Meeting of the Economic History Association, June 1996.

Borisova, L. V. *Trudovye otnosheniia v Sovetskoi Rossii (1918–1924).* Moskva: Sobranie, 2006.

Borovoi, S. Ya. *Kredit i banki Rossii.* Moskva: Gosfinizdat, 1958.

Bozherianov, I. N. *Graf Egor Frantsevich Kankrin, ego zhizn', literaturnye trudy i dvadtsatiletniaia deiatel'nost' upravlenia Ministerstvom Finansov.* St. Petersburg, 1897.

Brewer, John. *The Sinews of Power: War, Money, and the English State, 1688–1783.* Cambridge: Cambridge University Press, 1983.

Brown, Brendan. *Money Hard and Soft. On the International Currency Market.* New York: Wiley, 1978.

Budnitskii, O. V. *Den'gi russkoi emigratsii: Kolchakovskoe zoloto, 1918–1957.* Moskva: NLO, 2008.

Bugrov, A. V. "Gosudarstvennyi bank Rossiiskoi imperii: iz istorii melioratsionnogo kredita." *Den'gi i Kredit* 1 (2014).

Bugrov, A. V. *Kazennye Banki v Rossii 1754–1860.* Moskva: Tsentralnyi Bank RF, 2017.

Bukovetskii, A. I. "Svobodnaia nalichnost' i zolotoi zapas." *Monopolii i inostrannyi capital v Rossii.* Leningrad: Izd-vo AN SSSR, 1962.

Bukovetskii, A. I. "Kratkii obzor prepodavaniia finansovoi nauki i finansovogo prava v Peterburgskom (Petrogradskom) universitete v XIX—pervoi chetverti XX veka." *Vestnik Sankt-Peterburgskogo universiteta, Ser. 5. Ekonomika,* 1993, vyp. 1.

Camcastle, Cara. *More Moderate Side of Joseph de Maistre: Views on Political Liberty and Political Economy.* Montreal: McGill-Queen University Press, 2005.

Carr, E. H. *The Bolshevik Revolution 1917–1923,* vol. 2. New York: W. W. Norton, 1985.

Chernukha, V. G. *Vnutrenniaia politika tsarizma s serediny 50-kh do nachala 80-kh gg. XIX v.* Leningrad: Izd-vo AN SSSR, 1978.

Christian, David. "The Political Ideals of Michael Speransky." *Slavonic and East European Review* 54, no. 2 (Ap.il 1976).

Chudnov, I. A. *Denezhnaia reforma 1947 goda.* Moskva: ROSSPEN, 2018.

Clay, Christopher. *Gold for the Sultan: Western Bankers and Ottoman Finance 1856–1881: A Contribution to Ottoman and to International Financial History.* London: I. B. Tauris, 2000.

Cohen, Stephen F. *Bukharin and the Bolshevik Revolution: A Political Biography, 1888–1938.* New York: Oxford University Press, 1971.

Conway, Patrick. *Currency Proliferation: The Monetary Legacy of the Soviet Union.* Princeton, NJ: International Finance Section, Dept. of Economics, Princeton University, 1995.

Crisp, Olga. "Russian Financial Policy and the Gold Standard at the End of the Nineteenth Century." *Economic History Review,* new series,6, no.2 (1953).

Davies, R.W., and O. Khlevniuk. "Gosplan." In *Decision-making in the Stalinist Command Economy, 1932–37*, edited by E. A. Rees. New York: St. Martin's Press, 1997.

Davison, Roderic H. "The First Ottoman Experiment with Paper Money." In *Essays in Ottoman and Turkish History, 1774–1923*. Austin: University of Texas Press, 1990.

Davydov, A. Yu. *Meshochniki i diktatura v Rossii, 1917–1921*. St. Petersburg: Aleteiia, 2007.

Denisov, A. E. *Bumazhnye denezhnye znaki Rossii, 1769–1917*. Ch.1–3. Moskva: Numizmaticheskaia literatura, 2002–2004.

Desan, Christine. "The Constitutional Approach to Money." *Money Talks: Explaining How Money Really Works*, edited by Nina Bandelj, Frederick F. Wherry, and Viviana A. Zelizer. Princeton: Princeton University Press, 2017.

Desan, Christine. *Making Money: Coin, Currency, and the Coming of Capitalism*. Oxford: Oxford University Press, 2014.

Dickson, P. G. M. *The Financial Revolution: A Study in the Development of Public Credit*. London: Macmilan, 1967.

Ditiatovskii, I. D. "Malen'kie svideteli velikoi smuty." *Almanakh Obshchestva ROI*, kn. 3. Moskva, 2017.

Dodd, Nigel. *The Social Life of Money*. Princeton: Princeton University Press, 2016.

Dragan, O. V. "Gosudarstvennyi Bank i mery po stabilizatsii kursa rublia nakanune denezhnoi reformy 1897 g." In *Rossiia i Mir v kontse XIX—pervoi polovine XX v. Sbornik k 85-letiiu Borisa Vasilievicha Ananicha*. St. Petersburg: Liki Rossii, 2018.

Dragan, O. V. "Reforma Gosudarstvennnogo Banka 1892–1894: evropeiskii opyt i rossiiskaia praktika." *Ekonomicheskaia istoriia. Ezhegodnik, 2005*. Moskva: ROSSPEN, 2005.

Dragan, O. V. *Reforma Gosudarstvennogo Banka: tseli, proekty, resultaty. Konets 80kh—vtoraia polovina 90kh gg. XIX veka*. Dissertatsia na soiskanie stepeni kand ist.nauk. St. Petersburg: Sankt-Peterburgskii Institut Istorii RAN, 2008.

Eagly, Robert. "Monetary Policy and Politics in mid-Eighteenth Century Sweden." *Journal of Economic History* 29, no. 4 (December 1969): 739–757.

Eich, Stefan *The Currency of Politics: The Political Theory of Money from Aristotle to Keynes*. Princeton: Princeton University Press, 2022.

Eichengreen, Barry, and Marc Flandreau. "The Geography of the Gold Standard." *Currency Convertibility: The Gold Standard and Beyond*, edited by Jorge Braga de Macedo, Barry Eichengreen, and Jaime Reis. New York: Routledge, 1996.

Emery, Jacob. "Species of Legitimacy: The Rhetoric of Succession around Russian Coins." *Slavic Review* 75, no.1 (Spring 2016).

Engelstein, Laura. "Combined Underdevelopment: Discipline and the Law in Imperial and Soviet Russia." *American Historical Review* 98, no. 2 (1993).

Fan-Jung, N. "La reforme de la circulation monétaire en Russie." *Revue d'économie politique* 12, no.12 (1898).

Ferguson, Niall. *The Pity of War: Explaining World War I*. New York: Basic Books, 2001.

Fisk, Harvey. *The Inter-Ally Debts. An Analysis of War and Post-war Public Finance, 1914–1923*. New York: Bankers Trust Company, 1924.

Flandreau, Marc. "The French Crime 1873: An Essay on the Emergence of the International Gold Standard, 1870–1880." *Journal of Economic History* 56, no.4 (December 1996),

Flandreau, Marc. *The Glitter of Gold: France, Bimetallism, and the Emergence of the International Gold Standard, 1848–1873*. Oxford: Oxford University Press, 2004.

Foucault, Michel. *The Order of Things. An Archaeology of the Human Sciences*. New York: Routledge, 2002.

Frank, Carole. *The Genoa Conference: European Diplomacy, 1921–22*. Chapel Hill: University of North Carolina Press, 1984.

Frieden, Jeffrey. *Currency Politics. The Political Economy of Exchange Rate Policy*, Princeton: Princeton University Press, 2015.

Friedman, Milton. "Real and Pseudo Gold Standards." *Journal of Law & Economics* 4 (October 1961).

Friedman, Milton. "The Crime of 1873." *Journal of Political Economy*. 98, no. 6 (December, 1990).

Ganelin, R. Sh. "Gosudarstvennaia Duma i antisemitskie tsirkuliary 1915–1916 gg." *Vestnik Evreiskogo Universiteta v Moskve* 3, no. 10 (1995).

Garvy, George. "The Origins of Lenin's Views on the Role of Banks in the Socialist Transformation of Society." *History of Political Economy* 4, no. 1 (1972).

Gattrell, Peter, and Mark Harrison "The Russian and Soviet Economies in Two World Wars: A Comparative View." *Economic History Review*, new series, 46, no. 3 (August1993).

Gattrell, Peter. *Russia's First World War. A Social and Economic History*. Hoboken: Taylor and Francis, 2014.

Gimpelson E. G. *Sovetskie upravlentsy, 1917–1920*. Moskva: IRI RAN, 1998

Gimpelson, E. G. *"Voennyi Kommunizm": Politika, Praktika, Ideologiia* Moskva: Mysl', 1973.

Gimpelson, E. G. *Sovetskii rabochii klass, 1917–1920*. Moskva: Nauka, 1974.

Gindin, A. M. *Kak bolsheviki natsionalizirovali chastnye banki*. Moskva: Gosfinizdat, 1962.

Gindin, A. M. *Kak bolsheviki ovladeli Gosudarstvennym Bankom*. Moskva: Gosfinizdat, 1961.

Gindin, I. F. "S.Iu. Vitte kak gosudarstvennyi deiatel'." *Serguei Iulievich Vitte—gosudarstvennyi deiatel', reformator, ekonomist (k stopiatidesiteletiiu so dnia rozhdeniia)*. Moskva: In-t Ekonomiki, 1999.

Gindin, I. F. "Neustavnye ssudy Gosudarstvennogo Banka i ekonomicheskaia politika tsarskogo pravitelstva," *Istoricheskie Zapiski* 35 (1950).

Godsey, William D. *The Sinews of Habsburg Power. Lower Austria in a Fiscal-Military State*. Oxford: Oxford University Press, 2018.

Goland, Yu. M. "Currency Regulation in the NEP period," *Europe-Asia studies* 46, no. 8 (2007).

Goland, Yu. M. *Diskussii ob ekonomicheskoi politike v gody denezhnoi reformy 1921–1924.* Moskva: Ekonomika, 2006.

Gooding, John. "The Liberalism of Michael Speransky." *Slavonic and East European Review* 64, no. 3 (July 1986).

Graeber, David. *The Debt: The First 5,000 Years.* Brooklyn: Melville House Publishing, 2014.

Gray, Richard T. *Money Matters: Economics and the German Cultural Imagination, 1770–1850.* Seattle: University of Washington Press, 2008.

Graziosi, Andrea. "G. L. Piatakov (1890-1937): A Mirror of Soviet History." *Harvard Ukrainian Studies* 16, nos.1–2 (June 1992),

Gregory, Paul, and Aleksei Tikhonov. "Central Planning and Unintended Consequences: Creating the Soviet Financial System, 1930–1939." *Journal of Economic History* (60, no. 4 (December 2000).

Gregory, Paul. "Russian Monetary Policy and Industrialization, 1861–1913." *Journal of Economic History* 36 (December 1976).

Grinev, A. V. *Aliaska pod krylom dvuglavogo orla (rossiiskaia kolonizatsiia Novogo Sveta v kontekste otechestvennoi i mirovoi istorii).* Moskva: Akademia, 2016.

Gross, Stephen. "Confidence and Gold: German War Finance, 1914-1918." *Central European History* 42 (2009).

Grossman, Gregory. "Gold and the Sword: Money in the Soviet Command Economy." *Industrialization in Two Systems. Essays in Honor of Alexander Gerschenkron*, edited by Henry Rosovsky. New York: Wiley, 1966.

Grudina A. D. "Organizatsiia materialnoi podderzhki semei riadovogo sostava Pervoi mirovoi voiny i ee vliianie na razvitie protestnykh nastroenii v Petrograde." *Nauchnyi Dialog* 7 (2018).

Hacking, Ian. "Making Up People." *Reconstructing Individualism,* edited by P. Heller, M. Sosna, and D. Wellberry. Stanford, CA: Stanford University Press, 1986.

Hai-Nyzhnyk, Pavlo. "Dostavka dlia uriadu Direktori Ukrainskikh groshei s Nimetchiny i zagibel' Vitovskogo (1919)." *Gurzhivski historichni chitannia. Sbornik nauchnikh pratz,* Cherkasy, 2009.

Hai-Nyzhnyk, Pavlo. *Finansova politika uriadu Ukrain'skoi Derzhavi Get'mana Pavla Skoropads'kogo (29 kvitnia—14 grudnia 1918 r).* Kyiv [no publisher], 2001.

Herger, Nils. "An Empirical Assessment of the Swedish Bullionist Controversy." *Scandinavian Journal of Economics* 122, no. 3 (2020).

Hoch, Steven. "The Banking Crisis, Peasant Reform, and Economic Development in Russia, 18571861." *American Historical Review* 96, no. 3 (June 1991).

Holzman, Franklyn D., "The Ruble Exchange Rate and Soviet Foreign Trade Pricing Policies, 1929–1961." *American Economic Review* 58, no. 4 (1968).

Horn, Martin. *Britain, France, and the Financing of the First World War.* Montreal: McGill-Queen's University Press, 2002.

Hsu, Chia Yin. "The "Color" of Money: The Ruble, Competing Currencies, and Conceptions of Citizenship in Manchuria and the Russian Far East, 1890s–1920s." *Russian Review* 73, no. 1 (January 2014).

Ironside, Kristy. *A Full-Value Ruble: The Promise of Prosperity in the Postwar Soviet Union.* Cambridge, MA: Harvard University Press, 2021.

Iroshnikov, M. I. *Sozdanie sovetskogo tsentralnogo gosudarstvennogo apparata*, Leningrad: Nauka, 1967.

Iukht, A. I. *Russkie den'gi ot Petra Velikogo do Aleksandra I.* Moskva: Finansy i Statistika, 1994.

Ivanova, A. S. *Magaziny "Beriozka." Paradoksy potrebleniia v pozdnem SSSR.* Moskva: NLO, 2018.

Kahan, Arcadius. *The Plow, the Hammer, and the Knout. An Economic History of Eighteenth-century Russia.* Chicago: University of Chicago Press, 1985.

Kahan, Arcadius. "Government Policies and the Industrialization of Russia." *Journal of Economic History* 27 (December 1967).

Kahan, Arcadius. "The Costs of "Westernization" in Russia: The Gentry and the Economy in the Eighteenth Century." *Slavic Review* 25, no. 1 (March 1966).

Kaiser, Thomas. "Money, Despotism, and Public Opinion in Early Eighteenth-century France: John Law and the Debate on Royal Credit." *Journal of Modern History*, 63 (March 1991).

Kelner, V. E. "Politicheskoe biuro pri evreiiskikh deputatakh IV Gosudarstvennoi Dumy." *Peterburgskii Istoricheskii Zhurnal* 1 (2015).

Kennan, George F. *The Decline of Bismarck's European Order: Franco-Russian Relations, 1875–1890.* Princeton: Princeton University Press, 1980.

Khlevniuk, O. V. "Finansiruia voinu. Formirovamnie gosudarsvennogo biudzheta SSSR v 1941–1945 gg." *Rossiiskaia Istoriia* 3 (2020).

Khlevniuk, O. V. " 'Tolkachi,' Parallel'nye stimuly v stalinskoi ekonomicheskoi sisteme 1930-e –1950-e gody." *Cahiers du monde russe* 59, nos. 2–3 (2018).

Khodiakov, M. V. "Iz'atie iz denezhnogo obrashcheniia i unichtozhenie kreditnykh biletov v Sankt-Peterburge v nachale XX veka." *Trudy Istoricheskogo fakulteta Sankt-Peterburgskogo universiteta.* St. Petersburg: SPbGU, 2010.

Khodiakov, M. V. "Kerenki" i ikh izgotovlenie v Petrograde v 1917 godu." In *Istoria, Universitet, Istorik.* St. Petersburg: SPbGU, 2014.

Khodiakov, M. V. *Den'gi Revoliutsii i Grazhdanskoi voiny.* St. Petersburg: SPbGU, 2018.

Khrolenok, S. F. *Zolotopromyshlennost' Sibiri (1832–1917). Istoriko-ekonomicheskii ocherk.* Irkutsk: Izd-vo Irkutskogo universiteta, 1999.

Koenker, Diane. *Moscow Workers and the 1917 Revolution.* Princeton: Princeton University Press, 1981.

Kolonitskii, B. I. "The Desacralization of the Monarchy: Rumours and the Downfall of the Romanov." In *Interpreting the Russian Revolution: The Language and Symbols of 1917.* New Haven: Yale University Press, 1999.

Kopelev, D.N, "Dzon Lo, frantsuzskie kolonialnye proekty epokhi Regentstva i Petr Velikii." *Prirodnoe i kulturnoe nasledie: mezhdistsiplinarnye issledovaniia, sokhranenie i razvitie.* St. Petersburg: RGPU im. A. I. Gertsena, 2017.

Korchmina, Elena. "Peer Pressure: The Puzzle of Aristocrats' Tax Compliance in Early Nineteenth-century Moscow." *Economic History Review* 10 (2021).

Korkina, T. D. "Traktat Dzhona Lo "Den'gi i kupechestvo": Istoriia russkogo perevoda 1720 i tekstologicheskii analiz spiskov." *Acta Linguistica Petropolitana. Trudy instituta lingvisticheskikh issledovanii* 16, no. 3 (2020).

Kotkin, Stephen. *Armageddon Averted. The Soviet Collapse, 1970–2000.* New York: Oxford University Press, 2001.

Kotkin, Stephen. *Stalin. The Paradoxes of Power, 1878–1928.* New York: Penguin Books, 2014.

Kotsonis, Yanni. *Making Peasants Backward: Agricultural Cooperatives and the Agrarian Question in Russia, 1861–1914.* New York: Palgrave Macmillan, 1999.

Kotsonis, Yanni. *States of Obligation: Taxes and Citizenship in the Russian Empire and Early Soviet Republic.* Toronto: University of Toronto Press, 2014.

Kredit i banki v Rossii do nachala XX veka. Sankt-Peterburg i Moskva. St. Petersburg: Izd-vo S.-Peterburgskogo universiteta, 2005.

Kuusterä, Antti, and Juha Tarkka. *Bank of Finland: 200 Years. I. Imperial Cashier to Central Bank.* Helsinki: Suomen Pankki—Bank of Finland and Otava Publishing, 2011.

Kwass, Michael. *Privilege and the Politics of Taxations in Eeighteenth-century France.* Cambridge: Cambridge University Press, 2000.

Laue, Theodore von. *Sergei Witte and the Industrialization of Russia.* New York: Atheneum 1969.

Lebedev, S. K. *S.-Peterburgskii mezhdunarodnyi kommercheskii bank vo vtoroi polovine XIX veka: evropeiskie i russkie sviazi.* St. Petersburg: ROSSPEN, 2003.

Levy, Jonathan. *Ages of American Capitalism: A History of the United States.* New York: Random House, 2021.

Lizunov, P. V. "Birzhevaia spekuliatsiia na kurse kreditnogo rublia i mery protivodeistviia ei Ministerstva finansov." *Trudy Istoricheskogo fakul'teta Sankt-Peterburgskogo universiteta* 5 (2011).

Lizunov, P. V. "Neudachnoe nachalo "novoi ery" russkikh finansov." *Stranitsy russkoi istorii. Problemy, sobytiia, liudi. Sbornik statei v chest' B.V. Ananicha.* St. Petersburg: Liki Rossii, 2003.

Lizunov, P. V. "Regulirovanie denezhnogo obrashcheniia. Vypusk vnutrennikh vyigryshnykh zaimov 1864 i 1866 g." In *Gosudarsvtennyi Bank Rossiiskoi Imperii,* edited by Yu.A. Petrov and S.V. Tatarinov, vol. 1. Moskva: Tsentralnyi Bank Rossii, 2010.

Lizunov, P. V. *Sankt-Peterburgskaia birzha i rossiiskii rynok tsennykh bumag.* St. Petersburg: Blitz, 2004.

Lotman, Yu. M., and Uspenskii, B. A. "Spory o iazyke nachala XIX veka kak fakt russkoi kul'tury." *Istoriia i tipologiia russkoi kultury.* St. Petersburg: Iskusstvo-SPb, 2002.

Luckett, Thomas. "Imaginary Currency and Real Guillotines: The Intellectual Origins of the Financial Terror in France." *Historical Reflections/Réflexions Historique* 31, no.1 (Spring 2005).

Luehrmann, Sonja. "Russian Colonialism and the Asiatic Mode of Production: (Post-) Soviet Ethnography Goes to Alaska." *Slavic Review* 64, no. 4 (Winter, 2005).

Lukoianov, I. V. "S. F. Sharapov i S.Yu.Witte." *Otechestvennaia istoriia i istoricheskaia mysl' Rossii XIX—XX vekov.* St. Petersburg: Nestor-Istoriia, 2006.

Makarov, V. V. *Obshchestvenno-politicheskaia deiatelnost' A.I. Shingareva.* Diss. na soiskanie stepeni kand. ist. nauk. Voronezh, 2003.

Makushev, A. A. *Predprinimatelskaia deiatelnost' Maltsovykh vo vtoroi polovine XVIII—nachale XX veka: industrialnoe nasledie.* Saransk: Mordovskoe knizhnoe izd-vo, 2006.

Malle, Silvana. *The Economic Organization of War Communism, 1918–1921.* Cambridge: Cambridge University Press, 1985.

Mannheim, Karl. "Conservative Thought." *From Karl Mannheim,* edited with an introduction by K. H. Wolff. New York: Oxford University Press, 1971.

Markevich, Andrei, and Mark Harrison. "Great War, Civil War, and Recovery: Russia's National Income, 1913–1928." *Journal of Economic History* 71, no.3 (September 2011).

Marks, Steven. *Road to Power: The Trans-Siberian Railroad and the Colonization of Asian Russia, 1850–1917.* Ithaca, NY: Cornell University Press, 1991.

Marnei, L. P. *D. A. Guryev i finansovaia politika Rossii v nachale XIX veka.* Moskva: Indrik, 2009.

Martin, Felix. *Money: The Unauthorised Biography.* London: Bodley Head, 2013.

Mel'nikov, M. V. "Sud'ba zolotogo rublia. Spory mezhdu storonnikami i protivnikami denezhnoi reformy S.Iu. Vitte, 1895-1897 gg." *Novyi istoricheskii vestnik* 1, no. 23 (2010).

Mel'nikova, A. S. *Russkie monety on Ivana Groznogo do Petra Pervogo.* Moskva: Finansy i Statistika, 1989.

Metzler, Mark. *Lever of Empire. The International Gold Standard and the Crisis of Liberalism in Prewar Japan.* Berkeley: University of California Press, 2006.

Michelson, Alexander M., Paul Apostol, and Michael Bernatzky. *Russian Public Finance during the War.* New Haven: Yale University Press,1928.

Mil'china, Vera, and Alexander Ospovat. *Kommentarii k knige Astolfa de Kustina "Rossiia v 1839 godu."* St. Petersburg: Kriga, 2008.

Miller, Edward S. "Japan's Other Victory: Overseas Financing of the Russo-Japanese War." *The Russo-Japanese War in Global Perspective: World War Zero,* edited by John W. Steinberg et al. Leiden: Brill, 2005.

Monday, Chris, "Kameralizm kak istochnik nauchnogo apparata Kankrina," in E. F. Kankrin, *Mirovoe bogatstvo i natsional'naia ekonomika,* Moskva: Delo, 2018.

Monetary Standards in the Periphery: Paper, Silver, and Gold, 1854–1933, edited by Pablo Martin Aceña and Jaime Reis. New York: St. Martin's Press, 2000.

Morozan, V. V. *Istoriia bankovskogo dela v Rossii, vtoraia polovina XVIII—pervaia polovina XIX veka*. St. Petersburg: Kriga, 2004.

Nemanov, L. M. *Finansovaia politika Ukrainy 7 noiabria 1917—4 fevralia 1919*. Moskva: Koop. izd-vo, 1919.

Nikolaev, A. B. *Dumskaia Revoliutsiia. 27 fevralia—3 marta 1917*. Vol. 1. St. Petersburg: Izdatel'stvo RGPU im. A. I. Gertsena, 2017.

Nikolaev, M. G. "Bankir voleiu partii: stranitsy biografii A.P. Spunde (1892–1962)." *Ezhegodnik Ekonomicheskaia Istoriia 2019*. Moskva: ROSSPEN, 2020.

Nikolaev, M. G. "Koshelek "na udachu": K istorii odnogo iz novopriobretennykh eksponatov muzeino-ekspozitsionnogo fonda Banka Rossii." *Den'gi i Kredit* 50 (2017).

North, Douglas C., and Barry R. Weingast. "Constitutions and Commitment: The Evolution of Institutions Governing Public Choice in 17th-century England." *Journal of Economic History* 49, no. 4 (1989).

Nussbaum, Arthur. "The Legal Status of Gold." *American Journal of Comparative Law* 3, no. 3 (Summer, 1954).

Ögren, Anders, and Lars Fredrik Øksendal, eds. *The Gold Standard Peripheries. Monetary Policy, Adjustment and Flexibility in a Global Setting*. New York: Palgrave Macmillan, 2012.

Osokina, Elena. *Zoloto dlia industrializatsii: Torgsin. Istoriia Stalinizma*. Moskva: ROSSPEN, 2009.

Owen, Thomas C. "The Moscow Merchants and the Public Press, 1858–1868." *Jahrbuecher fuer Geschichte Osteuropas* 23, 1975, ch.1.

Owen, Thomas C. *Dilemmas of Russian Capitalism. Fedor Chizhov and Corporate Enterprise in the Railroad Age*. Cambridge, MA: Harvard University Press, 2005.

Palyi, Melchior. *The Twilight of Gold, 1914–1936*. Chicago: H. Regnery, 1972.

Pamuk, Sevket. *A Monetary History of the Ottoman Empire*. Cambridge: Cambridge University Press, 2000.

Petrov, Yu. A. "Nemetskie predprinimateli v dorevoliutsionnoi Moskve: torgovyi dom "Vogau i Ko." *Ekonomicheskaia Istoriia, Ezhegodnik 2000*, Moskva: ROSSPEN, 2001.

Pintner, Walter M. "Government and Industry during the Ministry of Count Kankrin, 1823–1844." *Slavic Review* 23, no. 1 (March 964).

Pogrebetskii, A. I. *Denezhnoe obrashchenie i denezhnye znaki Dal'nego Vostoka za period voiny i revoliutsii (1914–1924)*. Kharbin: Ob-vo izucheniia Man'chzhurskogo kraia, 1924.

Pogrebinskii, A. P. "Stroitel'stvo zheleznykh dorog i finansovaia politika tsarisma (60–90 e gody XIX veka)." *Istoricheskie zapiski* 47 (1954).

Poovey, Mary. *Genres of the Credit Economy: Mediating Value in Eighteenth- and Nineteenth-Century Britain*. Chicago: University of Chicago Press, 2008.

Porter, Jillian. *Economies of Feeling: Russian Literature under Nicholas I*. Evanston, IL: Northwestern University Press, 2017.

Pravilova, Ekaterina. "River of Empire: Geopolitics, Irrigation, and the Amu Darya in the Late 19th Century." In *Cahiers d'Asie Central* 17–18 (2009).

Pravilova, Ekaterina. "Truth, Facts, and Authenticity in Russian Imperial Jurisprudence and Historiography." In *Kritika: Explorations in Russian and Eurasian History* 21, no. 1 (Winter 2020).

Pravilova, Ekaterina. A *Public Empire: Property and the Quest for the Common Good in Imperial Russia*. Princeton: Princeton University Press, 2014.

Predtechenskii, A. V. *Ocherki obshchestvenno-politicheskoi istorii Rossii v pervoi chetverti XIX veka*. Moskva: Izd-vo Akademii Nauk SSSR, 1957.

Proskuriakova, N. A. *Zemel'nye banki Rossiiskoi Imperii*. Moskva: ROSSPEN, 2002.

Quinn, Stephen, and William Roberds. "A Policy Framework for the Bank of Amsterdam, 1736–1791." *Journal of Economic History* 79, no. 3 (September 2019).

Radziszewski, Henryk. *Bank Polski*. Poznan: Ostoja, 1919.

Raeff, Marc. *Michael Speransky: A Statesman of Russia*. The Hague: M. Nijhoff, 1969.

Razmanova, N. A. "Dmitrii Petrovich Bogolepov v Narkomfine v 1917–1918 godakh." *Vestnik Finansovoi Akademii* 2 (2001).

Rieber, Alfred. *Merchants and Entrepreneurs in Imperial Russia*. Chapel Hill: University of North Carolina Press, 1982.

Rieber, Alfred. *The Imperial Russian Project. Autocratic Politics, Economic Development, and Social Fragmentation*. Toronto: University of Toronto Press, 2017.

Ritter, Gretchen. *Goldbugs and Greenbacks. The Antimonopoly Tradition and the Politics of Finance in America, 1865–1896*. Cambridge: Cambridge University Press, 1997.

Rogova, O., and L. Moiseeva. "Denezhnaia sistema: Mekhanizm i napravlenie stabilizatsii." *Voprosy Ekonomiki* 7 (1990).

Rose, Carol M. "Property as the Keystone Right?" *Notre Dame Law Review* 71, no. 3 (1996).

Rosenberg, William. "The Democratization of Russia's Railroads in 1917." *American Historical Review* 86, no. 5 (December 1981).

Samokhvalov, F. M. *Sovety narodnogo khoziaistva v 1917–1932 gg*. Moskva: Nauka, 1964.

Sanchez-Sibony, Oscar. "Global Money and Bolshevik Authority: The NEP as the First Socialist Project." *Slavic Review* 78, no 3 (2019).

Sapogovskaia, L. V. "Zoloto v politike Rossii (1917–1921)." *Voprosy Istorii* 6 (2004).

Sapogovskaia, L. V. "Zolotye resursy SSSR v voenno-ekonomicheskom protivostoianii 1939–1945 godov (postanovka problemy)." *Voprosy Istorii* 5 (2005).

Schoppe, Seigfried G., and Michel Vale. "Changes in the Function of Gold within the Soviet Foreign Trade System since 1945–46." *Soviet and Eastern European Foreign Trade* 15, no. 3 (Fall 1979).

Scott, James C. *Weapons of the Weak: Everyday Forms of Peasant Resistance*. New Haven: Yale University Press, 1985.

Sementkovskii, R. I. *E. F. Kankrin: Ego zhizn' i gosudarstvennaia deiatelnost'*. St. Petersburg, 1893.

Semevskii, V. I. "Padenie Speranskogo." *Otechestvennaia voina i russkoe obshchestvo*, vol. 2. Moskva, 1911.

Shell, Marc. *The Economy of Literature*. Baltimore: Johns Hopkins University Press, 1978.

Sherratt, Simon. *Credit and Power: The Paradox at the Heart of the British National Debt*. London: Routledge, 2021.

Shevliakov, M. V. "Na rozyske. Po rasskazam byvshego nachal'nikia Sankt-Peterburgskoi sysknoi politsii I. D. Putilina." *Ivan Putilin. Russkii Sherlock Holmes. Zapiski nachal'nika Sankt-Peterburgskogo syska*. Moskva: Eksmo-Press, 2001.

Shikanova, I. S. "Novye materialy o denezhnykh znakakh Rossiisko-Amerikanskoi Kompanii." *Rossiia+Amerika=200. K iubileiu Rossiisko-Amerikanskoi kompanii, 1799–1999*. Moskva: Gos. Ist. Muzei, 1999.

Shishanov, V. A. "'Kostry iz assignatsii' ili pervye meropriiatiia Pavla I v otnoshenii bumazhnykh deneg." *Den'gi v rossiiskoi istorii. Sbornik materialo*, edited by Andrei Bogdanov. St. Petersburg: Goznak, 2019.

Sidorov, A. L. *Finansovoe polozhenie Rossii v gody Pervoi Mirovoi voiny*. Moskva: Akademia Nauk SSSR, 1960.

Siegel, Jennifer. *For Peace and Money: French and British Finance in the Service of Tsars and Commissars*. New York: Oxford University Press, 2014.

Siegelbaum, Lewis H. "Another 'Yellow Peril': Chinese Migrants in the Russian Far East and the Russian Reaction before 1917." *Modern Asian Studies* 12, no. 2 (1978).

Sivkov, K. V. "Finansy Rossii posle voin s Napoleonom." *Otechestvennaia Voina i Russkoe Obshchestvo*, vol. 7. Moskva, 1912.

Smith, S. A. *Red Petrograd: Revolution in the Factories*. Cambridge: Cambridge University Press, 1983.

Sokolov, E. N. *Denezhnaia i biudzhetnaia politika Sovetskoi respubliki*. Riazan': Riazanskii universitet im. S. A. Yesenina, 2012.

Spang, Rebecca. "Money, Art, and Representation: The Look and Sound of Money," in *A Cultural History of Money in the Age of Enlightenment*, edited by Christine Desan London: Bloomsbury Academic, 2021

Spang, Rebecca. *Stuff and Money in the Time of the French Revolution*. Cambridge, MA: Harvard University Press, 2015.

Spasskii, I. G "Ocherki po istorii russkoi numizmatiki." *Trudy Gosudarstvennogo Istoricheskogo Muzeia*, vyp.25. *Numizmaticheskii sbornik*, ch.1. Moskva: Gos. Ist. Muzei, 1955.

Startsev, V. I. *Vnutrenniaia politika Vremennogo Pravitel'stva pervogo sozyva*. Leningrad: Nauka, 1980.

Stasavage, David. *Public Debt and the Birth of the Democratic State, France and Great Britain, 1688–1789*. Cambridge: Cambridge University Press, 2003.

Stepanov, V. L. "I. A. Vyshnegradskii i Witte. Partnery i konkurenty." *Rossiiskaia istoriia* 6 (2014).

Stepanov, V.L. "Tsena pobedy: Russko-Turetskaia voina i ekonomika Rossii." *Rossiiskaia Istoriia* 6 (2015).

Stepanov, V. L. *N. Kh. Bunge. Sudba reformatora.* Moskva: ROSSPEN, 1998.

Strachan, Hew. *The First World War.* Oxford: Oxford University Press, 2001.

Strakhov, V. V. "Vnutrennie zaimy v Rossii v Pervuiu Mirovuiu Voinu." *Voprosy Istorii* 9 (2003).

Thiveaud, Jean-Marie. "1814: La Banque de France au défi de son indépendance. La question cruciale de la confiance." *Revue d'économie financière* 22 (Automne 1992).

Tribe, Keith. "Staatswirtschaft," "Staatswissenschaft," and "Nationaloekonomie": German Economic Discourse in the Time of Geothe." In *Goethe and Money. The Writer and Modern Economics,* edited by Vera Hierholzer and Sandra Richter. Frankfurt: Freies Deutsches Hochstift, 2012.

Troitskii, S. M. "Sistema" Dzhona Lo i ee russkie posledovateli." In *Franko-Russkie ekonomicheskie sviazi,* edited by Fernand Braudel. Moskva: Nauka, 1970.

Uspenskii, B. A. "Yazykovaia programma karamzinistov: zapadnoevropeiskie istoki," *Vokrug Trediakovskogo. Trudy po istorii russkogo iazyka i russkoi kultury.* Moskva: Indrik, 2008.

Valentino, Russell Scott. "'What's a Person Worth': Character and Commerce in Dostoevskii's Double." *American Contributions to the 13th International Congress of Slavists, Ljubljana, August 2003.* edited by Robert Maguire and Alan Timberlake, vol. 2. Bloomington: Indiana University Press, 2003.

Veksler, A. G., and A. Mel'nikova. *Rossiiskaia istoriia v moskovskikh kladakh.* Moskva: Zhiraf, 1999.

Verdery, Katherine. "After Socialism." In *A Companion to the Anthropology of Politics,* edited by Joan Vincent and David Nugent. Malden, MA: Blackwell, 2004.

Volobuev, P. V. *Ekonomicheskaia politika Vremennogo pravitel'stva.* Moskva, 1962

Vse ministry finansov Rossii, 1802–2004. Moskva: REO, 2004.

Waller, Joseph. "La naissance du rouble-or." *Cahiers du monde russe et soviétique* 20, nos. 3–4 (Julliet-Decembre 1979).

Wcislo, Francis W. *Tales of Imperial Russia: The Life and Times of Sergei Witte, 1849–1915.* Oxford: Oxford University Press, 2011.

White, Michael V., and Kurt Schuler. "Retrospectives: Who Said "Debauch the Currency": Keynes or Lenin?" *Journal of Economic Perspectives* 23, no. 2 (2009).

White, Stephen, *The Origins of the Détente. The Genoa Conference and Soviet-Western Relations, 1921–1922.* Cambridge: Cambridge University Press, 1985.

Woodruff, David M. "The Politburo on Gold, Industrialization, and the International Economy, 1925–1926." In *The Lost Politburo Transcripts: From Collective Rule to Stalin's Dictatorship,* edited by Paul R. Gregory and Norman Naimark. New Haven: Yale University Press, 2008.

Woodruff, David. *Money Unmade: Barter and the Fate of Russian Capitalism.* Ithaca, NY: Cornell University Press, 1999.

Yadryshnikov, K. S. "Vosstanovlenie Gosudarstvennogo Banka RSFSR v 1921 g. (pravovoi aspekt)." *Aktualnye problemy rossiiskogo prava* 3 (2009).

Yanin, V. L. *Denezhno-vesovye sistemy domongolskoi Rusi i ocherki istorii denezhnoi sistemy srednevekovogo Novgoroda.* Moskva: Yazyki slavianskikh kultur, 2009.

Zakharova, L. I., Yu. T. Trifankov, V. V. Dziuban, and N. G. Fedkina. *S.I. Maltsev: Sotsialnaia initsiativa v promyshlennom regione vo vtoroi polovine XIX veka.* Briansk: BGTU, 2014.

Zatlin, Jonathan R. *The Currency of Socialism.* Cambridge: Cambridge University Press, 2007.

Zauberman, Alfred. "Gold in Soviet Economic Theory and Policies." *American Economic Review* 41, no. 5 (December 1951).

Zelizer, Viviana A. *The Social Meaning of Money.* New York: Basic Books, 1994.

Zhivov, V. M. *Yazyk i kultura v Rossii XVIII veka.* Moskva: Shkola "Iazyki russkoi kul'tury," 1996.

Index

For the benefit of digital users, indexed terms that span two pages (e.g., 52–53) may, on occasion, appear on only one of those pages.

Tables, figures, and boxes are indicated by an italic t, f, and b following the page/paragraph number.